COMMENTARIES

ON

THE CATHOLIC EPISTLES

COMMENTARIES

ON

THE CATHOLIC EPISTLES

BY JOHN CALVIN

TRANSLATED AND EDITED

BY THE REV. JOHN OWEN,
VICAR OF THRUSSINGTON, AND RURAL DEAN, LEICESTERSHIRE

WIPF & STOCK · Eugene, Oregon

Wipf and Stock Publishers
199 W 8th Ave, Suite 3
Eugene, OR 97401

Commentaries on the Catholic Epistles
By Calvin, John and Owen, John
Softcover ISBN-13: 979-8-3852-1666-6
Hardcover ISBN-13: 979-8-3852-1667-3
eBook ISBN-13: 979-8-3852-1668-0
Publication date 2/13/2024
Previously published by Baker Book House, 2005

This edition is a scanned facsimile of the original edition published in 2005.

TRANSLATOR'S PREFACE.

THE Dedication to King Edward the Sixth is remarkably interesting, as it refers to the character of Popery at that day, and to its manœuvres with regard to a General Council. The language is strong, and perhaps rougher than what would be at present used, but still true according to all we gather from history as to the state of things in those days. The main principles of Popery are still the same, and similar are its proceedings, though they may be more disguised, and its spirit is equally intolerant and persecuting. Like Mahomedanism, it is exclusive, and ever injurious to the harmony and peace of society.

The order in which the Epistles are arranged is not the same as in our version. There has not been a uniformity in this respect among the ancients. The reason for the arrangement here adopted was probably this, that the First Epistle of Peter, and the First of John, had, from the beginning, been universally acknowledged as genuine, while the Epistle of James, the Second of Peter, and that of Jude, had not from the first been universally received as canonical, though they were eventually so received. The Second and the Third Epistle of John were evidently not deemed by Calvin as "catholic;" and for this reason, as it seems, he omitted them.

The word "Catholic," or General, as applied to the Epistles here explained, has been differently understood. Some have thought that they have been thus called, because they contain catholic truths; but other Epistles might, for this reason, be also called catholic. Others have supposed that catholic is synonymous with canonical; but in this case also there is no more reason for applying the word to these Epistles than to any other Epistles. But the more probable opinion is, that they were called Catholic, or General, because they were not written to any particular Church, but to Jewish or to Gentile Christians generally. Moreover, the term was not given them at first, but in subsequent ages.

The most probable *dates* of the *five* Epistles here explained are the following:—

The Epistle of James,	A.D. 61
The First Epistle of Peter,	64
The Second Epistle of Peter,	65
The Epistle of Jude,	66
The First Epistle of John,	68

This is the order according to the dates most approved by the learned. There is, for the most part, a unanimity as to the dates of the three first Epistles; but with regard to the Epistle of Jude, and the First Epistle of John, there is not the same agreement. There are many who fix later dates: to Jude, 90, and to John, 91 or 92. But this is a matter of no great consequence.

No doubt can be justly entertained but that JAMES, called the Less, was the author of the Epistle. He was the son of Alphæus or Cleopas, and of Mary, probably a cousin, not a sister, of Mary the mother of our Lord. Hence he is called our Lord's brother, (Gal. i. 19;) that is, a near relative, as the word brother is often taken in Scripture. He took a leading part in the council held at Jerusalem, mentioned in Acts xv.; and, according to *Jerome*, he resided there thirty years, and presided over the Church. He was put to death, as Hegesippus relates, who flourished in the second century, by a tumultuous mob, excited by Jewish zealots, in the year 62.

The canonicity of James's Epistle has been a subject of dispute, though almost universally allowed in the present day. The facts respecting it, according to *Basnage*, are these,—During the three first centuries it was not extensively known; in the fourth century its authenticity was by *some* disputed; but in the fifth century it was universally acknowledged as genuine; and it has ever since been so acknowledged, with a very few exceptions. What seems to be a sufficient evidence in its favour is the fact, that it is found as a part of Holy Scripture in the first Syriac Version, which was made early in the second century.

The occasion of writing the Epistle appears to have been the abuse made of the doctrine of free grace by professing Christians,—a subject referred to also by Paul in Romans vi., and in his other Epistles. Abounding grace is at one time despised and rejected; at another time it is turned into licentiousness: these are evils which have ever prevailed in the Church. The Pharisee is too proud to receive grace; the Antinomian pretends to receive and magnify grace, that he may gratify the inclinations of his sinful nature. It was against the Antinomian that James wrote his Epistle.

According to *Lardner* and *Macknight*, the Epistle was addressed to the whole Jewish nation, at home and abroad, believers and unbelievers; according to *Grotius* and *Wall*, to the Jews dispersed abroad indiscriminately, believing and unbelieving; according to *Michaelis*, to the believing Jews, while the unbelieving were not overlooked; but according to *Beza* and *Scott*, to the scattered Jews who professed the Christian faith. And this last opinion has the strongest reasons and evidence in its favour.[1]

With regard to the *First* Epistle of PETER, there has never been a doubt respecting its genuineness. This Apostle took a prominent part at first in the cause of Christianity, but of his labours after the council at Jerusalem, in the year 49, recorded in Acts xv., we have no account in Scripture. Mention is indeed made, in Gal. ii. 11, of his being afterwards at Antioch. It has been justly concluded from the superscription of this Epistle that he exercised his ministry in those parts which are here mentioned.

[1] See *Horne's* Introduction, vol. iv. part ii. chap. iv. sect. iii.

It was thought by *Beza* and *Grotius* that the Epistle was addressed to converted Jews; but by *Doddridge, Macknight,* and *Scott,* to Christians in general, both Jews and Gentiles. The latter opinion is the most probable. The arguments assigned by *Horne,* in his Introduction, in favour of the former opinion, are by no means satisfactory.

With regard to the *Second* Epistle of PETER, doubts have been entertained by some as to its authenticity. It appears that it was not at first so widely known as his First Epistle; and this was probably the reason why there were some during the first three centuries who did not regard it as genuine. But it has been quoted as a part of Scripture by some of the earliest Fathers, and fully acknowledged as authentic by those of the fourth and succeeding centuries.

The *First* Epistle of JOHN has from the beginning been uniformly received as a portion of Divine Revelation. Some difference has existed as to the persons for whom it was especially intended,—a matter of no great importance. Some have supposed it to have been written for the Jewish Christians in Judea; but others, with more probability, for Christians generally, both Jewish and Gentile.

Though there is no name attached to it, yet there has been universal consent from the beginning that John was its author; and indeed the style of it throughout is sufficient to shew that he was the writer of it; for his Gospel and the Book of Revelation are in this respect exactly alike; and it is a style peculiarly his own.

JUDE, or Judas, was, as he says, the brother of James, and therefore the son of Alphæus or Cleopas. Though he does not call himself an apostle, yet he proved himself to be so by saying that he was the brother of James. He is called, as James was, the brother of our Lord, Matt. xiii. 55. We have in Scripture no account of his ministry after the day of Pentecost.

His Epistle was not at first universally received as canonical. This is acknowledged by *Origen, Eusebius,* and *Jerome;* at the same time, they themselves so regarded it; and Jerome says that in his day it was by most received as genuine; and it has been quoted as a part of Scripture by *Clement* of Alexandria, *Tertullian, Cyril* of Jerusalem, *Athanasius, Ambrose,* and *Augustine.*[1]

That some of the Epistles were not universally received as authentic at first is no matter of wonder, when we consider the scattered condition of the Church, and the scanty means of communication. The fact, that *some* had doubts respecting them does not in the least degree invalidate their genuineness; on the contrary, it has conduced to strengthen the evidence in their favour; for the doubts of some must have occasioned a more minute inquiry as to their authenticity. And it was not long before all the Epistles, about which there had been some doubts, had attained the universal approbation of the Church; and what *Lardner* states is worthy of special attention,—That no writings, received by the primitive Church as genuine, have been since proved to be spurious; and that no writings, regarded by it as spurious, have been since proved to be genuine.

The Editor must mention here, what perhaps he ought to have mentioned before,—that in his translations he has not always retained what is called the historical present tense, which is often used by *Calvin,* according to the practice of Latin and Greek writers, and also of the Prophets and the Evangelists. This mode of writing does not accord with the usage of the present day.

Our translators have not been uniform in this respect either in the New or the Old Testament; for they sometimes departed from the original as to this tense, though, for the most part, they retained it. As, for instance, in John xi. 39, 40, the historical present is *not* retained in the 39th, while it is retained in the 40th verse. The anomalies as to

---

[1] See *Wolfius'* Prolegomena to this Epistle.

the tenses often met with, especially in the Psalms, have arisen from overlooking this peculiarity. The future in Hebrew is very often used for the present; and this is the historical present, and ought to be rendered in our language in the past tense.

J. O.

THRUSSINGTON, *Sept.* 29, 1855.

DEDICATION.

TO HIS MOST SERENE HIGHNESS,

EDWARD THE SIXTH,

THE KING OF ENGLAND, THE LORD OF IRELAND, AND A MOST CHRISTIAN PRINCE,

JOHN CALVIN.

BEHOLD, I return to you again, most excellent King. For though I did not expect that the Commentaries on Isaiah, which I lately dedicated to your Majesty, were a worthy gift, yet it was offered with my hearty good wishes. I have, therefore, thought of adding the Catholic Epistles, as they are commonly called, as a supplement to make up a full measure, so that both might come to your hands at the same time. And doubtless, since they were written either to Gentiles far distant, or to such as inhabited various countries far asunder, it is nothing new to them to pass over the sea, and to make a long circuit in coming to your Majesty. At the same time I thus as a private individual offer to you, most illustrious King, my labours, that being published under your name, they may profit all.

And truly, if there has ever been a time when the truth of God ought to have been freely and boldly maintained, it has never been more necessary than in the present day, as all must see. Not to mention the atrocious cruelty exercised towards its professors, to omit also all those machinations by which Satan fights against it, sometimes covertly and sometimes openly, there are places in which the pure doctrine of Religion lately prevailed, but where now the satellites of the Roman Antichrist by their spurious deformations so mock Christ as though they gave a reed in his hand instead of a sceptre, and laid a crown of thorns on his head. When these crafty corrupters of the purity of the Gospel hope by their arts gradually to extinguish it, with what cowardice do they connive at these mockeries offered to Christ, who ought to have hazarded their life a hundred times rather than to redeem it for a very short time by their perfidious silence?

In the meantime, the Pope himself, to complete the last tragedy of crucifying the Son of God, is said to have summoned again his own masked council. Though he marches with his savage soldiery to obliterate the name of Christ and to destroy his Church, yet every kind of council is to him as a sacred sword, to make slaughter as it were a solemn rite. Thus Paulus the Third, when he had resolved to kill and destroy all by whom the defence of truth was preferred to their own life, made a show at Trent of that odious spectre, though disguised in fine colours, that he might put an end to the Gospel as it were by its thunders. But all that preparation, when the good fathers had begun, through some gleams emitted at the sessions, to dazzle the eyes of the simple, was put an end to by a secret and sudden blast from the holy seat, and vanished into smoke, except that for the purpose of continuing the terror, a little cloud rested for a time on Bononia.

Hence Julius, his successor, who had performed his part previously at Trent, is said to be preparing himself now for this stratagem, as though this only remained as means to obliterate the Gospel from the memory of men, that is, to fulminate against us with the horrible and terrific decrees of council; though many think that he only makes a pretence. But it signifies but little whether he pretends or really means to call a council. It is indeed a thing clear and well proved, that since the Papacy began to decline through the efforts of Luther, whoever occupied that citadel of tyranny, though they might hope to obtain some support from a council, they yet have shunned this kind of remedy in way similar to a sick man, who, being all over full of ulcers, dreads even the touch of the most tender physician. Therefore common even among children is the saying, that the Papacy cannot otherwise be assisted by a council than by cauterizing or amputation.

But I see no cause why the Popes dread councils so much, except that fear is an inseparable companion of a bad conscience. For what, I pray, was the late rabble at Trent, (to which yet they gave the name of a holy, general, and ecumenical synod,) but a sort of empty apparition, which no more disturbed the pleasures of the Pope than the clangor of trumpets, or the sound of drums, with which he daily amuses himself? Were, indeed, a synod from all parts really assembled, there might be some cause of fear, lest a disturbance, arising in so great a multitude, should occasion a greater tumult. But by such fictitious councils as that of Trent, who can believe that a Pope could be terrified any more than by children's rattles, but that on the contrary he would sweetly slumber as through the blandishments of a quieter sleep? For example, two or three cardinals shall be chosen by the Pope, being his bosom friends, who shall wield all the authority. The same tyrant will hire from his courtiers some greedy fellow for a few ducats a month, who, being clothed in the mask of a patriarch, will servilely declare as his own opinion what had been dictated to him. Such was that blind Robert at Trent, whom I saw some time ago at Ratisbon, busying himself, not less foolishly than wickedly, in behalf of the Pope, when by his inveiglements he tried to draw me to a conference with Contarenus. There will fly together from all Italy the three-halfpenny bishops, of whom there will be a vast abundance. There will come also from France and Spain some of the light-headed and fatuitous, and others infamous for the vices of their former life; who afterwards returning home will boast that they had rendered a good and faithful service to the Catholic Church. Moreover, there will come forth from the caves of monks a great conflux of frogs into that marsh, who by their eager croaking will banish far away every truth. What! do I imagine here a new thing, or do I not, on the contrary, correctly describe the assembly which was lately seen at Trent?

Why then is it that the Pope dreads these guardians of his own tribunal, who are all, in the *first* place, his own servile creatures; and who, in the *second* place, seek no other thing than to gain by any means his favour?

Our Julius especially, who is a veteran in matters of this kind, can in mockery, whenever he pleases, compose such a council as this, so as, in the meantime, to leave as usual the thing undone. And, indeed, as he has given to many of the Dominicans the red cap, it seems to be no obscure prelude of such an event. This order, as they say, has ever been in favour with him; but such profusion arises from a higher cause. He, indeed, knows well, that none are more shameless than these beggarly fellows, as he has often employed at his nod their illiberal and sordid services. When he raised them again to this dignity, he knew that whatever he might bid them to do, none would be more audacious or more cruel than they. Besides, he is not ignorant that most of these hungry dogs, feeding on the same rewards, would rush into any contentions he wishes. I do not, however, say that they are mistaken who declare that he does not desire a council. But when he has arranged his own theatre, some sudden storm will be raised with no great trouble, which will disturb the whole proceeding. Hence, at the very beginning, if his own advantage so require it, he will fold up the curtains. A council, however, though an empty phantom, he thinks to be to him like Hercules's club, to lay Christ prostrate, and to break in pieces the remnant of the Church.

When this prince of impiety so wickedly tramples upon the glory of our God and the salvation of men, does it become us by silence to betray the sacred cause? nay, we ought to undergo hundred deaths, were that possible, rather than to suffer so unworthy, wicked, and barbarous oppression of sound doctrine to continue unknown through our sloth.

But let us grant what is hardly credible, that the Pope with his band does seriously intend to call a council. In that case Christ will not, at the first view, be so grossly mocked; yet in this way a wicked conspiracy would be formed against him: nay, the greater the fame of the gravity and splendour of the Papal council, the more injurious would it be to the Church, and a more dreadful pest would it prove. For it cannot possibly be hoped, that an assembly gathered under the authority of Antichrist, should be governed by the Spirit, or that the slaves of Satan should exercise any moderation. In the first place, the Pope, the professed and sworn enemy of Christ, would occupy there the chief place of authority. Though he would especially pretend to ask the opinions of the Fathers sitting there, yet being terrified by his presence, they would all follow what would please him. But in an assembly fully agreeing in every impiety, what need would there be of dissimulation? Such, I have no doubt, is every one of the cardinals. In that very college, which pretends to be a holier senate, there prevails, it is evident, an Epicurean contempt of God, a savage hatred of truth, a rabid fury against all the pious. Then the order of bishops, does it not consist nearly of the same monsters? except that many among them are slothful asses, who neither openly despise God, nor hostilely oppose sound doctrine; yet they are so enamoured with their own depraved state, that they cannot endure any reformation. Add to this, that authority will reside almost wholly with the few, who, being indeed altogether destitute of any concern for true religion, will shew themselves the most fierce supporters of the Roman See: others will make up the number. As every one of these will speak the most atrocious things against us, there will be many not only of those who may only give their votes, but also of the princes, who will subscribe either willingly and gladly according to their own inclinations, or from ambition, or from fear.

I am not, however, so unjust as not to concede that some of these have a sounder judgment, and are not otherwise ill disposed; but they do not possess so much courage, that they will dare to resist the wickedness of the whole body. There will be perhaps, amidst a thousand, two or three who may dare to give a half-uttered word for Christ, (as Peter Paul Vergerius at Trent,) but the holy council of the Fathers will have a remedy at hand, so that such may not create any further trouble; for being cast into prison, they will be presently driven to a recantation, or they will have to pay the penalty of death for too much freedom of speech, or they will have to drink the cup of perpetual silence.

But such is the equity with which we are treated, that we are untameable and hopelessly perverse heretics, except we seek from the holy council the rule for the necessary reformation, except we acquiesce without any demur in its decrees, whatever they may be. We, indeed, do not shun the authority of a legitimate council, (if such could be had,) as we have already made sufficiently evident by clear proofs. But when they require that we are to bow to the judgment of the chief adversary of Christ without any appeal, and indeed on this condition, that religion is to be defined at their will and pleasure, and not by the Word of God, what reason have we for submission, except we are prepared willingly and knowingly to deny Christ? There is no reason for any one to object and say, that we distrust before the time. Let them give us a council in which there will be a free liberty given to defend the cause of truth: if to that we refuse to come, and to give a reason for all that we have done, then they will justly charge us with contumacy. But so far will a permission be given us freely to speak, that there is no doubt but that we shall be prevented from making even a suitable defence. For how can they listen to the clear-sounding thunders of truth, who can by no means bear warnings however bland and conveyed in soft whispers? But this they publicly do— They invite us; is it that they may grant us some place on the lowest seats? Nay, they declare that it is not lawful to admit any one to their sittings except the anointed and the mitred. Then let them sit, provided we are heard, declaring the truth while standing. They answer, that they freely promise a hearing; that is, that having presented a suppliant petition, being ordered immediately to depart, after the turbulent clamours of some days, we shall be recalled for the purpose of being condemned. I say clamours, not that any altercation of dissidents is to be in that assembly, but that the sacred ears of bishops having been so irreverently offended by us, the indignity will appear to them intolerable. It is not unknown how tumultuous is their violence. Surely, when they ought to determine the cause with reason, this can never be obtained from them, when not even a slight hearing can be hoped for.

We shall endeavour to restore God's worship to its purity, purged from the innumerable superstitions by which it has been corrupted. Here the profane orators will chatter about nothing but the institutes, the old rites and ceremonies of the Fathers, as though the Church taught by the celestial ministry of the prophets and of Christ knew no other way of worshipping God than by adopting, in brutal stupidity, the dregs of Romulus, made fascinating by the anile dotages of Numa Pompilius. But where is that simplicity of obedience which the Lord everywhere makes so much of and so distinctly requires?

If the controversy be concerning the depravity of human nature, the miserable and lost state of mankind, the grace and power of Christ, or the freeness of our salvation, they will immediately bring forward and dogmatically allege the putid axioms of the schools, as things that ought to be received without dispute. The Holy Spirit teaches us in Scripture, that our mind is smitten with so much blindness, that the affections of our heart are so depraved and perverted, that our whole nature is so vitiated, that we can do nothing but sin, until he forms a new will within us. He constrains us, condemned to eternal death, to renounce all confidence in our own works, and to flee to our only asylum, the mercy of God, and to trust in it for all our righteousness. He also, inviting us to God, testifies that God is reconciled to us only through the blood of Christ, and bids us to rely on Christ's merits, and to come boldly to the heavenly tribunal. That none of these things may be heard, those endless decrees are adduced, to violate which is deemed more unlawful than to disbelieve God and all his angels.

Of the sacraments they will not permit a word to be said, differing from the notions entertained of them. And what else is this but to preclude the possibility of any reformation? But it is easy to show how preposterous is the administration of the sacraments under the Papacy, so that hardly anything bears an affinity to the genuine doctrine of Christ. What spurious corruptions have crept in, nay, what disgraceful sacrileges have entered! It is not lawful to move a question on this subject. Hence it is a common saying with theologians, which they have published everywhere in their books: That the Church may remain safe, care must especially be taken that the council should not admit a doubt respecting the chief controversies of the present day. Come forth also has lately, in the Italian language, the insipid book of one Mutius, witlessly breathing nothing but carnage, in which he dwells profusely on this point, that nothing else is to be done by the reverend Fathers, when they meet in council, but to pronounce what already appears to them right on the whole subject, and to compel us to subscribe to their sanguinary edicts. I should not indeed have thought it necessary to mention the hoarse chatterings of this unlucky owl, had not Pope Julius recommended the work. Hence readers may judge what sort of council Mutius recommends, and is to be expected from Julius his approver.

As then we see that these antichrists rush on with desperate pertinacity in order to destroy sound doctrine, and with equal insolence boldly exult that they will set up a masked council for no other purpose than that, having put to flight the gospel, they may celebrate their own victory; let us also in our turn gather courage to follow the banner of our leader, having put on the armour of truth. Were only the pure and simple doctrine of Scripture to shine forth as it ought, every one, who refuses not to open his eyes, would acknowledge the Papacy to be a savage and an execrable monster, made up, through Satan's arts, of innumerable masses of errors. For we make it evident by the most solid proofs, that the glory of God is so distributed by a sacrilegious rending among fictitious idols, that hardly a hundredth portion of his right remains to him. And further, when they reserve for him some portion of worship, we can show that no part of it is sincere, inasmuch as all things are full of the superstitious inventions of men; the law of God is also loaded with similar devices, for miserable consciences are held bound under the yoke of men, rather than ruled by God's commandments; and they groan and toil under the unjust burden of so many traditions, nay, they are oppressed with a cruel tyranny. We declare that prevaricating obedience can avail nothing except to lead men to a deeper labyrinth. We shew clearly from Scripture, that Christ's power under the Papacy is almost abolished, that his grace is in a great measure made void, that unhappy souls removed from him, are inflated with a fatal confidence in their own power and works. We prove that prayer to God, such as is prescribed by his word, (which yet is the only true asylum of salvation) is wholly subverted. We plainly shew that the sacraments are adulterated by extraneous inventions, and are also transferred to a foreign purpose; for the power of the Spirit is impiously tied to them, and what is peculiar to Christ is ascribed to them. Then we disown the number *seven*, which they have presumptuously adopted. The mass also, which they imagine to be a sacrifice, we prove to be a disgraceful denial of the sacrifice of Christ. There are many other sacrilegious things of which we make it evident that they are guilty.

Doubtless, were only the Scripture allowed its own authority, there are none of these things respecting which our adversaries would not be constrained to be mute. And this is what they by no means dissemble, when they contend that owing to the ambiguous meaning of Scripture, we ought to stand solely on the judgment of the Church. Who, I pray, does not see, that by laying aside the word of God, the whole right of defining things is thus transferred to them? Though they may kiss the closed copies of the Scripture as a kind of worship, when yet they charge it with being obscure and ambiguous, they allow it no more authority than if no part of it existed in writing. Let them assume specious titles as they please, that they may not appear to allege anything besides the dictates of the Spirit, (as they are wont to boast,) yet it is a settled and fixed thing with them, that all reasons being laid aside, their will alone ought to be believed ($αὐτόπιστος$.)

Then, lest the faithful should be carried about by every wind of imposture, lest they should be exposed to the crafty cavils of the ungodly, being taught by the sure experiment of faith, let them know that nothing is more firm or certain than the teaching of Scripture, and on that support let them confidently recumb. And since we see that it is shamefully deformed by the false comments of the Sophists, and that at this day the hired rabble of the Pope are bent on this artifice, in order that by their smoke they may obscure the light, it behoves us to be more intent on the restoration of its brightness.

I, indeed, have in an especial manner resolved to devote myself to this work, as long as I live, whenever time and opportunity shall be afforded me. In the first place, the Church to which I belong shall thus receive the fruit of this labour, so that it may hereafter continue the longer; for though a small portion of time remains to me from the duties of my office, yet that, how small soever it may be, I have determined to devote to this kind of writing.

But to return to you, most illustrious King, here you have a small pledge, my Commentaries on the Catholic Epistles, where many things have been deemed obscure and recondite, which I have endeavoured so to explain, that an easy access to the true meaning might be open to a reader not altogether slothful. And as interpreters of Scripture, according to their opportunity, are to supply weapons to fight against Antichrist, so also you must bear in mind that it is a duty which belongs to your Majesty, to vindicate from unworthy calumnies the true and genuine interpretation of Scripture, so that pure religion may flourish. It was not without reason that God commanded by Moses, that as soon as a king was appointed over his people, he should take care to have a copy of the Law written out for himself. Why so, if he had, as a private individual, already exercised himself diligently in this work, but that he might know that kings have themselves need of this remarkable doctrine, and are especially enjoined to defend and maintain it; the Lord has assigned to his Law a sacred habitation in their palaces. Moreover, since the heroic greatness of your mind far surpasses the measure of your age, there is no reason why I should add more words to stimulate you.

Farewell, most noble King. May the Lord protect your Majesty as he has already done, govern you and your counsellors with the spirit of wisdom and fortitude, and keep your whole kingdom in safety and peace.

GENEVA. *Jan.* 24, 1551.

COMMENTARIES

ON

THE FIRST EPISTLE OF PETER.

THE ARGUMENT.

The design of Peter in this Epistle is to exhort the faithful to a denial of the world and a contempt of it, so that being freed from carnal affections and all earthly hindrances, they might with their whole soul aspire after the celestial kingdom of Christ, that being elevated by hope, supported by patience, and fortified by courage and perseverance, they might overcome all kinds of temptations, and pursue this course and practice throughout life.

Hence at the very beginning he proclaims in express words the grace of God made known to us in Christ; and at the same time he adds, that it is received by faith and possessed by hope, so that the godly might raise up their minds and hearts above the world. Hence he exhorts them to holiness, lest they should render void the price by which they were redeemed, and lest they should suffer the incorruptible seed of the Word, by which they had been regenerated into eternal life, to be destroyed or to die. And as he had said, that they had been born again by God's Word, he makes mention of their spiritual infancy. Moreover, that their faith might not vacillate or stagger, because they saw that Christ was despised and rejected almost by the whole world, he reminds them that this was only the fulfilment of what had been written of him, that he would be the stone of stumbling. But he further teaches them that he would be a firm foundation to those who believe in him. Hence he again refers to the great honour to which God had raised them, that they might be animated by the contemplation of their former state, and by the perception of their present benefits, to devote themselves to a godly life.

He afterwards comes to particular exhortations,—that they were to conduct themselves in humility and obedience under the government of princes, that servants were to be subject to their masters, that wives were to obey their husbands and to be modest and chaste, and that, on the other hand, husbands were to treat their wives with kindness. And then he commands them to observe what was just and right towards one another; and that they might do this the more willingly, he sets before them what would be the fruit —a peaceable and happy life.

As, however, it happened to Christians, that how much soever they sought peace, they were often harassed by many injuries, and had the world for no just cause inimical to them, he exhorts them calmly to bear their persecutions, which they knew would promote their salvation. For this purpose he brings forward the example of Christ. On the other hand, he reminds them what unhappy end awaits the ungodly, whilst in the meantime God wonderfully delivers his Church from death by death. He still further refers to the example of Christ to enforce the mortification of the flesh. To this exhortation he adds various and brief sentences; but shortly after he returns to the doctrine of patience, so that the faithful might mingle consolation with their evils, regarding it as good for them to be chastised by the paternal hand of God.

At the beginning of the fifth chapter he reminds the elders of their duty, that they were not to tyrannize over the Church, but to preside under Christ with moderation. He recommends to the young modesty and teachableness. At length, after a short exhortation, he closes the Epistle with a prayer.

As to the place from which he wrote, all do not agree. There is, however, no reason that I see why we should doubt that he was then at Babylon, as he expressly declares.[1] But

[1] *Horne*, in his Introduction, vol. iv. p. 425, mentions four opinions on this subject. According to Bishop Pearson, Mill, and Le Clerc, it was

as the persuasion had prevailed, that he had moved from Antioch to Rome, and that he died at Rome, the ancients, led by this sole argument, imagined that Rome is here allegorically called Babylon. But as without any probable conjecture they rashly believed what they have said of the Roman episcopate of Peter, so also this allegorical figment ought to be regarded as nothing. It is indeed much more probable that Peter, according to the character of his apostleship, travelled over those parts in which most of the Jews resided; and we know that a great number of them were in Babylon and in the surrounding countries.

CHAPTER I.

1. Peter, an apostle of Jesus Christ, to the strangers scattered throughout Pontus, Galatia, Cappadocia, Asia, and Bithynia,	1. Petrus, apostolus Jesu Christi, electis inquilinis qui dispersi sunt per Pontum, Galatiam, Cappadociam, Asiam et Bithyniam,
2. Elect according to the foreknowledge of God the Father, through sanctification of the Spirit, unto obedience and sprinkling of the blood of Jesus Christ: Grace unto you, and peace, be multiplied.	2. Secundum præcognitionem Dei Patris in sanctificatione Spiritus, in obedientiam et aspersionem sanguinis Jesu Christi; Gratia vobis et pax multiplicetur.

1. *Peter, an apostle.* What in this salutation is the same with those of Paul, requires no new explanation. When Paul prayed for *grace* and *peace*, the verb is left out; but Peter adds it, and says, *be multiplied;* still the meaning is

---

Babylon in Egypt; according to Erasmus, Drusius, Beza, Dr. Lightfoot, Basnage, Beausobre, Dr. Cave, Wetstein, Drs. Benson and A. Clarke, it was Babylon in Assyria; according to Michaelis, it was Babylon in Mesopotamia; and according to Grotius, Drs. Whitby, Lardner, Macknight, and Hales, Bishop Tomline, and all the learned of the Romish communion, it is to be taken figuratively for Rome, according to what was done by John in Rev. xvii. and xviii. What renders the last opinion very improbable is, that to date an epistle at a place to which a figurative name is given, is without another instance in Scripture, and the thing itself seems quite absurd. The language of prophecy is quite a different matter. Paul wrote several of his epistles at Rome, and in no instance did he do anything of this kind. Such an opinion would have never gained ground, had there not been from early times a foolish attempt to connect Peter with Rome. And it is to be regretted that some learned Protestants have been duped on this subject by a mass of fictitious evidence which has been collected by the partisans of the Romish Church.—*Ed.*

the same; for Paul did not wish to the faithful the beginning of grace and peace, but the increase of them, that is, that God would complete what he had begun.

To the elect, or the elected. It may be asked, how could this be found out, for the election of God is hid, and cannot be known without the special revelation of the Spirit; and as every one is made sure of his own election by the testimony of the Spirit, so he can know nothing certain of others. To this I answer, that we are not curiously to inquire about the election of our brethren, but ought on the contrary to regard their calling, so that all who are admitted by faith into the church, are to be counted as the elect; for God thus separates them from the world, which is a sign of election. It is no objection to say that many fall away, having nothing but the semblance; for it is the judgment of charity and not of faith, when we deem all those elect in whom appears the mark of God's adoption. And that he does not fetch their election from the hidden counsel of God, but gathers it from the effect, is evident from the context; for afterwards he connects it with the *sanctification of the Spirit.* As far then as they proved that they were regenerated by the Spirit of God, so far did he deem them to be the elect of God, for God does not sanctify any but those whom he has previously elected.

However, he at the same time reminds us whence that election flows, by which we are separated for salvation, that we may not perish with the world; for he says, *according to the foreknowledge of God.* This is the fountain and the first cause: God knew before the world was created whom he had elected for salvation.

But we ought wisely to consider what this precognition or foreknowledge is. For the sophists, in order to obscure the grace of God, imagine that the merits of each are foreseen by God, and that thus the reprobate are distinguished from the elect, as every one proves himself worthy of this or that lot. But Scripture everywhere sets the counsel of God, on which is founded our salvation, in opposition to our merits. Hence, when Peter calls them elect according to the precognition of God, he intimates that the cause of it depends on nothing else but on God alone, for he of his own free will has chosen us. Then the foreknowledge of God excludes every worthiness on the part of man. We have treated this subject more at large in the first chapter of the Epistle to the Ephesians, and in other places.

As however in our election he assigns the first place to the gratuitous favour of God, so again he would have us to know it by the effects, for there is nothing more dangerous or more preposterous than to overlook our calling and to seek for the certainty of our election in the hidden prescience of God, which is the deepest labyrinth. Therefore to obviate this danger, Peter supplies the best correction; for though in the first place he would have us to consider the counsel of God, the cause of which is alone in himself; yet he invites us to notice the effect, by which he sets forth and bears witness to our election. That effect is the sanctification of the Spirit, even effectual calling, when faith is added to the outward preaching of the gospel, which faith is begotten by the inward operation of the Spirit.

To the sojourners.[1] They who think that all the godly are thus called, because they are strangers in the world, and are advancing towards the celestial country, are much mistaken, and this mistake is evident from the word *dispersion* which immediately follows; for this can apply only to the Jews, not only because they were banished from their own country and scattered here and there, but also because they had been driven out of that land which had been promised to them by the Lord as a perpetual inheritance. He indeed afterwards calls all the faithful sojourners, because they are pilgrims on the earth; but the reason here is different. They were sojourners, because they had been dispersed, some in Pontus, some in Galatia, and some in Bithynia. It is nothing strange that he designed this Epistle more especially for the Jews, for he knew that he was appointed in a particular manner their apostle, as Paul teaches us in Gal. ii. 8.

---

[1] *Inquilinis;* they are those who dwell in a hired house, tenants. The original, παρεπιδήμοις, means those who dwell among a people, that is, not their own. Sojourners or pilgrims would be the best word. The sentence literally is, " To the sojourners of the dispersion of Pontus." &c. —*Ed.*

In the countries he enumerates, he includes the whole of Asia Minor, from the Euxine to Cappadocia.[1]

Unto obedience. He adds two things to sanctification, and seems to understand newness of life by *obedience*, and by the *sprinkling* of the blood of Christ the remission of sins. But if these be parts or effects of sanctification, then sanctification is to be taken here somewhat different from what it means when used by Paul, that is, more generally. God then sanctifies us by an effectual calling; and this is done when we are renewed to an obedience to his righteousness, and when we are sprinkled by the blood of Christ, and thus are cleansed from our sins. And there seems to be an implied allusion to the ancient rite of sprinkling used under the law. For as it was not then sufficient for the victim to be slain and the blood to be poured out, except the people were sprinkled; so now the blood of Christ which has been shed will avail us nothing, except our consciences are by it cleansed. There is then to be understood here a contrast, that, as formerly under the law the sprinkling of blood was made by the hand of the priest; so now the Holy Spirit sprinkles our souls with the blood of Christ for the expiation of our sins.

Let us now state the substance of the whole; which is, that our salvation flows from the gratuitous election of God; but that it is to be ascertained by the experience of faith, because he sanctifies us by his Spirit; and then that there are two effects or ends of our calling, even renewal into obedience and ablution by the blood of Christ; and further, that both are the work of the Holy Spirit.[2] We hence

[1] On this question both ancient and modern divines have differed. It is to be decided by the contents of the Epistle only. There is nothing *decisive* in favour of the opinion that it was written only to believing Jews; but there is a passage, chap. iv. 3, which seems clearly to shew that Peter included the believing Gentiles; for " the abominable idolatries" could only refer to them, as the Jews, since the Babylonian captivity, had never fallen into idolatry.—*Ed.*

[2] The meaning would be more clear, were we to make a change in the order of the words, " Elected, according to the foreknowledge of God, unto obedience and the sprinkling of the blood of Jesus Christ, through (*or*, by) the sanctification of the Spirit," that is, they were elected in order that they might obey the gospel, and be cleansed from the guilt of sin by the blood of Christ, through the sanctifying power of the Spirit. It was not their

conclude, that election is not to be separated from calling, nor the gratuitous righteousness of faith from newness of life.

3. Blessed *be* the God and Father of our Lord Jesus Christ, which, according to his abundant mercy, hath begotten us again unto a lively hope, by the resurrection of Jesus Christ from the dead,	3. Benedictus Deus et Pater Domini nostri Jesu Christi, qui secundum multam suam misericordiam regenuit nos in spem vivam, per resurrectionem Jesu Christi ex mortuis,
4. To an inheritance incorruptible, and undefiled, and that fadeth not away, reserved in heaven for you,	4. In hæreditatem incorruptibilem et incontaminatam et immarcescibilem, repositum in cælis erga vos,
5. Who are kept by the power of God through faith unto salvation, ready to be revealed in the last time.	5. Qui virtute Dei custodimini per fidem in salutem, quæ parata est revelari tempore ultimo.

Blessed be God. We have said that the main object of this epistle is to raise us above the world, in order that we may be prepared and encouraged to sustain the spiritual contests of our warfare. For this end, the knowledge of God's benefits avails much; for, when their value appears to us, all other things will be deemed worthless, especially when we consider what Christ and his blessings are; for everything without him is but dross. For this reason he highly extols the wonderful grace of God in Christ, that is, that we may not deem it much to give up the world in order that we may enjoy the invaluable treasure of a future life; and also that we may not be broken down by present troubles, but patiently endure them, being satisfied with eternal happiness.

Further, when he gives thanks to God, he invites the faithful to spiritual joy, which can swallow up all the opposite feelings of the flesh.

And Father of our Lord Jesus Christ. Understand the words thus,—" Blessed be God who is the Father of Jesus Christ." For, as formerly, by calling himself the God of Abraham, he designed to mark the difference between him and all fictitious gods; so after he has mani-

---

obedience that made them the elect, but they were chosen that they might obey, and thus obey through the influence of the Spirit. This is clearly the doctrine of this passage. See 2 Thess. ii. 13.—*Ed.*

fested himself in his own Son, his will is, not to be known otherwise than in him. Hence they who form their ideas of God in his naked majesty apart from Christ, have an idol instead of the true God, as the case is with the Jews and the Turks. Whosoever, then, seeks really to know the only true God, must regard him as the Father of Christ; for, whenever our mind seeks God, except Christ be thought of, it will wander and be confused, until it be wholly lost. Peter meant at the same time to intimate how God is so bountiful and kind towards us; for, except Christ stood as the middle person, his goodness could never be really known by us.

Who hath begotten us again. He shews that supernatural life is a gift, because we are born the children of wrath; for had we been born to the hope of life according to the flesh, there would have been no necessity of being begotten again by God. Therefore Peter teaches us, that we who are by nature destined to eternal death, are restored to life by God's mercy. And this is, as it were, our second creation, as it is said in the first chapter of the Epistle to the Ephesians. *Lively* or *living hope,* means the hope of life.[1] At the same time there seems to be an implied contrast between the hope fixed on the incorruptible kingdom of God, and the fading and transient hopes of man.

According to his abundant mercy. He first mentions the efficient cause, and then he points out the mediating cause, as they say. He shews that God was induced by no merits

---

[1] " This is a Hebraism," says Macknight, " for *a hope of life.* Accordingly, the Syriac version hath here, *in spem vitæ—to a hope of life."* The begetting again seems not to refer to inward renovation, but to what God did by raising Christ from the dead. To beget, sometimes means to put one in a new state or condition; as the expression, " This day have I begotten thee," means, that God had then constituted his Son a king, publicly invested him, as it were, with that office. Similar is the meaning here: God through the resurrection of Christ restored to the hope of life his desponding followers: hence the import of the word " again;" though *Macknight* thinks the reference to be to the covenant of grace made with our first parents after the fall, and that believers were begotten the second time to the same hope by the resurrection of Christ. The word for " begetting again," is only found here, and in a passive sense in the 23d verse, where it has a different meaning, as it evidently refers to the renovation of the heart.—*Ed.*

of ours to regenerate us unto a living hope, because he assigns this wholly to his mercy. But that he might more completely reduce the merits of works to nothing, he says, *great (multam) mercy.* All, indeed, confess that God is the only author of our salvation, but they afterwards invent extraneous causes, which take away so much from his mercy. But Peter commends mercy alone; and he immediately connects the way or manner, *by the resurrection of Christ;* for God does not in any other way discover his mercy; hence Scripture ever directs our attention to this point. And that Christ's death is not mentioned, but his resurrection, involves no inconsistency, for it is included; because a thing cannot be completed without having a beginning; and he especially brought forward the resurrection, because he was speaking of a new life.

4. *To an inheritance.*[1] The three words which follow are intended to amplify God's grace; for Peter (as I have before said) had this object in view, to impress our minds thoroughly as to its excellency. Moreover, these two clauses, " to an inheritance incorruptible," &c., and " to salvation ready to be revealed," I deem as being in apposition, the latter being explanatory of the former; for he expresses the same thing in two ways.

Every word which follows is weighty. The inheritance is said to be *reserved*, or preserved, that we may know that it is beyond the reach of danger. For, were it not in God's hand, it might be exposed to endless dangers. If it were in this world, how could we regard it as safe amidst so many changes? That he might then free us from every fear, he testifies that our salvation is placed in safety beyond the harms which Satan can do. But as the certainty of salvation can bring us but little comfort, except each one knows that it belongs to himself, Peter adds, *for you.* For consciences will calmly recumb here, that is, when the Lord cries

---

[1] *Pareus* puts, " that is, *to an inheritance,*" making this sentence explanatory of " the hope," as hope here is a metonymy for its object. It is an inheritance " incorruptible," not to be destroyed by a flood or by fire,— " undefiled," not like the land of Canaan, its type, which was defiled by its inhabitants,—" unfading," different from any worldly inheritance, for the world passeth away.—*Ed.*

to them from heaven, " Behold, your salvation is in my hand and is kept for you." But as salvation is not indiscriminately for all, he calls our attention to faith, that all who are endued with faith, might be distinguished from the rest, and that they might not doubt but that they are the true and legitimate heirs of God. For, as faith penetrates into the heavens, so also it appropriates to us the blessings which are in heaven.

5. *Who are kept by the power of God.* We are to notice the connexion when he says, that we are kept while in the world, and at the same time our inheritance is reserved in heaven; otherwise this thought would immediately creep in, " What does it avail us that our salvation is laid up in heaven, when we are tossed here and there in this world as in a turbulent sea ? What can it avail us that our salvation is secured in a quiet harbour, when we are driven to and fro amidst thousand shipwrecks ?" The apostle, therefore, anticipates objections of this kind, when he shews, that though we are in the world exposed to dangers, we are yet kept by faith; and that though we are thus nigh to death, we are yet safe under the guardianship of faith. But as faith itself, through the infirmity of the flesh, often quails, we might be always anxious about the morrow, were not the Lord to aid us.[1]

And, indeed, we see that under the Papacy a diabolical opinion prevails, that we ought to doubt our final perseverance, because we are uncertain whether we shall be to-morrow in the same state of grace. But Peter did not thus leave us in suspense; for he testifies that we stand by the power of God, lest any doubt arising from a consciousness of our own infirmity, should disquiet us. How weak soever we may then be, yet our salvation is not uncertain, because it is sustained by God's power. As, then, we are begotten by faith, so faith itself receives its stability from God's power. Hence is its security, not only for the present, but also for the future.

---

[1] The meaning would be somewhat different, but the sentence would be more intelligible, were we to render it thus, " Who are kept by faith in the power of God unto salvation." Salvation here means that of the body as well as of the soul at the resurrection.—*Ed.*

Unto salvation. As we are by nature impatient of delay, and soon succumb under weariness, he therefore reminds us that salvation is not deferred because it is not yet prepared, but because the time of its revelation is not yet come. This doctrine is intended to nourish and sustain our hope. Moreover, he calls the day of judgment *the last time,* because the restitution of all things is not to be previously expected, for the intervening time is still in progress. What is elsewhere called the last time, is the whole from the coming of Christ; it is so called from a comparison with the preceding ages. But Peter had a regard to the end of the world.

6. Wherein ye greatly rejoice, though now for a season (if need be) ye are in heaviness through manifold temptations;	6. In quo exultatis, paulisper nunc, si opus esti, contristati in variis tentationibus;
7. That the trial of your faith, being much more precious than of gold that perisheth, though it be tried with fire, might be found unto praise, and honour, and glory, at the appearing of Jesus Christ:	7. Ut probatio fidei vestræ multo pretiosior auro, quod perit et tamen per ignem probatur, reperiatur in laudem et honorem et gloriam, quum revelabitur Jesus Christus:
8. Whom having not seen, ye love; in whom, though now ye see *him* not, yet believing, ye rejoice with joy unspeakable, and full of glory:	8. Quem quum non videritis, diligitis, in quem nunc credentes, quum eum non aspicitis, exultatis gaudio inenarrabili et glorificato;
9. Receiving the end of your faith, *even* the salvation of *your* souls.	9. Reportantes finem fidei vestræ, salutem animarum.

6. *Wherein ye greatly rejoice,* or, In which ye exult. Though the termination of the Greek verb is doubtful, yet the meaning requires that we read, "ye exult," rather than "exult ye." *In which* refers to the whole that is said of the hope of salvation laid up in heaven. But he rather exhorts than praises them; for his object was to shew what fruit was to come from the hope of salvation, even spiritual joy, by which not only the bitterness of all evil might be mitigated, but also all sorrow overcome. At the same time to exult is more expressive than to rejoice.[1]

---

[1] Some take the verb in a future sense, "At which (time) ye shall exult;" and some as being an imperative, "On account of which exult ye;" but neither of these comports with the context; for the 8th verse proves that he speaks of present joy, and that he states the case as it was among them. It is better with *Calvin* to refer "wherein," or, "on ac-

But it seems somewhat inconsistent, when he says that the faithful, who exulted with joy, were at the same time sorrowful, for these are contrary feelings. But the faithful know by experience, how these things can exist together, much better than can be expressed in words. However, to explain the matter in a few words, we may say that the faithful are not logs of wood, nor have they so divested themselves of human feelings, but that they are affected with sorrow, fear danger, and feel poverty as an evil, and persecutions as hard and difficult to be borne. Hence they experience sorrow from evils; but it is so mitigated by faith, that they cease not at the same time to rejoice. Thus sorrow does not prevent their joy, but, on the contrary, give place to it. Again, though joy overcomes sorrow, yet it does not put an end to it, for it does not divest us of humanity. And hence it appears what true patience is; its beginning, and, as it were, its root, is the knowledge of God's blessings, especially of that gratuitous adoption with which he has favoured us; for all who raise hither their minds, find it an easy thing calmly to bear all evils. For whence is it that our minds are pressed down with grief, except that we have no participation of spiritual things? But all they who regard their troubles as necessary trials for their salvation, not only rise above them, but also turn them to an occasion of joy.

Ye are in heaviness, or, Ye are made sorrowful. Is not sorrow also the common lot of the reprobate? for they are not free from evils. But Peter meant that the faithful endure sorrow willingly, while the ungodly murmur and perversely contend with God. Hence the godly bear sorrow, as the tamed ox the yoke, or as a horse, broken in, the bridle, though held by a child. God by sorrow afflicts the reprobate, as when a bridle is by force put in the mouth of a ferocious and refractory horse; he kicks and offers every resistance, but all in vain. Then Peter commends the faithful, because they willingly undergo sorrow, and not as though forced by necessity.

count of which," to the fact stated in the previous verse, that they were kept by God's power for salvation ready to be revealed.—*Ed.*

By saying, *though now for a season,* or, a little while, he supplied consolation; for the shortness of time, however hard evils may be, does not a little lessen them; and the duration of the present life is but a moment of time. *If need be;* the condition is to be taken for a cause; for he purposed to shew, that God does not, without reason, thus try his people; for, if God afflicted us without a cause, to bear it would be grievous. Hence Peter took an argument for consolation from the design of God; not that the reason always appears to us, but that we ought to be fully persuaded that it ought to be so, because it is God's will.

We must notice that he does not mention one temptation, but many; and not temptations of one kind, but *manifold temptations.* It is, however, better to seek the exposition of this passage in the first chapter of James.

7. *Much more precious than of gold.* The argument is from the less to the greater; for if gold, a corruptible metal, is deemed of so much value that we prove it by fire, that it may become really valuable, what wonder is it that God should require a similar trial as to faith, since faith is deemed by him so excellent? And though the words seem to have a different meaning, he yet compares faith to gold, and makes it more precious than gold, that hence he might draw the conclusion, that it ought to be fully proved.[1] It is moreover uncertain how far he extends the meaning of the words, "tried" (δοκιμάζεσθαι) and "trial" (δοκίμιον.) Gold is, indeed, tried twice by fire; first when it is separated from its dross; and then, when a judgment is to be formed of its purity. Both modes of trial may very suitably be applied to faith; for when there is much of the dregs of unbelief remaining in us, and when by various afflictions we are refined as it were in God's furnace, the dross of our faith is removed, so that it becomes pure and clean before God; and, at the same time, a trial of it is made, as to whether it be true or fictitious. I am disposed

---

[1] The seeming difference in meaning referred to, arises from this, that the Apostle uses two nouns (a common thing in Scripture) instead of a noun and an adjective or participle—" the trial of your faith," instead of " your tried faith," or, " your faith when tried."—*Ed.*

to take these two views, and what immediately follows seems to favour this explanation; for as silver is without honour or value before it. be refined, so he intimates that our faith is not to be honoured and crowned by God until it be duly proved.

At the appearing of Jesus Christ, or, when Jesus Christ shall be revealed. This is added, that the faithful might learn to hold on courageously to the last day. For our life is now hidden in Christ, and will remain hidden, and as it were, buried, until Christ shall appear from heaven; and the whole course of our life leads to the destruction of the external man, and all the things we suffer are, as it were, the preludes of death. It is hence necessary, that we should cast our own eyes on Christ, if we wish in our afflictions to behold glory and praise. For trials as to us are full of reproach and shame, and they become glorious in Christ; but that glory in Christ is not yet plainly seen, for the day of consolation is not yet come.[1]

8. *Whom having not seen*, or, Whom though ye have not seen. He lays down two things, that they loved Christ whom they had not seen, and that they believed on him whom they did not then behold. But the first arises from the second; for the cause of love is faith, not only because the knowledge of those blessings which Christ bestows on us, moves us to love him, but because he offers us perfect felicity, and thus draws us up to himself. He then commends the Jews, because they believed in Christ whom they did not see, that they might know that the nature of faith is to acquiesce in those blessings which are hid from our eyes. They had indeed given some proof of this very thing, though he rather directs what was to be done by praising them.

The first clause in order is, that faith is not to be measured by sight. For when the life of Christians is apparently miserable, they would instantly fail, were not their happiness dependent on hope. Faith, indeed, has also its

[1] The "praise, honour, and glory," refer to tried faith; it will be praised or approved by the Judge, honoured before men and angels, and followed by eternal glory.—*Ed.*

eyes, but they are such as penetrate into the invisible kingdom of God, and are contented with the mirror of the Word; for it is the demonstration of invisible things, as it is said in Heb. xi. 1. Hence true is that saying of Paul, that we are absent from the Lord while we are in the flesh; for we walk by faith and not by sight. (2 Cor. v. 6, 7.)

The second clause is, that faith is not a cold notion, but that it kindles in our hearts love to Christ. For faith does not (as the sophists prattle) lay hold on God in a confused and implicit manner, (for this would be to wander through devious paths;) but it has Christ as its object. Moreover, it does not lay hold on the bare name of Christ, or his naked essence, but regards what he is to us, and what blessings he brings; for it cannot be but that the affections of man should be led there, where his happiness is, according to that saying, "Where your treasure is, there is also your heart." (Matt. vi. 21.)

Ye rejoice, or, Ye exult. He again refers to the fruit of faith which he had mentioned, and not without reason; for it is an incomparable benefit, that consciences are not only at peace before God, but confidently exult in the hope of eternal life. And he calls it *joy unspeakable*, or unutterable, because the peace of God exceeds all comprehension. What is added, *full of glory*, or glorified, admits of two explanations. It means either what is magnificent and glorious, or what is contrary to that which is empty and fading, of which men will soon be ashamed. Thus "glorified" is the same with what is solid and permanent, beyond the danger of being brought to nothing.[1] Those who are not elevated by this joy above the heavens, so that being content with Christ alone, they despise the world, in vain boast that they have faith.

9. *Receiving the end of your faith.* He reminds the faith-

---

[1] After "unspeakable," "glorified" must mean something greater, or it may be viewed as more specific, it is a joy unspeakable, it being a glorified joy in a measure, or the joy of the glorified in heaven. According to this view the words may be thus rendered, "with joy unspeakable and heavenly." *Doddridge* gives this paraphrase, "With unutterable and even glorified joy, with such a joy as seems to anticipate that of the saints in glory."—*Ed.*

ful where they ought to direct all their thoughts, even to eternal salvation. For this world holds all our affections ensnared by its allurements; this life and all things belonging to the body are great impediments, which prevent us from applying our minds to the contemplation of the future and spiritual life. Hence the Apostle sets before us this future life as a subject of deep meditation, and he indirectly intimates that the loss of all other things is to be deemed as nothing, provided our souls be saved. By saying *receiving*, he takes away all doubt, in order that they might more cheerfully go on, being certain of obtaining salvation.¹ In the meantime, however, he shews what the end of faith is, lest they should be over-anxious, because it is as yet deferred. For our adoption ought now to satisfy us; nor ought we to ask to be introduced before the time into the possession of our inheritance. We may also take *the end* for reward; but the meaning would be the same. For we learn from the Apostle's words, that salvation is not otherwise obtained than by faith; and we know that faith leans on the sole promise of gratuitous adoption; but if it be so, doubtless salvation is not owing to the merits of works, nor can it be hoped for on their account.

But why does he mention *souls* only, when the glory of a resurrection is promised to our bodies? As the soul is immortal, salvation is properly ascribed to it, as Paul sometimes is wont to speak,—"That the soul may be saved in the day of the Lord." (1 Cor. v. 5.) But it is the same as though he had said "Eternal salvation." For there is an implied comparison between it and the mortal and fading life which belongs to the body. At the same time, the body is not excluded from a participation of glory when annexed to the soul.

10. Of which salvation the prophets have enquired and searched

10. De qua salute exquisierunt et scrutati sunt prophetæ, qui de

---

¹ It is necessary either to give a future meaning to this participle, "Being about to receive;" or to view the Apostle as speaking of the salvation of the soul now, as distinct from the salvation of the soul and body hereafter. The latter view seems most appropriate to the passage. The soul is now saved by faith. The end of faith, its object and accomplishment, is reconciliation with God, and reconciliation is salvation.—*Ed.*

diligently, who prophesied of the grace *that should come* unto you:	futura erga nos gratia vaticinati sunt;
11. Searching what, or what manner of time, the Spirit of Christ which was in them did signify, when it testified beforehand the sufferings of Christ, and the glory that should follow.	11. Scrutantes in quem aut cujusmodi temporis articulum significaret qui in illis erat Spiritus Christi; prius testificans venturas in Christum afflictiones, et quæ sequuturæ erant glorias;
12. Unto whom it was revealed, that not unto themselves, but unto us, they did minister the things which are now reported unto you by them that have preached the gospel unto you with the Holy Ghost sent down from heaven; which things the angels desire to look into.	12. Quibus revelatum est quod non sibi ipsis, sed nobis ministrabant hæc, quæ nunc annunciata sunt vobis per eos qui vobis prædicarunt evangelium, per Spiritum sanctum missum e cœlo; in quæ desiderant angeli prospicere.

He hence commends the value of salvation, because the prophets had their minds intensely fixed on it; for it must have been a great matter, and possessing peculiar excellency, which could have thus kindled in the prophets a spirit of inquiry respecting it. But still more clearly does God's goodness toward us shine forth in this case, because much more is now made known to us than what all the prophets attained by their long and anxious inquiries. At the same time he confirms the certainty of salvation by this very antiquity; for from the beginning of the world it had received a plain testimony from the Holy Spirit.

These two things ought to be distinctly noticed: he declares that more has been given to us than to the ancient fathers, in order to amplify by this comparison the grace of the gospel; and then, that what is preached to us respecting salvation, cannot be suspected of any novelty, for the Spirit had formerly testified of it by the prophets. When, therefore, he says that the prophets searched and sedulously inquired, this does not belong to their writings or doctrine, but to the private desire with which every one boiled over. What is said afterwards is to be referred to their public office.

But that each particular may be more evident, the passage must be arranged under certain propositions. Let the first then be this,—that the Prophets who foretold of the grace which Christ exhibited at his coming, diligently inquired as to the time when full revelation was to be made. The second is,—that the Spirit of Christ predicted by them of the future condition of Christ's kingdom, such as it is now, and such as it is expected yet to be, even that it is destined that Christ and his whole body should, through various sufferings, enter into glory. The third is,—that the prophets ministered to us more abundantly than to their own age, and that this was revealed to them from above; for in Christ only is the full exhibition of those things of which God then presented but an obscure image. The fourth is,—that in the Gospel is contained a clear confirmation of prophetic doctrine, but also a much fuller and plainer explanation; for the salvation which he formerly proclaimed as it were at a distance by the prophets, he now reveals openly to us, and as it were before our eyes. The last proposition is,—that it hence appears evident how wonderful is the glory of that salvation promised to us in the Gospel, because even angels, though they enjoy God's presence in heaven, yet burn with the desire of seeing it. Now all these things tend to shew this one thing, that Christians, elevated to the height of their felicity, ought to surmount all the obstacles of the world; for what is there which this incomparable benefit does not reduce to nothing?

10. *Of which salvation.* Had not the fathers the same salvation as we have? Why then does he say that the fathers *inquired*, as though they possessed not what is now offered to us? The answer to this is plain, that salvation is to be taken here for that clear manifestation of it which we have through the coming of Christ. The words of Peter mean no other thing than those of Christ, when he said, "Many kings and prophets have desired to see the things which ye see, and have not seen them." (Matt. xiii. 17.) As then the prophets had but a limited knowledge of the grace brought by Christ, as to its revelation they justly desired something more. When Simeon, after seeing Christ, prepared himself calmly and with a satisfied mind for death, he shewed that he was before unsatisfied and anxious. Such was the feeling of all the godly.

11. And what they inquired is pointed out when he adds, *Searching what, or what manner of time.* There was a dif-

ference between the law and the gospel, a veil as it were being interposed, that they might not see those things nearer which are now set before our eyes. Nor was it indeed proper, while Christ the Sun of righteousness was yet absent, that the full light should shine as at mid-day. And though it was their duty to confine themselves within their prescribed limits, yet it was no superstition to sigh with a desire of having a nearer sight. For when they wished that redemption should be hastened, and desired daily to see it, there was nothing in such a wish to prevent them patiently to wait as long as it pleased the Lord to defer the time. Moreover, to seek as to prophecies the particular time, seems to me unprofitable; for what is spoken of here is not what the prophets taught, but what they wished. Where the Latin interpreters render, " of future grace," it is literally, " of the grace which is to you." But as the meaning remains the same, I was not disposed to make any change.

It is more worthy of observation, that he does not say that the prophets searched according to their own understanding as to the time when Christ's kingdom would come, but that they applied their minds to the revelation of the Spirit. Thus they have taught us by their example a sobriety in learning, for they did not go beyond what the Spirit taught them. And doubtless there will be no limits to man's curiosity, except the Spirit of God presides over their minds, so that they may not desire anything else than to speak from him. And further, the spiritual kingdom is a higher subject than what the human mind can succeed in investigating, except the Spirit be the guide. May we also therefore submit to his guidance.

11. *The Spirit of Christ which was in them.* First, " who was in them," and secondly, " testifying," that is, giving a testimony, by which expression he intimates that the prophets were endued with the Spirit of knowledge, and indeed in no common manner, as those who have been teachers and witnesses to us, and that yet they were not partakers of that light which is exhibited to us. At the same time, a high praise is given to their doctrine, for it was the testimony of the Holy Spirit; the preachers and ministers were men, but

he was the teacher. Nor does he declare without reason that the Spirit of Christ then ruled; and he makes the Spirit, sent from heaven, to preside over the teachers of the Gospel, for he shews that the Gospel comes from God, and that the ancient prophecies were dictated by Christ.

The sufferings of Christ. That they might bear submissively their afflictions, he reminds them that they had been long ago foretold by the Spirit. But he includes much more than this, for he teaches us, that the Church of Christ has been from the beginning so constituted, that the cross has been the way to victory, and death a passage to life, and that this had been clearly testified. There is, therefore, no reason why afflictions should above measure depress us, as though we were miserable under them, since the Spirit of God pronounces us blessed.

The order is to be noticed; he mentions sufferings first, and then adds the glories which are to follow. For he intimates that this order cannot be changed or subverted; afflictions must precede glory. So there is to be understood a twofold truth in these words,—that Christians must suffer many troubles before they enjoy glory,—and that afflictions are not evils, because they have glory annexed to them. Since God has ordained this connexion, it does not behove us to separate the one from the other. And it is no common consolation, that our condition, such as we find it to be, has been foretold so many ages ago.

Hence we learn, that it is not in vain that a happy end is promised to us; secondly, we hence know that we are not afflicted by chance, but through the infallible providence of God; and lastly, that prophecies are like mirrors to set forth to us in tribulations the image of celestial glory.

Peter, indeed, says, that the Spirit had testified of the coming afflictions of Christ; but he does not separate Christ from his body. This, then, is not to be confined to the person of Christ, but a beginning is to be made with the head, so that the members may in due order follow, as Paul also teaches us, that we must be conformed to him who is the first-born among his brethren. In short, Peter does not speak of what is peculiar to Christ, but of the universal state of the Church. But it is much fitted to confirm our faith, when he sets forth our afflictions as viewed in Christ, for we thereby see better the connexion of death and life between us and him. And, doubtless, this is the privilege and manner of the holy union, that he suffers daily in his members, that after his sufferings shall be completed in us, glory also may have its completion. See more on this subject in the third chapter of the Epistle to the Colossians, and in the fourth of the first Epistle to Timothy.

12. *Unto whom it was revealed.* This passage has been strangely perverted by fanatics, so as to exclude the fathers who lived under the law from the hope of eternal salvation. For it does not deny that the prophets usefully ministered to their own age, and edified the church, but teaches us that their ministry is more useful to us, because we are fallen on the ends of the world. We see how highly they extolled the kingdom of Christ, how assiduous they were in adorning it, how diligently they stimulated all to seek it; but they were by death deprived of the privilege of seeing it as it now is. What else then was this, but that they spread the table, that others might afterwards feed on the provisions laid on it. They indeed tasted by faith of those things which the Lord has by their hands transmitted to be enjoyed by us; and they also partook of Christ as the real food of their souls. But what is spoken of now is the exhibition of this blessing, and we know that the prophetic office was confined as it were within limits, in order that they might support themselves and others with the hope of Christ, who was to come. They therefore possessed him as one hidden, and as it were absent—absent, I say, not in power or grace, but because he was not yet manifested in the flesh. Therefore his kingdom also was as yet hid as it were under coverings. At length descending on earth, he in a manner opened heaven to us, so that we might have a near view of those spiritual riches, which before were under types exhibited at a distance. This fruition then of Christ as manifested, forms the difference between us and the prophets. Hence we learn how they ministered to us rather than to themselves.

But though the prophets were admonished from above

that the grace which they proclaimed would be deferred to another age, yet they were not slothful in proclaiming it, so far were they from being broken down with weariness. But if their patience was so great, surely we shall be twice and thrice ungrateful, if the fruition of the grace denied to them will not sustain us under all the evils which are to be endured.

Which are now reported to you, or announced to you. He again marks the difference between the ancient doctrine and the preaching of the gospel. For as the righteousness of God is revealed in the gospel, having a testimony from the law and the prophets, so also the glory of Christ, of which the Spirit testified formerly, is now openly proclaimed. And at the same time he hence proves the certainty of the gospel, because it contains nothing but what had been long ago testified by the Spirit of God. He further reminds them, that under the banner of the same Spirit, by his dictation and guidance, the gospel was preached, lest they might think of anything human in this case.

Which things the angels desire to look into. It is indeed the highest praise to the gospel, that it contains treasures of wisdom, as yet concealed and hidden from angels. But some one may object, and say that it is not reasonable that things should be open and known to us which are hidden from angels, who always see the face of God, and are his ministers in ruling the church, and in the administration of all his blessings. To this I answer, that things are open to us as far as we see them in the mirror of the word; but our knowledge is not said to be higher than that of angels; Peter only means that such things are promised to us as angels desire to see fulfilled. Paul says that by the calling of the Gentiles the wonderful wisdom of God was made known to angels: for it was a spectacle to them, when Christ gathered into one body the lost world, alienated for so many ages from the hope of life. Thus daily they see with admiration the magnificent works of God in the government of his church. How much greater will their admiration be, at witnessing the last display of divine justice, when the kingdom of Christ shall be completed! This is as yet hidden, the revelation of which they still expect and justly wish to see.

The passage indeed admits of a twofold meaning; either that the treasure we have in the gospel fills the angels with a desire to see it, as it is a sight especially delightful to them; or that they anxiously desire to see the kingdom of Christ, the living image of which is set forth in the gospel. But the last seems to me to be the most suitable meaning.

13. Wherefore gird up the loins of your mind, be sober, and hope to the end, for the grace that is to be brought unto you at the revelation of Jesus Christ:	13. Quare succincti lumbis mentis vestræ, sobrii, perfecte sperate in eam quæ ad vos defertur gratiam, in revelatione Jesu Christi;
14. As obedient children, not fashioning yourselves according to the former lusts in your ignorance:	14. Tanquam filii obedientes, non conformati pristinis, quæ in ignorantia vestra regnarunt, cupiditatibus:
15. But as he which hath called you is holy, so be ye holy in all manner of conversation:	15. Sed quemadmodum is qui vos vocavit sanctus est, ita ipsi sancti in tota conversatione reddamini;
16. Because it is written, Be ye holy; for I am holy.	16. Propterea quòd scriptum est, Sancti estote, quia ego sanctus sum. (Lev. xi. 44; xix. 2; xx. 7.)

From the greatness and excellency of grace he draws an exhortation, that it surely behoved them the more readily to receive the grace of God, as the more bountifully he bestowed it upon them. And we must notice the connexion: he had said, that so elevated was the kingdom of Christ, to which the gospel calls us, that even angels in heaven desire to see it; what then ought to be done by us who are in the world? Doubtless, as long as we live on earth, so great is the distance between us and Christ, that in vain he invites us to himself. It is hence necessary for us to put off the image of Adam and to cast aside the whole world and all hinderances, that being thus set at liberty we may rise upwards to Christ. And he exhorted those to whom he wrote, to be prepared and sober, and to hope for the graces offered to them, and also to renounce the world and their former life, and to be conformed to the will of God.[1]

Then the first part of the exhortation is, to gird up the

---

[1] *Pareus* observes, that the Apostle, in this part of the chapter, exhorted the faithful to sobriety, holiness, humility, and brotherly love, by five reasons: 1, because they were the children of God, ver. 14; 2, because God is holy, and requires holiness, ver. 15; 3, because God is no respecter of persons, ver. 17; 4, because of the value of the price for their redemption, ver. 18; and 5, because they had been born again of an immortal seed, ver. 23.—*Ed.*

loins of their mind and to direct their thoughts to the hope of the grace presented to them. In the second part, he prescribes the manner, that having their minds changed, they were to be formed after the image of God.

13. *Wherefore gird up the loins of your mind.* It is a similitude taken from an ancient custom; for when they had long garments, they could not make a journey, nor conveniently do any work, without being girded up. Hence these expressions, to gird up one's-self for a work or an undertaking. He then bids them to remove all impediments, that being set at liberty they might go on to God. Those who philosophize more refinedly about the loins, as though he commanded lusts to be restrained and checked, depart from the real meaning of the Apostle, for these words mean the same with those of Christ, "Let your loins be girded about, and burning lamps in your hands," (Luke xii. 35,) except that Peter doubles the metaphor by ascribing loins to the mind. And he intimates that our minds are held entangled by the passing cares of the world and by vain desires, so that they rise not upward to God. Whosoever, then, really wishes to have this hope, let him learn in the first place to disentangle himself from the world, and gird up his mind that it may not turn aside to vain affections. And for the same purpose he enjoins sobriety, which immediately follows; for he commends not temperance only in eating and drinking, but rather spiritual sobriety, when all our thoughts and affections are so kept as not to be inebriated with the allurements of this world. For since even the least taste of them stealthily draws us away from God, when one plunges himself into these, he must necessarily become sleepy and stupid, and he forgets God and the things of God.

Hope to the end, or, Perfectly hope. He intimates that those who let their minds loose on vanity, did not really and sincerely hope for the grace of God; for though they had some hope, yet as they vacillated and were tossed to and fro in the world, there was no solidity in their hope. Then he says, *for the grace which will be brought to you,* in order that they might be more prompt to receive it. God ought to be sought, though far off; but he comes of his own will to meet us. How great, then, must be our ingratitude if we neglect the grace that is thus set before us! This amplification, then, is especially intended to stimulate our hope.

What he adds, *At the revelation of Jesus Christ,* may be explained in two ways: that the doctrine of the Gospel reveals Christ to us; and that, as we see him as yet only through a mirror and enigmatically, a full revelation is deferred to the last day. The first meaning is approved by Erasmus, nor do I reject it. The second seems, however, to be more suitable to the passage. For the object of Peter was to call us away beyond the world; for this purpose the fittest thing was the recollection of Christ's coming. For when we direct our eyes to this event, this world becomes crucified to us, and we to the world. Besides, according to this meaning, Peter used the expression shortly before. Nor is it a new thing for the apostles to employ the preposition ἐν in the sense of εἰς. Thus, then, I explain the passage,—" You have no need to make a long journey that you may attain the grace of God; for God anticipates you; inasmuch as he brings it to you." But as the fruition of it will not be until Christ appears from heaven, in whom is hid the salvation of the godly, there is need, in the meantime, of hope; for the grace of Christ is now offered to us in vain, except we patiently wait until the coming of Christ.

14. *As obedient children.* He first intimates that we are called by the Lord to the privilege and honour of adoption through the Gospel; and, secondly, that we are adopted for this end, that he might have us as his obedient children. For though obedience does not make us children, as the gift of adoption is gratuitous, yet it distinguishes children from aliens. How far, indeed, this obedience extends, Peter shews, when he forbids God's children to conform to or to comply with the desires of this world, and when he exhorts them, on the contrary, to conform to the will of God. The sum of the whole law, and of all that God requires of us, is this, that his image should shine forth in us, so that we should not be degenerate children. But this cannot be except we be renewed and put off the image of old Adam.

Hence we learn what Christians ought to propose to themselves as an object throughout life, that is, to resemble God in holiness and purity. But as all the thoughts and feelings of our flesh are in opposition to God, and the whole bent of our mind is enmity to him, hence Peter begins with the renunciation of the world; and certainly, whenever the Scripture speaks of the renewal of God's image in us, it begins here, that the old man with his lusts is to be destroyed.

In your ignorance. The time of ignorance he calls that before they were called into the faith of Christ. We hence learn that unbelief is the fountain of all evils. For he does not use the word ignorance, as we commonly do; for that Platonic dogma is false, that ignorance alone is the cause of sin. But yet, how much soever conscience may reprove the unbelieving, nevertheless they go astray as the blind in darkness, because they know not the right way, and they are without the true light. According to this meaning, Paul says, "Ye henceforth walk not as the Gentiles, in the vanity of their mind, who have the mind darkened, being alienated from the life of God, because of the ignorance that is in them." (Eph. iv. 17.) Where the knowledge of God is not, there darkness, error, vanity, destitution of light and life, prevail. These things, however, do not render it impossible that the ungodly should be conscious of doing wrong when they sin, and know that their judge is in heaven, and feel an executioner within them. In short, as the kingdom of God is a kingdom of light, all who are alienated from him must necessarily be blind and go astray in a labyrinth.

We are in the meantime reminded, that we are for this end illuminated as to the knowledge of God, that we may no longer be carried away by roving lusts. Hence, as much progress any one has made in newness of life, so much progress has he made in the knowledge of God.

Here a question arises,—Since he addressed the Jews, who were acquainted with the law, and were brought up in the worship of the only true God, why did he charge them with ignorance and blindness, as though they were heathens? To this I answer, that it hence appears how profitless is all knowledge without Christ. When Paul exposed the vain boasting of those who wished to be wise apart from Christ, he justly said in one short sentence, that they did not hold the head. (Col. ii. 19.) Such were the Jews; being otherwise imbued with numberless corruptions, they had a veil over the eyes, so that they did not see Christ in the Law. The doctrine in which they had been taught was indeed a true light; but they were blind in the midst of light, as long as the Sun of Righteousness was hid to them. But if Peter declares that the literal disciples even of the Law were in darkness like the heathens, as long as they were ignorant of Christ, the only true wisdom of God, with how much greater care it behoves us to strive for the knowledge of him!

15. *He who hath called you is holy.* He reasons from the end for which we are called. God sets us apart as a peculiar people for himself; then we ought to be free from all pollutions. And he quotes a sentence which had been often repeated by Moses. For as the people of Israel were on every side surrounded by heathens, from whom they might have easily adopted the worst examples and innumerable corruptions, the Lord frequently recalled them to himself, as though he had said, "Ye have to do with me, ye are mine; then abstain from the pollutions of the Gentiles." We are too ready to look to men, so as to follow their common way of living. Thus it happens, that some lead others in troops to all kinds of evil, until the Lord by his calling separates them.

In bidding us to be *holy* like himself, the proportion is not that of equals; but we ought to advance in this direction as far as our condition will bear. And as even the most perfect are always very far from coming up to the mark, we ought daily to strive more and more. And we ought to remember that we are not only told what our duty is, but that God also adds, "I am he who sanctify you."

It is added, *In all manner of conversation,* or, in your whole conduct. There is then no part of our life which is not to be redolent with this good odour of holiness. For we see that in the smallest things and almost insignificant, the Lord accustomed his people to the practice of holiness, in order that they might exercise a more diligent care as to themselves.

17. And if ye call on the Father, who without respect of persons judgeth according to every man's work, pass the time of your sojourning *here* in fear:

18. Forasmuch as ye know that ye were not redeemed with corruptible things, *as* silver and gold, from your vain conversation *received* by tradition from your fathers;

19. But with the precious blood of Christ, as of a lamb without blemish and without spot:

20. Who verily was fore-ordained before the foundation of the world, but was manifest in these last times for you,

21. Who by him do believe in God, that raised him up from the dead, and gave him glory; that your faith and hope might be in God.

22. Seeing ye have purified your souls in obeying the truth through the Spirit unto unfeigned love of the brethren, *see that ye* love one another with a pure heart fervently.

17. Et si Patrem invocatis, eum qui sine personæ acceptione secundum cujusque opus judicat, in timore conversantes, tempus incolatus vestri transigite;

18. Scientes quòd non corruptibilibus, argento vel auro, redempti sitis à vana conversatione à patribus tradita;

19. Sed pretioso sanguine velut agni immaculati et incontaminati Christi;

20. Qui præordinatus quidem fuerat ante conditum mundum, manifestatus autem est extremis temporibus propter vos;

21. Qui per ipsum creditis in Deum, qui eum suscitavit ex mortuis, et gloriam illi dedit, ut fides vestra et spes sit in Deum;

22. Purificantes animas vestras in obedientia veritatis per Spiritum, in fraternam charitatem non fictam, ex puro corde diligite vos mutuò impensè.

17. *And if ye call on the Father.* They are said here to call on God the Father, who professed themselves to be his children, as Moses says, that the name of Jacob was called on Ephraim and Manasseh, that they might be counted his children. (Gen. xlviii. 16.) According to this meaning also, we say in French *reclamer.* But he had a regard to what he had said before, "as obedient children." And from the character of the Father himself, he shews what sort of obedience ought to be rendered. He *judges,* he says, *without looking on the person,* that is, no outward mask is of any account with him, as the case is with men, but he sees the heart, (1 Sam. xvi. 7;) and his eyes look on faithfulness. (Jer. v. 3.) This also is what Paul means when he says that God's judgment is according to truth, (Rom. ii. 2;) for he there inveighs against hypocrites, who think that they deceive God by a vain pretence. The meaning is, that we by no means discharge our duty towards God, when we obey

him only in appearance; for he is not a mortal man, whom the outward appearance pleases, but he reads what we are inwardly in our hearts. He not only prescribes laws for our feet and hands, but he also requires what is just and right as to the mind and spirit.

By saying, *According to every man's work,* he does not refer to merit or to reward; for Peter does not speak here of the merits of works, nor of the cause of salvation, but he only reminds us, that there will be no looking to the person before the tribunal of God, but that what will be regarded will be the real sincerity of the heart. In this place faith also is included in the work. It hence appears evident how foolish and puerile is the inference that is drawn,—" God is such that he judges every one of us by the integrity of his conscience, not by the outward appearance; then we obtain salvation by works."

The *fear* that is mentioned, stands opposed to heedless security, such as is wont to creep in, when there is a hope of deceiving with impunity. For, as God's eyes are such that they penetrate into the hidden recesses of the heart, we ought to walk with him carefully and not negligently. He calls the present life a *sojourning,* not in the sense in which he called the Jews to whom he was writing sojourners, at the beginning of the Epistle, but because all the godly are in this world pilgrims. (Heb. xi. 13, 38.)

18. *Forasmuch as ye know,* or, knowing. Here is another reason, drawn from the price of our redemption, which ought always to be remembered when our salvation is spoken of. For to him who repudiates or despises the grace of the gospel, not only his own salvation is worthless, but also the blood of Christ, by which God has manifested its value. But we know how dreadfully sacrilegious it is to regard as common the blood of the Son of God. There is hence nothing which ought so much to stimulate us to the practice of holiness, as the memory of this price of our redemption.

Silver and gold. For the sake of amplifying he mentions these things in contrast, so that we may know that the whole world, and all things deemed precious by men, are nothing to the excellency and value of this price.

But he says that they had been *redeemed from* their *vain conversation*,[1] in order that we might know that the whole life of man, until he is converted to Christ, is a ruinous labyrinth of wanderings. He also intimates, that it is not through our merits that we are restored to the right way, but because it is God's will that the price, offered for our salvation, should be effectual in our behalf. Then the blood of Christ is not only the pledge of our salvation, but also the cause of our calling.

Moreover, Peter warns us to beware lest our unbelief should render this price void or of no effect. As Paul boasts that he worshipped God with a pure conscience from his forefathers, (1 Tim. i. 3,) and as he also commends to Timothy for his imitation the piety of his grandmother Lois, and of his mother Eunice, (2 Tim. i. 5,) and as Christ also said of the Jews that they knew whom they worshipped (John iv. 22,) it may seem strange that Peter should assert that the Jews of his time learnt nothing from their fathers but mere vanity. To this I answer, that Christ, when he declared that the way or the knowledge of true religion belonged to the Jews, referred to the law and the commandments of God rather than to the people; for the temple had not to no purpose been built at Jerusalem, nor was God worshipped there according to the fancies of men, but according to what was prescribed in the Law; he, therefore, said that the Jews were not going astray while observing the Law. As to Paul's forefathers, and as to Lois, Eunice, and similar cases, there is no doubt but that God ever had at least a small remnant among that people, in whom sincere piety continued, while the body of the people had become wholly corrupt, and had plunged themselves into all kinds of errors. Innumerable superstitions were followed, hypocrisy prevailed, the hope of salvation was built on the merest trifles; they were not only imbued with false opinions, but also fascinated with the grossest dotages; and

---

[1] The verb λυτρόω means properly to redeem by a price from tyranny or bondage, but its meaning here, and in Luke xxiv. 21, and Tit. ii. 14, is merely to deliver. "Vain conversation" signifies a useless, profitless mode of living.—*Ed.*

they who had been scattered to various parts of the world, were implicated in still greater corruptions. In short, the greater part of that nation had either wholly fallen away from true religion, or had much degenerated. When, therefore, Peter condemned the doctrine of the fathers, he viewed it as unconnected with Christ, who is the soul and the truth of the Law.

But we hence learn, that as soon as men depart from Christ, they go fatally astray. In vain is pretended in this case the authority of the Fathers or an ancient custom. For the Prophet Ezekiel cried to the Jews, "Walk ye not in the statutes of your fathers." (Ezek. xx. 18.) This ought also to be no less attended to by us in the present day; for, in order that the redemption of Christ may be effectual and useful to us, we must renounce our former life, though derived from the teaching and practice of our fathers. Thrice foolish, then, are the Papists, who think that the name of Fathers is a sufficient defence for all their superstitions, so that they boldly reject whatever is brought forward from the Word of God.

19. *As of a lamb.* He means by this similitude, that we have in Christ whatever had been shadowed forth by the ancient sacrifices, though he especially alludes to the Paschal lamb. But let us hence learn what benefit the reading of the Law brings us in this respect; for, though the rite of sacrificing is abolished, yet it assists our faith not a little, to compare the reality with the type, so that we may seek in the former what the latter contains. Moses ordered a whole or perfect lamb, without blemish, to be chosen for the Passover. The same thing is often repeated as to the sacrifices, as in Leviticus, the third and twenty-second chapters; in Numbers, the twenty-eighth chapter; and in other places. Peter, by applying this to Christ, teaches us that he was a suitable victim, and approved by God, for he was perfect, without any blemish; had he had any defect in him, he could not have been rightly offered to God, nor could he pacify his wrath.

20. *Who verily was foreordained.* He again by a comparison amplifies the grace of God, with which he had

peculiarly favoured the men of that age. For it was not a common or a small favour that God deferred the manifestation of Christ to that time, when yet he had ordained him in his eternal council for the salvation of the world. At the same time, however, he reminds us, that it was not a new or a sudden thing as to God that Christ appeared as a Saviour; and this is what ought especially to be known. For, in addition to this, that novelty is always suspicious, what would be the stability of our faith, if we believed that a remedy for mankind had suddenly occurred at length to God after some thousands of years? In short, we cannot confidently recumb on Christ, except we are convinced that eternal salvation is in him, and always has been in him. Besides, Peter addressed the Jews, who had heard that he had already been long ago promised; and though they understood nothing true or clear or certain respecting his power and office, yet there remained among them a persuasion, that a Redeemer had been promised by God to the fathers.

It may yet be asked, As Adam did not fall before the creation of the world, how was it that Christ had been appointed the Redeemer? for a remedy is posterior to the disease. My reply is, that this is to be referred to God's foreknowledge; for doubtless God, before he created man, foresaw that he would not stand long in his integrity. Hence he ordained, according to his wonderful wisdom and goodness, that Christ should be the Redeemer, to deliver the lost race of man from ruin. For herein shines forth more fully the unspeakable goodness of God, that he anticipated our disease by the remedy of his grace, and provided a restoration to life before the first man had fallen into death. If the reader wishes for more on this subject, he may find it in my Institutes.

But was manifest, or manifested. Included in these words, as I think, is not only the personal appearance of Christ, but also the proclamation of the Gospel. For, by the coming of Christ, God executed what he had decreed; and what he had obscurely indicated to the fathers is now clearly and plainly made known to us by the Gospel. He says that this was done *in these last times*, meaning the same as when Paul says, "In the fulness of time," (Gal. iv. 4;) for it was the mature season and the full time which God in his counsel had appointed. *For you.* He does not exclude the fathers, to whom the promise had not been useless; but as God has favoured us more than them, he intimates that the greater the amplitude of grace towards us, the more reverence and ardour and care are required of us.

21. *Who believe.* The manifestation of Christ refers not to all indiscriminately, but belongs to those only on whom he by the Gospel shines. But we must notice the words, *Who by him believe in God:* here is shortly expressed what faith is. For, since God is incomprehensible, faith could never reach to him, except it had an immediate regard to Christ. Nay, there are two reasons why faith could not be in God, except Christ intervened as a Mediator: first, the greatness of the divine glory must be taken to the account, and at the same time the littleness of our capacity. Our acuteness is doubtless very far from being capable of ascending so high as to comprehend God. Hence all knowledge of God without Christ is a vast abyss which immediately swallows up all our thoughts. A clear proof of this we have, not only in the Turks and the Jews, who in the place of God worship their own dreams, but also in the Papists. Common is that axiom of the schools, that God is the object of faith. Thus of hidden majesty, Christ being overlooked, they largely and refinedly speculate; but with what success? They entangle themselves in astounding dotages, so that there is no end to their wanderings. For faith, as they think, is nothing else but an imaginative speculation. Let us, therefore, remember, that Christ is not in vain called the image of the invisible God, (Col. i. 15;) but this name is given to him for this reason, because God cannot be known except in him.

The second reason is, that as faith unites us to God, we shun and dread every access to him, except a Mediator comes who can deliver us from fear. For sin, which reigns in us, renders us hateful to God and him to us. Hence, as soon as mention is made of God, we must necessarily be filled with dread; and if we approach him, his justice is like fire, which will wholly consume us.

It is hence evident that we cannot believe in God except through Christ, in whom God in a manner makes himself little, that he might accommodate himself to our comprehension; and it is Christ alone who can tranquillize consciences, so that we may dare to come in confidence to God.

That raised him up from the dead. He adds, that Christ had been raised up from the dead, in order that their faith and hope, by which they were supported, might have a firm foundation. And hereby again is confuted the gloss respecting universal and indiscriminate faith in God; for had there been no resurrection of Christ, still God would remain in heaven. But Peter says that he would not have been believed in, except Christ had risen. It is then evident, that faith is something else than to behold the naked majesty of God. And rightly does Peter speak in this manner; for it belongs to faith to penetrate into heaven, that it may find the Father there: how could it do so, except it had Christ as a leader? "By him," says Paul, "we have confidence of access." (Eph. iii. 12.) It is said also, in Heb. iv. 16, that relying on our high priest, we can come with confidence to the throne of grace. Hope is the anchor of the soul, which enter into the inner part of the sanctuary; but not without Christ going before. (Heb. vi. 19.) Faith is our victory against the world, (1 John v. 4:) and what is it that makes it victorious, except that Christ, the Lord of heaven and earth, has us under his guardianship and protection?

As, then, our salvation depends on the resurrection of Christ and his supreme power, faith and hope find here what can support them. For, except he had by rising again triumphed over death, and held now the highest sovereignty, to protect us by his power, what would become of us, exposed to so great a power as that of our enemies, and to such violent attacks? Let us, therefore, learn to what mark we ought to direct our aim, so that we may really believe in God.

22. *Seeing ye have purified your souls*, or, Purifying your souls. Erasmus badly renders the words, "Who have puri-

fied," &c. For Peter does not declare what they had done, but reminds them of what they ought to do. The participle is indeed in the past tense, but it may be rendered as a gerund, " By purifying, &c." The meaning is, that their souls would not be capable of receiving grace until they were purified, and by this our uncleanness is proved.[1] But that he might not seem to ascribe to us the power of purifying our souls, he immediately adds, *through the Spirit;* as though he had said, " Your souls are to be purified, but as ye cannot do this, offer them to God, that he may take away your filth by his Spirit." He only mentions souls, though they needed to be cleansed also from the defilements of the flesh, as Paul bids the Corinthians, (2 Cor. vii. 1;) but as the principal uncleanness is within, and necessarily draws with it that which is outward, Peter was satisfied with mentioning only the former, as though he had said, that not outward actions only ought to be corrected, but the very hearts ought to be thoroughly reformed.

He afterwards points out the manner, for purity of soul consists in obedience to God. *Truth* is to be taken for the rule which God prescribes to us in the Gospel. Nor does he speak only of works, but rather faith holds here the primacy. Hence Paul specially teaches us in the first and last chapter of the Epistle to the Romans, that faith is that by which we obey God; and Peter in Acts, the fifteenth chapter, bestows on it this eulogy, that God by it purifies the heart.

Unto love of the brethren, or, Unto brotherly love. He briefly reminds us what God especially requires in our life, and the mark to which all our endeavours should be directed. So Paul in the first chapter of the Epistle to the Ephesians, when speaking of the perfection of the faithful, makes it to consist in love. And this is what we ought the more carefully to notice, because the world makes its own sanctity to

---

[1] It is better to keep the tense of the participle,—" Having purified (or, since ye have purified) your souls by obeying the truth through the Spirit to an unfeigned love of the brethren, love ye one another fervently from a pure heart; having been born again," &c.

The order here is similar to what is often found in Scripture; purification is mentioned before regeneration, as being the most visible and the effect; then what goes before it as being in a manner the cause.—*Ed.*

consist of the veriest trifles, and almost overlooks this the chief thing. We see how the Papists weary themselves beyond measure with thousand invented superstitions: in the meantime, the last thing is that love which God especially commends. This, then, is the reason why Peter calls our attention to it, when speaking of a life rightly formed.

He had before spoken of the mortification of the flesh, and of our conformity with the will of God; but he now reminds us of what God would have us to cultivate through life, that is, mutual love towards one another; for by that we testify also that we love God; and by this evidence God proves who they are who really love him.

He calls it *unfeigned*, (ἀνυπόκριτον,) as Paul calls faith in 1 Tim. i. 5; for nothing is more difficult than to love our neighbours in sincerity. For the love of ourselves rules, which is full of hypocrisy; and besides, every one measures his love, which he shews to others, by his own advantage, and not by the rule of doing good. He adds, *fervently;* for the more slothful we are by nature, the more ought every one to stimulate himself to fervour and earnestness, and that not only once, but more and more daily.

23. Being born again, not of corruptible seed, but of incorruptible, by the word of God, which liveth and abideth for ever.	23. Regeniti non ex semine corruptibili, sed incorruptibili, per sermonem viventis Dei et manentis in æternum.
24. For all flesh *is* as grass, and all the glory of man as the flower of grass. The grass withereth, and the flower thereof falleth away:	24. Quandoquidem omnis caro tanquam herba, et omnis gloria ejus tanquam flos herbæ; exaruit herba et flos ejus decidit:
25. But the word of the Lord endureth for ever. And this is the word which by the gospel is preached unto you.	25. Verbum autem Domini manet in æternum; hoc autem est verbum quod annuntiatum est vobis.

23. *Being born again.* Here is another reason for an exhortation,—that since they were new men and born again of God, it behoved them to form a life worthy of God and of their spiritual regeneration. And this seems to be connected with a verse in the next chapter respecting the milk of the word, which they were to seek, that their way of living might correspond with their birth. It may, however, be extended wider, so as to be connected also with what has gone before; for Peter collected together those things

which may lead us to an upright and a holy life. The object, then, of Peter was to teach us that we cannot be Christians without regeneration; for the Gospel is not preached, that it may be only heard by us, but that it may, as a seed of immortal life, altogether reform our hearts.[1] Moreover, the *corruptible seed* is set in opposition to God's word, in order that the faithful might know that they ought to renounce their former nature, and that it might be more evident how much is the difference between the children of Adam who are born only into the world, and the children of God who are renewed into a heavenly life. But as the construction of the Greek text is doubtful, we may read, "the living word of God," as well as, "the word of the living God." As, however, the latter reading is less forced, I prefer it; though it must be observed, that the term is applied to God owing to the character of the passage. For, as in Heb. iv. 12, because God sees all things, and nothing is hid from him, the apostle argues that the word of God penetrates into the inmost marrow, so as to discern thoughts and feelings; so, when Peter in this place calls him the living God, who abides for ever, he refers to the word, in which the perpetuity of God shines forth as in a living mirror.

24. *For all flesh.* He aptly quotes the passage from Isaiah to prove both clauses; that is, to make it evident how fading and miserable is the first birth of man, and how great is the grace of the new birth. For as the Prophet there speaks of the restoration of the Church, to prepare

---

[1] Most commentators, like *Calvin*, represent the *seed* as the word; but the construction does not admit this; the words are, "Having been begotten from a seed, not corruptible, but incorruptible, through the living word of God, and for-ever abiding." The "seed" denotes evidently the vital principle of grace, the new nature, the restored image of God; it is the same with what John means when he says, "His seed (that is, of God) remaineth in him." (1 John iii. 9.) Then "the word" is set forth as the means or instrument by which this seed is implanted. The "living" here does not mean life-giving, as some interpret it, but stands opposed to what ceases to be valid: and "for-ever abiding" more fully expresses its meaning. The metaphor in the parable of the sower is quite different: the word there is compared to a seed sown on bad or good ground; but here the turning of a bad into a good ground is the subject; and in this process the word is employed as an instrument.—*Ed.*

the way for it, he reduces men to nothing lest they should flatter themselves. I know that the words are wrongly turned by some to another sense; for some explain them of the Assyrians, as though the Prophet said, that there was no reason for the Jews to fear so much from flesh, which is like a fading flower. Others think that the vain confidence which the Jews reposed in human aids, is reproved. But the Prophet himself disproves both these views, by adding, that the people were as grass; for he expressly condemns the Jews for vanity, to whom he promised restoration in the name of the Lord. This, then, is what I have already said, that until their own emptiness has been shewn to men, they are not prepared to receive the grace of God. In short, such is the meaning of the Prophet: as exile was to the Jews like death, he promised them a new consolation, even that God would send prophets with a command of this kind. The Lord, he says, will yet say, "Comfort ye my people;" and that in the desert and the waste, the prophetic voice would yet be heard, in order that a way might be prepared for the Lord. (Isaiah xl. 6.)

And as the obstinate pride which filled them, must have been necessarily purged from their minds, in order that an access might be open for God, the Prophet added what Peter relates here respecting the vanishing glory of the flesh. What is man? he says—grass; what is the glory of man? the flower of the grass. For as it was difficult to believe that man, in whom so much excellency appears, is like grass, the Prophet made a kind of concession, as though he had said, "Be it, indeed, that flesh has some glory; but lest that should dazzle your eyes, know that the flower soon withers." He afterwards shews how suddenly everything that seems beautiful in men vanishes, even through the blowing of the Spirit of God; and by this he intimates, that man seems to be something until he comes to God, but that his whole brightness is as nothing in his presence; that, in a word, his glory is in this world, and has no place in the heavenly kingdom.

The grass withereth, or, has withered. Many think that this refers only to the outward man; but they are mistaken; for we must consider the comparison between God's word and man. For if he meant only the body and what belongs to the present life, he ought to have said, in the second place, that the soul was far more excellent. But what he sets in opposition to the grass and its flower, is the word of God. It then follows, that in man nothing but vanity is found. Therefore, when Isaiah spoke of flesh and its glory, he meant the whole man, such as he is in himself; for what he ascribed as peculiar to God's word, he denied to man. In short, the Prophet speaks of the same thing as Christ does in John iii. 3, that man is wholly alienated from the kingdom of God, that he is nothing but an earthly, fading, and empty creature, until he is born again.

25. *But the word of God.* The Prophet does not shew what the word of God is in itself, but what we ought to think of it; for since man is vanity in himself, it remains that he ought to seek life elsewhere. Hence Peter ascribes power and efficacy to God's word, according to the authority of the Prophet, so that it can confer on us what is real, solid, and eternal. For this was what the Prophet had in view, that there is no permanent life but in God, and that this is communicated to us by the word. However fading, then, is the nature of man, yet he is made eternal by the word; for he is re-moulded and becomes a new creature.

This is the word which by the gospel is preached unto you, or, which has been declared to you. He first reminds us, that when the word of God is mentioned, we are very foolish if we imagine it to be remote from us in the air or in heaven; for we ought to know that it has been revealed to us by the Lord. What, then, is this word of the Lord, which gives us life? Even the Law, the Prophets, the Gospel. Those who wander beyond these limits of revelation, find nothing but the impostures of Satan and his dotages, and not the word of the Lord. We ought the more carefully to notice this, because impious and Luciferian men, craftily allowing to God's word its own honour, at the same time attempt to draw us away from the Scriptures, as that unprincipled man, Agrippa, who highly extols the eternity of God's word, and yet treats with scurrility the Prophets, and thus indirectly laughs to scorn the Word of God.

In short, as I have already reminded you, no mention is here made of the word which lies hid in the bosom of God, but of that which has proceeded from his mouth, and has come to us. So again it ought to be borne in mind, that God designed by the Apostles and Prophets to speak to us, and their mouths is the mouth of the only true God.

Then, when Peter says, *Which has been announced*, or declared, *to you*, he intimates that the word is not to be sought elsewhere than in the Gospel preached to us ; and truly we know not the way of eternal life otherwise than by faith. But there can be no faith, except we know that the word is destined for us.

To the same purpose is what Moses said to the people, "Say not in thine heart, Who shall ascend into heaven, &c. ; nigh is the word, in thy mouth and in thy heart." (Deut. xxx. 12.) That these words agree with what Peter says, Paul shews in Rom. x. 6, where he teaches us that it was the word of faith which he preached.

There is here, besides, no common eulogy on preaching ; for Peter declares that what is preached is the life-giving word. God alone is indeed he who regenerates us ; but for that purpose he employs the ministry of men ; and on this account Paul glories that the Corinthians had been spiritually begotten by him. (1 Cor. iv. 15.) It is indeed certain that those who plant and those who water, are nothing ; but whenever God is pleased to bless their labour, he makes their doctrine efficacious by the power of his Spirit ; and the voice which is in itself mortal, is made an instrument to communicate eternal life.

CHAPTER II.

1. Wherefore, laying aside all malice, and all guile, and hypocrisies, and envies, and all evil speakings,

2. As new-born babes, desire the sincere milk of the word, that ye may grow thereby;

1. Proinde deposita omni malitia et omni dolo et simulationibus et invidiis et omnibus obtrectationibus,

2. Tanquam modò geniti infantes, lac rationale et dolo vacuum appetite, ut per illud subolescatis :

3. If so be ye have tasted that the Lord *is* gracious:	3. Si quidem gustastis quòd benignus sit Dominus;
4. To whom coming, *as unto* a living stone, disallowed indeed of men, but chosen of God, *and* precious,	4. Ad quem accedentes, qui est lapis vivus, ab hominibus quidem reprobatus, apud Deum vero electus ac pretiosus;
5. Ye also, as lively stones, are built up a spiritual house, an holy priesthood, to offer up spiritual sacrifices, acceptable to God by Jesus Christ.	5. Ipsi quoque tanquam vivi lapides, ædificamini, domus spiritualis, sacerdotium sanctum, ad offerendas spirituales hostias, acceptas Deo per Jesum Christum.

After having taught the faithful that they had been regenerated by the word of God, he now exhorts them to lead a life corresponding with their birth. For if we live in the Spirit, we ought also to walk in the Spirit, as Paul says. (Gal. v. 25.) It is not, then, sufficient for us to have been once called by the Lord, except we live as new creatures. This is the meaning. But as to the words, the Apostle continues the same metaphor. For as we have been born again, he requires from us a life like that of infants; by which he intimates that we are to put off the old man and his works. Hence this verse agrees with what Christ says, "Except ye become like this little child, ye shall not enter into the kingdom of God." (Matt. xviii. 2.)

Infancy is here set by Peter in opposition to the ancientness of the flesh, which leads to corruption; and under the word *milk*, he includes all the feelings of spiritual life. For there is also in part a contrast between the vices which he enumerates and the sincere milk of the word; as though he had said, "Malice and hypocrisy belong to those who are habituated to the corruptions of the world; they have imbibed these vices: what pertains to infancy is sincere simplicity, free from all guile. Men, when grown up, become imbued with envy, they learn to slander one another, they are taught the arts of mischief; in short, they become hardened in every kind of evil: infants, owing to their age, do not yet know what it is to envy, to do mischief, or the like things." He then compares the vices, in which the oldness of the flesh indulges, to strong food; and milk is called that way of living suitable to innocent nature and simple infancy.

1. *All malice.* There is not here a complete enumeration of all those things which we ought to lay aside; but when

the Apostles speak of the old man, they lay down as examples some of those vices which mark his whole character. "Known," says Paul, "are the works of the flesh, which are these," (Gal. v. 19;) and yet he does not enumerate them all; but in those few things, as in a mirror, we may see that immense mass of filth which proceeds from our flesh. So also in other passages, where he refers to the new life, he touches only on a few things, by which we may understand the whole character.

What, then, he says amounts to this,—"Having laid aside the works of your former life, such as malice, deceit, dissimulations, envyings, and other things of this kind, devote yourselves to things of an opposite character, cultivate kindness, honesty," &c. He, in short, urges this, that new morals ought to follow a new life.

2. *The sincere milk of the word.* This passage is commonly explained according to the rendering of Erasmus, "Milk not for the body but for the soul;" as though the Apostle reminded us by this expression that he spoke metaphorically. I rather think that this passage agrees with that saying of Paul, "Be ye not children in understanding, but in malice." (1 Cor. xiv. 20.) That no one might think that infancy, void of understanding and full of fatuity, was commended by him, he in due time meets this objection; so he bids them to desire milk free from guile, and yet mixed with right understanding. We now see for what purpose he joins these two words, *rational and guileless,* (λογικὸν καὶ ἄδολον.) For simplicity and quickness of understanding are two things apparently opposite; but they ought to be mixed together, lest simplicity should become insipid, and lest malicious craftiness should creep in for want of understanding. This mingling, well regulated, is according to what Christ says, "Be ye wise as serpents, and harmless as doves." (Matt. x. 16.) And thus is solved the question which might have been otherwise raised.[1]

---

[1] Our version here seems to convey the most suitable meaning, by taking λογικὸν for τοῦ λόγου; see similar instances in ver. 13 and chap. iii. 7. It is the wordy milk, or milk made up of the word; the word is the milk. Then ἄδολον is to be taken in its secondary meaning: when applied to per-

Paul reproves the Corinthians because they were like children, and therefore they could not take strong food, but were fed with milk. (1 Cor. iii. 1.) Almost the same words are found in Heb. v. 12. But in these passages those are compared to children who remain always novices and ignorant scholars in the doctrine of religion, who continued in the first elements, and never penetrated into the higher knowledge of God. *Milk* is called the simpler mode of teaching, and one suitable to children, when there is no progress made beyond the first rudiments. Justly, then, does Paul charge this as a fault, as well as the author of the Epistle to the Hebrews. But milk, here, is not elementary doctrine, which one perpetually learns; and never comes to the knowledge of the truth, but a mode of living which has the savour of the new birth, when we surrender ourselves to be brought up by God. In the same manner infancy is not set in opposition to manhood, or full age in Christ, as Paul calls it in Eph. iv. 13, but to the ancientness of the flesh and of former life. Moreover, as the infancy of the new life is perpetual, so Peter recommends milk as a perpetual aliment, for he would have those nourished by it to grow.

3. *If so be that ye have tasted;* or, If indeed ye have tasted. He alludes to Ps. xxxiv. 8, " Taste and see that the Lord is good." But he says that this taste is to be had in Christ, as, doubtless, our souls can find no rest anywhere but in him. But he has drawn the ground of his exhortation from the goodness of God, because his kindness, which we perceive in Christ, ought to allure us ; for what follows,

To whom coming, is not to be referred simply to God, but to him as he is revealed to us in the person of Christ. Now, it cannot be but that the grace of God must powerfully draw

---

sons, it means undeceitful, or guileless; but when to things, genuine, pure, unadulterated, unmixed with anything deleterious. We may, therefore, render the words, " Desire the pure milk of the word." It is a milk not adulterated by water or by anything poisonous. There is no contrast here between milk and strong food; but it includes all that is necessary as an aliment for the soul, when renewed. The Word had before been represented as the instrument of the new birth; it is now spoken of as the food and aliment of the new-born.—*Ed.*

us to himself and inflame us with the love of him by whom we obtain a real perception of it. If Plato affirmed this of his Beautiful, of which a shadowy idea only he beheld afar off, much more true is this with regard to God.

Let it then be noticed, that Peter connects an access to God with the taste of his goodness. For as the human mind necessarily dreads and shuns God, as long as it regards him as rigid and severe; so, as soon as he makes known his paternal love to the faithful, it immediately follows that they disregard all things and even forget themselves and hasten to him. In short, he only makes progress in the Gospel, who in heart comes to God.

But he also shews for what end and to what purpose we ought to come to Christ, even that we may have him as our foundation. For since he is constituted a stone, he ought to be so to us, so that nothing should be appointed for him by the Father in vain or to no purpose. But he obviates an offence when he allows that Christ is rejected by men; for, as a great part of the world reject him, and even many abhor him, he might for this reason be despised by us; for we see that some of the ignorant are alienated from the Gospel, because it is not everywhere popular, nor does it conciliate favour to its professors. But Peter forbids us to esteem Christ the less, however despised he may be by the world, because he, notwithstanding, retains his own worth and honour before God.

5. *Ye also, as lively* or *living stones, are built up.* The verb may be in the imperative as well as in the indicative mood, for the termination in Greek is ambiguous. But in whatever way it is taken, Peter no doubt meant to exhort the faithful to consecrate themselves as a spiritual temple to God; for he aptly infers from the design of our calling what our duty is. We must further observe, that he constructs one house from the whole number of the faithful. For though every one of us is said to be the temple of God, yet all are united together in one, and must be joined together by mutual love, so that one temple may be made of us all. Then, as it is true that each one is a temple in which God dwells by his Spirit, so all ought to be so fitted together,

that they may form one universal temple. This is the case when every one, content with his own measure, keeps himself within the limits of his own duty; all have, however, something to do with regard to others.

By calling us *living stones* and *spiritual* building, as he had before said that Christ is a living stone, he intimates a comparison between us and the ancient temple; and this serves to amplify divine grace. For the same purpose is what he adds as to *spiritual sacrifices*. For by how much the more excellent is the reality than the types, by so much the more all things excel in the kingdom of Christ; for we have that heavenly exemplar, to which the ancient sanctuary was conformable, and everything instituted by Moses under the Law.

A holy priesthood. It is a singular honour, that God should not only consecrate us as a temple to himself, in which he dwells and is worshipped, but that he should also make us priests. But Peter mentions this double honour, in order to stimulate us more effectually to serve and worship God. Of the spiritual sacrifices, the first is the offering of ourselves, of which Paul speaks in Romans xii. 1; for we can offer nothing, until we offer to him ourselves as a sacrifice; which is done by denying ourselves. Then, afterwards follow prayers, thanksgiving, almsdeeds, and all the duties of religion.

Acceptable to God. It ought also to add not a little to our alacrity, when we know that the worship we perform to God is pleasing to him, as doubt necessarily brings sloth with it. Here, then, is the third thing that enforces the exhortation; for he declares that what is required is acceptable to God, lest fear should make us slothful. Idolaters are indeed under the influence of great fervour in their fictitious forms of worship; but it is so, because Satan inebriates their minds, lest they should come to consider their works; but whenever their consciences are led to examine things, they begin to stagger. It is, indeed, certain that no one will seriously and from the heart devote himself to God, until he is fully persuaded that he shall not labour in vain.

But the Apostle adds, *through Jesus Christ.* There is

never found in our sacrifices such purity, that they are of themselves acceptable to God; our self-denial is never entire and complete, our prayers are never so sincere as they ought to be, we are never so zealous and so diligent in doing good, but that our works are imperfect, and mingled with many vices. Nevertheless, Christ procures favour for them. Then Peter here obviates that want of faith which we may have respecting the acceptableness of our works, when he says, that they are accepted, not for the merit of their own excellency, but through Christ. And it ought to kindle the more the ardour of our efforts, when we hear that God deals so indulgently with us, that in Christ he sets a value on our works, which in themselves deserve nothing. At the same time, the words, *by* or through *Christ*, may be fitly connected with offering; for a similar phrase is found in Heb. xiii. 15, "Through him let us offer the sacrifice of praise to God." The sense, however, will remain the same; for we offer sacrifices through Christ, that they may be acceptable to God.

6. Wherefore also it is contained in the Scripture, Behold, I lay in Sion a chief corner stone, elect, precious: and he that believeth on him shall not be confounded.
7. Unto you therefore which believe *he is* precious: but unto them which be disobedient, the stone which the builders disallowed, the same is made the head of the corner,
8. And a stone of stumbling, and a rock of offence, *even to them* which stumble at the word, being disobedient; whereunto also they were appointed.

6. Propterea etiam continet scriptura, Ecce pono in Sion lapidem angularem, electum, pretiosum, et qui crediderit in illo, non pudefiet.
7. Vobis ergo qui creditis, pretiosus; incredulis vero, Lapis quem reprobaverunt ædificantes, hic positus est in caput anguli;
8. Et Lapis impactionis, et petra offendiculi iis qui impingunt in Sermonem, nec credunt; in quod etiam ordinati fuerant.

6. *Wherefore also it is contained in Scripture;* or, Wherefore also the Scripture contains.[1] They who refer the verb "contain" (περιέχειν) to Christ, and render it "embrace," because through him all these unite together, wholly depart from the meaning of the Apostle. No better is another

---

[1] Several copies have ἡ γραφὴ instead of ἐν τῇ γραφῇ; and this reading *Calvin* has followed. But the verb περιέχω is used by *Josephus* and others in a passive sense.—*Ed.*

exposition, that Christ excels others ; for Peter simply intended to quote the testimony of Scripture.[1] He then shews what had been taught by the Holy Spirit in the Scriptures, or, which is the same thing, that what he adds is contained in them. Nor is it an unsuitable confirmation of the preceding verse. For we see for what slight reasons, and almost for none, many reject Christ, and some fall away from him ; but this is a stumblingblock which above all other things stands in the way of some ; they are drawn away, because not only the common people despise and reject Christ, but also those who are high in dignity and honour, and seem to excel others. This evil has almost ever prevailed in the world, and at this day it prevails much ; for a great part of mankind judge of Christ according to the false opinion of the world. Moreover, such is the ingratitude and impiety of men, that Christ is everywhere despised. Thus it is, that while they regard one another, few pay him his due honour. Hence Peter reminds us of what had been foretold of Christ, lest the contempt or the rejection of him should move us from the faith.

Now, the first passage, which he adduces, is taken from Isaiah xxviii. 16 ; where the Prophet, after having inveighed against the desperate wickedness of his own nation, at length adds, "Your perfidy shall not prevent God from restoring his church, which now through you lies wholly in a ruinous state." The manner of restoration he thus describes, "I will lay in Sion a stone." We hence learn that there is no building up of the Church without Christ ; for there is no other foundation but he, as Paul testifies, (1 Cor. iii. 11.) This is no matter of wonder, for all our salvation is found only in him. Whosoever, then, turns away from him in the least degree, will find his foundation a precipice.

Therefore the Prophet not only calls him a corner-stone, which connects the whole edifice, but also a stone of trial, according to which the building is to be measured and regulated ; and farther, he calls him a solid foundation,

---

[1] The quotation is not exactly either from the Hebrew or from the *Sept*. The Apostle seems to have taken what was suitable to his purpose.—*Ed*.

which sustains the whole edifice. He is thus, then, a corner-stone, that he might be the rule of the building, as well as the only foundation. But Peter took from the words of the Prophet what was especially suitable to his argument, even that he was a chosen stone, and in the highest degree valuable and excellent, and also that on him we ought to build. This honour is ascribed to Christ, that how much soever he may be despised by the world, he may not be despised by us; for by God he is regarded as very precious. But when he calls him a corner-stone, he intimates that those have no concern for their salvation who do not recumb on Christ. What some have refined on the word "corner," as though it meant that Christ joins together Jews and Gentiles, as two distinct walls, is not well founded. Let us, then, be content with a simple explanation, that he is so called, because the weight of the building rests on him.

We must further observe, that the Prophet introduces God as the speaker, for he alone forms and plans his own Church, as it is said in Psalm lxxviii. 69, that his hand had founded Sion. He, indeed, employs the labour and ministry of men in building it; but this is not inconsistent with the truth that it is his own work. Christ, then, is the foundation of our salvation, because he has been ordained for this end by the Father.

And he says *in Sion*, because there God's spiritual temple was to have its beginning. That our faith, therefore, may firmly rest on Christ, we must come to the Law and to the Prophets. For though this stone extends to the extreme parts of the world, it was yet necessary for it to be located first in Sion, for there at that time was the seat of the Church. But it is said to have been then set, when the Father revealed him for the purpose of restoring his Church. In short, we must hold this, that those only rest on Christ, who keep the unity of the Church, for he is not set as a foundation-stone except in Sion. As from Sion the Church went forth, which is now everywhere spread, so also from Sion our faith has derived its beginning, as Isaiah says, "From Sion shall go forth the law, and the word of the

Lord from Jerusalem." (Isa. ii. 3.) Corresponding with this is what is said in the Psalms, "The sceptre of thy power will the Lord send forth from Sion." (Ps. cx. 2.)

He that believeth. The Prophet does not say *in him,* but declares generally, "He that believeth shall not make haste." As, however, there is no doubt but that God sets forth Christ there as the object of our faith, the faith of which the Prophet speaks must look on him alone. And, doubtless, no one can rightly believe, but he who is fully convinced that in Christ he ought wholly to trust.

But the words of the Prophet may be taken in two ways, either as a promise or as an exhortation. The future time is referred to, "He shall not make haste;" but in Hebrew the future is often to be taken for an imperative, "Let him not make haste." Thus the meaning would be, "Be ye not moved in your minds, but quietly entertain your desires, and check your feelings, until the Lord will be pleased to fulfil his promise." So he says in another place, "In silence and in quietness shall be your strength," (Isaiah xxx. 15.) But as the other reading seems to come nearer to Peter's interpretation, I give it the preference. Then the sense would not be unsuitable, "He who believeth shall not waver" or vacillate; for he has a firm and permanent foundation. And it is a valuable truth, that relying on Christ, we are beyond the danger of falling. Moreover, to be ashamed (*pudefieri*) means the same thing. Peter has retained the real sense of the Prophet, though he has followed the Greek version.[1]

7. *Unto you therefore which believe.* God having pronounced Christ to be a precious and a chosen stone, Peter draws the inference that he is so to us. For, no doubt, Christ is there described such as we apprehend him by faith, and such as he proves himself to be by real evidences. We ought, then, carefully to notice this inference: Christ is a

---

[1] As to this verb he has, but in the previous parts he comes nearer to the Hebrew than to the *Sept.* Paul quotes this sentence twice, Rom. ix. 33; x. 11, and follows the *Sept.* as Peter does. Indeed, the difference between יחיש, he shall make haste, and יבש, he shall be ashamed, is very small; and further, the former verb admits of a similar meaning with the latter.—*Ed.*

precious stone in the sight of God; then he is such to the faithful. It is faith alone which reveals to us the value and excellency of Christ.

But as the design of the Apostle was to obviate the offence which the multitude of the ungodly creates, he immediately adds another clause respecting the unbelieving, that by rejecting Christ, they do not take away the honour granted him by the Father. For this purpose a verse in Ps. cxviii. 22, is quoted, that the stone which the builders rejected, is become, nevertheless, the head of the corner. It hence follows, that Christ, though opposed by his enemies, yet continues in that dignity to which he has been appointed by the Father. But we must take notice of the two things here said,—the first is, that Christ was rejected by those who bore rule in the Church of God; and the other, that their efforts were all in vain, because necessarily fulfilled must have been what God had decreed, that is, that he, as the corner-stone, should sustain the edifice.

Moreover, that this passage ought properly to be understood of Christ, not only the Holy Spirit is a witness, and Christ himself, who has thus explained it, (Matt. xxi. 42;) but it appears also evident from this, that it was thus commonly understood before Christ came into the world; nor is there a doubt but this exposition had been delivered as it were from hand to hand from the fathers. We hence see that this was, as it were, a common saying even among children respecting the Messiah. I shall, therefore, no longer discuss this point. We may take it as granted, that David was thus rejected by his own age, that he might typify Christ.

Let us now, then, return to the first clause: Christ was rejected by the builders. This was first shadowed forth in David; for they who were in power counted him as condemned and lost. The same was fulfilled in Christ; for they who ruled in the Church, rejected him as far as they could. It might have greatly disturbed the weak, when they saw that Christ's enemies were so many, even the priests, the elders, and teachers, in whom alone the Church was conspicuously seen. In order to remove this offence, Peter reminded the faithful that this very thing had been predicted by David. He especially addressed the Jews, to whom this properly applied; at the same time, this admonition is very useful at this day. For they who arrogate to themselves the first place of authority in the Church, are Christ's most inveterate enemies, and with diabolical fury persecute his Gospel.

The Pope calls himself the vicar of Christ, and yet we know how fiercely he opposes him. This spectacle frightens the simple and ignorant. Why is this? even because they consider not that what David has predicted happens now. Let us, then, remember that not those only were by this prophecy warned who saw Christ rejected by the Scribes and Pharisees; but that we are also by it fortified against daily offences, which might otherwise upset our faith. Whenever then, we see those who glory in the title of prelates, rising up against Christ, let it come to our minds, that the stone is rejected by the builders, according to the prediction of David. And as the metaphor of building is common, when political or spiritual government is spoken of, so David calls them builders, to whom is committed the care and power of governing; not because they build rightly, but because they have the name of builders, and possess the ordinary power. It hence follows, that those in office are not always God's true and faithful ministers. It is, therefore, extremely ridiculous in the Pope and his followers to arrogate to themselves supreme and indubitable authority on this sole pretence, that they are the ordinary governors of the Church. In the first place, their vocation to govern the Church is in no way more just or more legitimate than that of Heliogabalus to govern the empire. But though we should allow them what they unblushingly claim, that they are rightly called, yet we see what David declares respecting the ordinary rulers of the Church, that they rejected Christ, so that they built a stye for swine rather than a temple for God. The other part follows, that all the great, proud of their power and dignity, shall not prevail, so that Christ should not continue in his own place.

And a stone of stumbling. After having comforted the

faithful, that they would have in Christ a firm and permanent foundation, though the greater part, and even the chief men, allowed him no place in the building, he now denounces the punishment which awaits all the unbelieving, in order that they might be terrified by their example. For this purpose he quotes the testimony of Isaiah (viii. 14.) The Prophet there declares that the Lord would be to the Jews a stone of stumbling and rock of offence. This properly refers to Christ, as it may be seen from the context; and Paul applies it to Christ, (Rom. ix. 32.) For in him the God of hosts has plainly manifested himself.

Here, then, the terrible vengeance of God is denounced on all the ungodly, because Christ would be to them an offence and a stumbling, inasmuch as they refused to make him their foundation. For as the firmness and stability of Christ is such that it can sustain all who by faith recumb on him; so his hardness is so great that it will break and tear in pieces all who resist him. For there is no medium between these two things,—we must either build on him, or be dashed against him.[1]

8. *Which stumble at the word.* He points out here the manner in which Christ becomes a stumbling, even when men perversely oppose the word of God. This the Jews did; for though they professed themselves willing to receive the Messiah, yet they furiously rejected him when presented to them by God. The Papists do the same in the present day; they worship only the name of Christ, while they cannot endure the doctrine of the Gospel. Here Peter intimates that all who receive not Christ as revealed in the Gospel, are adversaries to God, and resist his word, and also that

---

[1] There are in this verse two quotations, one from Ps. cxviii. 22, and the other from Isa. viii. 14. That from the Psalms is literally the *Sept.*, and is the same as quoted in Matt. xxi. 42; Mark xii. 10; and Luke xx. 17. In all these instances it is λίθον, and not λίθος, according to the Hebrew. It is therefore necessary to consider κατὰ, *as to*, or, *with respect to*, as understood, a thing not uncommon in Greek. With regard to ἡ τιμὴ, a noun for an adjective, it refers to the stone, or to *him*, in the preceding verse; but as the metaphor of stone is still continued in this verse, it is better to retain it here, " it is precious," that is, the stone; and especially as Christ is represented before, in verse 4, as a stone " precious" in the sight of God.—*Ed.*

Christ is to none for destruction, but to those who, through headstrong wickedness and obstinacy, rush against the word of God.

And this is especially what deserves to be noticed, lest our fault should be imputed to Christ; for, as he has been given to us as a foundation, it is as it were an accidental thing that he becomes a rock of offence. In short, his proper office is to prepare us for a spiritual temple to God; but it is the fault of men that they stumble at him, even because unbelief leads men to contend with God. Hence Peter, in order to set forth the character of the conflict, said that they were the unbelieving.

Whereunto also they were appointed, or, to which they had been ordained. This passage may be explained in two ways. It is, indeed, certain that Peter spoke of the Jews; and the common interpretation is, that they were appointed to believe, for the promise of salvation was destined for them. But the other sense is equally suitable, that they had been appointed to unbelief; as Pharaoh is said to have been set up for this end, that he might resist God, and all the reprobate are destined for the same purpose. And what inclines me to this meaning is the particle καὶ (also) which is put in.[1] If, however, the first view be preferred, then it is a vehement upbraiding; for Peter does hence enhance the sin of unbelief in the people who had been chosen by God, because they rejected the salvation that had been peculiarly ordained for them. And no doubt this circumstance rendered them doubly inexcusable, that having been called in preference to others, they had refused to hear God.

---

[1] The most obvious meaning is, to consider the phrase, "who stumble at the word," as the antecedent to εἰς ὅ, "to which:" they being disobedient or unbelieving were destined to stumble at the word, and thereby to fall and to be broken. (Isa. viii. 14, 15.) To the believing it was precious, but to the unbelieving it became the stone of stumbling; and this stumbling is a judgment to which all the unpersuaded (literally) or the unbelieving, are destined. I would render the two verses thus,—

"To you then who believe it is precious; but to the unbelieving (*with regard to* the stone which the builders have rejected, the same *which* has become the head of the corner) even a stone of stumbling and rock of offence; that is, *to those* who stumble at the word, being unbelieving; to which also they have been appointed:" that is, according to the testimony of Scripture.—*Ed.*

But, by saying that they were appointed to believe, he refers only to their outward call, even according to the covenant which God had made generally with the whole nation. At the same time their ingratitude, as it has been said, was sufficiently proved, when they rejected the word preached to them.

9. But ye *are* a chosen generation, a royal priesthood, an holy nation, a peculiar people; that ye should shew forth the praises of him who hath called you out of darkness into his marvellous light:	9. Vos autem genus electum, regale sacerdotium, gens sancta, populus in acquisitionem, ut virtutes enarretis ejus qui vos ex tenebris vocavit in admirabile lumen suum:
10. Which in time past *were* not a people, but *are* now the people of God: which had not obtained mercy, but now have obtained mercy.	10. Qui aliquando non populus, nunc autem populus Dei, qui non consequuti eratis misericordiam, nunc misericordiam consequuti estis.

9. *But ye are a chosen generation,* or race. He again separates them from the unbelieving, lest driven by their example (as it is often the case) they should fall away from the faith. As, then, it is unreasonable that those whom God has separated from the world, should mix themselves with the ungodly, Peter here reminds the faithful to what great honour they had been raised, and also to what purpose they had been called. But with the same high titles which he confers on them, Moses honoured the ancient people, (Ex. xix. 6;) but the Apostle's object was to shew that they had recovered again, through Christ, the great dignity and honour from which they had fallen. It is at the same time true, that God gave to the fathers an earthly taste only of these blessings, and that they are really given in Christ.

The meaning then is, as though he had said, "Moses called formerly your fathers a holy nation, a priestly kingdom, and God's peculiar people: all these high titles do now far more justly belong to you; therefore you ought to beware lest your unbelief should rob you of them."

In the meantime, however, as the greater part of the nation was unbelieving, the Apostle indirectly sets the believing Jews in opposition to all the rest, though they exceeded them in number, as though he had said, that those only were the children of Abraham, who believed in Christ, and that they only retained possession of all the blessings which God had by a singular privilege bestowed on the whole nation.

He calls them *a chosen race*, because God, passing by others, adopted them as it were in a special manner. They were also *a holy nation;* for God had consecrated them to himself, and destined that they should lead a pure and holy life. He further calls them *a peculiar people*, or, a people for acquisition, that they might be to him a peculiar possession or inheritance; for I take the words simply in this sense, that the Lord hath called us, that he might possess us as his own, and devoted to him. This meaning is proved by the words of Moses, "If ye keep my covenant, ye shall be to me a peculiar treasure beyond all other nations." (Ex. xix. 5.)

There is in the *royal priesthood* a striking inversion of the words of Moses; for he says, "a priestly kingdom," but the same thing is meant. So what Peter intimated was this, "Moses called your fathers a sacred kingdom, because the whole people enjoyed as it were a royal liberty, and from their body were chosen the priests; both dignities were therefore joined together: but now ye are royal priests, and, indeed, in a more excellent way, because ye are, each of you, consecrated in Christ, that ye may be the associates of his kingdom, and partakers of his priesthood. Though, then, the fathers had something like to what you have, yet ye far excel them. For after the wall of partition has been pulled down by Christ, we are now gathered from every nation, and the Lord bestows these high titles on all whom he makes his people."

There is further, as to these benefits, a contrast between us and the rest of mankind, to be considered: and hence it appears more fully how incomparable is God's goodness towards us; for he sanctifies us, who are by nature polluted; he chose us, when he could find nothing in us but filth and vileness; he makes his peculiar possession from worthless dregs; he confers the honour of the priesthood on the profane; he brings the vassals of Satan, of sin, and of death, to the enjoyment of royal liberty.

That ye should shew forth, or declare. He carefully

points out the end of our calling, that he might stimulate us to give the glory to God. And the sum of what he says is, that God has favoured us with these immense benefits and constantly manifests them, that his glory might by us be made known : for by *praises*, or virtues, he understands wisdom, goodness, power, righteousness, and everything else, in which the glory of God shines forth. And further, it behoves us to declare these virtues or excellencies not only by our tongue, but also by our whole life. This doctrine ought to be a subject of daily meditation, and it ought to be continually remembered by us, that all God's blessings with which he favours us are intended for this end, that his glory may be proclaimed by us.

We must also notice what he says, that we have been *called* out of darkness into God's marvellous or wonderful light; for by these words he amplifies the greatness of divine grace. If the Lord had given us light while we were seeking it, it would have been a favour; but it was a much greater favour, to draw us out of the labyrinth of ignorance and the abyss of darkness. We ought hence to learn what is man's condition, before he is translated into the kingdom of God. And this is what Isaiah says, "Darkness shall cover the earth, and gross darkness the people; but over thee shall the Lord be seen, and his glory shall in thee shine forth." (Isa. lx. 2.) And truly we cannot be otherwise than sunk in darkness, after having departed from God, our only light. See more at large on this subject in the second chapter of the Epistle to the Ephesians.

10. *Which in time past were not a people.* He brings for confirmation a passage from Hosea, and well accommodates it to his own purpose. For Hosea, after having in God's name declared that the Jews were repudiated, gives them a hope of a future restoration. Peter reminds us that this was fulfilled in his own age; for the Jews were scattered here and there, as the torn members of a body; nay, they seemed to be no longer God's people, no worship remained among them, they were become entangled in the corruptions of the heathens; it could not then be said otherwise of them, but that they were repudiated by the Lord. But

when they are gathered in Christ, from no people they really become the people of God. Paul, in Rom. ix. 26, applies also this prophecy to the Gentiles, and not without reason ; for from the time the Lord's covenant was broken, from which alone the Jews derived their superiority, they were put on a level with the Gentiles. It hence follows, that what God had promised, to make a people of no people, belongs in common to both.

Which had not obtained mercy. This was added by the Prophet, in order that the gratuitous covenant of God, by which he takes them to be his people, might be more clearly set forth ; as though he had said, " There is no other reason why the Lord counts us his people, except that he, having mercy on us, graciously adopts us." It is then God's gratuitous goodness, which makes of no people a people to God, and reconciles the alienated.[1]

11. Dearly beloved, I beseech *you,* as strangers and pilgrims, abstain from fleshly lusts, which war against the soul ;	11. Amici, adhortor vos tanquam inquilinos et peregrinos, ut abstineatis à carnalibus desideriis, quæ militant adversus animam ;
12. Having your conversation honest among the Gentiles ; that, whereas they speak against you as evil-doers, they may, by *your* good works, which they shall behold, glorify God in the day of visitation.	12. Conversationem vestram inter gentes bonam habentes, ut in quo detrahunt de vobis tanquam maleficis, ex bonis operibus æstimantes (*vel*, considerantes) glorificent Deum in die visitationis.

11. *As strangers,* or sojourners. There are two parts to this exhortation,—that their souls were to be free within from wicked and vicious lusts ; and also, that they were to live honestly among men, and by the example of a good life not only to confirm the godly, but also to gain over the unbelieving to God.

And first, to call them away from the indulgence of carnal lusts, he employs this argument, that they were sojourners and strangers. And he so calls them, not because they

[1] This verse is a quotation from Hos. ii. 23, only the two clauses are inverted. The same is quoted by Paul in Rom. ix. 25, in the same inverted form, and with this difference, that Peter follows the Hebrew, and Paul the Septuagint. The Hebrew is, " I will have mercy upon her that had not obtained mercy;" but according to the Septuagint, " I will love her that had not been loved." The meaning is the same, though the words are different.—*Ed.*

were banished from their country, and scattered into various lands, but because the children of God, wherever they may be, are only guests in this world. In the former sense, indeed, he called them sojourners at the beginning of the Epistle, as it appears from the context; but what he says here is common to them all. For the lusts of the flesh hold us entangled, when in our minds we dwell in the world, and think not that heaven is our country; but when we pass as strangers through this life, we are not in bondage to the flesh.

By the *lusts* or desires *of the flesh* he means not only those gross concupiscences which we have in common with animals, as the Sophists hold, but also all those sinful passions and affections of the soul, to which we are by nature guided and led. For it is certain that every thought of the flesh, that is, of unrenewed nature, is enmity against God. (Rom. viii. 7.)

Which war against the soul. Here is another argument, that they could not comply with the desires of the flesh, except to their own ruin. For he refers not here to the contest described by Paul in the seventh chapter of Romans, and in the fifth of the Galatians, as he makes the soul to be an antagonist to the flesh: but what he says here is, that the desires of the flesh, whenever the soul consents to them, lead to perdition. He proves our carelessness in this respect, that while we anxiously shun enemies from whom we apprehend danger to the body, we willingly allow enemies hurtful to the soul to destroy us; nay, we as it were stretch forth our neck to them.

12. *Your conversation.* The second part of the exhortation is, that they were to conduct themselves honestly towards men. What, indeed, precedes this in order is, that their minds should be cleansed before God; but a regard should also be had to men, lest we should become a hindrance to them. And he expressly says *among the Gentiles;* for the Jews were not only hated everywhere, but were also almost abhorred. The more carefully, therefore, ought they to have laboured to wipe off the odium and infamy attached to their name by a holy life and a well-regulated con-

duct.[1] For that admonition of Paul ought to be attended to, "To give no occasion to those who seek occasion." Therefore the evil speakings and the wicked insinuations of the ungodly ought to stimulate us to lead an upright life ; for it is no time for living listlessly and securely, when they sharply watch us in order to find out whatever we do amiss.

That they—may glorify God. He intimates that we ought thus to strive, not for our own sake, that men may think and speak well of us ; but that we may glorify God, as Christ also teaches us. And Peter shews how this would be effected, even that the unbelieving, led by our good works, would become obedient to God, and thus by their own conversion give glory to him ; for this he intimates by the words, *in the day of visitation.* I know that some refer this to the last coming of Christ ; but I take it otherwise, even that God employs the holy and honest life of his people, as a preparation, to bring back the wandering to the right way. For it is the beginning of our conversion, when God is pleased to look on us with a paternal eye ; but when his face is turned away from us, we perish. Hence the day of visitation may justly be said to be the time when he invites us to himself.

13. Submit yourselves to every ordinance of man for the Lord's sake : whether it be to the king, as supreme ;	13. Subditi ergo estote omni humanæ ordinationi propter Dominum ; sive regi tanquam supereminenti ;
14. Or unto governors, as unto them that are sent by him for the punishment of evil-doers, and for the praise of them that do well.	14. Sive præsidibus, tanquam iis qui per ipsum mittuntur, in vindictam quidem maleficorum, laudem verò benè agentium.
15. For so is the will of God, that with well-doing ye may put to silence the ignorance of foolish men :	15. Sic enim est voluntas Dei, ut benefaciendo obstruatis ignorantiam stultorum hominum :
16. As free, and not using *your* liberty for a cloak of maliciousness, but as the servants of God.	16. Ut liberi, et non quasi prætextum habentes malitiæ, libertatem ; sed tanquam servi Dei.

13. *Submit yourselves.* He now comes to particular exhortations : and as obedience with regard to magistrates is a part of honest or good conversation, he draws this infer-

---

[1] Neither "conversation" nor "honest" are suitable words. It is difficult to find a proper word in English for ἀναστροφὴ, which means deportment, behaviour, carriage, conduct, manner of life : perhaps life would be the best word, "Having your life good among the Gentiles ;" that is, morally good (καλὴν) right, or upright.—*Ed.*

ence as to their duty, "Submit yourselves," or, Be ye subject; for by refusing the yoke of government, they would have given to the Gentiles no small occasion for reproaching them. And, indeed, the Jews were especially hated and counted infamous for this reason, because they were regarded on account of their perverseness as ungovernable. And as the commotions which they raised up in the provinces, were causes of great calamities, so that every one of a quiet and peaceable disposition dreaded them as the plague,—this was the reason that induced Peter to speak so strongly on subjection. Besides, many thought the gospel was a proclamation of such liberty, that every one might deem himself as free from servitude. It seemed an unworthy thing that God's children should be servants, and that the heirs of the world should not have a free possession, no, not even of their own bodies. Then there was another trial,—All the magistrates were Christ's adversaries; and they used their own authority, so that no representation of God, which secures the chief reverence, appeared in them. We now perceive the design of Peter: he exhorted the Jews, especially for these reasons, to shew respect to the civil power.

To every ordinance of man. Some render the words, "to every creature;" and from a rendering so obscure and ambiguous, much labour has been taken to elicit some meaning. But I have no doubt but that Peter meant to point out the distinct manner in which God governs mankind: for the verb κτίζειν in Greek, from which κτίσις comes, means to form and to construct a building. Suitable, then, is the word "ordination;" by which Peter reminds us, that God the maker of the world has not left the human race in a state of confusion, that they might live after the manner of beasts, but as it were in a building regularly formed, and divided into several compartments. And it is called a *human ordination*, not because it has been invented by man, but because a mode of living, well arranged and duly ordered, is peculiar to men.[1]

[1] The words literally are, "Submit ye to every human creation:" but, as Calvin says, the Greek verb means sometimes to form, to construct;

Whether it be to the king. So he calls Cæsar, as I think, whose empire extended over all those countries mentioned at the beginning of the Epistle. For though "king" was a name extremely hated by the Romans, yet it was in use among the Greeks. They, indeed, often called him autocrat, (αὐτοκράτορα ;) but sometimes he was also called by them king, (βασιλεύς.) But as he subjoins a reason, that he ought to be obeyed because he excelled, or was eminent or supreme, there is no comparison made between Cæsar and other magistrates. He held, indeed, the supreme power; but that eminence which Peter extols, is common to all who exercise public authority. And so Paul, in Rom. xiii. 1, extends it to all magistrates. Now the meaning is, that obedience is due to all who rule, because they have been raised to that honour not by chance, but by God's providence. For many are wont to inquire too scrupulously by what right power has been attained; but we ought to be satisfied with this alone, that power is possessed and exercised. And so Paul cuts off the handle of useless objections when he declares that there is no power but from God. And for this reason it is that Scripture so often says, that it is God who girds kings with a sword, who raises them on high, who transfers kingdoms as he pleases.

As Peter referred especially to the Roman Emperor, it was necessary to add this admonition; for it is certain that the Romans through unjust means rather than in a legitimate way penetrated into Asia and subdued these countries. Besides, the Cæsars, who then reigned, had possessed themselves of the monarchy by tyrannical force. Hence Peter as it were forbids these things to be controverted, for he shews that subjects ought to obey their rulers without hesi-

and so does ברא, to create, in Hebrew. The noun may hence be rendered "institution," what is formed. As in the second verse, so here, the Apostle, in a way almost peculiar to himself, and the reverse of what is commonly done in Scripture, uses an adjective for a noun, "human" for "of man;" and he does the same in chap. iii. 7, "the womanish weaker vessel," instead of "the woman (or wife) the weaker vessel." We may then render the words, "Submit ye to every institution of man." The reference is clearly to government. The ostensible agent in the formation of all governments is man; but God is the overruler of all things.—*Ed.*

tation, because they are not made eminent, unless elevated by God's hand.

14. *Or unto governors,* or, Whether to presidents. He designates every kind of magistrates, as though he had said, that there is no kind of government to which we ought not to submit. He confirms this by saying that they are God's ministers; for they who apply *him* to the king, are greatly mistaken. There is then a common reason, which extols the authority of all magistrates, that they rule by the command of God, and are sent by him. It hence follows (as Paul also teaches us) that they resist God, who do not obediently submit to a power ordained by him.

For the punishment. This is the second reason why it behoves us reverently to regard and to respect civil authority, and that is, because it has been appointed by the Lord for the common good of mankind; for we must be extremely barbarous and brutal, if the public good is not regarded by us. This, then, in short, is what Peter means, that since God keeps the world in order by the ministry of magistrates, all they who despise their authority are enemies to mankind.

Now he assumes these two things, which belong, as Plato says, to a commonwealth, that is, reward to the good and punishment to the wicked; for, in ancient times, not only punishment was allotted to evil-doers, but also rewards to the doers of good. But though it often happens that honours are not rightly distributed, nor rewards given to the deserving, yet it is an honour, not to be despised, that the good are at the least under the care and protection of magistrates, that they are not exposed to the violence and injuries of the ungodly, that they live more quietly under laws and better retain their reputation, than if every one, unrestrained, lived as he pleased. In short, it is a singular blessing of God, that the wicked are not allowed to do what they like.

It may, however, be objected here and said, that kings and magistrates often abuse their power, and exercise tyrannical cruelty rather than justice. Such were almost all the magistrates, when this Epistle was written. To this I answer, that tyrants and those like them, do not produce such effects by their abuse, but that the ordinance of God ever remains in force, as the institution of marriage is not subverted though the wife and the husband were to act in a way not becoming them. However, therefore, men may go astray, yet the end fixed by God cannot be changed.

Were any one again to object and say, that we ought not to obey princes who, as far as they can, pervert the holy ordinance of God, and thus become savage wild beasts, while magistrates ought to bear the image of God. My reply is this, that government established by God ought to be so highly valued by us, as to honour even tyrants when in power. There is yet another reply still more evident,—that there has never been a tyranny, (nor can one be imagined,) however cruel and unbridled, in which some portion of equity has not appeared; and further, some kind of government, however deformed and corrupt it may be, is still better and more beneficial than anarchy.

15. *For so is the will of God.* He returns to his former doctrine, lest an occasion should be given to the unbelieving to speak evil, though he expresses less than what he had said before; for he says only that the mouths of the foolish ought to be stopped. The phrase which he adopts, "to stop up ignorance," though it may seem harsh on account of its novelty, does not yet obscure the sense.[1] For he not only calls the unbelieving foolish, but also points out the reason why they slandered, even because they were ignorant of God. But inasmuch as he makes the unbelieving to be without understanding and reason, we hence conclude, that a right understanding cannot exist without the knowledge of God. How much soever, then, the unbelieving may boast of their own acuteness, and may seem to themselves to be wise and prudent, yet the Spirit of God charges them with folly, in order that we may know that, apart from God, we cannot be really wise, as without him there is nothing perfect.

But he prescribes the way in which the evil-speaking of the unbelieving is to be restrained, even by *well-doing,* or,

---

[1] The word properly means to muzzle; "that ye, by doing good, should muzzle the ignorance of foolish men;" according to what is done to savage animals, in order to prevent them to do harm.—*Ed.*

by doing good. In this expression he includes all the duties of humanity and kindness which we ought to perform towards our neighbours. And in these is included obedience to magistrates, without which concord among men cannot be cultivated. Were any one to object and say, that the faithful can never be so careful to do good, but that they will be evil-spoken of by the unbelieving: to this the obvious answer is, that the Apostle here does not in any degree exempt them from calumnies and reproaches; but he means that no occasion of slandering ought to be given to the unbelieving, however much they may desire it. And lest any one should further object and say, that the unbelieving are by no means worthy of so much regard that God's children should form their life to please them, Peter expressly reminds us that we are bound by God's command to shut up their mouths.

16. *As free.* This is said by way of anticipation, that he might obviate those things which are usually objected to with regard to the liberty of God's children. For as men are naturally ingenious in laying hold on what may be for their advantage, many, at the commencement of the Gospel, thought themselves free to live only for themselves. This doting opinion, then, is what Peter corrects; and he briefly shews how much the liberty of Christians differed from unbridled licentiousness. And, in the first place, he denies that there is any veil or pretext for wickedness, by which he intimates, that there is no liberty given us to hurt our neighbours, or to do any harm to others. True liberty, then, is that which harms or injures no one. To confirm this, he declares that those are free who serve God. It is obvious, hence, to conclude, that we obtain liberty, in order that we may more promptly and more readily render obedience to God; for it is no other than a freedom from sin; and dominion is taken away from sin, that men may become obedient to righteousness.

In short, it is a free servitude, and a serving freedom. For as we ought to be the servants of God, that we may enjoy this benefit, so moderation is required in the use of it. In this way, indeed, our consciences become free; but this prevents us not to serve God, who requires us also to be subject to men.

| 17. Honour all *men*. Love the brotherhood. Fear God. Honour the king. | 17. Omnes honorate, fraternitatem diligite, Deum timete, regem honorate. |

This is a summary of what is gone before; for he intimates that God is not feared, nor their just right rendered to men, except civil order prevails among us, and magistrates retain their authority. That he bids honour to be rendered to all, I explain thus, that none are to be neglected; for it is a general precept, which refers to the social intercourse of men.[1] The word *honour* has a wide meaning in Hebrew, and we know that the apostles, though they wrote in Greek, followed the meaning of words in the former language. Therefore, this word conveys no other idea to me, than that a regard ought to be had for all, since we ought to cultivate, as far as we can, peace and friendship with all; there is, indeed, nothing more adverse to concord than contempt.

What he adds respecting the love of brethren is special, as contrasted with the first clause; for he speaks of that particular love which we are bidden to have towards the household of faith, because we are connected with them by a closer relationship. And so Peter did not omit this connexion; but yet he reminds us, that though brethren are to be specially regarded, yet this ought not to prevent our love from being extended to the whole human race. The word *fraternity*, or brotherhood, I take collectively for brethren.

Fear God. I have already said that all these clauses are applied by Peter to the subject he was treating. For he means, that honour paid to kings proceeds from the fear of God and the love of man; and that, therefore, it ought to be connected with them, as though he had said, "Whosoever fears God, loves his brethren and the whole human race as he ought, and will also give honour to kings." But, at the same time, he expressly mentions *the king*, because that form of

---

[1] It is better to take it in this wide sense, than to limit it, as some have done, to rulers or magistrates, because honour to magistrates is included in the last clause, "Honour the king."—*Ed.*

government was more than any other disliked; and under it other forms are included.

18. Servants, *be* subject to *your* masters with all fear; not only to the good and gentle, but also to the froward.	18. Famuli, subjecti sint cum omni timore dominis *suis*, non solum bonis et humanis, sed etiam pravis.
19. For this *is* thankworthy, if a man for conscience towards God endure grief, suffering wrongfully.	19. Hæc enim est gratia, si propter conscientiam Dei quispiam molestias ferat patiens injustè.
20. For what glory *is it*, if, when ye be buffeted for your faults, ye shall take it patiently? but if, when ye do well, and suffer *for it*, ye take it patiently, this *is* acceptable with God.	20. Qualis enim gloria, si quum peccantes alapis cædemini, suffertis? sed si bene facientes et in aliis affecti suffertis, hæc gratia apud Deum.

18. *Servants, be subject.* Though this is a particular admonition, yet it is connected with what is gone before, as well as the other things which follow; for the obedience of servants to masters, and of wives also to their husbands, forms a part of civil or social subjection.[1]

He first would have servants to be subject *with all fear;* by which expression he means that sincere and willing reverence, which they acknowledge by their office to be due. He then sets this fear in opposition to dissimulation as well as to forced subjection; for an eye-service (ὀφθαλμοδουλεία, Col. iii. 21,) as Paul calls it, is the opposite of this fear; and further, if servants clamour against severe treatment, being ready to throw off the yoke if they could, they cannot be said properly to fear. In short, fear arises from a right knowledge of duty. And though no exception is added in this place, yet, according to other places, it is to be understood. For subjection due to men is not to be so far extended as to lessen the authority of God. Then servants are to be subject to their masters, only as far as God permits, or as far as the altars, as they say. But as the word here is not δοῦλοι, slaves, but οἰκέται, domestics, we may understand the free as well as the bond servants to be meant, though it be a difference of little moment.

Not only to the good. Though as to the duty of servants

---

[1] The word for "servants," οἰκέται, properly means "domestics," or household servants. They are mentioned as they came more in contact with their masters, and were more liable to be ill-treated.—*Ed.*

to obey their masters, it is wholly a matter of conscience ; if, however, they are unjustly treated, as to themselves, they ought not to resist authority. Whatever, then, masters may be, there is no excuse for servants for not faithfully obeying them. For when a superior abuses his power, he must indeed hereafter render an account to God, yet he does not for the present lose his right. For this law is laid on servants, that they are to serve their masters, though they may be unworthy. For *the froward* he sets in opposition to the equitable or humane; and by this word he refers to the cruel and the perverse, or those who have no humanity and kindness.[1]

It is a wonder what could have induced an interpreter to change one Greek word for another, and render it "wayward." I should say nothing of the gross ignorance of the Sorbons, who commonly understand by wayward, (*dyscolos,*) the dissolute or dissipated, were it not that they seek by this absurd rendering to build up for us an article of faith, that we ought to obey the Pope and his horned wild beasts, however grievous and intolerable a tyranny they may exercise. This passage, then, shews how boldly they trifle with the Word of God.

19. *For this is thankworthy.* The word grace or favour, has the meaning of praise; for he means that no grace or praise shall be found before God, if we bear the punishment which we have by our faults deserved; but that they who patiently bear injuries and wrongs are worthy of praise and accepted by God.[2] To testify that it was acceptable to God, when any one from conscience towards God persevered in doing his duty, though unjustly and unworthily treated, was at that time very necessary; for the condition of servants was very

---

[1] "Good," ἀγαθοῖς, the kind, benevolent; "gentle," ἐπιεικέσιν, the yielding, mild, patient; "froward," σκολιοῖς, the crooked, perverse, untoward, those of a cross disposition, self-willed, and hence cruel, being neither kind nor meek.—*Ed.*

[2] Literally, "this is favour," that is, with God, as at the end of the next verse. To "find favour with God" is a similar phrase, Luke i. 30, which means to find acceptance with him. We may render the words, "This is acceptable:" with whom acceptable, is afterwards explained. So the word חֵן in Hebrew means a favourable acceptance, or approbation. See Gen. vi. 8; xxxii. 5.—*Ed.*

hard: they were counted no better than cattle. Such indignity might have driven them to despair; the only thing left for them was to look to God.

For *conscience towards God* means this, that one performs his duty, not from a regard to men, but to God. For, when a wife is submissive and obedient to her husband, in order to please him, she has her reward in this world, as Christ says of the ambitious, who looked to the praise of men, (Matt. vi. 16.) The same view is to be taken of other cases: When a son obeys his father in order to secure his favour and bounty, he will have his reward from his father, not from God. It is, in short, a general truth, that what we do is approved by God, if our object be to serve him, and if we are not influenced by a regard to man alone. Moreover, he who considers that he has to do with God, must necessarily endeavour to overcome evil with good. For, God not only requires that we should be such to every one as he is to us, but also that we should be good to the unworthy and to such as persecute us.

It is not, however, an assertion without its difficulty, when he says, that there is nothing praiseworthy in him who is justly punished; for, when the Lord punishes our sins, patience is certainly a sacrifice of sweet odour to him, that is, when we bear with a submissive mind our punishment. But to this I reply, that Peter does not here speak simply but comparatively; for it is a small and slender praise to bear with submission a just punishment, in comparison with that of an innocent man, who willingly bears the wrongs of men, only because he fears God. At the same time he seems indirectly to refer to the motive; because they who suffer punishment for their faults, are influenced by the fear of men. But the reply already given is sufficient.

21. For even hereunto were ye called: because Christ also suffered for us, leaving us an example, that ye should follow his steps:	21. In hoc enim vocati estis; quoniam Christus quoque passus est pro vobis, relinquens vobis exemplum, ut sequeremini vestigia ejus:
22. Who did no sin, neither was guile found in his mouth:	22. Qui quum peccatum non fecisset, nec inventus esset dolus in ore ejus;
23 Who, when he was reviled,	23. Quum probro afficeretur, non

| reviled not again; when he suffered, he threatened not; but committed *himself* to him that judgeth righteously: | regerebat; quum pateretur, non comminabatur; causam vero commendabat ei qui juste judicat. |

21. *For even hereunto were ye called.* For though his discourse was respecting servants, yet this passage ought not to be confined to that subject. For the Apostle here reminds all the godly in common as to what the condition of Christianity is, as though he had said, that we are called by the Lord for this end, patiently to bear wrongs; and as he says in another place that we are appointed to this. Lest, however, this should seem grievous to us, he consoles us with the example of Christ. Nothing seems more unworthy, and therefore less tolerable, than undeservedly to suffer; but when we turn our eyes to the Son of God, this bitterness is mitigated; for who would refuse to follow him going before us?

But we must notice the words, *Leaving us an example.*[1] For as he treats of imitation, it is necessary to know what in Christ is to be our example. He walked on the sea, he cleansed the leprous, he raised the dead, he restored sight to the blind: to try to imitate him in these things would be absurd. For when he gave these evidences of his power, it was not his object that we should thus imitate him. It has hence happened that his fasting for forty days has been made without reason an example; but what he had in view was far otherwise. We ought, therefore, to exercise in this respect a right judgment; as also Augustine somewhere reminds us, when explaining the following passage, "Learn of me, for I am meek and lowly in heart." (Matt. xi. 29.) And the same thing may be learnt from the words of Peter; for he marks the difference by saying that Christ's patience is what we ought to follow. This subject is handled more at large by Paul in Romans viii. 29, where he teaches us that all the children of God are foreordained to be made

[1] Calvin has "you" instead of "us," and has also "you" after "suffered." The authority as to *MSS.* is nearly equal; but the verse reads better with having "you" in both instances, as the verb "follow" is in the second person plural, "that *ye* may follow in his footsteps." The word for "example" is ὑπογραμμόν, a copy set before scholars to be imitated, and may be rendered "a pattern."—*Ed.*

conformable to the image of Christ, in order that he might be the first-born among many brethren. Hence, that we may live with him, we must previously die with him.

22. *Who did no sin.* This belongs to the present subject; for, if any one boasts of his own innocence, he must know that Christ did not suffer as a malefactor. He, at the same time, shews how far we come short of what Christ was, when he says, that there was *no guile found in his mouth;* for he who offends not by his tongue, says James, is a perfect man. (James iii. 2.) He then declares that there was in Christ the highest perfection of innocency, such as no one of us can dare claim for himself. It hence appears more fully how unjustly he suffered beyond all others. There is, therefore, no reason why any one of us should refuse to suffer after his example, since no one is so conscious of having acted rightly, as not to know that he is imperfect.

23. *When he was reviled,* or, reproached. Here Peter points out what we are to imitate in Christ, even calmly to bear wrongs, and not to avenge wrongs. For such is our disposition, that when we receive injuries, our minds immediately boil over with revengeful feelings; but Christ abstained from every kind of retaliation. Our minds, therefore, ought to be bridled, lest we should seek to render evil for evil.

But committed himself, or, his cause. The word *cause* is not expressed, but it is obviously understood. And Peter adds this for the consolation of the godly, that is, that if they patiently endured the reproaches and violence of the wicked, they would have God as their defender. For it would be a very hard thing for us, to be subjected to the will of the ungodly, and not to have God caring for our wrongs. Peter, therefore, adorns God with this high attribute, that he *judgeth righteously,* as though he had said, "It behoves us calmly to bear evils; God in the meantime will not neglect what belongs to him, but will shew himself to be a righteous judge." However wanton then the ungodly may be for a time, yet they shall not be unpunished for the wrongs done now to the children of God. Nor is there any cause for the godly to fear, as though they were without any protection; for since it belongs to God to defend them and to undertake their cause, they are to possess their souls in patience.

Moreover, as this doctrine brings no small consolation, so it avails to allay and subdue the inclinations of the flesh. For no one can recumb on the fidelity and protection of God, but he who in a meek spirit waits for his judgment; for he who leaps to take vengeance, intrudes into what belongs to God, and suffers not God to perform his own office. In reference to this Paul says, "Give place to wrath," (Rom. xii. 19;) and thus he intimates that the way is closed up against God that he might not himself judge, when we anticipate him. He then confirms what he had said by the testimony of Moses, "Vengeance is mine." (Deut. xxxii. 35.) Peter in short meant this, that we after the example of Christ shall be more prepared to endure injuries, if we give to God his own honour, that is, if we, believing him to be a righteous judge, refer our right and our cause to him.

It may however be asked, How did Christ commit his cause to the Father; for if he required vengeance from him, this he himself says is not lawful for us; for he bids us to do good to those who injure us, to pray for those who speak evil of us. (Matt. v. 44.) To this my reply is, that it appears evident from the gospel-history, that Christ did thus refer his judgment to God, and yet did not demand vengeance to be taken on his enemies, but that, on the contrary, he prayed for them, "Father," he said, "forgive them." (Luke xxiii. 34.) And doubtless the feelings of our flesh are far from being in unison with the judgment of God. That any one then may commit his cause to him who judgeth righteously, it is necessary that he should first lay a check on himself, so that he may not ask anything inconsistent with the righteous judgment of God. For they who indulge themselves in looking for vengeance, concede not to God his office of a judge, but in a manner wish him to be an executioner. He then who is so calm in his spirit as to wish his adversaries to become his friends, and endeavours to bring them to the right way, rightly commits to God his own cause, and his prayer is, "Thou, O Lord, knowest my heart, how I wish them to be saved who seek to destroy me: were they converted, I should congratulate them; but if they continue obstinate in their wickedness, for I know that thou watchest over my safety, I commit my cause to thee." This meekness was manifested by Christ; it is then the rule to be observed by us.

24. Who his own self bare our sins in his own body on the tree, that we, being dead to sins, should live unto righteousness: by whose stripes ye were healed.	24. Qui peccata nostra ipse pertulit in corpore suo super lignum, ut peccatis mortui, justitiæ vivamus: cujus livori sanati estis.
25. For ye were as sheep going astray; but are now returned unto the Shepherd and Bishop of your souls.	25. Eratis enim tanquam oves errantes; sed conversi estis nunc ad Pastorem et Episcopum animarum vestrarum.

Had he commended nothing in Christ's death except as an example, it would have been very frigid: he therefore refers to a fruit much more excellent. There are then three things to be noticed in this passage. The first is, that Christ by his death has given us an example of patience; the second, that by his death he restored us to life; it hence follows, that we are so bound to him, that we ought cheerfully to follow his example. In the third place, he refers to the general design of his death, that we, being dead to sins, ought to live to righteousness. And all these things confirm his previous exhortation.

24. *Who his own self bare our sins.* This form of speaking is fitted to set forth the efficacy of Christ's death. For as under the Law, the sinner, that he might be released from guilt, substituted a victim in his own place; so Christ took on himself the curse due to our sins, that he might atone for them before God. And he expressly adds, *on the tree,* because he could not offer such an expiation except on the cross. Peter, therefore, well expresses the truth, that Christ's death was a sacrifice for the expiation of our sins; for being fixed to the cross and offering himself a victim for us, he took on himself our sin and our punishment. Isaiah, from whom Peter has taken the substance of his doctrine, employs various forms of expression,—that he was smitten by God's hand for our sins, that he was wounded for our iniquities, that he was afflicted and broken for our sake,

that the chastisement of our peace was laid on him. But Peter intended to set forth the same thing by the words of this verse, even that we are reconciled to God on this condition, because Christ made himself before his tribunal a surety and as one guilty for us, that he might suffer the punishment due to us.

This great benefit the Sophists in their schools obscure as much as they can; for they prattle that by the sacrifice of the death of Christ we are only freed after baptism from guilt, but that punishment is redeemed by satisfactions. But Peter, when he says that he bore our sins, means that not only guilt was imputed to him, but that he also suffered its punishment, that he might thus be an expiatory victim, according to that saying of the Prophet, " The chastisement of our peace was upon him." If they object and say, that this only avails before baptism, the context here disproves them, for the words are addressed to the faithful.

But this clause and that which follows, *by whose stripes ye were healed*, may be also applied to the subject in hand, that is, that it behoves us to bear on our shoulders the sins of others, not indeed to expiate for them, but only to bear them as a burden laid on us.

Being dead to sins.[1] He had before pointed out another end, even an example of patience; but here, as it has been stated, it is made more manifest, that we are to live a holy and righteous life. The Scripture sometimes mentions both, that is, that the Lord tries us with troubles and adversities, that we might be conformed to the death of Christ, and also that the old man has been crucified in the death of Christ, that we might walk in newness of life. (Phil. iii. 10;

[1] Or, " Being freed from sins:" ἀπογινόμενοι, being away from, having departed from, or, being removed from. *Beza* renders it " being separated from." Freedom from the power or dominion of sin seems more expressly to be intended, as the end of this freedom is, that we may live to righteousness; the end of forgiveness on the other hand is, that we may have peace with God. *Beza, Estius, Grotius,* and *Scott*, take this view of the sentence. The subject in hand is not the removal of guilt, but holiness of life, and Christ in his sufferings is set forth as the pattern to us. Then in what follows, our diseased state and our wandering from the right way, are the things referred to. Christ's death was intended to answer two great ends,—to remove guilt and to remove or to destroy sin in us. The latter is the subject of this passage.—*Ed.*

Rom. vi. 4.) At the same time, this end of which he speaks, differs from the former, not only as that which is general from what is particular; for in patience there is simply an example; but when he says that Christ suffered, that we being dead to sins should live to righteousness, he intimates that there is power in Christ's death to mortify our flesh, as Paul explains more fully in the sixth chapter of the Epistle to the Romans. For he has not only brought this great benefit to us, that God justifies us freely, by not imputing to us our sins; but he also makes us to die to the world and to the flesh, that we may rise again to a new life: not that one day makes complete this death; but wherever it is, the death of Christ is efficacious for the expiation of sins, and also for the mortification of the flesh.

25. *For ye were as sheep.* This also has Peter borrowed from Isaiah, except that the Prophet makes it a universal statement, "All we like sheep have gone astray." (Isaiah liii. 6.) But on the word *sheep* there is no particular stress; he indeed compares us to sheep, but the emphasis is on what the Prophet adds, when he says that every one had turned to his own way. The meaning then is, that we are all going astray from the way of salvation, and proceeding in the way of ruin, until Christ brings us back from this wandering.

And this appears still more evident from the clause which follows, *but are now returned to the Shepherd,* &c.;[1] for all who are not ruled by Christ, are wandering like lost sheep in the ways of error. Thus, then, is condemned the whole wisdom of the world, which does not submit to the government of Christ. But the two titles given here to Christ are remarkable, that he is the *Shepherd and Bishop of souls.* There is then no cause to fear, but that he will faithfully watch over the safety of those who are in his fold and under his care. And it is his office to keep us safe both in body and

---

[1] I would render the clause thus, "But you have been now restored," that is, from your wandering, "to the shepherd and the bishop (or, overseer) of your souls." *Macknight* thinks, that our Lord took the title of shepherd in order to shew that he is the person foretold in Ezek. xxxiv. 23, and that Peter alludes, in calling him bishop or overseer, to the eleventh verse of that chapter, the latter clause of which, according to the *Sept.* is, " I will oversee them," (ἐπισκέψομαι.)—*Ed.*

soul; yet Peter mentions only souls, because this celestial Shepherd keeps us under his own spiritual protection unto eternal life.

CHAPTER III.

1. Likewise, ye wives, *be* in subjection to your own husbands : that, if any obey not the word, they also may without the word be won by the conversation of the wives;
2. While they behold your chaste conversation *coupled* with fear.
3. Whose adorning, let it not be that outward *adorning* of plaiting the hair, and of wearing of gold, or of putting on of apparel;
4. But *let it be* the hidden man of the heart, in that which is not corruptible, *even the ornament* of a meek and quiet spirit, which is in the sight of God of great price.

1. Similiter mulieres subjectæ sint propriis maritis; ut etiam siqui sunt increduli sermoni, per uxorum conversationem absque sermone lucrifiant;
2. Considerantes puram (*vel*, castam) vestram in timore conversationem;
3. Quarum ornatus sit non externus, in plicatura capillorum et circumpositione auri, aut palliorum amictu;
4. Sed interior cordis homo, qui in incorruptione situs est placidi et quieti spiritus, qui spiritus coram Deo pretiosus est (*vel*, quod est coram Deo pretiosum.)

HE proceeds now to another instance of subjection, and bids wives to be subject to their husbands. And as those seemed to have some pretence for shaking off the yoke, who were united to unbelieving men, he expressly reminds them of their duty, and brings forward a particular reason why they ought the more carefully to obey, even that they might by their probity allure their husbands to the faith. But if wives ought to obey ungodly husbands, with much more promptness ought they to obey, who have believing husbands.

But it may seem strange that Peter should say, that a husband might be *gained* to the Lord *without the word;* for why is it said, that "faith cometh by hearing?" Rom. x. 17. To this I reply, that Peter's words are not to be so understood as though a holy life alone could lead the unbelieving to Christ, but that it softens and pacifies their minds, so that they might have less dislike to religion; for as bad examples create offences, so good ones afford no small help. Then Peter shews that wives by a holy and pious life could do so much as to prepare their husbands, without speaking to them on religion, to embrace the faith of Christ.

2. *While they behold.* For minds, however alienated from the true faith, are subdued, when they see the good conduct of believers; for as they understood not the doctrine of Christ, they form an estimate of it by our life. It cannot, then, be but that they will commend Christianity, which teaches purity and fear.

3. *Whose adorning.* The other part of the exhortation is, that wives are to adorn themselves sparingly and modestly: for we know that they are in this respect much more curious and ambitious than they ought to be. Then Peter does not without cause seek to correct in them this vanity. And though he reproves generally sumptuous or costly adorning, yet he points out some things in particular,—that they were not artificially to curl or wreath their hair, as it was usually done by crisping-pins, or otherwise to form it according to the fashion; nor were they to set gold around their head: for these are the things in which excesses especially appear.

It may be now asked, whether the Apostle wholly condemns the use of gold in adorning the body. Were any one to urge these words, it may be said, that he prohibits precious garments no less than gold; for he immediately adds, *the putting on of apparel,* or, of clothes. But it would be an immoderate strictness wholly to forbid neatness and elegance in clothing. If the material is said to be too sumptuous, the Lord has created it; and we know that skill in art has proceeded from him. Then Peter did not intend to condemn every sort of ornament, but the evil of vanity, to which women are subject. Two things are to be regarded in clothing, usefulness and decency; and what decency requires is moderation and modesty. Were, then, a woman to go forth with her hair wantonly curled and decked, and make an extravagant display, her vanity could not be excused. They who object and say, that to clothe one's-self in this or that manner is an indifferent thing, in which all are free to do as they please, may be easily confuted; for excessive elegance and superfluous display, in short, all excesses, arise from a corrupted mind. Besides, ambition, pride, affectation of display, and all things of this kind, are not indifferent things. Therefore they whose minds are purified from all vanity, will duly order all things, so as not to exceed moderation.

4. *But* let it be *the hidden man of the heart.* The contrast here ought to be carefully observed. Cato said, that they who are anxiously engaged in adorning the body, neglect the adorning of the mind: so Peter, in order to restrain this desire in women, introduces a remedy, that they are to devote themselves to the cultivation of their minds. The word *heart,* no doubt means the whole soul. He at the same time shews in what consists the spiritual adorning of women, even in *the incorruptness of a meek and quiet spirit.* "Incorruptness," as I think, is set in opposition to things which fade and vanish away, things which serve to adorn the body. Therefore the version of Erasmus departs from the real meaning. In short, Peter means that the ornament of the soul is not like a fading flower, nor consists in vanishing splendour, but is incorruptible. By mentioning a *quiet* and a tranquil *spirit,* he marks out what especially belongs to women; for nothing becomes them more than a placid and a sedate temper of mind.[1] For we know how outrageous a being is an imperious and a self-willed woman. And further, nothing is more fitted to correct the vanity of which Peter speaks than a placid quietness of spirit.

What follows, that it is *in the sight of God of great price,* may be referred to the whole previous sentence as well as to the word *spirit;* the meaning indeed will remain the same. For why do women take so much care to adorn themselves, except that they may turn the eyes of men on themselves? But Peter, on the contrary, bids them to be more anxious for what is before God of a great price.

5. For after this manner in the old time the holy women also, who

5. Sic enim aliquando et sanctæ mulieres quæ sperabant in Deum,

---

[1] The best construction is to regard "adorning," or ornament, as understood after "incorruptible:"

"But the hidden man of the heart, *clothed* in (or with) the incorruptible *adorning* of a mild and quiet spirit."

"Mild" or meek, not given to passion or wrath, patient, not proud nor arrogant; "quiet," peaceable, not garrulous, not turbulent, nor given to strife and contention.—*Ed.*

trusted in God, adorned themselves, being in subjection unto their own husbands :

ornabant seipsas, subjectæ propriis maritis :

6. Even as Sarah obeyed Abraham, calling him lord: whose daughters ye are as long as ye do well, and are not afraid with any amazement.

6. Quemadmodum et Sara obediebat Abrahæ, dominum ipsum appellans, cujus filiæ estis factæ, si benefeceritis, et non terreamini ullo pavore.

He sets before them the example of pious women, who sought for spiritual adorning rather than outward meretricious ornaments. But he mentions Sarah above all others, who, having been the mother of all the faithful, is especially worthy of honour and imitation on the part of her sex. Moreover, he returns again to subjection, and confirms it by the example of Sarah, who, according to the words of Moses, called her husband Lord. (Gen. xviii. 12.) God, indeed, does not regard such titles ; and it may sometimes be, that one especially petulant and disobedient should use such a word with her tongue ; but Peter means, that Sarah usually spoke thus, because she knew that a command had been given her by the Lord, to be subject to her husband. Peter adds, that they who imitated her fidelity would be her daughters, that is, reckoned among the faithful.

6. *And are not afraid.* The weakness of the sex causes women to be suspicious and timid, and therefore morose ; for they fear lest by their subjection, they should be more reproachfully treated. It was this that Peter seems to have had in view in forbidding them to be disturbed by any fear, as though he had said, " Willingly submit to the authority of your husbands, nor let fear prevent your obedience, as though your condition would be worse, were you to obey." The words may be more general, " Let them not raise up commotions at home." For as they are liable to be frightened, they often make much of a little thing, and thus disturb themselves and the family. Others think that the timidity of women, which is contrary to faith, is generally reproved, as though Peter exhorted them to perform the duties of their calling with a courageous and intrepid spirit. However, the first explanation is what I prefer, though the last does not differ much from it.[1]

[1] The words are, " Whose daughters ye become, when ye do well and

7. Likewise, ye husbands, dwell with *them* according to knowledge, giving honour unto the wife, as unto the weaker vessel, and as being heirs together of the grace of life; that your prayers be not hindered.

7. Viri similiter cohabitent secundum scientiam, tanquam infirmiori vasi, muliebri impertientes honorem, tanquam etiam cohæredes gratiæ vitæ (*vel*, multiplicis gratiæ et vitæ,) ne preces vestræ interrumpantur.

7. *Likewise, ye husbands, dwell with* them. From husbands he requires prudence; for dominion over their wives is not given them, except on this condition, that they exercise authority prudently. Then let husbands remember that they need prudence to do rightly their duty. And doubtless many foolish things must be endured by them, many unpleasant things must be borne with; and they must at the same time beware lest their indulgence should foster folly. Hence the admonition of Peter is not in vain, that the husbands ought to cohabit with them as with a *weaker vessel*. Part of the prudence which he mentions, is, that the husbands honour their wives. For nothing destroys the friendship of life more than contempt; nor can we really love any but those whom we esteem; for love must be connected with respect.

Moreover, he employs a twofold argument, in order to persuade husbands to treat their wives honourably and kindly. The first is derived from the weakness of the sex; the other, from the honour with which God favours them. These things seem indeed to be in a manner contrary,—that honour ought to be given to wives, because they are weak, and because they excel; but these things well agree together where love exists. It is evident, that God is despised in his gifts, except we honour those on whom he has conferred any excellency. But when we consider that we are members of the same body, we learn to bear with one another, and mutually to cover our infirmities. This is what Paul means when he says that greater honour is given to the weaker members, (1 Cor. xii. 23;) even because we are more careful in protecting them from shame. Then Peter does

fear no terror." Terror here stands for what terrifies. The paraphrase of *Macknight* seems to give the real and simple meaning of the passage, "Whose daughters ye Christian women have become, by behaving well towards your husbands, and not being frightened to actions contrary to your religion through fear of displeasing them."

not without reason command that women should be cared for, and that they should be honoured with a kind treatment, because they are weak. And then as we more easily forgive children, when they offend through inexperience of age; so the weakness of the female sex ought to make us not to be too rigid and severe towards our wives.

The word *vessel*, as it is well known, means in Scripture any sort of instrument.

Being heirs together (or *co-heirs*) *of the grace of life.* Some copies have " of manifold grace;" others, instead of " life," have the word " living." Some read " co-heirs" in the dative case, which makes no difference in the sense. A conjunction is put by others between manifold grace and life; which reading is the most suitable.[1] For since the Lord is pleased to bestow in common on husbands and wives the same graces, he invites them to seek an equality in them; and we know that those graces are manifold in which wives are partakers with their husbands. For some belong to the present life, and some to God's spiritual kingdom. He afterwards adds, that they are co-heirs also of life, which is the chief thing. And though some are strangers to the hope of salvation, yet as it is offered by the Lord to them no less than to their husbands, it is a sufficient honour to the sex.

That your prayers be not hindered. For God cannot be rightly called upon, unless our minds be calm and peaceable. Among strifes and contentions there is no place for prayer. Peter indeed addresses the husband and the wife, when he bids them to be at peace one with another, so that they might with one mind pray to God. But we may hence gather a general doctrine—that no one ought to come to God except he is united to his brethren. Then as this reason ought to restrain all domestic quarrels and strifes, in order that each one of the family may pray to God; so in common life it ought to be as it were a bridle to check all contentions. For we are more than insane, if we knowingly and wilfully close up the way to God's presence by prayer, since this is the only asylum of our salvation.

---

[1] The received text is the most approved, and there is no different reading of any importance.—*Ed.*

Some give this explanation, that an intercourse with the wife ought to be sparing and temperate, lest too much indulgence in this respect should prevent attention to prayer, according to that saying of Paul, " Defraud not one another, unless by consent for a time, that ye may give yourselves to fasting and prayer." (1 Cor. vii. 5.) But the doctrine of Peter extends wider: and then Paul does not mean that prayers are interrupted by mutual cohabitation. Therefore the explanation which I have given ought to be retained.

8. Finally, *be ye* all of one mind, having compassion one of another; love as brethren, *be* pitiful, *be* courteous:	8. Denique sitis omnes idem sentientes, compatientes, fraternè vos diligentes, misericordes, humiles;
9. Not rendering evil for evil, or railing for railing: but contrariwise blessing; knowing that ye are thereunto called, that ye should inherit a blessing.	9. Non reddentes malum pro malo, vel convitium pro convitio; imo potius benedicentes, scientes quod in hoc vocati sitis, ut benedictionem hereditate consequamini.

Now follow general precepts which indiscriminately belong to all.[1] Moreover he summarily mentions some things which

---

[1] In the previous statements of particular duties belonging to various relations in life, the duty of masters towards their servants is omitted. Some have hence inferred that there were no masters who were Christians among those to whom Peter wrote. But this could not have been the case, and for this reason, because Paul, in his Epistles to the Ephesians and Colossians, expressly specifies the duty of masters towards their servants; and Ephesus and Colosse were included in Asia Minor, and it was to Christians scattered throughout that country that Peter wrote his Epistle.

But this omission is somewhat singular. At the same time, though the master's duty is not specifically mentioned, we may yet consider this verse as having a special reference to masters, as sympathy, brotherly love, and compassion or commiseration, are here inculcated.

The construction of the whole passage, beginning at the 17th verse of the last chapter, and ending at the 12th of this (for at the 13th of this, he resumes the subject he left off at the end of the 16th of the last) deserves to be noticed. " Honour all," is the injunction which he afterwards exemplifies as to servants, wives, and husbands; for the construction is " Honour all—the servants being subject, &c.—in like manner, the wives being subject, &c.—in like manner, the husbands, cohabiting according to knowledge, giving honour, &c." Then follows this verse in the same form, " And finally, all being of one mind, sympathizing, loving the brethren, compassionate, friendly-minded (or humble-minded,) not rendering, &c." And thus he proceeds to the end of the 12th verse. Afterwards he resumes the subject respecting the treatment the Christians met with from the world.

May we not then conclude, that as the duty of masters does not come under the idea of *honouring*, he did not specifically mention them, but referred only to the spirit and temper they ought to have exhibited?—*Ed.*

are especially necessary to foster friendship and love. The first is, *Be ye all of one mind,* or, think ye all the same thing. For though friends are at liberty to think differently, yet to do so is a cloud which obscures love; yea, from this seed easily arises hatred. Sympathy (συμπάθεια) extends to all our faculties, when concord exists between us; so that every one condoles with us in adversity as well as rejoices with us in prosperity, so that every one not only cares for himself, but also regards the benefit of others.

What next follows, *Love as brethren,* belongs peculiarly to the faithful; for where God is known as a Father, there only brotherhood really exists. Be *pitiful,* or merciful, which is added, means that we are not only to help our brethren and relieve their miseries, but also to bear with their infirmities. In what follows there are two readings in Greek; but what seems to me the most probable is the one I have put as the text; for we know that it is the chief bond to preserve friendship, when every one thinks modestly and humbly of himself; as there is nothing on the other hand which produces more discords than when we think too highly of ourselves. Wisely then does Peter bid us to be humble-minded (ταπεινόφρονες,) lest pride and haughtiness should lead us to despise our neighbours.[1]

9. *Not rendering evil for evil.* In these words every kind of revenge is forbidden; for in order to preserve love, we must bear with many things. At the same time he does not speak here of mutual benevolence, but he would have us to endure wrongs, when provoked by ungodly men. And though it is commonly thought that it is an instance of a weak and abject mind, not to avenge injuries, yet it is counted before God as the highest magnanimity. Nor is it indeed enough to abstain from revenge; but Peter requires also that we should pray for those who reproach us; for to *bless* here means to pray, as it is set in opposition to the second clause. But Peter teaches us in general, that evils are to be overcome by acts of kindness. This is indeed very hard, but we ought to imitate in this case our heavenly Father, who makes

[1] *Griesbach* has given the preference to ταπεινόφρονες, and has introduced it into the text.—*Ed.*

his sun to rise on the unworthy. What the sophists imagine to be the meaning, is a futile evasion; for when Christ said, "Love your enemies," he at the same time confirmed his own doctrine by saying, "That ye might be the children of God."

Knowing that ye are thereunto called. He means that this condition was required of the faithful when they were called by God, that they were not only to be so meek as not to retaliate injuries, but also to bless those who cursed them; and as this condition may seem almost unjust, he calls their attention to the reward; as though he had said, that there is no reason why the faithful should complain, because their wrongs would turn to their own benefit. In short, he shews how much would be the gain of patience; for if we submissively bear injuries, the Lord will bestow on us his blessing.

The verb, κληρονόμειν, to inherit, seems to express perpetuity, as though Peter had said, that the blessing would not be for a short time, but perpetual, if we be submissive in bearing injuries. But God blesses in a way different from men; for we express our wishes to him, but he confers a blessing on us. And on the other hand, Peter intimates that they who seek to revenge injuries, attempt what will yield them no good, for they thus deprive themselves of God's blessing.

10. For he that will love life, and see good days, let him refrain his tongue from evil, and his lips that they speak no guile:	10. Qui enim vult vitam diligere, et videre dies bonos, contineat linguam suam à malo, et labia sua, ne loquantur dolum;
11. Let him eschew evil, and do good; let him seek peace, and ensue it.	11. Declinet à malo et faciat bonum, quærat pacem et persequatur eam:
12. For the eyes of the Lord *are* over the righteous, and his ears *are open* unto their prayers: but the face of the Lord *is* against them that do evil.	12. Quoniam oculi Domini super justos, et aures ejus in preces eorum; vultus autem Domini super facientes mala.
13. And who *is* he that will harm you, if ye be followers of that which is good?	13. Et quis est qui vobis malè faciat, si boni æmuli sitis?
14. But and if ye suffer for righteousness' sake, happy *are ye:* and be not afraid of their terror, neither be troubled;	14. Verùm etiam si patiamini propter justitiam, beati; timorem vero eorum ne timeatis neque turbemini;

15. But sanctify the Lord God in your hearts.	15. Sed Dominum exercituum sanctificate in cordibus vestris.

10. *For he.* He confirms the last sentence by the testimony of David. The passage is taken from the thirty-fourth Psalm, where the Spirit testifies that it will be well with all who keep themselves from all evil-doing and wrong-doing. The common feeling indeed favours what is very different; for men think that they expose themselves to the insolence of enemies, if they do not boldly defend themselves. But the Spirit of God promises a happy life to none except to the meek, and those who endure evils; and we cannot be happy except God prospers our ways; and it is the good and the benevolent, and not the cruel and inhuman, that he will favour.

Peter has followed the Greek version, though the difference is but little. David's words are literally these,—" He who loves life and desires to see good days," &c. It is indeed a desirable thing, since God has placed us in this world, to pass our time in peace. Then, the way of obtaining this blessing is to conduct ourselves justly and harmlessly towards all.

The first thing he points out are the vices of the tongue; which are to be avoided, so that we may not be contumelious and insolent, nor speak deceitfully and with duplicity. Then he comes to deeds, that we are to injure none, or cause loss to none, but to endeavour to be kind to all, and to exercise the duties of humanity.

11. *Let him seek peace.* It is not enough to embrace it when offered to us, but it ought to be followed when it seems to flee from us. It also often happens, that when we seek it as much as we can, others will not grant it to us. On account of these difficulties and hindrances, he bids us to seek and pursue it.

12. *For the eyes of the Lord are over the righteous,* or, on the righteous. It ought to be a consolation to us, sufficient to mitigate all evils, that we are looked upon by the Lord, so that he will bring us help in due time. The meaning then is, that the prosperity which he has mentioned depends on the protection of God; for were not the Lord to care for his people, they would be like sheep exposed to wolves.

And that we for little reason raise a clamour, that we suddenly kindle unto wrath, that we burn with the passion of revenge, all this, doubtless, happens, because we do not consider that God cares for us, and because we do not acquiesce in his aid. Thus in vain we shall be taught patience, except our minds are first imbued with this truth, that God exercises such care over us, that he will in due time succour us. When, on the contrary, we are fully persuaded that God defends the cause of the righteous, we shall first attend simply to innocence, and then, when molested and hated by the ungodly, we shall flee to the protection of God. And when he says, that the *ears* of the Lord are open to our prayers, he encourages us to pray.

But the face of the Lord. By this clause he intimates that the Lord will be our avenger, because he will not always suffer the insolence of the ungodly to prevail; and at the same time he shews how it will be, if we seek to defend our life from injuries, even that God will be an adversary to us. But it may, on the other hand, be objected and said, that we experience it daily far otherwise, for the more righteous any one is, and the greater lover of peace he is, the more he is harassed by the wicked. To this I reply, that no one is so attentive to righteousness and peace, but that he sometimes sins in this respect. But it ought to be especially observed, that the promises as to this life do not extend further than as to what is expedient for us to be fulfilled. Hence, our peace with the world is often disturbed, that our flesh may be subdued, in order that we may serve God, and also for other reasons; so that nothing may be a loss to us.

13. *Who is he that will harm you.* He further confirms the previous sentence by an argument drawn from common experience. For it happens for the most part, that the ungodly disturb us, or are provoked by us, or that we do not labour to do them good as it behoves us; for they who seek to do good, do even soften minds which are otherwise hard as iron. This very thing is mentioned by Plato in his first book on the Republic, " Injustice," he says, " causes seditions and hatreds and fightings one with another; but

justice, concord and friendship."[1] However, though this commonly happens, yet it is not always the case; for the children of God, how much soever they may strive to pacify the ungodly by kindness, and shew themselves kind towards all, are yet often assailed undeservedly by many.

14. Hence Peter adds, *But if ye suffer for righteousness' sake.* The meaning is, that the faithful will do more towards obtaining a quiet life by kindness, than by violence and promptitude in taking revenge; but that when they neglect nothing to secure peace, were they to suffer, they are still blessed, because they suffer for the sake of righteousness. Indeed, this latter clause differs much from the judgment of our flesh; but Christ has not without reason thus declared; nor has Peter without reason repeated the sentence from his mouth; for God will at length come as a deliverer, and then openly will appear what now seems incredible, that is, that the miseries of the godly have been blessed when endured with patience.

To suffer *for righteousness,* means not only to submit to some loss or disadvantage in defending a good cause, but also to suffer unjustly, when any one is innocently in fear among men on account of the fear of God.

Be not afraid of their terror. He again points out the fountain and cause of impatience, that we are beyond due measure troubled, when the ungodly rise up against us. For such a dread either disheartens us, or degrades us, or kindles within us a desire for revenge. In the meantime, we do not acquiesce in the defence of God. Then the best remedy for checking the turbulent emotions of our minds will be, to conquer immoderate terrors by trusting in the aid of God.

But Peter no doubt meant to allude to a passage in the eighth chapter of Isaiah; for when the Jews against the prohibition of God sought to fortify themselves by the aid of the Gentile world, God warned his Prophet not to fear after their example. Peter at the same time seems to have turned "fear" into a different meaning; for it is taken passively by the Prophet, who accused the people of un-

[1] Στάσις γάρ που ἤγε ἀδικία καὶ μίσεα καὶ μάχας ἐν ἀλλήλοις παρέχει, ἡδὲ δικαιοσύνη ὁμόνοιαν καὶ φιλίαν.—Rep. lib. 1.

belief, because, at a time when they ought to have relied on the aid of God and to have boldly despised all dangers, they became so prostrate and broken down with fear, that they sent to all around them for unlawful help. But Peter takes fear in another sense, as meaning that terror which the ungodly are wont to fill us with by their violence and cruel threatenings. He then departs from the sense in which the word is taken by the Prophet; but in this there is nothing unreasonable; for his object was not to explain the words of the Prophet; he wished only to shew that nothing is fitter to produce patience than what Isaiah prescribes, even to ascribe to God his honour by recumbing in full confidence on his power.

I do not, however, object, if any one prefers to render Peter's words thus, *Fear ye not their fear;* as though he had said, "Be ye not afraid as the unbelieving, or the children of this world are wont to be, because they understand nothing of God's providence." But this, as I think, would be a forced explanation. There is, indeed, no need for us to toil much on this point, since Peter here did not intend to explain every word used by the Prophet, but only referred to this one thing, that the faithful will firmly stand, and can never be moved from a right course of duty by any dread or fear, if they will sanctify the Lord.

But this sanctification ought to be confined to the present case. For whence is it that we are overwhelmed with fear, and think ourselves lost, when danger is impending, except that we ascribe to mortal man more power to injure us than to God to save us? God promises that he will be the guardian of our salvation; the ungodly, on the other hand, attempt to subvert it. Unless God's promise sustain us, do we not deal unjustly with him, and in a manner profane him? Then the Prophet teaches us that we ought to think honourably of the Lord of hosts; for how much soever the ungodly may contrive to destroy us, and whatever power they may possess, he alone is more than sufficiently powerful to secure our safety.[1] Peter then adds, *in your hearts.* For if this

[1] "Sanctify" here, seems to have the same meaning as in our Lord's prayer, "Hallowed," or sanctified "be thy name;" where it means honoured

conviction takes full possession of our minds, that the help promised by the Lord is sufficient for us, we shall be well fortified to repel all the fears of unbelief.

15. And *be* ready always to *give* an answer to every man that asketh you a reason of the hope that is in you with meekness and fear:	15. Parati autem sitis ad responsionem cuivis poscenti à vobis rationem ejus quæ in vobis est spei;
16. Having a good conscience; that, whereas they speak evil of you, as of evil-doers, they may be ashamed that falsely accuse your good conversation in Christ.	16. Cum mansuetudine et timore, conscientiam habentes bonam; ut in quo de vobis obtrectant, tanquam maleficis, pudefiant dum infamant bonam vestram in Christo conversationem.

Though this is a new precept, it yet depends on what is gone before, for he requires such constancy in the faithful, as boldly to give a reason for their faith to their adversaries. And this is a part of that sanctification which he had just mentioned; for we then really honour God, when neither fear nor shame hinders us from making a profession of our faith. But Peter does not expressly bid us to assert and proclaim what has been given us by the Lord everywhere, and always and among all indiscriminately, for the Lord gives his people the spirit of discretion, so that they may know when and how far and to whom it is expedient to speak. He bids them only to be ready to give an answer, lest by their sloth and the cowardly fear of the flesh they should expose the doctrine of Christ, by being silent, to the derision of the ungodly. The meaning then is, that we ought to be prompt in avowing our faith, so as to set it forth whenever necessary, lest the unbelieving through our silence should condemn the religion we follow.

But it ought to be noticed, that Peter here does not command us to be prepared to solve any question that may be mooted; for it is not the duty of all to speak on every subject. But it is the general doctrine that is meant, which belongs to the ignorant and the simple. Then Peter had in view no other thing, than that Christians should make it evident to unbelievers that they truly worshipped God, and had a holy and good religion. And in this there is no diffi-

or glorified. And to honour or glorify God in our hearts is what Calvin very correctly explains.—*Ed.*

culty, for it would be strange if we could bring nothing to defend our faith when any one made inquiries respecting it. For we ought always to take care that all may know that we fear God, and that we piously and reverently regard his legitimate worship.

This was also required by the state of the times: the Christian name was much hated and deemed infamous; many thought the sect wicked and guilty of many sacrileges. It would have been, therefore, the highest perfidy against God, if, when asked, they had neglected to give a testimony in favour of their religion. And this, as I think, is the meaning of the word *apology*, which Peter uses, that is, that the Christians were to make it evident to the world that they were far off from every impiety, and did not corrupt true religion, on which account they were suspected by the ignorant.

Hope here is by a metonymy to be taken for faith. Peter, however, as it has been said, does not require them to know how to discuss distinctly and refinedly every article of the faith, but only to shew that their faith in Christ was consistent with genuine piety. And hence we learn how all those abuse the name of Christians, who understand nothing certain respecting their faith, and have nothing to give as an answer for it. But it behoves us again carefully to consider what he says, when he speaks of *that hope that is in you;* for he intimates that the confession which flows from the heart is alone that which is approved by God; for except faith dwells within, the tongue prattles in vain. It ought then to have its roots within us, so that it may afterwards bring forth the fruit of confession.

16. *With meekness.* This is a most necessary admonition; for unless our minds are endued with meekness, contentions will immediately break forth. And meekness is set in opposition to pride and vain ostentation, and also to excessive zeal. To this he justly adds *fear;* for where reverence for God prevails, it tames all the ferocity of our minds, and it will especially cause us to speak calmly of God's mysteries. For contentious disputes arise from this, because many think less honourably than they ought of the greatness of divine

wisdom, and are carried away by profane audacity. If, then, we would render approved of God the confession of our faith, all boasting must be put aside, all contention must be relinquished.

Having a good conscience. What we say without a corresponding life has but little weight; hence he joins to confession a good conscience. For we see that many are sufficiently ready with their tongue, and prate much, very freely, and yet with no fruit, because the life does not correspond. Besides, the integrity of conscience alone is that which gives us confidence in speaking as we ought; for they who prattle much about the gospel, and whose dissolute life is a proof of their impiety, not only make themselves objects of ridicule, but also expose the truth itself to the slanders of the ungodly. For why did he before bid us to be ready to defend the faith, should any one require from us a reason for it, except that it is our duty to vindicate the truth of God against those false suspicions which the ignorant entertain respecting it? But the defence of the tongue will avail but little, except the life corresponds with it.

He therefore says, *that they may be ashamed,* who blame your good conversation in Christ, and who speak against you as evil-doers; as though he had said, " If your adversaries have nothing to allege against you, except that you follow Christ, they will at length be ashamed of their malicious wickedness, or at least, your innocence will be sufficient to confute them."

17. For *it is* better, if the will of God be so, that ye suffer for well-doing, than for evil-doing. 18. For Christ also hath once suffered for sins, the just for the unjust, that he might bring us to God, being put to death in the flesh, but quickened by the Spirit:	17. Præstat enim benefaciendo (si ita fert voluntas Dei) pati quàm malefaciendo: 18. Quia et Christus semel pro peccatis passus est, justus pro injustis, ut nos adduceret Deo; mortificatus quidem carne, vivificatus autem spiritu.

17. *For it is better.* This belongs not only to what follows but to the whole context. He had spoken of the profession of faith, which at that time was attended with great danger; he says now that it is much better, if they sustained any loss in defending a good cause, to suffer thus

unjustly than to be punished for their evil deeds. This consolation is understood rather by secret meditation, than by many words. It is what indeed occurs everywhere in profane authors, that there is a sufficient defence in a good conscience, whatever evils may happen, and must be endured. These have spoken courageously ; but then the only really bold man is he who looks to God. Therefore Peter added this clause, *If the will of God be so.* For in these words he reminds us, that if we suffer unjustly, it is not by chance, but according to the divine will ; and he assumes, that God wills nothing or appoints nothing but for the best reason. Hence the faithful have always this comfort in their miseries, that they know that they have God as their witness, and that they also know that they are led by him to the contest, in order that they may under his protection give a proof of their faith.

18. *For Christ also.* It is another comfort, that if in our afflictions we are conscious of having done well, we suffer according to the example of Christ; and it hence follows that we are blessed. At the same time he proves, from the design of Christ's death, that it is by no means consistent with our profession that we should suffer for our evil deeds. For he teaches us that Christ suffered in order to bring us to God. What does this mean, except that we have been thus consecrated to God by Christ's death, that we may live and die to him ?

There are, then, two parts in this sentence ; the first is, that persecutions ought to be borne with resignation, because the Son of God shews the way to us ; and the other is, that since we have been consecrated to God's service by the death of Christ, it behoves us to suffer, not for our faults, but for righteousness' sake.

Here, however, a question may be raised, Does not God chastise the faithful, whenever he suffers them to be afflicted? To this I answer, that it indeed often happens, that God punishes them according to what they deserve ; and this is not denied by Peter ; but he reminds us what a comfort it is to have our cause connected with God. And how God does not punish sins in them who endure persecution for the sake of righteousness, and in what sense they are said to be innocent, we shall see in the next chapter.

Being put to death in the flesh. Now this is a great thing, that we are made conformable to the Son of God, when we suffer without cause; but there is added another consolation, that the death of Christ had a blessed issue; for though he suffered through the weakness of the flesh, he yet rose again through the power of the Spirit. Then the cross of Christ was not prejudicial, nor his death, since life obtained the victory. This was said (as Paul also reminds us in 2 Cor. iv. 10) that we may know that we are to bear in our body the dying of Christ, in order that his life may be manifested in us. *Flesh* here means the outward man; and *Spirit* means the divine power, by which Christ emerged from death a conqueror.

19. By which also he went and preached unto the spirits in prison;

20. Which sometime were disobedient, when once the long-suffering of God waited in the days of Noah, while the ark was a preparing, wherein few, that is, eight souls, were saved by water.

21. The like figure whereunto *even* baptism doth also now save us, (not the putting away of the filth of the flesh, but the answer of a good conscience toward God,) by the resurrection of Jesus Christ:

22. Who is gone into heaven, and is on the right hand of God; angels, and authorities, and powers, being made subject unto him.

19. In quo et iis qui in specula (*vel*, in excubiis, *vel*, carcere) erant spiritibus, profectus prædicavit;

20. Quum increduli fuissent olim, quum semel expectabatur Dei patientia in diebus Noe; dum apparabatur arca, in qua paucæ, hoc est, octo animæ servatæ sunt per aquam.

21. Cujus figura respondens baptismus, nos quoque salvos reddit, non abjectio sordium carnis, sed bonæ conscientiæ examen apud Deum, per resurrectionem Jesu Christi:

22. Qui est in dextera Dei profectus in cœlum, subjectis sibi angelis, et potestatibus et virtutibus.

19. *By which also.* Peter added this, that we might know that the vivifying power of the Spirit of which he spoke, was not only put forth as to Christ himself, but is also poured forth with regard to us, as Paul shews in Rom. v. 5. He then says, that Christ did not rise only for himself, but that he made known to others the same power of his Spirit, so that it penetrated to the dead. It hence follows, that we shall not less feel it in vivifying whatever is mortal in us.

But as the obscurity of this passage has produced, as usual, various explanations, I shall first disprove what has been brought forward by some, and secondly, we shall seek its genuine and true meaning.

Common has been the opinion that Christ's descent into hell is here referred to ; but the words mean no such thing ; for there is no mention made of the soul of Christ, but only that he went by the Spirit : and these are very different things, that Christ's soul went, and that Christ preached by the power of the Spirit. Then Peter expressly mentioned *the Spirit*, that he might take away the notion of what may be called a real presence.

Others explain this passage of the apostles, that Christ by their ministry appeared to the dead, that is, to unbelievers. I, indeed, allow that Christ by means of his apostles went by his Spirit to those who were kept as it were in prison ; but this exposition appears incorrect on several accounts : First, Peter says that Christ went *to spirits*, by which he means souls separated from their bodies, for living men are never called spirits ; and secondly, what Peter repeats in the fourth chapter on the same subject, does not admit of such an allegory. Therefore the words must be properly understood of the dead. Thirdly, it seems very strange, that Peter, speaking of the apostles, should immediately, as though forgetting himself, go back to the time of Noah. Certainly this mode of speaking would be most unsuitable. Then this explanation cannot be right.

Moreover, the strange notion of those who think that unbelievers as to the coming of Christ, were after his death freed from their sin, needs no long refutation ; for it is an indubitable doctrine of Scripture, that we obtain not salvation in Christ except by faith ; then there is no hope left for those who continue to death unbelieving. They speak what is somewhat more probable, who say, that the redemption obtained by Christ availed the dead, who in the time of Noah were long unbelieving, but repented a short time before they were drowned by the deluge. They then understood that they suffered in the flesh the punishment due to their perverseness, and yet were saved by Christ, so that they did not perish for ever. But this interpretation cannot stand ; it is indeed inconsistent with the words of the passage, for Peter ascribes salvation only to the family of Noah, and gives over to ruin all who were not within the ark.

I therefore have no doubt but Peter speaks generally, that the manifestation of Christ's grace was made to godly spirits, and that they were thus endued with the vital power of the Spirit. Hence there is no reason to fear that it will not flow to us. But it may be inquired, Why he puts in prison the souls of the godly after having quitted their bodies? It seems to me that φυλακή rather means a watchtower in which watchmen stand for the purpose of watching, or the very act of watching: for it is often so taken by Greek authors; and the meaning would be very appropriate, that godly souls were watching in hope of the salvation promised them, as though they saw it afar off. Nor is there a doubt but that the holy fathers in life, as well as after death, directed their thoughts to this object. But if the word *prison* be preferred, it would not be unsuitable; for, as while they lived, the Law, according to Paul, (Gal. iii. 23,) was a sort of prison in which they were kept; so after death they must have felt the same desire for Christ; for the spirit of liberty had not as yet been fully given. Hence this anxiety of expectation was to them a kind of prison.

Thus far the Apostle's words seem to agree together, and with the thread of the argument; but what follows is attended with some difficulty; for he does not mention the faithful here, but only the unbelieving; and this seems to overturn the preceding exposition. Some have for this reason been led to think that no other thing is said here, but that the unbelieving, who had formerly persecuted the godly, found the Spirit of Christ an accuser, as though Peter consoled the faithful with this argument, that Christ, even when dead, punished them. But their mistake is discovered by what we shall see in the next chapter, that the Gospel was preached to the dead, that they might live according to God in the spirit, which peculiarly applies to the faithful. And it is further certain that he repeats there what he now says. Besides, they have not considered that what Peter meant was especially this, that as the power of the Spirit of

Christ shewed itself to be vivifying in him, and was known as such by the dead, so it will be towards us.

Let us, however, see why it is that he mentions only the unbelieving; for he seems to say, that Christ in spirit appeared to those who formerly were unbelieving; but I understand him otherwise, that then the true servants of God were mixed together with the unbelieving, and were almost hidden on account of their number. I allow that the Greek construction is at variance with this meaning, for Peter, if he meant this, ought to have used the genitive case absolute. But as it was not unusual with the Apostles to put one case instead of another, and as we see that Peter here heaps together many things, and no other suitable meaning can be elicited, I have no hesitation in giving this explanation of this intricate passage; so that readers may understand that those called unbelieving are different from those to whom he said the Gospel was preached.

After having then said that Christ was manifested to the dead, he immediately adds, *When there were formerly unbelievers;* by which he intimated, that it was no injury to the holy fathers that they were almost hidden through the vast number of the ungodly. For he meets, as I think, a doubt, which might have harassed the faithful of that day. They saw almost the whole world filled with unbelievers, that they enjoyed all authority, and that life was in their power. This trial might have shaken the confidence of those who were shut up, as it were, under the sentence of death. Therefore Peter reminds them, that the condition of the fathers was not different, and that though the multitude of the ungodly then covered the whole earth, their life was yet preserved in safety by the power of God.

He then comforted the godly, lest they should be cast down and destroyed because they were so few; and he chose an example the most remarkable in antiquity, even that of the world drowned by the deluge; for then in the common ruin of mankind, the family of Noah alone escaped. And he points out the manner, and says that it was a kind of baptism. There is then in this respect also nothing unsuitable.

The sum of what is said is this, that the world has always been full of unbelievers, but that the godly ought not to be terrified by their vast number; for though Noah was surrounded on every side by the ungodly, and had very few as his friends, he was not yet drawn aside from the right course of his faith.[1]

When once the long-suffering of God waited. This ought to be applied to the ungodly, whom God's patience rendered more slothful; for when God deferred his vengeance and did not immediately execute it, the ungodly boldly disregarded all threatenings; but Noah, on the contrary, being warned by God, had the deluge for a long time before his eyes. Hence his assiduity in building the ark; for being terrified by God's judgment, he shook off all torpidity.

21. *The like figure whereunto.* I fully think that the relative ought to be read in the dative case, and that it has happened, through a mistake, that ὅ is put, and not ᾧ. The meaning, however, is not ambiguous, that Noah, saved by water, had a sort of baptism. And this the Apostle mentions, that the likeness between him and us might appear more evident. It has already been said that the design of this clause is to shew that we ought not to be led away by wicked examples from the fear of God, and the right way of salvation, and to mix with the world. This is

---

[1] The most satisfactory explanation of this passage is that of *Beza, Doddridge, Macknight,* and *Scott;* that the reference is to what was done in the time of Noah, that is, that Christ by his Spirit employed him as a preacher of righteousness, though with no success, as the spirits of the men to whom he preached were then in prison, reserved, as the fallen angels are represented to be, for the judgment of the last day. The Apostle had before said that Christ's Spirit was in the prophets who foretold his coming, chap. i. 11. The passage may be thus rendered,—

19. " By which also he, having gone, preached to the spirits who are in prison, formerly disobedient, when the long-suffering of God waited in the days of Noah," &c.; or, according to *Macknight,* "to the spirits *now* in prison, who formerly were disobedient," &c. The word "formerly" seems to require "now" in the previous clause, or, "who are," as rendered by *Beza.* " He, having gone, preached," is similar to a phrase in Eph. ii. 17, " And came and preached," &c.; or, literally, " And having come he preached," &c. Paul does not speak of his coming personally, but by his ministers: and Peter evidently speaks of his going in the same sense.

For ἅπαξ ἐξεδέχετο, *Griesbach* substitutes ἀπεξεδέχετο, as being the most approved reading.—*Ed.*

made evident in baptism, in which we are buried together with Christ, so that, being dead to the world, and to the flesh, we may live to God. On this account, he says that our baptism is an antitype (ἀντίτυπον) to the baptism of Noah, not that Noah's baptism was the first pattern, and ours an inferior figure, as the word is taken in the Epistle to the Hebrews, where the ceremonies of the law are said to be antitypes of heavenly things, (Heb. ix. 4.) Greek writers apply the same word to sacraments, so that, when they speak of the mystical bread of the holy Supper, they call it the antitype. But here there is no comparison made between the greater and the less; the Apostle only means that there is a likeness, and as they commonly say, a correspondence. Perhaps it might more properly be said to be correspondency, (ἀντίστροφον,) as Aristotle makes Dialectics to be the antistrophè of Rhetoric. But we need not labour about words, when there is an agreement about the thing itself. As Noah, then, obtained life through death, when in the ark, he was enclosed not otherwise than as it were in the grave, and when the whole world perished, he was preserved together with his small family; so at this day, the death which is set forth in baptism, is to us an entrance into life, nor can salvation be hoped for, except we be separated from the world.

Not the putting away of the filth of the flesh. This was added, because it might be that the greatest part of men would profess the name of Christ; and so it is with us, almost all are introduced into the church by baptism. Thus, what he had said before would not be appropriate, that few at this day are saved by baptism, as God saved only eight by the ark. This objection Peter anticipates, when he testifies that he speaks not of the naked sign, but that the effect must also be connected with it, as though he had said, that what happened in the age of Noah would always be the case, that mankind would rush on to their own destruction, but that the Lord would in a wonderful way deliver His very small flock.

We now see what this connexion means; for some one might object and say, " Our baptism is widely different from that of Noah, for it happens that most are at this day baptized." To this he replies, that the external symbol is not sufficient, except baptism be received really and effectually: and the reality of it will be found only in a few. It hence follows that we ought carefully to see how men commonly act when we rely on examples, and that we ought not to fear though we may be few in number.

But the fanatics, such as Schuencfeldius, absurdly pervert this testimony, while they seek to take away from sacraments all their power and effect. For Peter did not mean here to teach that Christ's institution is vain and inefficacious, but only to exclude hypocrites from the hope of salvation, who, as far as they can, deprave and corrupt baptism. Moreover, when we speak of sacraments, two things are to be considered, the sign and the thing itself. In baptism the sign is water, but the thing is the washing of the soul by the blood of Christ and the mortifying of the flesh. The institution of Christ includes these two things. Now that the sign appears often inefficacious and fruitless, this happens through the abuse of men, which does not take away the nature of the sacrament. Let us then learn not to tear away the thing signified from the sign. We must at the same time beware of another evil, such as prevails among the Papists; for as they distinguish not as they ought between the thing and the sign, they stop at the outward element, and on that fix their hope of salvation. Therefore the sight of the water takes away their thoughts from the blood of Christ and the power of the Spirit. They do not regard Christ as the only author of all the blessings therein offered to us; they transfer the glory of his death to the water, they tie the secret power of the Spirit to the visible sign.

What then ought we to do? Not to separate what has been joined together by the Lord. We ought to acknowledge in baptism a spiritual washing, we ought to embrace therein the testimony of the remission of sin and the pledge of our renovation, and yet so as to leave to Christ his own honour, and also to the Holy Spirit; so that no part of our salvation should be transferred to the sign. Doubtless when Peter, having mentioned baptism, immediately made this exception, that it is not the putting off of the filth of the flesh, he sufficiently shewed that baptism to some is only the outward act, and that the outward sign of itself avails nothing.

But the answer of a good conscience. The word *question*, or questioning, is to be taken here for " answer," or testimony. Now Peter briefly defines the efficacy and use of baptism, when he calls attention to conscience, and expressly requires that confidence which can sustain the sight of God and can stand before his tribunal. For in these words he teaches us that baptism in its main part is spiritual, and then that it includes the remission of sins and renovation of the old man; for how can there be a good and pure conscience until our old man is reformed, and we be renewed in the righteousness of God? and how can we answer before God, unless we rely on and are sustained by a gratuitous pardon of our sins? In short, Peter intended to set forth the effect of baptism, that no one might glory in a naked and dead sign, as hypocrites are wont to do.

But we must notice what follows, *by the resurrection of Jesus Christ.* By these words he teaches us that we are not to cleave to the element of water, and that what is thereby typified flows from Christ alone, and is to be sought from him. Moreover, by referring to the resurrection, he has regard to the doctrine which he had taught before, that Christ was vivified by the Spirit; for the resurrection was victory over death and the completion of our salvation. We hence learn that the death of Christ is not excluded, but is included in his resurrection. We then cannot otherwise derive benefit from baptism, than by having all our thoughts fixed on the death and the resurrection of Christ.

22. *Who is on the right hand of God.* He recommends to us the ascension of Christ unto heaven, lest our eyes should seek him in the world; and this belongs especially to faith. He commends to our notice his session on the Father's right hand, lest we should doubt his power to save us. And what his *sitting* at the right hand of the Father means, we have elsewhere explained, that is, that Christ exercises supreme power everywhere as God's representative. And an explanation of this is what follows, *angels being made subject to*

him; and he adds *powers* and *authorities* only for the sake of amplification, for angels are usually designated by such words. It was then Peter's object to set forth by these high titles the sovereignty of Christ.

CHAPTER IV.

1. Forasmuch then as Christ hath suffered for us in the flesh, arm yourselves likewise with the same mind: for he that hath suffered in the flesh hath ceased from sin;
2. That he no longer should live the rest of *his* time in the flesh to the lusts of men, but to the will of God.
3. For the time past of *our* life may suffice us to have wrought the will of the Gentiles, when we walked in lasciviousness, lusts, excess of wine, revellings, banquetings, and abominable idolatries:
4. Wherein they think it strange that ye run not with *them* to the same excess of riot, speaking evil of *you;*
5. Who shall give account to him that is ready to judge the quick and the dead.

1. Christo igitur passo pro nobis carne, vos quoque eadem cogitatione armamini ; quod scilicet qui passus est in carne, destitit à peccato ;
2. Ne amplius hominum concupiscentiis, sed voluntati Dei, quod residuum est temporis in carne, vivat.
3. Satis enim nobis est quod anteacto vitæ tempore voluntatem gentium patraverimus, quum ambularemus in lasciviis, concupiscentiis, comessationibus, potationibus et nefariis idololatriis:
4. Quod illis videtur insolens, quòd non concurratis in eandem luxus profusionem, ideoque malè loquuntur ;
5. Qui reddituri sunt rationem ei qui paratus est judicare vivos et mortuos.

1. *Forasmuch then as Christ.* When he had before set forth Christ before us, he only spoke of the suffering of the cross ; for sometimes the cross means mortification, because the outward man is wasted by afflictions, and our flesh is also subdued. But he now ascends higher; for he speaks of the reformation of the whole man. The Scripture recommends to us a twofold likeness to the death of Christ, that we are to be conformed to him in reproaches and troubles, and also that the old man being dead and extinct in us, we are to be renewed to a spiritual life. (Phil. iii. 10 ; Rom. vi. 4.) Yet Christ is not simply to be viewed as our example, when we speak of the mortification of the flesh ; but it is by his Spirit that we are really made conformable to his death, so that it becomes effectual to the crucifying of our flesh. In short, as Peter at the end of the last chapter exhorted us to patience

after the example of Christ, because death was to him a passage to life; so now from the same death he deduces a higher doctrine, that we ought to die to the flesh and to the world, as Paul teaches us more at large in the sixth chapter of his Epistle to the Romans. He therefore says, *arm yourselves,* or be ye armed, intimating that we are really and effectually supplied with invincible weapons to subdue the flesh, if we partake as we ought of the efficacy of Christ's death.

For he that hath suffered. The particle ὅτι does not, I think, denote here the cause, but is to be taken as explanatory; for Peter sets forth what that thought or mind is with which Christ's death arms us, even that the dominion of sin ought to be abolished in us, so that God may reign in our life. Erasmus has incorrectly, as I think, rendered the word "he who did suffer," (*patiebatur*) applying it to Christ. For it is an indefinite sentence, which generally extends to all the godly, and has the same meaning with the words of Paul in Rom. vi. 7, "He who is dead is justified or freed from sin;" for both the Apostles intimate, that when we become dead to the flesh, we have no more to do with sin, that it should reign in us, and exercise its power in our life.[1]

It may, however, be objected, that Peter here speaks unsuitably in making us to be conformable to Christ in this

[1] The subject of this passage, from ch. iii. 14 to ch. iv. 6, is suffering unjustly, or for righteousness' sake, and Christ is brought as an example, he being just, suffered for the unjust. After a digression at the 19th verse of the third chapter, the Apostle returns here to his former subject, the example of Christ suffering in the flesh or in his body and in order to retain still the idea that he was just when he suffered, this clause seems to have been put in parenthetically, " For he who suffered ceased from sin," that is, had no sin, but was just. And hence in the following verses he exhorts them to lead a holy life whatever might be the opposition from the world, so that they might be like their Saviour, suffering unjustly, they themselves being innocent.

1. " Christ then having suffered for us in the flesh, arm ye also yourselves with the same mind, (for he who suffered in the flesh ceased from sin;) 2. so as to live no longer the remaining time in the flesh to the lusts of men, but to the will of God."

They were exhorted to resolve to follow the example of Christ, but in such a way as not to suffer for their sins, but for righteousness' sake. It is implied that they had been evil-doers, but they were no longer to be so, otherwise their suffering in the flesh would not be like that of Christ. To suffer as well-doers, and not as evil-doers, was to suffer as Christ did.—*Ed.*

respect, that we suffer in the flesh; for it is certain that there was nothing sinful in Christ which required to be corrected. But the answer is obvious, that it is not necessary that a comparison should correspond in all its parts. It is then enough that we should in a measure be made conformable to the death of Christ. In the same way is also explained, not unfitly, what Paul says, that we are planted in the likeness of his death, (Rom. vi. 5;) for the manner is not altogether the same, but that his death is become in a manner the type and pattern of our mortification.

We must also notice that the word *flesh* is put here twice, but in a different sense; for when he says that Christ suffered in the flesh, he means that the human nature which Christ had taken from us was made subject to death, that is, that Christ as a man naturally died. In the second clause, which refers to us, *flesh* means the corruption and the sinfulness of our nature; and thus suffering in the flesh signifies the denying of ourselves. We now see what is the likeness between Christ and us, and what is the difference; that as he suffered in the flesh taken from us, so the whole of our flesh ought to be crucified.

2. *That he no longer.* Here he sets forth the way of ceasing from sin, that renouncing the covetings of men we should study to form our life according to the will of God. And thus he includes here the two things in which renovation consists, the destruction of the flesh and the vivification of the spirit. The course of good living is thus to begin with the former, but we are to advance to the latter.

Moreover, Peter defines here what is the rule of right living, even when man depends on the will of God. It hence follows, that nothing is right and well ordered in man's life as soon as he wanders from this rule. We ought further to notice the contrast between *God's will* and the *covetings* or lusts of *men*. We hence understand how great is our depravity, and how we ought to strive to become obedient to God. When he says, *the rest of time in the flesh*, the word *flesh* means the present life, as in Heb. v. 7.

3. *For the time past of our life may suffice.* Peter does not mean that we ought to be wearied with pleasures, as

those are wont to be who are filled with them to satiety; but that on the contrary the memory of our past life ought to stimulate us to repentance. And doubtless it ought to be the sharpest goad to make us run on well, when we recollect that we have been wandering from the right way the greatest part of our life. And Peter reminds us, that it would be most unreasonable were we not to change the course of our life after having been enlightened by Christ. For he makes a distinction here between the time of ignorance and the time of faith, as though he had said that it was but right that they should become new and different men from the time that Christ had called them. But instead of the *lusts* or covetings of men, he now mentions *the will of the Gentiles*, by which he reproves the Jews for having mixed with the Gentiles in all their pollutions, though the Lord had separated them from the Gentiles.

In what follows he shews that those vices ought to be put off which prove men to be blind and ignorant of God. And there is a peculiar emphasis in the words, *the time past of our life*, for he intimates that we ought to persevere to the end, as when Paul says, that Christ was raised from the dead, to die no more. (Rom. vi. 6.) For we have been redeemed by the Lord for this end, that we may serve him all the days of our life.

In lasciviousness. He does not give the whole catalogue of sins, but only mentions some of them, by which we may briefly learn what those things are which men, not renewed by God's Spirit, desire and seek, and to which they are inclined. And he names the grosser vices, as it is usually done when examples are adduced. I shall not stop to explain the words, for there is no difficulty in them.

But here a question arises, that Peter seems to have done wrong to many, in making all men guilty of lasciviousness, dissipation, lusts, drunkenness, and revellings; for it is certain that all were not involved in these vices; nay, we know that some among the Gentiles lived honourably and without a spot of infamy. To this I reply, that Peter does not so ascribe these vices to the Gentiles, as though he charged every individual with all these, but that we are by nature inclined to all these evils, and not only so, but that we are so much under the power of depravity, that these fruits which he mentions necessarily proceed from it as from an evil root. There is indeed no one who has not within him the seed of all vices, but all do not germinate and grow up in every individual. Yet the contagion is so spread and diffused through the whole human race, that the whole community appears infected with innumerable evils, and that no member is free or pure from the common corruption.

The last clause may also suggest another question, for Peter addressed the Jews, and yet he says that they had been immersed in abominable idolatries; but the Jews then living in every part of the world carefully abstained from idols. A twofold answer may be adduced here, either that by mentioning the whole for a part, he declares of all what belonged to a few, (for there is no doubt but the Churches to which he wrote were made up of Gentiles as well as of Jews,) or that he calls those superstitions in which the Jews were then involved, idolatries; for though they professed to worship the God of Israel, yet we know that no part of divine worship was genuine among them. And how great must have been the confusion in barbarous countries and among a scattered people, when Jerusalem itself, from whose rays they borrowed their light, had fallen into extreme impiety! for we know that dotages of every kind prevailed with impunity, so that the high-priesthood, and the whole government of the Church, were in the power of the Sadducees.

4. *Wherein they think it strange.* The words of Peter literally are these, "In which they are strangers, you not running with them into the same excess of riot, blaspheming." But the word, to be strangers, means to stop at a thing as new and unusual. This is a way of speaking which the Latins also sometimes use, as when Cicero says that he was a stranger in the city, because he knew not what was carried on there. But in this place, Peter fortifies the faithful, lest they should suffer themselves to be disturbed or corrupted by the perverse judgments or words of the ungodly. For it is no light temptation, when they among whom we live, charge us that our life is different from that of man-

kind in general. "These," they say, "must form for themselves a new world, for they differ from all mankind." Thus they accuse the children of God, as though they attempted a separation from the whole world.

Then the Apostle anticipated this, and forbade the faithful to be discouraged by such reproaches and calumnies; and he proposed to them, as a support, the judgment of God: for this it is that can sustain us against all assaults, that is, when we patiently wait for that day, in which Christ will punish all those who now presumptuously condemn us, and will shew that we and our cause are approved by Him. And he expressly mentions *the living and the dead*, lest we should think that we shall suffer any loss, if they remain alive when we are dead; for they shall not, for this reason, escape the hand of God. And in what sense he calls them the living and the dead, we may learn from the fifteenth chapter of the first Epistle to the Corinthians.

6. For, for this cause was the gospel preached also to them that are dead, that they might be judged according to men in the flesh, but live according to God in the spirit.

7. But the end of all things is at hand: be ye therefore sober, and watch unto prayer.

8. And above all things, have fervent charity among yourselves: for charity shall cover the multitude of sins.

9. Use hospitality one to another without grudging.

10. As every man hath received the gift, *even so* minister the same one to another, as good stewards of the manifold grace of God.

11. If any speak, *let him speak* as the oracles of God; if any man minister, *let him do it* as of the ability which God giveth; that God in all things may be glorified through Jesus Christ: to whom be praise and dominion for ever and ever. Amen.

6. In hoc enim et mortuis evangelizatus fuit (*vel*, prædicatum fuit evangelium,) ut judicentur quidem secundum homines carne, vivant autem secundum Deum spiritu.

7. Porro omnium finis propinquus est: sobrii itaque estote, et vigilantes ad precandum.

8. Ante omnia vero charitatem inter vos intentam habentes; quia charitas operiet multitudinem peccatorum.

9. Invicem hospitales sine murmurationibus.

10. Ut quisque accepit donum, ministrantes illud inter vos, tanquam boni dispensatores multiplicis gratiæ Dei.

11. Siquis loquitur, loquatur tanquam eloquia Dei; siquis ministrat, tanquam ex virtute quam suppeditat Deus; ut in omnibus glorificetur Deus per Jesum Christum; cui est gloria et imperium in secula seculorum. Amen.

6. *For for this cause was the gospel preached also to them that are dead*, or, He has been evangelized to the dead. We see in what sense he takes the former passage in the third

chapter, even that death does not hinder Christ from being always our defender. It is then a remarkable consolation to the godly, that death itself brings no loss to their salvation. Though Christ, then, may not appear a deliverer in this life, yet his redemption is not void, or without effect; for his power extends to the dead. But as the Greek word is doubtful, it may be rendered in the masculine, or in the neuter gender; but the meaning is almost the same, that is, that Christ had been made known as a redeemer to the dead, or that salvation had been made known to them by the gospel. But if the grace of Christ once penetrated to the dead, there is no doubt but that we shall partake of it when dead. We then set for it limits much too narrow, if we confine it to the present life.

That they might be judged. I omit the explanations of others, for they seem to me to be very remote from the Apostle's meaning. This has been said, as I think, by way of anticipation, for it might have been objected, that the gospel is of no benefit to the dead, as it does not restore them to life. Peter concedes a part of this objection, and yet in such a way, that they are not deprived of the salvation obtained by Christ. Therefore, in the first clause, when he says, "that they might be judged in the flesh, according to men," it is a concession; and "judged" means here, as often elsewhere, condemned; and *flesh* is the outward man. So that the meaning is, that though according to the estimation of the world the dead suffer destruction in their flesh, and are deemed condemned as to the outward man, yet they cease not to live with God, and that in their spirit, because Christ quickens them by his Spirit.

But we ought to add what Paul teaches us in Rom. viii. 10, that the Spirit is life; and hence it will be, that he will at length absorb the relics of death which still cleave to us. The sum of what he says is, that though the condition of the dead in the flesh is worse, according to man, yet it is enough that the Spirit of Christ revives them, and will eventually lead them to the perfection of life.[1]

[1] *Whitby, Doddridge,* and *Macknight,* regard *the dead* here as the dead in sins, according to Eph. ii. 1. The first thus paraphrases what follows,

7. *But*, or, moreover, *the end of all things is at hand.* Though the faithful hear that their felicity is elsewhere than in the world, yet, as they think that they should live long, this false thought renders them careless, and even slothful, so that they direct not their thoughts to the kingdom of God. Hence the Apostle, that he might rouse them from the drowsiness of the flesh, reminds them that the end of all things was nigh; by which he intimates that we ought not to sit still in the world, from which we must soon remove. He does not, at the same time, speak only of the end of individuals, but of the universal renovation of the world; as though he had said, "Christ will shortly come, who will put an end to all things."

It is, then, no wonder that the cares of this world overwhelm us, and make us drowsy, if the view of present things dazzles our eyes: for we promise, almost all of us, an eternity to ourselves in this world; at least, the end never comes to

---

"That they might condemn their former life, and live a better;" the second, "That they might be brought to such a state of life as their carnal neighbours will look upon it as a kind of condemnation and death;" and the third, "That *although* they might be condemned, indeed, by men in the flesh, yet they might live *eternally* by God in the Spirit."

Beza, Hammond, and *Scott,* consider that *the dead* were those already dead, that is, when the Apostle wrote, and even before the coming of Christ, taking the *dead* in the same sense as in the former verse: but they differ as to the clause which follows. The two first interpret it as signifying the same as dying to sin and living to God, a meaning which the former part of the clause can hardly bear: but the view of *Scott* is, that the gospel had been preached to those at that time dead, that they might be condemned by carnal men, or in the flesh, as evil-doers, but live to God through the Holy Spirit. The only fault, perhaps, with this rendering is as to the word *flesh*, which seems to mean here the same as *flesh* in chap. iii. 18, that is, the body; and the word *spirit* is also in the same form, for *Griesbach* in that verse regards the article $\tau\tilde{\varphi}$ as spurious. Then the rendering would be, "That they might be condemned in the flesh by men, but live as to God through the Spirit." There are two previous instances of the word *spirit*, when denoting the Holy Spirit, being without the article, that is, in chap. i. 2 and 22.

It seems an objection, that the gospel had been preached to them for *this end*, that they might be condemned to die by wicked men; but this had been expressly stated before, in chap. ii. 21: "For even hereunto, (that is, suffering, mentioned in the former verse) were ye called;" or, "For to this end ye have been called." Then Christ in his suffering is mentioned as one whom they ought to follow.

There is no other view so consistent with the whole tenor of the Apostle's argument. —*Ed.*

our mind. But were the trumpet of Christ to sound in our ears, it would powerfully rouse us and not suffer us to lie torpid.

But it may be objected and said, that a long series of ages has passed away since Peter wrote this, and yet that the end is not come. My reply to this is, that the time seems long to us, because we measure its length by the spaces of this fleeting life; but if we could understand the perpetuity of future life, many ages would appear to us like a moment, as Peter will also tell us in his second epistle. Besides, we must remember this principle, that from the time when Christ once appeared, there is nothing left for the faithful, but with suspended minds ever to look forward to his second coming.[1]

The *watchfulness* and the *sobriety* to which he exhorted them, belong, as I think, to the mind rather than to the body. The words are similar to those of Christ: "Watch ye, for ye know neither the day nor the hour wherein the Son of Man cometh." (Matt. xxv. 13.) For as an indulgence in surfeiting and sleep renders the body unfit for its duties, so the vain cares and pleasures of the world inebriate the mind and render it drowsy.

By adding *prayer*, he points out an exercise especially necessary, in which the faithful ought to be particularly occupied, since their whole strength depends on the Lord; as though he had said, "Since ye are in yourselves extremely weak, seek of the Lord to strengthen you." He yet reminds them that they were to pray earnestly, not formally.

8. *And above all things.* He commends charity or love as the first thing, for it is the bond of perfection. And he bids it to be *fervent*, or intense, or vehement, which is the same thing; for whosoever is immoderately fervent in self-love, loves others coldly. And he commends it on account of its fruit, because it buries innumerable sins, than which nothing is more desirable.

---

[1] There is no ground to suppose, as *Hammond, Macknight,* and some others have supposed, that "the end of all things" was the end of the Jews as a nation, the destruction of the temple and its worship. And it is strange that such a notion should be entertained, especially when we consider that the Apostle refers to the same subject in his Second Epistle, where the end of the world is plainly spoken of.—*Ed.*

But the sentence is taken from Solomon, whose words are found in Prov. x. 12, "Hatred discovers reproaches, but love covers a multitude of sins." What Solomon meant is sufficiently clear, for the two clauses contain things which are set in contrast the one with the other. As then he says in the first clause that hatred is the cause why men traduce and defame one another, and spread whatever is reproachful and dishonourable; so it follows that a contrary effect is ascribed to love, that is, that men who love one another, kindly and courteously forgive one another; hence it comes that, willingly burying each other's vices, one seeks to preserve the honour of another.[1] Thus Peter confirms his exhortation, that nothing is more necessary than to cherish mutual love. For who is there that has not many faults? Therefore all stand in need of forgiveness, and there is no one who does not wish to be forgiven.

This singular benefit love brings to us when it exists among us, so that innumerable evils are covered in oblivion. On the other hand, where loose reins are given to hatred, men by mutual biting and tearing must necessarily consume one another, as Paul says (Gal. v. 15.)

And it ought to be noticed that Solomon does not say that only a few sins are covered, but a multitude of sins, according to what Christ declares, when he bids us to forgive our brethren seventy times seven, (Matt. xviii. 22.) But the more sins love covers, the more evident appears its usefulness for the wellbeing of mankind.

This is the plain meaning of the words. It hence appears how absurd are the Papists, who seek to elicit from this passage their own satisfactions, as though almsgiving and other duties of charity were a sort of a compensation to God for blotting out their sins.[2] It is enough to point out by

---

[1] The quotation is from the Hebrew, and the sentence in the *Sept.* is evidently different. The same words are found also in James v. 20.

[2] " Though charity, or benevolence, hides the faults of *others* from the severity of our censure, yet charity or almsgiving is totally unable to conceal *our own* from the observance of our all-righteous Judge. Indeed, the only cover for these, or to speak more properly, the discharge of all their stains, is *faith*,—is the *blood* of Christ, working with repentance towards God."—*Bishop Warburton*, quoted by *Bloomfield.—Ed.*

the way their gross ignorance, for in a matter so clear it would be superfluous to add many words.

9. *Use hospitality*, or, Be hospitable. After having generally exhorted them to love one another, he specially mentions one of the duties of love. At that time hospitality was commonly used, and it was deemed in a manner a sacred kind of humanity, as we have stated elsewhere. He then bids them mutually to exercise it, so that no one might require more from others than what he himself was prepared to render. He adds, *without murmurings,* for it is a rare example that one spends himself and his own on his neighbour without any disparaging reflection. Then the Apostle would have us to show kindness willingly and with a cheerful mind.

10. *As every one hath received.* He reminds us what we ought to bear in mind when we do good to our neighbours; for nothing is more fitted to correct our murmurings than to remember that we do not give our own, but only dispense what God has committed to us. When therefore he says, " Minister the gift which every one has received," he intimates that to each had been distributed what they had, on this condition, that in helping their brethren they might be the ministers of God. And thus the second clause is an explanation of the first, for instead of ministry he mentions stewardship; and for what he had said, " as every one hath received the gift," he mentions the manifold graces which God variously distributes to us, so that each might confer in common his own portion. If then we excel others in any gift, let us remember that we are as to this the stewards of God, in order that we may kindly impart it to our neighbours as their necessity or benefit may require. Thus we ought to be disposed and ready to communicate.

But this consideration is also very important, that the Lord hath so divided his manifold graces, that no one is to be content with one thing and with his own gifts, but every one has need of the help and aid of his brother. This, I say, is a bond which God hath appointed for retaining friendship among men, for they cannot live without mutual assistance. Thus it happens, that he who in many things seeks the aid of his brethren, ought to communicate to them more freely what he has received. This bond of unity has been observed and noticed by heathens. But Peter teaches us here that God had designedly done this, that he might bind men one to another.

11. *If any man speak.* As he had spoken of the right and faithful use of gifts, he specifies two things as examples, and he has chosen those which are the most excellent or the most renowned. The office of teaching in the Church is a remarkable instance of God's favour. He then expressly commands those called to this office to act faithfully; though he does not speak here only of what we owe to men, but also of what we owe to God, so that we may not deprive him of his glory.

He who speaks, then, that is, who is rightly appointed by public authority, *let him speak as the oracles of God;* that is, let him reverently in God's fear and in sincerity perform the charge committed to him, regarding himself as engaged in God's work, and as ministering God's word and not his own. For he still refers to the doctrine, that when we confer any thing on the brethren, we minister to them by God's command what he has bestowed on us for that purpose. And truly, were all those who profess to be teachers in the Church duly to consider this one thing, there would be in them much more fidelity and devotedness. For how great a thing is this, that in teaching the oracles of God, they are representatives of Christ! Hence then comes so much carelessness and rashness, because the sacred majesty of God's word is not borne in mind but by a few; and so they indulge themselves as in a worldly stewardship.

In the meantime, we learn from these words of Peter, that it is not lawful for those who are engaged in teaching to do anything else, but faithfully to deliver o others, as from hand to hand, the doctrine received from God; for he forbids any one to go forth, except he who is instructed in God's word, and who proclaims infallible oracles as it were from his mouth. He, therefore, leaves no room for human inventions; for he briefly defines the doctrine which ought to be taught in the Church. Nor is the particle of similitude introduced here for the purpose of modifying the sentence, as though it were sufficient to profess that it is God's word that is taught. This was, indeed, commonly the case formerly with false prophets; and we see at this day how arrogantly the Pope and his followers cover with this pretence all their impious traditions. But Peter did not intend to teach pastors such hypocrisy as this, to pretend that they had from God whatever doctrine it pleased them to announce, but he took an argument from the subject itself, that he might exhort them to sobriety and meekness, to a reverence for God, and to an earnest attention to their work.

If any man minister. This second clause extends wider, it includes the office of teaching. But as it would have been too long to enumerate each of the ministerial works, he preferred summarily to speak of them all together, as though he had said, "Whatever part of the burden thou bearest in the Church, know that thou canst do nothing but what has been given thee by the Lord, and that thou art nothing else but an instrument of God: take heed, then, not to abuse the grace of God by exalting thyself; take heed not to suppress the power of God, which puts forth and manifests itself in the ministry for the salvation of the brethren." Let him then minister *as by God's power*, that is, let him regard nothing as his own, but let him humbly render service to God and his Church.

That God in all things may be glorified. When he says, *In all*, the word may be in the masculine or in the neuter gender; and thus men or gifts may be meant, and both meanings are equally suitable. The sense is, that God does not adorn us with his gifts, that he may rob himself and make himself as it were an empty idol by transferring to us his own glory, but that, on the contrary, his own glory may everywhere shine forth; and that it is therefore a sacrilegious profanation of God's gifts when men propose to themselves any other object than to glorify God. He says *through Jesus Christ*, because whatever power we have to minister, he alone bestows it on us; for he is the head, with which the whole body is connected by joints and bindings, and maketh increase in the Lord, according as he supplieth strength to every member.

To whom be praise, or glory. Some refer this to Christ; but the context requires that it should be rather applied to God; for he confirms the last exhortation, because God justly claims all the glory; and, therefore, men wickedly take away from him what is his own, when they obscure in anything, or in any part, his glory.

12. Beloved, think it not strange concerning the fiery trial which is to try you, as though some strange thing happened unto you:	12. Dilecti, ne miramini quum exploramini per ignem ad probationem vestri, perinde ac si novum aliquid vobis obtingat:
13. But rejoice, inasmuch as ye are partakers of Christ's sufferings; that, when his glory shall be revealed, ye may be glad also with exceeding joy.	13. Sed quatenus consortes estis passionum Christi gaudete; ut in revelatione quoque gloriæ ejus gaudeatis exultantes.
14. If ye be reproached for the name of Christ, happy *are ye;* for the Spirit of glory and of God resteth upon you: on their part he is evil spoken of, but on your part he is glorified.	14. Si probris afficimini in nomine Christi, beati estis, quoniam Spiritus gloriæ et Dei super vos requiescit; secundum ipsos quidem contumelia afficitur, secundum vos autem glorificatur.
15. But let none of you suffer as a murderer, or *as* a thief, or *as* an evil-doer, or *as* a busy-body in other men's matters.	15. Ne quis enim vestrum patiatur, ut homicida, aut fur, aut maleficus, aut cupidè rebus alienis inhians.
16. Yet if *any man suffer* as a Christian, let him not be ashamed; but let him glorify God on this behalf.	16. Si autem ut Christianus, ne pudefiat, imo glorificet Deum in hac parte.
17. For the time *is come* that judgment must begin at the house of God:—	17. Quandoquidem et tempus est, ut judicium incipiat a domo Dei:—

12. *Beloved, think it not strange,* or, wonder not. There is a frequent mention made in this Epistle of afflictions; the cause of which we have elsewhere explained. But this difference is to be observed, that when he exhorts the faithful to patience, he sometimes speaks generally of troubles common to man's life; but here he speaks of wrongs done to the faithful for the name of Christ. And first, indeed, he reminded them that they ought not to have deemed it strange as for a thing sudden and unexpected; by which he intimates, that they ought by a long meditation to have been previously prepared to bear the cross. For whosoever has resolved to fight under Christ's banner, will not be dismayed

when persecution happens, but, as one accustomed to it, will patiently bear it. That we may then be in a prepared state of mind when the waves of persecutions roll over us, we ought in due time to habituate ourselves to such an event by meditating continually on the cross.

Moreover, he proves that the cross is useful to us by two arguments,—that God thus tries our faith,—and that we become thus partakers with Christ. Then, in the first place, let us remember that the trial of our faith is most necessary, and that we ought thus willingly to obey God who provides for our salvation. However, the chief consolation is to be derived from a fellowship with Christ. Hence Peter not only forbids us to think it strange, when he sets this before us, but also bids us to rejoice. It is, indeed, a cause of joy, when God tries our faith by persecution; but the other joy far surpasses it, that is, when the Son of God allots to us the same course of life with himself, that he might lead us with himself to a blessed participation of heavenly glory. For we must bear in mind this truth, that we have the dying of Christ in our flesh, that his life may be manifested in us. The wicked also do indeed bear many afflictions; but as they are separated from Christ, they apprehend nothing but God's wrath and curse: thus it comes that sorrow and dread overwhelm them.

Hence, then, is the whole consolation of the godly, that they are associates with Christ, that hereafter they may be partakers of his glory; for we are always to bear in mind this transition from the cross to the resurrection. But as this world is like a labyrinth, in which no end of evils appears, Peter refers to the future revelation of Christ's glory, as though he had said, that the day of its revelation is not to be overlooked, but ought to be expected. But he mentions a twofold joy, one which we now enjoy in hope, and the other the full fruition of which the coming of Christ shall bring to us; for the first is mingled with grief and sorrow, the second is connected with exultation. For it is not suitable in the midst of afflictions to think of joy, which can free us from all trouble; but the consolations of God moderate evils, so that we can rejoice at the same time.

14. *If ye be reproached.* He mentions reproaches, because there is often more bitterness in them than in the loss of goods, or in the torments or agonies of the body; there is therefore nothing which is more grievous to ingenuous minds. For we see that many who are strong to bear want, courageous in torments, nay, bold to meet death, do yet succumb under reproach. To obviate this evil, Peter pronounces those blessed, according to what Christ says, (Mark viii. 35,) who are reproached for the sake of the Gospel. This is very contrary to what men commonly think and feel; but he gives a reason, *Because the Spirit of God*, called also the *Spirit of glory, rests* on them. Some read the words separately, "that which belongs to glory," as though the words were, "glory and the Spirit of God." But the former reading is more suitable as to the sense, and, as to language, more simple. Then Peter shews, that it is no hindrance to the happiness of the godly, that they sustain reproach for the name of Christ, because they nevertheless retain a complete glory in the sight of God, while the Spirit, who has glory ever connected with him, dwells in them. So, what seems to the flesh a paradox, the Spirit of God makes consistent by a sure perception in their minds.

On their part. This is a confirmation of the last sentence; for he intimates that it is enough for the godly, that the Spirit of God testifies that the reproaches endured for the sake of the Gospel, are blessed and full of glory. The wicked, however, attempted to effect a far different object; as though he had said, "Ye can boldly despise the insolence of the ungodly, because the testimony respecting your glory, which God's Spirit gives you, remains fixed within." And he says that the *Spirit* of God was reproached, because the unbelieving expose to ridicule whatever he suggests and dictates for our consolation. But this is by anticipation; for however the world in its blindness may see nothing but what is disgraceful in the reproaches of Christ, he would not have the eyes of the godly to be dazzled with this false opinion; but on the contrary they ought to look up to God. Thus he does not conceal what men commonly think; but he sets the hidden perception of faith, which God's children possess in their own hearts, in opposition to their presumption and insolence. Thus Paul boasted that he had the marks of Christ, and he gloried in his bonds. (Gal. vi. 17.) He had at the same time sufficiently found out what was the judgment formed of them by the world; and yet he intimates that it thought foolishly, and that those are blind together with the world, who esteem the slanders of the flesh glorious.

15. *But* (or, *For*) *let none of you.* Here also he anticipates an objection. He had exhorted the faithful to patience, if it happened to them to be persecuted for the cause of Christ; he now adds the reason why he had only spoken of that kind of trouble, even because they ought to have abstained from all evil-doing. Here, then, is contained another exhortation, lest they should do anything for which they might seem to be justly punished. Therefore the causal particle is not here superfluous, since the Apostle wished to give a reason why he so much exhorted the faithful to a fellowship with the sufferings of Christ, and at the same time to remind them by the way to live justly and harmlessly, lest they should bring on themselves a just punishment through their own faults; as though he had said, that it behoved Christians to deserve well of all, even when they were badly and cruelly treated by the world.

Were any one to object and say, that no one can be found to be so innocent, but that he deserves for many faults to be chastised by God; to this I reply, that Peter here speaks of sins from which we ought to be entirely freed, such as thefts and murders; and I give further this reply, that the Apostle commands Christians to be such as they ought to be. It is, then, no wonder, that he points out a difference between us and the children of this world, who being without God's Spirit, abandon themselves to every kind of wickedness. He would not have God's children to be in the same condition, so as to draw on themselves by a wicked life the punishment allotted by the laws. But we have already said elsewhere, that though there are always many sins in the elect, which God might justly punish, yet according to his paternal indulgence he spares his own children, so that he does not inflict the punishment they deserve, and that in the meantime, for honour's sake, he adorns them with his own tokens and those of his Christ, when he suffers them to be afflicted for the testimony of the Gospel.

The word ἀλλοτριοεπίσκοπος seems to me to designate one who covets what belongs to another. For they who gape after plunder or fraud, inquire into affairs of others with tortuous or crooked eyes, as Horace says;[1] but the despiser of money, as the same says elsewhere, looks on vast heaps of gold with a straight eye.[2]

16. *Yet if* any man suffer *as a Christian.* After having forbidden the Christians to do any hurt or harm, lest for their evil deeds, like the unbelieving, they should become hateful to the world, he now bids them to give thanks to God, if they suffered persecutions for the name of Christ. And truly it is no common kindness from God, that he calls us, freed and exempted from the common punishment of our sins, to so honourable a warfare as to undergo for the testimony of his Gospel either exiles, or prisons, or reproaches, or even death itself. Then he intimates that those are ungrateful to God, who clamour or murmur on account of persecutions, as though they were unworthily dealt with, since on the contrary they ought to regard it as gain and to acknowledge God's favour.

But when he says, *as a Christian*, he regards not so much the name as the cause. It is certain that the adversaries of Christ omitted nothing in order to degrade the Gospel. Therefore, whatever reproachful words they made use of, it was enough for the faithful, that they suffered for nothing else but for the defence of the Gospel.

[1] Sic tamen ut limis rapias quid prima secundo
Cera velit versu. . . . Sat. lib. ii. 5, 53.
[2] Quisquis ingentes oculo irretorto
Spectat acervos.—Carm. lib. ii. Od. ii. 23.

The sin here referred to must have some public act, punishable by law. The word means an observer of other people's affairs, but he must have done so for some sinister purpose. He was probably a pryer into matters of state or government in order to create discontent and to raise commotions; and this was an evil which prevailed much at the time among the Jews. Hence "seditions," or factions, would convey probably the right meaning.—*Ed.*

On this behalf, or, In this respect. For since all afflictions derive their origin from sin, this thought ought to occur to the godly, "I am indeed worthy to be visited by the Lord with this and even with greater punishment for my sins; but now he would have me to suffer for righteousness, as though I were innocent." For how much soever the saints may acknowledge their own faults, yet as in persecutions they regard a different end, such as the Lord sets before them, they feel that their guilt is blotted out and abolished before God. *On this behalf,* then, they have reason to glorify God.

17. *For the time is come,* or, Since also the time is come. He amplifies the consolation, which the goodness of the cause for which we suffer brings to us, while we are afflicted for the name of Christ. For this necessity, he says, awaits the whole Church of God, not only to be subject to the common miseries of men, but especially and mainly to be chastised by the hand of God. Then, with more submission, ought persecutions for Christ to be endured. For except we desire to be blotted out from the number of the faithful, we must submit our backs to the scourges of God. Now, it is a sweet consolation, that God does not execute his judgments on us as on others, but that he makes us the representatives of his own Son, when we do not suffer except for his cause and for his name.

Moreover, Peter took this sentence from the common and constant teaching of Scripture; and this seems more probable to me than that a certain passage, as some think, is referred to. It was formerly usual with the Lord, as all the prophets witness, to exhibit the first examples of his chastisements in his own people, as the head of a family corrects his own children rather than those of strangers. (Isa. x. 12.) For though God is the judge of the whole world, yet he would have his providence to be especially acknowledged in the government of his own Church. Hence, when he declares that he would rise up to be the judge of the whole world, he adds that this would be after he had completed his work on Mount Sion. He indeed puts forth his hand indifferently against his own people and against strangers; for we see that both are in common subjected to adversities;

and if a comparison be made, he seems in a manner to spare the reprobate, and to be severe towards the elect. Hence the complaints of the godly, that the wicked pass their life in continual pleasures, and delight themselves with wine and the harp, and at length descend without pains in an instant into the grave—that fatness covers their eyes—that they are exempt from troubles—that they securely and joyfully spend their life, looking down with contempt on others, so that they dare to set their mouth against heaven. (Job xxi. 13; Ps. lxxiii. 3-9.) In short, God so regulates his judgments in this world, that he fattens the wicked for the day of slaughter. He therefore passes by their many sins, and, as it were, connives at them. In the meantime, he restores by corrections his own children, for whom he has a care, to the right way, whenever they depart from it.

In this sense it is that Peter says that judgment begins at the house of God; for judgment includes all those punishments which the Lord inflicts on men for their sins, and whatever refers to the reformation of the world.

But why does he say that it was *now the time?* He means, as I think, what the prophets declare concerning his own time, that it especially belonged to Christ's kingdom, that the beginning of the reformation should be in the Church. Hence Paul says that Christians, without the hope of a resurrection, would of all men be the most miserable, (1 Cor. xv. 19;) and justly so, because, while others indulge themselves without fear, the faithful continually sigh and groan; while God connives at the sins of others, and suffers them to continue torpid, he deals rigidly with his own people, and subjects them to the discipline of the cross.

17. — And if *it* first *begin* at us, what shall the end *be* of them that obey not the gospel of God?

18. And if the righteous scarcely be saved, where shall the ungodly and the sinner appear?

19. Wherefore, let them that suffer according to the will of God commit the keeping of their souls *to him* in well-doing, as unto a faithful Creator.

17. — Si autem primum a nobis, quis finis eorum qui non obediunt evangelio Dei?

18. Et si justus vix servatur, impius et peccator ubi apparebunt?

19. Itaque qui patiuntur secundum Dei voluntatem, tanquam fideli possessori commendent animas suas benefaciendo.

When the faithful see that it is well with the wicked, they are necessarily tempted to be envious; and this is a very dangerous trial; for present happiness is what all desire. Hence the Spirit of God carefully dwells on this, in many places, as well as in the thirty-seventh Psalm, lest the faithful should envy the prosperity of the ungodly. The same is what Peter speaks of, for he shews that afflictions ought to be calmly borne by the children of God, when they compare the lot of others with their own. But he takes it as granted that God is the judge of the world, and that, therefore, no one can escape his hand with impunity. He hence infers, that a dreadful vengeance will soon overtake those whose condition seems now favourable. The design of what he says, as I have already stated, is to shew that the children of God should not faint under the bitterness of present evils, but that they ought, on the contrary, calmly to bear their afflictions for a short time, as the issue will be salvation, while the ungodly will have to exchange a fading and fleeting prosperity for eternal perdition.

But the argument is from the less to the greater; for if God spares not his own children whom he loves and who obey him, how dreadful will be his severity against enemies and such as are rebellious! There is, then, nothing better than to obey the Gospel, so that God may kindly correct us by his paternal hand for our salvation.

18. *And if the righteous.* It has been thought that this sentence is taken from Prov. xi. 31; for the Greek translators have thus rendered what Solomon says, "Behold, the just shall on the earth be recompensed; how much more the ungodly and the sinner?" Now, whether Peter intended to quote this passage, or repeated a common and a proverbial saying, (which seems to me more probable,[1]) the meaning is,

[1] It certainly *appears* as a quotation, as the words are literally the same. It is to be observed that the Hebrew has " on earth," which seems to confirm the view that *saved* here refers to deliverances from the troubles, trials, and persecutions, which the righteous have to go through during life; and that *scarcely*, or hardly, or with difficulty, as rendered by *Doddridge* and *Macknight*, is to be limited to the time of the Christian's course in this world; for, as *Macknight* observes, the Apostle speaks in his Second Epistle of an abundant entrance into the heavenly kingdom being vouchsafed to all faithful Christians. See 2 Peter i. 11.—*Ed.*

that God's judgment would be dreadful against the ungodly, since the way to salvation was so thorny and difficult to the elect. And this is said, lest we should securely indulge ourselves, but carefully proceed in our course, and lest we should also seek the smooth and easy road, the end of which is a terrible precipice.

But when he says, that a *righteous man is scarcely saved*, he refers to the difficulties of the present life, for our course in the world is like a dangerous sailing between many rocks, and exposed to many storms and tempests; and thus no one arrives at the port, except he who has escaped from thousand deaths. It is in the meantime certain that we are guided by God's hand, and that we are in no danger of shipwreck as long as we have him as our pilot.

Absurd, then, are those interpreters who think that we shall be hardly and with difficulty saved, when we shall come before God in judgment; for it is the present and not the future time that Peter refers to; nor does he speak of God's strictness or rigour, but shews how many and what arduous difficulties must be surmounted by the Christian before he reaches the goal. *Sinner* here means a wicked man;[1] and the righteous are not those who are altogether perfect in righteousness, but who strive to live righteously.

19. *Wherefore let them that suffer.* He draws this conclusion, that persecutions ought to be submissively endured, for the condition of the godly in them is much happier than that of the unbelieving, who enjoy prosperity to their utmost wishes. He, however, reminds us that we suffer nothing except according to the permission of God, which tends much to comfort us; when he says, *Let them commit themselves to God*, it is the same as though he had said, "Let them deliver themselves and their life to the safe keeping of God." And he calls him a *faithful possessor*, because he

---

[1] The two words, "ungodly," ἀσιβὴς, and "sinner," ἁμαρτωλὸς, exactly correspond with רשע and חוטא in Hebrew; the first is he who is not pious, not a worshipper of God, having neither fear nor love towards him; and the second is the wicked, and open and shameless transgressor, who regards not what is just and right. *Grotius* says, that the first is he who shews no piety towards God; and that the second is one who observes no justice towards man.— *Ed.*

faithfully keeps and defends whatever is under his protection or power. Some render the word "Creator;" and the term κτίστης means both; but the former meaning I prefer, for by bidding us to deposit our life with God, he makes him its safe keeper. He adds, *in well-doing*, lest the faithful should retaliate the wrongs done to them, but that they might on the contrary contend with the ungodly, who injured them, by well-doing.

CHAPTER V.

1. The elders which are among you I exhort, who am also an elder, and a witness of the sufferings of Christ, and also a partaker of the glory that shall he revealed: 2. Feed the flock of God which is among you, taking the oversight *thereof*, not by constraint, but willingly; not for filthy lucre, but of a ready mind; 3. Neither as being lords over *God's* heritage, but being ensamples to the flock: 4. And when the chief Shepherd shall appear, ye shall receive a crown of glory that fadeth not away.	1. Presbyteros qui inter vos sunt, hortor ego qui simul sum presbyter, et testis passionum Christi, et gloriæ quæ revelabitur particeps: 2. Pascite, quantum in vobis est, gregem Dei (*vel*, Christi, *vel*, Domini,) episcopatu fungentes, non coactè, sed voluntariè; neque turpis lucri causâ, sed liberaliter; 3. Nec tanquam dominium exercentes adversus cleros, sed ut sitis exemplaria gregis. 4. Et quum apparuerit Princeps pastorum, reportabitis immarcescibilem gloriæ coronam.

In exhorting pastors to their duty, he points out especially three vices which are found to prevail much, even sloth, desire of gain, and lust for power. In opposition to the first vice he sets alacrity or a willing attention; to the second, liberality; to the third, moderation and meekness, by which they are to keep themselves in their own rank or station.

He then says that pastors ought not to exercise care over the flock of the Lord, as far only as they are constrained; for they who seek to do no more than what constraint compels them, do their work formally and negligently. Hence he would have them to do willingly what they do, as those who are really devoted to their work. To correct avarice, he bids them to perform their office with a ready mind; for whosoever has not this end in view, to spend himself and his labour disinterestedly and gladly in behalf of the Church, is not a minister of Christ, but a slave to his own stomach and his purse. The third vice which he condemns is a lust for exercising power or dominion. But it may be asked, what kind of power does he mean? This, as it seems to me, may be gathered from the opposite clause, in which he bids them to be examples to the flock. It is the same as though he had said that they are to preside for this end, to be eminent in holiness, which cannot be, except they humbly subject themselves and their life to the same common rule. What stands opposed to this virtue is tyrannical pride, when the pastor exempts himself from all subjection, and tyrannizes over the Church. It was for this that Ezekiel condemned the false prophets, that is, that they ruled cruelly and tyrannically. (Ezek. xxxiv. 4.) Christ also condemned the Pharisees, because they laid intolerable burdens on the shoulders of the people which they would not touch, no, not with a finger. (Matt. xxiii. 4.) This imperious rigour, then, which ungodly pastors exercise over the Church, cannot be corrected, except their authority be restrained, so that they may rule in such a way as to afford an example of a godly life.

1. *The elders.* By this name he designates pastors and all those who are appointed for the government of the Church. But they called them presbyters or elders for honour's sake, not because they were all old in age, but because they were principally chosen from the aged, for old age for the most part has more prudence, gravity, and experience. But as sometimes hoariness is not wisdom, according to a Greek proverb, and as young men are found more fit, such as Timothy, these were also usually called presbyters, after having been chosen into that order. Since Peter calls himself in like manner a *presbyter*, it appears that it was a common name, which is still more evident from many other passages. Moreover, by this title he secured for himself more authority, as though he had said that he had a right to admonish pastors, because he was one of themselves, for there ought to be mutual liberty between colleagues. But if he had the right of primacy he would have claimed it; and this would have been most suitable on the present occa-

sion. But though he was an Apostle, he yet knew that authority was by no means delegated to him over his colleagues, but that on the contrary he was joined with the rest in the participation of the same office.

A witness of the sufferings of Christ. This may be explained of doctrine, yet I prefer to regard it as referring to his own life. At the same time both may be admitted; but I am more disposed to embrace the latter view, because these two clauses will be more in harmony,—that Peter speaks of the sufferings of Christ in his own flesh, and that he would be also a partaker of his glory. For the passage agrees with that of Paul, "If we suffer together, we shall also reign together." Besides, it avails much to make us believe his words, that he gave a proof of his faith by enduring the cross. For it hence appears evident that he spoke in earnest; and the Lord, by thus proving his people, seals as it were their ministry, that it might have more honour and reverence among men. Peter, then, had probably this in view, so that he might be heard as the faithful minister of Christ, a proof of which he gave in the persecutions he had suffered, and in the hope which he had of future life.[1]

But we must observe that Peter confidently declares that he would be a partaker of that glory which was not yet revealed; for it is the character of faith to acquiesce in hidden blessings.

2. *Feed the flock of God.* We hence learn what the word presbyter imports, even that it includes the office of feeding. It is for a far different end that the Pope makes presbyters, even that they may daily slay Christ, there being no mention made of feeding in their ordination. Let us then remember to distinguish between the institution of Christ and the confusion of the Pope, it being as different as light is from darkness. Let us also bear in mind the definition given of the word; for the flock of Christ cannot be fed except with pure doctrine, which is alone our spiritual food.

---

[1] The most obvious meaning is, that Peter had been an *eye-witness* of Christ's sufferings. So the word "witness" is taken by *Grotius, Macknight, Doddridge,* and *Scott.*—*Ed.*

Hence pastors are not mute hypocrites, nor those who spread their own figments, which, like deadly poison, destroy the souls of men.

The words, *as much as it is in you*, mean the same as though he had said, "Apply all your strength to this very thing, and whatever power God has conferred on you." The old interpreter has given this rendering, "Which is among you;" and this may be the sense of the words: more correct, however, is the rendering of Erasmus, which I have followed, though I do not reject nor disapprove of the other.[1]

The flock of God, or, of the Lord, or, of Christ: it matters little which you take, for the three readings are found in different copies.[2]

Taking the oversight, or, discharging the office of a bishop. Erasmus renders the words, "Taking care of it," (*curam illius agentes;*) but as the Greek word is ἐπισκοποῦντες, I doubt not but that Peter meant to set forth the office and title of the episcopate. We may learn also from other parts of Scripture that these two names, bishop and presbyter, are synonymous. He then shews how they were rightly to perform the pastoral office, though the word ἐπισκοπεῖν generally means to preside or to oversee. What I have rendered "not constrainedly," is literally, "not necessarily;" for when we act according to what necessity prescribes, we proceed in our work slowly and frigidly, as it were by constraint.

3. *Neither as being lords*, or, as exercising dominion. The preposition κατὰ in Greek is taken, for the most part, in a bad sense: then Peter here condemns unreasonable exercise of power, as the case is with those who consider not themselves to be the ministers of Christ and his Church, but seek something higher. And he calls particular churches "lots," (*cleros;*) for as the whole body of the Church is the Lord's heritage, so the churches, scattered through towns and

---

[1] The *Vulgate*, called here and elsewhere, "the old interpreter," seems to be the most correct, as viewed by most critics. The same form of words is found in the first verse, "The elders *who are among you.*"—*Ed.*

[2] By far the most approved reading is "of God."—*Ed.*

villages, were as so many farms, the culture of which he assigns to each presbyter. Some very ignorantly think that those called clergy are meant here. It was, indeed, an ancient way of speaking, to call the whole order of ministers, clergy; but I wish that it had never occurred to the Fathers to speak thus; for what Scripture ascribes in common to the whole Church, it was by no means right to confine to a few men. And this way of speaking was spurious, at least it was a departure from apostolic usage.

Peter, indeed, expressly gives the churches this title, in order that we may know that whatever men ascribe to themselves is taken away from the Lord, as in many places he calls the Church his peculiar treasure, and the rod of his heritage, when he intends to claim his entire dominion over it; for he never delivers to pastors the government, but only the care, so that his own right remains still complete.

4. *When the chief Shepherd shall appear.* Except pastors retain this end in view, it can by no means be that they will in good earnest proceed in the course of their calling, but will, on the contrary, become often faint; for there are innumerable hindrances which are sufficient to discourage the most prudent. They have often to do with ungrateful men, from whom they receive an unworthy reward; long and great labours are often in vain; Satan sometimes prevails in his wicked devices. Lest, then, the faithful servant of Christ should be broken down, there is for him one and only one remedy,—to turn his eyes to the coming of Christ. Thus it will be, that he, who seems to derive no encouragement from men, will assiduously go on in his labours, knowing that a great reward is prepared for him by the Lord. And further, lest a protracted expectation should produce languor, he at the same time sets forth the greatness of the reward, which is sufficient to compensate for all delay: *An unfading crown of glory,* he says, awaits you.

It ought also to be observed, that he calls Christ the *chief Pastor;* for we are to rule the Church under him and in his name, in no other way but that he should be still really the Pastor. So the word *chief* here does not only mean the principal, but him whose power all others ought to submit to, as they do not represent him except according to his command and authority.

5. Likewise, ye younger, submit yourselves unto the elder: yea, all *of you* be subject one to another, and be clothed with humility; for God resisteth the proud, and giveth grace to the humble.

6. Humble yourselves therefore under the mighty hand of God, that he may exalt you in due time:

7. Casting all your care upon him; for he careth for you.

5. Similiter juniores, subjecti estote senioribus; sic et omnes, alii aliis subjiciamini; humilitatem animi induite; propterea quod Deus superbis resistit, humilibus vero dat gratiam.

6. Humiliamini ergo sub potenti manu Dei, ut vos extollat quum erit opportunum;

7. Omni cura vestra in eum conjecta; quoniam illi cura est vestri.

5. *Likewise, ye younger.* The word *elder* is put here in a sense different from what it had before; for it is necessary, when a contrast is made between them and the younger, that the two clauses should correspond. Then he refers to the elders in age, having before spoken of the office; and thus he comes from the particular to the general. And in short, he bids every one that is inferior in age to obey the counsels of the elders, and to be teachable and humble; for the age of youth is inconstant, and requires a bridle. Besides, pastors could not have performed their duty, except this reverential feeling prevailed and was cultivated, so that the younger suffered themselves to be ruled; for if there be no subjection, government is overturned. When they have no authority who ought by right or order of nature to rule, all will immediately become insolently wanton.

Yea, all. He shews the reason why the younger ought to submit to the elder, even that there might be an equable state of things and due order among them. For, when authority is granted to the elders, there is not given them the right or the liberty of throwing off the bridle, but they are also themselves to be under due restraint, so that there may be a mutual subjection. So the husband is the head of the wife, and yet he in his turn is to be in some things subject to her. So the father has authority over his children, and still he is not exempt from all subjection, but something is due to them. The same thing, also, is to be thought of others. In short, all ranks in society have to defend the whole body, which cannot be done, except all the members are joined together by the bond of mutual subjection. Nothing is more adverse to the disposition of man than subjection. For it was formerly very truly said, that every one has within him the soul of a king. Until, then, the high spirits, with which the nature of men swells, are subdued, no man will give way to another; but, on the contrary, each one, despising others, will claim all things for himself.

Hence the Apostle, in order that humility may dwell among us, wisely reproves this haughtiness and pride. And the metaphor he uses is very appropriate, as though he had said, "Surround yourselves with humility on every side, as with a garment which covers the whole body." He yet intimates that no ornament is more beautiful or more becoming, than when we submit one to another.

For, or, because. It is a most grievous threatening, when he says, that all who seek to elevate themselves, shall have God as their enemy, who will lay them low. But, on the contrary, he says of the humble, that God will be propitious and favourable to them. We are to imagine that God has two hands; the one, which like a hammer beats down and breaks in pieces those who raise up themselves; and the other, which raises up the humble who willingly let down themselves, and is like a firm prop to sustain them. Were we really convinced of this, and had it deeply fixed in our minds, who of us would dare by pride to urge war with God? But the hope of impunity now makes us fearlessly to raise up our horn to heaven. Let, then, this declaration of Peter be as a celestial thunderbolt to make men humble.

But he calls those *humble,* who being emptied of every confidence in their own power, wisdom, and righteousness, seek every good from God alone. Since there is no coming to God except in this way, who, having lost his own glory, ought not willingly to humble himself?

6. *Humble yourselves therefore.* We must ever bear in mind for what end he bids us to be humble before God, even that we may be more courteous and kind to our brethren, and not refuse to submit to them as far as love demands. Then they who are haughty and refractory towards men, are, he says, acting insolently towards God. He therefore exhorts all the godly to submit to God's authority; and he

calls God's power his *hand,* that he might make them to fear the more. For though hand is often applied to God, yet it is to be understood here according to the circumstances of the passage. But as we are wont commonly to fear, lest our humility should be a disadvantage to us, and others might for this reason grow more insolent, Peter meets this objection, and promises eminency to all who humble themselves.

But he adds, *in due time,* that he might at the same time obviate too much haste. He then intimates that it is necessary for us to learn humility now, but that the Lord well knows when it is expedient for us to be elevated. Thus it behoves us to yield to his counsel.

7. *Casting all our care.* He more fully sets forth here the providence of God. For whence are these proverbial sayings, " We shall have to howl among wolves," and, "They are foolish who are like sheep, exposing themselves to wolves to be devoured," except that we think that by our humility we set loose the reins to the audacity of the ungodly, so that they insult us more wantonly? But this fear arises from our ignorance of divine providence. Now, on the other hand, as soon as we are convinced that God cares for us, our minds are easily led to patience and humility. Lest, then, the wickedness of men should tempt us to a fierceness of mind, the Apostle prescribes to us a remedy, and also David does in the thirty-seventh Psalm, so that having cast our care on God, we may calmly rest. For all those who recumb not on God's providence must necessarily be in constant turmoil and violently assail others. We ought the more to dwell on this thought, that God cares for us, in order, first, that we may have peace within ; and, secondly, that we may be humble and meek towards men.

But we are not thus bidden to cast all our care on God, as though God wished us to have strong hearts, and to be void of all feeling ; but lest fear or anxiety should drive us to impatience. In like manner, the knowledge of divine providence does not free men from every care, that they may securely indulge themselves ; for it ought not to encourage the torpidity of the flesh, but to bring rest to faith.

8. Be sober, be vigilant; because your adversary the devil, as a roaring lion, walketh about seeking whom he may devour:

9. Whom resist steadfast in the faith, knowing that the same afflictions are accomplished in your brethren that are in the world.

10. But the God of all grace, who hath called us unto his eternal glory by Christ Jesus, after that ye have suffered a while, make you perfect, stablish, strengthen, settle *you:*

11. To him *be* glory and dominion for ever and ever. Amen.

8. Sobrii estote, vigilate, quia adversarius vester diabolus, tanquam leo rugiens, circuit, quærens quem devoret (*vel,* quempiam devorare;)

9. Cui resistite firmi fide, scientes easdem passiones, vestræ quæ in mundo fraternitati adimpleri.

10. Deus autem omnis gratiæ, qui nos vocavit in æternam suam gloriam per Christum Jesum, paulisper afflictos ipse vos perficiat, confirmet, corroboret, stabiliat:

11. Ei gloria et imperium in secula seculorum. Amen.

8. *Be sober.* This explanation extends wider, that as we have war with a most fierce and most powerful enemy, we are to be strenuous in resisting him. But he uses a twofold metaphor, that they were to be sober, and that they were to exercise watchfulness. Surfeiting produces sloth and sleep; even so they who indulge in earthly cares and pleasures, think of nothing else, being under the power of spiritual lethargy.

We now perceive what the meaning of the Apostle is. We must, he says, carry on a warfare in this world; and he reminds us that we have to do with no common enemy, but one who, like a lion, runs here and there, ready to devour. He hence concludes that we ought carefully to watch. Paul stimulates us with the same argument in the sixth chapter of the Epistle to the Ephesians, where he says that we have a contest not with flesh and blood, but with spiritual wickedness, &c. But we too often turn peace into sloth, and hence it comes that the enemy then circumvents and overwhelms us; for, as though placed beyond the reach of danger, we indulge ourselves according to the will of the flesh.

He compares the devil to a lion, as though he had said, that he is a savage wild beast. He says that he *goes round* to devour, in order to rouse us to wariness. He calls him the *adversary* of the godly, that they might know that they worship God and profess faith in Christ on this condition, that they are to have continual war with the devil, for he does not spare the members who fights with the head.

9. *Whom resist.* As the power of an enemy ought to stimulate us and make us more careful, so there would be danger

lest our hearts failed through immoderate fear, except the hope of victory were given us. This then is what the Apostle speaks of; he shows that the issue of the war will be prosperous, if we indeed fight under the banner of Christ; for whosoever comes to this contest, endued with faith, he declares that he will certainly be a conqueror.

Resist, he says; but some one may ask, how? To this he answers, there is sufficient strength in faith. Paul, in the passage which I have already quoted, enumerates the various parts of our armour, but the meaning is the same, (Eph. vi. 13,) for John testifies that faith alone is our victory over the world.

Knowing that the same afflictions, or sufferings. It is another consolation, that we have a contest in common with all the children of God; for Satan dangerously tries us, when he separates us from the body of Christ. We have heard how he attempted to storm the courage of Job, " Look to the saints, has any one of them suffered such a thing?" Job v. 1. The Apostle on the other hand, reminds us here that nothing happens to us but what we see does happen to other members of the Church. Moreover a fellowship, or a similar condition, with all the saints, ought by no means to be refused by us.

By saying that the same sufferings are *accomplished,* he means what Paul declares in Col. i. 24, that what remains of the sufferings of Christ is daily fulfilled in the faithful.

The words, *that are in the world,* may be explained in two ways, either that God proves his faithful people indiscriminately everywhere in the world, or that the necessity of fighting awaits us as long as we are in the world. But we must observe that having said before that we are assailed by Satan, he then immediately refers to every kind of afflictions. We hence gather that we have always to do with our spiritual enemy, however adversities may come, or whatever they may be, whether diseases oppress us, or the barrenness of the land threatens us with famine, or men persecute us.

10. *But the God of all grace.* After having sufficiently dwelt on admonitions, he now turns to prayer; for doctrine is in vain poured forth into the air, unless God works by his Spirit. And this example ought to be followed by all the

ministers of God, that is, to pray that he may give success to their labours; for otherwise they effect nothing either by planting or by watering.

Some copies have the future tense, as though a promise is made; but the other reading is more commonly received. At the same time, the Apostle, by praying God, confirms those to whom he was writing, for when he calls God the author of *all grace,* and reminds them that they were called to eternal glory, his purpose no doubt was, to confirm them in the conviction, that the work of their salvation, which he had begun, would be completed.

He is called the *God of all grace* from the effect, from the gifts he bestows, according to the Hebrew manner.[1] And he mentions expressly *all grace,* first that they might learn that every blessing is to be ascribed to God; and secondly, that one grace is connected with another, so that they might hope in future for the addition of those graces in which they were hitherto wanting.

Who hath called us. This, as I have said, serves to increase confidence, because God is led not only by his goodness, but also by his gracious benevolence, to aid us more and more. He does not simply mention calling, but he shews wherefore they were called, even that they might obtain eternal glory. He further fixes the foundation of calling in Christ. Both these things serve to give perpetual confidence, for if our calling is founded on Christ, and refers to the celestial kingdom of God and a blessed immortality, it follows that it is not transient nor fading.

It may also be right, by the way, to observe that when he says that we are called *in Christ,* first, our calling is established, because it is rightly founded; and secondly, that all respect to our worthiness and merit is excluded; for that God, by the preaching of the gospel, invites us to himself, it is altogether gratuitous; and it is still a greater grace that he efficaciously touches our hearts so as to lead us to obey his voice. Now Peter especially addresses the faithful;

---

[1] We read in chap. iv. 10, of " the manifold grace of God," which may be viewed as explanatory of " the God of all grace."—*Ed.*

he therefore connects the efficacious power of the Spirit with the outward doctrine.

As to the three words which follow, some copies have them in the ablative case, which may be rendered in Latin by gerunds (*fulciendo, roborando, stabiliendo*) by supporting, by strengthening, by establishing.[1] But in this there is not much importance with regard to the meaning. Besides, Peter intends the same thing by all these words, even to confirm the faithful; and he uses these several words for this purpose, that we may know that to follow our course is a matter of no common difficulty, and that therefore we need the special grace of God. The words *suffered a while*, inserted here, shew that the time of suffering is but short, and this is no small consolation.

11. *To him be glory.* That he might add more confidence to the godly, he breaks out into thanksgiving. Though this be read in the indicative as well as in the optative mood, still the meaning is nearly the same.

12. By Silvanus, a faithful brother unto you, (as I suppose,) I have written briefly, exhorting, and testifying that this is the true grace of God wherein ye stand.	12. Per Silvanum vobis fidum fratrem (ut arbitror) paucis scripsi, exhortans et testificans hanc esse veram gratiam in qua statis.
13. The *church that is* at Babylon, elected together with *you*, saluteth you; and *so doth* Marcus my son.	13. Salutat vos quæ in Babylone est Ecclesia, simul vobiscum electa, et Marcus filius meus.
14. Greet ye one another with a kiss of charity. Peace *be* with you all that are in Christ Jesus. Amen.	14. Salutate vos invicem in osculo charitatis. Gratia vobis omnibus qui estis in Christo Jesu.

12. *By Silvanus.* He exhorts them at the conclusion of

---

[1] It seems that the preponderance as to readings is in favour of this construction, for *Griesbach* has introduced into his text these three words as nouns, στηρίξει, σθενώσει, θεμελιώσει, but it is a harsh construction. The probability is, that this reading has been introduced because of the sense, as it was not seen how these words could come after " make perfect." But the order is according to the usual style of the prophets, examples of which are also found in the New Testament: the ultimate object is mentioned first, and then what leads to it. The writer, as it were, retrogrades instead of going forward. See on this subject the preface to the third volume of *Calvin's* Commentaries on Jeremiah.

Divested of this peculiarity, the words would run thus: " may he establish, strengthen, confirm, perfect you;" that is, to give the words more literally, "may he put you on a solid foundation, render you strong, render you firm, make you perfect."—*Ed.*

the Epistle to constancy in the faith : yea, he declares that his design in writing, was to retain them in obedience to the doctrine which they had embraced. But he first commends the brevity of his Epistle, lest the reading of it should be tedious to them ; and, secondly, he adds a short commendation of his messenger, that the living voice might be added to what was written ; for this was the design of the testimony he bears to his fidelity. But the exception, *as I suppose*, or think, was added, either as token of modesty or to let them surely know, that he spoke according to the conviction of his own mind ; and it was unreasonable for them not to assent to the judgment of so great an apostle.

Exhorting and testifying. How difficult it is to continue in the faith ! evidences of this are the daily defections of many : nor, indeed, is such a thing to be wondered at, when we consider how great is the levity and inconsistency of men, and how great is their inclination to vanity. But as no doctrine can strike firm and perpetual roots in men's hearts, if it be accompanied with any doubt, he testifies that God's truth, in which they had been taught, was certain. And, doubtless, except its certainty appears to our minds, we must at all times necessarily vacillate, and be ready to turn at every wind of new doctrine. By the *grace of God*, he means faith with all its effects and fruits.

13. *That is at Babylon.* Many of the ancients thought that Rome is here enigmatically denoted. This comment the Papists gladly lay hold on, that Peter may appear to have presided over the Church of Rome : nor does the infamy of the name deter them, provided they can pretend to the title of an apostolic seat ; nor do they care for Christ, provided Peter be left to them. Moreover, let them only retain the name of Peter's chair, and they will not refuse to set Rome in the infernal regions. But this old comment has no colour of truth in its favour ; nor do I see why it was approved by Eusebius and others, except that they were already led astray by that error, that Peter had been at Rome. Besides, they are inconsistent with themselves. They say that Mark died at Alexandria, in the eighth year of Nero ; but they imagine that Peter, six years after this, was put to death at Rome by

Nero. If Mark formed, as they say, the Alexandrian Church, and had been long a bishop there, he could never have been at Rome with Peter. For Eusebius and Jerome extend the time of Peter's presidency at Rome to twenty-five years; but this may be easily disproved by what is said in the first and the second chapter of the Epistle to the Galatians.

Since, then, Peter had Mark as his companion when he wrote this Epistle, it is very probable that he was at Babylon : and this was in accordance with his calling ; for we know that he was appointed an apostle especially to the Jews. He therefore visited chiefly those parts where there was the greatest number of that nation.

In saying that the Church there was a partaker of the same election, his object was to confirm others more and more in the faith ; for it was a great matter that the Jews were gathered into the Church, in so remote a part of the world.

My son. So he calls Mark for honour's sake ; the reason, however, is, because he had begotten him in the faith, as Paul did Timothy. Of the *kiss of love* we have spoken elsewhere. Now he bids this to be the kiss of love,[1] so that the sincerity of the heart might correspond with the external act.

[1] See a Note in the Epistle to the Romans, p. 547.—*Ed.*

END OF THE FIRST EPISTLE OF PETER

COMMENTARIES

ON

THE FIRST EPISTLE OF JOHN.

THE ARGUMENT.

This Epistle is altogether worthy of the spirit of that disciple who, above others, was loved by Christ, that he might exhibit him as a friend to us. But it contains doctrines mixed with exhortations; for he speaks of the eternal Deity of Christ, and at the same time of the incomparable grace which he brought with him when he appeared in the world, and generally of all his blessings; and he especially commends and extols the inestimable grace of divine adoption.

On these truths he grounds his exhortations; and at one time he admonishes us in general to lead a pious and holy life, and at another time he expressly enjoins love. But he does none of these things in a regular order; for he everywhere mixes teaching with exhortation. But he particularly urges brotherly love: he also briefly touches on other things, such as to beware of impostors, and similar things. But each particular shall be noticed in its own place.

CHAPTER I.

1. That which was from the beginning, which we have heard, which we have seen with our eyes, which we have looked upon, and our hands have handled, of the Word of life;

2. (For the life was manifested, and we have seen *it*, and bear wit-

1. Quod erat ab initio, quod audivimus, quod vidimus oculis nostris, quod intuiti sumus, quod manus nostræ contrectaverunt, de Sermone vitæ;

2. Et vita manifesta est, et vidimus et testamur et annuntiamus

ness, and shew unto you that eternal life which was with the Father, and was manifested unto us.) | vobis vitam æternam, quæ erat apud Patrem, et manifesta est nobis.

He shews, first, that life has been exhibited to us in Christ; which, as it is an incomparable good, ought to rouse and inflame all our powers with a marvellous desire for it, and with the love of it. It is said, indeed, in a few and plain words, that life is manifested; but if we consider how miserable and horrible a condition death is, and also what is the kingdom and the glory of immortality, we shall perceive that there is something here more magnificent than what can be expressed in any words.

Then the Apostle's object, in setting before us the vast good, yea, the chief and only true happiness which God has conferred on us, in his own Son, is to raise our thoughts above; but as the greatness of the subject requires that the truth should be certain, and fully proved, this is what is here much dwelt upon. For these words, *What we have seen, what we have heard, what we have looked upon*, serve to strengthen our faith in the gospel. Nor does he, indeed, without reason, make so many asseverations; for since our salvation depends on the gospel, its certainty is in the highest degree necessary; and how difficult it is for us to believe, every one of us knows too well by his own experience. To believe is not lightly to form an opinion, or to assent only to what is said, but a firm, undoubting conviction, so that we may dare to subscribe to the truth as fully proved. It is for this reason that the Apostle heaps together so many things in confirmation of the gospel.

1. *That which was from the beginning.* As the passage is abrupt and involved, that the sense may be made clearer, the words may be thus arranged; "We announce to you the word of life, which was from the beginning and really testified to us in all manner of ways, that life has been manifested in him;" or, if you prefer, the meaning may be thus given, "What we announce to you respecting the word of life, has been from the beginning, and has been openly shewed to us, that life was manifested in him." But the words, *That which was from the beginning*, refer doubtless to

the divinity of Christ, for God manifested in the flesh was not from the beginning; but he who always was life and the eternal Word of God, appeared in the fulness of time as man. Again, what follows as to the looking on and the handling of the hands, refers to his human nature. But as the two natures constitute but one person, and Christ is one, because he came forth from the Father that he might put on our flesh, the Apostle rightly declares that he is the same, and had been invisible, and afterwards became visible.[1]

Hereby the senseless cavil of Servetus is disproved, that the nature and essence of Deity became one with the flesh, and that thus the Word was transformed into flesh, because the life-giving Word was seen in the flesh.

Let us then bear in mind, that this doctrine of the Gospel is here declared, that he who in the flesh really proved himself to be the Son of God, and was acknowledged to be the Son of God, was always God's invisible Word, for he does not refer here to the beginning of the world, but ascends much higher.

Which we have heard, which we have seen. It was not the hearing of a report, to which little credit is usually given, but John means, that he had faithfully learnt from his Master those things which he taught, so that he alleged nothing thoughtlessly and rashly. And, doubtless, no one is a fit teacher in the Church, who has not been the disciple of the Son of God, and rightly instructed in his school, since his authority alone ought to prevail.

When he says, we have seen *with our eyes*, it is no redundancy, but a fuller expression for the sake of amplifying; nay, he was not satisfied with seeing only, but added, *which we have looked upon, and our hands have handled.* By these words he shews that he taught nothing but what had been really made known to him.

It may seem, however, that the evidence of the senses

---

[1] It is more consistent with the passage to take "from the beginning" here as from the beginning of the Gospel, from the beginning of the ministry of our Saviour, because what had been from the beginning was what the apostles had *heard* and *seen*. That another view has been taken of these words has been owing to an over-anxiety on the part of many, especially of the Fathers, to establish the divinity of our Saviour; but this is what is sufficiently evident from the second verse. See ch. ii. 7, 24.—*Ed.*

little availed on the present subject, for the power of Christ could not be perceived by the eyes nor felt by the hands. To this I answer, that the same thing is said here as in the first chapter of the Gospel of John, "We have seen his glory, the glory as of the only-begotten of the Father;" for he was not known as the Son of God by the external form of his body, but because he gave illustrious proofs of his Divine power, so that in him shone forth the majesty of the Father, as in a living and distinct image. As the words are in the plural number, and the subject equally applies to all the apostles, I am disposed to include them, especially as the authority of testimony is what is treated of.

But no less frivolous (as I have before said) than impudent is the wickedness of Servetus, who urges these words to prove that the Word of God became visible and capable of being handled; he either impiously destroys or mingles together the twofold nature of Christ. It is, therefore, a pure figment. Thus deifying the humanity of Christ, he wholly takes away the reality of his human nature, at the same time denying that Christ is for any other reason called the Son of God, except that he was conceived of his mother by the power of the Holy Spirit, and taking away his own subsistence in God. It hence follows that he was neither God nor man, though he seems to form a confused mass from both. But as the meaning of the Apostle is evident to us, let us pass by that unprincipled man.

Of the Word of life. The genitive here is used for an adjective, vivifying, or life-giving; for in him, as it is said in the first chapter of John's Gospel, was life. At the same time, this distinction belongs to the Son of God on two accounts, because he has infused life into all creatures, and because he now restores life to us, which had perished, having been extinguished by the sin of Adam. Moreover, the term *Word* may be explained in two ways, either of Christ, or of the doctrine of the Gospel, for even by this is salvation brought to us. But as its substance is Christ, and as it contains no other thing than that he, who had been always with the Father, was at length manifested to men, the first view appears to me the more simple and genuine. Moreover, it appears more fully from the Gospel that the wisdom which dwells in God is called the Word.

2. *For* (or, and) *the life was manifested.* The copulative is explanatory, as though he had said, "We testify of the vivifying Word, as life has been manifested." The sense may at the same time be twofold, that Christ, who is life and the fountain of life, has been manifested, or, that life has been openly offered to us in Christ. The latter, indeed, necessarily follows from the former. Yet as to the meaning, the two things differ, as cause and effect. When he repeats, *We shew,* or announce *eternal life,* he speaks, I have no doubt, of the effect, even that he announces that life is obtained for us in Christ.

We hence learn, that when Christ is preached to us, the kingdom of heaven is opened to us, so that being raised from death we may live the life of God.

Which was with the Father. This is true, not only from the time when the world was formed, but also from eternity, for he was always God, the fountain of life; and the power and the faculty of vivifying was possessed by his eternal wisdom: but he did not actually exercise it before the creation of the world, and from the time when God began to exhibit the Word, that power which before was hid, diffused itself over all created things. Some manifestation had already been made; the Apostle had another thing in view, that is, that life was then at length manifested in Christ, when he in our flesh completed the work of redemption. For though the fathers were even under the law associates and partakers of the same life, yet we know that they were shut up under the hope that was to be revealed. It was necessary for them to seek life from the death and resurrection of Christ; but the event was not only far remote from their eyes, but also hid from their minds. They depended, then, on the hope of revelation, which at length in due time followed. They could not, indeed, have obtained life, except it was in some way manifested to them; but the difference between us and them is, that we hold him already revealed as it were in our hands, whom they sought obscurely promised to them in types.

But the object of the Apostle is, to remove the idea of novelty, which might have lessened the dignity of the Gospel; he therefore says, that life had not now at length began to be, though it had but lately appeared, for it was always with the Father.

3. That which we have seen and heard declare we unto you, that ye also may have fellowship with us: and truly our fellowship *is* with the Father, and with his Son Jesus Christ.

4. And these things write we unto you, that our joy may be full.

5. This then is the message which we have heard of him, and declare unto you, that God is light, and in him is no darkness at all.

6. If we say that we have fellowship with him, and walk in darkness, we lie, and do not the truth:

7. But if we walk in the light, as he is in the light, we have fellowship one with another, and the blood of Jesus Christ his Son cleanseth us from all sin.

3. Quod vidimus et audivimus, annuntiamus vobis, ut et vos societatem habeatis nobiscum, et societas nostra sit cum Patre et cum filio ejus Jesu Christo.

4. Et hæc scribimus vobis, ut gaudium vestrum sit completum.

5. Et hæc est promissio quam annuntiamus, quòd Deus lux est, et tenebræ in eo non sunt ullæ.

6. Si dixerimus quòd societatem habemus cum eo, et in tenebris ambulamus, mentimur, et veritatem non facimus.

7. Si autem in luce ambulamus, sicut ipse in luce est, societatem habemus inter nos mutuam, et sanguis Jesu Christi filii ejus emundat nos ab omni peccato.

3. *That which we have seen.* He now repeats the third time the words, *seen* and *heard*, that nothing might be wanting as to the real certainty of his doctrine. And it ought to be carefully noticed, that the heralds of the Gospel chosen by Christ were those who were fit and faithful witnesses of all those things which they were to declare. He also testifies of the feeling of their heart, for he says that he was moved by no other reason to write except to invite those to whom he was writing to the participation of an inestimable good. It hence appears how much care he had for their salvation; which served not a little to induce them to believe; for extremely ungrateful we must be, if we refuse to hear him who wishes to communicate to us a part of that happiness which he has obtained.

He also sets forth the fruit received from the Gospel, even that we are united thereby to God, and to his Son Christ, in whom is found the chief good. It was necessary for him to add this second clause, not only that he might represent the doctrine of the Gospel as precious and lovely, but that he might also shew that he wished them to be his associates for no other end but to lead them to God, so that they might be all one in him. For the ungodly have also a mutual union between themselves, but it is without God, nay, in order to alienate themselves more and more from God, which is the extreme of all evils. It is, indeed, as it has been stated, our only true happiness, to be received into God's favour, so that we may be really united to him in Christ; of which John speaks in the seventeenth chapter of his gospel.

In short, John declares, that as the apostles were adopted by Christ as brethren, that being gathered into one body, they might together be united to God, so he does the same with other colleagues; though many, they are yet made partakers of this holy and blessed union.

4. *That your joy may be full.* By full joy, he expresses more clearly the complete and perfect happiness which we obtain through the Gospel; at the same time he reminds the faithful where they ought to fix all their affections. True is that saying, "Where your treasure is, there will be your heart also." (Matt. vi. 21.) Whosoever, then, really perceives what fellowship with God is, will be satisfied with it alone, and will no more burn with desires for other things. "The Lord is my cup," says David, "and my heritage; the lines have fallen for me on an excellent lot." (Ps. xvi. 5, 6.) In the same manner does Paul declare that all things were deemed by him as dung, in comparison with Christ alone. (Phil. iii. 8.) He, therefore, has at length made a proficiency in the Gospel, who esteems himself happy in having communion with God, and acquiesces in that alone; and thus he prefers it to the whole world, so that he is ready for its sake to relinquish all other things.

5. *This then is the message,* or promise. I do not disapprove of the rendering of the old interpreter, "This is the annunciation," or message; for though ἐπαγγελία means for the most part a promise, yet, as John speaks here generally of the testimony before mentioned, the context seems to require the other meaning, except you were to

give this explanation, " The promise which we bring to you, includes this, or has this condition annexed to it." Thus, the meaning of the Apostle would become evident to us.[1] For his object here was not to include the whole doctrine of the Gospel, but to shew that if we desire to enjoy Christ and his blessings, it is required of us to be conformed to God in righteousness and holiness. Paul says the same thing in the second chapter of the Epistle to Titus, " Appeared has the saving grace of God to all, that denying ungodliness and worldly lusts, we may live soberly and righteously and holily in this world ;" except that here he says metaphorically, that we are to walk in the light, because God is light.

But he calls God *light,* and says that he is *in the light ;* such expressions are not to be too strictly taken. Why Satan is called the prince of darkness is sufficiently evident. When, therefore, God on the other hand is called the Father of light, and also light, we first understand that there is nothing in him but what is bright, pure, and unalloyed ; and, secondly, that he makes all things so manifest by his brightness, that he suffers nothing vicious or perverted, no spots or filth, no hypocrisy or fraud, to lie hid. Then the sum of what is said is, that since there is no union between light and darkness, there is a separation between us and God as long as we walk in darkness ; and that the fellowship which he mentions, cannot exist except we also become pure and holy.

In him is no darkness at all. This mode of speaking is commonly used by John, to amplify what he has affirmed by a contrary negation. Then, the meaning is, that God is such a light, that no darkness belongs to him. It hence follows, that he hates an evil conscience, pollution, and wickedness, and everything that pertains to darkness.

6. *If we say.* It is, indeed, an argument from what is inconsistent, when he concludes that they are alienated from God, who walk in darkness. This doctrine, however, depends

---

[1] *Griesbach* has substituted ἀγγελία for the word here used, as being most approved ; but the other, ἐπαγγελία, has also a similar meaning, announcement, or message, or command, though in the New Testament it is mostly taken in the sense of a promise.—*Ed.*

on a higher principle, that God sanctifies all who are his. For it is not a naked precept that he gives, which requires that our life should be holy; but he rather shews that the grace of Christ serves for this end to dissipate darkness, and to kindle in us the light of God; as though he had said, " What God communicates to us is not a vain fiction; for it is necessary that the power and effect of this fellowship should shine forth in our life; otherwise the possession of the gospel is fallacious." What he adds, *and do not the truth*, is the same as if he had said, " We do not act truthfully. We do not regard what is true and right." And this mode of speaking, as I have before observed, is frequently used by him.

7. *But if we walk in the light.* He now says, that the proof of our union with God is certain, if we are conformable to him; not that purity of life conciliates us to God, as the prior cause; but the Apostle means, that our union with God is made evident by the effect, that is, when his purity shines forth in us. And, doubtless, such is the fact; wherever God comes, all things are so imbued with his holiness, that he washes away all filth; for without him we have nothing but filth and darkness. It is hence evident, that no one leads a holy life, except he is united to God.

In saying, *We have fellowship one with another*, he does not speak simply of men; but he sets God on one side, and us on the other.

It may, however, be asked, " Who among men can so exhibit the light of God in his life, as that this likeness which John requires should exist; for it would be thus necessary, that he should be wholly pure and free from darkness?" To this I answer, that expressions of this kind are accommodated to the capacities of men: he is therefore said to be like God, who aspires to his likeness, however distant from it he may as yet be. The example ought not to be otherwise applied than according to this passage. He walks in darkness who is not ruled by the fear of God, and who does not, with a pure conscience, devote himself wholly to God, and seek to promote his glory. Then, on the other hand, he who in sincerity of heart spends his life, yea, every part of it, in the fear and service of God, and faithfully worships him, walks in the light, for he keeps the right way, though he may in many things offend and sigh under the burden of the flesh. Then, integrity of conscience is alone that which distinguishes light from darkness.

And the blood of Jesus Christ. After having taught what is the bond of our union with God, he now shews what fruit flows from it, even that our sins are freely remitted. And this is the blessedness which David describes in the thirty-second Psalm, in order that we may know that we are most miserable until, being renewed by God's Spirit, we serve him with a sincere heart. For who can be imagined more miserable than that man whom God hates and abominates, and over whose head is suspended both the wrath of God and eternal death?

This passage is remarkable; and from it we first learn, that the expiation of Christ, effected by his death, does then properly belong to us, when we, in uprightness of heart, do what is right and just: for Christ is no redeemer except to those who turn from iniquity, and lead a new life. If, then, we desire to have God propitious to us, so as to forgive our sins, we ought not to forgive ourselves. In short, remission of sins cannot be separated from repentance, nor can the peace of God be in those hearts, where the fear God does not prevail.

Secondly, this passage shews that the gratuitous pardon of sins is given us not only once, but that it is a benefit perpetually residing in the Church, and daily offered to the faithful. For the Apostle here addresses the faithful; as doubtless no man has ever been, nor ever will be, who can otherwise please God, since all are guilty before him; for however strong a desire there may be in us of acting rightly, we always go haltingly to God. Yet what is half done obtains no approval with God. In the meantime, by new sins we continually separate ourselves, as far as we can, from the grace of God. Thus it is, that all the saints have need of the daily forgiveness of sins; for this alone keeps us in the family of God.

By saying, *from all sin,* he intimates that we are, on many accounts, guilty before God ; so that doubtless there is no one who has not many vices. But he shews that no sins prevent the godly, and those who fear God, from obtaining his favour. He also points out the manner of obtaining pardon, and the cause of our cleansing, even because Christ expiated our sins by his blood ; but he affirms that all the godly are undoubtedly partakers of this cleansing.

The whole of his doctrine has been wickedly perverted by the sophists ; for they imagine that pardon of sins is given us, as it were, in baptism. They maintain that there only the blood of Christ avails ; and they teach, that after baptism, God is not otherwise reconciled than by satisfactions. They, indeed, leave some part to the blood of Christ ; but when they assign merit to works, even in the least degree, they wholly subvert what John teaches here, as to the way of expiating sins, and of being reconciled to God. For these two things can never harmonize together, to be cleansed by the blood of Christ, and to be cleansed by works : for John assigns not the half, but the whole, to the blood of Christ.

The sum of what is said, then, is, that the faithful know of a certainty, that they are accepted by God, because he has been reconciled to them through the sacrifice of the death of Christ. And sacrifice includes cleansing and satisfaction. Hence the power and efficiency of these belong to the blood of Christ alone.

Hereby is disproved and exposed the sacrilegious invention of the Papists as to indulgences; for as though the blood of Christ were not sufficient, they add, as a subsidy to it, the blood and merits of martyrs. At the same time, this blasphemy advances much further among us ; for as they say that their keys, by which they hold as shut up the remission of sins, open a treasure made up partly of the blood and merits of martyrs, and partly of the works of supererogation, by which any sinner may redeem himself, no remission of sins remains for them but what is derogatory to the blood of Christ ; for if their doctrine stands, the blood of Christ does not clease us, but comes in, as it were, as a partial aid. Thus consciences are held in suspense, which the Apostle here bids to rely on the blood of Christ.

8. If we say that we have no sin, we deceive ourselves, and the truth is not in us. 9. If we confess our sins, he is faithful and just to forgive us *our* sins, and to cleanse us from all unrighteousness. 10. If we say that we have not sinned, we make him a liar, and his word is not in us.	8. Si dixerimus quòd peccatum non habemus, nos ipsos decipimus, et veritas non est in nobis. 9. Si confitemur peccata nostra, fidelis est et justus, ut nobis peccata remittat; et purget nos ab omni injustitia. 10. Si dixerimus quòd non peccavimus, mendacem facimus eum, et sermo ejus non est in nobis.

8. *If we say.* He now commends grace from its necessity; for as no one is free from sin, he intimates that we are all lost and undone, except the Lord comes to our aid with the remedy of pardon. The reason why he so much dwells on the fact, that no one is innocent, is, that all may now fully know that they stand in need of mercy, to deliver them from punishment, and that they may thus be more roused to seek the necessary blessing.

By the word *sin*, is meant here not only corrupt and vicious inclination, but the fault or sinful act which really renders us guilty before God. Besides, as it is a universal declaration, it follows, that none of the saints, who exist now, have been, or shall be, are exempted from the number. Hence most fitly did Augustine refute the cavil of the Pelagians, by adducing against them this passage: and he wisely thought that the confession of guilt is not required for humility's sake, but lest we by lying should deceive ourselves.

When he adds, *and the truth is not in us,* he confirms, according to his usual manner, the former sentence by repeating it in other words; though it is not a simple repetition, (as elsewhere,) but he says that they are deceived who glory in falsehood.

9. *If we confess.* He again promises to the faithful that God will be propitious to them, provided they acknowledge themselves to be sinners. It is of great moment to be fully persuaded, that when we have sinned, there is a reconciliation with God ready and prepared for us: we shall otherwise carry always a hell within us. Few, indeed, consider how miserable and wretched is a doubting conscience; but the truth is, that hell reigns where there is no peace with God. The more, then, it becomes us to receive with the whole heart

this promise which offers free pardon to all who confess their sins. Moreover, this is founded even on the justice of God, because God who promises is true and just. For they who think that he is called *just*, because he justifies us freely, reason, as I think, with too much refinement, because justice or righteousness here depends on fidelity, and both are annexed to the promise. For God might have been just, were he to deal with us with all the rigour of justice; but as he has bound himself to us by his word, he would not have himself deemed just except he forgives.[1]

But this confession, as it is made to God, must be in sincerity; and the heart cannot speak to God without newness of life: it then includes true repentance. God, indeed, forgives freely, but in such a way, that the facility of mercy does not become an enticement to sin.

And to cleanse us. The verb, to cleanse, seems to be taken in another sense than before; for he had said, that we are cleansed by the blood of Christ, because through him sins are not imputed; but now, having spoken of pardon, he also adds, that God cleanses us from iniquity: so that this second clause is different from the preceding. Thus he intimates that a twofold fruit comes to us from confession,—that God being reconciled by the sacrifice of Christ, forgives us,—and that he renews and reforms us.

Were any one to object and say, that as long as we sojourn in the world, we are never cleansed from all unrighteousness, with regard to our reformation: this is indeed true; but John does not refer to what God now performs in us. He is faithful, he says, to cleanse us, not to-day or to-morrow;

---

[1] "Faithful" and "just" are nearly of the same import, having both a regard to God's *promise*, only the latter affords a stronger or an additional ground of confidence, inasmuch as the fulfilment of God's gracious promise is set forth as an act of justice. So that the penitent has here two of God's attributes, faithfulness and justice, to encourage and support his faith.

We may, at the same time, consider "just" as having reference to forgiveness, and "faithful" to cleansing, according to a very common mode of stating things both in the Old and New Testament, the order in the second clause being reversed. Then "just" means the same as when Paul says, "that he might be just and the justifier of him that believeth in Jesus," Rom. iii. 26. Forgiveness is thus an act of justice, then, not to us, but to Christ, who made an atonement for sins.—*Ed.*

for as long as we are surrounded with flesh, we ought to be in a continual state of progress; but what he has once begun, he goes on daily to do, until he at length completes it. So Paul says, that we are chosen, that we may appear without blame before God, (Col. i. 22;) and in another place he says, that the Church is cleansed, that it might be without spot or wrinkle. (Eph. v. 27.)

If yet any one prefers another explanation, that he says the same thing twice over, I shall not object.[1]

10. *We make him a liar.* He goes still further, that they who claim purity for themselves blaspheme God. For we see that he everywhere represents the whole race of man as guilty of sin.

Whosoever then tries to escape this charge carries on war with God, and accuses him of falsehood, as though he condemned the undeserving. To confirm this he adds, *and his word is not in us;* as though he had said, that we reject this great truth, that all are under guilt.

We hence learn, that we then only make a due progress in the knowledge of the word of the Lord, when we become really humbled, so as to groan under the burden of our sins and learn to flee to the mercy of God, and acquiesce in nothing else but in his paternal favour.

CHAPTER II.

1. My little children, these things write I unto you, that ye sin not. And if any man sin, we have an advocate with the Father, Jesus Christ the righteous:

2. And he is the propitiation for our sins; and not for ours only, but also for *the sins of* the whole world.

1. Filioli mei, hæc scribo vobis, ut non peccetis; quòd si quis peccaverit, advocatum habemus apud Patrem, Jesum Christum justum:

2. Et ipse est propitiatio pro peccatis nostris, non pro nostris autem solum, sed etiam pro totius mundi.

1. *My little children.* It is not only the sum and substance of the preceding doctrine, but the meaning of almost the whole gospel, that we are to depart from sin; and yet, though we are always exposed to God's judgment, we are

---

[1] That is, that he refers to forgiveness in the two clauses.—*Ed.*

certain that Christ so intercedes by the sacrifice of his death, that the Father is propitious to us. In the meantime, he also anticipates an objection, lest any one should think that he gave license to sin when he spoke of God's mercy, and shewed that it is presented to us all. He then joins together two parts of the gospel, which unreasonable men separate, and thus lacerate and mutilate. Besides, the doctrine of grace has always been calumniated by the ungodly. When the expiation of sins by Christ is set forth, they boastingly say that a license is given to sin.

To obviate these calumnies, the Apostle testifies first that the design of his doctrine was to keep men from sinning; for when he says, *that ye sin not,* his meaning only is, that they, according to the measure of human infirmity, should abstain from sins. And to the same purpose is what I have already said respecting fellowship with God, that we are to be conformable to him. He is not, however, silent as to the gratuitous remission of sins; for though heaven should fall and all things be confounded, yet this part of truth ought never to be omitted; but, on the contrary, what Christ is ought to be preached clearly and distinctly.

So ought we also to do at this day. As the flesh is inclined to wantonness, men ought to be carefully warned, that righteousness and salvation are provided in Christ for this end, that we may become the holy possession of God. Yet whenever it happens that men wantonly abuse the mercy of God, there are many snarlish men who load us with calumny, as though we gave loose reins to vices. We ought still boldly to go on and proclaim the grace of Christ, in which especially shines forth the glory of God, and in which consists the whole salvation of men. These barkings of the ungodly ought, I repeat it, to be wholly disregarded; for we see that the apostles were also by these barkings assailed.

For this reason he immediately adds the second clause, that when we sin we have an *advocate.* By these words he confirms what we have already said, that we are very far from being perfectly righteous, nay, that we contract new guilt daily, and that yet there is a remedy for reconciling us to God, if we flee to Christ; and this is alone that in which consciences can acquiesce, in which is included the righteousness of men, in which is founded the hope of salvation.

The conditional particle, *if*, ought to be viewed as causal; for it cannot be but that we sin. In short, John means, that we are not only called away from sin by the gospel, because God invites us to himself, and offers to us the Spirit of regeneration, but that a provision is made for miserable sinners, that they may have God always propitious to them, and that the sins by which they are entangled, do not prevent them from becoming just, because they have a Mediator to reconcile them to God. But in order to shew how we return into favour with God, he says that Christ is our advocate; for he appears before God for this end, that he may exercise towards us the power and efficacy of his sacrifice. That this may be better understood, I will speak more homely: The intercession of Christ is a continual application of his death for our salvation. That God then does not impute to us our sins, this comes to us, because he has regard to Christ as intercessor.

But the two names, by which he afterwards signalizes Christ, properly belong to the subject of this passage. He calls him *just* and a *propitiation*. It is necessary for him to be both, that he might sustain the office and person of an Advocate; for who that is a sinner could reconcile God to us? For we are excluded from access to him, because no one is pure and free from sin. Hence no one is fit to be a high priest, except he is innocent and separated from sinners, as it is also declared in Heb. vii. 26. *Propitiation* is added, because no one is fit to be a high priest without a sacrifice. Hence, under the Law, no priest entered the sanctuary without blood; and a sacrifice, as a usual seal, was wont, according to God's appointment, to accompany prayers. By this symbol it was God's design to shew, that whosoever obtains favour for us, must be furnished with a sacrifice; for when God is offended, in order to pacify him a satisfaction is required. It hence follows, that all the saints who have ever been and shall be, have need of an advocate, and that no one except Christ is equal to undertake this office. And doubtless John ascribed these two things to Christ, to shew that he is the only true advocate.

Now, as no small consolation comes to us, when we hear that Christ not only died for us to reconcile us to the Father, but that he continually intercedes for us, so that an access in his name is open to us, that our prayers may be heard; so we ought especially to beware, lest this honour, which belongs peculiarly to him, should be transferred to another.

But we know that under the Papacy this office is ascribed indiscriminately to the saints. Thirty years ago, this so remarkable an article of our faith, that Christ is our advocate, was nearly buried; but at this day they allow that he is indeed one of many, but not the only one. They among the Papists who have a little more modesty, do not deny that Christ excels others; but they afterwards join with him a vast number of associates. But the words clearly mean that he cannot be an advocate who is not a priest; and the priesthood belongs to none but to Christ alone. In the meantime we do not take away the mutual intercessions of saints, which they exercise in love towards one another; but this has nothing to do with the dead who have removed from their intercourse with men; and nothing with that patronage which they feign for themselves, that they may not be dependent on Christ alone. For though brethren pray for brethren, yet they all, without exception, look to one advocate. There is, then, no doubt but the Papists set up against Christ so many idols as the patrons or advocates they devise for themselves.

We must also notice by the way, that those err very grossly, who imagine that Christ falls on his knees before the Father to pray for us. Such thoughts ought to be renounced, for they detract from the celestial glory of Christ; and the simple truth ought to be retained, that the fruit of his death is ever new and perpetual, that by his intercession he renders God propitious to us, and that he sanctifies our prayers by the odour of his sacrifice, and also aids us by pleading for us.

2. *And not for ours only.* He added this for the sake of

amplifying, in order that the faithful might be assured that the expiation made by Christ, extends to all who by faith embrace the gospel.

Here a question may be raised, how have the sins of the whole world been expiated? I pass by the dotages of the fanatics, who under this pretence extend salvation to all the reprobate, and therefore to Satan himself. Such a monstrous thing deserves no refutation. They who seek to avoid this absurdity, have said that Christ[1] suffered sufficiently for the whole world, but efficiently only for the elect. This solution has commonly prevailed in the schools. Though then I allow that what has been said is true, yet I deny that it is suitable to this passage; for the design of John was no other than to make this benefit common to the whole Church. Then under the word *all* or whole, he does not include the reprobate, but designates those who should believe as well as those who were then scattered through various parts of the world. For then is really made evident, as it is meet, the grace of Christ, when it is declared to be the only true salvation of the world.

3. And hereby we do know that we know him, if we keep his commandments.	3. Atque in hoc cognoscimus quòd cognovimus eum, si præcepta ejus servamus.
4. He that saith, I know him, and keepeth not his commandments, is a liar, and the truth is not in him.	4. Qui dicit, Novi eum, et præcepta ejus non servat, mendax est, et in eo veritas non est.
5. But whoso keepeth his word, in him verily is the love of God perfected: hereby know we that we are in him.	5. Qui verò servat ejus sermonem, verè in ipso charitas Dei perfecta est; in hoc cognoscimus quòd in ipso sumus.
6. He that saith he abideth in him, ought himself also so to walk, even as he walked.	6. Qui dicit se in eo manere, debet, sicut ille ambulavit, ita et ipse ambulare.

3. *And hereby*, or by this. After having treated of the doctrine respecting the gratuitous remission of sins, he comes to the exhortations which belong to it, and which depend on it. And first indeed he reminds us that the knowledge of God, derived from the gospel, is not ineffectual, but that obedience proceeds from it. He then shews what God espe-

---

[1] " It seems to me that the Apostle is to be understood as speaking only of all those who believe, whether Jews or Gentiles, over the whole world." —*Doddridge.*—*Ed.*

cially requires from us, what is the chief thing in life, even love to God. What we read here of the living knowledge of God, the Scripture does not without reason repeat everywhere; for nothing is more common in the world than to draw the doctrine of religion to frigid speculations. In this way theology has been adulterated by the Sorbonian sophists, so that from their whole science not even the least spark of true religion shines forth. And curious men do everywhere learn so much from God's word, as enables them to prattle for the sake of display. In short, no evil has been more common in all ages than vainly to profess God's name.

John then takes this principle as granted, that the knowledge of God is efficacious. He hence concludes, that they by no means know God who keep not his precepts or commandments. Plato, though groping in darkness, yet denied that " the beautiful" which he imagined, could be known, without filling man with the admiration of itself; so he says in his Phædrus and in other places. How then is it possible for thee to know God, and to be moved by no feeling? Nor does it indeed proceed only from God's nature, that to know him is immediately to love him; but the Spirit also, who illuminates our minds, inspires our hearts with a feeling conformable to our knowledge. At the same time the knowledge of God leads us to fear him and to love him. For we cannot know him as Lord and Father, as he shews himself, without being dutiful children and obedient servants. In short, the doctrine of the gospel is a lively mirror in which we contemplate the image of God, and are transformed into the same, as Paul teaches us in 2 Cor. iii. 18. Where, therefore, there is no pure conscience, nothing can be there but an empty phantom of knowledge.

We must notice the order when he says, *We do know that we know him;* for he intimates that obedience is so connected with knowledge, that the last is yet in order the first, as the cause is necessarily before its effect.

If we keep his commandments. But there is no one who in everything keeps them; there would thus be no knowledge of God in the world. To this I answer, that the Apostle is by no means inconsistent with himself; since he has before shewed that all are guilty before God, he does not understand that those who keep his commandments wholly satisfy the law (no such example can be found in the world;) but that they are such as strive, according to the capacity of human infirmity, to form their life in conformity to the will of God. For whenever Scripture speaks of the righteousness of the faithful, it does not exclude the remission of sins, but on the contrary begins with it.

But we are not hence to conclude that faith recumbs on works; for though every one receives a testimony to his faith from his works, yet it does not follow that it is founded on them, since they are added as an evidence. Then the certainty of faith depends on the grace of Christ alone ; but piety and holiness of life distinguish true faith from that knowledge of God which is fictitious and dead ; for the truth is, that those who are in Christ, as Paul says, have put off the old man. (Col. iii. 9.)

4. *He that saith, I know him.* How does he prove that they are liars who boast that they have faith without piety ? even by the contrary effect ; for he has already said, that the knowledge of God is efficacious. For God is not known by a naked imagination, since he reveals himself inwardly to our hearts by the Spirit. Besides, as many hypocrites vainly boast that they have faith, the Apostle charges all such with falsehood ; for what he says would be superfluous, were there no false and vain profession of Christianity made by man.

5. *But whoso keepeth.* He now defines what a true keeping of God's law is, even to love God. This passage is, I think, incorrectly explained by those who understand that they please the true God who keep his word. Rather take this as its meaning, " to love God in sincerity of heart, is to keep his commandments." For he intended, as I have before reminded you, briefly to shew what God requires from us, and what is the holiness of the faithful. Moses also said the same thing, when he stated the sum of the law. " Now, O Israel, what does the Lord require of thee, but to fear and love him, and to walk in his precepts ?" (Deut. x. 12.) And again he says, in chap. xxx. 19, 20, " Choose life, even to love the Lord thy God, to serve him and to cleave to him." For

the law, which is spiritual, does not command only external works, but enjoins this especially, to love God with the whole heart.

That no mention is here made of what is due to men, ought not to be viewed as unreasonable; for brotherly love flows immediately from the love of God, as we shall hereafter see. Whosoever, then, desires that his life should be approved by God, must have all his doings directed to this end. If any one objects and says, that no one has ever been found who loved God thus perfectly; to this I reply, that it is sufficient, provided every one aspired to this perfection according to the measure of grace given unto him. In the meantime, the definition is, that the perfect love of God is the complete keeping of his law. To make progress in this as in knowledge, is what we ought to do.

Hereby know we that we are in him. He refers to that fruit of the gospel which he had mentioned, even fellowship with the Father and the Son; and he thus confirms the former sentence, by stating what follows, as a consequence: for if it be the end of the gospel to hold communion with God, and no communion can be without love, then no one makes a real progress in faith except he who cleaves from the heart to God.

6. *He that saith he abideth in him.* As he has before set before us God as light for an example, he now calls us also to Christ, that we may imitate him. Yet he does not simply exhort us to imitate Christ; but from the union we have with him, he proves that we ought to be like him. A likeness in life and deeds, he says, will prove that we abide in Christ. But from these words he passes on to the next clause, which he immediately adds respecting love to the brethren.

7. Brethren, I write no new commandment unto you, but an old commandment, which ye had from the beginning: the old commandment is the word which ye have heard from the beginning.	7. Fratres, non mandatum novum scribo vobis, sed mandatum vetus, quod habuistis ab initio: mandatum vetus est sermo quem audistis ab initio.
8. Again, a new commandment I write unto you, which thing is true in him and in you; because the	8. Rursum mandatum novum scribo vobis, quæ est veritas in ipso et in vobis; quia tenebræ

darkness is past, and the true light now shineth.	transeunt, et lumen verum jam lucet.
9. He that saith he is in the light, and hateth his brother, is in darkness even until now.	9. Quia dicit se in luce esse, et fratrem suum odit, in tenebris est adhuc.
10. He that loveth his brother abideth in the light, and there is none occasion of stumbling in him :	10. Qui diligit fratrem suum, in luce manet, et offendiculum in eo non est.
11. But he that hateth his brother is in darkness, and walketh in darkness, and knoweth not whither he goeth, because that darkness hath blinded his eyes.	11. Qui verò fratrem suum odit, in tenebris ambulat, nec scit quò vadat, quia tenebræ excæcarunt oculos ejus.

7. *Brethren, I write no new commandment.* This is an explanation of the preceding doctrine, that to love God is to keep his commandments. And not without reason did he largely dwell on this point. First, we know that novelty is disliked or suspected. Secondly, we do not easily undertake an unwonted yoke. In addition to these things, when we have embraced any kind of doctrine, we dislike to have anything changed or made new in it. For these reasons John reminds us, that he taught nothing respecting love but what had been heard by the faithful from the beginning, and had by long usage become old.

Some explain oldness differently, even that Christ now prescribes no other rule of life under the Gospel than what God did formerly under the Law. This is indeed most true ; nor do I object but that he afterwards calls in this sense the word of the gospel *the old commandment.* But I think that he now means only, that these were the first elements of the gospel, that they had been thus taught from the beginning, that there was no reason why they should refuse that as unusual by which they ought to have been long ago imbued. For the relative seems to be used in a causative sense. He calls it then *old,* not because it was taught the fathers many ages before, but because it had been taught them on their very entrance into a religious life. And it served much to claim their faith, that it had proceeded from Christ himself from whom they had received the gospel.[1]

---

[1] That this view is correct, appears evident from the words, " which *ye* had from the beginning ;" he calls it " old," because they had been taught it from " the beginning," that is, of the gospel. Then " new" can mean

The old commandment. The word *old*, in this place, probably extends further; for the sentence is fuller, when he says, *the word which ye have heard from the beginning is the old commandment.* And as I, indeed, think, he means that the gospel ought not to be received as a doctrine lately born, but what has proceeded from God, and is his eternal truth; as though he had said, "Ye ought not to measure the antiquity of the gospel which is brought to you, by time; since therein is revealed to you the eternal will of God: not only then has God delivered to you this rule of a holy life, when ye were first called to the faith of Christ, but the same has always been prescribed and approved by him." And, doubtless, this only ought to be deemed antiquity, and deserves faith and reverence, which has its origin from God. For the fictions of men, whatever long prescription of years they may have, cannot acquire so much authority as to subvert the truth of God.

8. *Again, a new commandment.* Interpreters do not appear to me to have attained the meaning of the Apostle. He says *new*, because God, as it were, renews it by daily suggesting it, so that the faithful may practise it through their whole life, for nothing more excellent can be sought for by them. The elements which children learn give place in time to what is higher and more solid. On the contrary, John denies that the doctrine respecting brotherly love is of this kind, is one which grows old with time, but that it is perpetually in force, so that it is no less the highest perfection than the very beginning.

It was, however, necessary that this should be added, for as men are more curious than what they ought to be, there are many who always seek something new. Hence there is a weariness as to simple doctrine, which produces innumerable prodigies of errors, when every one gapes continually for new mysteries. Now, when it is known that the Lord proceeds in the same even course, in order to keep us through life in that which we have learnt, a bridle is cast on desires of this kind. Let him, then, who would reach the goal of

no other thing than what *Calvin* states, that it continues still in force, it being, as it were, always new.—*Ed.*

wisdom, as to the right way of living, make proficiency in love.

Which thing is true, or which is truth. He proves by this reason what he had said; for this one command respecting love, as to our conduct in life, constitutes the whole truth of Christ. Besides, what other greater revelation can be expected? for Christ, doubtless, is the end and the completion of all things. Hence the word *truth* means this, that they stood, as it were at the goal, for it is to be taken for a completion or a perfect state. He joins Christ to them, as the head to the members, as though he had said, that the body of the Church has no other perfection, or, that they would then be really united to Christ, if holy love existed continually among them.

Some give another explanation, " That which is the truth in Christ, is also in you." But I do not see what the meaning of this is.

Because the darkness is past. The present time is here instead of the past; for he means, that as soon as Christ brings light, we have the full brightness of knowledge : not that every one of the faithful becomes wise the first day as much as he ought to be, (for even Paul testifies that he laboured to apprehend what he had not apprehended, (Phil. iii. 12,) but that the knowledge of Christ alone is sufficient to dissipate darkness. Hence, daily progress is necessary ; and the faith of every one has its dawn before it reaches the noon-day. But as God continues the inculcation of the same doctrine, in which he bids us to make advances, the knowledge of the Gospel is justly said to be the true light, when Christ, the Sun of righteousness, shines. Thus the way is shut up against the audacity of those men who try to corrupt the purity of the Gospel by their own fictions ; and we may safely denounce an anathema on the whole theology of the Pope, for it wholly obscures the true light.

9. *He that saith he is in the light.* He pursues the same metaphor : he said that love is the only true rule according to which our life is to be formed ; he said that this rule or law is presented to us in the Gospel ; he said, lastly, that it

is there as the meridian light, which ought to be continually looked on. Now, on the other hand, he concludes that all are blind and walk in darkness who are strangers to love. But that he mentioned before the love of God and now the love of the brethren, involves no more contrariety than there is between the effect and its cause. Besides, these are so connected together that they cannot be separated.

John says in the third chapter, that we falsely boast of love to God, except we love our brethren; and this is most true. But he now takes love to the brethren as a testimony by which we prove that we love God. In short, since love so regards God, that in God it embraces men, there is nothing strange in this, that the Apostle, speaking of love, should refer at one time to God, at another to the brethren; and this is what is commonly done in Scripture. The whole perfection of life is often said to consist in the love of God; and again, Paul teaches us, that the whole law is fulfilled by him who loves his neighbour, (Rom. xiii. 8;) and Christ declares that the main points of the law are righteousness, judgment, and truth. (Matt. xxiii. 23.) Both these things are true and agree well together, for the love of God teaches us to love men, and we also in reality prove our love to God by loving men at his command. However this may be, it remains always certain that love is the rule of life. And this ought to be the more carefully noticed, because all choose rather almost anything else than this one commandment of God.

To the same purpose is what follows, *and there is no occasion of stumbling in him*—that is, in him who acts in love; for, he who thus lives will never stumble.[1]

11. *But he that hateth his brother.* He again reminds us, that whatever specious appearance of excellency thou shew-

---

[1] Literally, "and to him there is not a stumblingblock;" that is, nothing that causes him to stumble or fall. He is not like him mentioned in the next verse, who "walks in darkness and knows not whither he goeth." The sentence seems to have been taken from Ps. cxix. 165, with this only difference, that it is "to them," instead of "to him." There is in the *Sept.* no preposition, but in Hebrew the preposition "to" is used; and ἐν has sometimes this meaning in the New Testament. See Col. i. 23; 1 Thess. iv. 7.—*Ed.*

est, there is yet nothing but what is sinful if love be absent. This passage may be compared with the thirteenth chapter of the First Epistle to the Corinthians, and no long explanation is needed. But this doctrine is not understood by the world, because the greater part are dazzled by all sorts of masks or disguises. Thus, fictitious sanctity dazzles the eyes of almost all men, while love is neglected, or, at least, driven to the farthest corner.

12. I write unto you, little children, because your sins are forgiven you for his name's sake. 13. I write unto you, fathers, because ye have known him *that is* from the beginning. I write unto you, young men, because ye have overcome the wicked one. I write unto you, little children, because ye have known the Father. 14. I have written unto you, fathers, because ye have known him *that is* from the beginning. I have written unto you, young men, because ye are strong, and the word of God abideth in you, and ye have overcome the wicked one.	12. Scribo vobis, filioli, quoniam remittuntur vobis peccata vestra propter nomen ejus. 13. Scribo vobis, patres, quoniam novistis eum qui est ab initio. Scribo vobis, adolescentes, quoniam vicistis malum illum. Scribo vobis, pueri, quoniam novistis Patrem. 14. Scripsi vobis, patres, quoniam novistis eum qui est ab initio. Scripsi vobis, adolescentes, quia fortes estis, et verbum Dei manet in vobis, et vicistis malum illum.

12. *Little children.* This is still a general declaration, for he does not address those only of a tender age, but by *little children* he means men of all ages, as in the first verse, and also hereafter. I say this, because interpreters have incorrectly applied the term to children. But John, when he speaks of children, calls them παιδία, a word expressive of age; but here, as a spiritual father, he calls the old as well as the young, τεκνία. He will, indeed, presently address special words to different ages; yet they are mistaken who think that he begins to do so here. But, on the contaray, lest the preceding exhortation should obscure the free remission of sins, he again inculcates the doctrine which peculiarly belongs to faith, in order that the foundation may with certainty be always retained, that salvation is laid up for us in Christ alone.

Holiness of life ought indeed to be urged, the fear of God ought to be carefully enjoined, men ought to be sharply goaded to repentance, newness of life, together with its fruits, ought to be commended; but still we ought ever to take heed, lest the doctrine of faith be smothered,—that doctrine which teaches that Christ is the only author of salvation and of all blessings; on the contrary, such moderation ought to be presented, that faith may ever retain its own primacy. This is the rule prescribed to us by John: having faithfully spoken of good works, lest he should seem to give them more importance than he ought to have done, he carefully calls us back to contemplate the grace of Christ.

Your sins are forgiven you. Without this assurance, religion would not be otherwise than fading and shadowy; nay, they who pass by the free remission of sins, and dwell on other things, build without a foundation. John in the meantime intimates, that nothing is more suitable to stimulate men to fear God than when they are rightly taught what blessing Christ has brought to them, as Paul does, when he beseeches by the bowels of God's mercies. (Phil. ii. 1.)

It hence appears how wicked is the calumny of the Papists, who pretend that the desire of doing what is right is frozen, when that is extolled which alone renders us obedient children to God. For the Apostle takes this as the ground of his exhortation, that we know that God is so benevolent to us as not to impute to us our sins.

For his name's sake. The material cause is mentioned, lest we should seek other means to reconcile us to God. For it would not be sufficient to know that God forgives us our sins, except we came directly to Christ, and to that price which he paid on the cross for us. And this ought the more to be observed, because we see that by the craft of Satan, and by the wicked fictions of men, this way is obstructed; for foolish men attempt to pacify God by various satisfactions, and devise innumerable kinds of expiations for the purpose of redeeming themselves. For as many means of deserving pardon we intrude on God, by so many obstacles are we prevented from approaching him. Hence John, not satisfied with stating simply the doctrine, that God remits to us our sins, expressly adds, that he is propitious to us from a regard to Christ, in order that he might exclude all other reasons. We also, that we may enjoy this blessing, must pass by and forget all other names, and rely only on the name of Christ.

13. *I write unto you, fathers.* He comes now to enumerate different ages, that he might shew that what he taught was suitable to every one of them. For a general address sometimes produces less effect; yea, such is our perversity, that few think that what is addressed to all belongs to them. The old for the most part excuse themselves, because they have exceeded the age of learning; children refuse to learn, as they are not yet old enough; men of middle age do not attend, because they are occupied with other pursuits. Lest, then, any should exempt themselves, he accommodates the Gospel to all. And he mentions three ages, the most common division of human life. Hence also, the Lacedemonian chorus had three orders; the first sang, "What ye are we shall be;" the last, "What ye are we have been;" and the middle, "We are what one of you have been and the other will be." Into these three degrees John divides human life.

He, indeed, begins with the old, and says that the Gospel is suitable to them, because they learnt from it to know the eternal Son of God. Moroseness is the character of the old, but they become especially unteachable, because they measure wisdom by the number of years. Besides, Horace in his Art of Poetry, has justly noticed this fault in them, that they praise the time of their youth and reject whatever is differently done or said. This evil John wisely removes, when he reminds us that the Gospel contains not only a knowledge that is ancient, but what also leads us to the very eternity of God. It hence follows that there is nothing here which they can dislike. He says that Christ was *from the beginning;* I refer this to his Divine presence, as being co-eternal with the Father, as well as to his power, of which the Apostle speaks in Heb. xiii. 8, that he was yesterday what he is to-day; as though he had said, "If antiquity delights you, ye have Christ, who is superior to all antiquity; therefore his disciples ought not to be ashamed of him who includes all ages in himself."

We must, at the same time, notice what that religion is which is really ancient, even that which is founded on Christ, for otherwise it will be of no avail, however long it may have existed, if it derives its origin from error.

I write unto you, young men. Though it be a diminutive word, νεανίσκοι,[1] yet there is no doubt but that he directs his word to all who were in the flower of their age. We also know that those of that age are so addicted to the vain cares of the world, that they think but little of the kingdom of God; for the vigour of their minds and the strength of their bodies in a manner inebriate them. Hence the Apostle reminds them where true strength is, that they might no more exult as usual in the flesh. *Ye are strong*, he says, *because ye have overcome* Satan. The copulative here is to be rendered causatively. And, doubtless, that strength is what we ought to seek, even that which is spiritual. At the same time he intimates that it is not had otherwise than from Christ, for he mentions the blessings which we receive through the Gospel. He says that they had conquered who were as yet engaged in the contest; but our condition is far otherwise than that of those who fight under the banners of men, for war is doubtful to them and the issue is uncertain; but we are conquerors before we engage with the enemy, for our head Christ has once for all conquered for us the whole world.

I write unto you, young children. They needed another direction. That the Gospel is well adapted to young children the Apostle concludes, because they find there the Father. We now see how diabolical is the tyranny of the Pope, which drives away by threats all ages from the doctrine of the Gospel, while the Spirit of God so carefully addresses them all.

But these things which the Apostle makes particular, are also general; for we should wholly fall off into vanity, except our infirmity were sustained by the eternal truth of God. There is nothing in us but what is frail and fading,

---

[1] The diminutive termination often expresses affection; hence νεανίσκοι may properly be rendered, "dear youth," or "dear young men;" and so τεκνία μου, in the first verse, may be rendered, "My dear children."—*Ed.*

except the power of Christ dwells in us. We are all like orphans until we attain the grace of adoption by the Gospel. Hence, what he declares respecting young children is also true as to the old. But yet his object was to apply to each what was most especially necessary for them, that he might shew that they all without exception stood in need of the doctrine of the Gospel. The particle ὅτι is explained in two ways, but the meaning I have given to it is the best, and agrees better with the context.

14. *I have written unto you, fathers.* These repetitions I deem superfluous; and it is probable that when unskilful readers falsely thought that he spoke twice of little children, they rashly introduced the other two clauses. It might at the same time be that John himself, for the sake of amplifying, inserted the second time the sentence respecting the young men, (for he adds, that they were strong, which he had not said before;) but that the copyists presumptuously filled up the number.[1]

15. Love not the world, neither the things *that are* in the world. If any man love the world, the love of the Father is not in him.
16. For all that *is* in the world, the lust of the flesh, and the lust of the eyes, and the pride of life, is not of the Father, but is of the world.
17. And the world passeth away, and the lust thereof: but he that doeth the will of God abideth for ever.

15. Ne diligatis mundum, neque ea quæ in mundo sunt: si quis diligit mundum non est charitas Patris in eo.
16. Quia quicquid est in mundo (nempe concupiscentia carnis, concupiscentia oculorum, et superbia vitæ) non est ex Patre, sed ex mundo est.
17. Atqui mundus transit, et concupiscentia ejus; qui autem facit voluntatem Dei manet in æternum.

15. *Love not.* He had said before that the only rule for living religiously, is to love God; but as, when we are occupied with the vain love of the world, we turn away all our thoughts and affections another way, this vanity must first

---

[1] There are no different readings that can justify the supposition of an interpolation. The only reading that *Griesbach* considers probable is ἔγραψα for γράφω at the end of the 13th verse. If that be adopted, then the three characters are twice mentioned, and in regular order. The objection that τεκνία in ver. 12, is παιδία in ver. 13, is not valid, for he uses the latter in the same sense as the former in ver. 18, as denoting Christians in general; while here, in connexion with "fathers" and "young men," they must mean those young in years or in the profession of the gospel. The repetition is for the sake of emphasis.— *Ed.*

be torn away from us, in order that the love of God may reign within us. Until our minds are cleansed, the former doctrine may be iterated a hundred times, but with no effect: it would be like pouring water on a ball; you can gather, no, not a drop, because there is no empty place to retain water.[1]

By the *world* understand everything connected with the present life, apart from the kingdom of God and the hope of eternal life. So he includes in it corruptions of every kind, and the abyss of all evils. In the world are pleasures, delights, and all those allurements by which man is captivated, so as to withdraw himself from God.[2]

Moreover, the love of the world is thus severely condemned, because we must necessarily forget God and ourselves when we regard nothing so much as the earth; and when a corrupt lust of this kind rules in man, and so holds him entangled that he thinks not of the heavenly life, he is possessed by a beastly stupidity.

If any man love the world. He proves by an argument from what is contrary, how necessary it is to cast away the love of the world, if we wish to please God; and this he afterwards confirms by an argument drawn from what is inconsistent; for what belongs to the world is wholly at vari-

---

[1] It is considered by many, such as *Macknight* and *Scott*, that the three former verses are connected with this—that the particulars stated with regard to little children, fathers, and young men, are adduced as reasons to enforce this exhortation, "Love not the world," &c. And this no doubt is the best view of the passage.—*Ed.*

[2] There are *two* things, the world, and the things that are in the world. The world, thus distinguished from what is in it, means, according to *Macknight*, the wicked and unbelieving, the men of the world, as when our Saviour says, "the world," that is, the unbelieving Jews, "hateth you," John xv. 19. According to this view, the contrast in verse 17 appears very suitable, "The world (the ungodly men of the world) passeth away, and its lust, (their lust;) but he that doeth the will of God abideth for ever." Others think that the blessings of the world are meant, the good things necessary for the support of man, and that these are not to be *loved*, though they may be rightly used. In this case, "in the world" must have a different meaning, a thing not unusual in Scripture; it must mean in the present state of things. But the most consistent view is the first, that is, to take "the world" throughout as signifying the ungodly men of the world. What prevail among them are the lusts here mentioned,—sensual gratification, avarice, and ambition,—the three gods who rule and reign in mankind.—*Ed.*

ance with God. We must bear in mind what I have already said, that a corrupt mode of life is here mentioned, which has nothing in common with the kingdom of God, that is, when men become so degenerated, that they are satisfied with the present life, and think no more of immortal life than mute animals. Whosoever, then, makes himself thus a slave to earthly lusts, cannot be of God.

16. *The lust of the flesh,* or, namely, the lust of the flesh. The old interpreter renders the verse otherwise, for from one sentence he makes two. Those Greek authors do better, who read these words together, "Whatever is in the world is not of God;" and then the three kinds of lusts they introduce parenthetically. For John, by way of explanation, inserted these three particulars as examples, that he might briefly shew what are the pursuits and thoughts of men who live for the world; but whether it be a full and complete division, it does not signify much; though you will not find a worldly man in whom these lusts do not prevail, at least one of them. It remains for us to see what he understands by each of these.

The first clause is commonly explained of all sinful lusts in general; for the flesh means the whole corrupt nature of man. Though I am unwilling to contend, yet I am unwilling to dissemble that I approve of another meaning. Paul, when forbidding, in Rom. xiii. 14, to make provision for the flesh as to its lusts, seems to me to be the best interpreter of this place. What, then, is the flesh there? even the body and all that belongs to it. What, then, is the lust or desire of the flesh, but when worldly men, seeking to live softly and delicately, are intent only on their own advantages? Well known from Cicero and others, is the threefold division made by Epicurus; for he made this difference between lusts; he made some natural and necessary, some natural and not necessary, and some neither natural nor necessary. But John, well knowing the insubordination ($\dot{a}\tau a\xi\acute{\iota}a$) of the human heart, unhesitantly condemns the lust of the flesh, because it always flows out immoderately, and never observes any due medium. He afterwards comes gradually to grosser vices.

The lust of the eyes. He includes, as I think, libidinous looks as well as the vanity which delights in pomps and empty splendour.

In the last place follows *pride* or haughtiness; with which is connected ambition, boasting, contempt of others, blind love of self, headstrong self-confidence.

The sum of the whole is, that as soon as the world presents itself, our lusts or desires, when our heart is corrupt, are captivated by it, like unbridled wild beasts; so that various lusts, all which are adverse to God, bear rule in us. The Greek word, βίος, rendered life, (*vita,*) means the way or manner of living.

17. *And the world passeth away.* As there is nothing in the world but what is fading, and as it were for a moment, he hence concludes that they who seek their happiness from it, make a wretched and miserable provision for themselves, especially when God calls us to the ineffable glory of eternal life; as though he had said, "The true happiness which God offers to his children, is eternal; it is then a shameful thing for us to be entangled with the world, which with all its benefits will soon vanish away." I take *lust* here metonymically, as signifying what is desired or coveted, or what captivates the desires of men. The meaning is, that what is most precious in the world and deemed especially desirable, is nothing but a shadowy phantom.

By saying that they who do the will of God shall abide *for ever*, or perpetually, he means that they who seek God shall be perpetually blessed. Were any one to object and say, that no one doeth what God commands, the obvious answer is, that what is spoken of here is not the perfect keeping of the law, but the obedience of faith, which, however imperfect it may be, is yet approved by God. The will of God is first made known to us in the law; but as no one satisfies the law, no happiness can be hoped from it. But Christ comes to meet the despairing with new aid, who not only regenerates us by his Spirit that we may obey God, but makes also that our endeavour, such as it is, should obtain the praise of perfect righteousness.

18. Little children, it is the last | 18. Filioli, novissima hora est; et

time: and as ye have heard that antichrist shall come, even now are there many antichrists; whereby we know that it is the last time.

19. They went out from us, but they were not of us; for if they had been of us, they would *no doubt* have continued with us; but *they went out,* that they might be made manifest that they were not all of us.

sicut audistis quòd Antichristus venturus sit, etiam nunc Antichristi multi cœperunt esse: unde scimus esse novissimam horam.

19. Ex nobis egressi sunt, sed non erant ex nobis; nam si fuissent ex nobis, permansissent utique nobiscum; sed ut manifesti fierent quòd non erant omnes ex nobis.

18. *It is the last time,* or hour. He confirms the faithful against offences by which they might have been disturbed. Already many sects had risen up, which rent the unity of faith and caused disorder in the churches. But the Apostle not only fortifies the faithful, lest they should falter, but turns the whole to a contrary purpose; for he reminds them that the last time had already come, and therefore he exhorts them to a greater vigilance, as though he had said, " Whilst various errors arise, it behoves you to be awakened rather than to be overwhelmed; for we ought hence to conclude that Christ is not far distant; let us then attentively look for him, lest he should come upon us suddenly." In the same way it behoves us to comfort ourselves at this day, and to see by faith the near advent of Christ, while Satan is causing confusion for the sake of disturbing the Church, for these are the signs of the last time.

But so many ages having passed away since the death of John, seem to prove that this prophecy is not true: to this I answer, that the Apostle, according to the common mode adopted in the Scripture, declares to the faithful, that nothing more now remained but that Christ should appear for the redemption of the world. But as he fixes no time, he did not allure the men of that age by a vain hope, nor did he intend to cut short in future the course of the Church and the many successions of years during which the Church has hitherto remained in the world. And doubtless, if the eternity of God's kingdom be borne in mind, so long a time will appear to us as a moment. We must understand the design of the Apostle, that he calls that the last time, during which all things shall be so completed, that nothing will remain except the last revelation of Christ.

As ye have heard that antichrist will come. He speaks as of a thing well known. We may hence conclude that the faithful had been taught and warned from the beginning respecting the future disorder of the Church, in order that they might carefully keep themselves in the faith they professed, and also instruct posterity in the duty of watchfulness. For it was God's will that his Church should be thus tried, lest any one knowingly and willingly should be deceived, and that there might be no excuse for ignorance. But we see that almost the whole world has been miserably deceived, as though not a word had been said about Antichrist.

Moreover, under the Papacy there is nothing more notorious and common than the future coming of Antichrist; and yet they are so stupid, that they perceive not that his tyranny is exercised over them. Indeed, the same thing happens altogether to them as to the Jews; for though they hold the promises respecting the Messiah, they are yet further away from Christ than if they had never heard his name; for the imaginary Messiah, whom they have invented for themselves, turns them wholly aside from the Son of God; and were any one to shew Christ to them from the Law and the Prophets, he would only spend his labour in vain. The Popes have imagined an Antichrist, who for three years and a half is to harass the Church. All the marks by which the Spirit of God has pointed out Antichrist, clearly appear in the Pope; but the triennial Antichrist lays fast hold on the foolish Papists, so that seeing they do not see. Let us then remember, that Antichrist has not only been announced by the Spirit of God, but that also the marks by which he may be distinguished have been mentioned.

Even now are there many antichrists. This may seem to have been added by way of correction, as they falsely thought that it would be some one kingdom; but it is not so. They who suppose that he would be only one man, are indeed greatly mistaken. For Paul, referring to a future defection, plainly shows that it would be a certain body or kingdom. (2 Thess. ii. 3.) He first predicts a defection that would prevail through the whole Church, as a universal evil; he then makes the head of the apostasy the adversary of Christ, who would sit in the temple of God, claiming for himself divinity and divine honours. Except we desire wilfully to err, we may learn from Paul's description to know Antichrist. That passage I have already explained; it is enough now to touch on it by the way.

But how can that passage agree with the words of John, who says that there were already many antichrists? To this I reply, that John meant no other thing than to say, that some particular sects had already risen, which were forerunners of a future Antichrist; for Cerinthus, Basilides, Marcion, Valentinus, Ebion, Arrius, and others, were members of that kingdom which the Devil afterwards raised up in opposition to Christ. Properly speaking, Antichrist was not yet in existence; but the mystery of iniquity was working secretly. But John uses the name, that he might effectually stimulate the care and solicitude of the godly to repel frauds.

But if the Spirit of God even then commanded the faithful to stand on their watch, when they saw at a distance only signs of the coming enemy, much less is it now a time for sleeping, when he holds the Church under his cruel and oppressive tyranny, and openly dishonours Christ.

19. *They went out from us.* He anticipates another objection, that the Church seemed to have produced these pests, and to have cherished them for a time in its bosom. For certainly it serves more to disturb the weak, when any one among us, professing the true faith, falls away, than when a thousand aliens conspire against us. He then confesses that they had gone out from the bosom of the Church; but he denies that they were ever of the Church. But the way of removing this objection is, to say, that the Church is always exposed to this evil, so that it is constrained to bear with many hypocrites who know not Christ really, however much they may by the mouth profess his name.

By saying, *They went out from us,* he means that they had previously occupied a place in the Church, and were counted among the number of the godly. He, however, denies that they were of them, though they had assumed the name of believers, as chaff though mixed with wheat on the same floor cannot yet be deemed wheat.

For if they had been of us. He plainly declares that those who fell away had never been members of the Church. And doubtless the seal of God, under which he keeps his own, remains sure, as Paul says, (2 Tim. ii. 19.) But here arises a difficulty, for it happens that many who seemed to have embraced Christ, often fall away. To this I answer, that there are three sorts of those who profess the Gospel; there are those who feign piety, while a bad conscience reproves them within; the hypocrisy of others is more deceptive, who not only seek to disguise themselves before men, but also dazzle their own eyes, so that they seem to themselves to worship God aright; the third are those who have the living root of faith, and carry a testimony of their own adoption firmly fixed in their hearts. The two first have no stability; of the last John speaks, when he says, that it is impossible that they should be separated from the Church, for the seal which God's Spirit engraves on their hearts cannot be obliterated; the incorruptible seed, which has struck roots, cannot be pulled up or destroyed.

He does not speak here of the constancy of men, but of God, whose election must be ratified. He does not then, without reason declare, that where the calling of God is effectual, perseverance would be certain. He, in short, means that they who fall away had never been thoroughly imbued with the knowledge of Christ, but had only a light and a transient taste of it.

That they might be made manifest. He shews that trial is useful and necessary for the Church. It hence follows, on the other hand, that there is no just cause for perturbation. Since the Church is like a threshing-floor, the chaff must be blown away that the pure wheat may remain. This is what God does, when he casts out hypocrites from the Church, for he then cleanses it from refuse and filth.

20. But ye have an unction from the Holy One, and ye know all things.

21. I have not written unto you because ye know not the truth, but

20. Et vos unctionem habetis à Sancto, et novistis omnia.

21. Non scripsi vobis, quia non noveritis veritatem; sed quia novis-

because ye know it, and that no lie is of the truth.

22. Who is a liar, but he that denieth that Jesus is the Christ? He is antichrist, that denieth the Father and the Son.

23. Whosoever denieth the Son, the same hath not the Father.

tis eam, et quia omne mendacium ex veritate non est.

22. Quis est mendax, nisi qui negat Jesum esse Christum? Hic est antichristus, qui negat Patrem et Filium.

23. Omnis qui negat Filium, neque Patrem habet.

20. *But ye have an unction.* The Apostle modestly excuses himself for having so earnestly warned them, lest they should think that they were indirectly reproved, as though they were rude and ignorant of those things which they ought to have well known. So Paul conceded wisdom to the Romans, that they were able and fit to admonish others. He at the same time shewed that they stood in need of being reminded, in order that they might rightly perform their duty. (Rom. xv. 14, 15.) The Apostles did not, however, speak thus in order to flatter them; but they thus wisely took heed lest their doctrine should be rejected by any, for they declared what was suitable and useful, not only to the ignorant, but also to those well instructed in the Lord's school.

Experience teaches us how fastidious the ears of men are. Such fastidiousness ought indeed to be far away from the godly; it yet behoves a faithful and wise teacher to omit nothing by which he may secure a hearing from all. And it is certain that we receive what is said with less attention and respect, when we think that he who speaks disparages the knowledge which has been given us by the Lord. The Apostle by this praise did at the same time stimulate his readers, because they who were endued with the gift of knowledge, had less excuse if they did not surpass others in their proficiency.

The state of the case is, that the Apostle did not teach them as though they were ignorant, and acquainted only with the first elements of knowledge, but reminded them of things already known, and also exhorted them to rouse up the sparks of the Spirit, that a full brightness might shine forth in them. And in the next words he explained himself, having denied that he wrote to them because they knew not the truth, but because they had been well taught in it;

for had they been wholly ignorant and novices, they could not have comprehended his doctrine.

Now, when he says that they knew *all things*, it is not to be taken in the widest sense, but ought to be confined to the subject treated of here. But when he says that they had *an unction from the Holy One,* he alludes, no doubt, to the ancient types. The oil by which the priests were anointed was obtained from the sanctuary; and Daniel mentions the coming of Christ as the proper time for anointing the Most Holy. (Dan. ix. 24.) For he was anointed by the Father, that he might pour forth on us a manifold abundance from his own fulness. It hence follows that men are not rightly made wise by the acumen of their own minds, but by the illumination of the Spirit; and further, that we are not otherwise made partakers of the Spirit than through Christ, who is the true sanctuary and our only high priest.[1]

21. *And that no lie is of the truth.* He concedes to them a judgment, by which they could distinguish truth from falsehood; for it is not the dialectic proposition, that falsehood differs from truth, (such as are taught as general rules in the schools;) but what is said is applied to that which is practical and useful; as though he had said, that they did not only hold what was true, but were also so fortified against the impostures and fallacies of the ungodly, that they wisely took heed to themselves. Besides, he speaks not of this or of that kind of falsehood; but he says, that whatever deception Satan might contrive, or in whatever way he might attack them, they would be able readily to distinguish between light and darkness, because they had the Spirit as their guide.

22. *Who is a liar.* He does not assert that they alone were liars who denied that the Son of God appeared in the flesh, lest no one in unloosing the knot should above measure torment himself; but that they surpassed all others, as

---

[1] "From the Holy One," from the Father, say some; from the Son, say others; from the Holy Spirit, according to a third party. By comparing this verse with the 27th and the 28th verse, we see reason to conclude that the "Holy One" is Christ, who had promised the Spirit to teach his people. The unction, or the anointing, is the act of the Spirit by which the truth is taught.—*Ed.*

though he had said, that except this be deemed a lie, no other could be so reckoned; as we are wont commonly to say, "If perfidy towards God and men is not a crime, what else can we call a crime?"[1]

What he had generally said of false prophets, he now applies to the state of his own time; for he points out, as by the finger, those who disturbed the Church. I readily agree with the ancients, who thought that Cerinthus and Carpocrates are here referred to. But the denial of Christ extends much wider; for it is not enough in words to confess that Jesus is the Christ, except he is acknowledged to be such as the Father offers him to us in the gospel. The two I have named gave the title of Christ to the Son of God, but imagined him to be man only. Others followed them, such as Arius, who, adorning him with the name of God, robbed him of his eternal divinity. Marcion dreamt that he was a mere phantom. Sabellius imagined that he differed nothing from the Father. All these denied the Son of God; for not one of them really acknowledged the true Christ; but, adulterating, as far as they could, the truth respecting him, they devised for themselves an idol instead of Christ. Then broke out Pelagius, who, indeed, raised no dispute respecting Christ's essence, but allowed him to be true man and God; yet he transferred to us almost all the honour that belongs to him. It is, indeed, to reduce Christ to nothing, when his grace and power are set aside.

So the Papists, at this day, setting up free-will in opposition to the grace of the Holy Spirit, ascribing a part of their righteousness and salvation to the merits of works, feigning for themselves innumerable advocates, by whom they render God propitious to them, have a sort of fictitious Christ, I know not what; but the lively and genuine image of God, which shines forth in Christ, they deform by their wicked inventions; they lessen his power, subvert and pervert his office.

We now see that Christ is denied, whenever those things which peculiarly belong to him, are taken away from him.

[1] Taking this view of the passage, we may give this rendering,—" Who is a liar, except it be he who denies that Jesus is the Christ?"—*Ed.*

And as Christ is the end of the law and of the gospel, and has in himself all the treasures of wisdom and knowledge, so he is the mark at which all heretics level and direct their arrows. Therefore the Apostle does not, without reason, make those the chief impostors, who fight against Christ, in whom the full truth is exhibited to us.

He is Antichrist. He speaks not of that prince of defection who was to occupy the seat of God; but all those who seek to overthrow Christ, he puts them among that impious band. And that he might amplify their crime, he asserts that the Father, no less than the Son, is denied by them; as though he had said, "They have no longer any religion, because they wholly cast away God." And this he afterwards confirms, by adding this reason, that the Father cannot be separated from the Son.

Now this is a remarkable sentence, and ought to be reckoned among the first axioms of our religion: yea, when we have confessed that there is one true God, this second article ought necessarily to be added, that he is no other but he who is made known in Christ. The Apostle does not here treat distinctly of the unity of essence. It is, indeed, certain, that the Son cannot be disunited from the Father, for he is of the same essence, ($\dot{o}\mu oo\acute{v}\sigma\iota o\varsigma$;) but another thing is spoken of here, that is, that the Father, who is invisible, has revealed himself only in his Son. Hence he is called the image of the Father, (Heb. i. 3,) because he sets forth and exhibits to us all that is necessary to be known of the Father. For the naked majesty of God would, by its immense brightness, ever dazzle our eyes; it is therefore necessary for us to look on Christ. This is to come to the light, which is justly said to be otherwise inaccessible.

I say, again, that there is not here a distinct discussion respecting the eternal essence of Christ, which he has in common with the Father. This passage is, indeed, abundantly sufficient to prove it: but John calls us to this practical part of faith, that as God has given himself to us to be enjoyed only in Christ, he is elsewhere sought for in vain; or (if any one prefers what is clearer) that as in Christ dwells all the fulness of the Deity, there is no God apart from him.

It hence follows, that Turks, Jews, and such as are like them, have a mere idol and not the true God. For by whatever titles they may honour the God whom they worship, still, as they reject him without whom they cannot come to God, and in whom God has really manifested himself to us, what have they but some creature or fiction of their own? They may flatter themselves as much as they please, with their own speculations, who, without Christ, philosophize on divine things; it is still certain that they do nothing but rave and rant, because, as Paul says, they hold not the Head. (Col. ii. 19.) It is obvious, hence, to conclude how necessary is the knowledge of Christ.

Many copies have the opposite sentence, " He who confesses the Son," &c. But as I think that a note by some copyist has crept into the text, I hesitated not to omit it.[1] But if its insertion be approved, the meaning would be, that there is no right confession of God except the Father be acknowledged in the Son.

Were any one to object and say, that many of the ancients thought rightly of God, to whom Christ was not known: I allow that the knowledge of Christ has not been always so explicitly revealed, nevertheless, I contend that it has been always true, that as the light of the sun comes to us by its rays, so the knowledge of God has been communicated through Christ.

24. Let that therefore abide in you which ye have heard from the beginning. If that which ye have heard from the beginning shall remain in you, ye also shall continue in the Son, and in the Father.

25. And this is the promise that he hath promised us, *even* eternal life.

26. These *things* have I written unto you concerning them that seduce you.

27. But the anointing which ye

24. Ergo quod audistis ab initio, in vobis maneat: si in vobis manserit quod ab initio audistis, et vos in Patre et Filio manebitis.

25. Atque hæc est promissio, quam ipse nobis promisit, nempe vitæ eternæ (*vel,* quam nobis pollicitus est vitam eternam.)

26. Hæc scripsi vobis de iis qui seducunt vos.

27. Et unctio quam accepistis ab

---

[1] The words are found in most of the MSS., and in most of the versions, and in many of the Fathers. Besides, they wholly comport with the usual style of the Apostle, whose common practice it was to state things positively and negatively, and *vice versa.* See especially chap. v. 12.—*Ed.*

have received of him abideth in you; and ye need not that any man teach you: but as the same anointing teacheth you of all things, and is truth, and is no lie, and even as it hath taught you, ye shall abide in him.

28. And now, little children, abide in him; that when he shall appear, we may have confidence, and not be ashamed before him at his coming.

29. If ye know that he is righteous, ye know that every one that doeth righteousness is born of him.

eo, in vobis manet; neque opus habetis ut quis vos doceat; sed quemadmodum unctio docet vos de omnibus, et veritas est, et non est mendacium; et quemadmodum docuit vos, manete in eo (*vel*, in ea.)

28. Et nunc filioli, manete in eo, ut quum apparuerit, habeamus fiduciam, neque pudefiamus ab ejus præsentia.

29. Si nostis quòd justus sit, cognoscite quòd quisquis facit justitiam ex eo genitus est.

24. *Let that therefore abide in you.* He annexes an exhortation to the former doctrine; and that it might have more weight, he points out the fruit they would receive from obedience. He then exhorts them to perseverance in the faith, so that they might retain fixed in their hearts what they had learnt.

But when he says, *from the beginning*, he does not mean that antiquity alone was sufficient to prove any doctrine true; but as he has already shewn that they had been rightly instructed in the pure gospel of Christ, he concludes that they ought of right to continue in it. And this order ought to be especially noticed; for were we unwilling to depart from that doctrine which we have once embraced, whatever it may be, this would not be perseverance, but perverse obstinacy. Hence, discrimination ought to be exercised, so that a reason for our faith may be made evident from God's word: then let inflexible perseverance follow.

The Papists boast of " a beginning," because they have imbibed their superstitions from childhood. Under this pretence they allow themselves obstinately to reject the plain truth. Such perverseness shews to us, that we ought always to begin with the certainty of truth.

If that which ye have heard. Here is the fruit of perseverance, that they in whom God's truth remains, remain in God. We hence learn what we are to seek in every truth pertaining to religion. He therefore makes the greatest proficiency, who makes such progress as wholly to cleave to God. But he in whom the Father dwells not through his Son, is altogether vain and empty, whatever knowledge he may possess. Moreover, this is the highest commendation of sound doctrine, that it unites us to God, and that in it is found whatever pertains to the real fruition of God.

In the last place, he reminds us that it is real happiness when God dwells in us. The words he uses are ambiguous. They may be rendered, " This is the promise which he has promised to us, even eternal life."[1] You may, however, adopt either of these renderings, for the meaning is still the same. The sum of what is said is, that we cannot live otherwise than by nourishing to the end the seed of life sown in our hearts. John insists much on this point, that not only the beginning of a blessed life is to be found in the knowledge of Christ, but also its perfection. But no repetition of it can be too much, since it is well known that it has ever been a cause of ruin to men, that being not content with Christ, they have had a hankering to wander beyond the simple doctrine of the gospel.

26. *These things have I written unto you.* The apostle excuses himself again for having admonished them who were well endued with knowledge and judgment. But he did this, that they might apply for the guidance of the Spirit, lest his admonition should be in vain; as though he had said, " I indeed do my part, but still it is necessary that the Spirit of God should direct you in all things; for in vain shall I, by the sound of my voice, beat your ears, or rather the air, unless he speaks within you."

When we hear that he wrote concerning seducers, we ought always to bear in mind, that it is the duty of a good and diligent pastor not only to gather a flock, but also to drive away wolves: for what will it avail to proclaim the pure gospel, if we connive at the impostures of Satan? No one, then, can faithfully teach the Church, except he is diligent in banishing errors whenever he finds them spread by seducers. What he says of the *unction* having been received *from him,* I refer to Christ.

---

[1] This, which is our version, is, no doubt, the best construction. " Promise" is a metonymy for what is promised: " This is the promise, which he hath promised to us, *even* eternal life." " Eternal life" is in apposition with " which."—*Ed.*

27. *And ye need not.* Strange must have been the purpose of John, as I have already said, if he intended to represent teaching as useless. He did not ascribe to them so much wisdom, as to deny that they were the scholars of Christ. He only meant that they were by no means so ignorant as to need things as it were unknown to be taught them, and that he did not set before them anything which the Spirit of God might not of himself suggest to them. Absurdly, then, do fanatical men lay hold on this passage, in order to exclude from the Church the use of the outward ministry. He says that the faithful, taught by the Spirit, already understood what he delivered to them, so that they had no need to learn things unknown to them. He said this, that he might add more authority to his doctrine, while every one repeated in his heart an assent to it, engraven as it were by the finger of God. But as every one had knowledge according to the measure of his faith, and as faith in some was small, in others stronger, and in none perfect, it hence follows, that no one knew so much, that there was no room for progress.

There is also another use to be made of this doctrine,—that when men really understand what is needful for them, we are yet to warn and rouse them, that they may be more confirmed. For what John says, that they were taught all things by the Spirit, ought not to be taken generally, but to be confined to what is contained in this passage. He had, in short, no other thing in view than to strengthen their faith, while he recalled them to the examination of the Spirit, who is the only fit corrector and approver of doctrine, who seals it on our hearts, so that we may certainly know that God speaks. For while faith ought to look to God, he alone can be a witness to himself, so as to convince our hearts that what our ears receive has come from him.

And the same is the meaning of these words, *As the same anointing teacheth you of all things, and is truth;* that is, the Spirit is like a seal, by which the truth of God is testified to you. When he adds, *and is no lie,* he points out another office of the Spirit, even that he endues us with judgment and discernment, lest we should be deceived by lies, lest we should hesitate and be perplexed, lest we should vacillate as in doubtful things.

As it hath taught you, ye shall abide in him, or, abide in him. He had said, that the Spirit abode in them; he now exhorts them to abide in the revelation made by him, and he specifies what revelation it was, " Abide," he says, " in Christ, as the Spirit hath taught you." Another explanation, I know, is commonly given, " Abide in it," that is, the unction. But as the repetition which immediately follows, cannot apply to any but to Christ, I have no doubt but that he speaks here also of Christ; and this is required by the context; for the Apostle dwells much on this point, that the faithful should retain the true knowledge of Christ, and that they should not go to God in any other way.

He at the same time shews, that the children of God are for no other end illuminated by the Spirit, but that they may know Christ. Provided they turned not aside from him, he promised them the fruit of perseverance, even confidence, so as not to be ashamed at his presence. For faith is not a naked and a frigid apprehension of Christ, but a lively and real sense of his power, which produces confidence. Indeed, faith cannot stand, while tossed daily by so many waves, except it looks to the coming of Christ, and, supported by his power, brings tranquillity to the conscience. But the nature of confidence is well expressed, when he says that it can boldly sustain the presence of Christ. For they who indulge securely in their vices, turn their backs as it were on God; nor can they otherwise obtain peace than by forgetting him. This is the security of the flesh, which stupifies men; so that turning away from God, they neither dread sin nor fear death; and in the meantime they shun the tribunal of Christ. But a godly confidence delights to look on God. Hence it is, that the godly calmly wait for Christ, nor do they dread his coming.

29. *If ye know that he is righteous.* He again passes on to exhortations, so that he mingles these continually with doctrine throughout the Epistle; but he proves by many arguments that faith is necessarily connected with a holy and pure life. The first argument is, that we are spiritually

begotten after the likeness of Christ ; it hence follows, that no one is born of Christ but he who lives righteously. It is at the same time uncertain whether he means Christ or God, when he says that they who are born of him do righteousness. It is a mode of speaking certainly used in Scripture, that we are born of God in Christ ; but there is nothing inconsistent in the other, that they are born of Christ, who are renewed by his Spirit.[1]

CHAPTER III.

1. Behold what manner of love the Father hath bestowed upon us, that we should be called the sons of God! therefore the world knoweth us not, because it knew him not.

2. Beloved, now are we the sons of God ; and it doth not yet appear what we shall be : but we know that, when he shall appear, we shall be like him ; for we shall see him as he is.

3. And every man that hath this hope in him purifieth himself, even as he is pure.

1. Videte (*vel*, videtis) qualem charitatem dedit nobis Pater, ut filii Dei nominenur : propterea mundus non novit nos, quia non novit ipsum.

2. Dilecti, nunc filii Dei sumus ; et nondum apparuit quid erimus : scimus autem quòd si apparuerit, similes ei erimus ; quia videbimus eum sicuti est.

3. Et omnis qui habet hanc spem in eo, purificat seipsum, quemadmodum ille purus est.

1. *Behold.* The second argument is from the dignity and excellency of our calling ; for it was not common honour, he says, that the heavenly Father bestowed on us, when he adopted us as his children. This being so great a favour, the desire for purity ought to be kindled in us, so as to be conformed to his image ; nor, indeed, can it be otherwise, but that he who acknowledges himself to be one of God's children should purify himself. And to make this exhor-

[1] It is the character of John's style that he often passes as it were abruptly from the Son to the Father, and from the Father to the Son ; and often the antecedent is not the next preceding word, but one at some distance : we find this to be the case by what the sentence contains, as in the present instance ; the new birth is never ascribed to the Son, referred to in the foregoing verse, but to the Father or to the Spirit. Hence we must conclude that the righteous one spoken of here, who together with the Son is mentioned in the 22d verse, is the Father. As the intervening verses, with the exception of the 23d, which is only explanatory of the previous verse, apply to the Son, so this verse seems to refer to the Father, consistently with a mode of writing common in Scripture.—*Ed.*

tation more forcible, he amplifies the favour of God; for when he says, that *love* has been *bestowed,* he means that it is from mere bounty and benevolence that God makes us his children; for whence comes to us such a dignity, except from the love of God? Love, then, is declared here to be gratuitous. There is, indeed, an impropriety in the language; but the Apostle preferred speaking thus rather than not to express what was necessary to be known. He, in short, means that the more abundantly God's goodness has been manifested towards us, the greater are our obligations to him, according to the teaching of Paul, when he besought the Romans by the mercies of God to present themselves as pure sacrifices to him. (Rom. xii. 1.) We are at the same time taught, as I have said, that the adoption of all the godly is gratuitous, and does not depend on any regard to works.

What the sophists say, that God foresees those who are worthy to be adopted, is plainly refuted by these words, for, in this way the gift would not be gratuitous. It behoves us especially to understand this doctrine; for since the only cause of our salvation is adoption, and since the Apostle testifies that this flows from the mere love of God alone, there is nothing left to our worthiness or to the merits of works. For why are we sons? even because God began to love us freely, when we deserved hatred rather than love. And as the Spirit is a pledge of our adoption, it hence follows, that if there be any good in us, it ought not to be set up in opposition to the grace of God, but, on the contrary, to be ascribed to him.

When he says that we are *called,* or named, the expression is not without its meaning; for it is God who with his own mouth declares us to be sons, as he gave a name to Abraham according to what he was.[1]

Therefore the world. It is a trial that grievously assaults our faith, that we are not so much regarded as God's children, or that no mark of so great an excellency appears in

---

[1] *Calvin,* like our version, renders τίκνα, "sons;" but the word would be better rendered "children," "That we should be called the children of God." The passage might be thus paraphrased, "See what great proof of love the Father hath given us, that we should be made the children of God!"—*Ed.*

us, but that, on the contrary, almost the whole world treats us with ridicule and contempt. Hence it can hardly be inferred from our present state that God is a Father to us, for the devil so contrives all things as to obscure this benefit. He obviates this offence by saying that we are not as yet acknowledged to be such as we are, because the world knows not God: a remarkable example of this very thing is found in Isaac and Jacob; for though both were chosen by God, yet Ishmael persecuted the former with laughter and taunts; and Esau, the latter with threats and the sword. However, then, we may be oppressed by the world, still our salvation remains safe and secure.

2. *Now are we the sons of God.* He comes now to what every one knows and feels himself; for though the ungodly may not entice us to give up our hope, yet our present condition is very short of the glory of God's children; for as to our body we are dust and a shadow, and death is always before our eyes; we are also subject to thousand miseries, and the soul is exposed to innumerable evils; so that we find always a hell within us. The more necessary it is that all our thoughts should be withdrawn from the present view of things, lest the miseries by which we are on every side surrounded and almost overwhelmed, should shake our faith in that felicity which as yet lies hid. For the Apostle's meaning is this, that we act very foolishly when we estimate what God has bestowed on us according to the present state of things, but that we ought with undoubting faith to hold to that which does not yet appear.

But we know that when he shall appear. The conditional particle ought to be rendered as an adverb of time, *when.* But the verb *appear* means not the same thing as when he used it before. The Apostle has just said, *it does not yet appear what we shall be,* because the fruit of our adoption is as yet hid, for in heaven is our felicity, and we are now far away travelling on the earth; for this fading life, constantly exposed to hundred deaths, is far different from that eternal life which belongs to the children of God; for being enclosed as slaves in the prison of our flesh, we are far distant from the full sovereignty of heaven and earth. But the verb now refers to Christ, *when he shall appear;* for he teaches the same thing with Paul, in Col. iii. 3, 4, where he says, " Your life is hid with Christ in God: when Christ, who is your life, shall appear, then shall ye also appear with him in glory." For our faith cannot stand otherwise than by looking to the coming of Christ. The reason why God defers the manifestation of our glory is this, because Christ is not manifested in the power of his kingdom. This, then, is the only way of sustaining our faith, so that we may wait patiently for the life promised to us. As soon as any one turns away the least from Christ, he must necessarily fail.[1]

The word to *know,* shews the certainty of faith, in order to distinguish it from opinion. Neither simple nor universal knowledge is here intended, but that which every one ought to have for himself, so that he may feel assured that he will be sometime like Christ. Though, then, the manifestation of our glory is connected with the coming of Christ, yet our knowledge of this is well founded.

We shall be like him. He does not understand that we shall be equal to him; for there must be some difference between the head and the members; but we shall be like him, because he will make our vile body conformable to his glorious body, as Paul also teaches us in Phil. iii. 21. For the Apostle intended shortly to shew that the final end of our adoption is, that what has in order preceded in Christ, shall at length be completed in us.

The reason that is added may, however, seem inappropriate: for if to see Christ makes us like him, we shall have this in common with the wicked, for they shall also see his glory. To this I reply, that this is to see him as a friend, which will not be the case with the wicked, for they will dread his presence; nay, they will shun God's presence, and be filled with terror; his glory will so dazzle their eyes, that

---

[1] "When he shall appear," refers to Christ, mentioned in the 28th verse of the last chapter; what intervenes seems to have been parenthetically introduced. This is often the manner of writing found in this apostle. The end of the 8th verse, in this chapter, is connected with the 16th; for the antecedent to ἐκεῖνος, *he,* in the latter verse, is "the Son of God" in the former.—*Ed.*

they will be stupified and confounded. For we see that Adam, conscious of having done wrong, dreaded the presence of God. And God declared this by Moses, as a general truth as to men, " No man shall see me and live." (Exod. xxxiii. 20.) For how can it be otherwise but that God's majesty, as a consuming fire, will consume us as though we were stubble, so great is the weakness of our flesh. But as far as the image of God is renewed in us, we have eyes prepared to see God. And now, indeed, God begins to renew in us his own image, but in what a small measure! Except then we be stripped of all the corruption of the flesh, we shall not be able to behold God face to face.

And this is also expressed here, *as he is.* He does not, indeed, say, that there is no seeing of God now; but as Paul says, " We see now through a glass, darkly." (1 Cor. xiii. 12.) But he elsewhere makes a difference between this way of living, and the seeing of the eye. In short, God now presents himself to be seen by us, not such as he is, but such as we can comprehend. Thus is fulfilled what is said by Moses, that we see only as it were his back, (Exod. xxxiii. 23;) for there is too much brightness in his face.

We must further observe, that the manner which the Apostle mentions is taken from the effect, not from the cause; for he does not teach us, that we shall be like him, because we shall see him; but he hence proves that we shall be partakers of the divine glory, for except our nature were spiritual, and endued with a heavenly and blessed immortality, it could never come so nigh to God: yet the perfection of glory will not be so great in us, that our seeing will enable us to comprehend all that God is; for the distance between us and him will be even then very great.

But when the Apostle says, that we shall see him as he is, he intimates a new and an ineffable manner of seeing him, which we enjoy not now; for as long as we walk by faith, as Paul teaches us, we are absent from him. And when he appeared to the fathers, it was not in his own essence, but was ever seen under symbols. Hence the majesty of God, now hid, will then only be in itself seen, when the veil of this mortal and corruptible nature shall be removed.

Refined questions I pass by: for we see how Augustine tormented himself with these, and yet never succeeded, both in his Epistles to Paulus and Fortunatus, and in his City of God, (ii. 2,) and in other places. What he says, however, is worthy of being observed, that the way in which we live avails more in this inquiry than the way in which we speak, and that we must beware, lest by wrangling as to the manner in which God can be seen, we lose that peace and holiness without which no one shall see him.

3. *And every man that hath this hope.* He now draws this inference, that the desire for holiness should not grow cold in us, because our happiness has not as yet appeared, for that hope is sufficient; and we know that what is hoped for is as yet hid. The meaning then is, that though we have not Christ now present before our eyes, yet if we hope in him, it cannot be but that this hope will excite and stimulate us to follow purity, for it leads us straight to Christ, whom we know to be a perfect pattern of purity.

4. Whosoever committeth sin transgresseth also the law; for sin is the transgression of the law.
5. And ye know that he was manifested to take away our sins; and in him is no sin.
6. Whosoever abideth in him sinneth not; whosoever sinneth hath not seen him, neither known him.

4. Quicunque facit peccatum, etiam iniquitatem facit; et peccatum est iniquitas.
5. Porrò nostis quòd ille apparuit ut peccata nostra tolleret; et peccatum in eo non est.
6. Quisquis in eo manet, non peccat; quisquis peccat, non vidit eum, nec novit eum.

4. *Whosoever committeth,* or doeth, *sin.* The Apostle has already shewn how ungrateful we must be to God, if we make but little account of the honour of adoption, by which he of his own good-will anticipates us, and if we do not, at least, render him mutual love. He, at the same time, introduced this admonition, that our love ought not to be diminished, because the promised happiness is deferred. But now, as men are wont to indulge themselves more than they ought, in evils, he reproves this perverse indulgence, declaring that all they who sin are wicked and transgressors of the law. For it is probable that there were then those who extenuated their vices by this kind of flattery, " It is no wonder if we sin, because we are men; but there is a great difference between sin and iniquity."

This frivolous excuse the Apostle now dissipates, when he defines sin to be a transgression of the divine law; for his object was to produce hatred and horror as to sin. The word *sin* seems light to some; but iniquity or transgression of the law cannot appear to be so easily forgiven. But the Apostle does not make sins equal, by charging all with iniquity who sin; but he means simply to teach us, that sin arises from a contempt of God, and that by sinning, the law is violated. Hence this doctrine of John has nothing in common with the delirious paradoxes of the Stoics.

Besides, to *sin* here, does not mean to offend in some instances; nor is the word *sin* to be taken for every fault or wrong a man may commit; but he calls that sin, when men with their whole heart run into evil, nor does he understand that men sin, except those who are given up to sin. For the faithful, who are as yet tempted by the lusts of the flesh, are not to be deemed guilty of iniquity, though they are not pure or free from sin: but as sin does not reign in them, John says that they do not sin, as I shall presently explain more fully.

The import of the passage is, that the perverse life of those who indulge themselves in the liberty of sinning, is hateful to God, and cannot be borne with by him, because it is contrary to his Law. It does not hence follow, nor can it be hence inferred, that the faithful are iniquitous; because they desire to obey God, and abhor their own vices, and that in every instance; and they also form their own life, as much as in them lieth, according to the law. But when there is a deliberate purpose to sin, or a continued course in sin, then the law is transgressed.[1]

---

[1] To do, or to commit, or to work, or to practise, sin, and to sin, are evidently used in the same sense by the Apostle: and to commit or practise sin, according to what he says in his Gospel, (chap. viii. 34,) is the same with being "the servant of sin." It is hence evident, that in the language of John, to do sin, or to sin, means a prevailing or an habitual course of sinning.

We might render the fourth verse thus,—

"Every doer of sin, is also the doer of unrighteousness; for sin is unrighteousness," or iniquity, as *Calvin* renders it.

The word ἀνομία, literally, is lawlessness, but it is never used strictly in this sense either in the *Sept.* or the New Testament. The terms by

5. *And ye know that he was manifested,* or, hath appeared. He shews by another argument how much sin and faith differ from one another; for it is the office of Christ to take away sins, and for this end was he sent by the Father; and it is by faith we partake of Christ's virtue. Then he who believes in Christ is necessarily cleansed from his sins. But it is said in John i. 29, that Christ takes away sins, because he atoned for them by the sacrifice of his death, that they may not be imputed to us before God : John means in this place that Christ really, and, so to speak, actually takes away sins, because through him our old man is crucified, and his Spirit, by means of repentance, mortifies the flesh with all its lusts. For the context does not allow us to explain this of the remission of sins; for, as I have said, he thus reasons, " They who cease not to sin, render void the benefits derived from Christ, since he came to destroy the reigning power of sin." This belongs to the sanctification of the Spirit.

And in him is no sin. He does not speak of Christ personally, but of his whole body.[1] Wherever Christ diffuses his efficacious grace, he denies that there is any more room for sin. He, therefore, immediately draws this inference, that they sin not who remain in Christ. For if he dwells in us by faith, he performs his own work, that is, he cleanses us from sins. It hence appears what it is to *sin.* For Christ by his Spirit does not perfectly renew us at once, or in an instant, but he continues our renovation throughout life. It cannot then be but that the faithful are exposed to sin as long as they live in the world; but as far as the kingdom of Christ prevails in them, sin is abolished. In the meantime they are designated according to the prevailing principle, that is, they are said to be righteous and to live righteously, because they sincerely aspire to righteousness.

which it is commonly expressed, are, wickedness, iniquity, transgression, unrighteousness. See verse 7.—*Ed.*

[1] It is generally taken as referring to Christ personally; he being mentioned here as having no sin, because he is in this respect an example to his people; or, according to some, because he was thereby fitted for the office of taking away our sins; or, because he had no sin of his own to take away. *Grotius* viewed the present as used here for the past tense,— " and sin was not in him." See a similar instance in John xv. 27 —*Ed.*

They are said *not to sin*, because they consent not to sin, though they labour under the infirmity of the flesh; but, on the contrary, they struggle with groaning, so that they can truly testify with Paul that they do the evil they would not.

He says that the faithful *abide* in Christ, because we are by faith united to him, and made one with him.

6. *Whosoever sinneth hath not seen him.* According to his usual manner he added the opposite clause, that we may know that faith in Christ and knowledge of him are vainly pretended, except there be newness of life. For Christ is never dormant where he reigns, but the Spirit renders effectual his power. And it may be rightly said of him, that he puts sin to flight, not otherwise than as the sun drives away darkness by its own brightness. But we are again taught in this place how strong and efficacious is the knowledge of Christ; for it transforms us into his image. So by *seeing* and *knowing* we are to understand no other thing than faith.

7. Little children, let no man deceive you: he that doeth righteousness is righteous, even as he is righteous.
8. He that committeth sin is of the devil; for the devil sinneth from the beginning. For this purpose the Son of God was manifested, that he might destroy the works of the devil.
9. Whosoever is born of God doth not commit sin; for his seed remaineth in him: and he cannot sin, because he is born of God.
10. In this the children of God are manifest, and the children of the devil:—

7. Filioli, nemo vos decipiat; qui facit justitiam justus est, quemadmodum ille justus est.
8. Qui facit peccatum, ex diabolo est; quia ab initio diabolus peccat: in hoc manifestus est Filius Dei, ut solvat opera diaboli.
9. Quisquis natus est ex Deo, peccatum non facit, quoniam semen ejus in ipso manet; et non potest peccare, quia ex Deo genitus est.
10. In hoc manifesti sunt filii Dei et filii Diaboli,—

7. *He that doeth righteousness.* The Apostle shews here that newness of life is testified by good works; nor does that likeness of which he has spoken, that is between Christ and his members, appear, except by the fruits they bring forth; as though he had said, "Since it behoves us to be conformed to Christ, the truth and evidence of this must appear in our life." The exhortation is the same with that of Paul in Gal. v. 25, "If ye live in the Spirit, walk also in the Spirit."

For many would gladly persuade themselves that they have this righteousness buried in their hearts, while iniquity evidently occupies their feet, and hands, and tongue, and eyes.

8. *He that committeth sin.* This word, to *commit*, or to do, refers also to outward works, so that the meaning is, that there is no life of God and of Christ, where men act perversely and wickedly, but that such are, on the contrary, the slaves of the devil; and by this way of speaking he sets forth more fully how unlike they are to Christ. For as he has before represented Christ as the fountain of all righteousness, so now, on the other hand, he mentions the devil as the beginning of sin. He denied that any one belongs to Christ except he who is righteous and shews himself to be such by his works; he now assigns to the devil all others, and subjects them to his government, in order that we may know that there is no middle condition, but that Satan exercises his tyranny where the righteousness of Christ possesses not the primacy.

There are not however two adverse principles, such as the Manicheans have imagined; for we know that the devil is not wicked by nature or by creation, but became so through defection. We know also that he is not equal to God, so that he can with equal right or authority contend with him, but that he is unwillingly under restraint, so that he can do nothing except at the nod and with the permission of his Creator. John, in the last place, in saying that some were born of God and some of the devil, imagined no traduction such as the Manicheans dreamt of; but he means that the former are governed and guided by the Spirit of God, and that the others are led astray by Satan, as God grants to him this power over the unbelieving.

For the Devil sinneth from the beginning. As before he spoke not of Christ personally, when he said that he is righteous, but mentioned him as the fountain and the cause of righteousness; so now, when he says that the Devil sins, he includes his whole body, even all the reprobate; as though he had said, this belongs to the Devil, to entice men to sin. It hence follows, that his members, and all who are ruled by him, give themselves up to commit sin. But the beginning which the Apostle mentions, is not from eternity, as when he says that the Word is from the beginning; for there is a wide difference between God and creatures. Beginning as to God, refers to no time. Since, then, the Word was always with God, you can find no point of time in which he began to be, but you must necessarily admit his eternity. But here John meant no other thing than that the Devil had been an apostate since the creation of the world, and that from that time he had never ceased to scatter his poison among men.

For this purpose the Son of God was manifested. He repeats in other words what he had before said, that Christ came to take away sins. Hence two conclusions are to be drawn, that those in whom sin reigns cannot be reckoned among the members of Christ, and that they can by no means belong to his body; for wherever Christ puts forth his own power, he puts the Devil to flight as well as sin. And this is what John immediately adds; for the next sentence, where he says that those who sin not are born of God, is a conclusion from what is gone before. It is an argument drawn from what is inconsistent, as I have already said; for the kingdom of Christ, which brings righteousness with it, cannot admit of sin. But I have already said what *not to sin* means. He does not make the children of God wholly free from all sin; but he denies that any can really glory in this distinction, except those who from the heart strive to form their life in obedience to God.

The Pelagians, indeed, and the Catharians did formerly make a wrong use of this passage, when they vainly imagined that the faithful are in this world endued with angelic purity; and in our own age some of the Anabaptists have renewed this dotage. But all those who dream of a perfection of this kind, sufficiently shew what stupid consciences they must have. But the words of the Apostle are so far from countenancing their error, that they are sufficient to confute it.

He says that they *sin not* who are born of God. Now, we must consider, whether God wholly regenerates us at once, or whether the remains of the old man continue in us until death. If regeneration is not as yet full and complete, it does not exempt us from the bondage of sin except in proportion to its own extent. It hence appears that it cannot be but that the children of God are not free from sins, and that they daily sin, that is, as far as they have still some remnants of their old nature. Nevertheless, what the Apostle contends for stands unalterable, that the design of regeneration is to destroy sin, and that all who are born of God lead a righteous and a holy life, because the Spirit of God restrains the lusting of sin.

The Apostle means the same thing by *the seed* of God; for God's Spirit so forms the hearts of the godly for holy affections, that the flesh and its lusts do not prevail, but being subdued and put as it were under a yoke, they are checked and restrained. In short, the Apostle ascribes to the Spirit the sovereignty in the elect, who by his power represses sin and suffers it not to rule and reign.

And he cannot sin. Here the Apostle ascends higher, for he plainly declares that the hearts of the godly are so effectually governed by the Spirit of God, that through an inflexible disposition they follow his guidance. This is indeed far removed from the doctrine of the Papists. The Sorbons, it is true, confess that the will of man, unless assisted by God's Spirit, cannot desire what is right; but they imagine such a motion of the Spirit as leaves to us the free choice of good and evil. Hence they draw forth merits, because we willingly obey the influence of the Spirit, which it is in our power to resist. In short, they desire the grace of the Spirit to be only this, that we are thereby enabled to choose right if we will. John speaks here far otherwise; for he not only shews that we cannot sin, but also that the power of the Spirit is so effectual, that it necessarily retains us in continual obedience to righteousness. Nor is this the only passage of Scripture which teaches us that the will is so formed that it cannot be otherwise than right. For God testifies that he gives a new heart to his children, and promises to do this, that they may walk in his commandments. Besides, John not only shews how efficaciously God works once in man, but plainly declares that the Spirit continues his grace in us to the last, so that inflexible perseverance is added to newness of life. Let us not, then, imagine with the Sophists that it is some neutral movement, which leaves men free either to follow or to reject; but let us know that our own hearts are so ruled by God's Spirit, that they constantly cleave to righteousness.

Moreover, what the Sophists absurdly object, may be easily refuted: they say that thus the will is taken away from man; but they say so falsely: for the will is a natural power; but, as nature is corrupted, it has only depraved inclinations. It is hence necessary that the Spirit of God should renew it, in order that it may begin to be good. And, then, as men would immediately fall away from what is good, it is necessary that the same Spirit should carry on what he has begun, to the end.

As to merit, the answer is obvious, for it cannot be deemed strange that men merit nothing; and yet good works, which flow from the grace of the Spirit, do not cease to be so deemed, because they are voluntary. They have also a reward, for they are by grace ascribed to men as though they were their own.

But here a question arises, Whether the fear and love of God can be extinguished in any one who has been regenerated by the Spirit of God? for that this cannot be, seems to be the import of the Apostle's words. They who think otherwise refer to the example of David, who for a time laboured under such a beastly stupor, that not a spark of grace appeared in him. Moreover, in the fifty-first Psalm, he prays for the restoration of the Spirit. It hence follows that he was deprived of him. I, however, doubt not but that the seed, communicated when God regenerates his elect, as it is incorruptible, retains its virtue perpetually. I, indeed, grant that it may sometimes be stifled, as in the case of David; but still, when all religion seemed to be extinct in him, a live coal was hid under the ashes. Satan, indeed, labours to root out whatever is from God in the elect; but when the utmost is permitted to him, there ever remains a hidden root, which afterwards springs up. But John does not speak of one act, as they say, but of the continued course of life.

Some fanatics dream of something I know not what, that is, of an eternal seed in the elect, which they always bring from their mother's womb; but for this purpose they very outrageously pervert the words of John; for he does not speak of eternal election, but begins with regeneration.

There are also those who are doubly frantic, who hold, under this pretence, that everything is lawful to the faithful, that is, because John says that they cannot sin. They then maintain that we may follow indiscriminately whatever our inclinations may lead us to. Thus they take the liberty to commit adultery, to steal, and to murder, because there can be no sin where God's Spirit reigns. But far otherwise is the meaning of the Apostle; for he denies that the faithful sin for this reason, because God has engraven his law on their hearts, according to what the Prophet says (Jer. xxxi. 33.)

10. *In this the children of God are manifest.* He shortly draws this conclusion, that those in vain claim a place and a name among the children of God, who do not prove themselves to be such by a pious and holy life, since by this evidence they shew that they differ from the children of the devil. But he does not mean that they are thus manifested, so as to be openly recognised by the whole world; but his meaning is only this, that the fruit and adoption always appear in the life.

10. — Whosoever doeth not righteousness is not of God, neither he that loveth not his brother.	10. — Quisquis non facit justitiam, non est ex Deo, et qui non diligit fratrem suum.
11. For this is the message that ye heard from the beginning, that we should love one another.	11. Quia hæc est prædicatio quam audistis ab initio, ut mutuò nos diligamus.
12. Not as Cain, *who* was of that wicked one, and slew his brother. And wherefore slew he him? Because his own works were evil, and his brother's righteous.	12. Non sicut Cain, qui ex maligno erat, occidit fratrem suum; et qua de causa eum occidit? Quia opera ejus mala erant, fratris autem justa.
13. Marvel not, my brethren, if the world hate you.	13. Ne miremini, fratres mei, si vos mundus odit.

10. *Whosoever doeth not righteousness.* To do righteous-

ness and to do sin, are here set in opposition the one to the other. Then, to do righteousness is no other thing than to fear God from the heart, and to walk in his commandments as far as human weakness will permit; for though righteousness in a strict sense is a perfect keeping of the law, from which the faithful are always far off; yet as offences and fallings are not imputed to them by God, righteousness is that imperfect obedience which they render to him. But John declares that all who do not live righteously are not of God, because all those whom God calls, he regenerates by his Spirit. Hence newness of life is a perpetual evidence of divine adoption.

Neither he who loveth not his brother. He accommodates a general doctrine to his own purpose. For hitherto he has been exhorting the faithful to brotherly love; now, for the same end, he refers to true righteousness. Hence this clause is added instead of an explanation. But I have already stated the reason why the whole of righteousness is included in brotherly love. The love of God holds, indeed, the first place; but as on it depends love towards men, it is often, as a part for the whole, comprehended under it, and also the latter under the former. Then he declares that every one who is endued with benevolence and humanity, is thus just, and is to be so deemed, because love is the fulfilment of the law. He confirms this declaration by saying that the faithful had been so *taught* from the beginning; for by these words he intimates that the statement which he made ought not to have appeared new to them.

12. *Not as Cain.* This is another confirmation, taken from what is contrary; for in the reprobate and the children of the devil hatred reigns, and it holds, as it were, the chief place in their life; and he brings forward Cain as an instance. It served in the meantime to give them consolation, as he at length concluded by saying, *Marvel not, if the world hate you.*

This explanation ought to be carefully noticed, for men ever blunder as to the way of living, because they make holiness to consist of fictitious works, and while they torment themselves with trifles, they think themselves doubly acceptable to God, as the monks, who proudly call their mode of living a state of perfection; nor is there any other worship of God under the Papacy but a mass of superstitions. But the Apostle testifies that this righteousness alone is approved by God, that is, if we love one another; and further, that the devil reigns where hatred, dissimulation, envy, and enmity prevail. We ought, however, at the same time, to bear in mind what I have already touched upon, that brotherly love, as it proceeds from the love of God as an effect from a cause, is not disjoined from it, but on the contrary is commended by John on this account, because it is an evidence of our love to God.

By saying that *Cain* was driven to slay his brother, because his works were evil, he intimates what I have already stated, that when impiety rules, hatred occupies the first place. He refers to Abel's righteous works, that we may learn to endure patiently when the world hates us gratuitously, without any just provocation.

14. We know that we have passed from death unto life, because we love the brethren: he that loveth not *his* brother abideth in death.
15. Whosoever hateth his brother is a murderer: and ye know that no murderer hath eternal life abiding in him.
16. Hereby perceive we the love *of God*, because he laid down his life for us: and we ought to lay down *our* lives for the brethren.
17. But whoso hath this world's good, and seeth his brother have need, and shutteth up his bowels *of compassion* from him, how dwelleth the love of God in him?
18. My little children, let us not love in word, neither in tongue; but in deed, and in truth.

14. Nos scimus quòd transierimus à morte in vitam, quia diligimus fratres: qui non diligit fratrem, manet in morte.
15. Omnis qui odit fratrem suum, homicida est; et nostis quòd omnis homicida, non habet vitam æternam in se manentem.
16. In hoc cognoscimus charitatem, quòd ille pro nobis animam suam posuit: et nos debemus pro fratribus animas ponere.
17. Si quis habeat victum mundi, et videat fratrem suum egentem, et claudat viscera sua ab eo, quomodo charitas Dei in ipso manet?
18. Filioli mei, ne diligamus sermone, neque lingua, sed opere et veritate.

14. *We know.* He commends love to us by a remarkable eulogy, because it is an evidence of a transition from death to life. It hence follows that if we love the brethren we are blessed, but that we are miserable if we hate them. There is no one who does not wish to be freed and delivered from death. Those then who by cherishing hatred willingly give

themselves up to death, must be extremely stupid and senseless. But when the Apostle says, that it is known by love that we have passed into life, he does not mean that man is his own deliverer, as though he could by loving the brethren rescue himself from death, and procure life for himself; for he does not here treat of the cause of salvation, but as love is the special fruit of the Spirit, it is also a sure symbol of regeneration. Then the Apostle draws an argument from the sign, and not from the cause. For as no one sincerely loves his brethren, except he is regenerated by the Spirit of God, he hence rightly concludes that the Spirit of God, who is life, dwells in all who love the brethren. But it would be preposterous for any one to infer hence, that life is obtained by love, since love is in order of time posterior to it.

The argument would be more plausible, were it said that love makes us more certain of life: then confidence as to salvation would recumb on works. But the answer to this is obvious; for though faith is confirmed by all the graces of God as aids, yet it ceases not to have its foundation in the mercy of God only. As for instance, when we enjoy the light, we are certain that the sun shines; if the sun shines on the place in which we are, we have a clearer view of it; but yet when the visible rays do not come to us, we are satisfied that the sun diffuses its brightness for our benefit. So when faith is founded on Christ, some things may happen to assist it, still it rests on Christ's grace alone.

15. *Is a murderer.* To stimulate us still more to love, he shews how detestable before God is hatred. There is no one who dreads not a murderer; nay, we all execrate the very name. But the Apostle declares that all who hate their brethren are murderers. He could have said nothing more atrocious; nor is what is said hyperbolical, for we wish him to perish whom we hate. It does not matter if a man keeps his hands from mischief; for the very desire to do harm, as well as the attempt, is condemned before God: nay, when we do not ourselves seek to do an injury, yet if we wish an evil to happen to our brother from some one else, we are murderers.

Then the Apostle defines the thing simply as it is, when

he ascribes murder to hatred. Hence is proved the folly of men, that though they abominate the name, they yet make no account of the crime itself. Whence is this? even because the external face of things engrosses our thoughts; but the inward feeling comes to an account before God. Let no one therefore extenuate any more so grievous an evil. Let us learn to refer our judgments to the tribunal of God.

16. *Hereby perceive we,* or, By this we know. He now shews what true love is; for it would not have been enough to commend it, unless its power is understood. As an instance of perfect love, he sets before us the example of Christ; for he, by not sparing his own life, testified how much he loved us. This then is the mark to which he bids them to advance. The sum of what is said is, that our love is approved, when we transfer the love of ourselves to our brethren, so that every one, in a manner forgetting himself, should seek the good of others.[1]

It is, indeed, certain, that we are far from being equal to Christ: but the Apostle recommends to us the imitation of him; for though we do not overtake him, it is yet meet that we should follow his steps, though at a distance. Doubtless, since it was the Apostle's object to beat down the vain boasting of hypocrites, who gloried that they had faith in Christ though without brotherly love, he intimated by these words, that except this feeling prevails in our hearts, we have no connexion with Christ. Nor does he yet, as I have said, set before us the love of Christ, so as to require us to be equal to him; for what would this be but to drive us all to despair? But he means that our feelings should be so formed and regulated, that we may desire to devote our life and also our death, first to God, and then to our neighbours.

There is another difference between us and Christ,—the virtue or benefit of our death cannot be the same. For the wrath of God is not pacified by our blood, nor is life pro-

---

[1] There is no authority for adding *of God* after *love* in this verse; nor indeed is it right, for what follows clearly shows that the love of Christ is what is referred to. The antecedent to "he," ("because he laid down," &c.) is "the Son of God" in the 8th verse. The passage may be thus rendered, "By this we know love, that he laid down his own life for us; and we ought to lay down *our* lives for *our* brethren."—*Ed.*

cured by our death, nor is punishment due to others suffered by us. But the Apostle, in this comparison, had not in view the end or the effect of Christ's death; but he meant only that our life should be formed according to his example.

17. *But whoso hath this world's good,* or, If any one has the world's sustenance. He now speaks of the common duties of love, which flow from that chief foundation, that is, when we are prepared to serve our neighbours even to death. He, at the same time, seems to reason from the greater to the less; for he who refuses to alleviate by his goods the want of his brother, while his life is safe and secure, much less would he expose for him his life to danger. Then he denies that there is love in us, if we withhold help from our neighbours. But he so recommends this external kindness, that at the same time he very fitly expresses the right way of doing good, and what sort of feeling ought to be in us.

Let this, then, be the first proposition, that no one truly loves his brethren, except he really shews this whenever an occasion occurs; the second, that as far as any one has the means, he is bound so far to assist his brethren, for the Lord thus supplies us with the opportunity to exercise love; the third, that the necessity of every one ought to be seen to, for as any one needs food and drink or other things of which we have abundance, so he requires our aid; the fourth, that no act of kindness, except accompanied with sympathy, is pleasing to God. There are many apparently liberal, who yet do not feel for the miseries of their brethren. But the Apostle requires that our bowels should be opened; which is done, when we are endued with such a feeling as to sympathize with others in their evils, no otherwise than as though they were our own.

The love of God. Here he speaks of loving the brethren; why then does he mention the love of God? even because this principle is to be held, that it cannot be but that the love of God will generate in us the love of the brethren.[1] And thus God tries our love to him, when he bids us to love men from a regard to himself, according to what is said in

---

[1] "The love of God" here is love of which God is the object, that is, love to God.—*Ed.*

Ps. xvi. 2, "My goodness reaches not to thee, but towards the saints who are on the earth is my will and my care."

18. *Let us not love in word.* There is a concession in this first clause; for we cannot love in tongue only; but as many falsely pretend this, the Apostle concedes, according to what is often done, the name of the thing to their dissimulation, though, in the second clause, he reproves their vanity, when he denies that there is reality except in the deed. For thus ought the words to be explained,—Let us not profess by the tongue that we love, but prove it by the deed; for this is the only true way of shewing love.[1]

19. And hereby we know that we are of the truth, and shall assure our hearts before him.	19. Et in hoc cognoscimus quòd ex veritate sumus, et coram ipso persuadebimus corda nostra.
20. For if our heart condemn us, God is greater than our heart, and knoweth all things.	20. Quòd si accuset nos cor nostrum, certè major est Deus corde nostro et novit omnia.
21. Beloved, if our heart condemn us not, *then* have we confidence toward God.	21. Dilecti, si cor nostrum non accuset, fiduciam habemus erga Deum:
22. And whatsoever we ask, we receive of him, because we keep his commandments, and do those things that are pleasing in his sight.	22. Et siquid petierimus, accipimus ab eo, quia præcepta ejus servamus, et quæ coram eo placent facimus.

19. *And hereby we know,* or, by this we know. The word *truth,* he takes now in a different sense; but there is a striking similarity in the words,—If we, in truth, love our neighbours, we have an evidence that we are born of God, who is truth, or that the truth of God dwells in us. But we must ever remember, that we have not from love the knowledge which the Apostle mentions, as though we were to seek from it the certainty of salvation. And doubtless we know not

---

[1] *Beza* and others regard "only," or "merely," as understood in the first clause, according to a mode of speaking which often occurs in Scripture, as "Labour not," &c., (John vi. 27.)

"My dear children, let us love, not only by word, or with the tongue, but by work and in truth."

That is, let us not love only by making in words fair promises, or by expressing sympathy with the tongue, but by giving effect to our sympathy by works, and by making our word true, by fulfilling it. Here we find the same arrangement as in many other instances; the "word" has its correspondence in "truth;" and "tongue" in "work."

It is justly observed by *Macknight,* that "the Apostle cannot be supposed to forbid our using affectionate speeches to our brethren in distress But he forbiddeth us to content ourselves with these."—*Ed.*

otherwise that we are the children of God, than as he seals his free adoption on our hearts by his own Spirit, and as we receive by faith the sure pledge of it offered in Christ. Then love is accessory or an inferior aid, a prop to our faith, not a foundation on which it rests.

Why then does the Apostle say, *We shall assure our hearts before God?* He reminds us in these words, that faith does not exist without a good conscience; not that assurance arises from it or depends on it, but that then only we are really and not falsely assured of our union with God, when by the efficacy of his Holy Spirit he manifests himself in our love. For it is ever meet and proper to consider what the Apostle handles; for as he condemns a feigned and false profession of faith, he says that a genuine assurance before God we cannot have, except his Spirit produces in us the fruit of love. Nevertheless, though a good conscience cannot be separated from faith, yet no one should hence conclude that we must look to our works in order that our assurance may be certain.

20. *For if our heart condemn us.* He proves, on the other hand, that they in vain possess the name and appearance of Christians, who have not the testimony of a good conscience. For if any one is conscious of guilt, and is condemned by his own heart, much less can he escape the judgment of God. It hence follows, that faith is subverted by the disquiet of an evil conscience.

He says, that *God is greater than our heart*, with reference to judgment, that is, because he sees much more keenly than we do, and searches more minutely and judges more severely. For this reason, Paul says, that though he was not conscious of wrong himself, yet he was not therefore justified, (1 Cor. iv. 4;) for he knew that however carefully attentive he was to his office, he erred in many things, and through inadvertence was ignorant of mistakes which God perceived. What then the Apostle means is, that he who is harassed and condemned by his own conscience, cannot escape the judgment of God.

To the same purpose is what immediately follows, that God *knoweth* or seeth *all things.* For how can those things be hid from him which we, who in comparison with him are dull and blind, are constrained to see? Then take this explanation, "Since God sees all things, he is far superior to our hearts." For to render a copulative as a causal particle is no new thing. The meaning is now clear, that since the knowledge of God penetrates deeper than the perceptions of our conscience, no one can stand before him except the integrity of his conscience sustains him.

But here a question may be raised. It is certain that the reprobate are sometimes sunk by Satan into such stupor, that they are no longer conscious of their own evils, and without alarm or fear, as Paul says, rush headlong into perdition; it is also certain, that hypocrites usually flatter themselves, and proudly disregard the judgment of God, for, being inebriated by a false conceit as to their own righteousness, they feel no convictions of sin. The answer to these things is not difficult; hypocrites are deceived because they shun the light; and the reprobate feel nothing, because they have departed from God; and, indeed, there is no security for an evil conscience but in hiding-places.

But the Apostle speaks here of consciences which God draws forth to the light, forces to his tribunal, and fills with an apprehension of his judgment. Yet it is at the same time generally true, that we cannot have a calm peace except that which God's Spirit gives to purified hearts; for those who, as we have said, are stupified, often feel secret compunctions, and torment themselves in their lethargy.

21. *If our heart condemn us not.* I have already explained that this refers not to hypocrites nor to the gross despisers of God. For how much soever the reprobate may approve of their own lives, yet the Lord, as Solomon says, weigheth their hearts. (Prov. xvi. 2.) This balance of God, by which he tries men, is such, that no one can boast that he has a clean heart. The meaning, then, of the Apostle's words is, that then only we come in calm confidence into God's presence, when we bring with us the testimony of a heart conscious of what is right and honest. That saying of Paul is indeed true, that by faith, which relies on the grace of Christ, an access to God with confidence is opened to us, (Eph. iii.

12;) and also, that peace is given us by faith, that our consciences may stand peaceably before God. (Rom. v. 1.) But there is not much difference between these sentences; for Paul shews the cause of confidence, but John mentions only an inseparable addition, which necessarily adheres to it, though it be not the cause.

Here, however, arises a greater difficulty, which seems to leave no confidence in the whole world; for who can be found whose heart reproves him in nothing? To this I answer, that the godly are thus reproved, that they may at the same time be absolved. For it is indeed necessary that they should be seriously troubled inwardly for their sins, that terror may lead them to humility and to a hatred of themselves; but they presently flee to the sacrifice of Christ, where they have sure peace. Yet the Apostle says, in another sense, that they are not condemned, because however deficient they may confess themselves to be in many things, they are still relieved by this testimony of conscience, that they truly and from the heart fear God and desire to submit to his righteousness. All who possess this godly feeling, and at the same time know that all their endeavours, how much soever they come short of perfection, yet please God, are justly said to have a calm or a peaceful heart, because there is no inward compunction to disturb their calm cheerfulness.

22. *And whatsoever we ask.* These two things are connected, confidence and prayer. As before he shewed that an evil conscience is inconsistent with confidence, so now he declares that none can really pray to God but those who with a pure heart fear and rightly worship him. The latter follows from the former. It is a general truth taught in Scripture, that the ungodly are not heard by God, but that on the contrary, their sacrifices and prayers are an abomination to him. Hence the door is here closed up against hypocrites, lest they should in contempt of him rush into his presence.

He does not yet mean that a good conscience must be brought, as though it obtained favour to our prayers. Woe to us if we look on works, which have nothing in them but what is a cause of fear and trembling. The faithful, then, cannot otherwise come to God's tribunal than by relying on Christ the Mediator. But as the love of God is ever connected with faith, the Apostle, in order that he might the more severely reprove hypocrites, deprives them of that singular privilege with which God favours his own children; that is, lest they should think that their prayers have an access to God.

By saying, *because we keep his commandments*, he means not that confidence in prayer is founded on our works; but he teaches this only, that true religion and the sincere worship of God cannot be separated from faith. Nor ought it to appear strange that he uses a causal particle, though he does not speak of a cause; for an inseparable addition is sometimes mentioned as a cause: as when one says, Because the sun shines over us at mid-day, there is more heat; but it does not follow that heat comes from light.

23. And this is his commandment, That we should believe on the name of his Son Jesus Christ, and love one another, as he gave us commandment.	23. Et hoc est præceptum ejus, ut credamus nomini Filii ejus Jesu Christi, et nos diligamus invicem, sicuti præceptum dedit nobis.
24. And he that keepeth his commandment dwelleth in him, and he in him: and hereby we know that he abideth in us, by the Spirit which he hath given us.	24. Qui servat præcepta ejus, in ipso manet, et ipse in eo; atque in hoc cognoscimus quòd manet in nobis, ex Spiritu quem nobis dedit.

23. *And this is his commandment.* He again accommodates a general truth to his own purpose. The meaning is, that such is the discord between us and God, that we are kept off from an access to him, except we are united by love to one another. At the same time he does not here commend love alone, as before, but joins it as the companion and attendant of faith.

The Sophists by their glosses distort these words, as though liberty to pray were obtained by us, partly by faith and partly by works. As John requires us to keep God's commandments that we may pray aright, and afterwards teaches us that this keeping refers to faith and love, they conclude, that from these two things ought we to derive confidence in prayer. But I have already several times reminded you, that the subject here is not how or by what means men may prepare themselves so that they may have confidence to pray to God, for he speaks not here of the cause of this or of any worthiness. John only shews, that God favours none with the honour and privilege of intercourse with himself but his own children, even those who have been regenerated by his Spirit. The import, then, of what is said is, Where the fear and love of God do not prevail, it cannot be that God will hear prayer.

But if it be our purpose to obey his commandments, let us see what he commands. He does not, however, separate faith from love; but he requires both together from us. And this is the reason why he uses the word *commandment* in the singular number.

But this is a remarkable passage; for he defines briefly as well as lucidly in what the whole perfection of a holy life consists. There is then no reason that we should allege any difficulty, since God does by no means lead us about through long labyrinths, but simply and shortly sets before us what is right and what he approves. Besides, in this brevity there is no obscurity, for he shews to us clearly the beginning and the end of a life rightly formed. But that a mention is here only made of brotherly love, while the love of God is omitted, the reason is, as we have elsewhere said, that as brotherly love flows from the love of God, so it is a sure and real evidence of it.

On the name of his Son. The name refers to preaching; and this connexion deserves to be noticed, for few understand what it is to believe on Christ; but from this mode of speaking, we may easily conclude that the only right faith is that which embraces Christ as he is set forth in the Gospel. Hence also it is, that there is no faith without teaching, as Paul also shews to us in Rom. x. 14. We must at the same time observe, that the Apostle includes faith in the knowledge of Christ; for he is the living image of the Father, and in him are laid up all the treasures of wisdom and knowledge. As soon, then, as we turn aside from him, we cannot do anything else but wander in error.

24. *And he that keepeth his commandments.* He con-

firms what I have already stated, that the union we have with God is evident when we entertain mutual love : not that our union begins thereby, but that it cannot be fruitless or without effect whenever it begins to exist. And he proves this by adding a reason, because God does not abide in us, except his Spirit dwells in us. But wherever the Spirit is, he necessarily manifests his power and efficiency. We hence readily conclude, that none abide in God and are united to him, but those who keep his commandments.

When, therefore, he says, *and by this we know*, the copulative, *and*, as a reason is here given, is to be rendered, "for," or, "because." But the character of the present reason ought to be considered ; for though the sentence in words agrees with that of Paul, when he says that the Spirit testifies to our hearts that we are the children of God, and that we through him cry to God, Abba, Father, yet there is some difference in the sense ; for Paul speaks of the certainty of gratuitous adoption, which the Spirit of God seals on our hearts ; but John here regards the effects which the Spirit produces while dwelling in us, as Paul himself does, when he says, that those are God's children who are led by the Spirit of God ; for there also he is speaking of the mortification of the flesh and newness of life.

The sum of what is said is, that it hence appears that we are God's children, that is, when his Spirit rules and governs our life. John at the same time teaches us, that whatever good works are done by us, proceed from the grace of the Spirit, and that the Spirit is not obtained by our righteousness, but is freely given to us.

CHAPTER IV.

1. Beloved, believe not every spirit, but try the spirits whether they are of God; because many false prophets are gone out into the world.

2. Hereby know ye the Spirit of God: Every spirit that confesseth

1. Dilecti, ne omni spiritui credatis, sed probate spiritus, an ex Deo sint; quia multi pseudoprophetæ exierunt in mundum.

2. In hoc cognoscite Spiritum Dei; omnis spiritus qui confitetur

that Jesus Christ is come in the flesh is of God:

3. And every spirit that confesseth not that Jesus Christ is come in the flesh is not of God: and this is that *spirit* of antichrist, whereof ye have heard that it should come; and even now already is it in the world.

Jesum Christum in carne venisse, ex Deo est:

3. Et omnis spiritus qui non confitetur Jesum Christum in carne venisse, ex Deo non est; et hic est antichristus, de quo audiistis quòd venturus sit; et nunc jam in mundo est.

HE returns to his former doctrine, which he had touched upon in the second chapter; for many (as it is usual in new things) abused the name of Christ for the purpose of serving their own errors. Some made a half profession of Christ; and when they obtained a place among his friends, they had more opportunity to injure his cause. Satan took occasion to disturb the Church, especially through Christ himself; for he is the stone of offence, against whom all necessarily stumble who keep not on the right way, as shewn to us by God.

But what the Apostle says consists of three parts. He first shews an evil dangerous to the faithful; and therefore he exhorts them to beware. He prescribes how they were to beware, that is, by making a distinction between the spirits; and this is the second part. In the third place, he points out a particular error, the most dangerous to them: he therefore forbids them to hear those who denied that the Son of God appeared in the flesh. We shall now consider each in order.

But though in the passage this reason is added, that many false prophets had gone forth into the world, yet it is convenient to begin with it. The announcement contains a useful admonition; for if Satan had then already seduced many, who under the name of Christ scattered their impostures, similar instances at this day ought not to terrify us. For it is the case perpetually with the Gospel, that Satan attempts to pollute and corrupt its purity by variety of errors. This our age has brought forth some horrible and monstrous sects; and for this reason many stand amazed; and not knowing where to turn, they cast aside every care for religion; for they find no more summary way for extricating themselves from the danger of errors. They thus, indeed, act most foolishly; for by shunning the light of truth, they cast themselves into the darkness of errors. Let, therefore, this fact remain fixed in our minds, that from the time the Gospel began to be preached, false prophets immediately appeared; and this fact will fortify us against such offences.

The antiquity of errors keeps many, as it were, fast bound, so that they dare not emerge from them. But John points out here an intestine evil which was then in the Church. Now, if there were impostors mixed then with the Apostles and other faithful teachers, what wonder is it, that the doctrine of the Gospel has been long ago suppressed, and that many corruptions have prevailed in the world? There is, then, no reason why antiquity should hinder us to exercise our liberty in distinguishing between truth and falsehood.

1. *Believe not every spirit.* When the Church is disturbed by discords and contentions, many, as it has been said, being frightened, depart from the Gospel. But the Spirit prescribes to us a far different remedy, that is, that the faithful should not receive any doctrine thoughtlessly and without discrimination. We ought, then, to take heed lest, being offended at the variety of opinions, we should discard teachers, and, together with them, the word of God. But this precaution is sufficient, that all are not to be heard indiscriminately.

The word *spirit* I take metonymically, as signifying him who boasts that he is endowed with the gift of the Spirit to perform his office as a prophet. For as it was not permitted to any one to speak in his own name, nor was credit given to speakers but as far as they were the organs of the Holy Spirit, in order that prophets might have more authority, God honoured them with this name, as though he had separated them from mankind in general. Those, then, were called spirits, who, giving only a language to the oracles of the Holy Spirit, in a manner represented him. They brought nothing of their own, nor came they forth in their own name But the design of this honourable title was, that God's word should not lose the respect due to it through the humble condition of the minister. For God would have his word to be always received from the mouth of man no otherwise than if he himself had appeared from heaven.

Here Satan interposed, and having sent false teachers to adulterate God's word, he gave them also this name, that they might more easily deceive. Thus false prophets have always been wont superciliously and boldly to claim for themselves whatever honour God had bestowed on his own servants. But the Apostle designedly made use of this name, lest they who falsely pretend God's name should deceive us by their masks, as we see at this day; for many are so dazzled by the mere name of a Church, that they prefer, to their eternal ruin, to cleave to the Pope, than to deny him the least part of his authority.

We ought, therefore, to notice this concession: for the Apostle might have said that every sort of men ought not to be believed; but as false teachers claimed the Spirit, so he left them to do so, having at the same time reminded them that their claim was frivolous and nugatory, except they really exhibited what they professed, and that those were foolish who, being astonished at the very sound of so honourable a name, dared not to make any inquiry on the subject.

Try the spirits. As all were not true prophets, the Apostle here declares that they ought to have been examined and tried. And he addresses not only the whole Church, but also every one of the faithful.

But it may be asked, whence have we this discernment? They who answer, that the word of God is the rule by which everything that men bring forward ought to be tried, say something, but not the whole. I grant that doctrines ought to be tested by God's word; but except the Spirit of wisdom be present, to have God's word in our hands will avail little or nothing, for its meaning will not appear to us; as, for instance, gold is tried by fire or touchstone, but it can only be done by those who understand the art; for neither the touchstone nor the fire can be of any use to the unskilful. That we may then be fit judges, we must necessarily be endowed with and directed by the Spirit of discernment. But as the Apostle would have commanded this in vain, were there no power of judging supplied, we may with certainty conclude, that the godly shall never be left destitute of the Spirit of wisdom as to what is necessary, provided they ask for him of the Lord. But the Spirit will only thus guide us to a right discrimination, when we render all our thoughts subject to God's word; for it is, as it has been said, like the touchstone, yea, it ought to be deemed most necessary to us; for that alone is true doctrine which is drawn from it.

But here a difficult question arises: If every one has the right and the liberty to judge, nothing can be settled as certain, but on the contrary the whole of religion will be uncertain. To this I answer, that there is a twofold trial of doctrine, private and public. The private trial is that by which every one settles his own faith, when he wholly acquiesces in that doctrine which he knows has come from God; for consciences will never find a safe and tranquil port otherwise than in God. Public trial refers to the common consent and polity of the Church; for as there is danger lest fanatics should rise up, who may presumptuously boast that they are endued with the Spirit of God, it is a necessary remedy, that the faithful meet together and seek a way by which they may agree in a holy and godly manner. But as the old proverb is too true, "So many heads, so many opinions," it is doubtless a singular work of God, when he subdues our perverseness and makes us to think the same thing, and to agree in a holy unity of faith.

But what Papists under this pretence hold, that whatever has been decreed in councils is to be deemed as certain oracles, because the Church has once proved them to be from God, is extremely frivolous. For though it be the ordinary way of seeking consent, to gather a godly and holy council, when controversies may be determined according to God's word; yet God has never bound himself to the decrees of any council. Nor does it necessarily follow, that as soon as a hundred bishops or more meet together in any place, they have duly called on God and inquired at his mouth what is true; nay, nothing is more clear that they have often departed from the pure word of God. Then in this case also the trial which the Apostle prescribes ought to take place, so that the spirits may be proved.

2. *Hereby*, or by this, *know ye.* He lays down a special mark by which they might more easily distinguish between true and false prophets. Yet he only repeats here what we have met with before, that as Christ is the object at which faith aims, so he is the stone at which all heretics stumble. As long then as we abide in Christ, there is safety; but when we depart from him, faith is lost, and all truth is rendered void.[1]

But let us consider what this confession includes; for when the Apostle says that Christ *came*, we hence conclude that he was before with the Father; by which his eternal divinity is proved. By saying that he came *in the flesh*, he means that by putting on flesh, he became a real man, of the same nature with us, that he might become our brother, except that he was free from every sin and corruption. And lastly, by saying that he came, the cause of his coming must be noticed, for he was not sent by the Father for nothing. Hence on this depend the office and merits of Christ.

As, then, the ancient heretics departed from the faith, in one instance, by denying the divine, and in another by denying the human nature of Christ; so do the Papists at this day: though they confess Christ to be God and man, yet they by no means retain the confession which the Apostle requires, because they rob Christ of his own merit; for where free-will, merits of works, fictitious modes of worship, satisfactions, the advocacy of saints, are set up, how very little remains for Christ!

---

[1] It appears that by "spirit" throughout this passage, we are to understand a teacher claiming, rightly or falsely, to be influenced by God's Spirit. Nor would it be improper, but suitable to the context, to consider "the spirit of God" in this verse as meaning a teacher guided by God. The meaning of the passage might be thus expressed,—
  2. "By this know ye the teacher of God; every teacher who confesses Jesus Christ as having come in the flesh, is from God; and
  3. every teacher who does not confess Jesus Christ as having come in the flesh, is not from God; and this is the teacher of Antichrist, (or, the Antichristian teacher,) of whom ye have heard that he is coming, and he is now already in the world."—*Ed.*

The Apostle then meant this, that since the knowledge of Christ includes the sum and substance of the doctrine respecting true religion, our eyes ought to be directed to and fixed on that, so that we may not be deceived. And doubtless Christ is the end of the law and the prophets; nor do we learn anything else from the gospel but his power and grace.

3. *And this is that spirit of Antichrist.* The Apostle added this, to render more detestable the impostures which lead us away from Christ. We have already said that the doctrine respecting the kingdom of Antichrist was well known; so that the faithful had been warned as to the future scattering of the Church, in order that they might exercise vigilance. Justly then did they dread the name as something base and ominous. The Apostle says now, that all those who depreciated Christ were members of that kingdom.

And he says that the spirit of *antichrist* would *come,* and that *it was* already in the world, but in a different sense. He means that it was already in the world, because it carried on in secret its iniquity. As, however, the truth of God had not as yet been subverted by false and spurious dogmas, as superstition had not as yet prevailed in corrupting the worship of God, as the world had not as yet perfidiously departed from Christ, as tyranny, opposed to the kingdom of Christ, had not as yet openly exalted itself, he therefore says, that it *would come.*

4. Ye are of God, little children, and have overcome them; because greater is he that is in you, than he that is in the world.	4. Vos ex Deo estis, filioli, et vicistis eos; quia major est qui est in vobis, quàm qui in mundo.
5. They are of the world; therefore speak they of the world, and the world heareth them.	5. Ipsi ex mundo sunt; propterea ex mundo loquuntur, et mundus eos audit.
6. We are of God: he that knoweth God heareth us; he that is not of God heareth not us. Hereby know we the spirit of truth, and the spirit of error.	6. Nos ex Deo sumus; qui novit Deum, audit nos; qui non est ex Deo, non audit nos: in hoc cognoscimus spiritum veritatis et spiritum erroris.

4. *Ye are of God.* He had spoken of one antichrist; he now mentions many. But the many were the false prophets

who had come forth before the head appeared.[1] But the Apostle's object was to animate the faithful, that they might courageously and boldly resist impostors, for alacrity is weakened when the issue of the contest is doubtful. Besides, it might have caused the good to fear, when they saw that hardly the kingdom of Christ had been set up, when enemies stood ready to suppress it. Though then they must contend, yet he says that they had conquered, because they would have a successful issue, as though he had said that they were already, though in the middle of the contest, beyond any danger, because they would surely be conquerors.

But this truth ought to be farther extended, for whatever contests we may have with the world and the flesh, a certain victory is to follow. Hard and fierce conflicts indeed await us, and some continually succeed others; but as by Christ's power we fight and are furnished with God's weapons, we even by fighting and striving become conquerors. As to the main subject of this passage, it is a great consolation, that with whatever wiles Satan may assail us, we shall stand through the power of God.

But we must observe the reason which is immediately added, *because greater*, or stronger, is he who is in you than he who is in the world. For such is our infirmity, that we succumb before we engage with an enemy, for we are so immersed in ignorance that we are open to all kinds of fallacies, and Satan is wonderfully artful in deceiving. Were we to hold out for one day, yet a doubt may creep into our minds as to what would be the case to-morrow; we should thus be in a state of perpetual anxiety. Therefore the Apostle reminds us that we become strong, not by our own power, but by that of God. He hence concludes, that we can no more be conquered than God himself, who has armed us with his own power to the end of the world. But in this whole spiritual warfare this thought ought to dwell in our hearts, that it would be all over with us immediately were

---

[1] When it is said, ye "have overcome them," the antecedent to "them" is no doubt "the false prophets" in the first verse. It is usual with John to refer to antecedents at some distance. See ch. iii. 16.—*Ed.*

we to fight in our own strength; but that as God repels our enemies while we are reposing, victory is certain.[1]

5. *They are of the world.* It is no small consolation that they who dare to assail God in us, have only the world to aid and help them. And by the world the Apostle means that portion of which Satan is the prince. Another consolation is also added, when he says that the world embraces through the false prophets that which it acknowledges as its own.[2] We see what great propensity to vanity and falsehood there is in men. Hence false doctrines easily penetrate and spread far and wide. The Apostle intimates that there is no reason why we should on this account be disturbed, for it is nothing new or unusual that the world, which is wholly fallacious, should readily hearken to what is false.

6. *We are of God.* Though this really applies to all the godly, yet it refers properly to the faithful ministers of the Gospel; for the Apostle, through the confidence imparted by the Spirit, glories here that he and his fellow-ministers served God in sincerity, and derived from him whatever they taught. It happens that false prophets boast of the same thing, for it is their custom to deceive under the mask of God; but faithful ministers differ much from them, who declare nothing of themselves but what they really manifest in their conduct.

We ought, however, always to bear in mind the subject which he here handles; small was the number of the godly,

---

[1] "The world" is in this verse identified with "the false prophets;" true Christians had overcome these for this reason, because greater was he that was in them than he that was in the world, that is, in the unbelieving and ungodly, of whom the false prophets formed a part. Hence it follows, "They are of the world," that is, they are of the number of those who are ungodly and wicked, who make up the kingdom of darkness.—*Ed.*

[2] The clause, "therefore speak they of the world," is hardly a true rendering, for ἐκ never means "of," in the sense of "concerning." *Macknight* renders it "from." *Grotius* paraphrases the sentence thus, "They preach things agreeable to the dispositions of the world;" and *Doddridge* thus, "They speak as of the world, as taking their instructions from it." But ἐκ, like *ex* in Latin, means sometimes "according to," as in Matt. xii. 37, "For by (or, according to) thy words thou shalt be justified." See also verse 34, "but of (or, according to) the abundance," &c. Then this sentence may be thus rendered, "Therefore speak they according to the world:" that is, according to the views and principles of the superstitious and ungodly men of the world.—*Ed.*

and unbelief prevailed almost everywhere; few really adhered to the Gospel, the greater part were running headlong into errors. Hence was the occasion of stumbling. John, in order to obviate this, bids us to be content with the fewness of the faithful, because all God's children honoured him and submitted to his doctrine. For he immediately sets in opposition to this a contrary clause, that they who are *not of God*, do not hear the pure doctrine of the Gospel. By these words he intimates that the vast multitude to whom the Gospel is not acceptable, do not hear the faithful and true servants of God, because they are alienated from God himself. It is then no diminution to the authority of the Gospel that many reject it.

But to this doctrine is added a useful admonition, that by the obedience of faith we are to prove ourselves to be of God. Nothing is easier than to boast that we are of God; and hence nothing is more common among men, as the case is at this day with the Papists, who proudly vaunt that they are the worshippers of God, and yet they no less proudly reject the word of God. For though they pretend to believe God's word, yet when they are brought to the test, they close their ears and will not hear, and yet to revere God's word is the only true evidence that we fear him. Nor can the excuse, made by many, have any place here, that they shun the doctrine of the Gospel when proclaimed to them, because they are not fit to form a judgment; for it cannot be but that every one who really fears and obeys God, knows him in his word.

Were any one to object and say, that many of the elect do not immediately attain faith, nay, that at first they stubbornly resist; to this I answer, that at that time they are not to be regarded, as I think, as God's children; for it is a sign of a reprobate man when the truth is perversely rejected by him.

And by the way, it must be observed, that the *hearing* mentioned by the Apostle, is to be understood of the inward and real hearing of the heart, which is done by faith.

Hereby know we. The antecedent to *hereby*, or, by this, is included in the two preceding clauses, as though he had said,

" Hence the truth is distinguished from falsehood, because some speak from God, others from the world." But by the *spirit of truth and the spirit of error,* some think that hearers are meant, as though he had said, that those who give themselves up to be deceived by impostors, were born to error, and had in them the seed of falsehood; but that they who obey the word of God shew themselves by this very fact to be the children of the truth. This view I do not approve of. For as the Apostle takes spirits here metonymically for teachers or prophets, he means, I think, no other thing than that the trial of doctrine must be referred to these two things, whether it be from God or from the world.[1]

However, by thus speaking he seems to say nothing; for all are ready to declare, that they do not speak except from God. So the Papists at this day boast with magisterial gravity, that all their inventions are the oracles of the Spirit. Nor does Mahomet assert that he has drawn his dotages except from heaven. The Egyptians also, in former times, pretended that all their mad absurdities, by which they infatuated themselves and others, had been revealed from above. But to all this I reply, that we have the word of the Lord, which ought especially to be consulted. When, therefore, false spirits pretend the name of God, we must inquire from the Scriptures whether things are so. Provided a devout attention be exercised, accompanied with humility and meekness, the spirit of discernment will be given us,

[1] According to this view, "the spirit of truth" means the teacher of truth, and "the spirit of error" the teacher of error; and this is agreeable to the whole tenor of the context, the spirit throughout denoting the person who claimed, rightly or falsely, to be under the direction of the divine Spirit. " By this," refers to what had been just stated, that is, that false teachers were of the world, and spake things agreeable to the worldly-minded, and were heard by the world, and that the true teachers were from God, and were heard or attended to by those who knew God, and were not attended to by such as were ignorant of him. It was by this statement which he had made, they could distinguish between the teacher of truth and the teacher of error. The teacher of truth was one from God, and was attended to by those who knew God, and not by those who knew him not; on the other hand, the teacher of error was from the world, preached what was agreeable to the men of the world, and was hearkened to by them. The order, as it is often the case, is inverted; the teacher of error, mentioned last, is described in the fifth verse, and the teacher of truth, mentioned first, at the beginning of the sixth.— *Ed.*

7. Beloved, let us love one another; for love is of God; and every one that loveth is born of God, and knoweth God.
8. He that loveth not, knoweth not God; for God is love.
9. In this was manifested the love of God toward us, because that God sent his only-begotten Son into the world, that we might live through him.
10. Herein is love, not that we loved God, but that he loved us, and sent his Son *to be* the propitiation for our sins.

7. Dilecti, diligamus nos mutuò, quia dilectio ex Deo est; et omnis qui diligit ex Deo genitus est, et cognoscit Deum.
8. Qui non diligit, non novit Deum; quia Deus dilectio est.
9. In hoc apparuit dilectio Dei in nobis, quòd Filium suum unigenitum misit Deus in mundum, ut per eum vivamus.
10. In hoc est dilectio, non quòd nos dilexerimus Deum, sed quòd nos ipse dilexit, et misit Filium propitiationem pro peccatis nostris.

7. *Beloved.* He returns to that exhortation which he enforces almost throughout the Epistle. We have, indeed, said, that it is filled with the doctrine of faith and exhortation to love. On these two points he so dwells, that he continually passes from the one to the other.

When he commands *mutual* love, he does not mean that we discharge this duty when we love our friends, because they love us; but as he addresses in common the faithful, he could not have spoken otherwise than that they were to exercise mutual love. He confirms this sentence by a reason often adduced before, even because no one can prove himself to be the son of God, except he loves his neighbours, and because the true knowledge of God necessarily produces love in us.

He also sets in opposition to this, according to his usual manner, the contrary clause, that there is no knowledge of God where there is no love. And he takes as granted a general principle or truth, that God is love, that is, that his nature is to love men. I know that many reason more refinedly, and that the ancients especially have perverted this passage in order to prove the divinity of the Spirit. But the meaning of the Apostle is simply this,—that as God is the fountain of love, this effect flows from him, and is diffused wherever the knowledge of him comes, as he had at the beginning called him light, because there is nothing dark in him, but on the contrary he illuminates all things by his own brightness. Here then he does not speak of the essence of God, but only shews what he is found to be by us.

But two things in the Apostle's words ought to be noticed, —that the true knowledge of God is that which regenerates and renews us, so that we become new creatures; and that hence it cannot be but that it must conform us to the image of God. Away, then, with that foolish gloss respecting unformed faith. For when any one separates faith from love, it is the same as though he attempted to take away heat from the sun.

9. *In this was manifested*, or, has appeared. We have the love of God towards us testified also by many other proofs. For if it be asked, why the world has been created, why we have been placed in it to possess the dominion of the earth, why we are preserved in life to enjoy innumerable blessings, why we are endued with light and understanding, no other reason can be adduced, except the gratuitous love of God. But the Apostle here has chosen the principal evidence of it, and what far surpasses all other things. For it was not only an immeasurable love, that God spared not his own Son, that by his death he might restore us to life; but it was goodness the most marvellous, which ought to fill our minds with the greatest wonder and amazement. Christ, then, is so illustrious and singular a proof of divine love towards us, that whenever we look upon him, he fully confirms to us the truth that God is love.

He calls him his *only begotten*, for the sake of amplifying. For in this he more clearly shewed how singularly he loved us, because he exposed his only Son to death for our sakes. In the meantime, he who is his only Son by nature, makes many sons by grace and adoption, even all who, by faith, are united to his body. He expresses the end for which Christ has been sent by the Father, even that we may live through him: for without him we are all dead, but by his coming he brought life to us; and except our unbelief prevents the effect of his grace, we feel it in ourselves.

10. *Herein is love.* He amplifies God's love by another

reason, that he gave us his own Son at the time when we were enemies, as Paul teaches us, in Rom. v. 8; but he employs other words, that God, induced by no love of men, freely loved them. He meant by these words to teach us that God's love towards us has been gratuitous. And though it was the Apostle's object to set forth God as an example to be imitated by us; yet the doctrine of faith which he intermingles, ought not to be overlooked. God freely loved us,—how so? because he loved us before we were born, and also when, through depravity of nature, we had hearts turned away from him, and influenced by no right and pious feelings.

Were the prattlings of the Papists entertained, that every one is chosen by God as he foresees him to be worthy of love, this doctrine, that he first loved us, would not stand; for then our love to God would be first in order, though in time posterior. But the Apostle assumes this as an evident truth, taught in Scripture (of which these profane Sophists are ignorant,) that we are born so corrupt and depraved, that there is in us as it were an innate hatred to God, so that we desire nothing but what is displeasing to him, so that all the passions of our flesh carry on continual war with his righteousness.

And sent his Son. It was then from God's goodness alone, as from a fountain, that Christ with all his blessings has come to us. And as it is necessary to know, that we have salvation in Christ, because our heavenly Father has freely loved us; so when a real and full certainty of divine love towards us is sought for, we must look nowhere else but to Christ. Hence all who inquire, apart from Christ, what is settled respecting them in God's secret counsel, are mad to their own ruin.

But he again points out the cause of Christ's coming and his office, when he says that he was sent to be a *propitiation for our sins.* And first, indeed, we are taught by these words, that we were all through sin alienated from God, and that this alienation and discord remains until Christ intervenes to reconcile us. We are taught, secondly, that it is the beginning of our life, when God, having been pacified by the death of his Son, receives us unto favour : for *propitiation* properly refers to the sacrifice of his death. We find, then, that this honour of expiating for the sins of the world, and of thus taking away the enmity between God and us, belongs only to Christ.

But here some appearance of inconsistency arises : For if God loved us before Christ offered himself to death for us, what need was there for another reconciliation ? Thus the death of Christ may seem to be superfluous. To this I answer, that when Christ is said to have reconciled the Father to us, this is to be referred to our apprehensions ; for as we are conscious of being guilty, we cannot conceive of God otherwise than as of one displeased and angry with us, until Christ absolves us from guilt. For God, wherever sin appears, would have his wrath, and the judgment of eternal death, to be apprehended. It hence follows, that we cannot be otherwise than terrified by the present prospect as to death, until Christ by his death abolishes sin, until he delivers us by his own blood from death. Further, God's love requires righteousness ; that we may then be persuaded that we are loved, we must necessarily come to Christ, in whom alone righteousness is to be found.

We now see that the variety of expressions, which occurs in Scripture, according to different aspects of things, is most appropriate and especially useful with regard to faith. God interposed his own Son to reconcile himself to us, because he loved us ; but this love was hid, because we were in the meantime enemies to God, continually provoking his wrath. Besides, the fear and terror of an evil conscience took away from us all enjoyment of life. Hence as to the apprehension of our faith, God began to love us in Christ. And though the Apostle here speaks of the first reconciliation, let us yet know that to propitiate God to us by expiating sins is a perpetual benefit proceeding from Christ.

This the Papists also in part concede ; but afterwards they extenuate and almost annihilate this grace, by introducing their fictitious satisfactions. For if men redeem themselves by their works, Christ cannot be the only true propitiation, as he is called here.

11. Beloved, if God so loved us, we ought also to love one another.

12. No man hath seen God at any time. If we love one another, God dwelleth in us, and his love is perfected in us.

13. Hereby know we that we dwell in him, and he in us, because he hath given us of his Spirit.

14. And we have seen, and do testify, that the Father sent the Son *to be* the Saviour of the world.

15. Whosoever shall confess that Jesus is the Son of God, God dwelleth in him, and he in God.

16. And we have known and believed the love that God hath to us. God is love; and he that dwelleth in love, dwelleth in God, and God in him.

11. Dilecti, si ita Deus nos dilexit, nos quoque debemus invicem diligere.

12. Deum nemo vidit unquam; si diligimus nos invicem, Deus in nobis manet, et dilectio ejus perfecta est in nobis.

13. In hoc cognoscimus, quòd in ipso manemus, et ipse in nobis, quia ex Spiritu suo dedit nobis.

14. Et nos vidimus et testamur, quòd Pater misit Filium servatorem mundi.

15. Qui confessus fuerit, quòd Jesus est Filius Dei, Deus in eo manet et ipse in Deo.

16. Et nos cognovimus et credimus dilectionem quam habet Deus in nobis: Deus charitas est; et qui manet in charitate, in Deo manet, et Deus in eo.

11. *Beloved.* Now the Apostle accommodates to his own purpose what he has just taught us respecting the love of God; for he exhorts us by God's example to brotherly love; as also Paul sets before us Christ, who offered himself to the Father a sacrifice of pleasant fragrance, that every one of us might labour to benefit his neighbours. (Eph. v. 2.) And John reminds us, that our love ought not to be mercenary, when he bids us to love our neighbours as God has loved us; for we ought to remember this, that we have been loved freely. And doubtless when we regard our own advantage, or return good offices to friends, it is self-love, and not love to others.

12. *No man hath seen God.* The same words are found in the first chapter of John's Gospel; but John the Baptist had not there exactly the same thing in view, for he meant only that God could not be otherwise known, but as he has revealed himself in Christ. The Apostle here extends the same truth farther, that the power of God is comprehended by us by faith and love, so as to know that we are his children and that he dwells in us.

He speaks, however, first of love, when he says, that God *dwells in us,* if we love one another; for perfected, or really proved to be, in us is then his love; as though he had said, that God shews himself as present, when by his Spirit he forms our hearts so that they entertain brotherly love. For the same purpose he repeats what he had already said, that we know by the Spirit whom he has given us that he dwells in us; for it is a confirmation of the former sentence, because love is the effect or fruit of the Spirit.

The sum, then, of what is said is, that since love is from the Spirit of God, we cannot truly and with a sincere heart love the brethren, except the Spirit puts forth his power. In this way he testifies that he dwells in us. But God by his Spirit dwells in us; then, by love we prove that we have God abiding in us. On the other hand, whosoever boasts that he has God and loves not the brethren, his falsehood is proved by this one thing, because he separates God from himself.

When he says, *and his love is perfected*, the conjunction is to be taken as a causative, *for*, or, *because*. And *love* here may be explained in two ways, either that which God shews to us, or that which he implants in us. That God has given his Spirit to us, or given us of his Spirit, means the same thing; for we know that the Spirit in a measure is given to each individual.

14. *And we have seen.* He now explains the other part of the knowledge of God, which we have referred to, that he communicates himself to us in his Son, and offers himself to be enjoyed in him. It hence follows, that he is by faith received by us. For the design of the Apostle is to shew, that God is so united to us by faith and love, that he really dwells in us and renders himself in a manner visible by the effect of his power, who otherwise could not be seen by us.

When the Apostle says, *We have seen and do testify*, he refers to himself and others. And by seeing, he does not mean any sort of seeing, but what belongs to faith, by which they recognised the glory of God in Christ, according to what follows, that he was *sent* to be the *Saviour of the world;* and this knowledge flows from the illumination of the Spirit.

15. *Whosoever shall confess.* He repeats the truth, that

we are united to God by Christ, and that we cannot be connected with Christ except God abides in us. *Faith* and *confession* are used indiscriminately in the same sense; for though hypocrites may falsely boast of faith, yet the apostle here acknowledges none of those who ordinarily confess, but such as truly and from the heart believe. Besides, when he says *that Jesus is the Son of God*, he briefly includes the sum and substance of faith; for there is nothing necessary for salvation which faith finds not in Christ.

After having said in general, that men are so united to Christ by faith, that Christ unites them to God, he subjoined what they themselves had seen; so that he accommodated a general truth to those to whom he was writing. Then follows the exhortation, to love one another as they were loved by God. Therefore the order and connexion of his discourse is this,—Faith in Christ makes God to dwell in men, and we are partakers of this grace; but as God is love, no one dwells in him except he loves his brethren. Then love ought to reign in us, since God unites himself to us.

16. *And we have known and believed.* It is the same as though he had said, "We have known by believing;" for such knowledge is not attained but by faith. But we hence learn how different is an uncertain or doubtful opinion from faith. Besides, though he meant here, as I have already said, to accommodate the last sentence to his readers, yet he defines faith in various ways. He had said before, that it is to confess that Jesus is the Son of God; but he now says, We know by faith God's love towards us. It hence appears, that the paternal love of God is found in Christ, and that nothing certain is known of Christ, except by those who know themselves to be the children of God by his grace. For the Father sets his own Son daily before us for this end, that he may adopt us in him.

God is love. This is as it were the minor proposition in an argument; for from faith to love he reasons in this way: By faith God dwells in us, and God is love; then, wherever God abides, love ought to be there. Hence it follows that love is necessarily connected with faith.

17. Herein is our love made perfect, that we may have boldness in the day of judgment: because as he is, so are we in this world.

18. There is no fear in love; but perfect love casteth out fear: because fear hath torment. He that feareth is not made perfect in love.

17. In hoc perfecta est charitas nobiscum, ut fiduciam habeamus in die judicii, quòd sicut ille est, nos quoque sumus in hoc mundo.

18. Timor non est in charitate; sed perfecta charitas foràs pellit timorem: quia timor tormentum habet; qui autem timet, non est perfectus in charitate.

17. Herein is our love made perfect. There are two clauses in this passage,—that we are then partakers of divine adoption, when we resemble God as children their father; and, secondly, that this confidence is invaluable, for without it we must be most miserable.

Then in the first place, he shews to what purpose God has in love embraced us, and how we enjoy that grace manifested to us in Christ. Then, God's love to us is what is to be understood here. He says it is *perfected*, because it is abundantly poured forth and really given, that it appears to be complete. But he asserts that no others are partakers of this blessing, but those who, by being conformed to God, prove themselves to be his children. It is, then, an argument taken from what is an inseparable condition.

That we may have boldness. He now begins to shew the fruit of divine love towards us, though he afterwards shews it more clearly from the contrary effect. It is, however, an invaluable benefit, that we can dare boldly to stand before God. By nature, indeed, we dread the presence of God, and that justly; for, as he is the Judge of the world, and our sins hold us guilty, death and hell must come to our minds whenever we think of God. Hence is that dread which I have mentioned, which makes men shun God as much as they can. But John says that the faithful do not fear, when mention is made to them of the last judgment, but that on the contrary they go to God's tribunal confidently and cheerfully, because they feel assured of his paternal love. Every one, then, has made so much proficiency in faith, as he is well prepared in his mind to look forward to the day of judgment.

As he is. By these words, as it has been already said, he means that it is required of us in our turn to resemble the image of God. What God then in heaven is, such he bids us to be in this world, in order that we may be deemed his children; for the image of God, when it appears in us, is as it were the seal of his adoption.

But he seems thus to place a part of our confidence on works. Hence the Papists raise their crests here, as though John denied that we, relying on God's grace alone, can have a sure confidence as to salvation without the help of works. But in this they are deceived, because they do not consider that the Apostle here does not refer to the cause of salvation, but to what is added to it. And we readily allow that no one is reconciled to God through Christ, except he is also renewed after God's image, and that the one cannot be disjoined from the other. Right then is what is done by the Apostle, who excludes from the confidence of grace all those in whom no image of God is seen; for it is certain that such are wholly aliens to the Spirit of God and to Christ. Nor do we deny that newness of life, as it is the effect of divine adoption, serves to confirm confidence, as a prop, so to speak, of the second order; but in the meantime we ought to have our foundation on grace alone.[1] Nor indeed does the doctrine of John appear otherwise consistent with itself; for experience proves, and even Papists are forced to confess, that as to works they always give an occasion for trembling. Therefore no one can come with a tranquil mind to God's tribunal, except he believes that he is freely loved.

But that none of these things please the Papists, there is no reason for any one to wonder, since being miserable they know no faith except that which is entangled with doubts. Besides, hypocrisy brings darkness over them, so that they do not seriously consider how formidable is God's judgment when Christ the Mediator is not present, and some of them regard the resurrection as fabulous. But that we may cheer-

---

[1] What is love? it is as much a gift, a grace, as faith; it constitutes a fitness for heaven, but is in no way meritorious; and were it perfect, there would be nothing of merit in it; for the highest degrees of it come far short of what is due to God. To set up merit of any kind on the part of man, betokens extreme blindness, for salvation from first to last is altogether gratuitous.—*Ed.*

fully and joyfully go forth to meet Christ, we must have our faith fixed on his grace alone.

18. *There is no fear.* He now commends the excellency of this blessing by stating the contrary effect, for he says that we are continually tormented until God delivers us from misery and anguish by the remedy of his own love towards us. The meaning is, that as there is nothing more miserable than to be harassed by continual inquietude, we obtain by knowing God's love towards us the benefit of a peaceful calmness beyond the reach of fear. It hence appears what a singular gift of God it is to be favoured with his love. Moreover from this doctrine, he will presently draw an exhortation; but before he exhorts us to duty, he commends to us this gift of God, which by faith removes our fear.

This passage, I know, is explained otherwise by many; but I regard what the Apostle means, not what others think. They say that there is no fear in love, because, when we voluntarily love God, we are not constrained by force and fear to serve him. Then according to them, servile fear is here set in opposition to voluntary reverence; and hence has arisen the distinction between servile and filial fear. I indeed allow it to be true, that when we willingly love God as a Father, we are no longer constrained by the fear of punishment; but this doctrine has nothing in common with this passage, for the Apostle only teaches us, that when the love of God is by us seen and known by faith, peace is given to our consciences, so that they no longer tremble and fear.

It may, however, be asked, when does perfect love expel fear, for since we are endued with some taste only of divine love towards us, we can never be wholly freed from fear? To this I answer, that though fear is not wholly shaken off, yet when we flee to God as to a quiet harbour, safe and free from all danger of shipwreck and of tempests, fear is really expelled, for it gives way to faith. Then fear is not so expelled, but that it assails our minds, but it is so expelled that it does not torment us nor impede that peace which we obtain by faith.

Fear hath torment. Here the Apostle amplifies still further the greatness of that grace of which he speaks; for as it is a most miserable condition to suffer continual torments, there is nothing more to be wished than to present ourselves before God with a quiet conscience and a calm mind. What some say, that servants fear, because they have before their eyes punishment and the rod, and that they do not their duty except when forced, has nothing to do, as it has been already stated, with what the Apostle says here. So in the next clause, the exposition given, that he who fears is not perfect in love, because he submits not willingly to God, but would rather free himself from his service, does not comport at all with the context. For the Apostle, on the contrary, reminds us, that it is owing to unbelief when any one fears, that is, has a disturbed mind; for the love of God, really known, tranquillizes the heart.[1]

19. We love him, because he first loved us.
20. If a man say, I love God, and hateth his brother, he is a liar: for he that loveth not his brother whom he hath seen, how can he love God whom he hath not seen?
21. And this commandment have we from him, That he who loveth God love his brother also.

19. Nos diligimus eum, quia prior dilexit nos.
20. Si quis dicit, Deum diligo; et proximum suum odio habeat, mendax est: qui enim non diligit fratrem suum quem videt; Deum quem non videt, quomodo potest diligere?
21. Et hoc præceptum habemus ab ipso, ut qui Deum diligit, diligat et fratrem suum.

19. *We love him.* The verb ἀγαπῶμεν may be either in the indicative or imperative mood; but the former is the more suitable here, for the Apostle, as I think, repeats the preceding sentence, that as God has anticipated us by his free love, we ought in return to render love to him, for he immediately infers that he ought to be loved in men, or that

---

[1] *Beza, Doddridge, Scott,* and most commentators, regard *love* here as that which is in us, and not the love of God as apprehended by faith. The *main* subject of the Apostle is love in us, and the words "perfected" and "perfect," as applied to it, seem inappropriate to God's love towards us; and this perfection is said in verse 17th to consist in this, that as God is, so are we in this world; that is, like him in love, as God is said in the previous verse to be love.

"Fear" is the fear of judgment, mentioned in verse 17th, and he who fears is said to be not perfected or made perfect in love, which obviously refers to love in us. And then it immediately follows, "We *love* him," and the reason is assigned, "because he first loved us." He afterwards proceeds to show the indispensable necessity of having love to God and to the brethren —*Ed.*

the love we have for him ought to be manifested towards men. If, however, the imperative mood be preferred, the meaning would be nearly the same, that as God has freely loved us, we also ought now to love him.

But this love cannot exist, except it generates brotherly love. Hence he says, that they are liars who boast that they love God, when they hate their brethren.

But the reason he subjoins seems not sufficiently valid, for it is a comparison between the less and the greater: If, he says, we love not our brethren whom we see, much less can we love God who is invisible. Now there are obviously two exceptions; for the love which God has to us is from faith and does not flow from sight, as we find in 1 Pet. i. 8; and secondly, far different is the love of God from the love of men; for while God leads his people to love him through his infinite goodness, men are often worthy of hatred. To this I answer, that the Apostle takes here as granted what ought no doubt to appear evident to us, that God offers himself to us in those men who bear his image, and that he requires the duties, which he does not want himself, to be performed to them, according to Ps. xvi. 2, where we read, " My goodness reaches not to thee, O Lord; towards the saints who are on the earth is my love." And surely the participation of the same nature, the need of so many things, and mutual intercourse, must allure us to mutual love, except we are harder than iron. But John meant another thing: he meant to shew how fallacious is the boast of every one who says that he loves God, and yet loves not God's image which is before his eyes.

21. *And this commandment.* This is a stronger argument, drawn from the authority and doctrine of Christ; for he not only gave a commandment respecting the love of God, but bade us also to love our brethren. We must therefore so begin with God, as that there may be at the same time a transition made to men.

CHAPTER V.

1. Whosoever believeth that Jesus is the Christ is born of God: and every one that loveth him that begat, loveth him also that is begotten of him.
2. By this we know that we love the children of God, when we love God, and keep his commandments.
3. For this is the love of God, that we keep his commandments: and his commandments are not grievous.
4. For whatsoever is born of God overcometh the world: and this is the victory that overcometh the world, *even* our faith.
5. Who is he that overcometh the world, but he that believeth that Jesus is the Son of God?

1. Omnis qui credit quòd Jesus est Christus, ex Deo genitus est; et omnis qui diligit eum qui genuit, diligit etiam eum qui genitus est ab eo.
2. In hoc cognoscimus quòd diligimus filios Dei, si Deum diligimus, et præcepta ejus servamus.
3. Hæc est dilectio Dei, ut præcepta ejus servemus, et præcepta ejus gravia non sunt.
4. Quoniam omne quod ex Deo genitum est, vincit mundum: et hæc est victoria quæ vincit mundum, fides nostra.
5. Quis est qui vincit mundum, nisi qui credit quòd Jesus est Filius Dei?

1. *Whosoever believeth.* He confirms by another reason, that faith and brotherly love are united; for since God regenerates us by faith, he must necessarily be loved by us as a Father; and this love embraces all his children. Then faith cannot be separated from love.

The first truth is, that all, born of God, believe that Jesus is the Christ; where, again, you see that Christ alone is set forth as the object of faith, as in him it finds righteousness, life, and every blessing that can be desired, and God in all that he is.[1] Hence the only true way of believing is when we direct our minds to him. Besides, to believe that he is the Christ, is to hope from him all those things which have been promised as to the Messiah.

Nor is the title, Christ, given him here without reason, for it designates the office to which he was appointed by the Father. As, under the Law, the full restoration of all things, righteousness and happiness, were promised through the Messiah; so at this day the whole of this is more clearly set forth in the gospel. Then Jesus cannot be received as Christ, except salvation be sought from him, since for this end he was sent by the Father, and is daily offered to us.

[1] Literally, " and the whole God—*totum Deum.*"—*Ed.*

Hence the Apostle declares that all they who really believe have been born of God ; for faith is far above the reach of the human mind, so that we must be drawn to Christ by our heavenly Father ; for not any of us can ascend to him by his own strength. And this is what the Apostle teaches us in his Gospel, when he says, that those who believe in the name of the only-begotten, were not born of blood nor of the flesh. (John i. 13.) And Paul says, that we are endued, not with the spirit of this world, but with the Spirit that is from God, that we may know the things given us by him. (1 Cor. ii. 12.) For eye hath not seen, nor ear heard, nor the mind conceived, the reward laid up for those who love God ; but the Spirit alone penetrates into this mystery. And further, as Christ is given to us for sanctification, and brings with him the Spirit of regeneration, in short, as he unites us to his own body, it is also another reason why no one can have faith, except he is born of God.

Loveth him also that is begotten of him. Augustine and some others of the ancients have applied this to Christ, but not correctly. For though the Apostle uses the singular number, yet he includes all the faithful ; and the context plainly shews that his purpose was no other than to trace up brotherly love to faith as its fountain. It is, indeed, an argument drawn from the common course of nature ; but what is seen among men is transferred to God.[1]

But we must observe, that the Apostle does not so speak of the faithful only, and pass by those who are without, as though the former are alone to be loved, and no care and no account to be had for the latter ; but he teaches us as it were by this first exercise to love all without exception, when he bids us to make a beginning with the godly.[2]

2. *By this we know.* He briefly shews in these words what true love is, even that which is towards God. He has

---

[1] The literal rendering of the verse is as follows,—

" Every one who believes that Jesus is the Christ has been begotten by God ; and every one who loves the begetter loves also the begotten by him."—*Ed.*

[2] The subject no doubt is love to the *brethren* throughout ; and this passage shews this most clearly. Love to all is evidently a duty, but it is not taught here.—*Ed.*

hitherto taught us that there is never a true love to God, except when our brethren are also loved; for this is ever its effect. But he now teaches us that men are rightly and duly loved, when God holds the primacy. And it is a necessary definition; for it often happens, that we love men apart from God, as unholy and carnal friendships regard only private advantages or some other vanishing objects. As, then, he had referred first to the effect, so he now refers to the cause; for his purpose is to shew that mutual love ought to be in such a way cultivated that God may be honoured.

To the love of God he joins the keeping of the law, and justly so; for when we love God as our Father and Lord, reverence must necessarily be connected with love. Besides, God cannot be separated from himself. As, then, he is the fountain of all righteousness and equity, he who loves him must necessarily have his heart prepared to render obedience to righteousness. The love of God, then, is not idle or inactive.[1]

But from this passage we also learn what is the keeping of the law. For if, when constrained only by fear, we obey God by keeping his commandments, we are very far off from true obedience. Then, the first thing is, that our hearts should be devoted to God in willing reverence, and then, that our life should be formed according to the rule of the law. This is what Moses meant when, in giving a summary of the law, he said, "O Israel, what does the Lord thy God require of thee, but to love him and to obey him?" (Deut. x. 12.)

3. *His commandments are not grievous.* This has been added, lest difficulties, as it is usually the case, should damp or lessen our zeal. For they who with a cheerful mind and great ardour have pursued a godly and holy life, afterwards grow weary, finding their strength inadequate. Therefore John, in order to rouse our efforts, says that God's commandments are not grievous.

But it may, on the other hand, be objected and said that we have found it far otherwise by experience, and that Scripture testifies that the yoke of the law is insupportable.

---

[1] "The love of God," here clearly means love to God: it is the love of which God is the object.—*Ed.*

(Acts xv. 2.) The reason also is evident, for as the denial of self is, as it were, a prelude to the keeping of the law, can we say that it is easy for a man to deny himself? nay, since the law is spiritual, as Paul, in Rom. vii. 14, teaches us, and we are nothing but flesh, there must be a great discord between us and the law of God. To this I answer, that this difficulty does not arise from the nature of the law, but from our corrupt flesh; and this is what Paul expressly declares; for after having said that it was impossible for the law to confer righteousness on us, he immediately throws the blame on our flesh.

This explanation fully reconciles what is said by Paul and by David, which apparently seems wholly contradictory. Paul makes the law the minister of death, declares that it effects nothing but to bring on us the wrath of God, that it was given to increase sin, that it lives in order to kill us. David, on the other hand, says that it is sweeter than honey, and more desirable than gold; and among other recommendations he mentions the following—that it cheers hearts, converts to the Lord, and quickens. But Paul compares the law with the corrupt nature of man; hence arises the conflict: but David shews how they think and feel whom God by his Spirit has renewed; hence the sweetness and delight of which the flesh knows nothing. And John has not omitted this difference; for he confines to God's children these words, *God's commandments are not grievous*, lest any one should take them generally; and he intimates that it comes through the power of the Spirit, that it is not grievous nor wearisome to us to obey God.

The question, however, seems not as yet to be fully answered; for the faithful, though ruled by the Spirit of God, yet carry on a hard contest with their own flesh; and how much soever they may toil, they yet hardly perform the half of their duty; nay, they almost fail under their burden, as though they stood, as they say, between the sanctuary and the steep. We see how Paul groaned as one held captive, and exclaimed that he was wretched, because he could not fully serve God. My reply to this is, that the law is said to be easy, as far as we are endued with heavenly power, and overcome the lusts of the flesh. For however the flesh may resist, yet the faithful find that there is no real enjoyment except in following God.

It must further be observed, that John does not speak of the law only, which contains nothing but commands, but connects with it the paternal indulgence of God, by which the rigour of the law is mitigated. As, then, we know that we are graciously forgiven by the Lord, when our works do not come up to the law, this renders us far more prompt to obey, according to what we find in Ps. cxxx. 4, "With thee is propitiation, that thou mayest be feared." Hence, then, is the facility of keeping the law, because the faithful, being sustained by pardon, do not despond when they come short of what they ought to be. The Apostle, in the meantime, reminds us that we must fight, in order that we may serve the Lord; for the whole world hinders us to go where the Lord calls us. Then, he only keeps the law who courageously resists the world.

4. *This is the victory.* As he had said that all who are born of God overcome the world, he also sets forth the way of overcoming it. For it might be still asked, whence comes this victory? He then makes the victory over the world to depend on faith.[1]

This passage is remarkable: for though Satan continually repeats his dreadful and horrible onsets, yet the Spirit of God, declaring that we are beyond the reach of danger, removes fear, and animates us to fight with courage. And

---

[1] The words literally are,—

"For every thing begotten by God overcomes the world," &c. The neuter gender is used for the masculine, "every thing" for "every one," as in the first verse; or according to כל in Hebrew, it is used in a plural sense, for πάντες, as in John xvii. 2, "that all (πᾶν) which thou hast given him, he should give them (αὐτοῖς) eternal life."

Macknight and others have said that the neuter gender is used in order to comprehend all sorts of persons, males and females, young and old, Jews and Gentiles, bond or free. Why, then, was not the neuter gender used in the first verse? It is clearly a peculiarity of style, and nothing else, and ought not to be retained in a translation.

"Victory" stands for that which brings victory, the effect for the cause; or it may designate the person, as νίκη means sometimes the goddess of victory.—"And this the conqueress who conquers the world, even our faith."—*Ed.*

the past time is more emphatical than the present or the future; for he says, *that has overcome*, in order that we might feel certain, as though the enemy had been already put to flight. It is, indeed, true, that our warfare continues through life, that our conflicts are daily, nay, that new and various battles are every moment on every side stirred up against us by the enemy; but as God does not arm us only for one day, and as faith is not that of one day, but is the perpetual work of the Holy Spirit, we are already partakers of victory, as though we had already conquered.

This confidence does not, however, introduce indifference, but renders us always anxiously intent on fighting. For the Lord thus bids his people to be certain, while yet he would not have them to be secure; but on the contrary, he declares that they have already overcome, in order that they may fight more courageously and more strenuously.

The term *world* has here a wide meaning, for it includes whatever is adverse to the Spirit of God: thus, the corruption of our nature is a part of the world; all lusts, all the crafts of Satan, in short, whatever leads us away from God. Having such a force to contend with, we have an immense war to carry on, and we should have been already conquered before coming to the contest, and we should be conquered a hundred times daily, had not God promised to us the victory. But God encourages us to fight by promising us the victory. But as this promise secures to us perpetually the invincible power of God, so, on the other hand, it annihilates all the strength of men. For the Apostle does not teach us here that God only brings some help to us, so that being aided by him, we may be sufficiently able to resist; but he makes victory to depend on faith alone; and faith receives from another that by which it overcomes. They then take away from God what is his own, who sing triumph to their own power.

5. *Who is he that overcometh the world.* This is a reason for the previous sentence; that is, we conquer by faith, because we derive strength from Christ; as Paul also says, "I can do all things through him that strengtheneth me," (Phil. iv. 13.) He only then can conquer Satan and the world, and

not succumb to his own flesh, who, diffident as to himself, recumbs on Christ's power alone. For by *faith* he means a real apprehension of Christ, or an effectual laying hold on him, by which we apply his power to ourselves.

6. This is he that came by water and blood, *even* Jesus Christ; not by water only, but by water and blood: and it is the Spirit that beareth witness, because the Spirit is truth.	6. Hic est qui venit per aquam et sanguinem, Jesum Christum ; non in aqua solum, sed in aqua et sanguine; et Spiritus est qui testificatur, quandoquidem Spiritus est veritas.
7. For there are three that bear record in heaven, the Father, the Word, and the Holy Ghost: and these three are one.	7. Nam tres sunt qui testificantur in cœlo, Pater, Sermo, et Spiritus Sanctus; et hi tres unum sunt.
8. And there are three that bear witness in earth, the spirit, and the water, and the blood: and these three agree in one.	8. Et tres sunt qui testificantur in terra, Spiritus, aqua et sanguis; et hi tres in unum conveniunt.
9. If we receive the witness of men, the witness of God is greater: for this is the witness of God which he hath testified of his Son.	9. Si testimonium hominum recipimus, testimonium Dei majus est; quoniam hoc est testimonium Dei, quod testificatus est de Filio suo.

6. *This is he that came.* That our faith may rest safely on Christ, he says the real substance of the shadows of the law appears in him. For I doubt not but that he alludes by the words *water and blood* to the ancient rites of the law. The comparison, moreover, is intended for this end, not only that we may know that the Law of Moses was abolished by the coming of Christ, but that we may seek in him the fulfilment of those things which the ceremonies formerly typified. And though they were of various kinds, yet under these two the Apostle denotes the whole perfection of holiness and righteousness, for by water was all filth washed away, so that men might come before God pure and clean, and by blood was expiation made, and a pledge given of a full reconciliation with God; but the law only adumbrated by external symbols what was to be really and fully performed by the Messiah.

John then fitly proves that Jesus is the Christ of the Lord formerly promised, because he brought with him that by which he sanctifies us wholly.

And, indeed, as to the blood by which Christ reconciled God, there is no doubt, but how he came by water may be questioned. But that the reference is to baptism is not probable. I certainly think that John sets forth here the fruit and effect of what he recorded in the Gospel history; for what he says there, that water and blood flowed from the side of Christ, is no doubt to be deemed a miracle. I know that such a thing does happen naturally to the dead; but it happened through God's purpose, that Christ's side became the fountain of blood and water, in order that the faithful may know that cleansing (of which the ancient baptisms were types) is found in him, and that they might know that what all the sprinklings of blood formerly presignified was fulfilled. On this subject we dwelt more at large on the ninth and tenth chapters of the Epistle to the Hebrews.

And it is the Spirit that beareth witness. He shews in this clause how the faithful know and feel the power of Christ, even because the Spirit renders them certain; and that their faith might not vacillate, he adds, that a full and real firmness or stability is produced by the testimony of the Spirit. And he calls the Spirit *truth,* because his authority is indubitable, and ought to be abundantly sufficient for us.

7. *There are three that bear record in heaven.* The whole of this verse has been by some omitted. Jerome thinks that this has happened through design rather than through mistake, and that indeed only on the part of the Latins. But as even the Greek copies do not agree, I dare not assert any thing on the subject. Since, however, the passage flows better when this clause is added, and as I see that it is found in the best and most approved copies, I am inclined to receive it as the true reading.[1] And the meaning would

[1] *Calvin* probably refers to printed copies in his day, and not to Greek MSS. As far as the authority of MSS. and versions and quotations goes, the passage is spurious, for it is not found in *any* of the Greek MSS prior to the 16th century, nor in *any* of the *early versions,* except the Latin, nor in some of the copies of that version; nor is it quoted by any of the early *Greek* fathers, nor by early *Latin* fathers, except a very few, and even their quotations have been disputed. These are *facts* which no refined conjectures can upset; and it is to be regretted that learned men, such as the late Bishop *Burgess,* should have laboured and toiled in an attempt so hopeless as to establish the genuineness of this verse, or rather of a part of this verse, and of the beginning of the following. The whole passage is as follows, the spurious part being put within crotchets,—

be, that God, in order to confirm most abundantly our faith in Christ, testifies in three ways that we ought to acquiesce in him. For as our faith acknowledges three persons in the one divine essence, so it is called in so many ways to Christ that it may rest on him.

When he says, *These three are one*, he refers not to essence, but on the contrary to consent; as though he had said, that the Father and his eternal Word and Spirit harmoniously testify the same thing respecting Christ. Hence some copies have εἰς ἕν, "for one." But though you read ἓν εἰσιν, as in other copies, yet there is no doubt but that the Father, the Word and the Spirit are said to be one, in the same sense in which afterwards the blood and the water and the Spirit are said to agree in one.

But as the Spirit, who is one witness, is mentioned twice, it seems to be an unnecessary repetition. To this I reply, that since he testifies of Christ in various ways, a twofold testimony is fitly ascribed to him. For the Father, together with his eternal Wisdom and Spirit, declares Jesus to be the Christ as it were authoritatively, then, in this case, the sole majesty of the Deity is to be considered by us. But as the Spirit, dwelling in our hearts, is an earnest, a pledge, and a seal, to confirm that decree, so he thus again speaks on earth by his grace.

But inasmuch as all do not receive this reading, I will therefore so expound what follows, as though the Apostle referred to the witnesses only on the earth.

8. *There are three.* He applies what had been said of water and blood to his own purpose, in order that they who reject Christ might have no excuse; for by testimonies abun-

---

7. " For there are three who bear witness [in heaven, the Father, the Word, and the Holy Ghost; and these three are one:
8. And there are three who bear witness in earth,] the Spirit and the water and the blood; and these three agree in one."

As to the construction of the passage, as far as grammar and sense are concerned, it may do with or without the interpolation equally the same. What has been said to the contrary on this point, seems to be nothing of a decisive character, in no way sufficient to shew that the words are not spurious. Indeed, the passage reads better without the interpolated words; and as to the sense, that is, the sense in which they are commonly taken by the advocates of their genuineness, it has no connexion whatever with the general drift of the passage.—*Ed.*

dantly strong and clear, he proves that it is he who had been formerly promised, inasmuch as water and blood, being the pledges and the effects of salvation, really testify that he had been sent by God. He adds a third witness, the Holy Spirit, who yet holds the first place, for without him the water and blood would have flowed without any benefit; for it is he who seals on our hearts the testimony of the water and blood; it is he who by his power makes the fruit of Christ's death to come to us; yea, he makes the blood shed for our redemption to penetrate into our hearts, or, to say all in one word, he makes Christ with all his blessings to become ours. So Paul, in Rom. i. 4, after having said that Christ by his resurrection manifested himself to be the Son of God, immediately adds, "Through the sanctification of the Spirit." For whatever signs of divine glory may shine forth in Christ, they would yet be obscure to us and escape our vision, were not the Holy Spirit to open for us the eyes of faith.

Readers may now understand why John adduced the Spirit as a witness together with the water and the blood, even because it is the peculiar office of the Spirit, to cleanse our consciences by the blood of Christ, to cause the cleansing effected by it to be efficacious. On this subject some remarks are made at the beginning of the Second Epistle of Peter, where he uses nearly the same mode of speaking, that is, that the Holy Spirit cleanses our hearts by the sprinkling of the blood of Christ.[1]

---

[1] If we exclude the words deemed interpolated, we may read the passage thus:—

" This is he who came with water and blood, even Jesus Christ; not with water only, but with water and blood: the Spirit also beareth witness, for (or seeing that) the Spirit is truth (or, is true); because there are three who bear witness, the Spirit, the water, and the blood, and these three agree in one."

We see hence a reason why the Spirit is said to be true, even because he is not alone, for the water and the blood concur with him. Thus a testimony is formed consistently with the requirement of the law. We hence also see the import of what is stated when the testimony of men is mentioned, as though he had said, The testimony of three men is received as valid, how much more valid is the testimony of God, which has three witnesses in its behalf? It is called God's testimony, because the witnesses have been ordered and appointed by him.

When it is said that he came with water and blood, the meaning is, that

But from these words we may learn, that faith does not lay hold on a bare or an empty Christ, but that his power is at the same time vivifying. For to what purpose has Christ been sent on the earth, except to reconcile God by the sacrifice of his death? except the office of washing had been allotted to him by the Father?

It may however be objected, that the distinction here mentioned is superfluous, because Christ cleansed us by expiating our sins; then the Apostle mentions the same thing twice. I indeed allow that cleansing is included in expiation; therefore I made no difference between the water and the blood, as though they were distinct; but if any one of us considers his own infirmity, he will readily acknowledge that it is not in vain or without reason that blood is distinguished from the water. Besides, the Apostle, as it has been stated, alludes to the rites of the law; and God, on account of human infirmity, had formerly appointed, not only sacrifices, but also washings. And the Apostle meant distinctly to show that the reality of both has been exhibited in Christ, and on this account he had said before, "Not by water only," for he means, that not only some part of our salvation is found in Christ, but the whole of it, so that nothing is to be sought elsewhere.

9. *If we receive the witness*, or testimony, *of men*. He proves, reasoning from the less to the greater, how ungrateful men are when they reject Christ, who has been approved, as he has related, by God; for if in worldly affairs we stand to the words of men, who may lie and deceive, how unreasonable it is that God should have less credit given to him, when sitting as it were on his own throne, where he is the supreme judge. Then our own corruption alone prevents us to receive Christ, since he gives us full proof for believing in his power. Besides, he calls not only that the testimony of

---

he came, having water and blood; the proposition διὰ has sometimes this meaning, and it is changed in the second clause into ἐν. We meet with similar instances in 2 Cor. iii. 11, and in iv. 11. See Rom. ii. 27; iv. 11.

According to this construction, the explanation of *Calvin* is alone the right one, that the water means cleansing, and the blood expiation, the terms being borrowed from the rites of the law; and a reference is also made to the law when the witness of men is mentioned.—*Ed.*

God which the Spirit imprints on our hearts, but also that which we derive from the water and the blood. For that power of cleansing and expiating was not earthly, but heavenly. Hence the blood of Christ is not to be estimated according to the common manner of men; but we must rather look to the design of God, who ordained it for blotting out sins, and also to that divine efficacy which flows from it.

9. —For this is the witness of God which he hath testified of his Son.
10. He that believeth on the Son of God hath the witness in himself: he that believeth not God hath made him a liar; because he believeth not the record that God gave of his Son.
11. And this is the record, that God hath given to us eternal life; and this life is in his Son.
12. He that hath the Son hath life; *and* he that hath not the Son of God hath not life.

9. —Porrò hoc est testimonium Dei, quod testificatus est de Filio suo.
10. Qui credit in Filium Dei, habet testimonium in seipso; qui non credit Deo, mendacem facit eum; quia non credidit in testimonium quod testificatus est Deus de Filio suo.
11. Et hoc est testimonium, quòd vitam æternam dedit nobis Deus; et hæc vita in Filio ejus est.
12. Qui habet Filium, habet vitam; qui non habet Filium Dei, vitam non habet.

9. *For this is the witness,* or testimony, *of God.* The particle ὅτι does not mean here the cause, but is to be taken as explanatory; for the Apostle, after having reminded us that God deserves to be believed much more than men, now adds, that we can have no faith in God, except by believing in Christ, because God sets him alone before us and makes us to stand in him. He hence infers that we believe safely and with tranquil minds in Christ, because God by his authority warrants our faith. He does not say that God speaks outwardly, but that every one of the godly feels within that God is the author of his faith. It hence appears how different from faith is a fading opinion dependent on something else.

10. *He that believeth not.* As the faithful possess this benefit, that they know themselves to be beyond the danger of erring, because they have God as their foundation; so he makes the ungodly to be guilty of extreme blasphemy, because they charge God with falsehood. Doubtless nothing is more valued by God than his own truth, therefore no wrong more atrocious can be done to him, than to rob him of this honour. Then in order to induce us to believe, he takes an argument from the opposite side; for if to make

God a liar be a horrible and execrable impiety, because then what especially belongs to him is taken away, who would not dread to withhold faith from the gospel, in which God would have himself to be counted singularly true and faithful? This ought to be carefully observed.

Some wonder why God commends faith so much, why unbelief is so severely condemned. But the glory of God is implicated in this; for since he designed to shew a special instance of his truth in the gospel, all they who reject Christ there offered to them, leave nothing to him. Therefore, though we may grant that a man in other parts of his life is like an angel, yet his sanctity is diabolical as long as he rejects Christ. Thus we see some under the Papacy vastly pleased with the mere mask of sanctity, while they still most obstinately resist the gospel. Let us then understand, that it is the beginning of true religion, obediently to embrace this doctrine, which he has so strongly confirmed by his testimony.

11. *That God hath given us eternal life.* Having now set forth the benefit, he invites us to believe. It is, indeed, a reverence due to God, immediately to receive, as beyond controversy, whatever he declares to us. But since he freely offers life to us, our ingratitude will be intolerable, except with prompt faith we receive a doctrine so sweet and so lovely. And, doubtless, the words of the Apostle are intended to shew, that we ought not only reverently to obey the gospel, lest we should affront God; but that we ought to love it, because it brings to us eternal life. We hence also learn what is especially to be sought in the gospel, even the free gift of salvation; for that God there exhorts us to repentance and fear, ought not to be separated from the grace of Christ.

But the Apostle, that he might keep us altogether in Christ, again repeats that life is found in him; as though he had said, that no other way of obtaining life has been appointed for us by God the Father. And the Apostle, indeed, briefly includes here three things: that we are all given up to death until God in his gratuitous favour restores us to life; for he plainly declares that life is a gift from God: and hence also it follows that we are destitute of it, and that it cannot be acquired by merits; secondly, he teaches us that this life is conferred on us by the gospel, because there the goodness and the paternal love of God is made known to us; lastly, he says that we cannot otherwise become partakers of this life than by believing in Christ.

12. *He that hath not the Son.* This is a confirmation of the last sentence. It ought, indeed, to have been sufficient, that God made life to be in none but in Christ, that it might be sought in him; but lest any one should turn away to another, he excludes all from the hope of life who seek it not in Christ. We know what it is to have Christ, for he is possessed by faith. He then shews that all who are separated from the body of Christ are without life.

But this seems inconsistent with reason; for history shews that there have been great men, endued with heroic virtues, who yet were wholly unacquainted with Christ; and it seems unreasonable that men of so great eminence had no honour. To this I answer, that we are greatly mistaken if we think that whatever is eminent in our eyes is approved by God; for, as it is said in Luke xvi. 15, "What is highly esteemed by men is an abomination with God." For as the filthiness of the heart is hid from us, we are satisfied with the external appearance; but God sees that under this is concealed the foulest filth. It is, therefore, no wonder if specious virtues, flowing from an impure heart, and tending to no right end, have an ill odour to him. Besides, whence comes purity, whence a genuine regard for religion, except from the Spirit of Christ? There is, then, nothing worthy of praise except in Christ.

There is, further, another reason which removes every doubt; for the righteousness of men is in the remission of sins. If you take away this, the sure curse of God and eternal death awaits all. Christ alone is he who reconciles the Father to us, as he has once for all pacified him by the sacrifice of the cross. It hence follows, that God is propitious to none but in Christ, nor is there righteousness but in him.

Were any one to object and say, that Cornelius, as mentioned by Luke, (Acts x. 2,) was accepted of God before he was called to the faith of the gospel : to this I answer shortly, that God sometimes so deals with us, that the seed of faith appears immediately on the first day. Cornelius had no clear and distinct knowledge of Christ ; but as he had some perception of God's mercy, he must at the same time understand something of a Mediator. But as God acts in ways hidden and wonderful, let us disregard those speculations which profit nothing, and hold only to that plain way of salvation, which he has made known to us.

13. These things have I written unto you that believe on the name of the Son of God, that ye may know that ye have eternal life, and that ye may believe on the name of the Son of God.	13. Hæc scripsi vobis credentibus in nomen Filii Dei, ut sciatis quòd vitam habetis æternam, et ut credatis in nomen Filii Dei.
14. And this is the confidence that we have in him, that, if we ask any thing according to his will, he heareth us.	14. Atque hæc est fiducia quam habemus erga eum, quòd si quid petierimus secundum voluntatem ejus, audit nos.
15. And if we know that he hear us, whatsoever we ask, we know that we have the petitions that we desired of him.	15 Si autem novimus quòd audit nos, quum quid petierimus ; novimus quòd habemus petitiones quas postulavimus ab eo.

13. *These things have I written unto you.* As there ought to be a daily progress in faith, so he says that he wrote to those who had already believed, so that they might believe more firmly and with greater certainty, and thus enjoy a fuller confidence as to eternal life. Then the use of doctrine is, not only to initiate the ignorant in the knowledge of Christ, but also to confirm those more and more who have been already taught. It therefore becomes us assiduously to attend to the duty of learning, that our faith may increase through the whole course of our life. For there are still in us many remnants of unbelief, and so weak is our faith that what we believe is not yet really believed except there be a fuller confirmation.

But we ought to observe the way in which faith is confirmed, even by having the office and power of Christ explained to us. For the Apostle says that he wrote these things, that is, that eternal life is to be sought nowhere else but in Christ, in order that they who were believers already might believe, that is, make progress in believing. It is therefore the duty of a godly teacher, in order to confirm disciples in the faith, to extol as much as possible the grace of Christ, so that being satisfied with that, we may seek nothing else.

As the Papists obscure this truth in various ways, and extenuate it, they shew sufficiently by this one thing that they care for nothing less than for the right doctrine of faith; yea, on this account, their schools ought to be more shunned than all the Scyllas and Charybdises in the world; for hardly any one can enter them without a sure shipwreck to his faith.

The Apostle teaches further in this passage, that Christ is the peculiar object of faith, and that to the faith which we have in his name is annexed the hope of salvation. For in this case the end of believing is, that we become the children and the heirs of God.

14. *And this is the confidence.* He commends the faith which he mentioned by its fruit, or he shews that in which our confidence especially is, that is, that the godly dare confidently to call on God; as also Paul speaks in Eph. iii. 12, that we have by faith access to God with confidence; and also in Rom. viii. 15, that the Spirit gives us a mouth to cry Abba, Father. And doubtless, were we driven away from an access to God, nothing could make us more miserable; but, on the other hand, provided this asylum be opened to us, we should be happy even in extreme evils; nay, this one thing renders our troubles blessed, because we surely know that God will be our deliverer, and relying on his paternal love towards us, we flee to him.

Let us, then, bear in mind this declaration of the Apostle, that calling on God is the chief trial of our faith, and that God is not rightly nor in faith called upon except we be fully persuaded that our prayers will not be in vain. For the Apostle denies that those who, being doubtful, hesitate, are endued with faith.

It hence appears that the doctrine of faith is buried and nearly extinct under the Papacy, for all certainty is taken away. They indeed mutter many prayers, and prattle much about praying to God; but they pray with doubtful and fluctuating hearts, and bid us to pray; and yet they even condemn this confidence which the Apostle requires as necessary.

According to his will. By this expression he meant by the way to remind us what is the right way or rule of praying, even when men subject their own wishes to God. For though God has promised to do whatsoever his people may ask, yet he does not allow them an unbridled liberty to ask whatever may come to their minds; but he has at the same time prescribed to them a law according to which they are to pray. And doubtless nothing is better for us than this restriction; for if it was allowed to every one of us to ask what he pleased, and if God were to indulge us in our wishes, it would be to provide very badly for us. For what may be expedient we know not; nay, we boil over with corrupt and hurtful desires. But God supplies a twofold remedy, lest we should pray otherwise than according to what his own will has prescribed; for he teaches us by his word what he would have us to ask, and he has also set over us his Spirit as our guide and ruler, to restrain our feelings, so as not to suffer them to wander beyond due bounds. For what or how to pray, we know not, says Paul, but the Spirit helpeth our infirmity, and excites in us unutterable groans. (Rom. viii. 26.) We ought also to ask the mouth of the Lord to direct and guide our prayers; for God in his promises has fixed for us, as it has been said, the right way of praying.

15. *And if we know.* This is not a superfluous repetition, as it seems to be; for what the Apostle declared in general respecting the success of prayer, he now affirms in a special manner that the godly pray or ask for nothing from God but what they obtain. But when he says that all the petitions of the faithful are heard, he speaks of right and humble petitions, and such as are consistent with the rule of obedience. For the faithful do not give loose reins to their desires, nor indulge in anything that may please them, but always regard in their prayers what God commands.

This, then, is an application of the general doctrine to the special and private benefit of every one, lest the faithful should doubt that God is propitious to prayers of each individual, so that with quiet minds they may wait until the Lord should perform what they pray for, and that being thus relieved from all trouble and anxiety, they may cast on God the burden of their cares. This ease and security ought not, however, to abate in them their earnestness in prayer, for he who is certain of a happy event ought not to abstain from praying to God. For the certainty of faith by no means generates indifference or sloth. The Apostle meant that every one should be tranquil in his necessities when he has deposited his sighs in the bosom of God.

16. If any man see his brother sin a sin *which is* not unto death, he shall ask, and he shall give him life for them that sin not unto death. There is a sin unto death: I do not say that he shall pray for it.	16. Si quis viderit fratrem suum peccantem peccato non ad mortem, petet; et dabit illi vitam peccanti, dico, non ad mortem: est peccatum ad mortem; non pro illo, dico, ut quis roget.
17. All unrighteousness is sin: and there is a sin not unto death.	17. Omnis injustitia peccatum est; et est peccatum non ad mortem.
18. We know that whosoever is born of God sinneth not; but he that is begotten of God keepeth himself, and that wicked one toucheth him not.	18. Novimus quòd quisquis ex Deo genitus est, non peccat; sed qui genitus est ex Deo servat seipsum, et malignus non tangit eum.

16. *If any man.* The Apostle extends still further the benefits of that faith which he has mentioned, so that our prayers may also avail for our brethren. It is a great thing, that as soon as we are oppressed, God kindly invites us to himself, and is ready to give us help; but that he hears us asking for others, is no small confirmation to our faith, in order that we may be fully assured that we shall never meet with a repulse in our own case.

The Apostle in the meantime exhorts us to be mutually solicitous for the salvation of one another; and he would also have us to regard the falls of the brethren as stimulants to prayer. And surely it is an iron hardness to be touched with no pity, when we see souls redeemed by Christ's blood going to ruin. But he shews that there is at hand a remedy, by which brethren can aid brethren. He who will pray for the perishing, will, he says, restore life to him; though the words, "he shall give," may be applied to God, as though it was said, God will grant to your prayers the life of a brother.

But the sense will still be the same, that the prayers of the faithful so far avail as to rescue a brother from death. If we understand man to be intended, that he will give life to a brother, it is a hyperbolical expression; it however contains nothing inconsistent; for what is given to us by the gratuitous goodness of God, yea, what is granted to others for our sake, we are said to give to others. So great a benefit ought to stimulate us not a little to ask for our brethren the forgiveness of sins. And when the Apostle recommends sympathy to us, he at the same time reminds us how much we ought to avoid the cruelty of condemning our brethren, or an extreme rigour in despairing of their salvation.

A sin which is not unto death. That we may not cast away all hope of the salvation of those who sin, he shews that God does not so grievously punish their falls as to repudiate them. It hence follows that we ought to deem them brethren, since God retains them in the number of his children. For he denies that sins are to death, not only those by which the saints daily offend, but even when it happens that God's wrath is grievously provoked by them. For as long as room for pardon is left, death does not wholly retain its dominion.

The Apostle, however, does not here distinguish between venial and mortal sin, as it was afterwards commonly done. For altogether foolish is that distinction which prevails under the Papacy. The Sorbons acknowledge that there is hardly a mortal sin, except there be the grossest baseness, such as may be, as it were, tangible. Thus in venial sins they think that there may be the greatest filth, if hidden in the soul. In short, they suppose that all the fruits of original sin, provided they appear not outwardly, are washed away by the slight sprinkling of holy water! And what wonder is it, since they regard not as blasphemous sins, doubts respecting God's grace, or any lusts or evil desires, except they are consented to? If the soul of man be assailed by unbelief, if impatience tempts him to rage against God, whatever monstrous lusts may allure him, all these are to the Papists lighter than to be deemed sins, at least after baptism. It is then no wonder, that they make venial offences of the greatest crimes ; for they weigh them in their own balance and not in the balance of God.

But among the faithful this ought to be an indubitable truth, that whatever is contrary to God's law is sin, and in its nature mortal ; for where there is a transgression of the law, there is sin and death.

What, then, is the meaning of the Apostle? He denies that sins are mortal, which, though worthy of death, are yet not thus punished by God. He therefore does not estimate sins in themselves, but forms a judgment of them according to the paternal kindness of God, which pardons the guilt, where yet the fault is. In short, God does not give over to death those whom he has restored to life, though it depends not on them that they are not alienated from life.

There is a sin unto death. I have already said that the sin to which there is no hope of pardon left, is thus called. But it may be asked, what this is ; for it must be very atrocious, when God thus so severely punishes it. It may be gathered from the context, that it is not, as they say, a partial fall, or a transgresssion of a single commandment, but apostasy, by which men wholly alienate themselves from God. For the Apostle afterwards adds, that the children of God do not sin, that is, that they do not forsake God, and wholly surrender themselves to Satan, to be his slaves. Such a defection, it is no wonder that it is mortal ; for God never thus deprives his own people of the grace of the Spirit ; but they ever retain some spark of true religion. They must then be reprobate and given up to destruction, who thus fall away so as to have no fear of God.

Were any one to ask, whether the door of salvation is closed against their repentance ; the answer is obvious, that as they are given up to a reprobate mind, and are destitute of the Holy Spirit, they cannot do anything else, than with obstinate minds, become worse and worse, and add sins to sins. Moreover, as the sin and blasphemy against the Spirit ever brings with it a defection of this kind, there is no doubt but that it is here pointed out.

But it may be asked again, by what evidences can we

know that a man's fall is fatal; for except the knowledge of this was certain, in vain would the Apostle have made this exception, that they were not to pray for a sin of this kind. It is then right to determine sometimes, whether the fallen is without hope, or whether there is still a place for a remedy. This, indeed, is what I allow, and what is evident beyond dispute from this passage; but as this very seldom happens, and as God sets before us the infinite riches of his grace, and bids us to be merciful according to his own example, we ought not rashly to conclude that any one has brought on himself the judgment of eternal death; on the contrary, love should dispose us to hope well. But if the impiety of some appear to us not otherwise than hopeless, as though the Lord pointed it out by the finger, we ought not to contend with the just judgment of God, or seek to be more merciful than he is.

17. *All unrighteousness.* This passage may be explained variously. If you take it adversatively, the sense would not be unsuitable, " Though all unrighteousness is sin, yet every sin is not unto death." And equally suitable is another meaning, " As sin is every unrighteousness, hence it follows that every sin is not unto death." Some take *all unrighteousness* for complete unrighteousness, as though the Apostle had said, that the sin of which he spoke was the summit of unrighteousness. I, however, am more disposed to embrace the first or the second explanation; and as the result is nearly the same, I leave it to the judgment of readers to determine which of the two is the more appropriate.

18. *We know that whosoever is born of God.* If you suppose that God's children are wholly pure and free from all sin, as the fanatics contend, then the Apostle is inconsistent with himself; for he would thus take away the duty of mutual prayer among brethren. Then he says that those *sin not* who do not wholly fall away from the grace of God; and hence he inferred that prayer ought to be made for all the children of God, because they sin not unto death. A proof is added, That every one, born of God, keeps himself, that is, keeps himself in the fear of God; nor does he suffer

himself to be so led away, as to lose all sense of religion, and to surrender himself wholly to the devil and the flesh.

For when he says, that he is not *touched* by *that wicked one*, reference is made to a deadly wound; for the children of God do not remain untouched by the assaults of Satan, but they ward off his strokes by the shield of faith, so that they do not penetrate into the heart. Hence spiritual life is never extinguished in them. This is not to sin. Though the faithful indeed fall through the infirmity of the flesh, yet they groan under the burden of sin, loathe themselves, and cease not to fear God.

Keepeth himself. What properly belongs to God he transfers to us; for were any one of us the keeper of his own salvation, it would be a miserable protection. Therefore Christ asks the Father to keep us, intimating that it is not done by our own strength. The advocates of free-will lay hold on this expression, that they may thence prove, that we are preserved from sin, partly by God's grace, and partly by our own power. But they do not perceive that the faithful have not from themselves the power of preservation of which the Apostle speaks. Nor does he, indeed, speak of their power, as though they could keep themselves by their own strength; but he only shews that they ought to resist Satan, so that they may never be fatally wounded by his darts. And we know that we fight with no other weapons but those of God. Hence the faithful keep themselves from sin, as far as they are kept by God. (John xvii. 11.)

19. *And* we know that we are of God, and the whole world lieth in wickedness.

20. And we know that the Son of God is come, and hath given us an understanding, that we may know him that is true; and we are in him that is true, *even* in his Son Jesus Christ. This is the true God, and eternal life.

21. Little children, keep yourselves from idols. Amen.

19. Novimus quòd ex Deo sumus, et mundus totus in maligno positus est.

20. Novimus autem quòd Filius Dei venit, et dedit nobis intelligentiam, ut cognoscamus illum verum; et sumus in ipso vero, in Filio ejus Jesu Christo: Hic est verus Deus, et vita æterna.

21. Filioli, custodite vos ab idolis. Amen.

19. *We are of God.* He deduces an exhortation from his previous doctrine; for what he had declared in common as to the children of God, he now applies to those he was writ-

ing to ; and this he did, to stimulate them to beware of sin, and to encourage them to repel the onsets of Satan.

Let readers observe, that it is only true faith, that applies to us, so to speak, the grace of God ; for the Apostle acknowledges none as faithful, but those who have the dignity of being God's children. Nor does he indeed put probable conjecture, as the Sophists speak, for confidence ; for he says that we *know*. The meaning is, that as we have been born of God, we ought to strive to prove by our separation from the world, and by the sanctity of our life, that we have not been in vain called to so great an honour.

Now, this is an admonition very necessary for all the godly ; for wherever they turn their eyes, Satan has his allurements prepared, by which he seeks to draw them away from God. It would then be difficult for them to hold on in their course, were they not so to value their calling as to disregard all the hindrances of the world. Then, in order to be well prepared for the contest, these two things must be borne in mind, that the world is wicked, and that our calling is from God.

Under the term *world*, the Apostle no doubt includes the whole human race. By saying that it *lieth in the wicked one*, he represents it as being under the dominion of Satan. There is then no reason why we should hesitate to shun the world, which contemns God and delivers up itself into the bondage of Satan : nor is there a reason why we should fear its enmity, because it is alienated from God. In short, since corruption pervades all nature, the faithful ought to study self-denial ; and since nothing is seen in the world but wickedness and corruption, they must necessarily disregard flesh and blood that they may follow God. At the same time the other thing ought to be added, that God is he who has called them, that under his protection they may oppose all the machinations of the world and Satan.

20. *And we know that the Son of God is come.* As the children of God are assailed on every side, he, as we have said, encourages and exhorts them to persevere in resisting their enemies, and for this reason, because they fight under the banner of God, and certainly know that they are ruled

by his Spirit; but he now reminds them where this knowledge is especially to be found.

He then says that God has been so made known to us, that now there is no reason for doubting. The Apostle does not without reason dwell on this point; for except our faith is really founded on God, we shall never stand firm in the contest. For this purpose the Apostle shews that we have obtained through Christ a sure knowledge of the true God, so that we may not fluctuate in uncertainty.

By *true* God he does not mean one who tells the truth, but him who is really God; and he so calls him to distinguish him from all idols. Thus *true* is in opposition to what is fictitious; for it is $ἀληθινὸς$, and not $ἀληθής$. A similar passage is in John xvii. 3, "This is eternal life, to know thee, the only true God, and him whom thou hast sent, Jesus Christ." And he justly ascribes to Christ this office of illuminating our minds as to the knowledge of God. For, as he is the only true image of the invisible God, as he is the only interpreter of the Father, as he is the only guide of life, yea, as he is the life and light of the world and the truth, as soon as we depart from him, we necessarily become vain in our own devices.

And Christ is said to have *given us an understanding*, not only because he shews us in the gospel what sort of being is the true God, and also illuminates us by his Spirit; but because in Christ himself we have God manifested in the flesh, as Paul says, since in him dwells all the fulness of the Deity, and are hid all the treasures of knowledge and wisdom. (Col. ii. 9.) Thus it is that the face of God in a manner appears to us in Christ; not that there was no knowledge, or a doubtful knowledge of God, before the coming of Christ, but that now he manifests himself more fully and more clearly. And this is what Paul says in 2 Cor. iv. 6, that God, who formerly commanded light to shine out of darkness at the creation of the world, hath now shone in our hearts through the brightness of the knowledge of his glory in the face of Christ.

And it must be observed, that this gift is peculiar to the elect. Christ, indeed, kindles for all indiscriminately the torch of his gospel; but all have not the eyes of their minds opened to see it, but on the contrary Satan spreads the veil of blindness over many. Then the Apostle means the light which Christ kindles within in the hearts of his people, and which when once kindled, is never extinguished, though in some it may for a time be smothered.

We are in him that is true. By these words he reminds us how efficacious is that knowledge which he mentions, even because by it we are united to Christ and become one with God; for it has a living root, fixed in the heart, by which it comes that God lives in us and we in him. As he says, without a copulative, that we are *in him that is true, in his Son*, he seems to express the manner of our union with God, as though he had said, that we are in God through Christ.[1]

This is the true God. Though the Arians have attempted to elude this passage, and some agree with them at this day, yet we have here a remarkable testimony to the divinity of Christ. The Arians apply this passage to the Father, as though the Apostle should again repeat that he is the true God. But nothing could be more frigid than such a repetition. He has already twice testified that the true God is he who has been made known to us in Christ, why should he again add, *This is the true God?* It applies, indeed, most suitably to Christ; for after having taught us that Christ is the guide by whose hand we are led to God, he now, by way of amplifying, affirms that Christ is that God, lest we should think that we are to seek further; and he confirms this view by what is added, *and eternal life.* It is doubtless the same that is spoken of, as being the true God and eternal life. I pass by this, that the relative οὗτος usually refers to the last person. I say, then, that Christ is properly called eternal life; and that this mode of speaking perpetually occurs in John, no one can deny.

---

[1] It is rendered by some, "through his Son Jesus Christ." Our version, "even in his Son Jesus Christ," seems not to be right, as it makes "him that is true," to be the Son, while the reference is to God, as in the previous clause. The true meaning would be thus conveyed, "And we are in the true *God, being* in his Son Jesus Christ;" for to be in Christ, is to be in God. Three MSS., the Vulgate, and several of the Fathers, read thus, "and we are in his true Son Jesus Christ."—*Ed.*

The meaning is, that when we have Christ, we enjoy the true and eternal God, for nowhere else is he to be sought; and, secondly, that we become thus partakers of eternal life, because it is offered to us in Christ though hid in the Father. The origin of life is, indeed, the Father; but the fountain from which we are to draw it, is Christ.

21. *Keep yourselves from idols.* Though this be a separate sentence, yet it is as it were an appendix to the preceding doctrine. For the vivifying light of the Gospel ought to scatter and dissipate, not only darkness, but also all mists, from the minds of the godly. The Apostle not only condemns idolatry, but commands us to beware of all images and idols; by which he intimates, that the worship of God cannot continue uncorrupted and pure whenever men begin to be in love with idols or images. For so innate in us is superstition, that the least occasion will infect us with its contagion. Dry wood will not so easily burn when coals are put under it, as idolatry will lay hold on and engross the minds of men, when an occasion is given to them. And who does not see that images are the sparks? What! sparks do I say? nay, rather torches, which are sufficient to set the whole world on fire.

The Apostle at the same time does not only speak of statues, but also of altars, and includes all the instruments of superstitions. Moreover, the Papists are ridiculous, who pervert this passage and apply it to the statues of Jupiter and Mercury and the like, as though the Apostle did not teach generally, that there is a corruption of religion whenever a corporeal form is ascribed to God, or whenever statues and pictures form a part of his worship. Let us then remember that we ought carefully to continue in the spiritual worship of God, so as to banish far from us everything that may turn us aside to gross and carnal superstitions.

END OF THE FIRST EPISTLE OF JOHN.

COMMENTARIES

ON

THE EPISTLE OF JAMES.

THE ARGUMENT.

It appears from the writings of Jerome and Eusebius, that this Epistle was not formerly received by many Churches without opposition. There are also at this day some who do not think it entitled to authority. I, however, am inclined to receive it without controversy, because I see no just cause for rejecting it. For what seems in the second chapter to be inconsistent with the doctrine of free justification, we shall easily explain in its own place. Though he seems more sparing in proclaiming the grace of Christ than it behoved an Apostle to be, it is not surely required of all to handle the same arguments. The writings of Solomon differ much from those of David; while the former was intent on forming the outward man and teaching the precepts of civil life, the latter spoke continually of the spiritual worship of God, peace of conscience, God's mercy and gratuitous promise of salvation. But this diversity should not make us to approve of one, and to condemn the other. Besides, among the evangelists themselves there is so much difference in setting forth the power of Christ, that the other three, compared with John, have hardly sparks of that full brightness which appears so conspicuous in him, and yet we commend them all alike.

It is enough to make men to receive this Epistle, that it contains nothing unworthy of an Apostle of Christ. It is indeed full of instruction on various subjects, the benefit of which extends to every part of the Christian life; for there are here remarkable passages on patience, prayer to God, the excellency and fruit of heavenly truth, humility, holy duties, the restraining of the tongue, the cultivation of peace, the repressing of lusts, the contempt of the world, and the like things, which we shall separately discuss in their own places.

But as to the author, there is somewhat more reason for doubting. It is indeed certain that he was not the son of Zebedee, for Herod killed him shortly after our Lord's resurrection. The ancients are nearly unanimous in thinking that he was one of the disciples named Oblias and a relative of Christ, who was set over the Church at Jerusalem; and they supposed him to have been the person whom Paul mentioned with Peter and John, who he says were deemed pillars, (Gal. ii. 9.) But that one of the disciples was mentioned as one of the three pillars, and thus exalted above the other Apostles, does not seem to me probable. I am therefore rather inclined to the conjecture, that he of whom Paul speaks was the son of Alpheus. I do not yet deny that another was the ruler of the Church at Jerusalem, and one indeed from the college of the disciples; for the Apostles were not tied to any particular place. But whether of the two was the writer of this Epistle, it is not for me to say. That Oblias was certainly a man of great authority among the Jews, appears even from this, that as he had been cruelly put to death by the faction of an ungodly chief-priest, Josephus hesitated not to impute the destruction of the city in part to his death.

CHAPTER I.

1. James, a servant of God and of the Lord Jesus Christ, to the twelve tribes which are scattered abroad, greeting.

2 My brethren, count it all joy when ye fall into divers temptations;

3. Knowing *this*, that the trying of your faith worketh patience.

4. But let patience have *her* perfect work, that ye may be perfect and entire, wanting nothing.

1. Jacobus, Dei ac Domini Jesu Christi servus, duodecim tribubus quæ in dispersione sunt, salutem.

2. Omne gaudium existimate, fratres mei, quum in tentationes varias incideritis;

3. Scientes quòd probatio fidei vestræ, patientiam operatur.

4. Patientia verò opus perfectum habeat, ut sitis perfecti et integri, in nullo deficientes.

1. *To the twelve tribes.* When the ten tribes were banished, the Assyrian king placed them in different parts. Afterwards, as it usually happens in the revolutions of kingdoms (such as then took place,) it is very probable that they moved here and there in all directions. And the Jews had been scattered almost unto all quarters of the world. He then wrote and exhorted all those whom he could not personally address, because they had been scattered far and wide. But that he speaks not of the grace of Christ and of faith in him, the reason seems to be this, because he addressed those who had already been rightly taught by others; so that they had need, not so much of doctrine, as of the goads of exhortations.[1]

2. *All joy.* The first exhortation is, to bear trials with a cheerful mind. And it was especially necessary at that time to comfort the Jews, almost overwhelmed as they were with troubles. For the very name of the nation was so infamous, that they were hated and despised by all people wherever they went; and their condition as Christians rendered them still more miserable, because they had their own nation as their most inveterate enemies. At the same time, this consolation was not so suited to one time, but that it is always useful to believers, whose life is a constant warfare on earth.

But that we may know more fully what he means, we must doubtless take *temptations* or trials as including all adverse

[1] The salutation is peculiar; but in the same form with the letter sent to Antioch by the Apostles, (of whom James was one,) and the Church at Jerusalem, Acts xv. 23. It is therefore apostolic, though adopted from a form commonly used by the heathen writers. See Acts xxiii. 26. John in his Second Epistle, verses 10 and 11, uses the verb χαίρειν in a similar sense; and it means properly to rejoice. It being an infinitive, the verb λέγω, to say or to bid, is put before it by John, and is evidently understood here. Hence the salutation may be thus rendered,—

"James, a servant of God and of the Lord Jesus Christ, bids, (or sends, or wishes) joy to the twelve tribes who are in their dispersion."

There had been an *eastern* and a *western* dispersion, the first at the Assyrian and Babylonian captivity, and the second during the predominancy of the Grecian power, which commenced with Alexander the Great. As this Epistle was written in Greek, it was no doubt intended more especially for those of the latter dispersion. But the benefit of the eastern dispersion was soon consulted, as the very *first* version of the New Testament was made into this language, that is, the Syriac; and this was done at the beginning of the second century.—*Ed.*

things; and they are so called, because they are the tests of our obedience to God. He bids the faithful, while exercised with these, to rejoice; and that not only when they fall into one temptation, but into many, not only of one kind, but of various kinds. And doubtless, since they serve to mortify our flesh, as the vices of the flesh continually shoot up in us, so they must necessarily be often repeated. Besides, as we labour under diseases, so it is no wonder that different remedies are applied to remove them.

The Lord then afflicts us in various ways, because ambition, avarice, envy, gluttony, intemperance, excessive love of the world, and the innumerable lusts in which we abound, cannot be cured by the same medicine.

When he bids us to *count it all joy*, it is the same as though he had said, that temptations ought to be so deemed as gain, as to be regarded as occasions of joy. He means, in short, that there is nothing in afflictions which ought to disturb our joy. And thus, he not only commands us to bear adversities calmly, and with an even mind, but shews that there is a reason why the faithful should rejoice when pressed down by them.

It is, indeed, certain, that all the senses of our nature are so formed, that every trial produces in us grief and sorrow; and no one of us can so far divest himself of his nature as not to grieve and be sorrowful whenever he feels any evil. But this does not prevent the children of God to rise, by the guidance of the Spirit, above the sorrow of the flesh. Hence it is, that in the midst of trouble they cease not to rejoice.

3. *Knowing* this, *that the trying.* We now see why he called adversities *trials* or temptations, even because they serve to try our faith. And there is here a reason given to confirm the last sentence. For it might, on the other hand, be objected, "How comes it, that we judge that sweet which to the sense is bitter?" He then shews by the effect that we ought to rejoice in afflictions, because they produce fruit that ought to be highly valued, even patience. If God then provides for our salvation, he affords us an occasion of rejoicing. Peter uses a similar argument at the beginning of his first Epistle, "That the trial of your faith, more precious

than gold, may be," &c. We certainly dread diseases, and want, and exile, and prison, and reproach, and death, because we regard them as evils; but when we understand that they are turned through God's kindness unto helps and aids to our salvation, it is ingratitude to murmur, and not willingly to submit to be thus paternally dealt with.

Paul says, in Rom. v. 3, that we are to glory in tribulations; and James says here, that we are to rejoice. "We glory," says Paul, "in tribulations, knowing that tribulation worketh patience." What immediately follows seems contrary to the words of James; for he mentions probation in the third place, as the effect of patience, which is here put first as though it were the cause. But the solution is obvious; the word there has an active, but here a passive meaning. Probation or trial is said by James to produce patience; for were not God to try us, but leave us free from trouble, there would be no patience, which is no other thing than fortitude of mind in bearing evils. But Paul means, that while by enduring we conquer evils, we experience how much God's help avails in necessities; for then the truth of God is as it were in reality manifested to us. Hence it comes that we dare to entertain more hope as to futurity; for the truth of God, known by experience, is more fully believed by us. Hence Paul teaches that by such a probation, that is, by such an experience of divine grace, hope is produced, not that hope then only begins, but that it increases and is confirmed. But both mean, that tribulation is the means by which patience is produced.

Moreover, the minds of men are not so formed by nature, that affliction of itself produces patience in them. But Paul and Peter regard not so much the nature of men as the providence of God through which it comes, that the faithful learn patience from troubles; for the ungodly are thereby more and more provoked to madness, as the example of Pharaoh proves.[1]

4. *But let patience have her perfect work.* As boldness

---

[1] The word used by James is δοκίμιον, trial, the act of testing, and by Paul δοκιμή, the result of testing, experience. James speaks of probation, and Paul of the experience gained thereby.—*Ed.*

and courage often appear in us and soon fail, he therefore requires perseverance. "Real patience," he says, "is that which endures to the end." For *work* here means the effort, not only to overcome in one contest, but to persevere through life. This perfection may also be referred to the sincerity of the soul, that men ought willingly and not feignedly to submit to God; but as the word *work* is added, I prefer to explain it of constancy. For there are many, as we have said, who shew at first an heroic greatness, and shortly after grow weary and faint. He therefore bids those who would be *perfect* and *entire*,[1] to persevere to the end.

But what he means by these two words, he afterwards explains, of those who fail not, or become not wearied: for they, who being overcome as to patience, are broken down, must, by degrees, be necessarily weakened, and at length wholly fail.

5. If any of you lack wisdom, let him ask of God, that giveth to all *men* liberally, and upbraideth not; and it shall be given him.	5. Porrò si quis vestrum destituitur sapientia, postulet à Deo, qui dat omnibus simpliciter, nec exprobrat; et dabitur ei.
6. But let him ask in faith, nothing wavering: for he that wavereth is like a wave of the sea driven with the wind and tossed.	6. Postulet autem in fide, nihil hæsitans; nam qui hæsitat similis est fluctui maris, qui vento agitur et circumfertur.
7. For let not that man think that he shall receive any thing of the Lord.	7. Non ergo existimet homo ille quòd sit quicquam accepturus à Domino.
8. A double-minded man *is* unstable in all his ways.	8. Vir duplici animo, instabilis est in omnibus viis suis.

5. *If any of you lack wisdom.* As our reason, and all our feelings are averse to the thought that we can be happy in the midst of evils, he bids us to ask of the Lord to give us wisdom. For *wisdom* here, I confine to the subject of the passage, as though he had said, "If this doctrine is higher than what your minds can reach to, ask of the Lord to illuminate you by his Spirit; for as this consolation alone is sufficient to mitigate all the bitterness of evils, that what is

---

[1] "Perfect, τέλειοι," fully grown, mature; "entire, ὁλόκληροι," complete, no part wanting. The first refers to the maturity of grace; and the second to its completeness, no grace being wanting. They were to be like men full grown, and not maimed or mutilated, but having all their members complete.— *Ed.*

grievous to the flesh is salutary to us; so we must necessarily be overcome with impatience, except we be sustained by this kind of comfort." Since we see that the Lord does not so require from us what is above our strength, but that he is ready to help us, provided we ask, let us, therefore, learn, whenever he commands anything, to ask of him the power to perform it.

Though in this place to be wise is to submit to God in the endurance of evils, under a due conviction that he so orders all things as to promote our salvation; yet the sentence may be generally applied to every branch of right knowledge.

But why does he say, *If any one*, as though all of them did not want wisdom? To this I answer, that all are by nature without it; but that some are gifted with the spirit of wisdom, while others are without it. As, then, all had not made such progress as to rejoice in affliction, but few there were to whom this had been given, James, therefore, referred to such cases; and he reminded those who were not as yet fully convinced that by the cross their salvation was promoted by the Lord, that they were to ask to be endued with wisdom. And yet there is no doubt, but that necessity reminds us all to ask the same thing; for he who has made the greatest progress, is yet far off from the goal. But to ask an increase of wisdom is another thing than to ask for it at first.

When he bids us to *ask of the Lord*, he intimates, that he alone can heal our diseases and relieve our wants.

That giveth to all men liberally. By *all*, he means those who ask; for they who seek no remedy for their wants, deserve to pine away in them. However, this universal declaration, by which every one of us is invited to ask, without exception, is very important; hence no man ought to deprive himself of so great a privilege.

To the same purpose is the promise which immediately follows; for as by this command he shews what is the duty of every one, so he affirms that they would not do in vain what he commands; according to what is said by Christ, " Knock, and it shall be opened." (Matt. vii. 7; Luke xi. 9.)

The word *liberally*, or freely, denotes promptitude in giving. So Paul, in Rom. xii. 8, requires simplicity in deacons. And in 2 Cor. viii. and ix., when speaking of charity or love, he repeats the same word several times. The meaning, then, is, that God is so inclined and ready to give, that he rejects none, or haughtily puts them off, being not like the niggardly and grasping, who either sparingly, as with a closed hand, give but little, or give only a part of what they were about to give, or long debate with themselves whether to give or not.[1]

And upbraideth not. This is added, lest any one should fear to come too often to God. Those who are the most liberal among men, when any one asks often to be helped, mention their former acts of kindness, and thus excuse themselves for the future. Hence, a mortal man, however open-handed he may be, we are ashamed to weary by asking too often. But James reminds us, that there is nothing like this in God; for he is ready ever to add new blessings to former ones, without any end or limitation.

6. *But let him ask in faith.* He shews here, first the right way of praying; for as we cannot pray without the word, as it were, leading the way, so we must believe before we pray; for we testify by prayer, that we hope to obtain from God the grace which he has promised. Thus every one who has no faith in the promises, prays dissemblingly. Hence, also, we learn what is true faith; for James, after having bidden us to ask in faith, adds this explanation, *nothing wavering,* or, doubting nothing. Then faith is that which relies on God's promises, and makes us sure of obtaining what we ask. It hence follows, that it is connected with confidence and certainty as to God's love towards us. The verb διακρίνεσθαι, which he uses, means properly to inquire into both sides of a question, after the manner of pleaders. He would have us then to be so convinced of what God has

---

[1] The literal meaning of ἁπλῶς is simply without any mixture; the noun, ἁπλότης, is used in the sense of sincerity, which has no mixture of hypocrisy or fraud, (2 Cor. i. 12,) and in the sense of liberality, or disposition free from what is sordid and parsimonious, having no mixture of niggardliness, (2 Cor. viii. 2.) This latter is evidently the meaning here, so that "liberally," according to our version, is the best word.—*Ed.*

once promised, as not to admit a doubt whether we shall be heard or not.

He that wavereth, or, doubteth. By this similitude he strikingly expresses how God punishes the unbelief of those who doubt his promises ; for, by their own restlessness, they torment themselves inwardly ; for there is never any calmness for our souls, except they recumb on the truth of God. He, at length, concludes, that such are unworthy to receive anything from God.

This is a remarkable passage, fitted to disprove that impious dogma which is counted as an oracle under the whole Papacy, that is, that we ought to pray doubtingly, and with uncertainty as to our success.

This principle, then, we hold, that our prayers are not heard by the Lord, except when we have a confidence that we shall obtain. It cannot indeed be otherwise, but that through the infirmity of our flesh we must be tossed by various temptations, which are like engines employed to shake our confidence ; so that no one is found who does not vacillate and tremble according to the feeling of his flesh ; but temptations of this kind are at length to be overcome by faith. The case is the same as with a tree, which has struck firm roots ; it shakes, indeed, through the blowing of the wind, but is not rooted up ; on the contrary, it remains firm in its own place.

8. *A double-minded man,* or, a man of a double mind. This sentence may be read by itself, as he speaks generally of hypocrites. It seems, however, to me to be rather the conclusion of the preceding doctrine ; and thus there is an implied contrast between the simplicity or liberality of God, mentioned before, and the double-mindedness of man ; for as God gives to us with a stretched-out hand, so it behoves us in our turn to open the bosom of our heart. He then says that the unbelieving, who have tortuous recesses, are *unstable ;* because they are never firm or fixed, but at one time they swell with the confidence of the flesh, at another they sink into the depth of despair.[1]

---

[1] "The double-minded," or the man with two souls, δίψυχος, means here no doubt the man who hesitates between faith and unbelief, because faith

9. Let the brother of low degree rejoice in that he is exalted;
10 But the rich, in that he is made low: because as the flower of the grass he shall pass away.
11. For the sun is no sooner risen with a burning heat, but it withereth the grass, and the flower thereof falleth, and the grace of the fashion of it perisheth : so also shall the rich man fade away in his ways.

9. Porrò glorietur frater humilis in sublimitate sua ;
10. Dives autem in humilitate sua, quia tanquam flos herbæ præteribit.
11. Nam sol exortus est cum æstu, et exarescit herba, et flos ejus cecidit, et decor aspectus ejus periit; sic et dives in suis viis (*vel*, copiis) marcescet.

9. *Let the brother of low degree.* As Paul, exhorting servants submissively to bear their lot, sets before them this consolation, that they were the free-men of God, having been set free by his grace from the most miserable bondage of Satan, and reminds them, though free, yet to remember that they were the servants of God ; so here James in the same manner bids the lowly to glory in this,—that they had been adopted by the Lord as his children ; and the rich, because they had been brought down into the same condition, the world's vanity having been made evident to them. Thus the first he would have to be content with their humble and low state ; and he forbids the rich to be proud.

Since it is incomparably the greatest dignity to be introduced into the company of angels, nay, to be made the associates of Christ, he who estimates this favour of God aright, will regard all other things as worthless. Then neither poverty, nor contempt, nor nakedness, nor famine, nor thirst, will make his mind so anxious, but that he will sustain himself with this consolation, " Since the Lord has conferred on me the principal thing, it behoves me patiently to bear the loss of other things, which are inferior."

Behold, how a lowly brother ought to glory in his elevation or exaltation ; for if he be accepted of God, he has sufficient consolation in his adoption alone, so as not to grieve unduly for a less prosperous state of life.

10. *But the rich, in that he is made low,* or, in his lowness. He has mentioned the particular for the general ; for this admonition pertains to all those who excel in honour, or in dignity, or in any other external thing. He bids them to

is the subject of the passage. When again used, in chap. iv. 8, it means a hesitation between God and the world.— *Ed.*

glory in their lowness or littleness, in order to repress the haughtiness of those who are usually inflated with prosperity. But he calls it *lowness*, because the manifested kingdom of God ought to lead us to despise the world, as we know that all the things we previously greatly admired, are either nothing or very little things. For Christ, who is not a teacher except of babes, checks by his doctrine all the haughtiness of the flesh. Lest, then, the vain joy of the world should captivate the rich, they ought to habituate themselves to glory in the casting down of their carnal excellency.[1]

As the flower of the grass. Were any one to say that James alludes to the words of Isaiah, I would not much object; but I cannot allow that he quotes the testimony of the Prophet, who speaks not only of the things of this life and the fading character of the world, but of the whole man, both body and soul; but here what is spoken of is the pomp of wealth or of riches. And the meaning is, that glorying in riches is foolish and preposterous, because they pass away in a moment. The philosophers teach the same thing; but the song is sung to the deaf, until the ears are opened by the Lord to hear the truth concerning the eternity of the celestial kingdom. Hence he mentions *brother*, intimating that there is no place for this truth, until we are admitted into the order of God's children.

Though the received reading is ἐν ταῖς πορείαις, yet I agree with Erasmus, and read the last word, πορίαις, without the diphthong, "in his riches," or, with his riches; and the latter I prefer.[2]

12. Blessed *is* the man that endureth temptation: for when he is tried, he shall receive the crown of life, which the Lord hath promised to them that love him.

12. Beatus vir qui suffert tentationem; quoniam quum probatus fuerit, accipiet coronam vitæ, quam promisit Deus diligentibus ipsum.

---

[1] The opinion of *Macknight* and some others, that the reference is to the lowness to which the rich were reduced by persecution, does not comport with the passage, for the Apostle afterwards speaks of the shortness of man's life and its uncertainty, and not of the fading nature of riches, which would have been most suitable, had he in view to comfort the rich at the loss of property. The Christian state was "lowness" according to the estimation of the world.—*Ed.*

[2] The received text is regarded as the best reading; the other is found in very few copies. —*Ed.*

13. Let no man say, when he is tempted, I am tempted of God: for God cannot be tempted with evil, neither tempteth he any man:	13. Nemo quum tentatur dicat, A Deo tentor; Deus enim nec tentari malis potest, nec quenquam tentat.
14. But every man is tempted, when he is drawn away of his own lust, and enticed.	14. Sed unusquisque tentatur, dum à sua concupiscentia abstrahitur, et inescatur.
15. Then, when lust hath conceived, it bringeth forth sin; and sin, when it is finished, bringeth forth death.	15. Postquam autem concupiscentia concepit, parit peccatum; peccatum verò perfectum generat mortem.

12. *Blessed is the man.* After having applied consolation, he moderated the sorrow of those who were severely handled in this world, and again humbled the arrogance of the great. He now draws this conclusion, that they are happy who magnanimously endure troubles and other trials, so as to rise above them. The word temptation may indeed be otherwise understood, even for the stings of lusts which annoy the soul within; but what is here commended, as I think, is fortitude of mind in enduring adversities. It is, however, a paradox, that they are not happy to whom all things come according to their wishes, but such as are not overcome with evils.

For when he is tried. He gives a reason for the preceding sentence; for the crown follows the contest. If, then, it be our chief happiness to be crowned in the kingdom of God, it follows, that the contests with which the Lord tries us, are aids and helps to our happiness. Thus the argument is from the end or the effect: hence we conclude, that the faithful are harassed by so many evils for this purpose, that their piety and obedience may be made manifest, and that they may be thus at length prepared to receive the crown of life.

But they reason absurdly who hence infer that we by fighting merit the crown; for since God has gratuitously appointed it for us, our fighting only renders us fit to receive it.

He adds, that it is *promised* to those who *love* God. By speaking thus, he means not that the love of man is the cause of obtaining the crown, (for God anticipates us by his gratuitous love;) but he only intimates that the elect who love him are alone approved by God. He yet reminds us that the conquerors of all temptations are those who love God, and that we fail not in courage when we are tried, for no other cause than because the love of the world prevails in us.

13. *Let no man, when he is tempted.* Here, no doubt, he speaks of another kind of temptation. It is abundantly evident that the external temptations, hitherto mentioned, are sent to us by God. In this way God tempted Abraham, (Gen. xxii. 1,) and daily tempts us, that is, he tries us as to what we are by laying before us an occasion by which our hearts are made known. But to draw out what is hid in our hearts is a far different thing from inwardly alluring our hearts by wicked lusts.

He then treats here of inward temptations, which are nothing else than the inordinate desires which entice to sin. He justly denies that God is the author of these, because they flow from the corruption of our nature.

This warning is very necessary, for nothing is more common among men than to transfer to another the blame of the evils they commit; and they then especially seem to free themselves, when they ascribe it to God himself. This kind of evasion we constantly imitate, delivered down to us as it is from the first man. For this reason James calls us to confess our own guilt, and not to implicate God, as though he compelled us to sin.

But the whole doctrine of Scripture seems to be inconsistent with this passage; for it teaches us that men are blinded by God, are given up to a reprobate mind, and delivered over to filthy and shameful lusts. To this I answer, that probably James was induced to deny that we are tempted by God by this reason, because the ungodly, in order to form an excuse, armed themselves with testimonies of Scripture. But there are two things to be noticed here: when Scripture ascribes blindness or hardness of heart to God, it does not assign to him the beginning of this blindness, nor does it make him the author of sin, so as to ascribe to him the blame: and on these two things only does James dwell.

Scripture asserts that the reprobate are delivered up to

depraved lusts; but is it because the Lord depraves or corrupts their hearts? By no means; for their hearts are subjected to depraved lusts, because they are already corrupt and vicious. But since God blinds or hardens, is he not the author or minister of evil? Nay, but in this manner he punishes sins, and renders a just reward to the ungodly, who have refused to be ruled by his Spirit. (Rom. i. 26.) It hence follows that the origin of sin is not in God, and no blame can be imputed to him as though he took pleasure in evils. (Gen. vi. 6.)

The meaning is, that man in vain evades, who attempts to cast the blame of his vices on God, because every evil proceeds from no other fountain than from the wicked lust of man. And the fact really is, that we are not otherwise led astray, except that every one has his own inclination as his leader and impeller. But that God tempts no one, he proves by this, because he is not *tempted with evils*.[1] For it is the devil who allures us to sin, and for this reason, because he wholly burns with the mad lust of sinning. But God does not desire what is evil: he is not, therefore, the author of doing evil in us.

14. *When he is drawn away by his own lust.* As the inclination and excitement to sin are inward, in vain does the sinner seek an excuse from an external impulse. At the same time these two effects of lust ought to be noticed—that it ensnares us by its allurements, and that it draws us away; each of which is sufficient to render us guilty.[2]

---

[1] Literally, "untemptable by evils," that is, not capable of being tempted or seduced by evils, by things wicked and sinful. He is so pure, that he is not influenced by any evil propensities, that he is not subject to any evil suggestions. It hence follows that he tempts or seduces no man to what is sinful. Being himself unassailable by evils, he cannot seduce others to what is evil. As God cannot be tempted to do what is sinful, he cannot possibly tempt others to sin. The words may be thus rendered,—
13. "Let no one, when seduced, say, 'By God am I seduced;' for God is not capable of being seduced by evils, and he himself seduceth no one."—*Ed.*

[2] The words are very striking,—"But every one is tempted (or, seduced) when, by his own lust, *he is* drawn away, (that is, from what is good,) and *is* caught by a bait (or, ensnared.)"

He is in the first drawn off from the line of duty, and then he is caught by something that is pleasing and plausible, but like the bait, it has in it a deadly hook.—*Ed.*

15. *Then when lust hath conceived.* He first calls that *lust* which is not any kind of evil affection or desire, but that which is the fountain of all evil affections; by which, as he shews, are conceived vicious broods, which at length break forth into sins. It seems, however, improper, and not according to the usage of Scripture, to restrict the word *sin* to outward works, as though indeed lust itself were not a sin, and as though corrupt desires, remaining closed up within and suppressed, were not so many sins. But as the use of a word is various, there is nothing unreasonable if it be taken here, as in many other places, for actual sin.

And the Papists ignorantly lay hold on this passage, and seek to prove from it that vicious, yea, filthy, wicked, and the most abominable lusts are not sins, provided there is no assent; for James does not shew when sin begins to be born, so as to be sin, and so accounted by God, but when it breaks forth. For he proceeds gradually, and shews that the consummation of sin is eternal death, and that sin arises from depraved desires, and that these depraved desires or affections have their root in lust. It hence follows that men gather fruit in eternal perdition, and fruit which they have procured for themselves.

By perfected sin, therefore, I understand, not any one act of sin perpetrated, but the completed course of sinning. For though death is merited by every sin whatever, yet it is said to be the reward of an ungodly and wicked life. Hence is the dotage of those confuted, who conclude from these words, that sin is not mortal until it breaks forth, as they say, into an external act. Nor is this what James treats of; but his object was only this, to teach that there is in us the root of our own destruction.

16. Do not err, my beloved brethren.	16. Ne erretis, fratres mei dilecti:
17. Every good gift and every perfect gift is from above, and cometh down from the Father of lights, with whom is no variableness, neither shadow of turning.	17. Omnis donatio bona et omne donum perfectum desursum est, descendens à Patre luminum; apud quem non est transmutatio, aut conversionis obumbratio.
18. Of his own will begat he us with the word of truth, that we should be a kind of firstfruits of his creatures.	18. Is sua voluntate genuit nos sermone veritatis, ut essemus primitiæ quædam suarum creaturarum.

16. *Do not err.* This is an argument from what is opposite; for as God is the author of all good, it is absurd to suppose him to be the author of evil. To do good is what properly belongs to him, and according to his nature; and from him all good things come to us. Then, whatever evil he does, is not agreeable to his nature. But as it sometimes happens, that he who quits himself well through life, yet in some things fails, he meets this doubt by denying that God is mutable like men. But if God is in all things and always like himself, it hence follows that well-doing is his perpetual work.

This reasoning is far different from that of Plato, who maintained that no calamities are sent on men by God, because he is good; for though it is just that the crimes of men should be punished by God, yet it is not right, with regard to him, to regard among evils that punishment which he justly inflicts. Plato, indeed, was ignorant; but James, leaving to God his right and office of punishing, only removes blame from him.

This passage teaches us, that we ought to be so affected by God's innumerable blessings, which we daily receive from his hand, as to think of nothing but of his glory; and that we should abhor whatever comes to our mind, or is suggested by others, which is not compatible with his praise.

God is called the *Father of lights*, as possessing all excellency and the highest dignity. And when he immediately adds, that there is in him *no shadow of turning*, he continues the metaphor, so that we may not measure the brightness of God by the irradiation of the sun which appears to us.[1]

---

[1] This verse must be taken in connexion with what is gone before. When he mentions "every good gift," it is in opposition to the evil of which he says God is not the author. See Matt. vii. 11. And "every perfect free-gift," as δώρημα means, has a reference to the correction of the evil which arises from man himself. And he calls free-gift perfect, because it has no mixture of evil, what he throughout denies that God is the author of. Then, the latter part of the verse bears a correspondence with the first. He calls God "the Father of lights." Light in the language of Scripture means especially two things, the light of truth, divine knowledge and holiness. God is the Father, the parent, the origin, the source of these lights. Hence from him descends every good, useful, necessary

18. *Of his own will.* He now brings forward a special proof of the goodness of God which he had mentioned, even that he has regenerated us unto eternal life. This invaluable benefit every one of the faithful feels in himself. Then the goodness of God, when known by experience, ought to remove from them all a contrary opinion respecting him.

When he says that God *of his own will,* or spontaneously, *hath begotten* us, he intimates that he was induced by no other reason, as the will and counsel of God are often set in opposition to the merits of men. What great thing, indeed, would it have been to say that God was not constrained to do this? But he expresses something more, that God according to his own good-will hath begotten us, and has been thus a cause to himself. It hence follows that it is natural to God to do good.

But this passage teaches us, that as our election before the foundation of the world was gratuitous, so we are illuminated by the grace of God alone as to the knowledge of the truth, so that our calling corresponds with our election. The Scripture shews that we have been gratuitously adopted by God before we were born. But James expresses here something more, that we obtain the right of adoption, because God does also call us gratuitously. (Eph. i. 4, 5.) Farther, we hence learn, that it is the peculiar office of God spiritually to regenerate us; for that the same thing is sometimes ascribed to the ministers of the gospel, means no other thing than this, that God acts through them; and it happens indeed through them, but he nevertheless alone doeth the work.

The word *begotten* means that we become new men, so that we put off our former nature when we are effectually called by God. He adds how God begets us, even by the

gift, to deliver men from evil, from ignorance and delusion, and every perfect free-gift to free men from their evil lusts, and to render them holy and happy. And to shew that God is ever the same, he adds, "with whom there is no variableness or the shadow (or shade, or the slightest appearance) of a change;" that is, who never varies in his dealings with men, and shews no symptom of any change, being the author and giver of all good, and the author of no evil, that is, of no sin.—*Ed.*

word of truth, so that we may know that we cannot enter the kingdom of God by any other door.

That we should be a kind of firstfruits of his creatures. The word τινὰ, "some," has the meaning of likeness, as though he had said, that we are in a manner firstfruits. But this ought not to be restricted to a few of the faithful; but it belongs to all in common. For as man excels among all creatures, so the Lord elects some from the whole mass and separates them as a holy offering to himself.[1] It is no common nobility into which God extols his own children. Then justly are they said to be excellent as firstfruits, when God's image is renewed in them.

19. Wherefore, my beloved brethren, let every man be swift to hear, slow to speak, slow to wrath:	19. Itaque, fratres mei dilecti, sit omnis homo celer ad audiendum, tardus autem ad loquendum, tardus ad iram:
20. For the wrath of man worketh not the righteousness of God.	20. Ira enim hominis justitiam Dei non operatur.
21. Wherefore, lay apart all filthiness, and superfluity of naughtiness, and receive with meekness the engrafted word, which is able to save your souls:	21. Quapropter deposita omni immunditie, et redundantia malitiæ, cum mansuetudine suscipite insitum sermonem qui potest servare animas vestras.

19. *Let every man.* Were this a general sentence, the inference would be far-fetched; but as he immediately adds a sentence respecting the word of truth suitable to the last verse, I doubt not but that he accommodates this exhortation peculiarly to the subject in hand. Having then set before us the goodness of God, he shews how it becomes us to be prepared to receive the blessing which he exhibits towards us. And this doctrine is very useful, for spiritual generation is not a work of one moment. Since some remnants of the old man ever abide in us, we must necessarily be through life renewed, until the flesh be abolished; for either our perverseness, or arrogance, or sloth, is a great impediment to God in perfecting in us his work. Hence, when James would have us to be swift to hear, he commends promptitude, as though he had said, "When God so freely

---

[1] The firstfruits being a part and a pledge of the coming harvest, to retain the metaphor, we must regard "creatures" here as including all the saved in future ages. Hence their opinion is to be preferred, who regard the first converts, who were Jews, as the firstfruits. — *Ed.*

and kindly presents himself to you, you also ought to render yourselves teachable, lest your slowness should cause him to desist from speaking."

But inasmuch as we do not calmly hear God speaking to us, when we seem to ourselves to be very wise, but by our haste interrupt him when addressing us, the Apostle requires us to be silent, to be *slow to speak*. And, doubtless, no one can be a true disciple of God, except he hears him in silence. He does not, however, require the silence of the Pythagorean school, so that it should not be right to inquire whenever we desire to learn what is necessary to be known; but he would only have us to correct and restrain our forwardness, that we may not, as it commonly happens, unseasonably interrupt God, and that as long as he opens his sacred mouth, we may open to him our hearts and our ears, and not prevent him to speak.

Slow to wrath. Wrath also, I think, is condemned with regard to the hearing which God demands to be given to him, as though making a tumult it disturbed and impeded him, for God cannot be heard except when the mind is calm and sedate. Hence, he adds, that as long as wrath bears rule there is no place for the righteousness of God. In short, except the heat of contention be banished, we shall never observe towards God that calm silence of which he has just spoken.

21. *Wherefore lay apart.* He concludes by saying how the word of life is to be received. And first, indeed, he intimates that it cannot be rightly received except it be implanted, or strike roots in us. For the expression, to receive the implanted word, ought to be thus explained, " to receive it, that it may be really implanted." For he alludes to seed often sown on arid ground, and not received into the moist bosom of the earth; or to plants, which being cast on the ground, or laid on dead wood, soon wither. He then requires that it should be a living implanting, by which the word becomes as it were united with our heart.

He at the same time shews the way and manner of this reception, even *with meekness*. By this word he means humility and the readiness of a mind disposed to learn, such as Isaiah describes when he says, "On whom does my Spirit rest, except on the humble and meek?" (Isa. lvii. 15.) Hence it is, that so few profit in the school of God, because hardly one in a hundred renounces the stubbornness of his own spirit, and gently submits to God; but almost all are conceited and refractory. But if we desire to be the living plantation of God, we must subdue our proud hearts and be humble, and labour to become like lambs, so as to suffer ourselves to be ruled and guided by our Shepherd.

But as men are never thus tamed, so as to have a calm and meek heart, except they are purged from depraved affections, so he bids us to *lay aside uncleanness and redundancy of wickedness*. And as James borrowed a comparison from agriculture, it was necessary for him to observe this order, to begin by rooting up noxious weeds. And since he addressed all, we may hence conclude that these are the innate evils of our nature, and that they cleave to us all; yea, since he addresses the faithful, he shews that we are never wholly cleansed from them in this life, but that they are continually sprouting up, and therefore he requires that care should be constantly taken to eradicate them. As the word of God is especially a holy thing, to be fitted to receive it, we must put off the filthy things by which we have been polluted.

Under the word κακία, he comprehends hypocrisy and obstinacy as well as unlawful desires or lusts. Not satisfied with specifying the seat of wickedness as being in the soul of man, he teaches us that so abounding is the wickedness that dwells there, that it overflows, or that it rises up as it were into a heap; and doubtless, whosoever will well examine himself will find that there is within him an immense chaos of evils.[1]

[1] What renders this passage unsatisfactory is the meaning given to περισσία, rendered by some "superfluity," and by others "redundancy." The verb περισσεύω means not only to abound, but also to be a residue, to remain, to be a remnant. See Matt. xiv. 20; Luke ix. 17. And its derivative περίσσευμα is used in the sense of a remnant or a remainder, Mark viii. 8; and this very word is used in the *Sept.* for יתר, which means a residue, a remnant, or, what remains, Eccl. vi. 8. Let it have this meaning here, and the sense will not only be clear, but very striking. James was addressing those who were Christians; and he exhorted them to throw

Which is able to save. It is a high eulogy on heavenly truth, that we obtain through it a sure salvation; and this is added, that we may learn to seek and love and magnify the word as a treasure that is incomparable. It is then a sharp goad to chastise our idleness, when he says that the word which we are wont to hear so negligently, is the means of our salvation, though for this purpose the power of saving is not ascribed to the word, as if salvation is conveyed by the external sound of the word, or as if the office of saving is taken away from God and transferred elsewhere; for James speaks of the word which by faith penetrates into the hearts of men, and only intimates that God, the author of salvation, conveys it by his Gospel.

22. But be ye doers of the word, and not hearers only, deceiving your own selves.
23. For if any be a hearer of the word, and not a doer, he is like unto a man beholding his natural face in a glass:
24. For he beholdeth himself, and goeth his way, and straightway forgetteth what manner of man he was.
25. But whoso looketh into the perfect law of liberty, and continueth *therein*, he being not a forgetful hearer, but a doer of the work, this man shall be blessed in his deed.
26. If any man among you seem to be religious, and bridleth not his tongue, but deceiveth his own heart, this man's religion *is* vain.
27. Pure religion, and undefiled, before God and the Father, is this, To visit the fatherless and widows in their affliction, *and* to keep himself unspotted from the world.

22. Estote factores sermonis, et non auditores solùm, fallentes vos ipsos.
23. Nam si quis auditor est sermonis, et non factor, hic similis est homini consideranti faciem nativitatis suæ in speculo:
24. Consideravit enim seipsum, et abiit, et protinus oblitus est qualis sit.
25. Qui verò intuitus fuerit in legem perfectam, quæ est libertatis, et permanserit, hic non auditor obliviosus, sed factor operis, beatus in opere suo erit.
26. Si quis videtur religiosus esse inter vos, nec refrænat linguam suam, sed decipit cor suum, hujus inanis est religio.
27. Religio pura et impolluta coram Deo et Patre, hæc est, Visitare pupillos et viduas in afflictione ipsorum, immaculatum servare se à mundo.

22. *Be ye doers of the word.* The doer here is not the same as in Rom. ii. 13, who satisfied the law of God and fulfilled it in every part, but the doer is he who from the heart embraces God's word and testifies by his life that he really

away every uncleanness and remnant of wickedness, or evil, as the word κακία more properly means. See Acts viii. 22; 1 Pet. ii. 16.

"Every uncleanness," or filthiness, means every kind of uncleanness arising from lustful and carnal indulgences; and "the remnant of wickedness," in thought and in deed, most suitably follows.—*Ed.*

believes, according to the saying of Christ, "Blessed are they who hear God's word and keep it," (Luke xi. 28;) for he shews by the fruits what that implanting is, before mentioned. We must further observe, that faith with all its works is included by James, yea, faith especially, as it is the chief work which God requires from us. The import of the whole is, that we ought to labour that the word of the Lord should strike roots in us, so that it may afterwards fructify.[1]

23. *He is like to a man.* Heavenly doctrine is indeed a mirror in which God presents himself to our view; but so that we may be transformed unto his image, as Paul says in 2 Cor. iii. 18. But here he speaks of the external glance of the eye, not of the vivid and efficacious meditation which penetrates into the heart. It is a striking comparison, by which he briefly intimates, that a doctrine merely heard and not received inwardly into the heart avails nothing, because it soon vanishes away.

25. *The perfect law of liberty.* After having spoken of empty speculation, he comes now to that penetrating intuition which transforms us to the image of God. And as he had to do with the Jews, he takes the word *law*, familiarly known to them, as including the whole truth of God.

But why he calls it a *perfect law,* and a law of *liberty,* interpreters have not been able to understand; for they have not perceived that there is here a contrast, which may be gathered from other passages of Scripture. As long as the law is preached by the external voice of man, and not inscribed by the finger and Spirit of God on the heart, it is but a dead letter, and as it were a lifeless thing. It is, then, no wonder that the law is deemed imperfect, and that it is the law of bondage; for as Paul teaches in Gal. iv. 24, separated from Christ, it generates to bondage; and as the same shews to us in Rom. viii. 13, it can do nothing but fill us with diffidence and fear. But the Spirit of regeneration, who inscribes it on our inward parts, brings also the grace of adoption. It is, then, the same as though James had

---

[1] *Calvin* takes no notice of the last sentence, "deceiving yourselves." The participle means deceiving by false reasoning; it may be rendered with *Doddridge,* "sophistically deceiving yourselves."—*Ed.*

said, "The teaching of the law, let it no longer lead you to bondage, but, on the contrary, bring you to liberty; let it no longer be only a schoolmaster, but bring you to perfection: it ought to be received by you with sincere affection, so that you may lead a godly and a holy life."

Moreover, since it is a blessing of the Old Testament that the law of God should reform us, as it appears from Jer. xxxi. 35, and other passages, it follows that it cannot be obtained until we come to Christ. And, doubtless, he alone is the end and perfection of the law; and James adds *liberty*, as an inseparable associate, because the Spirit of Christ never regenerates, but that he becomes also a witness and an earnest of our divine adoption, so as to free our hearts from fear and trembling.

And continueth. This is firmly to persevere in the knowledge of God; and when he adds, *this man shall be blessed in his deed*, or work, he means that blessedness is to be found in doing, not in cold hearing.[1]

26. *Seem to be religious.* He now reproves even in those who boasted that they were doers of the law, a vice under which hypocrites commonly labour, that is, the wantonness of the tongue in detraction. He has before touched on the duty of restraining the tongue, but for a different end; for he then bade silence before God, that we might be more fitted to learn. He speaks now of another thing, that the faithful should not employ their tongue in evil-speaking.

It was indeed needful that this vice should be condemned, when the subject was the keeping of the law; for they who have put off the grosser vices, are especially subject to this disease. He who is neither an adulterer, nor a thief, nor a drunkard, but, on the contrary, seems brilliant with some outward shew of sanctity, will set himself off by defaming others, and this under the pretence of zeal, but really through the lust of slandering.

The object here, then, was to distinguish between the true worshippers of God and hypocrites, who are so swollen with

---

[1] It may be rendered thus,—"The same shall be blessed in (or by) the doing of it," that is, the work. The very doing of the law of liberty, of what the gospel prescribes, makes a man blessed or happy.—*Ed.*

Pharisaic pride, that they seek praise from the defects of others. *If any one,* he says, *seems to be religious,* that is, who has a show of sanctity, and in the meantime flatters himself by speaking evil of others, it is hence evident that he does not truly serve God. For by saying that his religion is vain, he not only intimates that other virtues are marred by the stain of evil-speaking, but that the conclusion is, that the zeal for religion which appears is not sincere.

But deceiveth his own heart. I do not approve of the version of Erasmus—" but suffers his heart to err;" for he points out the fountain of that arrogance to which hypocrites are addicted, through which, being blinded by an immoderate love of themselves, they believe themselves to be far better than they really are ; and hence, no doubt, is the disease of slandering, because the wallet, as Æsop says in his Apologue, hanging behind, is not seen. Rightly, then, has James, wishing to remove the effect, that is, the lust of evil-speaking, added the cause, even that hypocrites flatter themselves immoderately. For they would be ready to forgive, were they in their turn to acknowledge themselves to be in need of forgiveness. Hence the flatteries by which they deceive themselves as to their own vices, make them such supercilious censors of others.

27. *Pure religion.* As he passes by those things which are of the greatest moment in religion, he does not define generally what religion is, but reminds us that religion without the things he mentions is nothing; as when one given to wine and gluttony boasts that he is temperate, and another should object, and say that the temperate man is he who does not indulge in excess as to wine or eating ; his object is not to express the whole of what temperance is, but to refer only to one thing, suitable to the subject in hand. For they are in vain religious of whom he speaks, as they are for the most part trifling pretenders.

James then teaches us that religion is not to be estimated by the pomp of ceremonies; but that there are important duties to which the servants of God ought to attend.

To *visit* in necessity is to extend a helping hand to alleviate such as are in distress. And as there are many others whom the Lord bids us to succour, in mentioning widows and orphans, he states a part for the whole. There is then no doubt but that under one particular thing he recommends to us every act of love, as though he had said, "Let him who would be deemed religious, prove himself to be such by self-denial and by mercy and benevolence towards his neighbours."

And he says, *before God*, to intimate that it appears indeed otherwise to men, who are led astray by external masks, but that we ought to seek what pleases him. By *God and Father*, we are to understand God who is a father.

CHAPTER II.

1. My brethren, have not the faith of our Lord Jesus Christ, *the Lord* of glory, with respect of persons.

2. For if there come unto your assembly a man with a gold ring, in goodly apparel, and there come in also a poor man in vile raiment;

3. And ye have respect to him that weareth the gay clothing, and say unto him, Sit thou here in a good place; and say to the poor, Stand thou there, or sit here under my footstool:

4. Are ye not then partial in yourselves, and are become judges of evil thoughts?

1. Fratres mei, ne in acceptionibus personarum fidem habeatis Domini Jesu Christi ex opinione, (*vel*, gloria.)

2. Si enim ingressus fuerit in cœtum vestrum vir aureos anulos gestans, veste indutus splendida; ingressus autem fuerit et pauper in sordida veste;

3. Et respexeritis in eum qui vestem fert splendidam, et ei dixeritis, Tu sede hic honeste, et pauperi dixeritis, Tu sta illic, vel, Sede hic sub scabello pedum meorum;

4. An non dijudicati estis in vobisipsis, et facti judices malarum cogitationum?

THIS reproof seems at first sight to be hard and unreasonable; for it is one of the duties of courtesy, not to be neglected, to honour those who are elevated in the world. Further, if respect of persons be vicious, servants are to be freed from all subjection; for freedom and servitude are deemed by Paul as conditions of life. The same must be thought of magistrates. But the solution of these questions is not difficult, if what James writes is not separated. For he does not simply disapprove of honour being paid to the rich, but that this should not be done in a way so as to despise or reproach the poor; and this will appear more clearly, when he proceeds to speak of the rule of love.

Let us therefore remember that the respect of persons here condemned is that by which the rich is so extolled, that wrong is done to the poor, which also he shews clearly by the context. And surely ambitious is that honour, and full of vanity, which is shewn to the rich to the contempt of the poor. Nor is there a doubt but that ambition reigns and vanity also, when the masks of this world are alone in high esteem. We must remember this truth, that he is to be counted among the heirs of God's kingdom, who disregards the reprobate and honours those who fear God. (Ps. xv. 4.)

Here then is the contrary vice condemned, that is, when from respect alone to riches, any one honours the wicked, and as it has been said, dishonours the good. If then thou shouldest read thus, "He sins who respects the rich," the sentence would be absurd; but if as follows, "He sins who honours the rich alone and despises the poor, and treats him with contempt," it would be a pious and true doctrine.

1. *Have not the faith*, &c., *with respect of persons.* He means that the respect of persons is inconsistent with the faith of Christ, so that they cannot be united together, and rightly so; for we are by faith united into one body, in which Christ holds the primacy. When therefore the pomps of the world become pre-eminent so as to cover over what Christ is, it is evident that faith hath but little vigour.

In rendering τῆς δόξης, "on account of esteem," (*ex opinione*,) I have followed Erasmus; though the old interpreter cannot be blamed, who has rendered it "glory," for the word means both; and it may be fitly applied to Christ, and that according to the drift of the passage. For so great is the brightness of Christ, that it easily extinguishes all the glories of the world, if indeed it irradiates our eyes. It hence follows, that Christ is little esteemed by us, when the admiration of worldly glory lays hold on us. But the other exposition is also very suitable, for when the esteem or value of riches or of honours dazzles our eyes, the truth is suppressed, which ought alone to prevail. To *sit becomingly* means to sit honourably.

4. *Are ye not then partial in yourselves?* or, Are ye not condemned in yourselves? This may be read affirmatively as well as interrogatively, but the sense would be the same, for he amplifies the fault by this, that they took delight and indulged themselves in so great a wickedness. If it be read interrogatively, the meaning is, " Does not your own conscience hold you convicted, so that you need no other judge?" If the affirmative be preferred, it is the same as though he had said, " This evil also happens, that ye think not that ye sin, nor know that your thoughts are so wicked as they are."[1]

5. Hearken, my beloved brethren, Hath not God chosen the poor of this world rich in faith, and heirs of the kingdom which he hath promised to them that love him?	5. Audite, fratres mei dilecti, nonne Deus elegit pauperes mundi hujus divites in fide et hæredes regni quod promisit iis qui diligunt eum?
6. But ye have despised the poor. Do not rich men oppress you, and draw you before the judgment-seats?	6. Vos autem contemptui habuistis pauperem: nonne divites tyrannidem in vos exercent et iidem trahunt vos ad tribunalia?
7. Do not they blaspheme that worthy name by the which ye are called?	7. Et iidem contumelia afficiunt bonum nomen quod invocatum est super vos?

5. *Hearken, my beloved brethren.* He proves now by a twofold argument, that they acted preposterously, when for the sake of the rich they despised the poor. The first is, that it is unbecoming and disgraceful to cast down those whom God exalts, and to treat reproachfully those whom he honours. As God honours the poor, then every one who repudiates them, reverses the order of God. The other argument is

[1] It is commonly admitted to be an interrogatory sentence: " And do ye not make a difference among (or, in) yourselves, and become judges, having evil thoughts?" literally, " judges of evil thoughts," it being, as they say, the genitive case of possession. Or the words may be rendered, " and become judges of evil (or, false) reasonings?" or, as *Beza* renders the sentence, " and become judges, reasoning falsely," concluding that the rich man was good and the poor man bad.

It is said by *Beza* and others, that διακρίνομαι never means to be judged or condemned, but to distinguish, to discriminate, to make a difference, and also to contend and to doubt. The difference made here was the respect of persons that was shewn, and they made this difference in themselves, in their own minds, through the perverse or false thoughts or reasonings which they entertained. But it appears that these preferences were shewn, not to the members of the Church, but to such strangers as might happen to come to their assemblies.—*Ed.*

taken from common experience; for since the rich are for the most part vexatious to the good and innocent, it is very unreasonable to render such a reward for the wrongs they do, so that they should be more approved by us than the poor, who aid us more than they wrong us. We shall now see how he proceeds with these two points.

Hath not God chosen the poor of this world? Not indeed alone, but he wished to begin with them, that he might beat down the pride of the rich. This is also what Paul says, that God hath chosen, not many noble, not many mighty in the world, but those who are weak, that he might make ashamed such as are strong. (1 Cor. i. 25.) In short, though God pours forth his grace on the rich in common with the poor, yet his will is to prefer these to those, that the mighty might learn not to flatter themselves, and that the ignoble and the obscure might ascribe all that they are to the mercy of God, and that both might be trained up to meekness and humility.

The rich in faith are not those who abound in the greatness of faith, but such as God has enriched with the various gifts of his Spirit, which we receive by faith. For, doubtless, since the Lord deals bountifully with all, every one becomes partaker of his gifts according to the measure of his own faith. If, then, we are empty or needy, that proves the deficiency of our faith; for if we only enlarge the bosom of faith, God is always ready to fill it.

He says, that a kingdom is *promised* to those who love God: not that the promise depends on love; but he reminds us that we are called by God unto the hope of eternal life, on this condition and to this end, that we may love him. Then the end, and not the beginning, is here pointed out.

6. *Do not the rich.* He seems to instigate them to vengeance by bringing forward the unjust rule of the rich, in order that they who were unjustly treated, might render like for like: and yet we are everywhere bid to do good to those who injure us. But the object of James was another; for he only wished to shew that they were without reason or judgment who through ambition honoured their executioners, and in the meantime injured their own friends, at least those

from whom they never suffered any wrong. For hence appeared more fully their vanity, that they were induced by no acts of kindness: they only admired the rich, because they were rich; nay, they servilely flattered those whom they found, to their own loss, to be unjust and cruel.

There are, indeed, some of the rich who are just, and meek, and hate all unrighteousness; but few of such men are to be found. James, then, mentions what for the most part usually happens, and what daily experience proves true. For as men commonly exercise their power in doing what is wrong, it hence happens, that the more power any one has, the worse he is, and the more unjust towards his neighbours. The more careful then ought the rich to be, lest they should contract any of the contagion which everywhere prevails among those of their own rank.

7. *Worthy*, or, good *name*. I doubt not but that he refers here to the name of God and of Christ. And he says, *by*, or, *on, the which ye are called;* not in prayer, as Scripture is wont sometimes to speak, but by profession; as the name of a father, in Gen. xlviii. 16, is said to be called on his offspring, and in Isa. iv. 1, the name of a husband is called on the wife. It is, then, the same as though he had said, "The good name in which ye glory, or which ye deem it an honour to be called by; but if they proudly calumniate the glory of God, how unworthy are they of being honoured by Christians!"

8. If ye fulfil the royal law according to the scripture, Thou shalt love thy neighbour as thyself, ye do well:

8. Si legem quidem regiam perficitis juxta scripturam, Diliges proximum tuum sicut teipsum, benefacitis. (Lev. xix. 18; Matt. xxii. 39; Mark xii. 31; Rom. xiii. 9; Gal. v. 14.)

9. But if ye have respect to persons, ye commit sin, and are convinced of the law as transgressors.

9. Sin personam respicitis, peccatum committitis, et redarguimini à lege veluti transgressores. (Lev. xix. 15; Deut. i. 17, 19.)

10. For whosoever shall keep the whole law, and yet offend in one *point*, he is guilty of all.

10. Quisquis enim totam legem servaverit, offenderit autem in uno, factus est omnium reus.

11. For he that said, Do not commit adultery, said also, Do not kill. Now, if thou commit no adultery, yet if thou kill, thou art become a transgressor of the law.

11. Nam qui dixit, Ne mœcheris, dixit etiam, Ne occidas. Quòd si non fueris mœchatus, occideris tamen, factus es transgressor legis.

Now follows a plainer declaration ; for he expressly points out the cause of the last reproof, for they were officiously attentive to the rich, not from love, but on the contrary, from a vain desire of attaining their favour. And it is an anticipation, by which he obviated an excuse on the other side ; for they might have objected and said, that he ought not to be blamed, who humbly submitted himself to the unworthy. James, indeed, concedes that this is true, but he shews that it was falsely pretended by them, because they shewed this submission of homage, not from love to their neighbours, but from respect of persons.

In the first clause, then, he acknowledges as right and praiseworthy, all the duties of love which we perform towards our neighbours. In the second, he denies that the ambitious respect of persons ought to be deemed as of this kind, for it widely differs from what the law prescribes. And the hinge of this answer turns on the words " neighbour" and " respect of persons," as though he had said, " If you pretend that there is a sort of love in what you do, this may be easily disproved ; for God bids us to love our neighbours, and not to shew respect of persons." Besides, this word "neighbour" includes all mankind : he, then, who says, that a very few, according to his own fancy, ought to be honoured, and others passed by, does not keep the law of God, but yields to the depraved desires of his own heart. God expressly commends to us strangers and enemies, and all, even the most contemptible. To this doctrine the respect of persons is wholly contrary. Hence, rightly does James assert, that respect of persons is inconsistent with love.

8. *If ye fulfil the royal law.* The law here I take simply as the rule of life ; and *to fulfil*, or perform it, is to keep it with real integrity of heart, and as they say, roundly, *(rotunde ;)* and he sets such a keeping in opposition to a partial observance of it. It is said, indeed, to be a *royal law*, as it is the royal way, or road ; that is, plain, straight, and level, which, by implication, is set in opposition to sinuous by-paths and windings.

Allusion however is made, as I think, to servile obedience which they rendered to the rich, when they might, by serving in sincerity their neighbours, be not only free men, but live as kings.

When, in the second place, he says, that those who had respect of persons were *convinced*, or reproved by the law, the law is taken according to its proper meaning. For since we are bidden by God's command to embrace all mortals, every one who, with a few exceptions, rejects all the rest, breaks the bond of God, and inverts also his order, and is, therefore, rightly called a transgressor of the law.

10. *For whosoever shall keep the whole law.* What alone he means is, that God will not be honoured with exceptions, nor will he allow us to cut off from his law what is less pleasing to us. At the first view, this sentence seems hard to some, as though the Apostle countenanced the paradox of the Stoics, which makes all sins equal, and as though he asserted that he who offends in one thing ought to be punished equally with him whose whole life has been sinful and wicked. But it is evident from the context that no such thing entered into his mind.

For we must always observe the reason why anything is said. He denies that our neighbours are loved, when a part only of them is through ambition chosen, and the rest neglected. This he proves, because it is no obedience to God, when it is not rendered equally according to his command. Then as the rule of God is plain and complete or perfect, so we ought to regard completeness; so that none of us should presumptuously separate what he has joined together. Let there be, therefore, a uniformity, if we desire rightly to obey God. As, for instance, were a judge to punish ten thefts, and leave one man unpunished, he would betray the obliquity of his mind, for he would thus shew himself indignant against men rather than against crimes; because what he condemns in one he absolves in another.

We now, then, understand the design of James, that is, that if we cut off from God's law what is less agreeable to us, though in other parts we may be obedient, yet we become guilty of all, because in one particular thing we violate the whole law. And though he accommodates what is said to the subject in hand, it is yet taken from a general principle,—that God has prescribed to us a rule of life, which it is not lawful for us to mutilate. For it is not said of a part of the law, "This is the way, walk ye in it;" nor does the law promise a reward except to universal obedience.

Foolish, then, are the schoolmen, who deem partial righteousness, as they call it, to be meritorious; for this passage, and many others, clearly shew that there is no righteousness except in a perfect obedience to the law.

11. *For he that said,* or, he who hath said. This is a proof of the former verse; because the Lawgiver is to be considered rather than each particular precept apart. The righteousness of God, as an indivisible body, is contained in the law. Whosoever, then, transgresses one article of the law, destroys, as far as he can, the righteousness of God. Besides, as in one part, so in every part, God's will is to try our obedience. Hence a transgressor of the law is every one who offends as to any one of its commandments, according to this saying, "Cursed is he who fulfils not all things." (Deut. xxvii. 26.) We further see, that the transgressor of the law, and the guilty of all, mean the same according to James.

| 12. So speak ye, and so do, as they that shall be judged by the law of liberty. | 12. Sic loquimini, et sic facite, ut per legem libertatis judicandi. |
| 13. For he shall have judgment without mercy that hath shewed no mercy; and mercy rejoiceth against judgment. | 13. Judicium enim sine misericordia ei qui non præstiterit misericordiam; et gloriatur misericordia adversus judicium. |

12. *So speak ye.* Some give this explanation, that as they flattered themselves too much, they are summoned to the right tribunal; for men absolve themselves according to their own notions, because they withdraw themselves from the judgment of the divine law. He then reminds them that all deeds and words are there to be accounted for, because God will judge the world according to his law. As, however, such a declaration might have smitten them with immoderate terror, to correct or mitigate what they might have thought severe, he adds, *the law of liberty.* For we know what Paul says, "Whosoever are under the law are under a curse." (Gal. iii. 10.) Hence the judgment of the

law in itself is condemnation to eternal death; but he means by the word *liberty*, that we are freed from the rigour of the law.

This meaning is not altogether unsuitable, though if one examines more minutely what immediately follows, he will see that James meant another thing; the sense is as though he had said, "Except ye wish to undergo the rigour of the law, ye must be less rigid towards your neighbours; for the law of liberty is the same as the mercy of God, which delivers us from the curse of the law." And so this verse ought to be read with what follows, where he speaks of the duty of bearing with infirmities. And doubtless the whole passage thus reads well: "Since none of us can stand before God, except we be delivered and freed from the strict rigour of the law, we ought so to act, that we may not through too much severity exclude the indulgence or mercy of God, of which we all have need to the last."

13. *For he shall have judgment.* This is an application of the last verse to the subject in hand, which confirms altogether the second explanation which I have mentioned: for he shews, that since we stand through God's mercy alone, we ought to shew that to those whom the Lord himself commends to us.

It is, indeed, a singular commendation of kindness and benevolence, that God promises that he will be merciful to us, if we be so to our brethren: not that our mercy, however great it may be, shewn towards men, merits the mercy of God; but that God would have those whom he has adopted, as he is to them a kind and an indulgent Father, to bear and exhibit his image on the earth, according to the saying of Christ, "Be ye merciful, as your heavenly Father is merciful." (Matt. v. 7.) We must notice, on the other hand, that he could denounce nothing on them more severe or more dreadful than the judgment of God. It hence follows, that all they are miserable and lost who flee not to the asylum of pardon.

And mercy rejoiceth. As though he had said, "God's mercy alone is that which delivers us from the dread and terror of judgment." He takes *rejoicing* or glorying in the sense of being victorious or triumphant ; for the judgment of condemnation is suspended over the whole world, and nothing but mercy can bring relief.

Hard and forced is the explanation of those who regard mercy as put here for the person, for man cannot properly be said to rejoice or glory against the judgment of God ; but mercy itself in a manner triumphs, and alone reigns when the severity of judgment gives way ; though I do not deny but that hence arises confidence in rejoicing, that is, when the faithful know that the wrath of God in a manner yields to mercy, so that being relieved by the latter, they are not overwhelmed by the former.

14. What *doth it* profit, my brethren, though a man say he hath faith, and have not works? can faith save him ?	14. Quid prodest, fratres mei, si fidem dicat aliquis se habere, opera autem non habeat ? nunquid potest fides salvum facere ipsum ?
15. If a brother or sister be naked, and destitute of daily food,	15. Quòd si frater aut soror nudi fuerint, et egentes quotidiano victu,
16. And one of you say unto them, Depart in peace, be *ye* warmed and filled ; notwithstanding ye give them not those things which are needful to the body, what *doth it* profit ?	16. Dicat autem aliquis vestrum illis, Abite cum pace, calescite et saturamini ; non tamen dederitis quæ sunt necessaria corpori, quæ utilitas ?
17. Even so faith, if it hath not works, is dead, being alone.	17. Sic et fides, si opera non habuerit, mortua est per se.

14. *What doth it profit.* He proceeds to commend mercy. And as he had threatened that God would be a severe Judge to us, and at the same time very dreadful, except we be kind and merciful towards our neighbours, and as on the other hand hypocrites objected and said, that faith is sufficient to us, in which the salvation of men consists, he now condemns this vain boasting. The sum, then, of what is said is, that faith without love avails nothing, and that it is therefore wholly dead.

But here a question arises, Can faith be separated from love ? It is indeed true that the exposition of this passage has produced that common distinction of the Sophists, between unformed and formed faith ; but of such a thing James knew nothing, for it appears from the first words, that he speaks of false profession of faith : for he does not begin thus, "If any one has faith ;" but, "If any says that he has faith ;" by which he certainly intimates that hypocrites boast of the empty name of faith, which really does not belong to them.

That he calls it then *faith*, is a concession, as the Rhetoricians say ; for when we discuss a point, it does no harm, nay, it is sometimes expedient, to concede to an adversary what he demands, for as soon as the thing itself is known, what is conceded may be easily taken away from him. James then, as he was satisfied that it was a false pretext by which hypocrites covered themselves, was not disposed to raise a dispute about a word or an expression. Let us, however, remember that he does not speak according to the impression of his own mind when he mentions faith, but that on the contrary he disputes against those who made a false pretence as to faith, of which they were wholly destitute.

Can faith save him ? This is the same as though he had said, that we do not attain salvation by a frigid and bare knowledge of God, which all confess to be most true ; for salvation comes to us by faith for this reason, because it joins us to God. And this comes not in any other way than by being united to the body of Christ, so that, living through his Spirit, we are also governed by him. There is no such thing as this in the dead image of faith. There is then no wonder that James denies that salvation is connected with it.[1]

15. *If a brother*, or, For if a brother. He takes an example from what was connected with his subject ; for he had been exhorting them to exercise the duties of love. If any one, on the contrary, boasted that he was satisfied with faith without works, he compares this shadowy faith to the saying of one who bids a famished man to be filled without supplying him with the food of which he is destitute. As, then, he who sends away a poor man with words, and offers

---

[1] When he says, " Can faith save him ?" his meaning is, " Can the faith which he says he has save him ?" that is, faith which is dead and produces no works; for that is the faith clearly intended here, as it appears from what follows. To make the meaning more evident *Macknight* renders the sentence thus,—" Can this faith save him ?" that is, the faith that has not works.—*Ed.*

him no help, treats him with mockery, so they who devise for themselves faith without works, and without any of the duties of religion, trifle with God.[1]

17. *Is dead, being alone.* He says that faith is dead, being by itself, that is, when destitute of good works. We hence conclude that it is indeed no faith, for when dead, it does not properly retain the name. The Sophists plead this expression and say, that some sort of faith is found by itself; but this frivolous cavilling is easily refuted; for it is sufficiently evident that the Apostle reasons from what is impossible, as Paul calls an angel anathema, if he attempted to subvert the gospel. (Gal. i. 8.)

18. Yea, a man may say, Thou hast faith, and I have works: shew me thy faith without thy works, and I will shew thee my faith by my works.	18. Quin dicat quispiam, Tu fidem habes, et ego opera habeo: ostende mihi fidem tuam sine operibus (*alias*, ex operibus) tuis, et ego tibi ex operibus meis ostendam fidem meam.
19. Thou believest that there is one God; thou doest well: the devils also believe, and tremble.	19. Tu credis quòd Deus unus est, bene facis; et dæmones credunt, ac contremiscunt.

18. *Yea, a man may say.* Erasmus introduces here two persons as speakers; one of whom boasts of faith without works, and the other of works without faith; and he thinks that both are at length confuted by the Apostle. But this view seems to me too forced. He thinks it strange, that this should be said by James, *Thou hast faith*, who acknowledges no faith without works. But in this he is much mistaken, that he does not acknowledge an irony in these words. Then ἀλλὰ I take for "nay rather;" and τὶς for "any one;" for the design of James was to expose the foolish boasting of those who imagined that they had faith when by their life they shewed that they were unbelievers; for he intimates that it would be easy for all the godly who led a holy life to strip hypocrites of that boasting with which they were inflated.[2]

Shew me. Though the more received reading is, "by

[1] This is adduced as an illustration: as the saying of a man to the naked, "Be ye clothed," when he does nothing, effects no good, is wholly useless, so is that faith that produces no works; it being as it were dead, it cannot save.—*Ed.*

I would render the verse thus,—

"But one may say, Thou hast faith, I have also works; shew me works," yet the old Latin is more suitable, and the reading is also found in some Greek copies. I therefore hesitated not to adopt it. Then he bids to shew faith without works, and thus reasons from what is impossible, to prove what does not exist. So he speaks ironically. But if any one prefers the other reading, it comes to the same thing, "Shew me by works thy faith;" for since it is not an idle thing, it must necessarily be proved by works. The meaning then is, "Unless thy faith brings forth fruits, I deny that thou hast any faith."[1]

But it may be asked, whether the outward uprightness of life is a sure evidence of faith? for James says, "I will shew thee my faith by my works." To this I reply, that the unbelieving sometimes excel in specious virtues, and lead an honourable life free from every crime; and hence works apparently excellent may exist apart from faith. Nor indeed does James maintain that every one who seems good possesses faith. This only he means, that faith, without the evidence of good works, is vainly pretended, because fruit ever comes from the living root of a good tree.

19. *Thou believest that there is one God.* From this one

> thy faith *that is* without works, and I will shew thee my faith by my works."
> It is the same as though he had said, "Thou hast faith only, I have also works in addition to my faith; now, prove to me that you have true faith without having works connected with it, (which was impossible, hence he is called 'vain man,' or empty-headed, in verse 20,) and I will prove my faith by its fruits, even good works."—*Ed.*

[1] *Griesbach* and others regard χωρὶς as the true reading, countenanced by most MSS., and found in the *Syr.* and *Vulg.*

This verse is a key to the meaning of James: faith is to be *proved* by works; then faith properly justifies and saves, and works prove its genuineness. When he says that a man is justified by works, the meaning according to this verse is, that a man is proved by works to be justified, his faith being thereby shewn to be a living and not a dead faith. We may well be surprised, as *Doddridge* was, that any, taking a view of this whole passage, should ever think that there is any contrariety in what is here said to the teaching of Paul. The doctrine of Paul, that man is justified by faith and not by works, that is, by a living faith, which works by love, is perfectly consistent with what James says, that is, that a man is not justified by a dead faith but by that faith which proves its living power by producing good works, or by rendering obedience to God. The sum of what James says is, that a dead faith cannot save, but a living faith, and that a living faith is a working faith—a doctrine taught by Paul as well as by James.—*Ed.*

sentence it appears evident that the whole dispute is not about faith, but of the common knowledge of God, which can no more connect man with God, than the sight of the sun carry him up to heaven; but it is certain that by faith we come nigh to God. Besides, it would be ridiculous were any one to say that the devils have faith; and James prefers them in this respect to hypocrites. The devil *trembles*, he says, at the mention of God's name, because when he acknowledges his own judge he is filled with the fear of him. He then who despises an acknowledged God is much worse.

Thou doest well, is put down for the purpose of extenuating, as though he had said, "It is, forsooth! a great thing to sink down below the devils."[1]

20. But wilt thou know, O vain man, that faith without works is dead?	20. Vis autem scire, O homo inanis! quòd fides absque operibus mortua sit?
21. Was not Abraham our father justified by works, when he had offered Isaac his son upon the altar?	21. Abraham pater noster, nonne ex operibus justificatus est, quum obtulit filium suum Isaac super altare?
22. Seest thou how faith wrought with his works, and by works was faith made perfect?	22. Vides quòd fides co-operata fuerit ejus operibus, et ex operibus fides perfecta fuerit?
23. And the scripture was fulfilled which saith, Abraham believed God, and it was imputed unto him for righteousness: and he was called the Friend of God.	23. Atque impleta fuit scriptura, quæ dicit, Credidit Abraham Deo, et imputatum illi fuit in justitiam, et Amicus Deo vocatus est?
24. Ye see then how that by works a man is justified, and not by faith only.	24. Videtis igitur quòd ex operibus justificatur homo, et non ex fide solùm.
25. Likewise also, was not Rahab the harlot justified by works, when she had received the messengers, and had sent *them* out another way?	25. Similiter et Rahab meretrix, nonnè ex operibus justificata est, quum excepit nuntios, et alia via ejecit?
26. For as the body without the spirit is dead, so faith without works is dead also.	26. Quemadmodum enim corpus sine anima mortuum est, ita et fides sine operibus mortua est.

[1] The design of alluding to the faith of devils seems to have been this, to shew that though a man may believe and tremble, yet if he does not obey God and do good works, he has no true evidence of faith. Obedient faith is that which saves, and not merely that which makes us tremble. The connexion with the preceding verse seems to be as follows,—

In the former verse the boaster of mere faith is challenged to prove that his faith is right and therefore saving; the challenger would prove his by his works. Then, in this verse, a test is applied—the very first article of faith is mentioned: "Be it that you believe this, yet this faith will not

20. *But wilt thou know.* We must understand the state of the question, for the dispute here is not respecting the cause of justification, but only what avails a profession of faith without works, and what opinion we are to form of it. Absurdly then do they act who strive to prove by this passage that man is justified by works, because James meant no such thing, for the proofs which he subjoins refer to this declaration, that no faith, or only a dead faith, is without works. No one will ever understand what is said, nor judge wisely of words, except he who keeps in view the design of the writer.

21. *Was not Abraham.* The Sophists lay hold on the word *justified,* and then they cry out as being victorious, that justification is partly by works. But we ought to seek out a right interpretation according to the general drift of the whole passage. We have already said that James does not speak here of the cause of justification, or of the manner how men obtain righteousness, and this is plain to every one; but that his object was only to shew that good works are always connected with faith; and, therefore, since he declares that Abraham was *justified by works,* he is speaking of the proof he gave of his justification.

When, therefore, the Sophists set up James against Paul, they go astray through the ambiguous meaning of a term. When Paul says that we are justified by faith, he means no other thing than that by faith we are counted righteous before God. But James has quite another thing in view, even to shew that he who professes that he has faith, must prove the reality of his faith by his works. Doubtless James did not mean to teach us here the ground on which our hope of salvation ought to rest; and it is this alone that Paul dwells upon.[1]

That we may not then fall into that false reasoning which has deceived the Sophists, we must take notice of the two-

save you: the devils have this faith, and instead of being saved they tremble.—*Ed.*

[1] It is justly observed by *Scott,* that there is the same difficulty in reconciling James with himself as with Paul. And this difficulty at once vanishes, when we take a view of the whole passage, and not confine ourselves to single expressions.— *Ed.*

fold meaning of the word *justified.* Paul means by it the gratuitous imputation of righteousness before the tribunal of God; and James, the manifestation of righteousness by the conduct, and that before men, as we may gather from the preceding words, "Shew to me thy faith," &c. In this sense we fully allow that man is justified by works, as when any one says that a man is enriched by the purchase of a large and valuable estate, because his riches, before hid, shut up in a chest, were thus made known.

22. *By works was faith made perfect.*[1] By this he again shews, that the question here is not respecting the cause of our salvation, but whether works necessarily accompany faith; for in this sense it is said to have been perfected by works, because it was not idle. It is said to have been perfected by works, not because it received thence its own perfection, but because it was thus proved to be true. For the futile distinction which the Sophists draw from these words, between formed and unformed faith, needs no laboured refutation; for the faith of Abraham was formed and therefore perfected before he sacrificed his son. And this work was not as it were the finishing or last work, for many things afterwards followed by which Abraham proved the increase of his faith. Hence this was not the perfection of his faith, nor did it then for the first time put on its form. James then understood no other thing than that the integrity of his faith then appeared, because it brought forth that remarkable fruit of obedience.

23. *And the Scripture was fulfilled.* They who seek to

[1] The previous sentence is hardly intelligible in our version or in *Calvin's.* "Seest thou how faith wrought (co-operated, by *C.*) with his works?" The verb is συνεργέω, which means properly to work together, to co-operate; and it means also, as the effect of co-operating, to aid, to help. "Seest thou how faith aided *him* in his works?" *Schleusner* gives this paraphrase, "Thou seest that Abraham was aided by his faith to do his remarkable works." *Beza's* version is, "Thou seest that faith was the assistant (*administer*) of his works." Some give the idea of combining to co-operating, "Thou seest that faith co-operated with his works," that is, in justification. It has been said, that if this combination had been intended, it ought to have been said that works co-operated with his faith, as faith, according to the testimony of Scripture and the nature of things, is the primary and the principal thing, and as there can be no good works without faith. But the first explanation is the most consonant with the words and with the drift of the passage.—*Ed.*

prove from this passage of James that the works of Abraham were imputed for righteousness, must necessarily confess that Scripture is perverted by him; for however they may turn and twist, they can never make the effect to be its own cause. The passage is quoted from Moses. (Gen. xv. 6.) The imputation of righteousness which Moses mentions, preceded more than thirty years the work by which they would have Abraham to have been justified. Since faith was imputed to Abraham fifteen years before the birth of Isaac, this could not surely have been done through the work of sacrificing him. I consider that all those are bound fast by an indissoluble knot, who imagine that righteousness was imputed to Abraham before God, because he sacrificed his son Isaac, who was not yet born when the Holy Spirit declared that Abraham was justified. It hence necessarily follows that something posterior is pointed out here.

Why then does James say that it was fulfilled? even because he intended to shew what sort of faith that was which justified Abraham; that is, that it was not idle or evanescent, but rendered him obedient to God, as also we find in Heb. xi. 8. The conclusion, which is immediately added, as it depends on this, has no other meaning. Man is not justified by faith alone, that is, by a bare and empty knowledge of God; he is justified by works, that is, his righteousness is known and proved by its fruits.

25. *Likewise also was not Rahab.* It seems strange that he connected together those who were so unlike. Why did he not rather choose some one from so large a number of illustrious fathers, and join him to Abraham? Why did he prefer a harlot to all others? He designedly put together two persons so different in their character, in order more clearly to shew, that no one, whatever may have been his or her condition, nation, or class in society, has ever been counted righteous without good works. He had named the patriarch, by far the most eminent of all; he now includes under the person of a harlot, all those who, being aliens, were joined to the Church. Whosoever, then, seeks to be counted righteous, though he may even be among the lowest, must yet shew that he is such by good works.

James, according to his manner of speaking, declares that Rahab was justified by works; and the Sophists hence conclude that we obtain righteousness by the merits of works. But we deny that the dispute here is concerning the mode of obtaining righteousness. We, indeed, allow that good works are required for righteousness; we only take away from them the power of conferring righteousness, because they cannot stand before the tribunal of God.[1]

CHAPTER III.

1. My brethren, be not many masters, knowing that we shall receive the greater condemnation.

2. For in many things we offend all. If any man offend not in word, the same *is* a perfect man, *and* able also to bridle the whole body.

3. Behold, we put bits in the horses' mouths, that they may obey us; and we turn about their whole body.

4. Behold also the ships, which, though *they be* so great, and *are* driven of fierce winds, yet are they turned about with a very small helm, whithersoever the governor listeth.

5. Even so the tongue is a little member, and boasteth great things.

1. Nolite plures magistri fieri, fratres mei; scientes quòd majus judicium sumpturi sumus.

2. In multis enim labimur omnes: si quis in sermone non labitur, hic perfectus est vir, ut qui possit fræno moderari totum etiam corpus.

3. Ecce equis fræna in ora injicimus, ut obediant nobis; et totum illorum corpus circumagimus:

4. Ecce etiam naves, cum tantæ sint, et à sævis ventis pulsentur, circumaguntur à minimo gubernaculo, quocunque affectus dirigentis voluerit:

5. Ita et lingua pusillum membrum est, et magna jactat.

1. *Be not many masters.* The common and almost universal interpretation of this passage is, that the Apostle discourages the desire for the office of teaching, and for this reason, because it is dangerous, and exposes one to a heavier judgment, in case he transgresses: and they think that he said, *Be not many masters*, because there ought to have been some. But I take masters not to be those who performed a

---

[1] The last verse is left unnoticed,—
26. "For as the body without the spirit is dead, so also faith without works (or, having no works) is dead."
The meaning is not, that works are to faith what the spirit is to the body, for that would make works to be the life of faith, the reverse of the fact; but the meaning is, that faith having no works is like a dead carcase without life.—*Ed.*

public duty in the Church, but such as took upon them the right of passing judgment upon others : for such reprovers sought to be accounted as masters of morals. And it was a mode of speaking usual among the Greeks as well as Latins, that they were called masters who superciliously animadverted on others.

And that he forbade them to be many, it was done for this reason, because many everywhere did thrust in themselves ; for it is, as it were, an innate disease in mankind to seek reputation by blaming others. And, in this respect, a twofold vice prevails,—though few excel in wisdom, yet all intrude indiscriminately into the office of masters; and then few are influenced by a right feeling, for hypocrisy and ambition stimulate them, and not a care for the salvation of their brethren. For it is to be observed, that James does not discourage those brotherly admonitions, which the Spirit so often and so much recommends to us, but that immoderate desire to condemn, which proceeds from ambition and pride, when any one exalts himself against his neighbour, slanders, carps, bites, and malignantly seeks for what he may turn to a sinister purpose : for this is usually done when impertinent censors of this kind insolently boast themselves in the work of exposing the vices of others.

From this outrage and annoyance James recalls us ; and he adds a reason, because they who are thus severe towards others shall undergo a heavier judgment : for he imposes a hard law on himself, who tries the words and deeds of others according to the rule of extreme rigour ; nor does he deserve pardon, who will pardon none. This truth ought to be carefully observed, that they who are too rigid towards their brethren, provoke against themselves the severity of God.

2. *For in many things we offend all.* This may be taken as having been said by way of concession, as though he had said, " Be it that thou findest what is blameable in thy brethren, for no one is free from sins ; but dost thou think that thou art perfect who usest a slanderous and virulent tongue ?" But James seems to me to exhort us by this argument to meekness, since we are ourselves also surrounded with many

infirmities; for he acts unjustly who denies to others the pardon he needs himself. So also Paul says, when he bids the fallen to be reproved kindly, and in the spirit of meekness; for he immediately adds, "considering thyself, lest thou also be tempted." (Gal. vi. 1.) For there is nothing which serves more to moderate extreme rigour than the knowledge of our own infirmity.

If any man offend not in word. After having said that there is no one who does not sin in many things, he now shews that the disease of evil-speaking is more odious than other sins; for by saying that he who offends not with his tongue is *perfect,* he intimates that the restraining of the tongue is a great virtue, and one of the chief virtues. Hence they act most perversely who curiously examine every fault, even the least, and yet so grossly indulge themselves.

He then indirectly touches here on the hypocrisy of censors, because in examining themselves they omitted the chief thing, and what was of great moment, even their evil-speaking; for they who reproved others pretended a zeal for perfect holiness; but they ought to have begun with the tongue, if they wished to be perfect. As they made no account of bridling the tongue, but, on the contrary, did bite and tear others, they exhibited only a fictitious sanctity. It is hence evident that they were the most reprehensible of all, because they neglected a primary virtue. This connexion renders the meaning of the Apostle plain to us.

3. *We put bits in the horses' mouths.* By these two comparisons he proves that a great part of true perfection is in the tongue, and that it exercises dominion, as he has just said, over the whole life. He compares the tongue, first, to a bridle, and then to a helm of a ship. Though a horse be a ferocious animal, yet he is turned about at the will of its rider, because he is bridled; no less can the tongue serve to govern man. So also with regard to the helm of a ship, which guides a large vessel and surmounts the impetuosity of winds. Though the tongue be a small member, yet it avails much in regulating the life of man.

And boasteth great things. The verb μεγαλαυχεῖν means to boast one's-self, or to vaunt. But James in this passage did not intend to reprove ostentation so much as to show that the tongue is the doer of great things; for in this last clause he applies the previous comparisons to his subject; and vain boasting is not suitable to the bridle and the helm. He then means that the tongue is endued with great power.

I have rendered what Erasmus has translated the *impetuosity*, the *inclination*, of the pilot or guide; for ὁρμὴ means desire. I indeed allow that among the Greeks it designates those lusts which are not subservient to reason. But here James simply speaks of the will of the pilot.

5. — Behold how great a matter a little fire kindleth!	5. — Ecce exiguus ignis quantam sylvam incendit.
6. And the tongue *is* a fire, a world of iniquity: so is the tongue among our members, that it defileth the whole body, and setteth on fire the course of nature; and it is set on fire of hell.	6. Et lingua ignis est, et mundus iniquitatis: sic inquam lingua constituta est in membris nostris, inquinans totum corpus, inflammans rotam nativitatis, et inflammatur à gehenna.

He now explains the evils which proceed from the neglect of restraining the tongue, in order that we may know that the tongue may do much good or much evil,—that if it be modest and well regulated, it becomes a bridle to the whole life, but that if it be petulant and violent, like a fire it destroys all things.

He represents it as a small or *little fire*, to intimate that this smallness of the tongue will not be a hindrance that its power should not extend far and wide to do harm.

6. By adding that it is *a world of iniquity*, it is the same as though he had called it the sea or the abyss. And he suitably connects the smallness of the tongue with the vastness of the world; according to this meaning, A slender portion of flesh contains in it the whole world of iniquity.

So is the tongue. He explains what he meant by the term *world*, even because the contagion of the tongue spreads through every part of life; or rather he shews what he understood by the metaphor *fire*, even that the tongue pollutes the whole man. He however immediately returns to the fire, and says, that the *whole course of nature* is set on fire by the tongue. And he compares human life to a *course* or a wheel: and γένεσις, as before, he takes for nature, (ch. i. 23.)

The meaning is, that when other vices are corrected by age or by the succession of time, or when at least they do not possess the whole man, the vice of the tongue spreads and prevails over every part of life ; except one prefers to take *setting on fire* as signifying a violent impulse, for we call that fervid which is accompanied with violence. And thus Horace speaks of wheels, for he calls chariots in battle fervid, on account of their rapidity. The meaning then would be, that the tongue is like untamed horses ; for as these draw violently the chariots, so the tongue hurries a man headlong by its own wantonness.[1]

When he says that it is *set on fire by hell,* it is the same as though he had said, that the outrageousness of the tongue is the flame of the infernal fire.[2] For as heathen poets imagined that the wicked are tormented by the torches of the Furies ; so it is true, that Satan by the fans of temptations kindles the fire of all evils in the world : but James means, that fire, sent by Satan, is most easily caught by the tongue, so that it immediately burns ; in short, that it is a material fitted for receiving, fostering, and increasing the fire of hell.

7. For every kind of beasts, and of birds, and of serpents, and of things in the sea, is tamed, and hath been tamed of mankind:	7. Omnis enim natura ferarum et volucrum et serpentum et marinorum, à natura humana domatur et domita est :
8. But the tongue can no man tame ; *it is* an unruly evil, full of deadly poison.	8. Linguam verò nullus hominum domare potest, incoercibile malum, plena veneno mortifero.
9. Therewith bless we God, even the Father ; and therewith curse we men, which are made after the similitude of God.	9. Per ipsam benedicimus Deum et Patrem ; et per ipsam execramur homines ad similitudinem ejus factos.
10. Out of the same mouth proceedeth blessing and cursing. My brethren, these things ought not so to be.	10. Ex eodem ore procedit benedictio et maledictio. Non convenit, fratres mei, hæc ita fieri.

[1] " The course of nature," or the compass of nature, that is, all that is included in nature, means evidently the same with " the whole body" in the preceding clause. There is no sense, compatible with the passage, in what some have suggested, " the whole course of life ;" for what idea is conveyed, when we say that the tongue inflames or sets in a flame the whole course of life? But there is an intelligible meaning, when it is said, that the tongue sets in a flame the whole machinery of our nature, every faculty that belongs to man.—*Ed.*

[2] " A bad tongue is the organ of the devil."—*Estius.*—*Ed.*

11. Doth a fountain send forth at the same place sweet water and bitter?
12. Can the fig-tree, my brethren, bear olive-berries? either a vine, figs? so *can* no fountain both yield salt water and fresh.

11. An fons ex eodem foramine ejicit dulce et amarum?
12. Non potest, fratres mei, ficus oleas proferre; aut vitis ficus; sic nullus fons salsam et dulcem gignere aquam.

7. *For every kind of beasts.* This is a confirmation of the last clause; for that Satan by the tongue rules most effectually he proves by this—that it can by no means be brought to due order, and he amplifies this by comparisons. For he says that there is no animal so savage or fierce, which is not tamed by the skill of man,—that fishes, which in a manner inhabit another world,—that birds, which are so quick and roving,—and that serpents, which are so inimical to mankind, are sometimes tamed. Since then the tongue cannot be restrained, there must be some secret fire of hell hidden in it.

What he says of wild beasts, of serpents, and of other animals, is not to be understood of them all; it is enough that the skill of man should subdue and tame some of the most ferocious of them, and also that serpents are sometimes tamed. He refers to present and to past time: the present regards power and capacity, and the past, usage or experience. He hence justly concludes that the tongue is full of deadly poison.

Though all these things most suitably refer in the first place to the subject of this passage—that they claim an unreasonable command over others, who labour under a worse vice; yet a universal doctrine may be understood as taught here,—that if we desire to form our life aright, we must especially strive to restrain the tongue, for no part of man does more harm.

9. *Therewith,* or, by it, *bless we God.* It is a clear instance of its deadly poison, that it can thus through a monstrous levity transform itself; for when it pretends to bless God, it immediately curses him in his own image, even by cursing men. For since God ought to be blessed in all his works, he ought to be so especially as to men, in whom his image and glory peculiarly shine forth. It is then a hypocrisy not to be borne, when man employs the same tongue in blessing

God and in cursing men. There can be then no calling on God, and his praises must necessarily cease, where evil-speaking prevails; for it is an impious profanation of God's name, when the tongue is virulent towards our brethren and pretends to praise him. That we may therefore rightly praise God, the vice of evil-speaking as to our neighbour must especially be corrected.

This particular truth ought also to be borne in mind, that severe censors discover their own virulence, when they suddenly vomit forth against their brethren whatever curses they can imagine, after having in sweet strains offered praises to God. Were any one to object and say, that the image of God in human nature has been blotted out by the sin of Adam; we must, indeed, confess that it has been miserably deformed, but in such a way that some of its lineaments still appear. Righteousness and rectitude, and the freedom of choosing what is good, have been lost; but many excellent endowments, by which we excel the brutes, still remain. He, then, who truly worships and honours God, will be afraid to speak slanderously of man.

11. *Doth a fountain.* He adduces these comparisons in order to shew that a cursing tongue is something monstrous, contrary to all nature, and subverts the order everywhere established by God. For God hath so arranged things which are contrary, that inanimate things ought to deter us from a chaotic mixture, such as is found in a double tongue.[1]

13. Who *is* a wise man, and endued with knowledge among you? let him shew out of a good conversation his works with meekness of wisdom.	13. Quis sapiens et intelligens inter vos? ostendat ex honesta conversatione opera sua in mansuetudine sapientiæ.
14. But if ye have bitter envying and strife in your hearts, glory not, and lie not against the truth.	14. Si verò æmulationem amaram habetis, et contentionem in corde vestro, ne gloriemini, et mentiamini adversus veritatem.
15. This wisdom descendeth not from above, but *is* earthly, sensual, devilish.	15. Non est hæc sapientia de sursum veniens, sed terrestris, animalis, dæmoniaca.

[1] There is a different reading at the end of the 12th verse, adopted by *Griesbach*, though rejected by *Mill* and others: οὕτως οὔτε ἁλυκὸν γλυκὺ ποιῆσαι ὕδωρ, "So neither can salt water produce sweet." This reading is favoured by the *Syr.* and *Vulg.*, though the words are somewhat different.—*Ed.*

16. For where envying and strife *is*, there *is* confusion, and every evil work.

17. But the wisdom that is from above is first pure, then peaceable, gentle, *and* easy to be entreated, full of mercy and good fruits, without partiality, and without hypocrisy.

18. And the fruit of righteousness is sown in peace of them that make peace.

16. Ubi enim æmulatio et contentio, ibi perturbatio et omne pravum opus.

17. Quæ autem è sursum est sapientia, primum pura est, deinde pacata, æqua, comis, plena misericordiæ et bonorum operum, sine disquisitione, sine simulatione.

18. Fructus autem justitiæ in pace seminatur facientibus pacem.

13. *Who is a wise man.* As the lust of slandering arises mostly from pride, and as the false conceit of wisdom for the most part generates pride, he therefore speaks here of wisdom. It is usual with hypocrites to exalt and shew off themselves by criminating all others, as the case was formerly with many of the philosophers, who sought glory for themselves by a bitter abuse of all other orders. Such haughtiness as slanderous men swell with and are blinded by, James checked, by denying that the conceit of wisdom, with which men flatter themselves, has in it anything divine; but, on the contrary, he declares that it proceeds from the devil.

Then the meaning is, that supercilious censors, who largely indulge themselves, and at the same time spare none, seem to themselves to be very wise, but are greatly mistaken; for the Lord teaches his people far otherwise, even to be meek, and to be courteous to others. They, then, are alone wise in the sight of God, who connect this meekness with an honest conversation; for they who are severe and inexorable, though they may excel others in many virtues, do not yet follow the right way of wisdom.[1]

14. *But if ye have bitter envying.* He points out the fruits which proceed from that extreme austerity which is contrary to meekness; for immoderate rigour necessarily

---

[1] " Who is wise and intelligent among you? let him by a good conduct shew his works in meekness of wisdom."

The arrangement here is according to what is common in Scripture: Wisdom the effect first, then knowledge the cause or what precedes it. In what follows the order is reversed; knowledge distinguishes between good and bad works, and the good ought to be exhibited with that meekness which wisdom dictates.—*Ed.*

begets mischievous emulations, which presently break forth into contentions. It is, indeed, an improper mode of speaking, to place contentions in the heart; but this affects not the meaning; for the object was to shew that the evil disposition of the heart is the fountain of these evils.

He has called *envying*, or emulation, *bitter;* for it prevails not, except when minds are so infected with the poison of malignity, that they turn all things into bitterness.[1]

That we may then really glory that we are the children of God, he bids us to act calmly and meekly towards our brethren; otherwise he declares that we are lying in assuming the Christian name. But it is not without reason that he has added the associate of envying, even *strife*, or contention, for contests and quarrels ever arise from malignity and envy.

15. *This wisdom descendeth not.* As hypocrites with difficulty give way, he sharply checked their haughtiness, denying that to be true wisdom with which they were inflated, while they were extremely morose in searching out the vices of others. Conceding to them, however, the term *wisdom*, he shews by the words he applies to it its true character, and says that it is *earthly, sensual, devilish*, or demoniac, while true wisdom must be heavenly, spiritual, divine; which three things are directly contrary to the three preceding ones. For James takes it as granted, that we are not wise, except when we are illuminated by God from above through his Spirit. However, then, the mind of man may enlarge itself, all its acuteness will be vanity; and not only so, but being at length entangled in the wiles of Satan, it will become wholly delirious.[2]

---

[1] A similar order as to the words is found here as in the former verse: bitter envying is occasioned by strife or contention. There may be envying without contention, but it is contention that commonly makes it bitter.—*Ed.*

[2] *Scott* considers that this wisdom was called "earthly," because it sought earthly distinctions, and was of an earthly origin,—" sensual," or rather " natural," as the word is rendered in 1 Cor. ii. 14, because it was the result of such principles as *natural* men are actuated by, such as envy and ambition,—" and devilish," because it came first from the devil, and constituted the image of his pride, ambition, malignity, and falsehood.

The word "sensual" has led some to suppose that the reference is to

Sensual, or animal, is in opposition to what is spiritual, as in 1 Cor. ii. 14, where Paul says that the sensual or animal man receives not the things of God. And the pride of man could not have been more effectually cast down, than when thus is condemned whatever wisdom he has from himself, without the Spirit of God; nay, when from himself a transition is made to the devil. For it is the same as though he had said, that men, following their own sense, or minds, or feelings, soon become a prey to the delusions of Satan.

16. *For where envying is.* It is an argument from what is contrary; for envying, by which hypocrites are influenced, produces effects contrary to wisdom. For wisdom requires a state of mind that is calm and composed, but envying disturbs it, so that in itself it becomes in a manner tumultuous, and boils up immoderately against others.

Some render ἀκαταστασία inconstancy, and sometimes it means this: but as it signifies also sedition and tumult, perturbation seems the most suitable to this passage. For James meant to express something more than levity, even that the malignant and the slanderer does everything confusedly and rashly, as though he were beside himself; and hence he adds, *every evil work.*

17. *But the wisdom which is from above.* He now mentions the effects of celestial wisdom, which are wholly contrary to the former effects. He says first that it is *pure;* by which term he excludes hypocrisy and ambition.[1] He, in the second place, calls it *peaceable,* to intimate that it is not contentious. In the third place, he calls it *kind* or humane, that we may know that it is far away from that immoderate austerity which tolerates nothing in our brethren. He also calls it *gentle* or tractable; by which he means that it widely differs from pride and malignity. In the last

---

sensuality, the gratification of carnal lusts: but there is nothing in the passage that favours this view. The only things mentioned are envy and a contentious spirit, things which belong to natural man.—*Ed.*

[1] "Pure," ἁγνή, is to be understood according to what the context contains. It means what is free from taint or pollution: the *kind* of taint must be learnt from the passage. The wisdom from above is contrasted with the wisdom from below: the latter has envy and contention; the former is "pure," being free from envy, and is "peaceable."—*Ed.*

place, he says that it is *full of mercy*, &c., while hypocrisy is inhuman and inexorable. By *good fruits* he generally refers to all those duties which benevolent men perform towards their brethren; as though he had said, It is full of benevolence. It hence follows, that they lie who glory in their cruel austerity.

But though he had sufficiently condemned hypocrisy, when he said that wisdom is *pure* or sincere; he yet makes it more clear by repeating the same thing at the end. We are hence reminded, that for no other reason are we beyond measure morose or austere, but this, because we too much spare ourselves, and connive at our own vices.

But what he says, *without discerning*, (*sine dijudicatione*,) seems strange; for the Spirit of God does not take away the difference between good and evil; nor does he render us so senseless as to be so void of judgment as to praise vice, and regard it as virtue. To this I reply, that James here, by *discerning* or distinguishing, refers to that over-anxious and over-scrupulous inquiry, such as is commonly carried on by hypocrites, who too minutely examine the sayings and doings of their brethren, and put on them the worst construction.[1]

18. *And the fruit of righteousness.* This admits of two meanings,—that fruit is sown by the peaceable, which after-

---

[1] The word ἀδιάκριτος is found only here, and has been variously rendered, because the verb from which it comes has various meanings,—to discern, to make a difference, to judge, to examine, to contend or litigate, and to doubt. It is rendered by the *Vulg.*, " not judging"—uncensorious; by *Beza*, " without contending"—incontroversial; by *Erasmus*, " making no difference"—impartial; and by *Hammond*, " not doubting," *i. e.*, as to the faith. " Uncensorious," or, " impartial," seems the most suitable rendering; not given to rashness in judging of others, or not shewing respect of persons, previously condemned in ch. ii. 1. Then follows " undissembling," not saying one thing and meaning another.

There seems to be a complete contrast between the two kinds of wisdom. The wisdom from above is not envious, but pure; is not contentious, but peaceable; does not create confusion, but is patient and conciliatory; and instead of producing " every evil work," it is full of mercy or benevolence, and of the fruits of benevolence, being not censorious or partial in judgment, and not dissembling, or acting dishonestly. By this comparison, we see what were some of the things included in " every evil work;" they were the reverse of mercy or benevolence, and its fruits, even censoriousness or partiality, and dissimulation. And yet those who exhibited all those evil things thought that they had wisdom! and even gloried in it!—*Ed.*

wards they gather,—or, that they themselves, though they meekly tolerate many things in their neighbours, do not yet cease to sow righteousness. It is, however, an anticipation of an objection; for they who are carried away to evil-speaking by the lust of slandering, have always this excuse, " What! can we then remove evil by our courteousness?" Hence James says, that those who are wise according to God's will, are so kind, meek, and merciful, as yet not to cover vices nor favour them; but on the contrary in such a way as to strive to correct them, and yet in a peaceable manner, that is, in moderation, so that union is preserved. And thus he testifies that what he had hitherto said tends in no degree to do away with calm reproofs; but that those who wish to be physicians to heal vices ought not to be executioners.

He therefore adds, *by those who make peace;* which ought to be thus explained : they who study peace, are nevertheless careful to sow righteousness; nor are they slothful or negligent in promoting and encouraging good works; but they moderate their zeal with the condiment of peace, while hypocrites throw all things into confusion by a blind and furious violence.

CHAPTER IV.

1. From whence *come* wars and fightings among you? *come they* not hence, *even* of your lusts that war in your members?

2. Ye lust, and have not: ye kill, and desire to have, and cannot obtain: ye fight and war, yet ye have not, because ye ask not.

3. Ye ask, and receive not, because ye ask amiss, that ye may consume *it* upon your lusts.

1. Unde bella et pugnæ inter vos? nonne hinc, ex voluptatibus vestris, quæ militant in membris vestris.

2. Concupiscitis et non habetis; invidetis et æmulamini, et non potestis obtinere; pugnatis et belligeramini, non habetis, propterea quòd non petitis;

3. Petitis, et non accipitis, quia malè petitis, ut in voluptates vestras insumatis.

1. *From whence* come *wars.* As he had spoken of peace, and had reminded them that vices are to be exterminated in such a way as to preserve peace, he now comes to their contentions, by which they created confusion among them-

selves; and he shews that these arose from their invidious desires and lusts, rather than from a zeal for what was just and right; for if every one observed moderation, they would not have disturbed and annoyed one another. They had their hot conflicts, because their lusts were allowed to prevail unchecked.

It hence appears, that greater peace would have been among them, had every one abstained from doing wrong to others; but the vices which prevailed among them were so many attendants armed to excite contentions. He calls our faculties *members*. He takes *lusts* as designating all illicit and lustful desires or propensities which cannot be satisfied without doing injury to others.

2. *Ye lust*, or covet, *and have not*. He seems to intimate that the soul of man is insatiable, when he indulges wicked lusts; and truly it is so; for he who suffers his sinful propensities to rule uncontrolled, will know no end to his lust. Were even the world given to him, he would wish other worlds to be created for him. It thus happens, that men seek torments which exceed the cruelty of all executioners. For that saying of Horace is true:

The tyrants of Sicily found no torment greater than envy.[1]

Some copies have φονεύετε, " ye kill;" but I doubt not but that we ought to read, φθονεῖτε, " ye envy," as I have rendered it; for the verb, to kill, does in no way suit the context.[2] *Ye fight:* he does not mean those wars and fight-

---

[1] Invidiâ Siculi non invenêre tyranni
Majus tormentum.—EPIST. Lib. I. II. 58.

[2] There is no MS. nor version in favour of φθονεῖτε. When it is said, " ye kill," the meaning is, that they did so as to the hatred or envy they entertained, for hatred is the root of murder, and arises often from envy. What has evidently led *Calvin* and others to conjecture a mistake here, has been the difficulty arising from the order of the words, " Ye kill and ye envy;" but this order is wholly consonant with the style of Scripture, where often the greater evil or good is mentioned first, and then that which precedes or leads to it. It is the same here as though the copulative, *and*, were rendered causatively, " ye kill because ye envy." Envy is murder in the sight of God.

The language of the whole passage is highly metaphorical. He calls their contentions " wars and fightings;" for the whole tenor of the passage is opposed to the supposition that he refers to actual wars. He adopts a military term as to inward lusts or ambitious desires, that they " carried on war" in their members; the expedition for their contests was prepared

ings, which men engage in with drawn swords, but the violent contentions which prevailed among them. They derived no benefit from contentions of this kind, for he affirms that they received the punishment of their own wickedness. God, indeed, whom they owned not as the author of blessings, justly disappointed them. For when they contended in ways so unlawful, they sought to be enriched through the favour of Satan rather than through the favour of God. One by fraud, another by violence, one by calumnies, and all by some evil or wicked arts, strove for happiness. They then sought to be happy, but not through God. It was therefore no wonder that they were frustrated in their efforts, since no success can be expected except through the blessing of God alone.

3. *Ye seek and receive not.* He goes farther; though they sought, yet they were deservedly denied; because they wished to make God the minister of their own lusts. For they set no bounds to their wishes, as he had commanded; but gave unbridled license to themselves, so as to ask those things of which man, conscious of what is right, ought especially to be ashamed. Pliny somewhere ridicules this impudence, that men so wickedly abuse the ears of God. The less tolerable is such a thing in Christians, who have had the rule of prayer given them by their heavenly Master.

And doubtless there appears to be in us no reverence for God, no fear of him, in short, no regard for him, when we dare to ask of him what even our own conscience does not approve. James meant briefly this,—that our desires ought to be bridled: and the way of bridling them is to subject them to the will of God. And he also teaches us, that what we in moderation wish, we ought to seek from God himself; which if it be done, we shall be preserved from wicked contentions, from fraud and violence, and from doing any injury to others.

within, mustered in their hearts. Then the character of this war is more plainly defined, " Ye covet," not, ye lust; " ye kill, or commit murder, for " ye envy ;" when ye cannot obtain your objects, " ye wage war and fight," that is, ye wrangle and quarrel. Avarice and ambition were the two prevailing evils, but especially avarice ; and avarice too for the purpose of gratifying the lusts and propensities of their sinful nature, as it appears from the third verse.—*Ed.*

4. Ye adulterers and adulteresses, know ye not that the friendship of the world is enmity with God? whosoever therefore will be a friend of the world is the enemy of God.

5. Do ye think that the scripture saith in vain, The spirit that dwelleth in us lusteth to envy?

6. But he giveth more grace:—

4. Adulteri et adulterae, an nescitis quòd amicitia mundi inimicitia Dei est? qui ergo voluerit amicus esse mundi, inimicus Dei constituitur.

5. An putatis quòd frustra dicat scriptura? An ad invidiam concupiscit spiritus qui habitat in nobis?

6. Quin majorem dat gratiam:—

4. *Ye adulterers.* I connect this verse with the foregoing verses: for he calls them *adulterers*, as I think, metaphorically; for they corrupted themselves with the vanities of this world, and alienated themselves from God; as though he had said, that they had become degenerated, or were become bastards. We know how frequent, in Holy Scripture, is that marriage mentioned which God forms with us. He would have us, then, to be like a chaste virgin, as Paul says, (2 Cor. xi. 2.) This chastity is violated and corrupted by all impure affections towards the world. James, then, does not without reason compare the love of the world to adultery.

They, then, who take his words literally, do not sufficiently observe the context: for he goes on still to speak against the lusts of men, which lead away those entangled with the world from God, as it follows,—

The friendship of the world. He calls it the friendship of the world, when men surrender themselves to the corruptions of the world, and become slaves to them. For such and so great is the disagreement between the world and God, that as much as any one inclines to the world, so much he alienates himself from God. Hence the Scripture bids us often to renounce the world, if we wish to serve God.

5. *Do ye think.* He seems to adduce from Scripture the next following sentence. Hence interpreters toil much, because none such, at least none exactly alike, is found in Scripture. But nothing hinders the reference to be made to what has been already said, that is, that the friendship of the world is adverse to God. Moreover, it has been rightly said, that this is a truth which occurs everywhere in Scripture. And that he has omitted the pronoun, which

would have rendered the sentence clearer, is not to be wondered at, for, as it is evident, he is everywhere very concise.

The Spirit, or, Does the Spirit? Some think that the soul of man is meant, and therefore read the sentence affirmatively, and according to this meaning,—that the spirit of man, as it is malignant, is so infected with envy, that it has ever a mixture of it. They, however, think better who regard the Spirit of God as intended; for it is he that is given to dwell in us.[1] I then take the Spirit as that of God, and read the sentence as a question; for it was his object to prove, that because they envied they were not ruled by the Spirit of God; because he teaches the faithful otherwise; and this he confirms in the next verse, by adding that he *giveth more* grace.

For it is an argument arising from what is contrary. Envy is a proof or sign of malignity; but the Spirit of God proves himself to be bountiful by the affluence of his blessings. There is then nothing more repugnant to his nature than envy. In short, James denies that the Spirit of God rules where depraved lusts prevail, which excite to mutual contention; because it is peculiarly the office of the Spirit to enrich men more and more continually with new gifts.

I will not stop to refute other explanations. Some give this meaning, that the Spirit lusteth against envy; which is too harsh and forced. Then they say that God *gives more grace* to conquer and subdue lust. But the meaning I have given is more suitable and simple,—that he restores us by

---

[1] There are waggon-loads of interpretations, says *Erasmus*, on this passage. The one given by *Calvin*, and adopted by *Whitby, Doddridge, Scholefield*, and others, is the most satisfactory, and what alone enables us to see a meaning in the words, "more grace," in the following verse. The Spirit dwells in God's people, and he dwells there to give more or increasing grace, according to the tenor of what is said in Isa. lvii. 15, where God is said to " dwell with him that is of a contrite and humble spirit," and for this purpose, " to revive the spirit of the humble," &c.

 5, 6. " Do ye think that the scripture speaketh *thus* in vain? doth the Spirit who dwells in us lust to envy? *nay*, but he giveth more (or, increasing) grace: he therefore saith, God sets himself in array against the insolent, but gives grace to the humble."

The humble are they who are made so by grace; but God promises to give them more grace, to perfect that which has been begun.—*Ed.*

his bounty from the power of malignant emulation. The continuative particle δὲ is to be taken adversatively, for ἀλλὰ or ἀλλά γε; so have I rendered it *quin*, but.

7. Submit yourselves therefore to God. Resist the devil, and he will flee from you.	7. Subjecti igitur estote Deo; Resistite diabolo, et fugiet à vobis;
8. Draw nigh to God, and he will draw nigh to you. Cleanse *your* hands, *ye* sinners; and purify *your* hearts, *ye* double-minded.	8. Appropinquate Deo, et appropinquabit vobis; mundate manus, peccatores; purificate corda duplici animo;
9. Be afflicted. and mourn, and weep: let your laughter be turned to mourning, and *your* joy to heaviness.	9. Affligimini, lugete et plorate; risus vester in luctum vertatur, et gaudium in mœrorem.
10. Humble yourselves in the sight of the Lord, and he shall lift you up.	10. Humiliamini coram Deo, et eriget vos.

7. *Submit yourselves.* The submission which he recommends is that of humility; for he does not exhort us generally to obey God, but requires submission; for the Spirit of God rests on the humble and the meek. (Isa. lvii. 15.) On this account he uses the illative particle. For as he had declared that God's Spirit is bountiful in increasing his gifts, he hence concludes that we ought to lay aside envy, and to submit to God.

Many copies have introduced here the following sentence: " Wherefore he saith, God resisteth the proud, but giveth grace unto the humble." But in others it is not found. Erasmus suspects that it was first a note in the margin, and afterwards crept into the text. It may have been so, though it is not unsuitable to the passage. For what some think, that it is strange that what is found only in Peter, should be quoted as Scripture, may be easily disposed of. But I rather conjecture that this sentence, which accords with the common doctrine of Scripture, had become then a sort of proverbial saying common among the Jews. And, indeed, it is no more than what is found in Ps. xviii. 27, " The humble, O Lord, thou wilt save; and the eyes of the proud wilt thou cast down:" and similar sentences are found in many other passages.[1]

---

[1] The passage is found in all MSS. and versions: there is, therefore, no ground to think it an interpolation. And it is taken literally from

Resist the devil. He shews what that contention is which we ought to engage in, as Paul says, that our contest is not with flesh and blood, but he stimulates us to a spiritual fight. Then, after having taught us meekness towards men, and submission towards God, he brings before us Satan as our enemy, whom it behoves us to fight against.

However, the promise which he adds, respecting the fleeing of Satan, seems to be refuted by daily experience; for it is certain, that the more strenuously any one resists, the more fiercely he is urged. For Satan, in a manner, acts playfully, when he is not in earnest repelled; but against those who really resist him, he employs all the strength he possesses. And further, he is never wearied with fighting; but when conquered in one battle, he immediately engages in another. To this I reply, that fleeing is to be taken here for putting to flight, or routing. And, doubtless, though he repeats his attacks continually, he yet always departs vanquished.

8. *Draw nigh to God.* He again reminds us that the aid of God will not be wanting to us, provided we give place to him. For when he bids us to draw nigh to God, that we may know him to be near to us, he intimates that we are destitute of his grace, because we withdraw from him. But as God stands on our side, there is no reason to fear succumbing. But if any one concludes from this passage, that the first part of the work belongs to us, and that afterwards the grace of God follows, the Apostle meant no such thing; for though we ought to do this, yet it does immediately follow that we can. And the Spirit of God, in exhorting us to our duty, derogates nothing from himself, or from his own power; but the very thing he bids us to do, he himself fulfils in us.

In short, James meant no other thing in this passage, than that God is never wanting to us, except when we alienate ourselves from him. He is like one who brings the hungry to a table, and the thirsty to a fountain. There is

Prov. iii, 34, according to the *Sept.*; though the first clause differs from the Hebrew in words, yet it is substantially the same. To " scorn the scorners," and to " resist (or, to stand in array against) the proud" or insolent, mean the same thing.—*Ed.*

this difference, that our steps must be guided and sustained by the Lord, for our feet fail us. But what some cavil at, and say, that God's grace is secondary to our preparation, and as it were the waiting-maid, is very frivolous; for we know that it is no new thing that he adds new to former graces, and thus enriches more and more those to whom he has already given much.

Cleanse your *hands*. He here addresses all those who were alienated from God. And he does not refer to two sorts of men, but he calls the same *sinners* and *double-minded*. Nor does he understand every kind of sinners, but the wicked and those of a corrupt life. It is said in John ix. 3, "God does not hear sinners;" in the same sense a woman is called a sinner by Luke. (Luke vii. 36.) It is said by the same and the other evangelists, "He drinketh and eateth with sinners." He, therefore, does not invite all indiscriminately to that sort of repentance mentioned here, but those who are wicked and corrupt in heart, and whose life is base and flagitious, or at least wicked; it is from these he requires a purity of heart and outward cleanliness.

We hence learn what is the true character of repentance. It is not only an outward amendment of life, but its beginning is the cleansing of the heart. It is also necessary, on the other hand, that the fruits of inward repentance should appear in the uprightness of our works.[1]

---

[1] In the seventh verse he seems still to continue military terms, " Se yourselves, therefore, in array under God ; stand up against the devil, an he will flee from you." It is especially to be observed, that the first thing is to be under the banner and protection of God, and then we can successfully stand up against the devil: apart from God, we have no power to resist him.

The order in the following verse, the eighth, is worthy of notice, as an example of what is very common in Scripture. The main thing is firs stated, to draw nigh to God; and then the things which are previously necessary, to cleanse their hands and to purify their hearts—an allusion probably to a practice among the priests under the law, of washing themselves before they engaged in the service of the temple. They were to wash their hands as though they had been stained with blood, as the crime of murder had been imputed to them in verse 2: and they were to purify their hearts from the covetings and ambitious desires which they had entertained. Except those things were done they could not draw nigh to God. And further, to draw nigh to God was necessary before they could set themselves in array under his authority, so that there is a connexi

9. *Be afflicted and mourn.* Christ denounces mourning on those who laugh, as a curse, (Luke vi. 25;) and James, in what shortly follows, alluding to the same words, threatens the rich with mourning. But here he speaks of that salutary mourning or sorrow which leads us to repentance. He addresses those who, being inebriated in their minds, did not perceive God's judgment. Thus it happened that they flattered themselves in their vices. That he might shake off from them this deadly torpor, he admonishes them to learn to mourn, that being touched with sorrow of conscience they might cease to flatter themselves and to exult on the verge of destruction. Then *laughter* is to be taken as signifying the flattering with which the ungodly deceive themselves, while they are infatuated by the sweetness of their sins and forget the judgment of God.

10. *Humble yourselves,* or, be ye humbled. The conclusion of what is gone before is, that the grace of God will then be ready to raise us up, when he sees that our proud spirits are laid aside. We emulate and envy, because we desire to be eminent. This is a way wholly unreasonable, for it is God's peculiar work to raise up the lowly, and especially those who willingly humble themselves. Whosoever, then, seeks a firm elevation, let him be cast down under a sense of his own infirmity, and think humbly of himself. Augustine well observes somewhere, As a tree must strike deep roots downwards, that it may grow upwards, so every one who has not his soul fixed deep in humility, exalts himself to his own ruin.

11. Speak not evil one of another, brethren. He that speaketh evil of *his* brother, and judgeth his brother, speaketh evil of the law, and judgeth the law: but if thou judge the law, thou art not a doer of the law, but a judge.	11. Ne detrahatis invicem, fratres; qui detrahit fratri, aut judicat fratrem suum, detrahit legi, et judicat legem; si autem judicas legem, non es factor legis sed judex.

between this verse and the former; the ultimate object, stated first, was submission to God, and to be under his protection; and all that follows was necessary for that purpose. The regular order would be, Purify your hearts, cleanse your hands, draw nigh to God, and be subject to him. But this mode of statement, by going backward instead of going forward, is to be met with in all parts of Scripture. See on this subject the Preface to the third volume of *Calvin's* Commentaries on Jeremiah.—*Ed.*

12. There is one lawgiver, who is able to save and to destroy: who art thou that judgest another?	12. Unus est legislator, qui potest servare et perdere: tu, quis es qui judicas alterum?

11. *Speak not evil,* or, defame not. We see how much labour James takes in correcting the lust for slandering. For hypocrisy is always presumptuous, and we are by nature hypocrites, fondly exalting ourselves by calumniating others. There is also another disease innate in human nature, that every one would have all others to live according to his own will or fancy. This presumption James suitably condemns in this passage, that is, because we dare to impose on our brethren our rule of life. He then takes *detraction* as including all the calumnies and suspicious words which flow from a malignant and perverted judgment. The evil of slandering takes a wide range; but here he properly refers to that kind of slandering which I have mentioned, that is, when we superciliously determine respecting the deeds and sayings of others, as though our own morosity were the law, when we confidently condemn whatever does not please us.

That such presumption is here reproved is evident from the reason that is immediately added, *He that speaketh evil of,* or defames his *brother, speaketh evil of,* or defames *the law.* He intimates, that so much is taken away from the law as one claims of authority over his brethren. Detraction, then, against the law is opposed to that reverence with which it behoves us to regard it.

Paul handles nearly the same argument in Rom. xiv., though on a different occasion. For when superstition in the choice of meats possessed some, what they thought unlawful for themselves, they condemned also in others. He then reminded them, that there is but one Lord, according to whose will all must stand or fall, and at whose tribunal we must all appear. Hence he concludes, that he who judges his brethren according to his own view of things, assumes to himself what peculiarly belongs to God. But James reproves here those who under the pretence of sanctity condemned their brethren, and therefore set up their own morosity in the place of the Divine law. He, however, employs the same reason with Paul, that is, that we act presumptuously when we assume authority over our brethren, while the law of God subordinates us all to itself without exception. Let us then learn that we are not to judge but according to God's law.

Thou art not a doer of the law, but a judge. This sentence ought to be thus explained : " When thou claimest for thyself a power to censure above the law of God, thou exemptest thyself from the duty of obeying the law." He then who rashly judges his brother, shakes off the yoke of God, for he submits not to the common rule of life. It is then an argument from what is contrary ; because the keeping of the law is wholly different from this arrogance, when men ascribe to their conceit the power and authority of the law. It hence follows, that we then only keep the law, when we wholly depend on its teaching alone, and do not otherwise distinguish between good and evil ; for all the deeds and words of men ought to be regulated by it.

Were any one to object and say, that still the saints will be the judges of the world, (1 Cor. vi. 2,) the answer is obvious, that this honour does not belong to them according to their own right, but inasmuch as they are the members of Christ ; and that they now judge according to the law, so that they are not to be deemed judges, because they only obediently assent to God as their own judge and the judge of all. With regard to God, he is not to be deemed the doer of the law, because his righteousness is prior to the law ; for the law has flown from the eternal and infinite righteousness of God as a river from its fountain.

12. *There is one lawgiver.*[1] When he connects the power of saving and destroying with the office of a lawgiver, he intimates that the whole majesty of God is forcibly assumed by those who claim for themselves the right of making a law ; and this is what is done by those who impose as a law on others their own nod or will. And let us remember that the subject here is not civil government, in which the edicts

---

[1] *Griesbach* adds, καὶ κριτής, " and judge," a reading favoured by many MSS. and the versions ; and doubtless it makes the passage more complete, especially as what follows belongs to the judge rather than to the lawgiver, that is, to save or destroy.—*Ed.*

and laws of magistrates have place, but the spiritual government of the soul, in which the word of God alone ought to bear rule. There is then one God, who has consciences subjected by right to his own laws, as he alone has in his own hand the power to save and to destroy.

It hence appears what is to be thought of human precepts, which cast the snare of necessity on consciences. Some indeed would have us to shew modesty, when we call the Pope Antichrist, who exercises tyranny over the souls of men, making himself a lawgiver equal to God. But we learn from this passage something far more, even that they are the members of Antichrist, who willingly submit to be thus ensnared, and that they thus renounce Christ, when they connect themselves with a man that is not only a mortal, but who also extols himself against Him. It is, I say, a prevaricating obedience, rendered to the devil, when we allow any other than God himself to be a lawgiver to rule our souls.

Who art thou. Some think that they are admonished here to become reprovers of their own vices, in order that they might begin to examine themselves, and that by finding out that they were not purer than others, they might cease to be so severe. I think that their own condition is simply suggested to men, so that they may think how much they are below that dignity which they assumed, as Paul also says, "Who art thou who judgest another?" (Rom. xiv. 4.)

13. Go to now, ye that say, To-day, or to-morrow, we will go into such a city, and continue there a year, and buy and sell, and get gain;

14. Whereas ye know not what *shall be* on the morrow: for what *is* your life? It is even a vapour, that appeareth for a little time, and then vanisheth away.

15. For that ye *ought* to say, If the Lord will, we shall live, and do this, or that.

16. But now ye rejoice in your boastings: all such rejoicing is evil.

17. Therefore to him that knoweth to do good, and doeth *it* not, to him it is sin.

13. Age nunc, qui dicitis, Hodie et cras eamus in civitatem, et transigamus illic annum unum, et mercemur et lucremur;

14. Qui nescitis quid cras futurum sit; quæ enim est vita nostra? vapor est scilicet ad exiguum tempus apparens, deinde evanescens:

15. Quum dicere debeatis, Si Dominus voluerit, et vixerimus, faciemus hoc vel illud.

16. Nunc autem gloriamini in superbiis vestris; omnia gloriatio talis, mala est.

17. Qui ergo novit facere bonum, nec facit, peccati reus est.

13. *Go to now.* He condemns here another kind of presumption, that many, who ought to have depended on God's providence, confidently settled what they were to do, and arranged their plans for a long time, as though they had many years at their own disposal, while they were not sure, no not even of one moment. Solomon also sharply ridicules this kind of foolish boasting, when he says that "men settle their ways in their heart, and that the Lord in the meantime rules the tongue." (Prov. xvi. 1.) And it is a very insane thing to undertake to execute what we cannot pronounce with our tongue. James does not reprove the form of speaking, but rather the arrogance of mind, that men should forget their own weakness, and speak thus presumptuously; for even the godly, who think humbly of themselves, and acknowledge that their steps are guided by the will of God, may yet sometimes say, without any qualifying clause, that they will do this or that. It is indeed right and proper, when we promise anything as to future time, to accustom ourselves to such words as these, "If it shall please the Lord," "If the Lord will permit." But no scruple ought to be entertained, as though it were a sin to omit them; for we read everywhere in the Scriptures that the holy servants of God spoke unconditionally of future things, when yet they had it as a principle fixed in their minds, that they could do nothing without the permission of God. Then as to the practice of saying, "If the Lord will or permit," it ought to be carefully attended to by all the godly.

But James roused the stupidity of those who disregarded God's providence, and claimed for themselves a whole year, though they had not a single moment in their own power; the gain which was afar off they promised to themselves, though they had no possession of that which was before their feet.

14. *For what is your life?* He might have checked this foolish license in determining things to come by many other reasons; for we see how the Lord daily frustrates those presumptuous men who promise what great things they will do. But he was satisfied with this one argument, Who has promised to thee a life for to-morrow? Canst thou, a dying man,

do what thou so confidently resolvest to do? For he who remembers the shortness of his life, will have his audacity easily checked so as not to extend too far his resolves. Nay, for no other reason do ungodly men indulge themselves so much, but because they forget that they are men. By the similitude of *vapour*, he strikingly shews that the purposes which are founded only on the present life, are altogether evanescent.

15. *If the Lord will.* A twofold condition is laid down, " If we shall live so long," and, " If the Lord will;" because many things may intervene to upset what we may have determined; for we are blind as to all future events.[1] By *will* he means not that which is expressed in the law, but God's counsel by which he governs all things.

16. *But now ye rejoice,* or, glory. We may learn from these words that James condemned something more than a passing speech. *Ye rejoice,* or, glory, he says, in your empty boastings. Though they robbed God of his government, they yet flattered themselves; not that they openly set themselves up as superior to God, though they were especially inflated with confidence in themselves, but that their minds were inebriated with vanity so as to disregard God. And as warnings of this kind are usually received with contempt by ungodly men—nay, this answer is immediately given, " Known to ourselves is what is offered to us, so that there is no need of such a warning;"—he alleges against them this knowledge in which they gloried, and declares that they sinned the more grievously, because they did not sin through ignorance, but through contempt.

CHAPTER V.

1. Go to now, *ye* rich men, weep and howl for your miseries that shall come upon *you*.

1. Agedum nunc divites, plorate, ululantes super miseriis vestris quæ advenient vobis.

---

[1] The words may be rendered thus, " If the Lord will, we shall both live and do this or that." So that living and doing are both dependent on God's will.—*Ed.*

2. Your riches are corrupted, and your garments are moth-eaten.

3. Your gold and silver is cankered; and the rust of them shall be a witness against you, and shall eat your flesh as it were fire. Ye have heaped treasure together for the last days.

4. Behold, the hire of the labourers which have reaped down your fields, which is of you kept back by fraud, crieth: and the cries of them which have reaped are entered into the ears of the Lord of Sabaoth.

5. Ye have lived in pleasure on the earth, and been wanton; ye have nourished your hearts, as in a day of slaughter.

6. Ye have condemned *and* killed the just; *and* he doth not resist you.

2. Divitiæ vestræ putrefactæ sunt, vestimenta vestra à tineis exesa sunt.

3. Aurum et argentum vestrum ærugine corruptum est; et ærugo eorum in testimonium vobis erit, et exedet carnes vestras sicut ignis: thesaurum congessistis in extremis diebus.

4. Ecce merces operariorum, qui messuerunt regiones vestras, quæ fraude aversa est à vobis, clamat; et clamores eorum qui messuerunt, in aures Domini Sabaoth introierunt.

5. In deliciis vixistis super terram; lascivistis, enutristis corda vestra, sicut in die mactationis.

6. Condemnastis et occidistis justum, et non resistit vobis.

1. *Go to now.* They are mistaken, as I think, who consider that James here exhorts the rich to repentance. It seems to me to be a simple denunciation of God's judgment, by which he meant to terrify them without giving them any hope of pardon; for all that he says tends only to despair. He, therefore, does not address them in order to invite them to repentance; but, on the contrary, he has a regard to the faithful, that they, hearing of the miserable end of the rich, might not envy their fortune, and also that knowing that God would be the avenger of the wrongs they suffered, they might with a calm and resigned mind bear them.¹

---

¹ Many commentators, such as *Grotius, Doddridge, Macknight,* and *Scott,* consider that the Apostle refers at the beginning of this chapter, not to professing Christians, but to unbelieving Jews. There is nothing said that can lead to such an opinion: and if the two preceding chapters were addressed (as admitted by all) to those who *professed* the faith, there is no reason why this should not have been addressed to them; the sins here condemned are not worse than those previously condemned. Indeed, we find by the Epistles of Peter, and by that of Jude, that there were men professing religion at that time, who were not a whit better (if not worse) than many who profess religion in our age.

Besides, it was not unusual, in epistles to Christians, to address unbelievers. Indeed, Paul expressly says, "What have I to do to judge them that are without?"

That there were rich men professing the gospel at that time, is evident from chap. i. 10. —*Ed.*

But he does not speak of the rich indiscriminately, but of those who, being immersed in pleasures and inflated with pride, thought of nothing but of the world, and who, like inexhaustible gulfs, devoured everything; for they, by their tyranny, oppressed others, as it appears from the whole passage.

Weep and howl, or, Lament, howling. Repentance has indeed its weeping, but being mixed with consolation, it does not proceed to howling. Then James intimates that the heaviness of God's vengeance will be so horrible and severe on the rich, that they will be constrained to break forth into howling, as though he had said briefly to them, "Woe to you!" But it is a prophetic mode of speaking: the ungodly have the punishment which awaits them set before them, and they are represented as already enduring it. As, then, they were now flattering themselves, and promising to themselves that the prosperity in which they thought themselves happy, would be perpetual, he declared that the most grievous miseries were nigh at hand.

2. *Your riches.* The meaning may be twofold:—that he ridicules their foolish confidence, because the riches in which they placed their happiness, were wholly fading, yea, that they could be reduced to nothing by one blast from God—or that he condemns their insatiable avarice, because they heaped together wealth only for this, that they might perish without any benefit. This latter meaning is the most suitable. It is, indeed, true that those rich men are insane who glory in things so fading as garments, gold, silver, and such things, since it is nothing else than to make their glory subject to rust and moths; and well known is that saying, "What is ill got is soon lost;" because the curse of God consumes it all, for it is not right that the ungodly or their heirs should enjoy riches which they have snatched, as it were, by violence from the hand of God.

But as James enumerates the vices by which the rich brought on themselves the calamity which he mentions, the context requires, as I think, that we should say, that what he condemns here is the extreme rapacity of the rich, in retaining everything they could lay hold on, that it might rot uselessly in their chests. For thus it was, that what God had created for the use of men, they destroyed, as though they were the enemies of mankind.[1]

But it must be observed, that the vices which he mentions here do not belong to all the rich; for some of them indulge themselves in luxury, some spend much in show and display, and some pinch themselves, and live miserably in their own filth. Let us, then, know that he here reproves some vices in some, and some vices in others. However, all those are generally condemned who unjustly accumulate riches, or who foolishly abuse them. But what James now says, is not only suitable to the rich of extreme tenacity, (such as Euclio of Plautus,) but to those also who delight in pomp and luxury, and yet prefer to heap up riches rather than to employ them for necessary purposes. For such is the malignity of some, that they grudge to others the common sun and air.

3. *A witness against you.* He confirms the explanation I have already given. For God has not appointed gold for rust, nor garments for moths; but, on the contrary, he has designed them as aids and helps to human life. Therefore, even spending without benefit is a witness of inhumanity. The rusting of gold and silver will be, as it were, the occasion of inflaming the wrath of God, so that it will, like fire, consume them.

Ye have heaped treasure together. These words may also admit of two explanations:—that the rich, as they would always live, are never satisfied, but weary themselves in heaping together what may be sufficient to the end of the world,—or, that they heap together the wrath and curse of God for the last day; and this second view I embrace.[2]

---

[1] Reference is here made to three *sorts* of riches,—stores of corn, which rotted,—garments, which were moth-eaten,—and precious metals, money, and jewels, &c., which rusted.—*Ed.*

[2] By "last days" are commonly meant the days of the gospel. The day of judgment is often called by John, in his Gospel, "the last day;" and the same seems to be called here "the last days." The reference made by some to the destruction of Jerusalem, has nothing in the passage to favour it. To "heap treasure," or to lay up a store, has an evident reference to the day of judgment, as Paul makes use of the same expression in Rom. ii. 5, only he adds "wrath" to it, which is also added here by the *Vulg.* The whole verse is comminatory, and in this sentence the rich are reminded

4. *Behold, the hire.* He now condemns cruelty, the invariable companion of avarice. But he refers only to one kind, which, above all others, ought justly to be deemed odious. For if a humane and a just man, as Solomon says in Prov. xii. 10, regards the life of his beast, it is a monstrous barbarity, when man feels no pity towards the man whose sweat he has employed for his own benefit. Hence the Lord has strictly forbidden, in the law, the hire of the labourer to sleep with us. (Deut. xxiv. 15.) Besides, James does not refer to labourers in common, but, for the sake of amplifying, he mentions husbandmen and reapers. For what can be more base than that they, who supply us with bread by their labour should be pined through want? and yet this monstrous thing is common; for there are many of such a tyrannical disposition, that they think that the rest of mankind live only for their benefit alone.

But he says that this hire *crieth,* for whatever men retain either by fraud or by violence, of what belongs to another, it calls for vengeance as it were by a loud voice. We ought to notice what he adds, that the *cries* of the poor come to the ears of God, so that we may know that the wrong done to them shall not be unpunished. They, therefore, who are oppressed by the unjust ought resignedly to sustain their evils, because they will have God as their defender. And they who have the power of doing wrong ought to abstain from injustice, lest they provoke God against them, who is the protector and patron of the poor. And for this reason also he calls God the Lord of Sabaoth, or of hosts, intimating thereby his power and his might, by which he renders his judgment more dreadful.

5. *In pleasure.* He comes now to another vice, even luxury and sinful gratifications; for they who abound in wealth seldom keep within the bounds of moderation, but abuse their abundance by extreme indulgences. There are, indeed, some rich men, as I have said, who pine themselves in the midst of their abundance. For it was not without

of the issue, the final issue of their conduct. The character of the store is to be learnt from the preceding part of the verse. In treasuring dishonest wealth, they were treasuring wrath for themselves.—*Ed.*

reason that the poets have imagined Tantalus to be hungry near a table well furnished. There have ever been Tantalians in the world. But James, as it has been said, does not speak of all rich men. It is enough that we see this vice commonly prevailing among the rich, that they are given too much to luxuries, to pomps and superfluities.

And though the Lord allows them to live freely on what they have, yet profusion ought to be avoided and frugality practised. For it was not in vain that the Lord by his prophets severely reproved those who slept on beds of ivory, who used precious ointments, who delighted themselves at their feasts with the sound of the harp, who were like fat cows in rich pastures. For all these things have been said for this end, that we may know that moderation ought to be observed, and that extravagance is displeasing to God.

Ye have nourished your hearts. He means that they indulged themselves, not only as far as to satisfy nature, but as far as their cupidity led them. He adds a similitude, *as in a day of slaughter*, because they were wont in their solemn sacrifices to eat more freely than according to their daily habits. He then says, that the rich feasted themselves every day of their life, because they immersed themselves in perpetual indulgences.

6. *Ye have condemned.* Here follows another kind of inhumanity, that the rich by their power oppressed and destroyed the poor and weak. He says by a metaphor that the just were condemned and killed; for when they did not kill them by their own hand, or condemn them as judges, they yet employed the authority which they had to do wrong, they corrupted judgments, and contrived various arts to destroy the innocent, that is, really to condemn and kill them.[1]

---

[1] Many have thought that what is referred to here is the condemnation of our Saviour by the Jewish nation, especially as he is called ὁ δίκαιος, "the just one." This is true, but the Christian is so called too, in 1 Pet. iv. 18. James very frequently individualizes the faithful, using the singular for the plural number. The whole context proves that he speaks here of the poor faithful who suffered injustice from the rich, professing the same faith. Besides, the death of Christ is not ascribed to the rich, but to the elders and chief priests.

The two first verbs, being aorists, may be rendered in the present tense,

By adding that the just did *not resist* them, he intimates that the audacity of the rich was greater, because those whom they oppressed were without any protection. He, however, reminds them that the more ready and prompt would be the vengeance of God, when the poor have no protection from men. But though the just did not resist, because he ought to have patiently endured wrongs, I yet think that their weakness is at the same time referred to, that is, he did not resist, because he was unprotected and without any help from men.

7. Be patient therefore, brethren, unto the coming of the Lord. Behold, the husbandman waiteth for the precious fruit of the earth, and hath long patience for it, until he receive the early and latter rain.	7. Patienter ergo agite, fratres, usque in adventum Domini. Ecce agricola expectat pretiosum fructum terræ, patienter se gerens erga eum, donec recipiat pluviam matutinam et vespertinam.
8. Be ye also patient; stablish your hearts; for the coming of the Lord draweth nigh.	8. Patienter ergo agite et vos; confirmate corda vestra, quoniam adventus Domini propinquus est.
9. Grudge not one against another, brethren, lest ye be condemned: behold, the Judge standeth before the door.	9. Ne ingemiscatis alii in alios, fratres, ne condemnemini: ecce judex stat pro foribus.

7. *Be patient therefore.* From this inference it is evident that what has hitherto been said against the rich, pertains to the consolation of those who seemed for a time to be exposed to their wrongs with impunity. For after having mentioned the causes of those calamities which were hanging over the rich, and having stated this among others, that they proudly and cruelly ruled over the poor, he immediately adds, that we who are unjustly oppressed, have this reason to be patient, because God would become the judge. For this is what he means when he says, *unto the coming of the Lord,* that is, that the confusion of things which is now seen in the world will not be perpetual, because the Lord at his

especially as the last verb is in that tense. For in the very next verse, the 7*th,* the aorist is so used. We may then give this version,—
  6. " Ye condemn, ye kill the righteous; he sets himself not in array
     against you."
Probably the aorist is used, as it expresses what was done habitually, or a continued act, like the future tense often in Hebrew. The preceding verse, the 5*th,* where all the verbs are aorists, would be better rendered in the same way, " Ye live in pleasure," &c.—*Ed.*

coming will reduce things to order, and that therefore our minds ought to entertain good hope; for it is not without reason that the restoration of all things is promised to us at that day. And though the day of the Lord is everywhere called in the Scriptures a manifestation of his judgment and grace, when he succours his people and chastises the ungodly, yet I prefer to regard the expression here as referring to our final deliverance.

Behold, the husbandman. Paul briefly refers to the same similitude in 2 Tim. ii. 6, when he says that the husbandman ought to labour before he gathers the fruit; but James more fully expresses the idea, for he mentions the daily patience of the husbandman, who, after having committed the seed to the earth, confidently, or at least patiently, waits until the time of harvest comes; nor does he fret because the earth does not immediately yield a ripe fruit. He hence concludes, that we ought not to be immoderately anxious, if we must now labour and sow, until the harvest as it were comes, even the day of the Lord.

The precious fruit. He calls it precious, because it is the nourishment of life and the means of sustaining it. And James intimates, that since the husbandman suffers his life, so precious to him, to lie long deposited in the bosom of the earth, and calmly suspends his desire to gather the fruit, we ought not to be too hasty and fretful, but resignedly to wait for the day of our redemption. It is not necessary to specify particularly the other parts of the comparison.

The early and the latter rain. By the two words, *early* and *latter*, two seasons are pointed out; the first follows soon after sowing; and the other when the corn is ripening. So the prophets spoke, when they intended to set forth the time for rain, (Deut. xxviii. 12; Joel ii. 23; Hos. vi. 3.) And he has mentioned both times, in order more fully to shew that husbandmen are not disheartened by the slow progress of time, but bear with the delay.

8. *Stablish your hearts.* Lest any should object and say, that the time of deliverance was too long delayed, he obviates this objection and says, that the Lord was at hand, or (which is the same thing) that his coming was drawing nigh.

In the meantime, he bids us to correct the softness of the heart, which weakens us, so as not to persevere in hope. And doubtless the time appears long, because we are too tender and delicate. We ought, then, to gather strength that we may become hardened : and this cannot be better attained than by hope, and as it were by a realizing view of the near approach of our Lord.

9. *Grudge not,* or, groan not. As the complaints of many were heard, that they were more severely treated than others, this passage is so explained by some, as though James bade each to be contented with his own lot, not to envy others, nor grudge if the condition of others was more tolerable. But I take another view ; for after having spoken of the unhappiness of those who distress good and quiet men by their tyranny, he now exhorts the faithful to be just towards one another and ready to pass by offences. That this is the real meaning may be gathered from the reason that is added : Be not querulous one against another, *lest ye be condemned.* We may, indeed, groan, when any evil torments us ; but he means an accusing groan, when one expostulates with the Lord against another. And he declares that thus they would all be condemned, because there is no one who does not offend his brethren, and afford them an occasion of groaning. Now, if every one complained, they would all have accused one another ; for no one was so innocent, that he did not do some harm to others.

God will be the common judge of all. What, then, will be the case, but that every one who seeks to bring judgment on others, must allow the same against himself ; and thus all will be given up to the same ruin. Let no one, then, ask for vengeance on others, except he wishes to bring it on his own head. And lest they should be hasty in making complaints of this kind, he declares that the judge was at the door. For as our propensity is to profane the name of God, in the slightest offences we appeal to his judgment. Nothing is a fitter bridle to check our rashness, than to consider that our imprecations vanish not into air, because God's judgment is at hand.

10. Take, my brethren, the pro- 10. Exemplum accipite afflictio-

phets, who have spoken in the name of the Lord, for an example of suffering affliction, and of patience.

11. Behold, we count them happy which endure. Ye have heard of the patience of Job, and have seen the end of the Lord; that the Lord is very pitiful, and of tender mercy.

nis, fratres mei, et tolerantiæ, prophetas, qui loquuti sunt nomine Domini.

11. Ecce beatos esse ducimus eos qui sustinent: patientiam Job audistis, et finem Domini vidistis, quòd multùm sit misericors et commiserans.

10. *Take, my brethren, the prophets.* The comfort which he brings is not that which is according to the common proverb, that the miserable hope for like companions in evils. But he set before them associates, in whose number it was desirable to be classed; and to have the same condition with them, was no misery. For as we must necessarily feel extreme grief, when any evil happens to us which the children of God have never experienced, so it is a singular consolation when we know that we suffer nothing different from them; nay, when we know that we have to sustain the same yoke with them.

When Job heard from his friends, "Turn to the saints, can you find any like to thee?" (Job v. 1,) it was the voice of Satan, because he wished to drive him to despair. When, on the other hand, the Spirit by the mouth of James designs to raise us up to a good hope, he shews to us all the foregoing saints, who as it were stretch out their hand to us, and by their example encourage us to undergo and to conquer afflictions.

The life of men is indeed indiscriminately subject to troubles and adversities; but James did not bring forward any kind of men for examples, for it would have availed nothing to perish with the multitude; but he chose the prophets, a fellowship with whom is blessed. Nothing so breaks us down and disheartens us as the feeling of misery; it is therefore a real consolation to know that those things commonly deemed evils are aids and helps to our salvation. This is, indeed, what is far from being understood by the flesh; yet the faithful ought to be convinced of this, that they are happy when by various troubles they are proved by the Lord. To convince us of this, James reminds us to consider the end or design of the afflictions endured by the prophets; for as in our own evils we are without judgment, being influenced by grief, sorrow, or some other immoderate feelings, as we see nothing under a foggy sky and in the midst of storms, and being tossed here and there as it were by a tempest, it is therefore necessary for us to cast our eyes to another quarter, where the sky is in a manner serene and bright. When the afflictions of the saints are related to us, there is no one who will allow that they were miserable, but, on the contrary, that they were happy.

Then James has done well for us; for he has laid before our eyes a pattern, that we may learn to look at it whenever we are tempted to impatience or to despair. And he takes this principle as granted, that the prophets were blessed in their afflictions, for they courageously sustained them. Since it was so, he concludes that the same judgment ought to be formed of us when afflicted.

And he says, *the prophets who have spoken in the name of the Lord;* by which he intimates that they were accepted and approved by God. If, then, it had been useful for them to have been free from miseries, doubtless God would have kept them free. But it was otherwise. It hence follows that afflictions are salutary to the faithful. He, therefore, bids them to be taken as an example of suffering affliction. But patience also must be added, which is a real evidence of our obedience. Hence he has joined them both together.

11. *The patience of Job.* Having spoken generally of the prophets, he now refers to an example remarkable above others; for no one, as far as we can learn from histories, has ever been overwhelmed with troubles so hard and so various as Job; and yet he emerged from so deep a gulf. Whosoever, then, will imitate his patience, will no doubt find God's hand, which at length delivered him, to be the same. We see for what end his history has been written. God suffered not his servant Job to sink, because he patiently endured his afflictions. Then he will disappoint the patience of no one.

If, however, it be asked, Why does the Apostle so much commend the patience of Job, as he had displayed many signs of impatience, being carried away by a hasty spirit? To this I reply, that though he sometimes failed through the infirmity of the flesh, or murmured within himself, yet he ever surrendered himself to God, and was ever willing to be restrained and ruled by him. Though, then, his patience was somewhat deficient, it is yet deservedly commended.

The end of the Lord. By these words he intimates that afflictions ought ever to be estimated by their end. For at first God seems to be far away, and Satan in the meantime revels in the confusion; the flesh suggests to us that we are forsaken of God and lost. We ought, then, to extend our view farther, for near and around us there appears no light. Moreover, he has called it the end of the Lord, because it is his work to give a prosperous issue to adversities. If we do our duty in bearing evils obediently, he will by no means be wanting in performing his part. Hope directs us only to the end; God will then shew himself very merciful, however rigid and severe he may seem to be while afflicting us.[1]

12. But above all things, my brethren, swear not; neither by heaven, neither by the earth, neither by any other oath: but let your yea be yea: and *your* nay, nay; lest ye fall into condemnation.

13. Is any among you afflicted? let him pray. Is any merry? let him sing psalms.

12. Ante omnia vero, fratres mei, Ne juretis, neque per cœlum, neque per terram, neque aliud quodvis jusjurandum; sit autem vestrum, Est, Est; Non, Non: ne in judicium (*vel*, simulationem) incidatis.

13. Affligitur quis inter vos? oret: hilari est animo? psallat.

12. *But above all things.* It has been a common vice almost in all ages, to swear lightly and inconsiderately. For so bad is our nature that we do not consider what an atrocious crime it is to profane the name of God. For though the Lord strictly commands us to reverence his name, yet men devise various subterfuges, and think that they can swear with impunity. They imagine, then, that there is no evil, provided they do not openly mention the name of God; and this is an old gloss. So the Jews, when they swore by heaven or earth, thought that they did not

---

[1] "The end of the Lord" seems a singular expression; but τέλος, properly the end, means also the issue, the upshot, the termination, the conclusion. It is genitive of the efficient cause, "the end (or issue) given by the Lord." See Job xlii. 12. According to *Griesbach* there are three MSS. which have ἔλεος, "mercy;" which would be very suitable,—" and ye have seen the mercy of the Lord, that the Lord is very full of pity, and compassionate." But the authority is not sufficient.—*Ed.*

profane God's name, because they did not mention it. But while men seek to be ingenious in dissembling with God, they delude themselves with the most frivolous evasions.

It was a vain excuse of this kind that Christ condemned in Matt. v. 34. James, now subscribing to the decree of his Master, commands us to abstain from these indirect forms of swearing: for whosoever swears in vain and on frivolous occasions, profanes God's name, whatever form he may give to his words. Then the meaning is, that it is not more lawful to swear by heaven or by the earth, than openly by the name of God. The reason is mentioned by Christ,—because the glory of God is everywhere inscribed, and everywhere shines forth : nay, men take the words, heaven and earth, in their oaths, in no other sense and for no other purpose, than if they named God himself; for by thus speaking they only designate the Worker by his works.

But he says, *above all things ;* because the profanation of God's name is not a slight offence. The Anabaptists, building on this passage, condemn all oaths, but they only shew their ignorance. For James does not speak of oaths in general, nor does Christ in the passage to which I have referred; but both condemn that evasion which had been devised, when men took the liberty to swear without expressing the name of God, which was a liberty repugnant to the prohibition of the law.

And this is what the words clearly mean, *Neither by heaven, neither by the earth.* For, if the question had been as to oaths in themselves, to what purpose were these forms mentioned ? It then appears evident that both by Christ and by James the puerile astuteness of those is reproved who taught that they could swear with impunity, provided they adopted some circuitous expressions. That we may, then, understand the meaning of James, we must understand first the precept of the law, "Thou shalt not take the name of God *in vain.*" It hence appears clear, that there is a right and lawful use of God's name. Now, James condemns those who did not indeed dare in a direct way to profane God's name, but endeavoured to evade the profanation which the law condemns, by circumlocutions.

But let your yea be yea. He brings the best remedy to correct the vice which he condemns, that is, that they were habitually to keep themselves to truth and faithfulness in all their sayings. For whence is the wicked habit of swearing, except that such is the falsehood of men, that their words alone are not believed? For, if they observed faithfulness, as they ought, in their words, there would have been no necessity of so many superfluous oaths. As, then, the perfidy or levity of men is the fountain from which the vice of swearing flows, in order to take away the vice, James teaches us that the fountain ought to be removed; for the right way of healing is to begin with the cause of illness.

Some copies have, "Let your word (or speech) be, yea, yea; no, no." The true reading, however, is what I have given, and is commonly received; and what he means I have already explained, that is, that we ought to tell the truth, and to be faithful in our words. To the same purpose is what Paul says in 2 Cor. i. 18, that he was not in his preaching yea and nay, but pursued the same course from the beginning.

Lest ye fall into condemnation. There is a different reading, owing to the affinity of the words ὑπὸ κρίσιν and ὑπόκρισιν.[1] If you read, "into judgment" or condemnation, the sense will clearly be, that to take God's name in vain will not be unpunished. But it is not unsuitable to say, "into hypocrisy;" because when simplicity, as it has been already said, prevails among us, the occasion for superfluous oaths is cut off. If, then, fidelity appears in all we say, the dissimulation, which leads us to swear rashly, will be removed.

13. *Is any among you afflicted?* He means that there is no time in which God does not invite us to himself. For afflictions ought to stimulate us to pray; prosperity supplies us with an occasion to praise God. But such is the perverseness of men, that they cannot rejoice without forgetting God, and that when afflicted they are disheartened

---

[1] For εἰς ὑπόκρισιν there are several MSS., but for ὑπὸ κρίσιν there are not only several MSS., but the earliest versions, *Syr.* and *Vulg.*; so *Griesbach* takes the latter as the true reading.—*Ed.*

and driven to despair. We ought, then, to keep within due bounds, so that the joy, which usually makes us to forget God, may induce us to set forth the goodness of God, and that our sorrow may teach us to pray. For he has set the *singing of psalms* in opposition to profane and unbridled joy; and thus they express their joy who are led, as they ought to be, by prosperity to God.

14. Is any sick among you? let him call for the elders of the church; and let them pray over him, anointing him with oil in the name of the Lord:	14. Infirmatur quis inter vos? advocet presbyteros ecclesiæ, et orent super eum, ungentes oleo in nomine Domini:
15. And the prayer of faith shall save the sick, and the Lord shall raise him up; and if he have committed sins, they shall be forgiven him.	15. Et oratio fidei servabit ægrotum, et excitabit eum Dominus; et si peccata admiserit, remittentur illi.

14. *Is any sick among you?* As the gift of healing as yet continued, he directs the sick to have recourse to that remedy. It is, indeed, certain that they were not all healed; but the Lord granted this favour as often and as far as he knew it would be expedient; nor is it probable that the oil was indiscriminately applied, but only when there was some hope of restoration. For, together with the power there was given also discretion to the ministers, lest they should by abuse profane the symbol. The design of James was no other than to commend the grace of God which the faithful might then enjoy, lest the benefit of it should be lost through contempt or neglect.

For this purpose he ordered the presbyters to be sent for, but the use of the anointing must have been confined to the power of the Holy Spirit.

The Papists boast mightily of this passage, when they seek to pass off their extreme unction. But how different their corruption is from the ancient ordinance mentioned by James, I will not at present undertake to shew. Let readers learn this from my Institutes. I will only say this, that this passage is wickedly and ignorantly perverted, when extreme unction is established by it, and is called a sacrament, to be perpetually observed in the Church. I indeed allow that it was used as a sacrament by the disciples of Christ, (for I cannot agree with those who think that it was medicine;) but as the reality of this sign continued only for a time in the Church, the symbol also must have been only for a time. And it is quite evident, that nothing is more absurd than to call that a sacrament which is void and does not really present to us that which it signifies. That the gift of healing was temporary, all are constrained to allow, and events clearly prove: then the sign of it ought not to be deemed perpetual. It hence follows, that they who at this day set anointing among the sacraments, are not the true followers, but the apes of the Apostles, except they restore the effect produced by it, which God has taken away from the world for more than fourteen hundred years. So we have no dispute, whether anointing was once a sacrament; but whether it has been given to be so perpetually. This latter we deny, because it is evident that the thing signified has long ago ceased.

The presbyters, or elders, *of the church.* I include here generally all those who presided over the Church; for pastors were not alone called presbyters or elders, but also those who were chosen from the people to be as it were censors to protect discipline. For every Church had, as it were, its own senate, chosen from men of weight and of proved integrity. But as it was customary to choose especially those who were endued with gifts more than ordinary, he ordered them to send for the elders, as being those in whom the power and grace of the Holy Spirit more particularly appeared.

Let them pray over him. This custom of praying over one was intended to shew, that they stood as it were before God; for when we come as it were to the very scene itself, we utter prayers with more feeling; and not only Elisha and Paul, but Christ himself, roused the ardour of prayer and commended the grace of God by thus praying over persons. (2 Kings iv. 32; Acts xx. 10; John xi. 41.)

15. But it must be observed, that he connects a promise with the prayer, lest it should be made without faith. For he who doubts, as one who does not rightly call on God, is unworthy to obtain anything, as we have seen in the first chapter. Whosoever then really seeks to be heard, must be fully persuaded that he does not pray in vain.

As James brings before us this special gift, to which the external rite was but an addition, we hence learn, that the oil could not have been rightly used without faith. But since it appears that the Papists have no certainty as to their anointing, as it is manifest that they have not the gift, it is evident that their anointing is spurious.

And if he have committed sins. This is not added only for the sake of amplifying, as though he had said, that God would give something more to the sick than health of body; but because diseases were very often inflicted on account of sins; and by speaking of their remission he intimates that the cause of the evil would be removed. And we indeed see that David, when afflicted with disease and seeking relief, was wholly engaged in seeking the pardon of his sins. Why did he do this, except that while he acknowledged the effect of his faults in his punishment, he deemed that there was no other remedy, but that the Lord should cease to impute to him his sins?

The prophets are full of this doctrine, that men are relieved from their evils when they are loosed from the guilt of their iniquities. Let us then know that it is the only fit remedy for our diseases and other calamities, when we carefully examine ourselves, being solicitous to be reconciled to God, and to obtain the pardon of our sins.

16. Confess *your* faults one to another, and pray one for another, that ye may be healed. The effectual fervent prayer of a righteous man availeth much.	16. Confitemini invicem peccata vestra, et orate invicem alii pro aliis, ut salvemini: multum valet precatio justi efficax.
17. Elias was a man subject to like passions as we are, and he prayed earnestly that it might not rain; and it rained not on the earth by the space of three years and six months.	17. Elias homo erat passionibus similiter obnoxius ut nos; et precatione precatus est, ne plueret; et non pluit super terram annos tres et sex menses.
18. And he prayed again, and the heaven gave rain, and the earth brought forth her fruit.	18. Et rursum oravit, et cœlum dedit pluviam, et terra protulit fructum suum.

16. *Confess your faults one to another.* In some copies the illative particle is given, nor is it unsuitable; for though when not expressed, it must be understood. He had said, that sins were remitted to the sick over whom the elders

prayed: he now reminds them how useful it is to discover our sins to our brethren, even that we may obtain the pardon of them by their intercession.[1]

This passage, I know, is explained by many as referring to the reconciling of offences; for they who wish to return to favour must necessarily know first their own faults and confess them. For hence it comes, that hatreds take root, yea, and increase and become irreconcilable, because every one pertinaciously defends his own cause. Many therefore think that James points out here the way of brotherly reconciliation, that is, by mutual acknowledgment of sins. But as it has been said, his object was different; for he connects mutual prayer with mutual confession; by which he intimates that confession avails for this end, that we may be helped as to God by the prayers of our brethren; for they who know our necessities, are stimulated to pray that they may assist us; but they to whom our diseases are unknown are more tardy to bring us help.

Wonderful, indeed, is the folly or the insincerity of the Papists, who strive to build their whispering confession on this passage. For it would be easy to infer from the words of James, that the priests alone ought to confess. For since a mutual, or to speak more plainly, a reciprocal confession is demanded here, no others are bidden to confess their own sins, but those who in their turn are fit to hear the confes-

---

[1] The illative οὖν, though found in some MSS., is not introduced into the text by *Griesbach*, there being no sufficient evidence in its favour. Nor does there appear a sufficient reason for the connexion mentioned by *Calvin*. The two cases seem to be different. The elders of the church were in the previous instance to be called in, who were to pray and anoint the sick, and it is said that the prayer of faith (*i. e.* of miraculous faith) would save the sick, and that his sins would be forgiven him. This was clearly a case of miraculous healing. But what is spoken of in this verse seems to be quite different. Prayer is alone mentioned, not by the elders, but by a righteous man, not saving as in the former case, but availing much. It seems then probable that the sins of the sick miraculously healed were more especially against God; and that the sins which they were to confess to one another were against the brethren, also visited with judgment; and the remedy for them was mutual confession and mutual prayer; but the success in this case was not as sure or as certain as in the former, only we are told that an earnest prayer avails much. Then to encourage this earnest or fervent prayer, the case of Elias is adduced; but it had nothing to do with miraculous healing.—*Ed.*

sion of others; but this the priests claim for themselves alone. Then confession is required of them alone. But since their puerilities do not deserve a refutation, let the true and genuine explanation already given be deemed sufficient by us.

For the words clearly mean, that confession is required for no other end, but that those who know our evils may be more solicitous to bring us help.

Availeth much. That no one may think that this is done without fruit, that is, when others pray for us, he expressly mentions the benefit and the effect of prayer. But he names expressly the *prayer of a righteous* or just *man;* because God does not hear the ungodly; nor is access to God open, except through a good conscience: not that our prayers are founded on our own worthiness, but because the heart must be cleansed by faith before we can present ourselves before God. Then James testifies that the righteous or the faithful pray for us beneficially and not without fruit.

But what does he mean by adding *effectual* or efficacious? for this seems superfluous; for if the prayer avails much, it is doubtless effectual. The ancient interpreter has rendered it "assiduous;" but this is too forced. For James uses the Greek participle, ἐνεργουμένη, which means "working." And the sentence may be thus explained, "It avails much, because it is effectual."[1] As it is an argument drawn from this principle, that God will not allow the prayers of the faithful to be void or useless, he does not therefore unjustly conclude that it avails much. But I would rather confine it to the present case: for our prayers may properly be said to be ἐνεργούμεναι, working, when some necessity meets us which excites in us earnest prayer. We pray daily for the whole Church, that God may pardon its sins; but then only

---

[1] This can hardly be admitted. The word expresses what sort of prayer is that which avails much. Besides, to avail much, and to be effectual, are two distinct things. The word as a verb and a participle has commonly an active sense. *Schleusner* gives only one instance in which it has a passive meaning, 2 Cor. i. 6; to which may be added 2 Cor. iv. 12. If taken passively, it may be rendered, " inwrought," that is, by the Spirit, according to *Macknight.* But it has been most commonly taken actively, and in the sense of the verbal adjective ἐνεργὴς, energetic, powerful, ardent, fervent.—*Ed.*

is our prayer really in earnest, when we go forth to succour those who are in trouble. But such efficacy cannot be in the prayers of our brethren, except they know that we are in difficulties. Hence the reason given is not general, but must be specially referred to the former sentence.

17. *Elias was a man.* There are innumerable instances in Scripture of what he meant to prove; but he chose one that is remarkable above all others; for it was a great thing that God should make heaven in a manner subject to the prayers of Elias, so as to obey his wishes. Elias kept heaven shut by his prayers for three years and a half; he again opened it, so that it poured down abundance of rain. Hence appeared the wonderful power of prayer. Well known is this remarkable history, and is found in 1 Kings xvii. and xviii. And though it is not there expressly said, that Elias prayed for drought, it may yet be easily gathered, and that the rain also was given to his prayers.

But we must notice the application of the example. James does not say that drought ought to be sought from the Lord, because Elias obtained it; for we may by inconsiderate zeal presumptuously and foolishly imitate the Prophet. We must then observe the rule of prayer, so that it may be by faith. He, therefore, thus accommodates this example,—that if Elias was heard, so also we shall be heard when we rightly pray. For as the command to pray is common, and as the promise is common, it follows that the effect also will be common.

Lest any one should object and say, that we are far distant from the dignity of Elias, he places him in our own rank, by saying, that he was a mortal *man* and *subject to the same passions* with ourselves. For we profit less by the examples of saints, because we imagine them to have been half-gods or heroes, who had peculiar intercourse with God; so that because they were heard, we receive no confidence. In order to shake off this heathen and profane superstition, James reminds us that the saints ought to be considered as having the infirmity of the flesh; so that we may learn to ascribe what they obtained from the Lord, not to their merits, but to the efficacy of prayer.

It hence appears how childish the Papists are, who teach men to flee to the protection of saints, because they had been heard by the Lord. For thus they reason, "Because he obtained what he asked as long as he lived in the world, he will be now after death our best patron." This sort of subtle refinement was altogether unknown to the Holy Spirit. For James on the contrary argues, that as their prayers availed so much, so we ought in like manner to pray at this day according to their example, and that we shall not do so in vain.

19. Brethren, if any of you do err from the truth, and one convert him;	19. Fratres mei, si quis inter vos erraverit à veritate, et converterit quispiam eum;
20. Let him know, that he which converteth the sinner from the error of his way shall save a soul from death, and shall hide a multitude of sins.	20. Cognoscat quòd qui converterit peccatorem ab errore viæ suæ, servabit animam à morte, et multitudinem operiet peccatorum.

20. *Let him know.* I doubt whether this ought rather to have been written, γινώσκετε, "know ye." In both ways the meaning however is the same. For James recommends to us the correction of our brethren from the effect produced, that we may more assiduously attend to this duty. Nothing is better or more desirable than to deliver a soul from eternal death; and this is what he does who restores an erring brother to the right way: therefore a work so excellent ought by no means to be neglected. To give food to the hungry, and drink to the thirsty, we see how much Christ values such acts; but the salvation of the soul is esteemed by him much more precious than the life of the body. We must therefore take heed lest souls perish through our sloth, whose salvation God puts in a manner in our hands. Not that we can bestow salvation on them; but that God by our ministry delivers and saves those who seem otherwise to be nigh destruction.

Some copies have *his soul*, which makes no change in the sense. I, however, prefer the other reading, for it has more force in it.

And shall hide a multitude of sins. He makes an allusion to a saying of Solomon, rather than a quotation. (Prov.

x. 12.) Solomon says that love covers sins, as hatred proclaims them. For they who hate burn with the desire of mutual slander; but they who love are disposed to exercise mutual forbearance. Love, then, buries sins as to men. James teaches here something higher, that is, that sins are blotted out before God; as though he had said, Solomon has declared this as the fruit of love, that it covers sins; but there is no better or more excellent way of covering them than when they are wholly abolished before God. And this is done when the sinner is brought by our admonition to the right way: we ought then especially and more carefully to attend to this duty.

END OF THE EPISTLE OF JAMES.

COMMENTARIES

ON

THE SECOND EPISTLE OF PETER.

THE ARGUMENT.

THE doubts respecting this Epistle mentioned by Eusebius, ought not to keep us from reading it. For if the doubts rested on the authority of men, whose names he does not give, we ought to pay no more regard to it than to that of unknown men. And he afterwards adds, that it was everywhere received without any dispute. What Jerome writes influences me somewhat more, that some, induced by a difference in the style, did not think that Peter was the author. For though some affinity may be traced, yet I confess that there is that manifest difference which distinguishes different writers. There are also other probable conjectures by which we may conclude that it was written by another rather than by Peter. At the same time, according to the consent of all, it has nothing unworthy of Peter, as it shews everywhere the power and the grace of an apostolic spirit. If it be received as canonical, we must allow Peter to be the author, since it has his name inscribed, and he also testifies that he had lived with Christ: and it would have been a fiction unworthy of a minister of Christ, to have personated another individual. So then I conclude, that if the Epistle be deemed worthy of credit, it must have proceeded from Peter; not that he himself wrote it, but that some one of his disciples set forth in writing, by his command, those things which the necessity of the times required. For it is probable that he was now in extreme old age, for he says, that he was near his end. And it may have been that at the request of the godly, he allowed this testimony of his mind to be recorded shortly before his death, because it might have somewhat availed, when he was dead, to support the good, and to repress the wicked. Doubtless, as in every part of the Epistle the majesty of the Spirit of Christ appears, to repudiate it is what I dread, though I do not here recognise the language of Peter. But since it is not quite evident as to the author, I shall allow myself the liberty of using the word Peter or Apostle indiscriminately.

I shall now come to the argument, which may be briefly stated.

The *design* is to shew, that those who have once professed the true faith of Christ, ought to respond to their calling to the last. After having then extolled, in high terms, the grace of God, he recommends to them holiness of life, because God usually punishes in hypocrites a false profession of his name, with dreadful blindness, and on the other hand he increases his gifts to those who truly and from the heart embrace the doctrine of religion. He, therefore, exhorts them to prove their calling by a holy life. And, to give a greater weight to his admonitions, he says that he is already near his end, and at the same time, excuses himself that he so often repeated the same things, his object being that they who should remain alive on the earth after his death, might have what he, when alive, wrote, more deeply fixed in their minds.

And as the foundation of true religion is the certainty or the truth of the gospel, he shews, first, how indubitable is its truth by this fact,—that he himself had been an eyewitness of all things which it contains, and especially that he had heard Christ proclaimed from heaven to be the Son of God; and, in the second place, it was God's will that it should be borne witness to, and approved by the oracles of the prophets.

He, however, predicts, at the same time, that danger was approaching from false teachers, who would spread impious inventions, as well as from the despisers of God, who would mock all religion; and he did this, that the faithful might learn to be watchful, and that they might be fortified. And he seems to have spoken thus designedly, lest they expected that the course of truth in the kingdom of Christ would be tranquil and peaceable, and free from all contention. He afterwards, as on a tablet, describes the character and manners of those who would, by their corruptions, pollute Christianity. But the description which he presents, especially suits the present age, as it will be more evident by a comparison. For he especially draws his pen against Lucianic men, who abandon themselves to every wickedness, and take a profane license to shew contempt to God, yea, and treat with ridicule the hope of a better life; and at this day we see that the world is everywhere full of such rabble.

He further exhorts the faithful, not only to look always for the coming of Christ with suspended and expectant minds, but also to regard that day as present before their eyes, and in the meantime to keep themselves unpolluted for the Lord : in which doctrine he makes Paul as his associate and approver; and to defend his writings from the calumnies of the ungodly, he severely reproves all those who pervert them.

CHAPTER I.

1. Simon Peter, a servant and an apostle of Jesus Christ, to them that have obtained like precious faith with us, through the righteousness of God and our Saviour Jesus Christ:

2. Grace and peace be multiplied unto you through the knowledge of God, and of Jesus our Lord,

3. According as his divine power hath given unto us all things that *pertain* unto life and godliness, through the knowledge of him that hath called us to glory and virtue :

4. Whereby are given unto us exceeding great and precious promises; that by these ye might be

1. Simeon Petrus, et servus et apostolus Jesu Christi, iis qui æquè pretiosam nobiscum sortiti sunt fidem, per justitiam Dei nostri et Servatoris Jesu Christi,

2. Gratia vobis et pax multiplicetur per cognitionem (*vel,* cum cognitione) Dei et Jesu Domini nostri;

3. Quemadmodum divina ejus potentia omnia nobis quæ spectant ad vitam et pietatem dedit per cognitionem ejus qui vocavit nos propria gloria et virtute (*vel,* per gloriam et virtutem):

4. Quibus et maximæ et pretiosæ promissiones nobis donatæ sunt, ut per hæc fieretis divinæ con-

partakers of the divine nature, having escaped the corruption that is in the world through lust.

sortes naturæ, ubi fugeritis corruptionem quæ in mundo est in concupiscentia.

1. *Simon Peter.* Prayer takes the first place at the beginning of this Epistle, and then follows thanksgiving, by which he excites the Jews to gratitude, lest they should forget what great benefits they had already received from God's hand. Why he called himself the *servant and an apostle* of Jesus Christ, we have elsewhere stated, even because no one is to be heard in the Church, except he speaks as from the mouth of Christ. But the word *servant* has a more general meaning, because it includes all the ministers of Christ, who sustain any public office in the Church. There was in the apostleship a higher rank of honour. He then intimates, that he was not one from the rank of ministers, but was made by the Lord an apostle, and therefore superior to them.[1]

Like precious faith. This is a commendation of the grace which God had indiscriminately shewed to all his elect people; for it was no common gift, that they had all been called to one and the same faith, since faith is the special and chief good of man. But he calls it *like* or equally *precious*, not that it is equal in all, but because all possess by faith the same Christ with his righteousness, and the same salvation. Though then the measure is different, that does not prevent the knowledge of God from being common to all, and the fruit which proceeds from it. Thus we have a real fellowship of faith with Peter and the Apostles.

He adds, *through the righteousness of God,* in order that they might know that they did not obtain faith through their own efforts or strength, but through God's favour alone. For these things stand opposed the one to the other, the righteousness of God (in the sense in which it is taken here) and the merit of man. For the efficient cause of faith is called God's righteousness for this reason, because no one is capable of conferring it on himself. So the righteousness that is to

---

[1] Simeon, and not Simon, is the name as here given, though a few copies and the *Vulg.* have Simon. His name is given both ways elsewhere; see **Luke v.** 8, and **Acts xv.** 14. Why he called himself Peter in the first Epistle, and Simeon Peter here, does not appear.—*Ed.*

be understood, is not that which remains in God, but that which he imparts to men, as in Rom. iii. 22. Besides, he ascribes this righteousness in common to God and to Christ, because it flows from God, and through Christ it flows down to us.[1]

2. *Grace and peace.* By grace is designated God's paternal favour towards us. We have indeed been once for all reconciled to God by the death of Christ, and by faith we come to the possession of this so great a benefit; but as we perceive the grace of God according to the measure of our faith, it is said to increase according to our perception, when it becomes more fully known to us.

Peace is added; for as the beginning of our happiness is when God receives us into favour; so the more he confirms his love in our hearts, the richer blessing he confers on us, so that we become happy and prosperous in all things,

Through the knowledge, literally, *in the knowledge;* but the preposition ἐν often means " through" or " with :" yet both senses may suit the context. I am, however, more disposed to adopt the former. For the more any one advances in the knowledge of God, every kind of blessing increases also equally with the sense of divine love. Whosoever then aspires to the full fruition of the blessed life which is mentioned by Peter, must remember to observe the right way. He connects together at the same time the knowledge of God and of Christ; because God cannot be rightly known except in Christ, according to that saying, " No one knoweth the Father but the Son, and he to whom the Son will reveal him." (Matt. xi. 27.)

3. *According as his divine power.* He refers to the infinite goodness of God which they had already experienced, that they might more fully understand it for the future. For he continues the course of his benevolence perpetually to the

---

[1] It has been maintained by many, that the rendering of these words ought to be, " of our God and Saviour Jesus Christ," the article before " God" being not repeated before " Saviour." In this case the ἐν before " righteousness" would be rendered " in;" for it is more suitable to say that faith is *in* than *through* the righteousness of Christ. Christ is thus called here God as well as Saviour; and so he is called " our Lord and Saviour Jesus Christ" in chap. iii. 18, the article being used in the same manner.—*Ed.*

end, except when we ourselves break it off by our unbelief; for he possesses exhaustless power and an equal will to do good. Hence the Apostle justly animates the faithful to entertain good hope by the consideration of the former benefits of God.[1] For the same purpose is the amplification which he makes; for he might have spoken more simply, "As he has freely given us all things." But by mentioning "divine power," he rises higher, that is, that God has copiously unfolded the immense resources of his power. But the latter clause may be referred to Christ as well as to the Father, but both are suitable. It may however be more fitly applied to Christ, as though he had said, that the grace which is conveyed to us by him, is an evidence of divinity, because it could not have done by humanity.

That pertain *to life and godliness,* or, as to life and godliness. Some think that the present life is meant here, as godliness follows as the more excellent gift; as though by those two words Peter intended to prove how beneficent and bountiful God is towards the faithful, that he brought them to light, that he supplies them with all things necessary for the preservation of an earthly life, and that he has also renewed them to a spiritual life by adorning them with godliness. But this distinction is foreign to the mind of Peter, for as soon as he mentioned life, he immediately added godliness, which is as it were its soul; for God then truly gives us life, when he renews us unto the obedience of righteousness. So Peter does not speak here of the natural gifts of God, but only mentions those things which he confers peculiarly on his own elect above the common order of nature.[2]

---

[1] The connexion here is variously regarded. Our version and *Calvin* seem to connect this verse with the foregoing, in this sense, that the Apostle prays for the increase of grace and peace from the consideration of what God had already done, or in conformity with his previous benefits. Others, perhaps more correctly, view this verse as connected with the 5th, and render ὡς, "since," and the beginning of the 5th verse, "Do ye also for this reason, giving all diligence, add," &c.; that is, "Since God has done so great things for you, ye also for this reason ought to be diligent in adding to your faith virtue, &c." But ὡς and καὶ may be rendered *as* and *so.* See Acts vii. 51. "As his divine power . . . . so for this reason, giving all diligence, add," &c.—*Ed.*

[2] The order is according to what is common in Scripture; the chief thing is mentioned first, and then that which leads to it.—*Ed.*

That we are born men, that we are endued with reason and knowledge, that our life is supplied with necessary support,—all this is indeed from God. As however men, being perverted in their minds and ungrateful, do not regard these various things, which are called the gifts of nature, among God's benefits, the common condition of human life is not here referred to, but the peculiar endowments of the new and spiritual life, which derive their origin from the kingdom of Christ. But since everything necessary for godliness and salvation is to be deemed among the supernatural gifts of God, let men learn to arrogate nothing to themselves, but humbly ask of God whatever they see they are wanting in, and to ascribe to him whatever good they may have. For Peter here, by attributing the whole of godliness, and all helps to salvation, to the divine power of Christ, takes them away from the common nature of men, so that he leaves to us not even the least particle of any virtue or merit.

Through the knowledge of him. He now describes the manner in which God makes us partakers of so great blessings, even by making himself known to us by the gospel. For the knowledge of God is the beginning of life and the first entrance into godliness. In short, spiritual gifts cannot be given for salvation, until, being illuminated by the doctrine of the gospel, we are led to know God. But he makes God the author of this knowledge, because we never go to him except when called. Hence the effectual cause of faith is not the perspicacity of our mind, but the calling of God. And he speaks not of the outward calling only, which is in itself ineffectual; but of the inward calling, effected by the hidden power of the Spirit, when God not only sounds in our ears by the voice of man, but draws inwardly our hearts to himself by his own Spirit.

To glory and virtue, or, by his own glory and power. Some copies have ἰδίᾳ δόξῃ, "by his own glory," and it is so rendered by the old interpreter; and this reading I prefer, because the sentence seems thus to flow better. For it was Peter's object expressly to ascribe the whole praise of our salvation to God, so that we may know that we owe every thing to him. And this is more clearly expressed by these words,—that he has called us *by his own glory and power.* However, the other reading, though more obscure, tends to the same thing; for he teaches us, that we are covered with shame, and are wholly vicious, until God clothes us with glory and adorns us with virtue. He further intimates, that the effect of calling in the elect, is to restore to them the glorious image of God, and to renew them in holiness and righteousness.

4. *Whereby are given to us.* It is doubtful whether he refers only to glory and power, or to the preceding things also. The whole difficulty arises from this,—that what is here said is not suitable to the glory and virtue which God confers on us; but if we read, "by his own glory and power," there will be no ambiguity nor perplexity. For what things have been promised to us by God, ought to be properly and justly deemed to be the effects of his power and glory.[1]

At the same time the copies vary here also; some have δι' ὃν, "on account of whom;" so the reference may be to Christ. Whichsoever of the two readings you choose, still the meaning will be, that first the promises of God ought to be most highly valued; and, secondly, that they are gratuitous, because they are offered to us as gifts. And he then shews the excellency of the promises, that they make us partakers of the divine nature, than which nothing can be conceived better.

---

[1] The received text no doubt contains the true reading. The word ἀρετή never means "power" either in the classics, or in the *Sept.*, or in the New Testament. *Beza* and also *Schleusner*, regard διά as expressing the final cause, *to;* it is also used in the sense of "for the sake of," or, "on account of." "Glory and virtue" are in a similar order as the previous words, "life and godliness," and also in the same order with the concluding words of the next verse, "partakers of the divine nature," and "escaping the corruptions of the world." So that there is a correspondence as to the order of the words throughout the whole passage.

With respect to δι' ὧν, the rendering may be, "for the sake of which," that is, for the purpose of leading us to "glory and virtue," many and precious promises have been given; and then the conclusion of the verse states the object in other words, that we might by these promises become partakers of the divine nature, having escaped the pollutions of the world. Escaping the corruption of the world is "godliness," is "virtue;" and partaking of the divine nature is "life," is "glory." This complete correspondence confirms the meaning which *Beza* and our version give to the preposition διά at the end of the third verse.— *Ed.*

For we must consider from whence it is that God raises us up to such a height of honour. We know how abject is the condition of our nature; that God, then, should make himself ours, so that all his things should in a manner become our things, the greatness of his grace cannot be sufficiently conceived by our minds. Therefore this consideration alone ought to be abundantly sufficient to make us to renounce the world and to carry us aloft to heaven. Let us then mark, that the end of the gospel is, to render us eventually conformable to God, and, if we may so speak, to deify us.

But the word *nature* is not here essence but quality. The Manicheans formerly dreamt that we are a part of God, and that after having run the race of life we shall at length revert to our original. There are also at this day fanatics who imagine that we thus pass over into the nature of God, so that his swallows up our nature. Thus they explain what Paul says, that God will be all in all (1 Cor. xv. 28,) and in the same sense they take this passage. But such a delirium as this never entered the minds of the holy Apostles; they only intended to say that when divested of all the vices of the flesh, we shall be partakers of divine and blessed immortality and glory, so as to be as it were one with God as far as our capacities will allow.

This doctrine was not altogether unknown to Plato, who everywhere defines the chief good of man to be an entire conformity to God; but as he was involved in the mists of errors, he afterwards glided off to his own inventions. But we, disregarding empty speculations, ought to be satisfied with this one thing,—that the image of God in holiness and righteousness is restored to us for this end, that we may at length be partakers of eternal life and glory as far as it will be necessary for our complete felicity.

Having escaped. We have already explained that the design of the Apostle was, to set before us the dignity of the glory of heaven, to which God invites us, and thus to draw us away from the vanity of this world. Moreover, he sets the corruption of the world in opposition to the divine nature; but he shews that this corruption is not in the elements which surround us, but in our heart, because there vicious and depraved affections prevail, the fountain and root of which he points out by the word *lust*. Corruption, then, is thus placed in the world, that we may know that the world is in us.

5. And besides this, giving all diligence, add to your faith, virtue; and to virtue, knowledge;

6. And to knowledge, temperance; and to temperance, patience; and to patience, godliness;

7. And to godliness, brotherly kindness; and to brotherly kindness, charity.

8. For if these things be in you, and abound, they make *you that ye shall* neither *be* barren nor unfruitful in the knowledge of our Lord Jesus Christ.

9. But he that lacketh these things is blind, and cannot see afar off, and hath forgotten that he was purged from his old sins.

5. Atque in hoc ipsum omne studium applicantes, subministrate in fide vestra virtutem, in virtute autem scientiam;

6. In scientia verò temperantiam, in temperantia autem patientiam, in patientia verò pietatem,

7. In pietate autem fraternum amorem, in fraterno verò amore charitatem.

8. Hæc enim si vobis adsint, et abundè suppetant, non otiosos neque infructuosos constituent vos in cognitione Domini nostri Jesu Christi.

9. Cui enim hæc non adsunt, cæcus est, manu palpans, purgationis oblitus veterum delictorum.

5. And besides this. As it is a work arduous and of immense labour, to put off the corruption which is in us, he bids us to strive and make every effort for this purpose. He intimates that no place is to be given in this case to sloth, and that we ought to obey God calling us, not slowly or carelessly, but that there is need of alacrity; as though he had said, "Put forth every effort, and make your exertions manifest to all." For this is what the participle he uses imports.

Add to your faith virtue, or, Supply to your faith virtue. He shews for what purpose the faithful were to strive, that is, that they might have faith adorned with good morals, wisdom, patience, and love. Then he intimates that faith ought not to be naked or empty, but that these are its inseparable companions. To supply to faith, is to add to faith. There is not here, however, properly a gradation as to the sense, though it appears as to the words; for love does not in order follow patience, nor does it proceed from it. Therefore the passage is to be thus simply explained, "Strive that virtue, prudence, temperance, and the things which follow, may be added to your faith."[1]

I take *virtue* to mean a life honest and rightly formed; for it is not here ἐνέργεια, energy or courage, but ἀρετή, virtue, moral goodness. *Knowledge* is what is necessary for acting prudently; for after having put down a general term, he mentions some of the principal endowments of a Christian. *Brotherly-kindness*, φιλαδελφία, is mutual affection among the children of God. *Love* extends wider, because it embraces all mankind.

It may, however, be here asked, Whether Peter, by assigning to us the work of supplying or adding virtue, thus far extolled the strength and power of free-will? They who seek to establish free-will in man, indeed concede to God the first place, that is, that he begins to act or work in us; but they imagine that we at the same time co-operate, and that it is thus owing to us that the movements of God are not rendered void and inefficacious. But the perpetual doctrine of Scripture is opposed to this delirious notion: for it plainly testifies, that right feelings are formed in us by God, and are rendered by him effectual. It testifies also that all our progress and perseverance are from God. Besides, it expressly declares that wisdom, love, patience, are the gifts of God and the Spirit. When, therefore, the Apostle requires these things, he by no means asserts that they are in our power, but only shews what we ought to have, and what ought to be done. And as to the godly, when conscious of their own infirmity, they find themselves

---

[1] Some, like *Bishop Warburton*, have very ingeniously attempted to shew that there is here a regular order and gradation; but it is not the order of cause and effect. Different things are mentioned, and what is added, has in some way or another a connexion with the previous word. To faith add virtue or moral conduct; that virtue may be rightly formed, add knowledge; that knowledge may be gained, add temperance; that temperance may continue, add patience or perseverance; that perseverance may be retained, add godliness or piety, that is, prayer to God; that godliness may not be alone, add brotherly-kindness; and that brotherly kindness may be enlarged, add love to all mankind. The word added has a connexion with the immediately previous word, as the way, means, or an addition.—*Ed*.

deficient in their duty, nothing remains for them but to flee to God for aid and help.¹

8. *For if these things be in you.* Then, he says, you will at length prove that Christ is really known by you, if ye be endued with virtue, temperance, and the other endowments. For the knowledge of Christ is an efficacious thing and a living root, which brings forth fruit. For by saying that these things would make them *neither barren nor unfruitful*, he shews that all those glory, in vain and falsely, that they have the knowledge of Christ, who boast of it without love, patience, and the like gifts, as Paul also says in Eph. iv. 20, " Ye have not so learned Christ, if so be that ye have heard him, and have been taught by him, as the truth is in Jesus, that ye put off the old man," &c. For he means that those who possess Christ without newness of life, have never been rightly taught his doctrine.

But he would not have the faithful to be only taught patience, godliness, temperance, love; but he requires a continual progress to be made as to these endowments, and that justly, for we are as yet far off from the goal. We ought, therefore, always to make advances, so that God's gifts may continually increase in us.

9. *But he that lacketh these things.* He now expresses more clearly that they who profess a naked faith are wholly without any true knowledge. He then says that they go astray like the blind in darkness, because they do not see the right way which is shewn to us by the light of the gospel.² This

---

¹ The question of free-will does not properly belong to this passage; for the Apostle writes, not to those in their natural state, but to those whom he considered to be new creatures. The question of free-will ought to be confined to conversion, and not extended to the state of those who have been converted. The tenth Article of the Church of England nearly meets the question, yet not wholly: it ascribes the will to turn most distinctly to God, and says that man cannot turn himself; but it does not expressly say whether man can resist the good-will given him, which is the very gist of the question. But it says further, that the grace of God by Christ " worketh with us when we have that good-will," which seems certainly to imply, that the good-will first given is made thereby effectual. If there be, then, a co-operation, (as no doubt there is,) it is the co-operation, according to this Article, of the good-will first given, and not of any thing in man by nature.—*Ed.*

² " He is blind, (*manu palpans*) stroking with the hand," is Calvin's;

he also confirms by adding this reason, because such have forgotten that through the benefit of Christ they had been cleansed from sin, and yet this is the beginning of our Christianity. It then follows, that those who do not strive for a pure and holy life, do not understand even the first rudiments of faith.

But Peter takes this for granted, that they who were still rolling in the filth of the flesh had forgotten their own purgation. For the blood of Christ has not become a washing bath to us, that it may be fouled by our filth. He, therefore, calls them *old sins*, by which he means, that our life ought to be otherwise formed, because we have been cleansed from our sins; not that any one can be pure from every sin while he lives in this world, or that the cleansing we obtain through Christ consists of pardon only, but that we ought to differ from the unbelieving, as God has separated us for himself. Though, then, we daily sin, and God daily forgives us, and the blood of Christ cleanses us from our sins, yet sin ought not to rule in us, but the sanctification of the Spirit ought to prevail in us; for so Paul teaches us in 1 Cor. vi. 11, " And such were some of you; but ye are washed," &c.

10. Wherefore the rather, brethren, give diligence to make your calling and election sure: for if ye do these things, ye shall never fall:

11. For so an entrance shall be ministered unto you abundantly into the everlasting kingdom of our Lord and Saviour Jesus Christ.

12. Wherefore I will not be negligent to put you always in remembrance of these things, though ye know *them*, and be established in the present truth.

13. Yea, I think it meet, as long as I am in this tabernacle, to stir you up, by putting *you* in remembrance;

14. Knowing that shortly I must put off *this* my tabernacle, even as our Lord Jesus Christ hath shewed me.

10. Quamobrem magis, fratres, studete firmam vestram vocationem et electionem facere: hæc enim si feceritis, non cadetis unquam :

11. Sic enim abundè subministrabitur vobis ingressus in regnum æternum Domini nostri et Servatoris Jesu Christi.

12. Itaque non negligam semper de iis commonefacere, etiamsi noveritis, et confirmati sitis in præsenti veritate.

13. Justum autem arbitror, quandiu sum in hoc tabernaculo, excitare vos admonitione;

14. Quum sciam brevi me depositurum hoc tabernaculum, quemadmodum et Dominus Jesus manifestavit mihi.

the *Vulgate* is *manu tentans*, " feeling with the hand:" but the original word means, " closing the eyes," according to the Greek grammarians, *Hesychius* and *Suidas:* " He is blind, closing his eyes."—*Ed.*

15. Moreover, I will endeavour that ye may be able after my decease to have these things always in remembrance.

15. Dabo autem operam, ut etiam semper post meum discessum possitis horum habere memoriam.

10. *Wherefore the rather, brethren, give diligence.* He draws this conclusion, that it is one proof that we have been really elected, and not in vain called by the Lord, if a good conscience and integrity of life correspond with our profession of faith. And he infers, that there ought to be more labour and diligence, because he had said before, that faith ought not to be barren.

Some copies have, "by good works;" but these words make no change in the sense, for they are to be understood though not expressed.[1]

He mentions *calling* first, though the last in order. The reason is, because election is of greater weight or importance; and it is a right arrangement of a sentence to subjoin what preponderates. The meaning then is, labour that you may have it really proved that you have not been called nor elected in vain. At the same time he speaks here of calling as the effect and evidence of election. If any one prefers to regard the two words as meaning the same thing, I do not object; for the Scripture sometimes merges the difference which exists between two terms. I have, however, stated what seems to me more probable.[2]

Now a question arises, Whether the stability of our calling and election depends on good works, for if it be so, it follows that it depends on us. But the whole Scripture teaches us, first, that God's election is founded on his eternal purpose; and secondly, that calling begins and is completed through his gratuitous goodness. The Sophists, in order to transfer what is peculiar to God's grace, to ourselves, usually pervert this evidence. But their evasions may be easily refuted.

[1] There is no sufficient authority for introducing them. Besides, there is no need of them, for the word ταῦτα, "these things," has been often previously repeated, and refers to the things mentioned in ver. 5, 6, and 7.—*Ed.*

[2] The order is such as we often meet with, the visible effect first, and then the cause, as in Rom. x. 9; confession, the ostensible act, is mentioned first, and then faith, which precedes it. So here, calling, the effect produced, is first mentioned, and then election, the cause of it; as though he had said, "Make your calling, which has proceeded from your election, sure."—*Ed.*

For if any one thinks that calling is rendered sure by men, there is nothing absurd in that; we may, however, go still farther, that every one confirms his calling by leading a holy and pious life. But it is very foolish to infer from this what the Sophists contend for; for this is a proof not taken from the cause, but on the contrary from the sign or the effect. Moreover, this does not prevent election from being gratuitous, nor does it shew that it is in our own hand or power to confirm election. For the matter stands thus,—God effectually calls whom he has preordained to life in his secret counsel before the foundation of the world; and he also carries on the perpetual course of calling through grace alone. But as he has chosen us, and calls us for this end, that we may be pure and spotless in his presence; purity of life is not improperly called the evidence and proof of election, by which the faithful may not only testify to others that they are the children of God, but also confirm themselves in this confidence, in such a manner, however, that they fix their solid foundation on something else.

At the same time, this certainty, mentioned by Peter, ought, I think, to be referred to the conscience, as though the faithful acknowledged themselves before God to be chosen and called. But I take it simply of the fact itself, that calling appears as confirmed by this very holiness of life. It may, indeed, be rendered, Labour that your calling may become certain; for the verb $\pi o \iota e \hat{\iota} \sigma \theta a \iota$ is transitive or intransitive. Still, however you may render it, the meaning is nearly the same.

The import of what is said is, that the children of God are distinguished from the reprobate by this mark, that they live a godly and a holy life, because this is the design and end of election. Hence it is evident how wickedly some vile unprincipled men prattle, when they seek to make gratuitous election an excuse for all licentiousness; as though, forsooth! we may sin with impunity, because we have been predestinated to righteousness and holiness!

For if ye do these things. Peter seems again to ascribe to the merits of works, that God furthers our salvation, and also that we continually persevere in his grace. But the explanation is obvious; for his purpose was only to shew that hypocrites have in them nothing real or solid, and that, on the contrary, they who prove their calling sure by good works, are free from the danger of falling, because sure and sufficient is the grace of God by which they are supported. Thus the certainty of our salvation by no means depends on us, as doubtless the cause of it is beyond our limits. But with regard to those who feel in themselves the efficacious working of the Spirit, Peter bids them to take courage as to the future, because the Lord has laid in them the solid foundation of a true and sure calling.

He explains the way or means of persevering, when he says, *an entrance shall be ministered to you.* The import of the words is this: "God, by ever supplying you abundantly with new graces, will lead you to his own kingdom." And this was added, that we may know, that though we have already passed from death into life, yet it is a passage of hope; and as to the fruition of life, there remains for us yet a long journey. In the meantime we are not destitute of necessary helps. Hence Peter obviates a doubt by these words, "The Lord will abundantly supply your need, until you shall enter into his eternal kingdom." He calls it the kingdom of *Christ*, because we cannot ascend to heaven except under his banner and guidance.

12. *Wherefore I will not be negligent.* As we seem to distrust either the memory or the attention of those whom we often remind of the same thing, the Apostle makes this modest excuse, that he ceased not to press on the attention of the faithful what was well known and fixed in their minds, because its importance and greatness required this. "Ye do, indeed," he says, "fully understand what the truth of the gospel is, nor have I to confirm as it were the wavering, but in a matter so great, admonitions are never superfluous; and, therefore, they ought never to be deemed vexatious." Paul also employs a similar excuse in Rom. xv. 14, "I am persuaded of you, brethren," he says, "that ye are full of knowledge, so as to be able to admonish one another: but I have more confidently written to you, as putting you in mind."

He calls that *the present truth,* into the possession of which they had already entered by a sure faith. He, then, commends their faith, in order that they might remain fixed in it more firmly.

13. *Yea, I think it meet,* or right. He expresses more clearly how useful and how necessary is admonition, because it is needful to arouse the faithful, for otherwise torpor will creep in from the flesh. Though, then, they might not have wanted teaching, yet he says that the goads of admonitions were useful, lest security and indulgence (as it is usually the case) should weaken what they had learned, and at length extinguish it.

He adds another cause why he was so intent on writing to them, because he knew that a short time remained for him. " I must diligently employ my time," he says ; " for the Lord has made known to me that my life in this world will not be long."

We hence learn, that admonitions ought to be so given, that the people whom we wish to benefit may not think that wrong is done to them, and also that offences ought to be so avoided, that yet the truth may have a free course, and exhortations may not be discontinued. Now, this moderation is to be observed towards those to whom a sharp reproof would not be suitable, but who ought on the contrary to be kindly helped, since they are inclined of themselves to do their duty. We are also taught by the example of Peter, that the shorter term of life remains to us, the more diligent ought we to be in executing our office. It is not commonly given to us to foresee our end ; but they who are advanced in years, or weakened by illness, being reminded by such indications of the shortness of their life, oug'it to be more sedulous and diligent, so that they may in d' time perform what the Lord has given them to do ; nay, those who are the strongest and in the flower of their age, as they do not render to God so constant a service as it behoves them to do, ought to quicken themselves to the same care and diligence by the recollection of approaching death ; lest the occasion of doing good may pass away, while they attend negligently and slothfully to their work.

At the same time, I doubt not but that it was Peter's object to gain more authority and weight to his teaching, when he said that he would endeavour to make them to remember these things after his death, which was then nigh at hand. For when any one, shortly before he quits this life, addresses us, his words have in a manner the force and power of a testament or will, and are usually received by us with greater reverence.

14. *I must put off this my tabernacle.* Literally the words are, "Short is the putting away of this tabernacle." By this mode of speaking, and afterwards by the word "departing," he designates death, which it behoves us to notice; for we are here taught how much death differs from perdition. Besides, too much dread of death terrifies us, because we do not sufficiently consider how fading and evanescent this life is, and do not reflect on the perpetuity of future life. But what does Peter say? He declares that death is departing from this world, that we may remove elsewhere, even to the Lord. It ought not, then, to be dreadful to us, as though we were to perish when we die. He declares that it is the putting away of a tabernacle, by which we are covered only for a short time. There is, then, no reason why we should regret to be removed from it.

But there is to be understood an implied contrast between a fading tabernacle and a perpetual habitation, which Paul explains in 2 Cor. v. 1.[1]

When he says that it had been revealed to him by Christ, he refers not to the kind of death, but to the time. But if he received the oracle at Babylon respecting his death being near, how was he crucified at Rome? It certainly appears that he died very far from Italy, except he flew in a moment over seas and lands.[2] But the Papists, in order to claim for

---

[1] Paul, at the beginning of this chapter, compares our state in this world in a fading body with our state above after the resurrection in a glorified body, and takes no account of the intervening time between death and the resurrection. By keeping this in view, the whole passage, otherwise obscure, will appear quite clear. He speaks of being unclothed and clothed, that is, of being divested of one body, and of putting on another; and consistently with this view he speaks of not being found naked, that is, without a body as a covering.—*Ed.*

[2] It has been disputed, whether he refers here to what is recorded in

themselves the body of Peter, make themselves Babylonians, and say that Rome is called Babylon by Peter: this shall be refuted in its proper place. What he says of remembering these things after his death, was intended to shew, that posterity ought to learn from him when dead. For the apostles had not regard only for their own age, but purposed to do us good also. Though, then, they are dead, their doctrine lives and prevails: and it is our duty to profit by their writings, as though they were manifestly present with us.

16. For we have not followed cunningly-devised fables, when we made known unto you the power and coming of our Lord Jesus Christ, but were eye-witnesses of his majesty.

17. For he received from God the Father honour and glory, when there came such a voice to him from the excellent glory, This is my beloved Son, in whom I am well pleased.

18. And this voice which came from heaven we heard, when we were with him in the holy mount.

16. Neque enim fabulas subtiliter excogitatas (*vel*, arte compositas) sequuti, notam vobis fecimus Domini nostri Jesu Christi potentiam et adventum; sed spectatores facti ejus magnificentiæ.

17. Accepit enim à Deo Patre honorem et gloriam, allata illi à magnifica gloria hujusmodi voce, Hic est Filius meus dilectus, in quo mihi complacui.

17. Et hanc vocem nos audivimus, dum essemus in monte sancto cum illo.

16. *For we have not followed cunningly-devised fables.* It gives us much courage, when we know that we labour in a matter that is certain. Lest, then, the faithful should think that in these labours they were beating the air, he now comes to set forth the certainty of the gospel; and he denies that anything had been delivered by him but what was altogether true and indubitable: and they were encouraged to persevere, when they were sure of the prosperous issue of their calling.

In the first place, Peter indeed asserts that he had been an eye-witness; for he had himself seen with his own eyes the glory of Christ, of which he speaks. This knowledge he sets in opposition to crafty fables, such as cunning men are wont to fabricate to ensnare simple minds. The old interpreter renders the word "feigned," (*fictas ;*) Erasmus,

John xxi. 18, 19, or to a new revelation. The latter was the opinion of some of the ancient fathers; and not without reason, for in John the *manner* of his death is what is mentioned, but here the *near approach* of it,—two things wholly distinct.—*Ed.*

"formed by art." It seems to me that what is subtle to deceive is meant: for the Greek word here used, σοφίζεσθαι, sometimes means this. And we know how much labour men bestow on frivolous refinements, and only that they may have some amusement. Therefore no less seriously ought our minds to be applied to know the truth which is not fallacious, and the doctrine which is not nugatory, and which discovers to us the glory of the Son of God and our own salvation.[1]

The power and the coming. No doubt he meant in these words to include the substance of the gospel, as it certainly contains nothing except Christ, in whom are hid all the treasures of wisdom. But he distinctly mentions two things, —that Christ had been manifested in the flesh,—and also that power was exhibited by him.[2] Thus, then, we have the whole gospel; for we know that he, the long-promised Redeemer, came from heaven, put on our flesh, lived in the world, died and rose again; and, in the second place, we perceive the end and fruit of all these things, that is, that he might be God with us, that he might exhibit in himself a sure pledge of our adoption, that he might cleanse us from the defilements of the flesh by the grace of his Spirit, and consecrate us temples to God, that he might deliver us from hell, and raise us up to heaven, that he might by the sacrifice of his death make an atonement for the sins of the world, that he might reconcile us to the Father, that he might become to us the author of righteousness and of life. He who knows and understands these things, is fully acquainted with the gospel.

Were eye-witnesses, or beholders.[3] We hence conclude, that they by no means serve Christ, nor are like the apostles,

---

[1] The verb σοφίζω, once used by Paul in 2 Tim. iii. 15, means "to make wise," and in this sense it is used in the *Sept.*; and it may properly have a similar meaning here, "myths (or, fables) made wise," or made to appear wise,—a trade still carried on in the world. The idea of craft and subtlety is what is given to it in the classics.—*Ed.*

[2] We have the same order as in several previous instances; "power" first, then "coming." It is the peculiar style of Scripture.—*Ed.*

[3] *Spectatores,* ἰπόπται, lookers on, inspectors, surveyors: it betokens those who not only see or behold a thing, but who attentively look on. It is more emphatical than αὐτόπται, "eye-witnesses."—*Ed.*

who presumptuously mount the pulpit to prattle of speculations unknown to themselves ; for he alone is the lawful minister of Christ, who knows the truth of the doctrine which he delivers : not that all obtain certainty in the same way ; for what Peter says is that he himself was present, when Christ was declared by a voice from heaven to be the Son of God. Three only were then present, but they were sufficient as witnesses ; for they had through many miracles seen the glory of Christ, and had a remarkable evidence of his divinity in his resurrection. But we now obtain certainty in another way ; for though Christ has not risen before our eyes, yet we know by whom his resurrection has been handed down to us. And added to this is the inward testimony of conscience, the sealing of the Spirit, which far exceeds all the evidence of the senses. But let us remember that the gospel was not at the beginning made up of vague rumours, but that the apostles were the authentic preachers of what they had seen.

17. *For he received from God the Father.* He chose one memorable example out of many, even that of Christ, when, adorned with celestial glory, he conspicuously displayed his divine majesty to his three disciples. And though Peter does not relate all the circumstances, yet he sufficiently designates them when he says, that *a voice came from the magnificent glory.* For the meaning is, that nothing earthly was seen there, but that a celestial majesty shone on every side. We may hence conclude what those displays of greatness were which the evangelists relate. And it was necessarily thus done, in order that the authority of that voice which came might be more awful and solemn, as we see that it was done all at once by the Lord. For when he spoke to the fathers, he did not only cause his words to sound in the air, but by adding some symbols or tokens of his presence, he proved the oracles to be his.

This is my beloved Son. Peter then mentions this voice, as though it was sufficient alone as a full evidence for the gospel, and justly so. For when Christ is acknowledged by us to be him whom the Father has sent, this is our highest wisdom. There are two parts to this sentence. When he says, "This is," the expression is very emphatical, intimating, that he was the Messiah who had been so often promised. Whatever, then, is found in the Law and the Prophets respecting the Messiah, is declared here, by the Father, to belong to him whom he so highly commended. In the other part of the sentence, he announces Christ as his own Son, in whom his whole love dwells and centres. It hence follows that we are not otherwise loved than in him, nor ought the love of God to be sought anywhere else. It is sufficient for me now only to touch on these things by the way.

18. *In the holy mount.* He calls it the holy mount, for the same reason that the ground was called holy where God appeared to Moses. For wherever the Lord comes, as he is the fountain of all holiness, he makes holy all things by the odour of his presence. And by this mode of speaking we are taught, not only to receive God reverently wherever he shews himself, but also to prepare ourselves for holiness, as soon as he comes nigh us, as it was commanded the people when the law was proclaimed on Mount Sinai. And it is a general truth, " Be ye holy, for I am holy, who dwell in the midst of you." (Lev. xi. 44; xix. 2.)

19. We have also a more sure word of prophecy; whereunto ye do well that ye take heed, as unto a light that shineth in a dark place, until the day dawn, and the day-star arise in your hearts;	19. Et habemus firmiorem propheticum sermonem, cui benè facitis attendentes, tanquam lucernæ apparenti in caliginoso loco, donec illuceat dies, et lucifer oriatur in cordibus vestris;
20. Knowing this first, that no prophecy of the scripture is of any private interpretation.	20. Hoc primùm cognito, quòd omnis prophetia scripturæ privatæ (*vel*, proprii motus) interpretationis non est:
21. For the prophecy came not in old time by the will of man; but holy men of God spake *as they were* moved by the Holy Ghost.	21. Neque enim voluntate hominis allata est quondam prophetia; sed à Spiritu Sancto impulsi, loquuti sunt sancti Dei homines.

19. *We have also.* He now shews that the truth of the gospel is founded on the oracles of the prophets, lest they who embraced it should hesitate to devote themselves wholly to Christ : for they who waver cannot be otherwise than remiss in their minds. But when he says, "We have," he refers to himself and other teachers, as well as to their dis-

ciples. The apostles had the prophets as the patrons of their doctrine; the faithful also sought from them a confirmation of the gospel. I am the more disposed to take this view, because he speaks of the whole Church, and makes himself one among others. At the same time, he refers more especially to the Jews, who were well acquainted with the doctrine of the prophets. And hence, as I think, he calls their word *more sure* or firmer.

For they who take the comparative for a positive, that is, " more sure," for " sure," do not sufficiently consider the whole context. The sense also is a forced one, when it is said to be " more sure," because God really completed what he had promised concerning his Son. For the truth of the gospel is here simply proved by a twofold testimony,—that Christ had been highly approved by the solemn declaration of God, and, then, that all the prophecies of the prophets confirmed the same thing. But it appears at first sight strange, that the word of the prophets should be said to be more sure or firmer than the voice which came from the holy mouth of God himself; for, first, the authority of God's word is the same from the beginning; and, secondly, it was more confirmed than previously by the coming of Christ. But the solution of this knot is not difficult: for here the Apostle had a regard to his own nation, who were acquainted with the prophets, and their doctrine was received without any dispute. As, then, it was not doubted by the Jews but that all the things which the prophets had taught, came from the Lord, it is no wonder that Peter said that their word was more sure. Antiquity also gains some reverence. There are, besides, some other circumstances which ought to be noticed; particularly, that no suspicion could be entertained as to those prophecies in which the kingdom of Christ had so long before been predicted.

The question, then, is not here, whether the prophets deserve more credit than the gospel; but Peter regarded only this, to shew how much deference the Jews paid to those who counted the prophets as God's faithful ministers, and had been brought up from childhood in their school.[1]

[1] Much has been written on this subject; and the difficulty has arisen

Whereunto ye do well. This passage is, indeed, attended with some more difficulty; for it may be asked, what is the *day* which Peter mentions? To some it seems to be the clear knowledge of Christ, when men fully acquiesce in the gospel; and the *darkness* they explain as existing, when they, as yet, hesitate in suspense, and the doctrine of the gospel is not received as indubitable; as though Peter praised those Jews who were searching for Christ in the Law and the Prophets, and were advancing, as by this preceding light towards Christ, the Sun of righteousness, as they were praised by Luke, who, having heard Paul preaching, searched the Scripture to know whether what he said was true. (Acts xvii. 11.)

But in this view there is, first, an inconsistency, because it thus seems that the use of the prophecies is confined to a short time, as though they would be superfluous when the gospel-light is seen. Were one to object and say, that this does not necessarily follow, because *until* does not always denote the end. To this I say, that in commands it cannot be otherwise taken: " Walk until you finish your course ;" " Fight until you conquer." In such expressions we doubtless see that a certain time is specified.[1] But were I to concede this point, that the reading of the prophets is not thus wholly cast aside; yet every one must see how frigid is this commendation, that the prophets are useful until Christ

---

from a wrong construction of the passage, which is literally as follows :—
" And we have more firm the prophetic word," Καὶ ἔχομεν βεβαιότερον τὸν προφητικὸν λόγον, that is, we have rendered more firm the prophetic word. This is confirmed by what follows; for the prophetic word is compared to " a light shining in a dark place," and, therefore, not clear nor firm until it be fulfilled; but they were doing well to attend to this light until the full light of the gospel shone in their hearts. As *Scott* maintains, the reference here is clearly to the experience of Christians, to their real knowledge of divine truths; for it was to be *in* their *hearts*, and not before their eyes.

A great deal of learning has been spent to no purpose on this passage. It has been by most taken as granted, that " the power and coming of our Lord," mentioned in verse 16th, is his second coming, when the whole passage refers only and expressly to his first coming. And on this gratuitous and even false supposition is grounded the elaborate exposition of *Sherlock, Horsley,* and others.—*Ed.*

[1] There is no command here: the Apostle only approves of what they were doing, " whereunto ye do well that ye take heed."—*Ed.*

is revealed to us; for their teaching is necessary to us until the end of life. Secondly, we must bear in mind who they were whom Peter addressed; for he was not instructing the ignorant and novices, who were as yet in the first rudiments; but even those respecting whom he had before testified, that they had obtained the same precious faith, and were confirmed in the present truth. Surely the gross darkness of ignorance could not have been ascribed to such people. I know what some allege, that all had not made the same progress, and that here beginners who were as yet seeking Christ, are admonished.

But as it is evident from the context, that the words were addressed to the same persons, the passage must necessarily be applied to the faithful who had already known Christ, and had become partakers of the true light. I therefore extend this darkness, mentioned by Peter, to the whole course of life, and *the day*, I consider will then *shine* on us when we shall see face to face, what we now see through a glass darkly. Christ, the Sun of righteousness, indeed, shines forth in the gospel; but the darkness of death will always, in part, possess our minds, until we shall be brought out of the prison of the flesh, and be translated into heaven. This, then, will be the brightness of day, when no clouds or mists of ignorance shall intercept the bright shining of the Sun.

And doubtless we are so far from a perfect day, as our faith is from perfection. It is, therefore, no wonder that the state of the present life is called darkness, since we are far distant from that knowledge to which the gospel invites us.[1]

In short, Peter reminds us that as long as we sojourn in this world, we have need of the doctrine of the prophets as a guiding light; which being extinguished, we can do nothing else but wander in darkness; for he does not disjoin the prophecies from the gospel, when he teaches us that

---

[1] The Apostle does not speak of the perfect day, but of the dawn of it, and the day-star is that which ushers in the perfect day. The gospel is the dawn and the day-star, compared with the glimmering light of prophecy, and compared too with the perfect day of the heavenly kingdom. Prophecy is useful still; for its fulfilment, found in the gospel, greatly strengthens faith.—*Ed.*

they shine to shew us the way. His object only was to teach us that the whole course of our life ought to be guided by God's word; for otherwise we must be involved on every side in the darkness of ignorance; and the Lord does not shine on us, except when we take his word as our light.

But he does not use the comparison, *light*, or lamp, to intimate that the light is small and sparing, but to make these two things to correspond,—that we are without light, and can no more keep on the right way than those who go astray in a dark night; and that the Lord brings a remedy for this evil, when he lights a torch to guide us in the midst of darkness.

What he immediately adds respecting *the day-star* does not however seem altogether suitable to this explanation; for the real knowledge, to which we are advancing through life, cannot be called the beginning of the day. To this I reply, that different parts of the day are compared together, but the whole day in all its parts is set in opposition to that darkness, which would wholly overspread all our faculties, were not the Lord to come to our help by the light of his word.

This is a remarkable passage: we learn from it how God guides us. The Papists have ever and anon in their mouth, that the Church cannot err. Though the word is neglected, they yet imagine that it is guided by the Spirit. But Peter, on the contrary, intimates that all are immersed in darkness who do not attend to the light of the word. Therefore, except thou art resolved wilfully to cast thyself into a labyrinth, especially beware of departing even in the least thing from the rule and direction of the word. Nay, the Church cannot follow God as its guide, except it observes what the word prescribes.

In this passage Peter also condemns all the wisdom of men, in order that we may learn humbly to seek, otherwise than by our own understanding, the true way of knowledge; for without the word nothing is left for men but darkness.

It further deserves to be noticed, that he pronounces on the clearness of Scripture; for what is said would be a false eulogy, were not the Scripture fit and suitable to shew to us with certainty the right way. Whosoever, then, will open his eyes through the obedience of faith, shall by experience know that the Scripture has not been in vain called a light. It is, indeed, obscure to the unbelieving; but they who are given up to destruction are wilfully blind. Execrable, therefore, is the blasphemy of the Papists, who pretend that the light of Scripture does nothing but dazzle the eyes, in order to keep the simple from reading it. But it is no wonder that proud men, inflated with the wind of false confidence, do not see that light with which the Lord favours only little children and the humble. With a similar eulogy David commends the law of God in Ps. xix. and cxix.

20. *Knowing this first.* Here Peter begins to shew how our minds are to be prepared, if we really wish to make progress in scriptural knowledge. There may at the same time be two interpretations given, if you read ἐπηλύσεως, as some do, which means occurrence, impulse; or, as I have rendered it, interpretation, ἐπιλύσεως. But almost all give this meaning, that we ought not to rush on headlong and rashly when we read Scripture, confiding in our own understanding. They think that a confirmation of this follows, because the Spirit, who spoke by the prophets, is the only true interpreter of himself.

This explanation contains a true, godly, and useful doctrine,—that then only are the prophecies read profitably, when we renounce the mind and feelings of the flesh, and submit to the teaching of the Spirit, but that it is an impious profanation of it, when we arrogantly rely on our own acumen, deeming that sufficient to enable us to understand it, though the mysteries contain things hidden to our flesh, and sublime treasures of life far surpassing our capacities. And this is what we have said, that the light which shines in it, comes to the humble alone.

But the Papists are doubly foolish, when they conclude from this passage, that no interpretation of a private man ought to be deemed authoritative. For they pervert what Peter says, that they may claim for their own councils the chief right of interpreting Scripture; but in this they act indeed childishly; for Peter calls interpretation *private*, not that of every individual, in order to prohibit each one to interpret; but he shews that whatever men bring of their own is profane. Were, then, the whole world unanimous, and were the minds of all men united together, still what would proceed from them, would be private or their own; for the word is here set in opposition to divine revelation; so that the faithful, inwardly illuminated by the Holy Spirit, acknowledge nothing but what God says in his word.

However, another sense seems to me more simple, that Peter says that Scripture came not from man, or through the suggestions of man. For thou wilt never come well prepared to read it, except thou bringest reverence, obedience, and docility; but a just reverence then only exists, when we are convinced that God speaks to us, and not mortal men. Then Peter especially bids us to believe the prophecies as the indubitable oracles of God, because they have not emanated from men's own private suggestions.[1]

To the same purpose is what immediately follows,—*but holy men of God spake* as they were *moved by the Holy Ghost*. They did not of themselves, or according to their own will,

[1] There are in the main three renderings of this passage:—1. " No prophecy of Scripture is of a private impulse," or invention;—2. " No prophecy of Scripture is of self-interpretation," that is, is its own interpreter; —3. No prophecy of Scripture is of private interpretation, that is, is not to be interpreted according to the fancies of men, but according to the word of God and the guidance of his Spirit. Now which of these corresponds with the context? Clearly the first, the two others have nothing in the passage to countenance them. The next verse is evidently explanatory of this sentence, which seems at once to determine its meaning; and, as it is often the case in Scripture, the explanation is given negatively and positively. Prophecy *did not* come from the will of man; it *did* come from the Spirit of God. Besides, the importance attached to the announcement, "Knowing this especially," is not so clearly borne out as by the first exposition, because the fact that prophecy did not come from man, is everything in the question, while the other expositions contain only things of subordinate importance. Thus what goes before and comes after tends to confirm the same view.

Whether we take the conjectural reading (which only differs from the other in one small letter) or that which is found in all the MSS., it may admit of the meaning that has been given. There is either an ἐκ, "from," understood, or the word *prophecy* is to be repeated: " No prophecy of Scripture is *from* one's own explanation;" or, " No prophecy of Scripture is a *prophecy* of one's own explanation," or interpretation, that is, as to things to come.

Calvin has been followed in his view of this passage, among others, by *Grotius, Doddridge,* and *Macknight.*—*Ed.*

foolishly deliver their own inventions. The meaning is, that the beginning of right knowledge is to give that credit to the holy prophets which is due to God. He calls them the *holy men of God,* because they faithfully executed the office committed to them, having sustained the person of God in their ministrations. He says that they were *moved*—not that they were bereaved of mind, (as the Gentiles imagined their prophets to have been,) but because they dared not to announce anything of their own, and obediently followed the Spirit as their guide, who ruled in their mouth as in his own sanctuary. Understand by *prophecy of Scripture* that which is contained in the holy Scriptures.

CHAPTER II.

1. But there were false prophets also among the people, even as there shall be false teachers among you, who privily shall bring in damnable heresies, even denying the Lord that bought them, and bring upon themselves swift destruction.

2. And many shall follow their pernicious ways; by reason of whom the way of truth shall be evil spoken of.

3. And through covetousness shall they with feigned words make merchandise of you: whose judgment now of a long time lingereth not, and their damnation slumbereth not.

1. Fuerunt autem et falsi prophetæ in populo, sicuti et inter vos erunt falsi doctores, qui subinducent sectas perditionis, et etiam Dominum qui eos redemit abnegantes, accersentes sibi celerem interitum.

2. Et multi sequentur eorum exitia, per quos via veritatis blasphemabitur;

3. Et in avaritia fictis sermonibus de vobis negotiabuntur; quorum judicium pridem non cessat, et quorum perditio non dormitat.

1. *But there were.* As weak consciences are usually very grievously and dangerously shaken, when false teachers arise, who either corrupt or mutilate the doctrine of faith, it was necessary for the Apostle, while seeking to encourage the faithful to persevere, to remove out of the way an offence of this kind. He, moreover, comforted those to whom he was writing, and confirmed them by this argument, that God has always tried and proved his Church by such a temptation as this, in order that novelty might not disturb their hearts. "Not different," he says, "will be the condition of the Church under the gospel, from what it was formerly

under the law ; false prophets disturbed the ancient Church ; the same thing must also be expected by us."

It was necessary expressly to shew this, because many imagined that the Church would enjoy tranquillity under the reign of Christ ; for as the prophets had promised that at his coming there would be real peace, the highest degree of heavenly wisdom, and the full restoration of all things, they thought that the Church would be no more exposed to any contests. Let us then remember that the Spirit of God hath once for all declared, that the Church shall never be free from this intestine evil ; and let this likeness be always borne in mind, that the trial of our faith is to be similar to that of the fathers, and for the same reason—that in this way it may be made evident, whether we really love God, as we find it written in Deut. xiii. 3.

But it is not necessary here to refer to every example of this kind ; it is enough, in short, to know that, like the fathers, we must contend against false doctrines, that our faith ought by no means to be shaken on account of discords and sects, because the truth of God shall remain unshaken notwithstanding the violent agitations by which Satan strives often to upset all things.

Observe also, that no one time in particular is mentioned by Peter, when he says *there shall be false teachers,* but that all ages are included ; for he makes here a comparison between Christians and the ancient people. We ought, then, to apply this truth to our own time, lest, when we see false teachers rising up to oppose the truth of God, this trial should break us down. But the Spirit reminds us, in order that we may take the more heed ; and to the same purpose is the whole description which follows.

He does not, indeed, paint each sect in its own colours, but particularly refers to profane men who manifested contempt towards God. The advice, indeed, is general, that we ought to beware of false teachers ; but, at the same time, he selected one kind of such from whom the greater danger arose. What is said here will hereafter become more evident from the words of Jude, who treats exactly of the same subject.

Who privily shall bring in. By these words he points out

the craftiness of Satan, and of all the ungodly who militate under his banner, that they would creep in by oblique turnings, and as through burrows under ground.¹ The more watchful, then, ought the godly to be, so that they may escape their hidden frauds : for however they may insinuate themselves, they cannot circumvent those who are carefully vigilant.

He calls them *opinions of perdition,* or destructive opinions, that every one, solicitous for his salvation, might dread such opinions as the most noxious pests. As to the word *opinions* or heresies, it has not, without reason, been always deemed infamous and hateful by the children of God ; for the bond of holy unity is the simple truth. As soon as we depart from that, nothing remains but dreadful discord.

Even denying the Lord that bought them. Though Christ may be denied in various ways, yet Peter, as I think, refers here to what is expressed by Jude, that is, when the grace of God is turned into lasciviousness ; for Christ redeemed us, that he might have a people separated from all the pollutions of the world, and devoted to holiness and innocency. They, then, who throw off the bridle, and give themselves up to all kinds of licentiousness, are not unjustly said to deny Christ by whom they have been redeemed. Hence, that the doctrine of the gospel may remain whole and complete among us, let this be fixed in our minds, that we have been redeemed by Christ, that he may be the Lord of our life and of our death, and that our main object ought to be, to live to him and to die to him. He then says, that their *swift destruction* was at hand, lest others should be ensnared by them.²

2. *And many shall follow.* It is, indeed, no slight offence to the weak, when they see that false doctrines are received by the common consent of the world, that a large number of

---

¹ " Peter intimated that the heresies of which he speaks were to be introduced under the colour of true doctrine, in the dark. as it were, and by little and little ; so that the people would not discern their real nature." —*Macknight.*

² The word here for "Lord" is δισπότης, which is more expressive of power and authority than Κύριος, commonly rendered " Lord." This seems to intimate the character of the men alluded to : they denied Christ as their sovereign, as they rendered no obedience to him, though they may have professed to believe in him as a Saviour.—*Ed.*

men are led astray, so that few continue in true obedience to Christ. So, at this day, there is nothing that more violently disturbs pious minds than such a defection. For hardly one in ten of those who have once made a profession of Christ, retains the purity of faith to the end. Almost all turn aside into corruptions, and being deluded by the teachers of licentiousness, they become profane. Lest this should make our faith to falter, Peter comes to our help, and in due time foretells that this very thing would be, that is, that false teachers would draw many to perdition.

But there is a double reading even in the Greek copies; for some read, " lasciviousness," and others, " perdition." I have, however, followed what has been mostly approved.[1]

By reason of whom the way of truth. This I consider to have been said for this reason, because as religion is adorned when men are taught to fear God, to maintain uprightness of life, a chaste and virtuous conduct, or when at least the mouth of the wicked is closed, that they do not speak evil of the gospel; so when the reins are let loose, and every kind of licentiousness is practised, the name and the doctrine of Christ are exposed to the reproaches of the ungodly. Others give a different explanation,—that these false teachers, like filthy dogs, barked at sound doctrine. But the words of Peter appear to me on the contrary to intimate, that these would give occasion to enemies insolently to assail the truth of God. Though then they would not themselves assail the Christian faith with calumnies, yet they would arm others with the means of reproaching it.

3. *With feigned words.* Peter endeavours by all means to render the faithful displeased with ungodly teachers, that they might resist them more resolutely and more constantly. It is especially an odious thing that we should be exposed to sale like vile slaves. But he testifies that this is done,

---

[1] Few copies have " perdition," or perditions, for the word is in the plural number; and very many have " lasciviousness," and also the *Vulg.* and *Syr.* versions. Having before mentioned their destructive opinions or heresies, which involved the denial of the Lord who bought them, he now refers to the immorality which accompanied their false doctrines; and that immorality is here referred to is evident from this, that the way of truth would be evil spoken of or calumniated.—*Ed.*

when any one seduces us from the redemption of Christ. He calls those *feigned words* which are artfully formed for the purpose of deceiving.[1] Unless then one is so mad as to sell the salvation of his soul to false teachers, let him close up every avenue that may lead to their wicked inventions. For the same purpose as before he repeats again, that their destruction delayed not, that is, that he might frighten the good from their society. For since they were given up to a sudden destruction, every one who connected himself with them, must have perished with them.

4. For if God spared not the angels that sinned, but cast *them* down to hell, and delivered *them* into chains of darkness, to be reserved unto judgment;

5. And spared not the old world, but saved Noah, the eighth *person*, a preacher of righteousness, bringing in the flood upon the world of the ungodly;

6. And turning the cities of Sodom and Gomorrha into ashes, condemned *them* with an overthrow, making *them* an ensample unto those that after should live ungodly;

7. And delivered just Lot, vexed with the filthy conversation of the wicked:

8. (For that righteous man dwelling among them, in seeing and hearing, vexed *his* righteous soul from day to day with *their* unlawful deeds;)

4. Si enim Angelis qui peccaverant, Deus non perpercit, sed catenis caliginis in tartarum præcipitatos tradidit servandos in judicium;

5. Et prisco mundo non pepercit, sed octavum justitiæ præconem Noe servavit, diluvio in mundum impiorum inducto;

6. Et civitates Sodomorum et Gomorrhæ in cinerem redactas, subversione damnavit, easque statuit exemplum iis qui impiè acturi forent;

7. Et justum Lot qui opprimebatur à nefariis per libidinosam conversationem eripuit;

8. Nam oculis et auribus justus ille, quum habitaret inter ipsos quotidie animam justam iniquis illorum operibus excruciabat;

For if. We have stated how much it behoves us to know that the ungodly, who by their mischievous opinions corrupt the Church, cannot escape God's vengeance; and this he

---

[1] Either "feigned" or "invented" may be meant by πλαστοῖς: if "feigned," then they were words used not conveying their real sentiments, but adopted for the purpose of alluring others, as is the case with those who pretend great zeal for truth and great love for souls, when their object is to gain adherents for filthy lucre's sake. But if "invented" be adopted, then λόγοι must mean narratives or fables,—"invented (or fictitious) fables," or tales. And this is the rendering of *Macknight*. And he says, that the Apostle had probably in view the fables concerning the visions of angels and the miracles performed at the sepulchres of departed saints, which the false teachers in the early ages, and the monks in latter times, fabricated, to draw money from the people. Similar are the devices of superstitious men, greedy of gain, in every age. —*Ed.*

proves especially by three remarkable examples of God's judgment,—that he spared not even angels, that he once destroyed the whole world by a deluge, that he reduced Sodom to ashes, and other neighbouring cities. But Peter thought it sufficient to take as granted what ought to be never doubted by us, that is, that God is the judge of the whole world. It hence follows that the punishment he formerly inflicted on the ungodly and wicked, he will now also inflict on the like characters. For he can never be unlike himself, nor does he shew respect of persons, so as to forgive the same wickedness in one which he has punished in another; but he hates injustice and wrong equally, whenever it is found.[1]

For we must always bear in mind that there is a difference between God and men; for men indeed judge unequally, but God keeps the same course in judging. For that he forgives sins, this is done because he blots them out through repentance and faith. He therefore does not otherwise reconcile himself to us than by justifying us; for until sin is taken away, there is always an occasion of discord between us and Him.

As to the *angels*. The argument is from the greater to the less; for they were far more excellent than we are, and yet their dignity did not preserve them from the hand of God; much less then can mortal men escape, when they follow them in their impiety. But as Peter mentions here but briefly the fall of angels, and as he has not named the time and the manner and other circumstances, it behoves us soberly to speak on the subject. Most men are curious and make no end of inquiries on these things; but since God in Scripture has only sparingly touched on them, and as it were by the way, he thus reminds us that we ought to be satisfied with this small knowledge. And indeed they who curiously

---

[1] The "if" at the beginning of the verse requires a corresponding clause. Some, as *Piscator* and *Macknight*, supply at the end of the seventh verse, "he will not spare thee," or, "will he spare thee?" But there is no need of this, the corresponding clause is in the ninth verse; and this is our version. The deliverance of the just is there first mentioned, as that of Lot was the subject of the previous verse, and then the reservation of the unjust for judgment, examples of which he had before given. This sort of arrangement is common in Scripture.—*Ed.*

inquire, do not regard edification, but seek to feed their souls with vain speculations. What is useful to us, God has made known, that is, that the devils were at first created, that they might serve and obey God, but that through their own fault they apostatized, because they would not submit to the authority of God ; and that thus the wickedness found in them was accidental, and not from nature, so that it could not be ascribed to God.

All this Peter declares very clearly, when he says that angels fell, though superior to men ; and Jude is still more express when he writes, that they kept not their first estate, or their pre-eminence. Let those who are not satisfied with these testimonies have recourse to the Sorbonian theology, which will teach them respecting angels to satiety, so as to precipitate them to hell together with the devils.

Chains of darkness. This metaphor intimates that they are held bound in darkness until the last day. And the comparison is taken from malefactors, who after having been condemned, suffer half of their punishment by the severity of the prison, until they are drawn forth to their final doom. We may hence learn, not only what punishment the wicked suffer after death, but also what is the condition of the children of God : for they calmly acquiesce in the hope of sure and perfect blessedness, though they do not as yet enjoy it ; as the former suffer dreadful agonies on account of the vengeance prepared for them.

5. *The old world.* The import of what he says is, that God, after having drowned the human race, formed again as it were a new world. This is also an argument from the greater to the less ; for how can the wicked escape the deluge of divine wrath, since the whole world was once destroyed by it ? For by saying that eight only were saved, he intimates that a multitude would not be a shield against God to protect the wicked ; but that as many as sin shall be punished, be they few or many in number.

But it may be asked why he calls Noah *the preacher of righteousness.* Some understand that he was the preacher of the righteousness of God, inasmuch as Scripture commends God's righteousness, because he defends his own and restores them, when dead, to life. But I rather think that he is called the preacher of righteousness, because he laboured to restore a degenerated world to a sound mind, and this not only by his teaching and godly exhortations, but also by his anxious toil in building the ark for the term of a hundred and twenty years. Now, the design of the Apostle is to set before our eyes God's wrath against the wicked, so as to encourage us at the same time to imitate the saints.[1]

6. *The cities of Sodom.* This was so memorable an example of Divine vengeance, that when the Scripture speaks of the universal destruction of the ungodly, it alludes commonly to this as the type. Hence Peter says, that these cities were made an example. This may, indeed, be truly said of others; but Peter points out something singular, because it was the chief and a lively image; yea, rather, because the Lord designed that his wrath against the ungodly should be made known to all ages; as when he redeemed his people from Egypt, he has set forth to us by that one favour the perpetual safety of his Church. Jude has also expressed the same thing, calling it the punishment of eternal fire.

8. *In seeing and hearing.* The common explanation is, that Lot was just in his eyes and ears, because all his senses abhorred the crimes of Sodom. However, another view may be taken of his seeing and hearing, so as to make this the meaning, that when the just man lived among the Sodomites, he tormented his soul by seeing and hearing; for we know that he was constrained to see and hear many things which greatly vexed his mind. The purport of what is said then is, that though the holy man was surrounded with every kind of monstrous wickedness, he yet never turned aside from his upright course.

But Peter expresses more than before, that is, that just

---

[1] There is a difference of opinion as to the word "eighth:" some think that the sense is, that Noah was the eighth person who was saved at the deluge, being one of the eight who were preserved. Others render the words, "Noah, the eighth preacher of righteousness," calculating from Enos, in whose time as it is said, " men began to call upon the name of the Lord." (Gen. iv. 26.) *Lightfoot* and some others, have held the latter opinion, though the former has been more generally approved.—*Ed.*

Lot underwent voluntary sorrows; as it is right that all the godly should feel no small grief when they see the world rushing into every kind of evil, so the more necessary it is that they should groan for their own sins. And Peter expressly mentioned this, lest when impiety everywhere prevails, we should be captivated and inebriated by the allurements of vices, and perish together with others, but that we might prefer this grief, blessed by the Lord, to all the pleasures of the world.

9. The Lord knoweth how to deliver the godly out of temptations, and to reserve the unjust unto the day of judgment to be punished;	9. Novit Dominus pios ex tentatione eripere; injustos autem in diem judicii puniendos servare;
10. But chiefly them that walk after the flesh in the lust of uncleanness, and despise government: presumptuous *are they*, self-willed, they are not afraid to speak evil of dignities:	10. Præsertim verò eos qui post carnem in concupiscentia pollutionis ambulant, dominationem despiciunt, audaces, præfracti, qui excellentias non verentur probro afficere;
11. Whereas angels, which are greater in power and might, bring not railing accusation against them before the Lord.	11. Quum angeli, qui sunt robore et potentia majores, non ferant adversus illas coram Domino contumeliosum judicium.

9. *The Lord knoweth.* What first offends the weak is, that when the faithful anxiously seek aid, they are not immediately helped by God; but on the contrary he suffers them sometimes as it were to pine away through daily weariness and languor; and secondly, when the wicked grow wanton with impunity, and God in the meantime is silent, as though he connived at their evil deeds. This double offence Peter now removes; for he testifies that the Lord knows when it is expedient to deliver the godly from temptation. By these words he reminds us that this office ought to be left to him, and that therefore we ought to endure temptations, and not to faint, when at any time he defers his vengeance against the ungodly.

This consolation is very necessary for us, for this thought is apt to creep in, "If the Lord would have his own to be safe, why does he not gather them all into some corner of the earth, that they may mutually stimulate one another to holiness? why does he mingle them with the wicked by whom they may be defiled?" But when God claims to himself the office of helping and protecting his own, that they may not fail in the contest, we gather courage to fight more strenuously. The meaning of the first clause is, that this law is prescribed by the Lord to all the godly, that they are to be proved by various temptations, but that they are to entertain good hope of success, because they are never to be deprived of his aid and help.

And to reserve the unjust. By this clause he shews that God so regulates his judgments as to bear with the wicked for a time, but not to leave them unpunished. Thus he corrects too much haste, by which we are wont to be carried headlong, especially when the atrocity of wickedness grievously wounds us, for we then wish God to fulminate without delay; when he does not do so, he seems no longer to be the judge of the world. Lest, then, this temporary impunity of wickedness should disturb us, Peter reminds us that a day of judgment has been appointed by the Lord; and that, therefore, the wicked shall by no means escape punishment, though it be not immediately inflicted.

There is an emphasis in the word *reserve,* as though he had said, that they shall not escape the hand of God, but be held bound as it were by hidden chains, that they may at a certain time be drawn forth to judgment. The participle κολαζομένους, though in the present tense, is yet to be thus explained, that they are reserved or kept to be punished, or, that they may be punished. For he bids us to rely on the expectation of the last judgment, so that in hope and patience we may fight till the end of life.

10. *But chiefly them.* He comes here to particulars, accommodating a general doctrine to his own purpose; for he had to do with men of desperate wickedness. He then shews that dreadful vengeance necessarily awaited them. For since God will punish all the wicked, how can they escape who abandon themselves like brute beasts to every kind of iniquity? *To walk after the flesh,* is to be given up to the flesh, like brute animals, who are not led by reason and judgment, but have the natural desire of their flesh as their chief guide. By the *lust of uncleanness* understand filthy and unbridled gratifications, when men, having cast away every

virtuous feeling, and shaken off shame, are carried away into every uncleanness.

This is the first mark by which he brands them, that they are impure men, given up to wickedness. Other marks follow, that they despised government, and feared not to calumniate and reproach men whom God had favoured with honourable stations in life. But these words refer to the same thing; for after having said that they held government in contempt, he immediately points out the fountain of this evil, that they were *presumptuous*, or audacious, and *self-willed*, or refractory;[1] and lastly, that he might more fully exhibit their pride, he says that they did not fear nor tremble when they treated dignities with contempt. For it is a monstrous arrogance to regard as nothing the glory which shines forth in dignities appointed by God.

But there is no doubt but that in these words he refers to the imperial and magisterial power; for though there is no lawful station in life which is not worthy of respect, yet we know that the magisterial office excels every other, because in governing mankind God himself is represented. Then truly glorious is that power in which God himself appears.

We now perceive what the Apostle meant in this second clause, even that they of whom he speaks were frantic men, lovers of tumults and confusion; for no one can introduce anarchy (ἀναρχίαν) into the world without introducing disorder (ἀταξίαν.) Now, these with bold effrontery vomited forth reproaches against magistrates, that they might take away every respect for public rights; and this was openly to fight against God by their blasphemies. There are also many turbulent men of this sort at the present day, who proudly declare that the power of the sword is heathen and unlawful, and furiously attempt to subvert all government. Such furies Satan excites, in order to disturb and prevent the progress of the gospel. But the Lord hath dealt favourably with us; for he hath not only warned us to beware of

---

[1] Rather, "self-pleasing," αὐθάδης, whose ruling principle was to please and gratify themselves, without regarding God's will or the good of others —whose god was self. In a secondary sense, the word designates those who are haughty, arrogant, supercilious, refractory; and such is commonly the character of selfish men.— *Ed.*

this deadly poison, but hath also by this ancient example fortified us against this scandal. Hence the Papists act very dishonestly, when they accuse us, and say that seditious men are made so by our doctrine. The same thing might indeed have been alleged against the apostles formerly; and yet they were as far as possible from encouraging any such wickedness.

11. *Whereas angels.* He hence shews their rash arrogance, because they dared to assume more liberty than even angels. But it seems strange that he says that angels do not bring a railing accusation against magistrates; for why should they be adverse to that sacred order, the author of which they know to be God? why should they oppose rulers whom they know to be exercising the same ministry with themselves? This reasoning has made some to think that the devils are meant; but they do not thus by any means escape the difficulty. For how could Satan be so moderate as to spare men, since he is the author of every blasphemy against God? And further, their opinion is refuted by what Jude says.

But when we consider the circumstances of the time, what is said applies very suitably to holy angels. For all the magistrates were then ungodly, and bloody enemies to the gospel. They must, therefore, have been hateful to angels, the guardians of the Church. He, however, says, that men deserving hatred and execration, were not condemned by them, in order that they might shew respect to a power divinely appointed. While such moderation, he says, is shewn by angels, these men fearlessly give vent to impious and unbridled blasphemies.

12. But these, as natural brute beasts, made to be taken and destroyed, speak evil of the things that they understand not; and shall utterly perish in their own corruption;	12. Isti autem tanquam bruta animalia, naturaliter genita in capturam et perniciem, in quibus nihil intelligunt maledicentes, in sua corruptione peribunt
13. And shall receive the reward of unrighteousness, *as* they that count it pleasure to riot in the daytime: spots *they are* and blemishes, sporting themselves with their own deceivings while they feast with you:	13. Recipientes mercedem injustitiæ, pro voluptate ducentes in diem frui deliciis, labes et maculæ, deliciantes in erroribus suis, conviventes vobiscum;

14. Having eyes full of adultery, and that cannot cease from sin; beguiling unstable souls: an heart they have exercised with covetous practices; cursed children:	14. Oculos habentes plenos adulteræ, et inquietos ad peccandum, inescantes animas instabiles, cor habentes exercitatum cupiditatibus, execrabiles filii;
15. Which have forsaken the right way, and are gone astray, following the way of Balaam *the son* of Bosor, who loved the wages of unrighteousness;	15. Qui relicta via aberraverunt, sequuti viam Balaam, filii Bozor, qui mercedem injustitiæ dilexit;
16. But was rebuked for his iniquity: the dumb ass, speaking with man's voice, forbade the madness of the prophet.	16. Sed redargutus fuit de sua iniquitate; animal subjugale mutum, humana voce loquens, prohibuit prophetæ dementiam. (Num. xxii. 16, 28.)

12. *But these.* He proceeds with what he had begun to say respecting impious and wicked corrupters. And, first, he condemns their loose manners and the obscene wickedness of their whole life; and then he says that they were audacious and perverse, so that by their scurrilous garrulity they insinuated themselves into the favour of many.

He especially compares them to those *brute animals*, which seem to have come to existence to be ensnared, and to be driven to their own ruin by their own instinct; as though he had said, that being induced by no allurements, they of themselves hasten to throw themselves into the snares of Satan and of death. For what we render, *naturally born,* Peter has literally, "natural born." But there is not much difference in the sense, whether one of the two has been by somebody else supplied, or by putting down both he meant more fully to express his meaning.[1]

What he adds, *speaking evil* of the things that they *understand not,* refers to the pride and presumption he mentioned in the preceding verse. He then says that all excellency was insolently despised by them, because they were become wholly stupified, so that they differed nothing

---

[1] The words may be thus rendered,—
 "But these, as natural unreasoning animals, born for capture and destruction, speaking evil of things which they understand not, shall utterly perish through their own corruption."
They are compared to animals which are by nature without reason, and such as live on prey, wild and rapacious, which seem to have been made to be taken and destroyed; and they are often taken and destroyed while committing plunder. So these men, their wickedness would be the means of ensnaring and destroying them.—*Ed.*

from beasts. But the word I have rendered *for destruction*, and afterwards *in corruption*, is the same, φθορὰ; but it is variously taken: but when he says that they would perish in their own corruption, he shews that their corruptions would be ruinous or destructive.

13. *Count it pleasure.*[1] As though he had said, "They place their happiness in their present enjoyments." We know that men excel brute animals in this, that they extend their thoughts much farther. It is, then, a base thing in man to be occupied only with present things. Here he reminds us that our minds ought to be freed from the gratifications of the flesh, except we wish to be reduced to the state of beasts.

The meaning of what follows is this, "These are filthy spots to you and your assembly; for while they feast with you, they at the same time luxuriate in their errors, and shew by their eyes and gestures their lascivious lusts and detestable incontinency." Erasmus has rendered the words thus, "Feasting in their errors, they deride you." But this is too forced. It may not unaptly be thus explained, "Feasting with you, they insolently deride you by their errors." I, however, have given the version which seems the most probable, "luxuriating in their errors, feasting with you." He calls the libidinous such as had *eyes full of adultery*, and who were incessantly led to sin without restraint, as it appears from what is afterwards said.

14. *Beguiling*, or baiting, *unstable souls.* By the metaphor of baiting he reminds the faithful to beware of their hidden and deceitful arts; for he compares their impostures to hooks

---

[1] It is better to connect the first words of this verse, "receiving the reward of unrighteousness," with the foregoing, and to begin another period with this clause, and to render this verse and the following thus,—

"Counting (or, deeming) riot in the day-time a pleasure, *they are* spots and stains, rioting in their own delusions, feasting together with 14 you; having eyes full of adultery and which cease not from sin, ensnaring unstable souls, having a heart inured to covetous desires, *being* children of the curse."

The various things said of them are intended to shew that they were "spots and stains," disgraceful and defiling: they rioted in carnal pleasure, and rioted in delusion, and associated with the faithful, feasting with them; they were libidinous, and led unstable souls to follow their ways; they were covetous, and shewed that they were heirs to the curse of God.—*Ed.*

which may catch the unwary to their destruction. By adding *unstable souls* he shews the reason for caution, that is, when we have not struck firm roots in faith and in the fear of the Lord: and he intimates at the same time, that they have no excuse who suffer themselves to be baited or allured by such flatteries; for this must have been ascribed to their levity. Let there be then a stability of faith, and we shall be safe from the artifices of the ungodly.

An heart they have exercised with covetous practices, or, with lusts. Erasmus renders the last word, "rapines." The word is of a doubtful meaning. I prefer "lusts." As he had before condemned incontinence in their eyes, so he now seems to refer to the vices latent in their hearts. It ought not, however, to be confined to covetousness. By calling them *cursed* or execrable *children*, he may be understood to mean, that they were so either actively or passively, that is, that they brought a curse with them wherever they went, or that they deserved a curse.

As he has hitherto referred to the injury they did by the example of a perverse and corrupt life, so he again repeats, that they spread by their teaching the deadly poison of impiety, in order that they might destroy the simple. He compares them to Balaam, the son of Bozor, who employed a venal tongue to curse God's people. And to shew that they were not worthy of a long refutation, he says that Balaam was reproved by an ass, and that thus his madness was condemned. But by this means also he restrains the faithful from associating with them. For it was a dreadful judgment of God, that the angel made himself known to the ass before he did to the prophet, so that the ass, perceiving God displeased, dared not to advance farther, but went back, when the prophet, under the blind impulse of his own avarice, pushed forward against the evident prohibition of the Lord. For what was afterwards answered to him, that he was to proceed, was an evidence of God's indignation rather than a permission. In short, as the greatest indignity to him, the mouth of the ass was opened, that he who had been unwilling to submit to God's authority might have that as his teacher. And by this miracle the Lord designed to show how monstrous a thing it was to change the truth to a lie.

It may be here asked, by what right Balaam had the name of a prophet, when it appears that he was addicted to many wicked superstitions. To this I reply, that the gift of prophecy was so special, that though he did not worship the true God, and had not true religion, he might yet have been endued with it. Besides, God has sometimes caused prophecy to exist in the midst of idolatry, in order that men might have less excuse.

Now, if any one considers the chief things which Peter says, he will see that his warning is equally suitable to the present age; for it is an evil which prevails everywhere, that men use scurrilous raillery for the purpose of deriding God and the Saviour; nay, they ridicule all religion under the cloak of wit; and when addicted, like beasts, to their own lusts, they will mingle with the faithful; they prattle something about the gospel, and yet they prostitute their tongue to the service of the devil, that they may bring the whole world, as far as they can, to eternal perdition. They are in this respect worse than Balaam himself, because they gratuitously pour forth their maledictions, when he, induced by reward, attempted to curse.

17. These are wells without water, clouds that are carried with a tempest; to whom the mist of darkness is reserved for ever.

18. For when they speak great swelling *words* of vanity, they allure through the lusts of the flesh, *through much* wantonness, those that were clean escaped from them who live in error.

19. While they promise them liberty, they themselves are the servants of corruption: for of whom a man is overcome, of the same is he brought in bondage.

17. Ii sunt fontes sine aqua, nebulæ quæ à turbine aguntur; quibus caligo tenebrarum in æternum parata est.

18. Nam ubi plusquàm fastuosa vanitatis verba sonuerint, inescant per concupiscentias carnis, lasciviis, eos qui verè aufugerant ab iis qui in errore versantur.

19. Dum libertatem illis promittunt, quum ipsi sint servi corruptionis: a quo enim quis superatus est, huic in servitutem est addictus.

17. *These are wells*, or fountains, *without water.* He shews by these two metaphors, that they had nothing within, though they made a great display. A fountain, by its appearance, draws men to itself, because it promises them water to drink,

and for other purposes ; as soon as clouds appear, they give hope of immediate rain to irrigate the earth. He then says that they were like fountains, because they excelled in boasting, and displayed some acuteness in their thoughts and elegance in their words ; but that yet they were dry and barren within : hence the appearance of a fountain was fallacious.

He says that they were *clouds carried* by the wind, either without rain, or which burst forth into a calamitous storm. He thereby denotes that they brought nothing useful, and that often they were very hurtful. He afterwards denounces on them the dreadful judgment of God, that fear might restrain the faithful. By naming the *mist* or the blackness *of darkness*, he alludes to the clouds which obscure the air; as though he had said, that for the momentary darkness which they now spread, there is prepared for them a much thicker darkness which is to continue for ever.

18. *For when they speak great swelling* words *of vanity.*[1] He means that they dazzled the eyes of the simple by high-flown stuff of words, that they might not perceive their deceit, for it was not easy to captivate their minds with such dotages, except they were first besotted by some artifice. He then says that they used an inflated kind of words and speech, that they might fill the unwary with admiration. And then this grandiloquence, which the ample lungs of the soul send forth, (as Persius says,[2]) was very suitable to cover their shifts and trumperies. There was formerly a craft of this kind in Valentinus, and in those like him, as we learn from the books of Irenæus. They made words unheard of before, by the empty sound of which, the unlearned being smitten, they were ensnared by their reveries.

There are fanatics of a similar kind at this day, who call

---

[1] The words are,—
" For uttering bombasts of vanity, they allure," &c.
The word ὑπέρογκα, being a neuter plural, may be rendered as a noun ; literally, " overswellings of vanity ;" but when applied to words, it means what is pompous, inflated, bombastic; but these bombasts were those of vanity, being empty, useless, unprofitable ; or as some render the words, they were the bombasts of falsehood, according to the meaning of the word as used often in the *Sept.* ; they spoke false things in a bombastic and inflated strain.—*Ed.*

[2] Sat. i. 14.

themselves by the plausible title of Libertines or free-men. For they talk most confidently of the Spirit and of spiritual things, as though they roared out from above the clouds, and fascinate many by their tricks and wiles, so that you may say that the Apostle has correctly prophesied of them. For they treat all things jocosely and scoffingly; and though they are great simpletons, yet as they indulge in all vices, they find favour with their own people by a sort of drollery. The state of the case is this, that when the difference between good and evil is removed, everything becomes lawful; and men, loosed from all subjection to laws, obey their own lusts. This Epistle, therefore, is not a little suitable to our age.

They allure, or bait, *through the lusts of the flesh.* He strikingly compares to hooks the allurements of the ungodly, when they make anything they please lawful; for as the lusts of men are headstrong and craving, as soon as liberty is offered, they lay hold on it with great avidity; but soon afterwards the strangling hook within is perceived. But we must consider the whole sentence of the Apostle.

He says that they who had really escaped from the society of those in error were again deceived by a new kind of error, even when the reins were let loose to them for the indulgence of every sort of intemperance. He hereby reminds us how dangerous are the wiles of these men. For it was already a dreadful thing that blindness and thick darkness possessed almost all mankind. It was, therefore, in a manner a double prodigy, that men, freed from the common errors of the world, should, after having received the light of God, be brought back to a beastly indifference. Let us be reminded of what we ought especially to beware of, after having been once enlightened, that is, lest Satan entice us under the pretence of liberty, so as to give ourselves up to lasciviousness to gratify the lusts of the flesh. But they are safe from this danger who seriously attend to the study of holiness.

19. *While they promise them liberty.* He shews their inconsistency, that they falsely promised liberty, while they themselves served sin, and were in the worst bondage; for

no one can give what he has not. This reason, however, does not seem to be sufficiently valid, because it sometimes happens that wicked men, and wholly unacquainted with Christ, preach usefully concerning the benefits and blessings of Christ. But we must observe, that what is condemned here is vicious doctrine, connected with impurity of life; for the Apostle's design was to obviate the deceptive allurements by which they ensnared the foolish. The name of liberty is sweet, and they abused it for this end, that the hearer, being loosed from the fear of the divine law, might abandon himself unto unbridled licentiousness. But the liberty which Christ has procured for us, and which he offers daily by the gospel, is altogether different, for he has exempted us from the yoke of the law as far as it subjects us to a curse, that he might also deliver us from the dominion of sin, as far as it subjects us to its own lusts. Hence, where lusts reign, and therefore where the flesh rules, there the liberty of Christ has no place whatever. The Apostle then declares this to all the godly, that they might not desire any other liberty but that which leads those, who are set free from sin, to a willing obedience to righteousness.

We hence learn that there have ever been depraved men who made a false pretence to liberty, and that this has been an old cunning trick of Satan. We need not wonder that at this day the same filth is stirred up by fanatical men.

The Papists turn and twist this passage against us, but they thereby betray their ridiculous impudence. For in the first place, men of the filthiest life, in public-houses and brothels, belch out this charge, that we are the servants of corruption, in the life of whom they cannot point out anything reproachful. In the second place, since we teach nothing respecting Christian liberty but what is derived from Christ and his Apostles, and at the same time require the mortification of the flesh, and the proper exercises for subduing it, much more strictly than they do who slander us, they vomit forth their curses, not so much against us as against the Son of God, whom we have as our certain teacher and authority.

For of whom a man is overcome. This sentence is derived

from military law; but yet it is a common saying among heathen writers, that there is no harder or a more miserable bondage than when lusts rule and reign. What then ought to be done by us, on whom the Son of God has bestowed his Spirit, not only that we may be freed from the dominion of sin, but that we may also become the conquerors of the flesh and the world?

20. For if after they have escaped the pollutions of the world, through the knowledge of the Lord and Saviour Jesus Christ, they are again entangled therein, and overcome, the latter end is worse with them than the beginning.	20. Nam si ii qui aufugerant ab inquinamentis mundi per cognitionem Domini et Servatoris Jesu Christi, rursum iisdem impliciti superantur, facta sunt illis postrema pejora prioribus.
21. For it had been better for them not to have known the way of righteousness, than, after they have known *it*, to turn from the holy commandment delivered unto them.	21. Melius enim ipsis esset non cognovisse viam justitiæ, quàm ubi cognoverunt converti ab eo, quod illis traditum fuit, sancto præcepto.
22. But it is happened unto them according to the true proverb, The dog *is* turned to his own vomit again; and the sow that was washed to her wallowing in the mire.	22. Sed accidit illis quod vero proverbio dicitur, Canis reversus ad proprium vomitum; et sus lota, ad volutabrum cœni.

20. *For if after.* He again shews how pernicious was the sect which led men consecrated to God back again to their old filth and the corruptions of the world. And he exhibits the heinousness of the evil by a comparison; for it was no common sin to depart from the holy doctrine of God. It would have been better for them, he says, not to have known the way of righteousness; for though there is no excuse for ignorance, yet the servant who knowingly and wilfully despises the commands of his lord, deserves a twofold punishment. There was besides ingratitude, because they wilfully extinguished the light of God, rejected the favour conferred on them, and having shaken off the yoke, became perversely wanton against God; yea, as far as they could, they profaned and abrogated the inviolable covenant of God, which had been ratified by the blood of Christ. The more earnest then ought we to be, to advance humbly and carefully in the course of our calling. We must now consider each sentence.

By naming *the pollutions of the world*, he shews that we roll in filth and are wholly polluted, until we renounce the world. By *the knowledge of Christ* he no doubt understands the gospel. He testifies that the design of it is, to deliver us from the defilements of the world, and to lead us far away from them. For the same reason he afterwards calls it *the way of righteousness*. He then alone makes a right progress in the gospel who faithfully learns Christ; and he truly knows Christ, who has been taught by him to put off the old man and to put on the new man, as Paul reminds us in Eph. iv. 22.[1]

21. By saying that having forsaken *the commandment delivered unto them*, they returned to their own pollutions, he intimates first, how inexcusable they were; and secondly, he reminds us that the doctrine of a holy and virtuous life, though common to all and indiscriminately belonging to all, is yet peculiarly taught to those whom God favours with the light of his gospel. But he declares that they who make themselves slaves again to the pollutions of the world fall away from the gospel. The faithful also do indeed sin; but as they allow not dominion to sin, they do not fall away from the grace of God, nor do they renounce the profession of sound doctrine which they have once embraced. For they are not to be deemed conquered, while they strenuously resist the flesh and its lusts.

22. *But it has happened unto them.* As the example disturbs many, when men who had submitted to the obedience of Christ, rush headlong into vices without fear or shame, the Apostle, in order to remove the offence, says that this happens through their own fault, and that because they are pigs and dogs. It hence follows that no part of the sin can be ascribed to the gospel.

For this purpose he quotes two ancient proverbs, the first of which is found as the saying of Solomon in Prov. xxvi. 11. But what Peter meant is briefly this, that the gospel is a medicine which purges us by wholesome vomiting, but that

---

[1] The end of this verse is not explained, but the words of the version, *facta sunt illis postrema pejora prioribus*, seem to mean, that their last pollutions would become worse to them than their former pollutions; and this is the rendering of *Macknight*. The sentence is commonly taken in the same sense as in Matt. xii. 45, but the words are somewhat different. —*Ed.*

there are many dogs who swallow again what they have vomited to their own ruin; and that the gospel is also a laver which cleanses all our uncleanness, but that there are many swine who, immediately after washing, roll themselves again in the mud. At the same time the godly are reminded to take heed to themselves, except they wish to be deemed dogs or swine.

CHAPTER III.

1. This second epistle, beloved, I now write unto you; in *both* which I stir up your pure minds by way of remembrance.

2. That ye may be mindful of the words which were spoken before by the holy prophets, and of the commandment of us the apostles of the Lord and Saviour:

3. Knowing this first, that there shall come in the last days scoffers, walking after their own lusts,

4. And saying, Where is the promise of his coming? for since the fathers fell asleep, all things continue as *they were* from the beginning of the creation.

1. Hanc jam, dilecti, secundam vobis scribo epistolam, in quibus excito per commonefactionem vestram puram mentem;

2. Ut memores sitis verborum quæ predicta sunt à sanctis prophetis, et præcepti nostri, qui sumus apostoli Domini et Servatoris;

3. Hoc primùm scientes, quòd venient in extremo dierum illusores, secundum suas ipsorum concupiscentias ambulantes,

4. Ac dicentes, Ubi est promissio adventus ejus? Ex quo enim patres dormierunt, omnia sic permanent ab initio creationis.

1. Lest they should be wearied with the Second Epistle as though the first was sufficient, he says that it was not written in vain, because they stood in need of being often stirred up. To make this more evident, he shews that they could not be beyond danger, except they were well fortified, because they would have to contend with desperate men, who would not only corrupt the purity of the faith, by false opinions, but do what they could to subvert entirely the whole faith.

By saying, *I stir up your pure mind,* he means the same as though he had said, "I wish to awaken you to a sincerity of mind." And the words ought to be thus explained, "I stir up your mind that it may be pure and bright." For the meaning is, that the minds of the godly become dim, and as it were contract rust, when admonitions cease. But we also hence learn, that men even endued with learning, become, in a manner, drowsy, except they are stirred up by constant warnings.¹

It now appears what is the use of admonitions, and how necessary they are; for the sloth of the flesh smothers the truth once received, and renders it inefficient, except the goads of warnings come to its aid. It is not then enough, that men should be taught to know what they ought to be, but there is need of godly teachers, to do this second part, deeply to impress the truth on the memory of their hearers. And as men are, by nature, for the most part, fond of novelty, and thus inclined to be fastidious, it is useful for us to bear in mind what Peter says, so that we may not only willingly suffer ourselves to be admonished by others, but that every one may also exercise himself in calling to mind continually the truth, so that our minds may become resplendent with the pure and clear knowledge of it.

2. *That ye may be mindful.* By these words he intimates that we have enough in the writings of the prophets, and in the gospel, to stir us up, provided we be as diligent as it behoves us, in meditating on them; and that our minds sometimes contract a rust, or become bedimmed through darkness, is owing to our sloth. That God may then continually shine upon us, we must devote ourselves to that study: let our faith at the same time acquiesce in witnesses so certain and credible. For when we have the prophets and apostles agreeing with us, nay, as the ministers of our faith, and God as the author, and angels as approvers, there is no reason that the ungodly, all united, should move us from our position. By the *commandment of the apostles* he means the whole doctrine in which they had instructed the faithful.²

---

¹ The Apostle evidently admits that they had a sincere or a pure mind, that is, freed from the pollutions referred to in the last chapter; but still they stood in need of being stirred up by admonitions: hence their minds were not, in a strict sense, perfect, though sincere.—*Ed.*

² The construction of the passage is as follows:—" In *both* which I, by admonition, arouse your sincere mind to remember the words, aforetime spoken by the holy prophets, and the doctrine of us, the apostles of our Lord and Saviour."

The verb μνσθῆναι is connected with " arouse;" and it is in this tense

3. *Knowing this first.* The participle *knowing* may be applied to the Apostle, and in this way, " I labour to stir you up for this reason, because I know what and how great is your impending danger from scoffers." I however prefer this explanation, that the participle is used in place of a verb, as though he had said, " Know ye this especially." For it was necessary that this should have been foretold, because they might have been shaken, had impious men attacked them suddenly with scoffs of this kind. He therefore wished them to know this, and to feel assured on the subject, that they might be prepared to oppose such men.

But he calls the attention of the faithful again to the doctrine which he touched upon in the second chapter. For by *the last days* is commonly meant the kingdom of Christ, or the days of his kingdom, according to what Paul says, " Upon whom the ends of the world are come." (1 Cor. x. 11.)[1] The meaning is, that the more God offers himself by the gospel to the world, and the more he invites men to his kingdom, the more audacious on the other hand will ungodly men vomit forth the poison of their impiety.

He calls those *scoffers,* according to what is usual in Scripture, who seek to appear witty by shewing contempt to God, and by a blasphemous presumption. It is, moreover, the very extremity of evil, when men allow themselves to treat the awful name of God with scoffs. Thus, the first Psalm speaks of the seat of scoffers. So David, in Ps. cxix. 51, complains that he was derided by the proud, because he attended to God's law. So Isaiah, in the 28th chapter, having referred to them, describes their supine security and insensibility. Let us therefore bear in mind, that there is nothing to be feared more than a contest with scoffers. On this subject we said something while explaining the third chapter of the Epistle to the Galatians. As, however, the

used actively as well as passively. See Matt. xxvi. 75, and Acts x. 31. There is in the noun, ἐντολὴ, a metonymy, the commandment for what was commanded to be taught, the doctrine. It has this meaning, according to *Schleusner,* in John xii. 50, and in this Epistle, ch. ii. 21.—*Ed.*

[1] It is literally, " the last of the days," according to the Hebrew form אחרית הימים, " the extremity of the days," (Isa. ii. 2 ;) but the meaning is the same as " the last days," as used in Heb. i. 1, and in other places, that is, the days of the gospel dispensation.— *Ed.*

holy Scripture has foretold that they would come, and has also given us a shield by which we may defend ourselves, there is no excuse why we should not boldly resist them whatever devices they may employ.

4. *Where is the promise.* It was a dangerous scoff when they insinuated a doubt as to the last resurrection ; for when that is taken away, there is no gospel any longer, the power of Christ is brought to nothing, the whole of religion is gone. Then Satan aims directly at the throat of the Church, when he destroys faith in the coming of Christ. For why did Christ die and rise again, except that he may some time gather to himself the redeemed from death, and give them eternal life ? All religion is wholly subverted, except faith in the resurrection remains firm and immovable. Hence, on this point Satan assails us most fiercely.

But let us notice what the scoff was. They set the regular course of nature, such as it seems to have been from the beginning, in opposition to the promise of God, as though these things were contrary, or did not harmonize together. Though the faith of the fathers, they said, was the same, yet no change has taken place since their death, and it is known that many ages have passed away. Hence they concluded that what was said of the destruction of the world was a fable ; because they conjectured, that as it had lasted so long, it would be perpetual.

5. For this they willingly are ignorant of, that by the word of God the heavens were of old, and the earth standing out of the water and in the water :

6. Whereby the world that then was, being overflowed with water, perished :

7. But the heavens and the earth which are now, by the same word are kept in store, reserved unto fire against the day of judgment and perdition of ungodly men.

8. But, beloved, be not ignorant of this one thing, that one day *is* with the Lord as a thousand years, and a thousand years as one day.

5. Nam hoc nesciunt volentes, quòd cœli jam olim fuerint, et terra ex aqua, et per aquam consistens, Dei sermone ;

6. Per quæ mundus qui tunc erat, aqua inundatus periit :

7. Qui autem nunc sunt cœli et terra, ejusdem sermone repositi sunt, et servantur igni in diem judicii et perditionis impiorum.

8. Porrò ne hoc unum nos lateat, dilecti, quòd unus dies apud Dominum perinde est ut mille anni, et mille anni ut dies unus.

5. *For this they willingly are ignorant of.* By one argu-

ment only he confutes the scoff of the ungodly, even by this, that the world once perished by a deluge of waters, when yet it consisted of waters. (Gen. i. 2.) And as the history of this was well known, he says that they *willingly*, or of their own accord, erred. For they who infer the perpetuity of the world from its present state, designedly close their eyes, so as not to see so clear a judgment of God. The world no doubt had its origin from waters, for Moses calls the chaos from which the earth emerged, waters; and further, it was sustained by waters; it yet pleased the Lord to use waters for the purpose of destroying it. It hence appears that the power of nature is not sufficient to sustain and preserve the world, but that on the contrary it contains the very element of its own ruin, whenever it may please God to destroy it.

For it ought always to be borne in mind, that the world stands through no other power than that of God's word, and that therefore inferior or secondary causes derive from him their power, and produce different effects as they are directed. Thus through water the world stood, but water could have done nothing of itself, but on the contrary obeyed God's word as an inferior agent or element. As soon then as it pleased God to destroy the earth, the same water obeyed in becoming a ruinous inundation. We now see how egregiously they err, who stop at naked elements, as though there was perpetuity in them, and their nature were not changeable according to the bidding of God.

By these few words the petulance of those is abundantly refuted, who arm themselves with physical reasons to fight against God. For the history of the deluge is an abundantly sufficient witness that the whole order of nature is governed by the sole power of God. (Gen. vii. 17.)

It seems, however, strange that he says that the *world* perished through the deluge, when he had before mentioned the heaven and the earth. To this I answer, that the heaven was then also submerged, that is, the region of the air, which stood open between the two waters. For the division or separation, mentioned by Moses, was then confounded. (Gen. i. 6;) and the word *heaven* is often taken in this sense. If any wishes for more on this subject, let him read Augustine on the City of God. *Lib.* 20.[1]

7. *But the heavens and the earth which are now.* He does not infer this as the consequence; for his purpose was no other than to dissipate the craftiness of scoffers respecting the perpetual state of nature; and we see many such at this day, who being slightly embued with the rudiments of philosophy, only hunt after profane speculations, in order that they may pass themselves off as great philosophers.

But it now appears quite evident from what has been said, that there is nothing unreasonable in the declaration made by the Lord, that the heaven and the earth shall hereafter

---

[1] The two verses, the fifth and the sixth, have been differently explained. "The earth," say some, "subsisting from water and through water," that is, emerging from water and made firm and solid by means of water; which is true, for through moisture the earth adheres together and becomes a solid mass. Others render the last clause, "in water," or in the midst of water, that is, surrounded by water; and this is the most suitable meaning.

The δι'ῶν at the beginning of the sixth verse, refers, according to *Beza, Whitby,* and others, to the heavens and the earth in the preceding verse, the deluge being occasioned by "the windows of heaven being opened," and "the fountains of the great deep being broken up." (Gen. vii. 11.) "By which (or by the means of which) the world at that time, being overflowed with water, was destroyed."

The objection to this view is, as justly stated by *Macknight,* that the correspondence between this verse and the following is thereby lost: the reservation of the world to be destroyed by fire is expressly ascribed, in verse seventh, to God's word; and to the same ought the destruction of the old world to be ascribed. This is doubtless the meaning required by the passage, but "which" being in the plural, creates a difficulty, and there is no different reading. *Macknight* solves the difficulty by saying that the plural "which" or whom, refers to "word," meaning Christ, and "God," as in the first verse of this chapter, "in both which," a reference is made to what is implied in "the second Epistle," that is, the first. He supposes that there is here the same anomalous mode of speaking. But the conjecture which has been made is not improbable, that it is a typographical mistake, ῶν being put for οὗ or for ὅν. Then the meaning would be evident; and the two parts would correspond the one with the other:

5. "For of this they are wilfully ignorant, that the heavens existed of old and the earth (*which* subsisted from water and in water,) by
6. the word of God; by which the world at that time, being over-
7. flowed with water, was destroyed. But the present heavens and the earth are by His word reserved, being kept for fire to the day of judgment and of the perdition of ungodly men."

By "word" here is meant command, or power, or the *fiat* by which the world was created; and by the same it was destroyed, and by the same it will be finally destroyed. Instead of αὐτῷ "the same," *Griesbach* has introduced into his text αὐτοῦ, "His."—*Ed.*

be consumed by fire, because the reason for the fire is the same as that for the water. For it was a common saying even among the ancients, that from these two chief elements all things have proceeded. But as he had to do with the ungodly, he speaks expressly of their destruction.

8. *But be not ignorant of this one thing.* He now turns to speak to the godly; and he reminds them that when the coming of Christ is the subject, they were to raise upwards their eyes, for by so doing, they would not limit, by their unreasonable wishes, the time appointed by the Lord. For waiting seems very long on this account, because we have our eyes fixed on the shortness of the present life, and we also increase weariness by computing days, hours, and minutes. But when the eternity of God's kingdom comes to our minds, many ages vanish away like so many moments.

This then is what the Apostle calls our attention to, so that we may know that the day of resurrection does not depend on the present flow of time, but on the hidden purpose of God, as though he had said, " Men wish to anticipate God for this reason, because they measure time according to the judgment of their own flesh ; and they are by nature inclined to impatience, so that celerity is even delay to them : do ye then ascend in your minds to heaven, and thus time will be to you neither long nor short."

9. The Lord is not slack concerning his promise, as some men count slackness; but is long-suffering to us-ward, not willing that any should perish, but that all should come to repentance.

10. But the day of the Lord will come as a thief in the night; in the which the heavens shall pass away with a great noise, and the elements shall melt with fervent heat, the earth also, and the works that are therein, shall be burnt up.

11. *Seeing* then *that* all these things shall be dissolved, what manner *of persons* ought ye to be in *all* holy conversation and godliness;

12. Looking for and hasting unto the coming of the day of God, where-

9. Non tardat Dominus in promissione, sicuti quidam tarditatem existimant; sed tolerantem se præbet erga nos, nolens ullos perire, sed omnes ad pœnitentiam recipere (*aut*, colligi, *vel*, aggregari.)

10. Veniet autem dies Domini tanquam fur in nocte, in qua cœli in modum procellæ transibunt, elementa autem ardore solventur ; et terra, quæque in ea sunt opera ardebunt.

11. Quum hæc igitur omnia solvantur, quales oportet nos esse in sanctis conversationibus et pietatibus;

12. Expectantes properando adventum diei Dei, propter quem cœli

in the heavens, being on fire, shall be dissolved, and the elements shall melt with fervent heat?	solventur, et elementa ardore consumentur?
13. Nevertheless we, according to his promise, look for new heavens and a new earth, wherein dwelleth righteousness.	13. Novos autem cœlos et terram novam juxta promissum ejus expectamus, in quibus habitat justitia.

9. *But the Lord is not slack,* or, delays not. He checks extreme and unreasonable haste by another reason, that is, that the Lord defers his coming, that he might invite all mankind to repentance. For our minds are always prurient, and a doubt often creeps in, why he does not come sooner. But when we hear that the Lord, in delaying, shews a concern for our salvation, and that he defers the time because he has a care for us, there is no reason why we should any longer complain of tardiness. He is tardy who allows an occasion to pass by through slothfulness : there is nothing like this in God, who in the best manner regulates time to promote our salvation. And as to the duration of the whole world, we must think exactly the same as of the life of every individual ; for God by prolonging time to each, sustains him that he may repent. In the like manner he does not hasten the end of the world, in order to give to all time to repent.

This is a very necessary admonition, so that we may learn to employ time aright, as we shall otherwise suffer a just punishment for our idleness.

Not willing that any should perish. So wonderful is his love towards mankind, that he would have them all to be saved, and is of his own self prepared to bestow salvation on the lost. But the order is to be noticed, that God is ready to receive all to repentance, so that none may perish ; for in these words the way and manner of obtaining salvation is pointed out. Every one of us, therefore, who is desirous of salvation, must learn to enter in by this way.

But it may be asked, If God wishes none to perish, why is it that so many do perish? To this my answer is, that no mention is here made of the hidden purpose of God, according to which the reprobate are doomed to their own ruin, but only of his will as made known to us in the gospel. For God there stretches forth his hand without a difference to all, but lays hold only of those, to lead them to himself, whom he has chosen before the foundation of the world.[1]

But as the verb χωρῆσαι is often taken passively by the Greeks, no less suitable to this passage is the verb which I have put in the margin, that God would have all, who had been before wandering and scattered, to be gathered or come together to repentance.

10. *But the day of the Lord will come.* This has been added, that the faithful might be always watching, and not promise to-morrow to themselves. For we all labour under two very different evils—too much haste, and slothfulness. We are seized with impatience for the day of Christ already expected; at the same time we securely regard it as afar off. As, then, the Apostle has before reproved an unreasonable ardour, so he now shakes off our sleepiness, so that we may attentively expect Christ at all times, lest we should become idle and negligent, as it is usually the case. For whence is it that flesh indulges itself except that there is no thought of the near coming of Christ?

What afterwards follows, respecting the burning of heaven and earth, requires no long explanation, if indeed we duly consider what is intended. For it was not his purpose to speak refinedly of fire and storm, and other things, but only that he might introduce an exhortation, which he immediately adds, even that we ought to strive after newness of life. For he thus reasons, that as heaven and earth are to be purged by fire, that they may correspond with the kingdom of Christ, hence the renovation of men is much more necessary. Mischievous, then, are those interpreters who consume much labour on refined speculations, since the Apostle applies his doctrine to godly exhortations.

Heaven and earth, he says, shall pass away for our sakes; is it meet, then, for us to be engrossed with the things of earth, and not, on the contrary, to attend to a holy and godly life? The corruptions of heaven and earth will be purged by fire, while yet as the creatures of God they are pure; what then ought to be done by us who are full of so many pollutions?

---

[1] A similar view was taken by *Estius*, *Piscator*, and *Beza*.—*Ed.*

As to the word *godlinesses* (*pietatibus*,) the plural number is used for the singular, except you take it as meaning the duties of godliness.[1] Of the elements of the world I shall only say this one thing, that they are to be consumed, only that they may be renovated, their substance still remaining the same, as it may be easily gathered from Rom. viii. 21, and from other passages.[2]

12. *Looking for and hasting unto*, or, waiting for by hastening; so I render the words, though they are two participles; for what we had before separately he gathers now into one sentence, that is, that we ought hastily to wait. Now this contrarious hope possesses no small elegance, like the proverb, "Hasten slowly," (*festina lentè*.) When he says, "Waiting for," he refers to the endurance of hope; and he sets hastening in opposition to torpor; and both are very apposite. For as quietness and waiting are the peculiarities of hope, so we must always take heed lest the security of the flesh should creep in; we ought, therefore, strenuously to labour in good works, and run quickly in the race of our calling.[3] What he before called the day of Christ (as it is everywhere called in Scripture) he now calls the day of God, and that rightly, for Christ will then restore the kingdom to the Father, that God may be all in all.

14. Wherefore, beloved, seeing that ye look for such things, be diligent, that ye may be found of him in peace, without spot, and blameless:	14. Quare, dilecti, quum hæc expectetis, studete incontaminati et irreprehensibiles ab eo inveniri in pace:

[1] The previous word is also in the plural number, "in holy conversations." What seems to be meant is, that every part of the conduct should be holy, and that every part of godliness should be attended to: "In every part of a holy life, and every act of godliness;" that is, we are not to be holy in part or pious in part, but attend to every branch of duty towards man, and every branch of duty towards God.—*Ed*.

[2] All that is said here is, that there will be new heavens and a new earth, and not that the present heavens and the present earth will be renovated. See Rev. xx. 11; xxi. 1.—*Ed*.

[3] The first meaning of σπευδω is to hasten, and it is often used, when connected with another verb, adverbially as proposed by *Calvin;* but when followed as here by an accusative case, it has often the secondary meaning of earnestly desiring a thing. It is so taken here by *Schleusner*, *Parkhurst*, and *Macknight;* "Expecting and earnestly desiring the coming of the day of God."—*Ed*.

15. And account *that* the long-suffering of our Lord *is* salvation; even as our beloved brother Paul also, according to the wisdom given unto him, hath written unto you;

16. As also in all *his* epistles, speaking in them of these things: in which are some things hard to be understood, which they that are unlearned and unstable wrest, as *they do* also the other scriptures, unto their own destruction.

17. Ye therefore, beloved, seeing ye know *these things* before, beware lest ye also, being led away with the error of the wicked, fall from your own stedfastness:

18. But grow in grace, and *in* the knowledge of our Lord and Saviour Jesus Christ. To him *be* glory both now and for ever. Amen.

15. Et Domini nostri tolerantiam salutem existimate, quemadmodum et dilectus frater noster Paulus, secundum datam sibi sapientiam scripsit vobis;

16. Sicuti in omnibus Epistolis, loquens de iis in quibus sunt quædam difficilia intellectu, quæ indocti et instabiles invertunt (ut et cæteras Scripturas) ad suam perniciem.

17. Vos igitur, dilecti, præmoniti cavete, ut ne simul nefariorum errore abacti, excidatis à vestra firmitate.

18. Crescite autem in gratia et notitia Domini nostri et Servatoris Jesu Christi; ipsi gloria et nunc et in diem æternitatis.

14. *Wherefore.* He justly reasons from hope to its effect, or the practice of a godly life; for hope is living and efficacious; therefore it cannot be but that it will attract us to itself. He, then, who waits for new heavens, must begin with renewal as to himself, and diligently aspire after it; but they who cleave to their own filth, think nothing, it is certain, of God's kingdom, and have no taste for anything but for this corrupt world.

But we must notice what he says, that we ought to be *found blameless* by Christ; for by these words he intimates, that while the world engages and engrosses the minds of others, we must cast our eyes on the Lord, and he shews at the same time what is real integrity, even that which is approved by his judgment, and not that which gains the praise of men.[1]

The word *peace* seems to be taken for a quiet state of conscience, founded on hope and patient waiting.[2] For as

---

[1] He says, "Expecting these things, be diligent," &c.; σπουδάσατι, hasten, make speed, diligently strive, earnestly labour, carefully endeavour:

"Therefore, beloved, since ye expect these things, diligently strive to be found by him in peace, unspotted and unblamable;" that is, having no stain, and not chargeable with crime.—*Ed.*

[2] Some say, "peace" with God; but the view of *Calvin* is more suitable here.—*Ed.*

so few turn their attention to the judgment of Christ, hence it is, that while they are carried headlong by their importunate lusts, they are at the same time in a state of disquietude. This peace, then, is the quietness of a peaceable soul, which acquiesces in the word of God.

It may be asked, how any one can be found blameless by Christ, when we all labour under so many deficiencies. But Peter here only points out the mark at which the faithful ought all to aim, though they cannot reach it, until having put off their flesh they become wholly united to Christ.

15. *The long-suffering of our Lord.* He takes it as granted that Christ defers the day of his coming, because he has a regard for our salvation. He hence animates the faithful, because in a longer delay they have an evidence as to their own salvation. Thus, what usually disheartens others through weariness, he wisely turns to a contrary purpose.

Even as our beloved brother Paul. We may easily gather from the Epistle to the Galatians, as well as from other places, that unprincipled men, who went about everywhere to disturb the churches, in order to discredit Paul, made use of this pretence, that he did not well agree with the other Apostles. It is then probable that Peter referred to Paul in order to shew their consent; for it was very necessary to take away the occasion for such a calumny. And yet, when I examine all things more narrowly, it seems to me more probable that this Epistle was composed by another, according to what Peter communicated, than that it was written by himself, for Peter himself would have never spoken thus. But it is enough for me that we have a witness of his doctrine and of his goodwill, who brought forward nothing contrary to what he would have himself said.

16. *In which are some things.* The relative *which* does not refer to *epistles*, for it is in the neuter gender.[1] The

---

[1] It is in the feminine gender in some MSS. The authority as to the copies and versions is nearly equal. The difference is not much as to the sense, only " in which epistles," reads better. So thought *Beza, Mill*, and others.

It has been a question as to the particular epistle referred to by Peter; for that he alludes to some particular epistle is evident from the manner

meaning is, that in the things which he wrote there was sometimes an obscurity, which gave occasion to the unlearned to go astray to their own ruin. We are reminded by these words, to reason soberly on things so high and obscure; and further, we are here strengthened against this kind of offence, lest the foolish or absurd speculations of men should disturb us, by which they entangle and distort simple truth, which ought to serve for edification.

But we must observe, that we are not forbidden to read Paul's Epistles, because they contain some things hard and difficult to be understood, but that, on the contrary, they are commended to us, provided we bring a calm and teachable mind. For Peter condemns men who are trifling and volatile, who strangely turn to their own ruin what is useful to all. Nay, he says that this is commonly done as to all the Scripture: and yet he does not hence conclude, that we are not to read it, but only shews, that those vices ought to be

in which he writes. The difficulty has arisen from connecting the reference made to Paul, only with the former part of the 15th verse, while that part ought to be viewed only as an addition to the former verse; and the former verse stands connected with the new heavens and the new earth. So that the subjects in hand are the day of judgment, the future state, and the necessity of being prepared for it; and that these are the things referred to is evident from this, that he says, that Paul speaks of them in all his epistles, which is not true, as to what is said at the beginning of the 15th verse. The passage then ought to be thus rendered:—

14. " Therefore, beloved, since ye expect these things, diligently strive to be found by him in peace, unspotted and unblamable;
15. and deem the long-suffering of our Lord *to be for* salvation: even as Paul, our beloved brother, has, according to the wisdom given
16. to him, written to you; as also in all his epistles, when speaking in them of these things; in which (epistles) there are some things difficult to be understood," &c.

Now the special epistle referred to was most probably the epistle to the Hebrews, one particular design of which was to direct the attention of the Jews to the country promised to their fathers. Some, indeed, hold that that epistle was written to the Jews in Judea; but others maintain that it was written to converted Hebrews generally, whether in Judea or elsewhere; and this passage seems to favour the latter opinion.

If the view given here is right, that is, that the subjects on which reference is made to Paul, are those mentioned in the 12th, the 13th, and 14th verses, then there is no epistle of Paul which could be more appropriately referred to than that to the Hebrews, as the new heavens and the new earth answer exactly to " the better and heavenly country," mentioned in the Epistle to the Hebrews. See Heb. xi. 16. Besides, the exhortations and warnings of that epistle wholly coincide with the exhortation given here by Peter.—*Ed.*

corrected which prevent improvement, and not only so, but render deadly to us what God has appointed for our salvation.

It may, however, be asked, Whence is this obscurity, for the Scripture shines to us like a lamp, and guides our steps? To this I reply, that it is nothing to be wondered at, if Peter ascribed obscurity to the mysteries of Christ's kingdom, and especially if we consider how hidden they are to the perception of the flesh. However, the mode of teaching which God has adopted, has been so regulated, that all who refuse not to follow the Holy Spirit as their guide, find in the Scripture a clear light. At the same time, many are blind who stumble at mid-day; others are proud, who, wandering through devious paths, and flying over the roughest places, rush headlong into ruin.

17. *Ye, therefore, beloved.* After having shewn to the faithful the dangers of which they were to beware, he now concludes by admonishing them to be wise. But he shews that there was need of being watchful, lest they should be overwhelmed. And, doubtless, the craft of our enemy, the many and various treacheries which he employs against us, the cavils of ungodly men, leave no place for security. Hence, vigilance must be exercised, lest the devices of Satan and of the wicked should succeed in circumventing us. It, however seems that we stand on slippery ground, and the certainty of our salvation is suspended, as it were, on a thread, since he declares to the faithful, that they ought to take heed lest they should fall from their own steadfastness.

What, then, will become of us, if we are exposed to the danger of falling? To this I answer, that this exhortation, and those like it, are by no means intended to shake the firmness of that faith which recumbs on God, but to correct the sloth of our flesh. If any one wishes to see more on this subject, let him read what has been said on the tenth chapter of the First Epistle to the Corinthians.

The meaning is this, that as long as we are in the flesh, our tardiness must be roused, and that this is fitly done by having our weakness, and the variety of dangers which surround us, placed before our eyes; but that the confidence which rests on God's promises ought not to be thereby shaken.

18. *But grow in grace.* He also exhorts us to make progress; for it is the only way of persevering, to make continual advances, and not to stand still in the middle of our journey; as though he had said, that they only would be safe who laboured to make progress daily.

The word *grace,* I take in a general sense, as meaning those spiritual gifts we obtain through Christ. But as we become partakers of these blessings according to the measure of our faith, *knowledge* is added to grace; as though he had said, that as faith increases, so would follow the increase of grace.[1]

To him be glory. This is a remarkable passage to prove the divinity of Christ; for what is said cannot belong to any but to God alone. The adverb of the present time, *now,* is designed for this end, that we may not rob Christ of his glory, during our warfare in the world. He then adds, *for ever,* that we may now form some idea of his eternal kingdom, which will make known to us his full and perfect glory.

[1] "Grace" is the attainment, and "the knowledge" of Christ is the way and means. The chief thing is often mentioned first in Scripture, and then that which leads to it, or the cause of it.—*Ed.*

END OF THE SECOND EPISTLE OF PETER.

COMMENTARIES

ON

THE EPISTLE OF JUDE

THE ARGUMENT.

THOUGH there was a dispute among the ancients respecting this Epistle, yet as the reading of it is useful, and as it contains nothing inconsistent with the purity of apostolic doctrine, and was received as authentic formerly, by some of the best, I willingly add it to the others. Its brevity, moreover, does not require a long statement of its contents; and almost the whole of it is nearly the same with the second chapter of the last Epistle.

As unprincipled men, under the name of Christians, had crept in, whose chief object was to lead the unstable and weak to a profane contempt of God, Jude first shews, that the faithful ought not to have been moved by agents of this kind, by which the Church has always been assailed; and yet he exhorts them carefully to beware of such pests. And to render them more hateful and detestable, he denounces on them the approaching vengeance of God, such as their impiety deserved. Now, if we consider what Satan has attempted in our age, from the commencement of the revived gospel, and what arts he still busily employs to subvert the faith, and the fear of God, what was a useful warning in the time of Jude, is more than necessary in our age. But this will appear more fully as we proceed in reading the Epistle.

1. Jude, the servant of Jesus Christ, and brother of James, to them that are sanctified by God the Father, and preserved in Jesus Christ, *and* called.	1. Judas Jesu Christi servus, frater autem Jacobi, vocatis qui in Deo Patre sanctificati sunt, et in Jesu Christo custoditi,
2. Mercy unto you, and peace, and love, be multiplied.	2. Misericordia vobis et pax et dilectio augeatur.

1. *Jude the servant of Jesus Christ.* He calls himself the servant of Christ, not as the name applies to all the godly, but with respect to his apostleship; for they were deemed peculiarly the servants of Christ, who had some public office committed to them. And we know why the apostles were wont to give themselves this honourable name. Whosoever is not called, arrogates to himself presumptuously the right and authority of teaching. Then their calling was an evidence to the apostles, that they did not thrust themselves into their office through their own will. It was not, however, of itself sufficient to be appointed to their office, except they faithfully discharged it. And, no doubt, he who declares himself to be the servant of God, includes both these things, that is, that God is the bestower of the office which he exercises, and that he faithfully performs what has been committed to him. Many act falsely, and falsely boast to be what they are very far from being: we ought always to examine whether the reality corresponds with the profession.

And brother of James. He mentions a name more celebrated than his own, and more known to the churches. For though faithfulness of doctrine and authority do not depend on the names of mortal men, yet it is a confirmation to the faith, when the integrity of the man who undertakes the office of a teacher is made certain to us. Besides, the authority of James is not here brought forward as that of a private individual, but because he was counted by all the Church as one of the chief apostles of Christ. He was the son of Alpheus, as I have said elsewhere. Nay, this very passage is a sufficient proof to me against Eusebius and others, who say, that he was a disciple, named Oblias, [James,] mentioned by Luke, in Acts xv. 13; xxi. 18, who was more eminent than the apostles in the Church.[1] But there is no

---

[1] Some have held, that James, mentioned in the forecited places in Acts,

doubt but that Jude mentions here his own brother, because he was eminent among the apostles. It is, then, probable, that he was the person to whom the chief honour was conceded by the rest, according to what Luke relates.

To them that are sanctified by God the Father, or, to the called who are sanctified, &c.[1] By this expression, " the called," he denotes all the faithful, because the Lord has separated them for himself. But as calling is nothing else but the effect of eternal election, it is sometimes taken for it. In this place it makes but little difference in which way you take it; for he, no doubt, commends the grace of God, by which he has been pleased to choose them as his peculiar treasure. And he intimates that men do not anticipate God, and that they never come to him until he draws them.

Of the same he says that they were *sanctified in God the Father*, which may be rendered, " by God the Father." I have, however, retained the very form of the expression, that readers may exercise their own judgment. For it may be, that this is the sense,—that being profane in themselves, they had their holiness in God. But the way in which God sanctifies is, by regenerating us by his Spirit.

Another reading, which the Vulgate has followed, is somewhat harsh, " To the beloved ($\dot{\eta}\gamma\alpha\pi\eta\mu\acute{e}\nu o\iota s$) in God the Father." I therefore regard it as corrupt; and it is, indeed, found but in a few copies.

He further adds, that they were *preserved in Jesus Christ*. For we should be always in danger of death through Satan, and he might take us at any moment as an easy prey, were we not safe under the protection of Christ, whom the Father has given to be our guardian, so that none of those whom he has received under his care and shelter should perish.

Jude then mentions here a threefold blessing, or favour of God, with regard to all the godly,—that he has made them

was not James the apostle, but another James, a disciple, and one of the seventy, who was also called Oblias: but this is not correct.—*Ed.*

[1] So *Beza* renders the words, " To the called, sanctified by God the Father, and preserved by Jesus Christ:" that is, to the effectually called, (as the word commonly means,) set apart and separated by God from the ungodly world, and kept by Christ, having been committed to his care and protection.—*Ed.*

by his calling partakers of the gospel; that he has regenerated them, by his Spirit, unto newness of life ; and that he has preserved them by the hand of Christ, so that they might not fall away from salvation.

2. *Mercy to you.* Mercy means nearly the same as grace in the salutations of Paul. Were any one to wish for a refined distinction, it may be said that grace is properly the effect of mercy ; for there is no other reason why God has embraced us in love, but that he pitied our miseries. *Love* may be understood as that of God towards men, as well as that of men towards one another.[1] If it be referred to God, the meaning is, that it might increase towards them, and that the assurance of divine love might be daily more confirmed in their hearts. The other meaning is, however, not unsuitable, that God would kindle and confirm in them mutual love.

3. Beloved, when I gave all diligence to write unto you of the common salvation, it was needful for me to write unto you, and exhort *you*, that ye should earnestly contend for the faith which was once delivered unto the saints.

4. For there are certain men crept in unawares, who were before of old ordained to this condemnation; ungodly men, turning the grace of our God into lasciviousness, and denying the only Lord God, and our Lord Jesus Christ.

3. Dilecti, quum omne studium adhiberem ad scribendum vobis de communi salute, necesse habui scribere vobis ad vos hortandos ut certando adjuvetis eam, quæ semel tradita est sanctis, fidem.

4. Subingressi enim sunt quidam homines, olim præscripti in hoc judicium, impii, Dei nostri gratiam transferentes in lasciviam, et Deum, qui solus est Herus, et Dominum nostrum Jesum Christum negantes.

3. *When I gave diligence.* I have rendered the words σπουδὴν ποιούμενος, " Applying care :" literally they are, " Making diligence." But many interpreters explain the sentence in this sense, that a strong desire constrained Jude to write, as we usually say of those under the influence of some strong feeling, that they cannot govern or restrain themselves. Then, according to these expounders, Jude was under a sort of necessity, because a desire to write suffered him not to rest. But I rather think that the two clauses are separate,

---

[1] As *mercy* is that of God, so it is more consistent to consider " peace" and " love" to be those of God : " may the mercy" of God, " and the peace" of God, " and the love" of God, " be increased (or multiplied) to you."— *Ed.*

that though he was inclined and solicitous to write, yet a necessity compelled him. He then intimates, that he was indeed glad and anxious to write to them, but yet necessity urged him to do so, even because they were assailed (according to what follows) by the ungodly, and stood in need of being prepared to fight with them.[1]

Then, in the first place, Jude testifies that he felt so much concern for their salvation, that he wished himself, and was indeed anxious to write to them; and, secondly, in order to rouse their attention, he says that the state of things required him to do so. For necessity adds strong stimulants. Had they not been forewarned how necessary his exhortation was, they might have been slothful and negligent; but when he makes this preface, that he wrote on account of the necessity of their case, it was the same as though he had blown a trumpet to awake them from their torpor.

Of the common salvation. Some copies add "your," but without reason, as I think; for he makes salvation common to them and to himself. And it adds not a little weight to the doctrine that is announced, when any one speaks according to his own feeling and experience; for vain is what we say, if we speak of salvation to others, when we ourselves have no real knowledge of it. Then, Jude professed himself to be (so to speak) an experimental teacher, when he associated himself with the godly in the participation of the same salvation.

And exhort you. Literally, "exhorting you;" but as he points out the end of his counsel, the sentence ought to be thus expressed. What I have rendered, "to help the faith by contending," means the same as to strive in retaining the faith, and courageously to sustain the contrary assaults

---

[1] Then the rendering would be, "Beloved, when I was applying all care to write to you of the common salvation, I deemed (or found) it necessary to write to you, in order to exhort you to contend for the faith once delivered to the saints." *Macknight* and some others give another meaning to the first clause, and one more literal: "Beloved, making all haste to write to you, concerning the common salvation, I have thought it necessary," &c. For this haste the Apostle gives a reason in the following verse, "For some men have stealthily crept in," &c. This is the most obvious meaning of the passage.—*Ed.*

of Satan.[1] For he reminds them that in order to persevere in the faith, various contests must be encountered and continual warfare maintained. He says that faith had been *once delivered*, that they might know that they had obtained it for this end, that they might never fail or fall away.

4. *For there are certain men crept in unawares.* Though Satan is ever an enemy to the godly, and never ceases to harass them, yet Jude reminds those to whom he was writing of the state of things at that time. Satan now, he says, attacks and harasses you in a peculiar manner; it is therefore necessary to take up arms to resist him. We hence learn that a good and faithful pastor ought wisely to consider what the present state of the Church requires, so as to accommodate his doctrine to its wants.

The word $\pi\alpha\rho\epsilon\iota\sigma\acute{\epsilon}\delta\upsilon\sigma\alpha\nu$, which he uses, denotes an indirect and stealthy insinuation, by which the ministers of Satan deceive the unwary; for Satan sows his tares in the night, and while husbandmen are asleep, in order that he may corrupt the seed of God. And at the same time he teaches us that it is an intestine evil; for Satan in this respect also is crafty, as he raises up those who are of the flock to do mischief, in order that they may more easily creep in.

Before of old ordained. He calls that judgment, or condemnation, or a reprobate mind, by which they were led astray to pervert the doctrine of godliness; for no one can do such a thing except to his own ruin. But the metaphor is taken from this circumstance, because the eternal counsel of God, by which the faithful are ordained unto salvation, is called a book: and when the faithful heard that these were given up to eternal death, it behoved them to take heed lest they should involve themselves in the same destruction. It was at the same time the object of Jude to obviate danger, lest the novelty of the thing should disturb and distress any of

---

[1] The meaning of the verb is, to combat for, to strive, fight or contend for. It is a word derived from the games, and expresses a strenuous effort. Our version conveys well its meaning, " earnestly contend for the faith;" or, the words may be rendered, " strenuously combat for the faith;" not with the sword, says *Beza*, but with sound doctrine and the example of a holy life.—*Ed.*

them; for if these were already long ago ordained, it follows that the Church is not tried or exercised but according to the infallible counsel of God.[1]

The grace of our God. He now expresses more clearly what the evil was; for he says that they abused the grace of God, so as to lead themselves and others to take an impure and profane liberty in sinning. But the grace of God has appeared for a far different purpose, even that, denying ungodliness and worldly lusts, we may live soberly, righteously, and godly in this world. Let us, then, know that nothing is more pestilential than men of this kind, who from the grace of Christ take a cloak to indulge in lasciviousness.[2]

Because we teach that salvation is obtained through God's mercy alone, the Papists accuse us of this crime. But why should we use words to refute their effrontery, since we everywhere urge repentance, the fear of God, and newness of life, and since they themselves not only corrupt the whole world with the worst examples, but also by their ungodly teaching take away from the world true holiness and the pure worship of God? Though I rather think, that those of whom Jude speaks, were like the libertines of our time, as it will be more evident from what follows.

The only Lord God, or, God who alone is Lord. Some old copies have, "Christ, who alone is God and Lord." And, indeed, in the Second Epistle of Peter, Christ alone is mentioned, and there he is called Lord.[3] But he means that

---

[1] The words literally are, "Who have been long ago (or, some time past) forewritten of for (or, as to) this judgment." The reference is to prophecy; such creepers in for the purpose of corrupting the truth had been foretold; and this creeping in for such a purpose was a judgment for yielding up themselves to the delusions of Satan. The word πάλαι refers indefinitely to what is past, either long ago, or some time past. See Matt. xi. 21, and Mark xv. 44. The reference may be to ancient prophecies, or to those of our Saviour and his Apostles.—*Ed.*

[2] "The grace of God" here is evidently the gospel. They transformed, says *Grotius,* the gospel to a libidinous doctrine.—*Ed.*

[3] *Griesbach* excludes Θεόν, "God," from the text: then the passage would correspond in sense with 2 Peter ii. 1; literally, "denying the only sovereign and Lord of us, Jesus Christ." The word δεσπότην, sovereign, or master, is used by Jude as well as by Peter. It was not the grace, but the ruling power of Christ that was denied; they boasted of his grace, but

Christ is *denied,* when they who had been redeemed by his blood, become again the vassals of the Devil, and thus render void as far as they can that incomparable price. That Christ, then, may retain us as his peculiar treasure, we must remember that he died and rose again for us, that he might have dominion over our life and death.

5. I will therefore put you in remembrance, though ye once knew this, how that the Lord, having saved the people out of the land of Egypt, afterward destroyed them that believed not.	5. Commonefacere autem vos volo, quum istud semel noveritis, quòd Dominus postquam ex terra Egypti populum servaverat, postea non credentes perdidit.
6. And the angels which kept not their first estate, but left their own habitation, he hath reserved in everlasting chains, under darkness, unto the judgment of the great day.	6. Angelos verò qui principatum (*vel,* initium) suum non servaverant, sed reliquerant suum domicilium, in judicium magnæ diei vinculis æternis sub caligine servavit.
7. Even as Sodom and Gomorrha, and the cities about them, in like manner, giving themselves over to fornication, and going after strange flesh, are set forth for an example, suffering the vengeance of eternal fire.	7. Quemadmodum Sodoma et Gomorrha, et quæ circum erant urbes, quum simili modo scortatæ essent, et abiissent post carnem alienam, propositæ sunt in exemplar, ignis æterni judicium sustinentes.

5. *I will therefore put you in remembrance,* or, remind you. He either modestly excuses himself, lest he should seem to teach as it were the ignorant things unknown to them; or, indeed, he openly declares in an emphatical manner, (which I approve more of,) that he adduced nothing new or unheard of before, in order that what he was going to say might gain more credit and authority. I only recall, he says, to your mind what you have already learnt. As he ascribes knowledge to them, so he says that they stood in need of warnings, lest they should think that the labour he undertook towards them was superfluous; for the use of God's word is not only to teach what we could not have otherwise known, but also to rouse us to a serious meditation of those things which we already understand, and not to suffer us to grow torpid in a cold knowledge.

Now, the meaning is, that after having been called by

---

did not submit to him as a king. Hence the word δισπότης is used—one exercising absolute power. We may render the words, " denying our only sovereign and Lord, Jesus Christ."—*Ed.*

God, we ought not to glory carelessly in his grace, but on the contrary, to walk watchfully in his fear; for if any trifles thus with God, the contempt of his grace will not be unpunished. And this he proves by three examples. He first refers to the vengeance which God executed on those unbelievers, whom he had chosen as his people, and delivered by his power. Nearly the same reference is made by Paul in the tenth chapter of the First Epistle to the Corinthians. The import of what he says is, that those whom God had honoured with the greatest blessings, whom he had extolled to the same degree of honour as we enjoy at this day, he afterwards severely punished. Then in vain were all they proud of God's grace, who did not live in a manner suitable to their calling.

The word *people* is by way of honour taken for the holy and chosen nation, as though he had said that it availed them nothing, that they by a singular favour had been taken into covenant. By calling them *unbelieving*, he denotes the fountain of all evils; for all their sins, mentioned by Moses, were owing to this, because they refused to be ruled by God's word. For where there is the subjection of faith, there obedience towards God necessarily appears in all the duties of life.

6. *And the angels.* This is an argument from the greater to the less; for the state of angels is higher than ours; and yet God punished their defection in a dreadful manner. He will not then forgive our perfidy, if we depart from the grace unto which he has called us. This punishment, inflicted on the inhabitants of heaven, and on such superior ministers of God, ought surely to be constantly before our eyes, so that we may at no time be led to despise God's grace, and thus rush headlong into destruction.

The word $ἀρχή$, in this place, may be aptly taken for beginning as well as for principality or dominion. For Jude intimates that they suffered punishment, because they had despised the goodness of God and deserted their first vocation. And there follows immediately an explanation, for he says that they had *left their own habitation;* for, like military deserters, they left the station in which they had been placed.

We must also notice the atrocity of the punishment which the Apostle mentions. They were not only free spirits but celestial powers; they are now held bound by perpetual chains. They not only enjoyed the glorious light of God, but his brightness shone forth in them, so that from them, as by rays, it spread over all parts of the universe; now they are sunk in darkness. But we are not to imagine a certain place in which the devils are shut up, for the Apostle simply intended to teach us how miserable their condition is, since the time they apostatized and lost their dignity. For whereever they go, they drag with them their own chains, and remain involved in darkness. Their extreme punishment is in the meantime deferred until the great day comes.

7. *Even as Sodom and Gomorrha.* This example is more general, for he testifies that God, excepting none of mankind, punishes without any difference all the ungodly. And Jude also mentions in what follows, that the fire through which the five cities perished was a type of the eternal fire. Then God at that time exhibited a remarkable example, in order to keep men in fear till the end of the world. Hence it is that it is so often mentioned in Scripture; nay, whenever the prophets wished to designate some memorable and dreadful judgment of God, they painted it under the figure of sulphurous fire, and alluded to the destruction of Sodom and Gomorrha. It is not, therefore, without reason that Jude strikes all ages with terror, by exhibiting the same view.

When he says, *the cities about them in like manner, giving themselves over to fornication,* I do not apply these words to the Israelites and the angels, but to Sodom and Gomorrha. It is no objection that the pronoun τούτοις is masculine; for Jude refers to the inhabitants and not to the places. To *go after strange flesh,* is the same as to be given up to monstrous lusts; for we know that the Sodomites, not content with the common manner of committing fornication, polluted themselves in a way the most filthy and detestable. We ought to observe, that he devotes them to eternal fire; for we hence learn, that the dreadful spectacle which Moses describes, was only an image of a much heavier punishment.

8. Likewise also these *filthy* dreamers defile the flesh, despise dominion, and speak evil of dignities.

9. Yet Michael the archangel, when contending with the devil, (he disputed about the body of Moses,) durst not bring against him a railing accusation, but said, The Lord rebuke thee.

10. But these speak evil of those things which they know not; but what they know naturally, as brute beasts, in those things they corrupt themselves.

8. Similiter isti quoque somniis delusi, carnem quidem contaminant, dominationem verò rejiciunt, et in glorias maledicta congerunt.

9. Atqui Michael archangelus, quando judicio disceptans cum diabolo, disputabat de corpore Mosis, non ausus fuit judicium inferre contumeliæ; sed dixit, Increpet te Dominus.

10. Isti verò quæcumque non noverunt, convitiis incessunt; quæcunque verò naturaliter tanquam bruta animalia sciunt, in iis corrumpuntur.

8. *Likewise also these.* This comparison is not to be pressed too strictly, as though he compared these whom he mentions in all things to the Sodomites, or to the fallen angels, or to the unbelieving people. He only shews that they were vessels of wrath appointed to destruction, and that they could not escape the hand of God, but that he would some time or another make them examples of his vengeance. For his design was to terrify the godly to whom he was writing, lest they should entangle themselves in their society.

But he begins here more clearly to describe these impostors. And he says first, that they polluted their flesh as it were by dreaming, by which words he denotes their stupid effrontery, as though he had said that they abandoned themselves to all kinds of filth, which the most wicked abhor, except sleep took away shame and also consciousness. It is then a metaphorical mode of speaking, by which he intimates that they were so dull and stupid as to give up themselves without any shame to every kind of baseness.[1]

---

[1] The "dreaming" is connected with the three things which follow, defiling the flesh, despising government, and slandering dignities. Hence the idea conveyed by our version, in which *filthy* is introduced, is by no means correct. Allusion seems to be made to the pretensions of false prophets in former times. See Jer. xxiii. 25-27. The false prophets taught what they pretended to see in dreams, as dreams as well as visions were vouchsafed to true prophets. See Joel ii. 28. It is not improbable that those referred to here pretended that they had received what they taught, by supernatural dreams; for how otherwise could they deceive others, especially respecting errors so gross and palpable as are here mentioned? The eighth verse is, as to its construction, connected with the seventh. The

There is a contrast to be noticed, when he says that they *defiled* or polluted *the flesh*, that is, that they degraded what was less excellent, and that yet they despised as disgraceful what is deemed especially excellent among mankind.

It appears from the second clause that they were seditious men, who sought anarchy, that, being loosed from the fear of the laws, they might sin more freely. But these two things are nearly always connected, that they who abandon themselves to iniquity, do also wish to abolish all order. Though, indeed, their chief object is to be free from every yoke, it yet appears from the words of Jude that they were wont to speak insolently and reproachfully of magistrates, like the fanatics of the present day, who not only grumble because they are restrained by the authority of magistrates, but furiously declaim against all government, and say that the power of the sword is profane and opposed to godliness; in short, they superciliously reject from the Church of God all kings and all magistrates. *Dignities* or glories are orders or ranks eminent in power or honour.

9. *Yet Michael the archangel.* Peter gives this argument shorter, and states generally, that angels, far more excellent than men, dare not bring forward a railing judgment.

But as this history is thought to have been taken from an apocryphal book, it has hence happened that less weight has been attached to this Epistle. But since the Jews at that time had many things from the traditions of the fathers, I see nothing unreasonable in saying that Jude referred to what had already been handed down for many ages. I know indeed that many puerilities had obtained the name of tradition, as at this day the Papists relate as traditions many

---

ὡς and the ὁμοίως are corresponding terms; "as Sodom and Gomorrha, &c., are set forth for an example, in like manner also these would be." This is the drift of the passage;—

8. "In like manner, indeed, *shall* also these dreamers *be* (that is, an example of divine vengeance,) *who* defile the flesh, despise dominion, and revile dignities."

Peter threatened them with "swift destruction," 2 Pet. ii. 1. There are here three things mentioned which apply to the three instances previously adduced: like the Sodomites they defiled the flesh; like the fallen angels they despised dominion; and like the Israelites in the wilderness, they reviled dignities; for it was especially by opposing the power given to Moses that the Israelites manifested their unbelief.—*Ed.*

of the silly dotages of the monks ; but this is no reason why they should not have had *some* historical facts not committed to writing.

It is beyond controversy that Moses was buried by the Lord, that is, that his grave was concealed according to the known purpose of God. And the reason for concealing his grave is evident to all, that is, that the Jews might not bring forth his body to promote superstition. What wonder then is it, when the body of the prophet was hidden by God, Satan should attempt to make it known ; and that angels, who are ever ready to serve God, should on the other hand resist him ? And doubtless we see that Satan almost in all ages has been endeavouring to make the bodies of God's saints idols to foolish men. Therefore this Epistle ought not to be suspected on account of this testimony, though it is not found in Scripture.

That Michael is introduced alone as disputing against Satan is not new. We know that myriads of angels are ever ready to render service to God ; but he chooses this or that to do his business as he pleases. What Jude relates as having been said by Michael, is found also in the book of Zechariah, " Let God chide (or check) thee, Satan." (Zech. iii. 2.) And it is a comparison, as they say, between the greater and the less. Michael dared not to speak more severely against Satan (though a reprobate and condemned) than to deliver him to God to be restrained ; but those men hesitated not to load with extreme reproaches the powers which God had adorned with peculiar honours.

10. *But these speak evil of those things which they know not.* He means that they had no taste for anything but what was gross, and as it were beastly, and therefore did not perceive what was worthy of honour ; and that yet they added audacity to madness, so that they feared not to condemn things above their comprehension ; and that they also laboured under another evil—for when like beasts they were carried away to those things which gratified the senses of the body, they observed no moderation, but gorged themselves excessively like the swine which roll themselves in stinking mud. The adverb *naturally* is set in opposition to reason and judg-

11. Woe unto them! for they have gone in the way of Cain, and ran greedily after the error of Balaam for reward, and perished in the gainsaying of Core.

12. These are spots in your feasts of charity, when they feast with you, feeding themselves without fear: clouds *they are* without water, carried about of winds; trees whose fruit withereth, without fruit, twice dead, plucked up by the roots;

13. Raging waves of the sea, foaming out their own shame; wandering stars, to whom is reserved the blackness of darkness for ever.

11. Væ illis, quoniam viam Cain ingressi sunt (Gen. iv. 12;) et deceptione mercedis Balaam effusi sunt (Num. xxii. 21;) et contradictione Core perierunt (Num. xxvi. 2.)

12. Ili sunt in fraternis vestris conviviis maculæ, inter se (*vel* vobiscum) convivantes, securè pascentes seipsos; nubes aqua carentes, quæ à ventis circum aguntur; arbores autumni emarcidæ, infrugiferæ, bis emortuæ, et eradicatæ;

13. Undæ efferatæ maris, despumantes sua ipsorum dedecora; stellæ erraticæ, quibus caligo tenebrarum in æternum servata est.

11. *Woe unto them.* It is a wonder that he inveighs against them so severely, when he had just said that it was not permitted to an angel to bring a railing accusation against Satan. But it was not his purpose to lay down a general rule. He only shewed briefly, by the example of Michael, how intolerable was their madness when they insolently reproached what God honoured. It was certainly lawful for Michael to fulminate against Satan his final curse; and we see how vehemently the prophets threatened the ungodly; but when Michael forbore extreme severity (otherwise lawful), what madness was it to observe no moderation towards those excelling in glory? But when he pronounced woe on them, he did not so much imprecate evil on them, but rather reminded them what sort of end awaited them; and he did so, lest they should carry others with them to perdition.

He says that they were the imitators of *Cain*, who being ungrateful to God, and perverting his worship through an ungodly and wicked heart, forfeited his birthright. He says that they were deceived like *Balaam* by a reward, because they adulterated the doctrine of true religion for the sake of filthy lucre. But the metaphor he uses, expresses something more; for he says that they *overflowed*, even because their excess was like overflowing water. He says in the third place, that they imitated the *contradiction of Core*, because they disturbed the order and quietness of the church.

12. *These are spots in your feasts of charity.* They who read, " among your charities," do not, as I think, sufficiently explain the true meaning. For he calls those feasts *charities*, (ἀγάπαις,) which the faithful had among themselves for the sake of testifying their brotherly unity. Such feasts, he says, were disgraced by impure men, who afterwards fed themselves to an excess; for in these there was the greatest frugality and moderation. It was then not right that these gorgers should be admitted, who afterwards indulged themselves to an excess elsewhere.

Some copies have, " Feasting with you," which reading, if approved, has this meaning, that they were not only a disgrace, but that they were also troublesome and expensive, as they crammed themselves without fear, at the public expense of the church. Peter speaks somewhat different, who says that they took delight in errors, and feasted together with the faithful, as though he had said that they acted inconsiderately who cherished such noxious serpents, and that they were very foolish who encouraged their excessive luxury. And at this day I wish there were more judgment in some good men, who, by seeking to be extremely kind to wicked men, bring great damage to the whole church.

Clouds they are *without water.* The two similitudes found in Peter are here given in one, but to the same purpose, for both condemn vain ostentation: these unprincipled men, though promising much, were yet barren within and empty, like clouds driven by stormy winds, which give hope of rain, but soon vanish into nothing. Peter adds the similitude of a dry and empty fountain; but Jude employs other metaphors for the same end, that they were *trees fading*, as the vigour of trees in autumn disappears. He then calls them trees *unfruitful, rooted up,* and *twice dead;*[1] as though he had said, that there was no sap within, though leaves might appear.

[1] " Twice dead" is deemed by some a proverbial expression to signify what is altogether dead; or, as by *Macknight*, it means that they were dead when professing Judaism, and dead after having made a profession of the gospel.—*Ed.*

13. *Raging waves of the sea.* Why this was added, we may learn more fully from the words of Peter: it was to shew, that being inflated with pride, they breathed out, or rather cast out the scum of high-flown stuff of words in grandiloquent style. At the same time they brought forth nothing spiritual, their object being on the contrary to make men as stupid as brute animals. Such, as it has been before stated, are the fanatics of our day, who call themselves Libertines. You may justly say that they make only rumbling sounds; for, despising common language, they form for themselves an exotic idiom, I know not what. They seem at one time to carry their disciples above heaven, then they suddenly fall down to beastly errors, for they imagine a state of innocency in which there is no difference between baseness and honesty; they imagine a spiritual life, when fear is extinguished, and when every one heedlessly indulges himself; they imagine that we become gods, because God absorbs the spirits when they quit their bodies. With the more care and reverence ought the simplicity of Scripture to be studied, lest, by reasoning more refinedly than is right, we should not draw men to heaven, but on the contrary be involved in manifold labyrinths. He therefore calls them *wandering stars,* because they dazzled the eyes by a sort of evanescent light.

14. And Enoch also, the seventh from Adam, prophesied of these, saying, Behold, the Lord cometh with ten thousand of his saints,

15. To execute judgment upon all, and to convince all that are ungodly among them of all their ungodly deeds which they have ungodly committed, and of all their hard *speeches* which ungodly sinners have spoken against him.

16. These are murmurers, complainers, walking after their own lusts; and their mouth speaketh great swelling *words,* having men's persons in admiration because of advantage.

14. Prius autem etiam de iis vaticinatus est septimus ab Adam Enoch, dicens, Ecce venit Dominus in sanctis millibus suis,

15. Ut faciat judicium adversus omnes, et redarguat ex eis omnes impios de factis omnibus impietatis quæ impiè patrarunt, deque omnibus duris quæ loquuti sunt adversus Deum peccatores impii.

16. Hi sunt murmuratores, queruli, juxta concupiscentias suas ambulantes, et os illorum loquitur tumida, admirantes personas, utilitatis gratia.

14. *And Enoch also.* I rather think that this prophecy was unwritten, than that it was taken from an apocryphal

book; for it may have been delivered down by memory to posterity by the ancients.[1] Were any one to ask, that since similar sentences occur in many parts of Scripture, why did he not quote a testimony written by one of the prophets? the answer is obvious, that he wished to repeat from the oldest antiquity what the Spirit had pronounced respecting them: and this is what the words intimate; for he says expressly that he was the *seventh* from Adam, in order to commend the antiquity of the prophecy, because it existed in the world before the flood.

But I have said that this prophecy was known to the Jews by being reported; but if any one thinks otherwise, I will not contend with him, nor, indeed, respecting the epistle itself, whether it be that of Jude or of some other. In things doubtful, I only follow what seems probable.

Behold, the Lord cometh, or came. The past tense, after the manner of the prophets, is used for the future. He says, that the Lord would *come with ten thousand of his saints;*[2] and by saints he means the faithful as well as angels; for both will adorn the tribunal of Christ, when he shall descend to judge the world. He says, *ten thousand,* as Daniel also mentions myriads of angels, (Dan. vii. 10;) in order that the multitude of the ungodly may not, like a violent sea, overwhelm the children of God; but that they may think of this, that the Lord will sometime collect his own people, a part of whom are dwelling in heaven, unseen by us, and a part are hid under a great mass of chaff.

But the vengeance suspended over the wicked ought to keep the elect in fear and watchfulness. He speaks of *deeds* and *words,* because their corrupters did much evil, not only by their wicked life, but also by their impure and false speech. And their words were *hard,* on account of the

---

[1] This is the most common opinion. There is no evidence of such a *book* being known for some time after this epistle was written; and the book so called was probably a forgery, occasioned by this reference to Enoch's prophecy. See *Macknight's* Preface to this Epistle. Until of late, it was supposed to be lost; but in 1821, the late Archbishop *Laurence,* having found an Ethiopic version of it, published it with a translation.—*Ed.*

[2] Literally, " with his holy myriads."—*Ed.*

refractory audacity, by which, being elated, they acted insolently.[1]

16. *These are murmurers.* They who indulge their depraved lusts, are hard to please, and morose, so that they are never satisfied. Hence it is, that they always murmur and complain, however kindly good men may treat them.[2] He condemns their proud language, because they haughtily made a boast of themselves; but at the same time he shews that they were mean in their disposition, for they were servilely submissive for the sake of gain. And, commonly, this sort of inconsistency is seen in unprincipled men of this kind. When there is no one to check their insolence, or when there is nothing that stands in their way, their pride is intolerable, so that they imperiously arrogate everything to themselves; but they meanly flatter those whom they fear, and from whom they expect some advantage. He takes *persons* as signifying eternal greatness and power.

17. But, beloved, remember ye the words which were spoken before of the apostles of our Lord Jesus Christ:

18. How that they told you there should be mockers in the last time, who should walk after their own ungodly lusts.

19. These be they which separate themselves, sensual, having not the Spirit.

17. Vos autem dilecti, memores estis (*vel,* estote) verborum quæ prædicta sunt ab apostolis Domini nostri Jesu Christi, nempe,

18. Quod vobis dixerunt, ultimo tempore futuros (*vel,* venturos) derisores, qui secundum concupiscentias suarum impietatum ambularent.

19. Hi sunt qui seipsos segregant, animales, Spiritum non habentes.

17. *But, beloved.* To a most ancient prophecy he now adds the admonitions of the apostles, the memory of whom was recent. As to the verb μνήσθητε, it makes no great difference, whether you read it as declarative or as an ex-

---

[1] There seems to be a want of due order in the 15th verse; the execution of judgment is mentioned first, and then the conviction of the ungodly; but it is an order which exactly corresponds with numberless passages in Scripture: the final action first, and then that which leads to it.—*Ed.*

[2] We may render the words "Grumblers and fault-finders," that is, as the word means, with their own lot: they grumbled or murmured against others, and were discontented with their own condition; and yet walked in such a way (that is, in indulging their lusts,) as made their lot worse and occasioned still more grumbling.—*Ed.*

hortation; for the meaning remains the same, that being fortified by the prediction he quotes, they ought to be terrified. By *the last time* he means that in which the renewed condition of the Church received a fixed form till the end of the world; and it began at the first coming of Christ.

After the usual manner of Scripture, he calls them scoffers who, being inebriated with a profane and impious contempt of God, rush headlong into a brutal contempt of the Divine Being, so that no fear nor reverence keeps them any longer within the limits of duty: as no dread of a future judgment exists in their hearts, so no hope of eternal life. So at this day the world is full of epicurean despisers of God, who having cast off every fear, madly scoff at the whole doctrine of true religion, regarding it as fabulous.

19. *These be they who separate themselves.* Some Greek copies have the participle by itself, other copies add ἑαυτοὺς, " themselves;" but the meaning is nearly the same. He means that they separated from the Church, because they would not bear the yoke of discipline, as they who indulge the flesh dislike spiritual life.[1] The word *sensual,* or animal, stands opposed to spiritual, or to the renovation of grace; and hence it means the vicious or corrupt, such as men are when not regenerated. For in that degenerated nature which we derive from Adam, there is nothing but what is gross and earthly; so that no part of us aspires to God, until we are renewed by his Spirit.

20. But ye, beloved, building up yourselves on your most holy faith, praying in the Holy Ghost,

20. Vos autem dilecti, sanctissimæ vestræ fidei vosmet superstruentes, in Spiritu Sancti precantes,

---

[1] This is the common interpretation, and yet it seems inconsistent with what is previously said of these men, that they crept in stealthily, and " feasted" with the members of the Church. The ἑαυτοὺς, though retained by *Griesbach,* is excluded by *Wetstein* and others, being absent from most of the MSS. The verb ἀποδιορίζω, means to separate by a boundary two portions from one another, and hence metaphorically to separate or cause divisions: " These be they who cause divisions." They were doing the same thing as those mentioned by Paul in Rom. xvi. 17. They were producing discords *in* the Church, and not separations *from* it; and by continuing in it, they became " spots and stains" to its members.—*Ed.*

21. Keep yourselves in the love of God, looking for the mercy of our Lord Jesus Christ unto eternal life.
22. And of some have compassion, making a difference.
23. And others save with fear, pulling *them* out of the fire; hating even the garment spotted by the flesh.
24. Now unto him that is able to keep you from falling, and to present *you* faultless before the presence of his glory with exceeding joy,
25. To the only wise God our Saviour, *be* glory and majesty, dominion and power, both now and ever. Amen.

21. Vosmet in charitate servate, expectantes misericordiam Domini nostri Jesu Christi in vitam eternam.
22. Et hos quidem miseramini, dijudicantes;
23. Illos verò per timorem servate, ex incendio rapientes, odio prosequentes etiam maculatam à carne tunicam.
24. Ei autem qui servare potest vos (*vel*, eos) à peccato immunes, et statuere in conspectu gloriæ suæ irreprehensibiles cum exultatione,—
25. Soli sapienti Deo, Servatori nostro, gloria et magnificentia et imperium et potestas, nunc, et in omnia secula. Amen.

20. *But ye, beloved.* He shews the manner in which they could overcome all the devices of Satan, that is, by having love connected with faith, and by standing on their guard as it were in their watch-tower, until the coming of Christ. But as he uses often and thickly his metaphors, so he has here a way of speaking peculiar to himself, which must be briefly noticed.

He bids them first to *build* themselves *on faith;* by which he means, that the foundation of faith ought to be retained, but that the first instruction is not sufficient, except they who have been already grounded on true faith, went on continually towards perfection. He calls their faith *most holy*, in order that they might wholly rely on it, and that, leaning on its firmness, they might never vacillate.

But since the whole perfection of man consists in faith, it may seem strange that he bids them to build upon it another building, as though faith were only a commencement to man. This difficulty is removed by the Apostle in the words which follow, when he adds, that men build on faith when love is added; except, perhaps, some one may prefer to take this meaning, that men build on faith, as far as they make proficiency in it, and doubtless the daily progress of faith is such, that itself rises up as a building.[1] Thus the Apostle

---

[1] It is better to take "faith" here metonymically for the word or doc-

teaches us, that in order to increase in faith, we must be instant in prayer and maintain our calling by love.

Praying in the Holy Ghost. The way of persevering is, when we are endued with the power of God. Hence whenever the question is respecting the constancy of faith, we must flee to prayer. And as we commonly pray in a formal manner, he adds, *In the Spirit;* as though he had said, that such is our sloth, and that such is the coldness of our flesh, that no one can pray aright except he be roused by the Spirit of God; and that we are also so inclined to diffidence and trembling, that no one dares to call God his Father, except through the teaching of the same Spirit; for from him is solicitude, from him is ardour and vehemence, from him is alacrity, from him is confidence in obtaining what we ask; in short, from him are those unutterable groanings mentioned by Paul (Rom. viii. 26.) It is not, then, without reason that Jude teaches us, that no one can pray as he ought without having the Spirit as his guide.

21. *Keep yourselves in the love of God.* He has made love as it were the guardian and the ruler of our life; not that he might set it in opposition to the grace of God, but that it is the right course of our calling, when we make progress in love. But as many things entice us to apostasy, so that it is difficult to keep us faithful to God to the end, he calls the attention of the faithful to the last day. For the hope of that alone ought to sustain us, so that we may at no time despond; otherwise we must necessarily fail every moment.

But it ought to be noticed, that he would not have us to hope for eternal life, except through the mercy of Christ: for he will in such a manner be our judge, as to have no

trine of faith, the gospel; and the sense would be more evident, were we to render ἑαυτοὺς, " one another," as it means in 1 Thess. v. 13.
  20. " But ye, beloved, building one another on your most holy faith, (on the most holy doctrine which you believe,) praying by the
  21. Holy Spirit, keep one another in love to God, waiting for the mercy of our Lord Jesus Christ to eternal life. And on some, indeed, have compassion, making a difference; but others save with fear, ' &c.

The whole passage would read thus better, when their duty towards one another is specifically pointed out.—*Ed.*

other rule in judging us than that gratuitous benefit of redemption obtained by himself.

22. *And of some have compassion.* He adds another exhortation, shewing how the faithful ought to act in reproving their brethren, in order to restore them to the Lord. He reminds them that such ought to be treated in different ways, every one according to his disposition: for to the meek and teachable we ought to use kindness; but others, who are hard and perverse, must be subdued by terror.[1] This is the *difference* which he mentions.

The participle διακρινόμενοι, I know not why this is rendered in a passive sense by Erasmus. It may, indeed, be rendered in either way, but its active meaning is more suitable to the context. The meaning then is, that if we wish to consult the wellbeing of such as go astray, we must consider the character and disposition of every one; so that they who are meek and tractable may in a kind manner be restored to the right way, as being objects of pity; but if any be perverse, he is to be corrected with more severity. And as asperity is almost hateful, he excuses it on the ground of necessity; for otherwise, they who do not willingly follow good counsels, cannot be saved.

Moreover, he employs a striking metaphor. When there is a danger of fire, we hesitate not to snatch away violently whom we desire to save; for it would not be enough to beckon with the finger, or kindly to stretch forth the hand. So also the salvation of some ought to be cared for, because they will not come to God, except when rudely drawn. Very different is the old translation, which reading is however found in many of the Greek copies; the Vulgate is, "Rebuke the judged," (*Arguite dijudicatos.*) But the first meaning is more suitable, and is, as I think, according to

[1] Though most agree that by "fear" here is meant terror, that is, that the persons referred to were to be terrified by the judgment which awaited them; yet what follows seems favourable to another view, that fear means the care and caution with which they were to be treated; for the act of saving them is compared to that of a man snatching anything from the fire, in doing which he must be careful lest he himself should be burnt; and then the other comparison, that of a man shunning an infected garment lest he should catch the contagion, favours the same view. Hence our version seems right—" *with* fear."—*Ed.*

the old and genuine reading. The word to *save*, is transferred to men, not that they are the authors, but the ministers of salvation.

23. *Hating even the garment.* This passage, which otherwise would appear obscure, will have no difficulty in it, when the metaphor is rightly explained. He would have the faithful not only to beware of contact with vices, but that no contagion might reach them, he reminds them that everything that borders on vices and is near to them ought to be avoided: as, when we speak of lasciviousness, we say that all excitements to lusts ought to be removed. The passage will also become clearer, when the whole sentence is filled up, that is, that we should hate not only the flesh, but also the garment, which, by a contact with it, is infected. The particle καὶ even serves to give greater emphasis. He, then, does not allow evil to be cherished by indulgence, so that he bids all preparations and all accessories, as they say, to be cut off.

24. *Now unto him that is able to keep you.* He closes the Epistle with praise to God; by which he shews that our exhortations and labours can do nothing except through the power of God accompanying them.[1]

Some copies have "them" instead of "you." If we receive this reading, the sense will be, "It is, indeed, your duty to endeavour to save them; but it is God alone who can do this." However, the other reading is what I prefer; in which there is an allusion to the preceding verse; for after having exhorted the faithful to save what was perish-

---

[1] The doxology is as follows,—
"To the only wise God (or, to the wise God alone) our Saviour, *be* glory and greatness, might and dominion, both now and through all ages."

"Dominion" (ἐξουσία) is the right to govern, imperial authority or power; "might" (κράτος) is strength to effect his purpose, omnipotence; "greatness" (μεγαλωσύνη) comprises knowledge, wisdom, holiness, and everything that constitutes what is really great and magnificent; and 'glory" (δόξα) is the result of all these things which belong to God; all terminate in his glory. The ultimate issue is first mentioned, then the things which lead to it. It is by acknowledging his sovereign power, his capacity to exercise that power—his omnipotence, and his greatness in everything that constitutes greatness, that we give him the glory, the honour, and the praise due to his name.—*Ed.*

ing, that they might understand that all their efforts would be vain except God worked with them, he testifies that they could not be otherwise saved than through the power of God. In the latter clause there is indeed a different verb, φυλάξαι, which means to guard; so the allusion is to a remoter clause, when he said, *Keep yourselves.*

END OF THE EPISTLE OF JUDE.

A TRANSLATION

OF

CALVIN'S VERSION

OF

THE CATHOLIC EPISTLES.

THE FIRST EPISTLE OF PETER.

CHAPTER I.

1 Peter, an apostle of Jesus Christ, to the sojourners who are scattered through Pontus, Galatia, Cappadocia, Asia, and
2 Bithynia, elected according to the foreknowledge of God the Father, through the sanctification of the Spirit, unto obedience and the sprinkling of the blood of Jesus Christ: Grace to you and peace be multiplied.
3 Blessed be God, even the Father of our Lord Jesus Christ, who, according to his great mercy hath begotten us again to a living hope, through the resurrection of Jesus Christ from the
4 dead, to an inheritance incorruptible, and undefiled, and unfad-
5 ing, laid up in heaven for you; who by the power of God are kept through faith unto salvation, which is ready to be revealed
6 at the last time: on account of which ye exult, though now for a little while, if it be necessary, ye are made sorrowful
7 through various temptations; that the probation of your faith, much more precious than gold which perisheth, though even it be proved by fire, may be found unto praise, and honour, and
8 glory, when Jesus Christ shall be revealed: whom, though ye have not seen, ye love; on whom believing, though ye see him not, ye exult with joy unspeakable and glorious; receiv-
9 ing the end of your faith, the salvation of your souls.
10 Of which salvation the prophets inquired and searched, who
11 prophesied of future grace to us; searching what or what manner of time the Spirit of Christ who was in them did signify, previously testifying of the sufferings of Christ, and of the
12 glories which were to follow: to whom it was revealed, that not to themselves, but to us they ministered the things which

have been now declared to you by those who have preached to you the gospel, through the Holy Spirit sent from heaven; into which things the angels desire to look.

13 Therefore, girding up the loins of your mind, being sober, perfectly hope for the grace which is to be brought to you at
14 the revelation of Jesus Christ; as obedient children, not conformed to former lusts which prevailed during your ignorance:
15 but as he who has called you is holy, be ye also yourselves holy
16 in *your* whole conduct; because it is written, "Be ye holy, for I am holy."
17 And since ye call on the Father, who, without respect of persons, judgeth the work of every one, pass in fear the time
18 of your sojourning; knowing that not with corruptible things, silver or gold, you have been redeemed from your vain way of
19 living, delivered down from the fathers; but with the precious
20 blood of Christ, as of a lamb unspotted and undefiled: who had been, indeed, foreordained before the world was founded,
21 but has been manifested in the last times for you, who through him believe in God, who has raised him from the dead, and has given him glory, that your faith and hope may be in God:
22 purifying your souls by obedience to the truth through the Spirit, with an unfeigned brotherly love, love ye one another
23 from a pure heart fervently; having been begotten again, not from a seed that is corruptible, but incorruptible, through the
24 word of the living God, which abideth for ever. For all flesh is as grass, and all his glory as the flower of the grass: wither
25 does the grass, and its flower fades; but the word of the Lord remains for ever: and this is the word which has been declared to you.

CHAPTER II.

1 Laying aside, therefore, all wickedness, and all guile, and
2 dissimulations, and envyings, and all slanderings, as infants lately born, desire the milk that is rational and guileless, that
3 by it ye may grow; if indeed ye have tasted that the Lord is
4 gracious: to whom coming as to a living stone, rejected indeed
5 by men, but chosen by God and precious, ye also yourselves as living stones are built up a spiritual house, a holy priesthood, to offer spiritual sacrifices, acceptable to God through
6 Jesus Christ. Therefore also the Scripture contains *this*, "Behold, I lay in Sion a corner-stone, chosen, precious; and he
7 who believeth in him shall not be ashamed." To you, then, who believe, he is precious; but to the unbelieving, the stone which the builders rejected, this has become the head of the
8 corner; and a stone of stumbling and a rock of offence to those who stumble at the word, being unbelieving; to which also

9 they had been appointed. But ye are a chosen race, a royal priesthood, a holy nation, a peculiar people, that ye may de-
10 clare the virtues of him who has called you out of darkness into his marvellous light: who sometimes were not a people, but now are the people of God; who had not obtained mercy, but now have obtained mercy.
11 Beloved, I exhort you as sojourners and strangers, to abstain
12 from carnal desires, which war against the soul; having your behaviour good among the Gentiles, that whereas they speak against you as evil-doers, they may, considering your good works, glorify God in the day of visitation.
13 Be then subject to every human ordinance for the Lord's
14 sake; whether to the king, as supreme; or to governors, as those who are sent by him, for the punishment indeed of evil-
15 doers, but for the praise of those who do well: *for so is the will of God, that by well-doing ye should put a stop to the*
16 *ignorance of foolish men;* as free, and not having liberty as a
17 cloak for wickedness, but as the servants of God. Honour all,
18 love the brotherhood, fear God, honour the king. The servants, let them be subject with all fear to *their* lords, not only
19 to the good and humane, but also to the perverse. For this is acceptable, if for conscience towards God any one bears sor-
20 rows, suffering unjustly: for what sort of glory is it, if ye bear it when having done evil ye be buffeted? but if, having done well and suffering, ye bear it, this is acceptable with God.
21 For to this end you have been called; because Christ also suffered for you, leaving you an example, that ye may follow
22 his footsteps; who did no sin, nor was guile found in his mouth;
23 who, when reviled, reviled not again; when suffering, threatened not; but committed his cause to him who judgeth right-
24 eously; who bare himself our sins in his own body on the tree, that we, being dead to sin, may live to righteousness; by
25 whose bruise have ye been healed. For ye were as sheep going astray; but ye have been now turned to the Shepherd and Bishop of your souls.

CHAPTER III.

1 In like manner the wives, let them be subject to their own husbands, that even if any believe not the word, they may without the word be gained by the behaviour of *their* wives,
2 while observing your pure behaviour and fear: whose adorning, let it not be the outward, in the plaiting of the hair and
3 the encircling of gold, or the putting on of cloaks; but the
4 inner man of the heart, which is in the incorruption of a placid
5 and quiet spirit, which before God is precious. For so formerly also holy women who hoped in God, adorned themselves, being

6 subject to their own husbands; as Sara, *who* obeyed Abraham, calling him lord; whose daughters ye become, when ye do well, and are not terrified by any dread.

7 Let husbands in like manner dwell with *them* according to knowledge, giving honour to the wife as the weaker vessel, and as joint-heirs of the grace of life, that your prayers may not be hindered.

8 Finally, *be ye* of one mind, compassionate, loving to the
9 brethren, merciful, humble-minded; not rendering evil for evil, or railing for railing, but on the contrary, bless ye, knowing that you have been called for this end, that ye may inherit a
10 blessing. For let him who would love life and see good days, keep his tongue from evil and his lips from speaking guile;
11 let him turn away from evil and do good; let him seek peace
12 and pursue it: because the eyes of the Lord are on the righteous, and his ears to their prayers; but the face of the Lord is
13 against them who do evil. And who is he who can do you
14 harm, if ye be followers of what is good? But if ye also suffer for righteousness, happy *are ye;* and the fear of them
15 fear not, nor be troubled; but sanctify the Lord of hosts in your hearts, and be ready always for an answer to any one asking you a reason for the hope that is in you, with meekness
16 and fear; having a good conscience, that whereas they speak against you as evil-doers, they may be ashamed who slander your good behaviour in Christ.
17 For it is better to suffer, if so be the will of God, for doing
18 good than for doing evil: because Christ also once suffered for sins, the just for the unjust, that he might bring us to God, having indeed been put to death in the flesh, but brought to
19 life by the Spirit: by whom having also gone, he preached to
20 the spirits who were in prison, when there were formerly unbelievers, when once the patience of God waited in the days of Noah, while the ark was prepared; in which a few, that is,
21 eight souls, were saved by water; corresponding to which, baptism saves us also now (not the casting away of the filth of the flesh, but the answer of a good conscience towards God)
22 through the resurrection of Jesus Christ; who is at the right hand of God, having gone into heaven, angels and dominions and powers being made subject to him.

CHAPTER IV.

1 Christ then having suffered for us in the flesh, be ye also armed with the same mind: because he who hath suffered in
2 the flesh hath ceased from sin; that he may no longer live the rest of his time in the flesh to the lusts of men, but to the will
3 of God. For it is enough for us, that we have wrought, in the

past time of life, the will of the Gentiles, when we walked in lasciviousness, lusts, excesses in wine, revellings, banquetings,
4 and wicked idolatries: on account of which they think it strange, that ye run not with *them* into the same excess of riot,
5 speaking evil *of you;* who shall give account to him who is
6 ready to judge the living and the dead. For the gospel has for this end been also preached to the dead, that they may indeed be judged according to men in the flesh, but live accord-
7 ing to God in the Spirit. But the end of all things is near;
8 be ye then sober, and watchful to pray; and above all things having fervent love among yourselves; for love will cover a
9 multitude of sins. Be hospitable towards one another, without murmurings.
10 As every one has received a gift, minister the same one to
11 another, as good dispensers of the manifold grace of God; if any one speak, *let him speak* as the oracles of God; if any one minister, *let him do so* as by the power which God supplies; that in all things God may be glorified through Jesus Christ; to whom be the glory and the dominion for ever and ever. Amen.
12 Beloved, think it not strange when ye are tried by fire for the purpose of proving you, as though some new thing had
13 happened to you; but inasmuch as ye are partakers of the sufferings of Christ, rejoice; that at the revelation also of his glory
14 ye may exultingly rejoice. If ye be reproached for the name of Christ, happy *are ye;* for the Spirit of glory and of God rests upon you: by them, indeed, he is slandered, but by you
15 he is glorified. But let none of you suffer as a murderer, or a thief, or an evil-doer, or as a coveter of another man's goods;
16 but if as a Christian, let him not be ashamed; nay, let him in
17 this case glorify God: for it is the time, when judgment begins at the house of God; but if it be first on us, what *will be* the
18 end of those who obey not the gospel of God? and if the righteous be hardly saved, the ungodly and the sinner, where will they appear?
19 Let therefore those who suffer according to the will of God, commit their souls to him, in doing good, as to a faithful possessor.

CHAPTER V.

1 The elders who are among you I exhort, who am also an elder and a witness of the sufferings of Christ, and a partaker
2 of the glory which shall be revealed: feed as much as in you lieth the flock of God, discharging the office of bishops, not constrainedly, but willingly; not for the sake of filthy lucre, but
3 liberally; and not as exercising tyranny over *God's* heritages,
4 but that ye may be patterns to the flock: and when the Chief

Shepherd shall appear, ye shall receive an unfading crown of glory.

5 In like manner the younger, be ye subject to the elder; yea, be ye all subject to one another: put ye on humility of mind; because God resisteth the proud, but giveth grace to
6 the humble. Be ye then humbled under the mighty hand of
7 God, that he may exalt you in due time; all your care being cast on him, for he cares for you.

8 Be sober, be vigilant, because your adversary, the Devil, as a roaring lion, goeth around, seeking whom he may devour:
9 whom resist ye, being firm in the faith, knowing that the same sufferings are accomplished in your brethren in the world.

10 Now the God of all grace, who hath called us to his eternal glory through Christ Jesus,—may he perfect you, while suffer-
11 ing for a short time, confirm, strengthen, *and* establish *you:* to him be the glory and the dominion, for ever and ever. Amen.

12 By Sylvanus, a faithful brother to you, as I suppose, I have written in a few words, exhorting *you* and testifying that this
13 is the true grace of God in which ye stand. The *church,* elected together with you, which is in Babylon, saluteth you,
14 and Marcus my son. Salute ye one another with the kiss of love. Grace *be* to you all who are in Christ Jesus. Amen.

THE FIRST EPISTLE OF JOHN.

CHAPTER I.

1 What has been from the beginning, what we have heard, what we have seen with our eyes, what we have looked on, what our hands have handled, concerning the word of life;
2 (and the life has been manifested, and we have seen, and do testify, and declare to you that eternal life, which was with
3 the Father, and has been manifested to us)—what we have seen and heard, declare we to you, that ye also may have fellowship with us; and our fellowship is with the Father, and
4 with his Son Jesus Christ: and we write these things to you, that your joy may be complete.

5 And this is the message which we have heard from him, and declare to you, that God is light, and in him there is not any
6 darkness. If we say that we have fellowship with him, and
7 walk in darkness, we lie, and do not tell the truth. But if we

walk in the light, as he is in the light, we have fellowship one with another, and the blood of Jesus Christ his Son cleanseth
8 us from all sin. If we say that we have no sin, we deceive
9 ourselves, and the truth is not in us: If we confess our sins, faithful is he and just, so as to forgive us *our* sins, and to cleanse
10 us from all unrighteousness: If we say that we have not sinned, we make him a liar, and his word is not in us.

CHAPTER II.

1 My little children, I write these things to you, that you may not sin; but if any one sin, we have an advocate with the
2 Father, Jesus Christ, the righteous one: and he is the propitiation for our sins, and not for ours only, but also for *the sins* of the whole world.

3 And by this we know that we have known him, if we keep
4 his commandments. He who says, "I know him," and keeps not his commandments, is a liar, and the truth is not in him:
5 but he who keeps his word, verily in him the love of God is
6 perfected; by this we know that we are in him. He who says that he abides in him, ought also himself so to walk as he walked.

7 Brethren, no new commandment do I write to you, but an old commandment, which you have had from the beginning: the old commandment is the word which you have heard from
8 the beginning. Again, a new commandment do I write to you; which is true in him and in you, because the darkness is passing away, and the true light now shines.

9 He who says that he is in the light, and hates his brother,
10 is still in darkness. He who loves his brother abides in the
11 light, and to him there is no stumbling: but he who hates his brother, walks in darkness; and he knows not where he goeth, because darkness hath blinded his eyes.

12 I write to you, little children, because your sins are forgiven you for his name's sake.

13 I write to you, fathers, because ye have known him who is from the beginning. I write to you, young men, because ye have overcome the wicked one. I write to you, children, be-
14 cause ye have known the Father. I have written to you, fathers, because ye have known him who is from the beginning. I have written to you, young men, because ye are strong, and the word of God abides in you, and ye have overcome the evil one.

15 Love not the world, nor the things which are in the world: if any one loves the world, the love of the Father is not in him.
16 For whatever is in the world, (*even* the lust of the flesh, and the lust of the eyes, and the pride of life,) is not from the

17 Father, but from the world. And the world passeth away, and the lust of it; but he who doeth the will of God, abides for ever.
18 Little children, it is the last hour; and as you have heard that Antichrist is to come, even now there are many Anti-
19 christs: hence we know that it is the last hour. From us have they gone out, but of us they were not, for had they been of us, they would *surely* have remained with us; but *they have gone out,* that they might be made manifest that they were not
20 of us. But ye have an unction from the Holy One, and ye know all things.
21 I have not written to you, because ye know not the truth, but because ye know it, and that everything false is not
22 from the truth. Who is a liar, but he who denies Jesus to be the Christ? He is an Antichrist, who denies the
23 Father and the Son: every one who denies the Son hath not the Father.
24 Let, then, what you have heard from the beginning remain in you: if what you have heard from the beginning remain in
25 you, ye shall also remain in the Son, and in the Father; and this is the promise which he hath promised to us. *even* eternal life.
26 These things have I written to you respecting them who
27 seduce you: but the unction which ye have received from him remains in you, so that ye have no need that any one should teach you; but as the unction teaches you all things, and is truth, and is not a lie, and as it has taught you, *so* remain in him.
28 And now, little children, continue in him, that when he shall appear, we may have confidence, and not be ashamed
29 at his presence. Since ye know that he is righteous, know ye that every one who doeth righteousness has been born of him.

CHAPTER III.

1 See what manner of love the Father hath bestowed on us, that we should be called the sons of God! the world for this
2 reason knoweth us not, because it did not know him. Beloved, we are now the sons of God, and it does not yet appear what we shall be; but we know, that when he shall appear, we
3 shall be like him; for we shall see him as he is: and every one who hath this hope in him purifieth himself, inasmuch as he is pure.
4 Whosoever doeth sin, doeth also iniquity; and sin is ini-
5 quity. But ye know that he appeared that he might take
6 away our sins, and sin is not in him. Whosoever abides in

him doth not sin; whosoever sins, hath not seen him, nor known him.

7, 8 Little children, let no one deceive you,—he who doeth righteousness is righteous, inasmuch as he is righteous: he who doeth sin, is of the devil, for the devil sins from the beginning. The Son of God was for this end manifested, that he might
9 undo the works of the devil. Whosoever has been born of God, doth not do sin, because his seed remains in him; and he
10 cannot sin, because he has been born of God. By this are made manifest the sons of God, and the sons of the devil,—every one who doeth not righteousness, is not of God, nor he who loves not his brother.

11 For this is the message that ye heard from the beginning,
12 that we love one another: not as Cain, who was of the wicked one, and slew his brother; and why did he slay him? because
13 his works were evil, and his brother's righteous. Wonder not,
14 my brethren, if the world hate you. We know that we have passed from death to life, because we love the brethren; he
15 who loves not his brother, remains in death. Every one who hates his brother, is a murderer; and ye know that no mur-
16 derer has eternal life abiding in him. By this we know love, that he laid down his own life for us; and we ought to lay
17 down *our* lives for the brethren. But when any one has this world's goods, and seeth his brother in want, and closeth up his bowels from him, how abideth the love of God in him?

18 My little children, let us not love in word, nor in tongue,
19 but in deed and in truth: and by this we know that we are of
20 the truth, and shall assure our hearts before him. For if our heart accuse us, doubtless God is greater than our heart, and
21 knoweth all things. Beloved, if our heart do not accuse us,
22 we have confidence towards God: and if we ask anything, we receive *it* from him, because we keep his commandments, and
23 do the things which are pleasing in his sight. And this is his commandment, that we believe on the name of his Son Jesus Christ, and love one another, as he gave us commandment.
24 And he who keepeth his commandment, abideth in him, and he in him; and by this we know that he abideth in us, *even* by the Spirit whom he hath given us.

CHAPTER IV.

1 Beloved, believe not every spirit, but prove the spirits whether they are from God; because many false prophets have
2 gone forth into the world. By this know ye the Spirit of God,—Every spirit that confesseth that Jesus Christ has come
3 in the flesh, is from God; and every spirit that confesses not

that Jesus Christ has come in the flesh, is not from God; and this is the Antichrist, of whom you have heard that
4 he is to come, and he is now already in the world. Ye are of God, little children, and have overcome them; because greater is he who is in you than he who is in the
5 world. They are of the world; therefore of the world do
6 they speak, and the world heareth them. We are of God; he who knoweth God heareth us; he who is not of God, doth not hear us: by this we know the spirit of truth and the spirit of error.
7 Beloved, let us love one another; because love is from God; and every one who loveth has been born of God, and know-
8 eth God. He who loveth not, knoweth not God, because God
9 is love. In this has appeared the love of God to us, that God has sent his only-begotten Son into the world, that we may
10 live through him. In this is love, not that we have loved God, but that God has loved us and sent his Son a propitia-
11 tion for our sins. Beloved, if God has so loved us, we ought
12 also to love one another. No one hath ever seen God: if we love one another, God abides in us, and his love has been per-
13 fected in us. By this we know that we abide in him, and he in us, because he hath given us of his Spirit.
14 And we have seen and do testify, that the Father has sent
15 his Son to be the Saviour of the world. He who shall confess that Jesus is the Son of God, God abideth in him, and he in
16 God. And we have known and have believed the love which God hath to us: God is love; and he who abideth in love,
17 abideth in God, and God in him. By this has love in us been perfected, that we may have confidence in the day of
18 judgment, because as He is, so are we in this world. Fear is not in love: but perfect love casteth out fear; because fear hath torment; and he who fears, has not been perfected in
19 love. We love him, because he has first loved us.
20 If any one say, "I love God," and hate his neighbour, he is a liar; for he who loves not his brother whom he sees,
21 how can he love God whom he sees not? And this commandment we have from Him, that he who loves God should also love his brother.

CHAPTER V.

1 Every one who believes that Jesus is the Christ has been born of God; and every one who loves Him who has be-
2 gotten, loves him also who has been begotten by Him. By this we know that we love the children of God, when we love
3 God and keep his commandments: for this is the love of God, that we keep his commandments; and his commandments are

4 not grievous. For, whatever has been born of God overcometh the world; and this is the victory which overcometh the world,
5 our faith. Who is he who overcomes the world, but he who believes that Jesus is the Son of God?
6 This is he who has come by water and blood, Jesus Christ; not by water only, but by water and blood; and the Spirit is
7 He who testifies, inasmuch as the Spirit is truth. For there are three who testify in heaven, the Father, the Word, and the
8 Holy Spirit; and these three are one. And there are three
9 who testify on earth, the Spirit, the water, and the blood; and these three agree in one. If we receive the testimony of men, the testimony of God is greater.
10 Moreover, this is the testimony of God, which he hath testified respecting his own Son (He who believes on the Son of God hath the testimony in himself; he who believes not God, makes him a liar, because he hath not believed the testimony
11 which God hath testified respecting his own Son,) even this is the testimony, that God hath given to us eternal life; and this
12 life is in his Son. He who hath the Son, hath life; he who hath not the Son of God, hath not life.
13 These things have I written to you who believe on the name of the Son of God, that ye may know that ye have eternal life, and that ye may believe on the name of the Son
14 of God. And this is the confidence which we have towards Him, that when we ask anything according to his will, he
15 heareth us: and if we know that he hears us when we ask anything, we know that we have the petitions which we have desired of him.
16 If any one see his brother sinning a sin not to death, he shall ask, and he will give to him life for him who sins not to death: there is a sin to death, I do not say that any one shall
17 pray for that. Every unrighteousness is sin; and there is a
18 sin not to death. We know that every one who has been born of God, sins not; but he who has been born of God, keeps himself, and the wicked one touches him not.
19 We know that we are of God; and the whole world lieth in
20 the wicked one. And we know that the Son of God has come, and has given to us an understanding, that we may know him who is true; and we are in him who is true, in his Son Jesus Christ: this is the true God and eternal life.
21 Little children, keep yourselves from idols. Amen.

THE EPISTLE OF JAMES.

CHAPTER I.

1 JAMES, a servant of God and of the Lord Jesus Christ, to the twelve tribes which are in the dispersion, health:
2 Count it all joy, my brethren, when ye fall into various
3 temptations; knowing that the trying of your faith works
4 patience: but let patience have its perfect work, so that ye may be perfect and entire, in nothing deficient.
5 But if any of you be deficient in wisdom, let him ask *it* from God, who giveth to all freely, and does not upbraid: and it
6 shall be given to him. But let him ask in faith, by no means doubting; for he who doubts, is like a wave of the sea, which
7 by the wind is driven and tossed to and fro. Let not, then, that man think that he shall receive anything from the Lord.
8 A man of a double mind is unstable in all his ways.
9 Now, let a brother who is low, rejoice in his exaltation;
10 and the rich, in his lowness: because as a flower of grass shall
11 he pass away: for the sun rises with heat and withers the grass, and the flower falls, and the beauty of its appearance perishes; so also shall the rich fade away in his riches.
12 Blessed *is* the man, who endures temptation; for when he is tried, he shall receive the crown of life, which the Lord hath promised to them who love him.
13 Let no one, when he is tempted, say, "By God I am tempted:" for God cannot be tempted by evils, nor does he
14 tempt any one. But every one is tempted, when he is drawn
15 away by his own lusts, and is ensnared. Then lust, having conceived, brings forth sin; and sin, being perfected, begets death.
16 Do not err, my beloved brethren: Every good gift and every
17 perfect gift is from above, descending from the Father of lights, with whom there is no change nor shadow of turning.
18 Of his own will has he begotten us by the word of truth, that
19 we might be some firstfruits of his creatures. Let every man, therefore, my beloved brethren, be swift to hear, slow to
20 speak, slow to wrath: for the wrath of man worketh not the
21 righteousness of God. Laying aside then all filthiness and redundancy of wickedness, receive with meekness the implanted word, which is able to save your souls.
22 And be ye doers of the word and not hearers only, deceiving
23 yourselves. For if any one be a hearer of the word and not a doer, he is like a man who looks on his natural face in a glass;
24 for he hath looked on himself and departed, and hath imme-

25 diately forgotten what manner of man he was. But he who attentively looks on the perfect law of liberty and continues *to do so*,—this *man*, being not a forgetful hearer, but a doer of the work, shall be blessed in his work.
26 If any one seems to be religious among you and bridleth not his tongue, but deceiveth his own heart, his religion is vain.
27 Pure religion and undefiled before God even the Father, is this,—To visit the orphans and widows in their affliction, to keep himself unspotted from the world.

CHAPTER II.

1 My brethren, have not the faith of our Lord Jesus Christ
2 with respect of persons on account of reputation. For if there enter into your assembly a man wearing gold rings, having on a splendid dress, and there enter in also a poor man in sordid
3 clothing; and ye have respect to him who wears a splendid dress, and say to him, "Sit thou here honourably," and ye say to the poor, " Stand thou there," or, " Sit here under my foot-
4 stool ;" are ye not condemned in yourselves, and become judges
5 of evil thoughts? Hear, my beloved brethren, Has not God chosen the poor of this world *to be* rich in faith and heirs of the kingdom which he hath promised to them who love Him?
6 But ye have despised the poor. Do not the rich domineer
7 over you, and draw you before judgment-seats? Do they not blaspheme the good name which is called on you?
8 If indeed ye fulfil the royal law, according to Scripture,
9 "Thou shalt love thy neighbour as thyself," ye do well: but if ye respect persons, ye commit sin, and are reproved by the
10 law as transgressors. For whosoever shall keep the whole
11 law, and yet offend in one thing, becomes guilty of all : for he who hath said, "Thou shalt not commit adultery," hath said also, "Thou shalt not kill." Now if thou committest no adultery, yet if thou killest, thou becomest a transgressor of the
12 law. So speak ye and so do, as those who shall be judged by
13 the law of liberty. For judgment will be without mercy to him who hath not shewed mercy ; and mercy glorieth against judgment.
14 What does it avail, my brethren, if any one say that he hath
15 faith, and have not works ? Can faith save him ? Now, if a
16 brother or a sister be naked and in want of daily bread, and one of you say to them, "Go away in peace, be warmed and be filled ;" though ye give them not those things which are
17 necessary for the body, what does it avail ? Even so faith, if
18 it hath no works, being by itself, is dead. Nay, rather, one may say, "Thou hast faith and I have works ; shew me thy faith without thy works, and I will by my works shew thee

19 my faith." Thou believest that there is one God; thou doest
20 right: the devils also believe and tremble. But wilt thou
know, O vain man, that faith without works is dead?
21 Abraham our father, was he not justified by works, when
22 he offered up Isaac his son on the altar? Seest thou that
faith co-operated with his works, and faith was by works made
23 perfect? And fulfilled was the Scripture which saith, "Abraham believed God, and it was counted to him for righteous-
24 ness:" and he was called the Friend of God. Ye then see,
25 that by works is man justified, and not by faith only. In like
manner also Rahab the harlot, was not she justified by works,
when she received the messengers, and sent them forth another
26 way? For as the body without the soul is dead, so also faith
without works is dead.

CHAPTER III.

1 Be not many masters, my brethren, knowing that we shall
2 receive greater judgment: for in many things we all offend.
If any one offend not in word, he is a perfect man, as one who
3 can bridle also the whole body. Behold, we put bridles in
horses' mouths, that they may obey us, and we turn about
4 their whole body. Behold also the ships, however large they
may be and driven by fierce winds, yet they are turned about
by a very small helm wherever the will of the pilot wishes.
5 So also the tongue is a very small member and boasts great
things.
6 Behold, a little fire, what quantity of wood it burns! And
the tongue is a fire, and a world of iniquity. So is the tongue
among our members; it defiles the whole body and sets on fire
7 the whole course of nature, and it is set on fire by hell. For
every kind of beasts, and of birds, and of serpents, and of
things in the sea, is tamed and has been tamed by mankind:
8 but the tongue no man can tame, an unrestrainable evil, full of
9 deadly poison. By it we bless God, even the Father; and by
10 it we curse men made after his likeness! From the same
mouth proceeds blessing and cursing! These things, my
11 brethren, ought not to be so. Does a fountain from the same
12 opening send forth the sweet and the bitter? Can a fig-tree,
my brethren, bear olive-berries; or a vine, figs? so no fountain can bring forth briny and sweet water.
13 Who is wise and intelligent among you? Let him shew by
14 a good conduct his works with meekness of wisdom. But if
ye have bitter emulation and contention in your heart, glory
15 not, and lie not against the truth. This is not the wisdom
16 which comes from above, but earthly, animal, demoniacal: for
where emulation and contention *are*, there is confusion and

17 every evil work. But the wisdom which is from above, is
first pure, then peaceable, humane, tractable, full of mercy and
18 of good works, not officiously prying, not dissembling : and the
fruit of righteousness is sown in peace by those who make
peace.

CHAPTER IV.

1 Whence wars and fightings among you? are they not
2 hence,—from your lusts which war in your members? Ye
covet and have not ; ye envy and emulate, and cannot obtain ;
3 ye fight and war, yet ye have not, because ye do not ask ; ye
ask and receive not, because ye ask amiss, that ye may spend
it on your lusts.
4 Adulterers and adulteresses! know ye not, that the friendship of the world is enmity to God? Whosoever then will
5 be a friend of the world, becomes the enemy of God. Do ye
think that the Scripture speaks in vain? Does the Spirit
6 who dwells in us, lust to envy? Nay, he giveth more grace :
hence He saith, God resists the proud, but giveth grace to
the humble.
7 Be ye then subject to God ; resist the devil and he will flee
8 from you. Draw nigh to God, and he will draw nigh to you:
cleanse your hands, ye sinners; and purify *your* hearts, ye
9 double-minded. Be afflicted and mourn and weep; let your
10 laughter be turned to mourning, and your joy to sorrow. Be
humbled before God, and he will exalt you.
11 Defame not one another, brethren ; he who defames a
brother and judges his brother, defames the law and judges the
law ; but if thou judge the law, thou art not a doer of the
12 law, but a judge. One is the lawgiver, who can save and
destroy ; who art thou who judgest another?
13 Come now ye who say, "To-day, or, to-morrow, we shall
go into the city and pass there a year, and trade and make
14 gain :" who know not what is to be to-morrow ; for what is
your life? It is indeed a vapour, which for a short time ap-
15 pears, and then vanishes away. On the contrary ye ought to
say, "If the Lord will, and we live, we shall do this or that."
But now ye glory in your presumptions : all such glorying is
evil. He then who knows to do good and doeth it not, is
guilty of sin.

CHAPTER V.

1 Come now ye rich, weep and howl for your miseries, which
2 shall come upon *you*. Your riches are become rotten, and
your garments are eaten by moths; your gold and silver are
3 rusted, and their rust will be a witness against you, and shall

eat all your flesh as fire : ye have heaped together a treasure for the last days.

4 Behold the wages of the workmen, who have reaped your fields, fraudulently kept back by you, loudly cry; and the cries of those who have been reaping have entered into the ears
5 of the Lord of Sabaoth. In pleasures have ye lived on the earth, and have been wanton; ye have nourished your hearts
6 as in a day of slaughter. Ye have condemned *and* killed the just; and he does not resist you.

7 Be patient then, brethren, until the coming of the Lord. Behold, the husbandman waits for the precious fruit of the earth, having long patience for it, until he receives the early
8 and the latter rain. Be ye then also patient; strengthen your hearts; because the coming of the Lord is nigh.

9 Groan not one against another, brethren, lest ye be con-
10 demned; behold, the Judge stands before the door. Take, my brethren, the prophets, who have spoken in the name of the Lord, as an example of suffering affliction, and of patience.
11 Behold, we count them blessed who endure : ye have heard of the patience of Job, and have seen the end of the Lord, that he is very merciful and compassionate.

12 But above all things, my brethren, swear not, neither by heaven, nor by the earth, nor by any other oath; but let yours be, yea, yea; no, no; lest ye fall into condemnation.

13 Is any one afflicted among you ? let him pray : is any cheer-
14 ful ? let him sing psalms : is any sick among you ? let him call for the elders of the church; and let them pray over him,
15 anointing him with oil in the name of the Lord; and the prayer of faith shall save the sick, and the Lord shall raise him up : and if he have committed sins, they shall be forgiven
16 him. Confess mutually your sins, and pray for one another, that ye may be healed : the efficacious prayer of a righteous
17 man availeth much. Elias was a man subject to passions in the like manner as we; and he earnestly prayed that it might not rain; and it rained not on the earth for three years and
18 six months : and he prayed again, and the heaven gave rain, and the earth brought forth its fruit.

19 My brethren, if any one among you err from the truth, and
20 some one convert him; let him know, that he who converts a sinner from the error of his way shall save a soul from death, and shall cover a multitude of sins.

THE SECOND EPISTLE OF PETER.

CHAPTER I.

1 SIMEON PETER, a servant and an apostle of Jesus Christ, to those who have obtained an equally precious faith with us, through the righteousness of our God and Saviour Jesus Christ;
2 Grace to you and peace be multiplied, through the knowledge
3 of God, and of Jesus our Lord; as his divine power has given us all things which *pertain* to life and godliness, through the knowledge of him who hath called us by his own glory and
4 power; by which also very great and precious promises have been freely given us, that through these ye might become partakers of the divine nature, having escaped the corruption that
5 is in the world through lust. And for this purpose using all diligence, add to your faith, virtue; and to virtue, knowledge;
6 and to knowledge, temperance; and to temperance, patience;
7 and to patience, godliness; and to godliness, brotherly affec-
8 tion; and to brotherly affection, love: for if these be in you, and be abounding, they make you to be neither idle nor un-
9 fruitful in the knowledge of our Lord Jesus Christ; but he in whom these things are wanting is blind, and cannot see afar
10 off, having forgotten the cleansing of his old sins. Therefore,
11 brethren, strive the more to make your calling and election
12 sure; for if ye do these things, ye shall never fall: for thus shall abundantly be supplied to you an entrance into the eternal kingdom of our Lord and Saviour Jesus Christ.

12   I will not, therefore, neglect always to remind you of these things, though ye know them, and have been confirmed in the
13 present truth. Yea, I think it right, as long as I am in this
14 tabernacle, to stir you up by reminding you; since I know that I am shortly to put away this tabernacle, as also our Lord
15 Jesus Christ hath made manifest to me. I will, however, endeavour, that ye may also be able to have these things always in remembrance after my departure.

16   For it was not cunningly-devised fables that we followed, when we made known to you the power and the coming of our Lord Jesus Christ; but we were eye-witnesses of his majesty:
17 for he received from God the Father honour and glory, when such a voice as this came to him from the magnificent glory, " This is my beloved Son, in whom I have been well pleased."
18 And this voice we heard, when we were with him on the holy
19 mount. And we have the more sure word of prophecy, to which ye do well in attending, as to a light shining in a dark place, until the day dawn, and the day-star arise in your

20 hearts; knowing this first, that no prophecy of the Scripture
21 is of a private suggestion: for prophecy came not formerly by the will of man; but holy men of God spoke, being moved by the Holy Spirit.

CHAPTER II.

1 There were, however, false prophets also among the people; as there will also be false teachers among you, who will stealthily bring in opinions of perdition, denying even the Lord who has redeemed them, bringing on themselves swift
2 destruction. And many shall follow their ruinous courses,
3 through whom the way of truth shall be blasphemed. And through avarice they shall make a trade of you by feigned words; whose judgment a long ago ceases not, and whose perdition does not slumber.
4 For if God spared not the angels who had sinned, but having cast them into hell in chains of darkness, delivered them
5 to be kept for judgment;—and *if* he spared not the old world, but saved Noah, the eighth *person*, a preacher of righteousness, having brought in the flood on the world of the ungodly;—
6 and *if* having turned into ashes the cities of the Sodomites and of Gomorrah, he condemned *them* with an overthrow, having
7 made them an example to those who would live ungodly, and delivered the righteous Lot, who was vexed by the wicked
8 through their lascivious conduct; for that righteous man, while dwelling among them, had by seeing and hearing his righteous
9 soul daily tormented by their iniquitous deeds;—the Lord knoweth how to deliver the godly out of temptations, and to reserve the unjust for the day of judgment to be punished;
10 and especially those who walk after the flesh in the lust of uncleanness, and despise government: audacious *and* refrac-
11 tory, they fear not to blaspheme dignities, when angels, who are greater in strength and power, bring no railing judgment against them before the Lord.
12 But these, as brute animals, naturally made to be taken and destroyed, blaspheming those things which they understand
13 not, shall perish in their own corruption, receiving the reward of unrighteousness; deeming riot in the day-time a pleasure, *they are* blots and stains, rioting in their own errors, while
14 feasting with you; having eyes full of adultery, which cease not from sin, ensnaring unstable souls, having a heart exercised
15 in lusts, accursed children; who having left the right way, have gone astray, following the way of Balaam, the son of
16 Bosor, who loved the reward of unrighteousness; but was reproved for his iniquity; a mute beast of burden, speaking with the human voice, restrained the madness of the prophet.

17 These are fountains without water, clouds driven by a tempest, for whom has been prepared thick darkness for ever.
18 For when they speak most haughty words of vanity, they ensnare through the lusts of the flesh, by lasciviousness, those
19 who had really escaped from such as live in error; while they promise them liberty, they themselves are the slaves of corruption; for by whom any one is overcome, to him is he brought into bondage.
20 For if they who had escaped from the pollutions of the world, through the knowledge of the Lord and Saviour Jesus Christ, become again entangled with these, and are overcome,
21 the last *pollutions* become worse to them than the former: for it would have been better for them not to have known the way of righteousness, than to have known *it*, and to turn away from
22 the holy commandment delivered to them. But what is said in the true proverb has happened to them, " The dog has returned to his own vomit, and the washen sow to *her* wallowing in the mire."

CHAPTER III.

1 This second Epistle, beloved, I now write to you; in both which I stir up your pure mind by admonition, that ye may
2 remember the words which have been foretold by the holy Prophets and the commandment of us who are the apostles of
3 the Lord and Saviour; knowing this first, that scoffers will come in the last days, walking according to their own lusts,
4 and saying, " Where is the promise of his coming? for since the fathers have slept, all things remain as from the beginning
5 of the creation." For of this they are wilfully ignorant, that by the word of God the heavens were formerly, and the earth,
6 subsisting by water and through water; through which the world, which then was, perished, being overflowed with water.
7 But the heavens and the earth, which are now, are reserved by the word of the same, and are kept for fire against the day of judgment and of the perdition of the ungodly.
8 But of this one thing, beloved, be ye not ignorant, that one day with the Lord is as a thousand years, and a thousand
9 years as one day. The Lord does not delay as to his promise, as some count delay, but is patient towards us, not willing that any should perish, but that all should come to repentance.
10 But the day of the Lord will come as a thief in the night, in which the heavens with a tempest shall pass away, and the elements shall melt with heat, and the earth and all its works shall be burnt up.
11 Since then all these things shall be dissolved, what ought we
12 to be in all holy conduct and all godliness; waiting in haste for the coming of the day of God; on account of which the

heavens being on fire, shall be dissolved, and the elements
13 shall be consumed with heat. But according to his promise
we look for new heavens and a new earth, in which righteousness dwells.
14 Therefore, beloved, since ye look for these things, labour to be found by him in peace, unpolluted and blameless; and
15 regard the patience of our Lord as salvation, as also our beloved brother Paul has written to you according to the wis-
16 dom given to him; as also in all his Epistles, speaking of these things; in which there are some things hard to be understood, which the unlearned and the unstable pervert, as also other
17 scriptures, to their own ruin. Do ye then, beloved, being forewarned, take heed, lest ye, being led away by the error of
18 the wicked, should fall from your own steadfastness. But grow in the grace and knowledge of our Lord and Saviour Jesus Christ: to him be glory both now and for ever. Amen.

THE EPISTLE OF JUDE.

1 JUDE, a servant of Jesus Christ, and the brother of James, to the called, who are sanctified by God the Father, and pre-
2 served by Jesus Christ; mercy to you and peace and love be increased.
3 Beloved, when I was applying all care to write to you of the common salvation, I deemed it necessary to write to you in order to exhort *you*, that ye should by contending help the
4 faith once delivered to the saints. For crept in stealthily have certain men, ordained of old to this judgment, ungodly, turning the grace of our God into lasciviousness, and denying God, the only sovereign, and our Lord Jesus Christ.
5 Now I wish to remind you, though ye once knew this, that the Lord, after having saved the people from the land of
6 Egypt, afterwards destroyed the unbelieving; and the angels, who had not kept their own pre-eminence, but left their own abode, he has reserved under darkness in eternal chains for the
7 judgment of the great day. As Sodom and Gomorrha, and the cities around them, having in like manner committed fornication and gone after strange flesh, have been set forth for an
8 example, undergoing the judgment of eternal fire: in like manner also do these, deluded with dreams, pollute the flesh,
9 reject government, and heap curses on dignities: yet Michael the archangel, when, contending with the devil, he disputed

about the body of Moses, dared not to bring against him a
10 reviling judgment, but said, "The Lord rebuke thee." But
these revile those things which they know not, but what
things they know naturally, as brute beasts; in these they cor-
11 rupt themselves. Woe to them! for they have gone in the way
of Cain, and abandoned themselves to the error of Balaam's
reward, and perished in the gainsaying of Core.
12 These are stains in your brotherly feasts, feasting with you,
heedlessly feeding themselves; clouds without water, driven
about by winds; withering trees of autumn, fruitless, twice
13 dead, rooted up; raging waves of the sea, foaming out their
own shame; wandering stars, for whom is reserved the black-
14 ness of darkness for ever: and Enoch also, the seventh from
Adam, formerly prophesied of these, saying,
"Behold, the Lord cometh with thousands of his saints, to
15 execute judgment on all, and to convict all the ungodly of the
ungodly deeds of ungodliness which they have in an ungodly
manner done, and of all the hard things which ungodly sinners
have spoken against God."
16 These are murmurers, complainers, walking after their own
lusts; and their mouth speaks swelling words, admiring persons
17 for the sake of gain. But ye, beloved, remember the words
which have been spoken before by the Apostles of our Lord
19 Jesus Christ; for they have told you, that in the last time
scoffers would come, walking after their own ungodly lusts.
19 These are they who separate themselves, being sensual, having
not the Spirit.
20 But ye, beloved, building up yourselves on your most holy
21 faith, praying in the Holy Spirit, keep yourselves in the love
of God, looking for the mercy of our Lord Jesus Christ unto
22 eternal life. And on some have mercy, making a difference;
23 but others save by fear, snatching them from the fire, hating
even the garment spotted by the flesh.
24 Now to him who can keep you free from sin and set you
25 faultless before the presence of his glory with exultation—to
the only wise God our Saviour, be glory and majesty, dominion and power, both now and to all ages. Amen.

TABLE I.

GREEK WORDS EXPLAINED.

	Page		Page
Ἀγάπαις,	441	κληρονόμειν,	103
ἀγαπῶμεν,	248	κολαζόμενος,	400
ἀκαταστασία,	326	κτίσις,	80
ἀληθινὸς, ἀληθής,	273	κτίστης,	142
ἀλλὰ,	311	μεγαλαυχεῖν,	319
ἀναρχία,	401	μνήσθητε,	444
ἀντίστροφον,	117	νεανίσκοι,	184
ἀντίτυπον,	117	οἰκέται,	86
ἀρχὴ,	435	ὁμοούσιος,	196
ἀταξία,	187, 401	ὁρμὴ,	320
αὐτοκράτορα,	81	ὅτι,	121, 185, 261
βασιλεὺς,	81	οὗτος,	274
βίος,	188	ὀφθαλμοδουλεία,	86
γένεσις,	320	παιδία,	181
γινώσκετε,	361	παρεισέδυσαν,	432
διακρίνεσθαι,	283	περιέχειν,	66
διακρινόμενοι,	448	ποιεῖσθαι,	377
δι' ὃν,	370	πορείαις, πορίαις,	286
δοκιμάζεσθαι,	33	σοφίζεσθαι,	382
δοκίμιον,	33	σπουδὴν ποιούμενος,	430
δοῦλοι,	86	συμπάθεια,	102
εἰς ἓν,	45	ταπεινόφρονες,	102
εἰς ἓν, ἓν εἰσιν,	258	τεκνία,	181
ἐνέργεια,	373	τῆς δόξης,	301
ἐνεργουμένη,	359	τίς,	311
ἐπαγγελία,	162	ὑπὸ κρίσιν,	354
ἐπιλύσεως,	389	ὑποκρισιν,	354
ἐπηλύσεως,	389	φθονεῖτε,	329
ἐπισκοποῦντες,	145	φθορὰ,	404
ἰδία δόξα,	369	φιλαδελφία,	373
καὶ,	73	φονεύετε,	329
κακία,	295	φυλάξαι,	450
κατὰ,	145		

TABLE II.

TEXTS QUOTED OR EXPLAINED.

GENESIS.			1 SAMUEL.			ISAIAH.			MATTHEW.		
Chap.	Ver.	Page	Chap.	Ver.	Page	Chap.	Ver.	Page	Chap.	Ver.	Page
i.	2	416	xvi.	7	48	ii.	3	69	v.	7	308
	6	416				iv.	1	304		84	353
iv.	12	440				viii.	14	72		44	91
vi.	6	289	1 KINGS.			x.	12	188	vi.	16	88
vii.	17	416				xxviii.	16	67		21	35, 162
xv.	6	316	xvii., xviii.		360	xxx.	15	69	vii.	7	282
xviii.	12	98				xl.	6	58	x.	16	62
xxii.	1	288				liii.	6	94	xi.	27	367
xlviii.	16	48, 304	2 KINGS.			lvii.	15	295, 333		29	89
						lx.	2	76	xiii.	17	38
			iv.	32	356				xviii.	2	61
EXODUS.										22	129
						JEREMIAH.			xxi.	42	70
xix.	5	75	JOB.						xxii.	39	304
	6	74				v.	3	48	xxiii.	4	143
xxxiii.	20, 23	206	v.	1	151, 350	xxxi.	33	215, 298		23	180
			xxi.	13	139				xxv.	10	128
LEVITICUS.						EZEKIEL.					
xi.	44	384	PSALMS.			xx.	18	51	MARK.		
xix.	2	384				xxxiv.	4	143			
	15	304	xv.	4	301				viii.	35	135
	18	304		5, 6	162				xii.	31	304
			xvi.	2	221, 249	DANIEL.					
			xviii.	27	333				LUKE.		
NUMBERS.			xxxiv.	8	63	vii.	10	443			
			lxxiii.	8-9	139	ix.	24	194	vi.	25	336
xxii.	21	440	lxxviii.	69	68				vii.	36	335
xxvi.	2	440	cx.	2	69				xi.	9	282
			cxviii.	22	70	HOSEA.				28	297
			cxix.	51	414				xii.	35	44
DEUTERONOMY.			cxxx.	4	254	vi.	8	348	xvi.	15	263
									xxiii.	34	91
i.	17, 19	304									
x.	12	175, 252	PROVERBS.			JOEL.			JOHN.		
xiii.	3	392									
xxiv.	15	345	x.	12	129, 362	ii.	23	848	i.	13	251
xxvii.	26	307	xi.	31	140					29	209
xxviii.	12	348	xii.	10	345				iii.	3	59
xxx.	12	60	xvi.	1	340	ZECHARIAH.			iv.	22	50
	19, 20	175		2	223				ix.	3	335
xxxii.	35	91	xxvi.	11	411	iii.	2	439			

Chap.	Ver.	Page
xi.	41	356
xvii.	3	273
	11	271

ACTS.

Chap.	Ver.	Page
x.	2	264
xv.	2	253
	13	428
xvii.	11	386
xx.	10	356
xxi.	18	428

ROMANS.

Chap.	Ver.	Page
i.	4	259
	26	289
ii.	2	48
	13	296
iii.	22	367
v.	1	224
	3	280
	5	112
	8	240
vi.	4	94, 120
	5	122
	6	123
vii.	14	253
viii.	7	78
	10	126
	13	297
	15	265
	26	266
	29	89
ix.	26	77
	32	72
x.	14	226
	17	95
xii.	1	65, 203

Chap.	Ver.	Page
xii.	8	283
	19	91
xiii.	1	81
	8	180
	14	187
xiv.	4	339
xv.	14, 15	193, 378

1 CORINTHIANS.

Chap.	Ver.	Page
i.	25	303
ii.	12	251
iii.	1	63
	11	67
iv.	4	222
	15	60
v.	1	380
	5	36
vi.	2	338
	11	375
vii.	5	101
x.	11	414
xii.	23	99
xiii.	12	206
xiv.	20	62
xv.	19	139
	28	371

2 CORINTHIANS.

Chap.	Ver.	Page
i.	18	354
iii.	18	174, 297
iv.	6	273
	10	112
v.	6, 7	35
vii.	1	55
viii., ix.		283
xi.	2	331

GALATIANS.

Chap.	Ver.	Page
i.	8	311
ii.	8	25
	9	277
iii.	10	307
	23	114
iv.	4	53
	24	297
v.	14	304
	15	129
	19	62
	25	61, 210
vi.	1	319
	17	136

EPHESIANS.

Chap.	Ver.	Page
i.	4, 5	292
iii.	12	54, 223, 265
iv.	13	63
	17	46
	22	411
v.	2	242
	27	169
vi.	13	151

PHILIPPIANS.

Chap.	Ver.	Page
ii.	1	182
iii.	8	162
	10	93, 120
	12	179
	21	205
iv.	13	255

COLOSSIANS.

Chap.	Ver.	Page
i.	22	169
	24	151
ii.	9	278
	19	47, 19
iii.	3, 4	205
	9	175

2 THESSALONIANS

Chap.	Ver.	Page
ii.	3	190

1 TIMOTHY.

Chap.	Ver.	Page
i.	3	50
	5	56

2 TIMOTHY.

Chap.	Ver.	Page
ii.	5	50
	19	192

HEBREWS.

Chap.	Ver.	Page
i.	3	196
iv.	16	55
v.	12	63
vi.	19	54
vii.	26	171
xi.	1	35
	8	316
	13, 38	49
xiii.	8	183
	15	66

GENERAL INDEX

TO THE COMMENTARIES ON THE CATHOLIC EPISTLES.

A

ABEL, his works righteous, 217.
Able, the ingrafted word is, to save souls, 296.
Ablutions, what they signified under the Law, 256.
Abraham, how justified, 314-316; the children of, believers only, 74; had a name according to what he was, 203.
Adam, the image of, must be put off, 43, 45; the fall of, posterior to God's purpose of redemption, 52; life lost by the sin of, 159.
Admonitions necessary, 413.
Adoption, gratuitous, 32; obedience a proof of, 45; an evidence of the Father's love, 202.
Adorning, the, of women, what it ought to be, 96.
Adulterers and adulteresses, the lovers of the world, 331.
Adultery, eyes full of, the false teachers had, 404.
Adversary, an, the devil is, to us, 150.
Advocate, Christ is our, 170.
Afflicted, the, exhorted to pray, 354.
Afflictions, have glory annexed to them, 40; a curse to the wicked, 134.
Alienation from God, the extremity of evil, 162.
Allure, false teachers did, through the lusts of the flesh, 408.
Alphæus, Jude the son of, 428.
Anabaptists, the, condemn all oaths, 353.
Angels, the, desire to look into the things of Christ's kingdom, 42; the, made subject to Christ, 119; the, who sinned, 396; the, bring no railing accusation, 402.
Anointed, the sick were to be, by the elders, 355.
Anointing, *see* Unction.
Answer, an, to be given for our hope, 108; the, of a good conscience, 119.
Antichrist, foretold, 190; an, who is, 196; the spirit of, how distinguished, 232, 233.
Antichrists, many, 190.
Antiquity, no sufficient proof of truth, 198.
Apostles, the, the commandment of, to be borne in mind, 413; the, the words of, ought to be remembered, 444.
Apparel, modesty in, required, 96.
Archangel, the, Michael, 438.
Arius, his false opinion, 195.
Arians, the, pervert 1 John v. 20, 274.
Ashamed, to suffer as Christians, none ought to be, 137.
Ask, to, we ought, in faith, 283; to, amiss, how done, 330.
Ass, the dumb, rebuked Balaam, 405.
Associates, the persecuted are, with Christ, 134.
Augustine, how he refuted the cavil of the Pelagians, 167; dealt in refinement, 207; incorrectly applied 1 John v. 1, 251; his saying on humility, 336.
Authority, the, of the Fathers, vainly pretended, 51.

B

BABES, the new born, believers compared to, 62.
Babylon, Peter wrote his Epistle from, 154.
Balaam, the way of, 405; the error of, 440.
Baptism, the sin after, redeemed, as the Sophists say, by satisfactions, 93; typified by the flood, 117.
Barren, or unfruitful, they are not, who add to faith virtue, &c., 374.
Beasts, every kind of, tamed, 322; brute, ungodly men compared to, 403, 439.
Beginning, from the, what it means, 157.

Begotten, to a living hope, 28 ; to an inheritance, 29 ; us, God has, of his own will, 292.

Beguiled, unstable souls are, 404.

Believe, to, difficult, 157.

Believers, are the born of God, 251.

Bishop, the, of souls, Christ is, 94 ; and Presbyter, the same, 145.

Blameless, to be found, in Christ, we must be diligent, 422.

Bless, to, its meaning, 102 ; to, God, with the tongue, 322.

Blind, who is, 374.

Blood, the, of Jesus Christ, cleanses from all sin, 165.

Boldness in the day of judgment, how attained, 245.

Born, the, of God, sins not, 212, 270 ; the, of God, loves his brother, 238.

Born again, the, exhorted to love, 56 ; the faithful are, not of a corruptible seed, 57.

Brother, he who hates his, is in darkness, 180, 181 ; he who loves not his, is not of God, 216 ; Cain slew his, 217 ; he who loves not his, abides in death, 217, 218 ; he who hates his, is a murderer, 218 ; a needy, he who sympathizes not with, has no love to God, 220 ; he who hates his, and says he loves God, is a liar, 248 ; to love our, is God's command, 249 ; the, of low degree is to rejoice for his exaltation, 285.

Brotherhood, ought to be loved, 85.

Buffeted, to be, for faults, not praiseworthy, 88.

Builders, the, rejected the chief cornerstone, 70.

C

Cain, an example of hatred, 216 ; followed by false teachers, 449.

Called, Christians are, to bear wrongs patiently, 89 ; the believers are, to inherit a blessing, 103.

Calling, the, of God, gratuitous, 152 ; and election, to be made sure, 376, 377.

Care, to be cast on God, 149.

Catharians, the, held angelic purity, 212.

Cato, his opinion of display in dress, 97.

Censors, severe, their hypocrisy, 323 ; deem themselves very wise, 324.

Cerinthus, a heresiarch, 191, 195.

Certainty, the, of faith, generates no indifference, 267.

Charity or love, the kiss of, 155 ; the feasts of, 441.

Chastity, spiritual, how violated, 331.

Children, little, the faithful so called by John, 181 ; the, of God and of the devil, how distinguished, 215.

Chorus, the Lacedemonian, 183.

Christ, not seen, yet loved, 34 ; the sufferings of, foretold by the prophets, 40 ; compared to a lamb, 51 ; called a stone, a corner-stone, 64, 67 ; rejected by professing builders in all ages, 67 ; an example, to bear wrongs patiently, 89 ; without sin and guile, 90 ; committed his cause to God, 91 ; bare our sins on the tree, 92 ; the shepherd and bishop of souls, 94 ; suffered for sins, the just for the unjust, 111 ; was put to death in the flesh, but quickened by the Spirit, 112 ; praise given to, 133 ; our advocate, 170 ; our propitiation, 171 ; was manifested to take away sins, 209 ; an example of love in laying down his life, 219 ; the true God and eternal life, 274 ; glory ascribed to, 426.

Christian, to suffer as a, none ought to be ashamed, 137.

Christians, ought not to be evil-doers, 136.

Church, the, ever had hypocrites, 191; the defection from, 192 ; the name of, many are dazzled by, 230 ; the, cannot err, the false opinion of the Papists, 388 ; the, under the Gospel, similar as to trials, to what it was under the Law, 391, 392.

Cicero, a saying of, 124.

Cleanse (see Blood) to, from all unrighteousness, God is faithful, 168 ; to, the hands, sinners exhorted, 335.

Clouds, false teachers likened to, 407, 441.

Coming, the, of the Lord, to be waited for, 347.

Commandment, new and old, 177, 178 ; the, of God, to believe and to love, 225, 226; the holy, the sin of turning away from, 411.

Commandments, the, kept by those who know God, 173 ; the, of God, not grievous, 252.

Comparison, a, corresponds not in all parts, 122.

Compassion, sympathy, 102 ; ought to be felt for others, 448.

GENERAL INDEX. 477

Complainers, the false teachers were, 444.
Condemnation, the false teachers ordained to, 432.
Confess, to, our faults, we ought, to one another, 357.
Confession, necessary to forgiveness, 167; must be sincere, 168; the, of Jesus as the Son of God, 244.
Confidence, connected with good conscience, 222-224; combined with prayer, 224; to be exercised in prayer, 265.
Contend, to, for the faith, 431.
Conversation, the, of Christians, ought to be holy, 47; vain, redeemed from, 50; among the Gentiles, ought to be honest, 78; good, in Christ, 110.
Convert, to, the erring, hides many sins, 361.
Core, the gainsaying of, 441.
Cornelius, his case referred to, 263, 264.
Corner-stone, Christ so called, 67.
Count, to, all joy, to fall into divers temptations, 279.
Courteous, Christians ought to be, 101.
Craftiness, the, of Satan, 393, 409.
Creator, or Possessor, a faithful, God is, 141.
Creatures, the, of God, the first-fruits, 293.
Cross, the, the way to victory, 40; the, means mortification, 120; the, useful in two ways, 134.
Crown, an unfading, of glory, to faithful pastors, 146; an unfading, of glory, promised to all who love God, 287.
Curiosity, the, of man, ought to be kept within the limits of revelation, 39.
Cursed children, the false teachers were, 405.

D

DARKNESS, Christians called out of, 76; none who know God walk in, 163; dissipated by the gospel, 179; in chains of, the fallen angels are kept, 397.
David, a type of Christ, 70; the fall of, referred to, 214.
Day, the dawning of, 386; one, as a thousand years, 418; the, of the Lord, is to come, 420; the, of God, to be looked for, 421.
Day-star, the, what it means, 388.

Days, in the last, scoffers will come, 414.
Death, the, of Christ, a twofold likeness to, 120; apprehended near, ought to make ministers more diligent, 379.
Destruction, swift, awaiting false teachers, 393.
Detraction, condemned, 337.
Devil, the, compared to a roaring lion, 150; the, sins from the beginning, 211; the, the works of, Christ came to destroy, 212; the, believes in one God, and trembles, 311; the, ought to be resisted, 334.
Dignities, evil spoken of, 401, 438.
Disallowed, the living stone, by men, 64.
Disobedient, the, Christ a stone of stumbling to, 71, 72; the, the unbelievers in Noah's time, 115.
Doer, a, of the work, blessed, 298; not a, of the law, is the evil-speaker, 338.
Doers, the, of the word, we ought to be, not hearers only, 296.
Dog, the, a proverb concerning, 411.
Dogma, a Platonic, referred to, 46.
Dominion, despised by false teachers, 439.
Double-minded, the, is unstable, 284; the, exhorted to purify their hearts, 335.
Draw nigh, to, we ought, to God, 334.
Dreamers, the false teachers were, 437.

E

EARS, the, of the Lord, open to prayers, 105; the, of the Lord of Sabaoth, 345.
Earthly, the wisdom that is, 325.
Elder, an, Peter was, 142; the, the younger ought to submit to, 147.
Elders, the, exhorted to feed God's flock, 143, 144; the, of the Church, to be sent for by the sick, 355.
Elect, the saints are, according to God's foreknowledge, 24; the chief corner-stone is, 66.
Election, not to be separated from calling, 27; to be made sure, 376, 377.
Elias, his case referred to, 360.
Emperor, the Roman, Peter is supposed to refer to, 81.
End, the, of all things, at hand, 127; the, of the Lord, what it means, 352.
Engrafted word, the, is able to save souls, 296.

Enmity, the friendship of the world, is to God, 331.
Entrance, an abundant, into our Lord's everlasting kingdom, 378.
Envying, bitter, proceeds from malignity, 325.
Envyings, or envies, to be laid aside, 60.
Episcopate, how its duties are to be discharged, 145.
Epistle, the First of Peter, the main object of, 27 ; the Second, why written, 412.
Epistles, the, of Paul, referred to, 423, 424.
Erasmus, his version disapproved, 54, 121 ; his version referred to, 145.
Err, not to, we are warned, 291.
Eusebius, what he says of Peter being at Rome, 155; his opinion of Peter's Second Epistle, 363.
Evil for evil, not to render, 102.
Evil-doers, Christians falsely charged as being, 79 ; are to be put to shame by well-doing, 110.
Evil-speaking, the, of the unbelieving, to be stopped by doing good, 83.
Excess, the, of riot, 140.
Eyes, the, of the Lord, on the righteous, 104.
Eye-witnesses, the apostles were, of Christ's majesty, 382.

F

Fables, cunningly-devised, the apostles did not follow, 381.
Face, the, of the Lord, against evil-doers, 105.
Faith, tried, more precious than gold, 35; penetrates into heaven, 34, 54; brings joy, 35; the end of, salvation, 36; reaches God through Christ, 53; unites to God, 53; unformed, a foolish gloss, 239, 309; gains the victory, 254; a daily progress to be made in, 264; we ought to ask in, 283; rich in, the poor chosen to be, 303; a dead, cannot save, 310; is to be shewn by works, 311, 312; made perfect by works, 315; the prayer of, saving the sick, 356; is precious, 366; obtained through the righteousness of God, 366; the, is to be earnestly contended for, 431; on the, to build, 446.
Faithful, the, mingle joy with sorrow, 32; a, Creator or Possessor, God is, 141; God is, to forgive sins, 168.
Fanatics, the, take away the sacrament, 118; the, extend salvation to all the reprobate, 173; exclude the ministry, 200; hold licentious doctrines, 215.
Father, with the, and the Son, our fellowship is, 161 ; with the, we have an advocate, 169; the, the love of, is not in those who love the world, 185; the, and the Son, are denied by Antichrist, 195; the, and the Son, cannot be separated, 196; the, the wonderful love of, 202; the, of lights, from whom comes every good gift, 291.
Fatherless, the, to visit, a part of pure religion, 299.
Fathers, the ancient, in what they differed from us, 38, 39, 41; were partakers of the same life with us, 160; the, in the Church, addressed by John, 183.
Faults, to be confessed to one another, 357.
Fear, opposed to security, 49; with all, servants ought to be subject to their masters, 86; coupled with, ought the chaste conduct of wives to be, 96; with, and meekness, ought a reason to be given of our hope, 108; none in love, 247; without, the false teachers feasted and fed themselves, 441 ; with, to save others, 448.
Feast, the false teachers did, with the Church, 404, 441.
Fellowship, one with another, 161, 164; with the Father and the Son, 162.
Fervent, the prayer that is, avails much, 359.
Fervently, we ought so to love one another, 56.
Filthiness, all, or uncleanness, ought to be laid aside, 295.
First-fruits, to be, of God's creatures, 293.
Flesh, all, fading, 57; the, the filth of, to be put away, 117; the, means the body, corruption, and the present life, 122; the, to walk after, what it means, 400 ; strange, to go after, 436.
Flock, the, of God, pastors ought to feed, 144.
Flower, the, of the grass, the rich compared to, 286.
Foreknowledge, the, of God, 24.
Forgiveness, the main thing in religion, 182.
Fornication, the cities around Sodom, given to, 436.

Fountain, a, sends not forth bitter and sweet water, 323.
Fraud, cries for vengeance, 305.
Free, Christians are, 84.
Free-will, set up by Papists, 195; the advocates of, their opinion, 373.
Friendship, the, of the world, is enmity to God, 331.
Froward, the, masters, ought to be obeyed, 87.
Frugality, ought to be practised, 346.

G

GARMENT, the, spotted by the flesh, is to be hated, 449.
Generation, or race, a chosen, believers are, 75.
Gift, the, received, ought to be ministered, 130; every good and perfect, is from above, 291.
Glass, in a, man beholds his natural face, 297.
Glory, an unfading crown of, promised to faithful ministers, 146; eternal, we are called to, 152; ascribed to God, 153; Christ has called us to, 369; ascribed to Christ, 426; ascribed to God, 449.
God, the Father, 24, 383, 429; ought to be worshipped according to his word, 50; the knowledge of, without Christ, not attainable, 53; ought to be feared, 85; is a righteous judge, 90; claims vengeance as his own, 91; to bring us to, Christ suffered, 110; ought to be glorified in all things, 132; cares for his people, 149; the, of all grace, 151; has called us to eternal glory, 152; is light, having no darkness, 163; is faithful and just to forgive sins, 168; is love, 238, 244; gives to all liberally and upbraids not, 282, 283; is not willing that any should perish, 419.
Godliness, what pertains to, given by divine power, 368; to be added to patience, 372; in all, it behoves all to be, who look for the dissolution of heaven and earth, 421.
Godly, the, the Lord knows how to deliver out of temptations, 399.
Gomorrha, *see* Sodom.
Gospel, the, preached with the Holy Ghost sent down from heaven, 42; the, is the word preached, 59; the, preached to the dead, 125.
Government, despised by false teachers, 401, 439.

Governors, we ought to be subject to, 82.
Grace, and peace, their increase prayed for, 23, 366; the, of the gospel, foretold by the prophets, 37, 38; the, that is to be brought at the resurrection, 43, 44; the, of life, 100; the manifold, of God, 130; God gives, to the humble, 148; the God of all, 151; the true, of God, 154; more, God gives to the humble, 332; to grow in, we are exhorted, 426; the, of God, turned into laciviousness, 433.
Grass, the, men compared to, 58.
Grievous, God's commandments are not, 252.
Grudge, or groan, to, we ought not, against one another, 349.
Grudging, hospitality to be exercised without, 130.

H

HABITATION, their own, the fallen angels left, 435.
Happiness, the, of heaven exceeds all our thoughts, 204.
Happy, they are, who suffer for righteousness' sake, 106; are those who are reproached for Christ's name, 135.
Hard to be understood, are some things said by Paul, 422.
Hatred, the, of the brethren, a proof of being in darkness, 180.
Heart, with a pure, to love one another, 55, 56; the, the hidden man of, 97; the condemning and not condemning, 222, 223; his own, he who seems only religious, deceives, 299; an, exercised with covetous practices, 405.
Hearts, in our, to sanctify the Lord, 107; our, assured before God, 222; in our, when the day-star arise, 388.
Heat, with a burning, the sun rises, 285; with fervent, the elements shall melt, 420.
Heavens, the, and the earth, reserved for fire, 417.
Heresies, damnable, stealthily brought in, 328.
Hire, the, of labourers, kept back by the rich, 345.
Holiness, fictitious works of, devised by monks, 216.
Holy, the *Holy* Ghost, 41; " be ye *holy*," 47; an *holy* priesthood, 65; *holy* women, 98; the *holy* One, 193; the *Holy* Ghost, 257; the *holy* mount,

884; *holy* men—the *Holy* Ghost, 890; the *holy* commandment, 411; the *holy* prophets, 413; *holy* conversation, 420; most *holy* faith, 446; the *Holy* Ghost, 447.
Honour, due to all, 85.
Hope, to, we ought, to the end, 44.
Hope, to a lively, God has begotten us, 28; that our, may be in God, 53: a reason to be given for, 109; the, of the Christian, purifies, 207.
Horace, on the liberal and the miser, 137; on old age, 183; on the word fervid, 321; on envy, 329.
Horses, the, are ruled by bits in their mouths, 319.
Hospitality, enjoined, 130.
House, a spiritual, 65; the, of God, judgment begins at, 138.
Humble, to, ourselves, we ought, under the mighty hand of God, 148; to, ourselves, we ought, in the sight of the Lord, 336.
Humble, the, God gives grace to, 148; the, shall be exalted, 336.
Humility, we are to be clothed with, 148.
Husbands, the, may be won by the conversation of their wives, 95; they ought to give honour to their wives, 99.
Husbandman, his example of patience referred to, 348.
Hypocrisy, is always presumptuous, 337.
Hypocrites, attempt to deceive God, 48; criminate others to exalt themselves, 324, 337; are keen-eyed as to the faults of others, 327.

I

IDOLATERS, shew great zeal and fervour, 65.
Idolatries, abominable, the heathens guilty of, 124.
Idols, to keep from, John exhorts all, 275.
Ignorance, the, of heathens, 46; the, of the foolish, to be stopped by doing good, 83; the, of scoffers, wilful, 416.
Image, the, of God, deformed by Adam's sin, 323. *See* Adam.
Inheritance, an incorruptible, &c., God has begotten us to, 29.
Iniquity, the tongue a world of, 320; for his, Balaam was rebuked, 405.

J

JAMES, a servant of God, 277.

Jerome, referred to, as to Peter, 155; his opinion of the Second Epistle of Peter, 363.
Jews, the, worship an idol, not the true God, 28, 53, 197.
Joy, the, of believers, unspeakable, 35; a twofold, given to Christians, 134; the fulness of, designed by John in writing his Epistle, 162; all, occasioned by various temptations, 278, 279; exceeding, to be presented faultless with, before God, 449.
Jude, a servant of Christ and James' brother, 428; an experimental teacher, 431; modestly excused himself for writing, 434; exhorted Christians to remember the words before spoken by the apostles, 444.
Judge, the Father does, without respect of persons, 49; God does, righteously, 90; to, a brother is to judge the law, 337-339.
Judged, we shall be, by the law of liberty, 307.
Judges, the, of evil thoughts, 302.
Judgment, begins at God's house, 138; shall be without mercy to those who shew no mercy, 308; the, of the false teachers, lingers not, 395; reserved for the fallen angels, 396, 435; to execute, the Lord comes, 443.
Just, the, suffered, for the unjust, 111; God is, to forgive sins, 168; the, condemned and killed by the rich, 346; Lot being, God delivered, 398.
Justified, Abraham was by works, 314; a man is, by works, not by faith only, 316; Rahab was, by works, 316, 317.

K

KEEP, to, God's commandments, a proof that we know him, 173; to, God's commandments, makes prayer successful, 224; to, God's commandments, a proof that we love his children, 251, 252; to, God's commandments, a proof that we love Him, 252; to, from idols, all are exhorted, 275; to, one's-self unspotted from the world, a part of pure religion, 300; to, the whole law, and to fail in one thing, makes us guilty, 306; to, in God's love, Jude exhorts us, 447; to, us from falling, God is able, 449.

GENERAL INDEX. 481

Kindness, brotherly, added to godliness, 373.
King, the, we are to be subject to, 81; the, we ought to honour, 85.
Kingdom, to be heirs of his, God has chosen the poor, 302, 303; into the everlasting, an entrance is abundantly ministered, 374.
Kiss, the, of charity or love, 155.
Knowledge, all, without Christ is profitless, 46; the, of God, combined with obedience, 173, 174; the true, of God, produces brotherly love, 238; through the, of God, grace and peace is multiplied, 367; to be added to virtue, 373; in the, of our Lord Jesus Christ, we are not to be barren nor unfruitful, 374; the, of our Lord and Saviour, pollutions are escaped through, 410; in the, of our Lord and Saviour Jesus Christ, we are exhorted to grow, 426.

L

LABOURERS, the hire of, withheld by the rich, 345.
Lack, he that doth, wisdom, is to ask wisdom of God, 281; he that doth, these things, is blind, 374.
Lamb, paschal, a type of Christ, 51.
Lasciviousness, the Christians walked in, when Gentiles, 123; the grace of God turned into, 433.
Last, the *last* time, 31, 189, 445; the *last* times, 52, 53; the *last* days, 344, 414.
Law, the, and the gospel, the difference between, 39; the, is transgressed by the doer of sin, 207; the perfect, of liberty, 297; the royal, ought to be fulfilled, 305; the whole is transgressed when violated in one thing, 306; by the, of liberty, we are to be judged, 307; the, to speak evil of, is to judge the law, 337; not a doer of, the detractor, 338.
Lawgiver, the, is one, 338.
Liar, a, God is made, by those who deny their sins, 169; a, the man is, who says he knows God and keeps not his commandments, 175; a, is he who denies Christ, 194; a, is he who says he loves God, and hates his brother, 249; a, is he who believes not God, 261.
Liberally, God gives, 283.
Liberty, is not to be made a pretext for evil, 84; the perfect law of, 297; promised by the slaves of corruption, 408; the, which Christ gives, 409.
Life, the grace of, the husband and the wife are co-heirs of, 100; what he who loves, must do, 104; of our, the time past, 122; the word of, 159; manifested and seen, 160; eternal, with the Father, 160; eternal, promised by the Father, 199; eternal, no murderer hath, 218; Christ laid down his, 219; he hath, who hath the Son, 263; the crown of, 287; our, a vapour, 340; things pertaining to, given us, 368.
Light, marvellous, believers are brought into, 76; God is, 163; the, God is in, so ought we to be, 164; the, he who says he is in, and hates his brother, is in darkness, 179; the, he is in, who loves his brother, 180; a, shining in a dark place, prophecy compared to, 386-388.
Lips, the, we ought to keep from speaking guile, 104.
Lively, a *lively* hope, 28; as *lively* stones, 65.
Lives, our, we ought to lay down for the brethren, 219.
Loins, the, of the mind, to be girded up, 44.
Long-suffering, the, of God, in Noah's time, 116; the, of the Lord is salvation, 423.
Lord, the, that bought them, denied by false teachers, 393; the only, denied, 439; the, the coming of, foretold by Enoch, 443.
Lords, elders are not to be, over God's heritage, 145.
Lot, delivered from Sodom's ruin, 398.
Love, brotherly, 55, 102; unfeigned, 56; fervent, 128; covers many sins, 129; to God, proved by keeping his law, 175; brotherly, flows from love to God, 176, 216; the, of God, and of the brethren, inseparable, 180; the, of the Father, in our adoption, 202; the, of the brethren, a proof of having passed from death to life, 217; an example of, in Christ when he laid down his life, 219; the, of the brethren, an evidence of knowing the truth, 221; God is, 238, 244; the, of God, an example to us, 242; the, of God, perfected in us, 243; in, no fear, 247; to God and to the brethren, combined, 252; the, of God, we are exhorted to keep in, 447.
Low, the brother of *low* degree, 285; the rich made *low*, 285, 286.

482   GENERAL INDEX.

Lust, the, of the flesh and of the eyes, 187 ; the, of the world, passeth away, 188 ; of his own, man is drawn, when tempted, 289 ; conceived, brings forth sin, 290 ; through, the corruption of the world comes, 372 ; the, of uncleanness, the ungodly walk in, 400.

Lusts, according to former, Christians are not to fashion themselves, 44, 45; fleshly, an exhortation to abstain from, 78 ; to the, of men, we are not to live, 122 ; in, Christians once walked, 123 ; the cause of wars and fightings, 328, 329 ; on, to consume blessings, 330 ; through, of the flesh, false teachers allured men, 408 ; after their own, scoffers walked, 414 ; after their, murmurers walked, 444 ; after their ungodly, mockers walked, 445.

Luxury, condemned, 345.

M

Mahomet, pretended a divine mission, 237.

Malice, guile, hypocrisies, envies, evil-speakings, to be laid aside, 62.

Manicheans, their opinions, 211, 371.

Mark, Peter's companion, 155.

Masters, servants ought to be subject to, 86 ; ought not to be many, 317.

Mediator, as necessary, 53.

Meekness, the, of spirit, esteemed by God, 97 ; joined with fear, 109 ; with, we ought to receive the word, 294.

Members, the faculties of the soul, 329.

Men, young, addressed by John, 184 ; holy, of God, spoke, being moved by the Holy Spirit, 390 ; the, who crept in unawares, 432.

Merchandise made of men, by feigned words, 304, 305.

Mercy, according to his abundant, 28 ; obtained by those who had not obtained mercy, 77 ; judgment without, to those who shew no mercy, 308 ; rejoices against judgment, 308, 309 ; full of, is the wisdom from above, 327 ; of tender, the Lord is, 352 ; and peace and love, be multiplied, 430 ; for the, of the Lord Jesus, the Church is to look, 447.

Message, the, which the apostles brought, 162.

Michael the archangel, 438.

Milk, the sincere, of the word, 62.

Mind, to be all of one, Christians ought, 102; with the same, as was in Christ, we ought to be armed, 120; of a ready, elders ought to be, in discharging their office, 145.

Minister, the prophets did, to us, 41; to, we ought, to one another, 130; to, every man ought, according to the ability which God grants, 131, 132.

Mire, in the, the sow wallowing, 411, 412.

Miseries, threatened to the rich, 342, 343.

Mockers, their coming in the last time, 444, 445.

Monks, the, vainly boast of perfection, 217.

Moses, the body of, disputed about, 439.

Moth-eaten, the garments of the rich were, 343.

Mount, the holy, where Christ was transfigured, 384.

Multiplied, grace and peace be, 23, 367; mercy and peace and love, be, 430.

Multitude, a, of sins, love covers, 128, 129; a, of sins, hidden by him who converts the erring, 261, 262.

Murderer, a, or a thief, a Christian ought not to be, 136; a, is he who hates his brother, 218.

Murmurers, the false teachers were, 444.

N

Name, for the, of Christ, if reproached, we are happy, 135; for the, of Christ, sins are forgiven, 182; on the, of God's Son, we are commanded to believe, 225, 226; on the, of God's Son, John wrote that we might believe, 264; the worthy, by which Christians are called, 334.

Nature, the course of, set on fire by the tongue, 320; the divine, to become partakers of, 370, 371.

New, *new* born babes, 61, 62; a *new* commandment, 177, 178; *new* heavens and a *new* earth, 419, 420.

Newness, the, of life, an evidence of faith, 210.

Noah, saved by water, 116, 117; a preacher of righteousness, 397.

Novelty, suspicious, 52; the idea of, removed, 161.

O

OATHS, all, objected to by Anabaptists, 353.
Obedience, elected to, 26; to the truth, required, 55.
Offend, to, in one point, 306; we all do, in many things, 318.
Offender, an, not in word, perfect, 319.
Offence, the rock of, Christ is, to unbelievers, 73; no slight, to the weak, when many follow false teachers, 393, 394.
Oil, the sick were to be anointed with, 355.
Old, the, their character, 183. *See* Commandment.
One, the wicked, overcome by young men, 183, 184; the holy, an unction from, 193, 194; of the wicked, Cain was, 216, 217; these three are,—these three agree in, 237-239; the wicked, touches not the born of God, 270, 271.
Oppress, the rich did, the poor, 303.
Oracles, the, of God, ought to be spoken alone by ministers, 131.
Ordinance, to every, of men, we ought to submit, 80.
Overcome, young men had, the wicked one, 184, 185; God's children had, the false teachers, 233, 234; the born of God do, the world, 254; faith does, the world, 255; of whom a man is, he is brought in bondage, 409; the end of those who are, is worse than their beginning, 410.

P

PAPISTS, the, foolish in boasting of the Fathers, 51; weary themselves with trifles, 56 ; worship the name of Christ and reject his gospel, 72, 236; pervert the Lord's supper, 118; hold satisfactions for sins, 119; believe in indulgences and in works of supererogation, 166, 182; make many advocates, 172; hold freewill, 213; deem decrees of Councils as God's oracles, 231, 237; foolishly ground extreme unction on Jam. v. 14, 355; absurdly build their whispering confession on Jam. v. 16, 358.
Partakers, the, of Christ's sufferings, exhorted to rejoice, 133, 134; the, of the divine nature, 370.
Partial, Christians are not to be, 302.
Patience, wrought by the trying of faith, 280; ought to have its perfect work, 281; the, of the husbandman, 348; an example of, the prophets, 350; the, cf Job, 351; is to be added to temperance, 372.
Patient, the poor exhorted to be, under oppression, 347.
Pastors, exposed to three vices, 142; the faithful, regard the exigencies of the Church, 432.
Paul, what is said by, and by David, as to the law, reconciled, 253; the epistles of, referred to, by Peter, 423.
Peace (*see* Grace) is to be sought by him who loves life, 104; sown in, is the fruit of righteousness, 327, 328; to be found in, by God, we must be diligent, 422.
Peaceable, the wisdom from above is, 327.
Pelagius, his false doctrine, 195.
Pelagians, the, refuted by Augustine, 167; the, hold angelic purity, 212.
People, a peculiar, the Christians are, 75; not a, made the people of God, 76; among the, there were false prophets, 391 ; the, the Lord having saved, destroyed the unbelieving, 434, 435.
Perdition, the, of ungodly men, 417, 418.
Perfect, God makes *perfect*, 152, 153; love made *perfect*, when we are like God, 245; *perfect* love casts out fear, 247; let patience have her *perfect* work, 280; that ye may be *perfect*, 281; every *perfect* gift from above, 291; the *perfect* law of liberty, 297; faith made *perfect* by works, 315; he who offends not in word is a *perfect* man, 319.
Perfected, the love of God is, in him who keeps his word, 175; the love of God is, in us when we love one another, 243.
Perseverance, enforced, 201.
Peter, his main design in his First Epistle, 21 ; an Apostle of Jesus Christ, 23; calls himself an elder or presbyter, 143; was a witness of Christ's sufferings, 144; a servant and an Apostle of Jesus Christ, 366; promised not to be negligent in reminding his brethren, 378; knew that his death was near, 379; was an eye-witness of Christ's majesty, 382, 383; the Second Epistle of, why written, 412; refers to Paul's Epistles, 423.

Pharisees and scribes, the, professing to be builders, rejected Christ, the chief corner-stone, 71.

Pilgrims, exhorted to abstain from fleshly lusts, 77.

Pitiful, or merciful, we ought to be, 102 ; the Lord is very, 352.

Plaiting, the, of the hair, discountenanced, 96.

Plato, his saying of the beautiful, 64, 174 ; on the duty of magistrates, 82 ; on justice and injustice, 105 ; was wrong as to his notion of evils, 291 ; defines the chief good, 371.

Pliny, on the prayer of the wicked, 330.

Pollutions, the, of the world, escaped through the knowledge of Christ, 410.

Poor, the, ought not to be despised in places of worship, 301 ; the, chosen by God to be rich in faith, 303 ; the, God is the patron of, 345; the, condemned by the rich, 346.

Pope, the, an enemy to Christ, calls himself his vicar, 71 ; the, the tyranny of, intolerable, 87 ; the, and his followers, teach traditions as God's oracles, 132 ; the, makes pastors to destroy the Church, 144 ; the, has all the marks of Antichrist, 190.

Power, by the, of God, saints are kept unto salvation, 30 ; divine, by which all things are given to us, 367; the, and the coming of Christ, made known by the apostles, 382; angels greater in, 402; ascribed to God our Saviour, 449.

Praise, unto, the trying of faith will be found, 33; for the, of those who do well, governors are sent, 82; ascribed to God, 133.

Praises, the, of God, those called out of darkness ought to set forth, 76.

Prayer, to watch unto, 128; to be according to God's will, 266; for a fallen brother, 267; not to be offered for sin unto death, 268, 269; recommended to the afflicted, 354; to be offered over the sick, 355; the, of faith, saving the sick, 356; the, of the righteous man, availing much, 359; the, of Elias, 360; to be offered through the aid of the Holy Spirit, 447.

Prayers, hindered by domestic strifes, 100; to the, of the righteous, the Lord's ears are open, 105.

Precepts, human, bring a snare on consciences, 339.

Precious; the trial of faith much more *precious* than gold, 33; redeemed with the *precious* blood of Christ, 51; Christ, a *precious* stone, 64 ; Christ *precious* to those who believe, 69 ; *precious* faith, 366; *precious* promises, 370, 371.

Presumption, as to the future, reproved, 340.

Presumptuous, the false teachers were, 401.

Price, a meek and quiet spirit is of great, in the sight of God, 97.

Pride, the, of life, 188.

Priesthood, a holy, 65; a royal, 75.

Primacy, the, faith holds, 55; the, not claimed by Peter, 143.

Principle, the prevailing, shews the character, 209.

Promise, the, of eternal life, 199; the, of a crown of life, 287; the, of liberty, by the servants of corruption, 409; the, of the Lord's coming, derided by scoffers, 415; concerning his, the Lord is not slack, 419; according to his, we look for new heavens and a new earth, 421.

Promises, great and precious, 370.

Prophecy, a more sure word of, 385; the word of, compared to a light shining in a dark place, 386; the, of Scripture, not of private interpretation or suggestion, 389; came not by man's will, 390; the gift of, special, 406; the, of Enoch, 443.

Prophets, the, prophesied of the grace that is come to us, 37; many false, gone out into the world, 230; the false ever boast that they are sent by God, 230; there were false, among the people of Israel, 391; the true, are to be taken as examples of patience, 350.

Propitiation, Christ is our, 171.

Proud, the, are resisted by God, 148, 333.

Proverb, according to the true, 411.

Psalms, he who is merry, is exhorted to sing, 355.

Punishment, for the, of evil doers, governors are sent, 12.

Pure, " as he is *pure*," 207; *pure* religion, 299; the wisdom from above is *pure*, 326; " I stir up your *pure* minds," 412.

Purify, the faithful do, their souls by obeying the truth, 54, 55; he who has hope does, himself, 207; to, their

hearts, the double-minded are exhorted, 335.
Purification, the, of the soul, by the Spirit, 55.
Purity, angelic, held by the Pelagians and Catharians, 212.

Q

QUICK, or living, the, and the dead, the Lord is ready to judge, 125.
Quickened, Christ was, by the Spirit, 111.

R

RAHAB, how justified, 316.
Rain, the early and the latter, waited for by the husbandman, 348; the, was stopped, and came, at the prayer of Elias, 360.
Reason, to give a, for our hope, we ought, with meekness, 108.
Rebuke, " the Lord *rebuke* thee," 439.
Rebuked, Balaam was, for his iniquity, 405.
Record, there are three who bear, in heaven, 257; the, of God, respecting his Son, 262.
Redeemed, we are, not with corruptible things, 49.
Rejoice, the saints do greatly, in the hope of salvation, 31.
Religion, pure, what it is, 299.
Religious, he who seems to be, 298.
Renovation, the, of the Christian, continues through life, 209.
Repentance, its true character, 335; we are led to, by sorrow, 336.
Reproach, bitterer than most evils, 135.
Reproached, the, for Christ's sake, are happy, 133.
Reserved, an inheritance is, in heaven, for the faithful, 29.
Resist, to, the devil, we are exhorted, 150, 334.
Respect of persons, the Father judges without, 43; not to be shewn by Christians in their assemblies, 301.
Resurrection, the, of Christ, gives a living hope, 29; the, salvation depends on, 54.
Reviled, Christ was, but reviled not again, 90.
Rich, the, is to rejoice in his lowness, 285; the, not to be honoured, and the poor despised in places of worship, 301; the, oppress the poor, 303; the, called to weep and howl, 343; the, condemned the poor when not resisting, 346.
Righteous, the, scarcely saved, 140.
Righteousness, the dead to sins are to live to, 93; those who suffer for, are happy, 106; he who doeth, is born of God, 201; the doer of, is righteous, 210; the, of God, not wrought by wrath, 294; the fruit of, sown in peace, 327, 328; the, of God, faith obtained through, 366; the way of, the great sin of forsaking, 411.
Riot, to, in the day-time, counted pleasure by the false teachers, 404.
Rule, the, of right living, is the will of God, 122.

S

SABAOTH, the Lord of, 345.
Sabellians, their false doctrine, 195.
Sacrifice, a, Christ's death was, 92.
Sacrifices, spiritual, offered by the faithful, 65; imperfect, rendered acceptable through Christ, 66.
Saints, the, faith once delivered to, 432; the Lord cometh with ten thousand of his, 443.
Salvation, flows from election, 26; unto, the faithful are kept through faith, 30; the, of the soul, the end of faith, 35; inquired of, by the prophets, 36; desired to be known by angels, 38; the long-suffering of the Lord is, 423; the common, 431.
Sanctify, to, the Lord in our hearts, 107.
Sanctified, the, by God the Father, 429.
Sanctity, the superstitious, of the Papists, 55, 56.
Sarah, an example of obedience to her husband, 98.
Satan, fights covertly and openly against the truth, xi.; inebriates the minds of men, 65; corrupts the Church with variety of errors, 228; the craftiness of, 393, 409; has ever attempted to make saints idols, 439.
Satellites, the, of Antichrist, are crafty corrupters of the gospel, xii.
Save, baptism does now, 116; able to, the word is, 296; " can faith *save* him ?" 309, 310; able to, and to destroy, the lawgiver is, 338, 339; "the prayer of faith shall *save* the sick," 356; " he shall *save* a soul from

death," 361; "others *save* with fear," 448.

Saviour, to be the, of the world, the Father sent his Son, 243; our, through the righteousness of, faith is obtained, 366; our, an entrance into the everlasting kingdom of, 378; the, through the knowledge of, men escape pollutions, 410, 411; the, the apostles of, 413; our, we are to grow in the knowledge of, 426; our, glory is ascribed to, 446.

Schools, the popish, more to be dreaded than any Scyllas or Charybdises, 265.

Scoffers, foretold, 414, 445; their ignorance, 416.

Scripture, the, it is contained in, "I lay in Sion," &c., 66; the, does it say in vain? 331; the, the clearness of, 388; the, the prophecy of, not of private interpretation, 389; the, not obscure to those taught by the Spirit, 425.

Scriptures, the, wrested by the unlearned and unstable, 424.

Seducers, to warn against, the duty of pastors, 199.

Seed, not corruptible, 57; the, of God, remaining in the faithful, 213.

Self-willed, the false teachers were, 401.

Sending, the, of his Son, a singular proof of God's love, 239.

Sensual, the wisdom from below, 325; the false teachers were, 445.

Servants, ought to be subject to their masters, 86.

Servetus, his cavils, 158.

Sheep, going astray, the unconverted compared to, 94.

Shepherd, the, of souls, Christ is, 94; the chief, his appearance, 146.

Ships, guided by a small helm, 319.

Sick, the, directed to send for the elders of the Church, 355.

Silver and gold, we are not redeemed with, 49.

Sin, he who doeth, transgresses the law, 207; none in Christ, 209; he that doeth, is of the devil, 211; finished, what it means, 290.

Sins, our, Christ bare on the tree, 92; dead to, what it means, 93; taken away by Christ, 209; the, of the sick, forgiven, 359; from old, to be purged, 375.

Sion, a stone laid in, 67.

Slackness, or delay, belongs not to the Lord, 419.

Slandering, the lust of, arises from pride, 324.

Slow, we ought to be, to speak and to wrath, 294.

Sobriety, enjoined, 44, 128, 150.

Sodom and Gomorrha, the cities of, destroyed, 398, 436.

Sojourners, the dispersed Jews, 25; the faithful in this world, 49; ought to abstain from fleshly lusts, 77.

Son, the, Christ, of God, 161, 212; the only-begotten, 238; the, of God, a propitiation for our sins, 240.

Sons, the, of God, made by adoption, 202.

Sophists, the, hold foreseen works as the cause of election, 24; the, obscure Christ's sacrifice, 93; the, the futile evasions of, 103; imagine pardon given in baptism, 166; make foreseen works as the cause of adoption, 203.

Soul, the, lust- war against, 78.

Souls, purified through the Spirit, 54; Christ, the bishop and shepherd of, 94; saved by the engrafted word, 296; unstable, beguiled by false teachers, 404.

Sow, the, a proverb concerning, 411.

Speak, to, evil of a brother, is to speak evil of the law, 337.

Spirit, not every, we ought to believe, 229; the, of truth and of error, how to distinguish, 235-237.

Spirit (the Holy), elect through the sanctification of, 24; the, of glory and of God, rests on the reproached, 135; the, dwells in those who keep God's commandments, 227; the, the witness of, 257; the, applies the water and the blood, 259; the, leads not to envy, 332; by the, holy men were moved, when they prophesied, 390.

Spirits, the, in prison, 113; the, we ought to try, 230.

Spots, the false teachers were, to the Church, 404, 441.

Stedfastness, a warning against falling from, 425.

Stewards, good, ministers ought to be, of God's manifold grace, 125, 130.

Stoics, their paradoxes, 208; the, make all sins equal, 306.

Stone, a, Christ compared to, 64.

Stones, living, believers are called, 64.

Strangers, *see* Sojourners.

Strife, connected with envy, 325.

Stumbling, a stone of, Christ is, to unbelievers, 71.

GENERAL INDEX.   487

Submission to God, required, 333.
Suffer, to, wrongs patiently, acceptable to God, 87.
Superfluity, the, of naughtiness, to be laid aside, 295.
Superstitions, prevailed among the Jews, 50.
Swearing in common conversation, forbidden, 352-354.
Swelling words of vanity, spoken by the false teachers, 407.
Swift, we ought to be, to hear, 293.
Sylvanus, Peter wrote by, 153.
Sympathy, without, there is no love to God, 220.

T

TABERNACLE, Peter was warned that he should soon put off his, 380.
Taste, to, that the Lord is God, 63.
Teachers, the false, ever claim to be deemed true, 230; the false, are of the world, 235; false, are to be expected in the Church, 291, 292; false, are followed by many, an offence to the weak, 393, 394.
Temple, a, every believer is, in which God dwells by his Spirit, 64.
Temptation, he who endures, is blessed, 287.
Temptations, various, ought to be borne with all joy, 278.
Tempted, no one is, by God, 288; he is, who is drawn away by his own lust, 289.
Terror, the, of the world, not to be dreaded, 106.
Time, the, of ignorance, and of faith, 123; compared to eternity, a moment, 128; the last, 189.
Times, the last, 52.
To-morrow, to presume on, reproved, 340, 341.
Tongue, the, ought to be restrained, 104; to love in, not sufficient, 221; the, boasts great things, 319; the, compared to fire, 320; the, is set on fire by hell, 321; with the, we bless God and curse men, 322.
Torment, fear brings, 247.
Treasure, a, heaped for the last day by the rich, 344.
Tree, on the, Christ bare our sins, 92.
Trees, withered, the false teachers compared to, 441.
Trial, the fiery, what it was, 133, 134; the, of doctrine, twofold, 231.
Trials necessary, 32; to be borne with all joy, 278.

Tribes, the twelve, James wrote to, 278.
Tried, the, shall receive a crown of glory, 287.
Truth, to do, what it means, 164; the way of, evil-spoken of, 394.
Trying, the, of faith, worketh patience, 279.
Turks, the, worship an idol instead of the true God, 28, 53, 197.
Turning, no shadow of, in God, 291.
Tyranny, though cruel, is better than anarchy, 83.

U

UNBELIEVING, the, the acuteness of, is folly, 83; the, were destroyed in the wilderness, 435.
Unction, an, from the Holy One, 193; the, teacheth all things, 200.
Understanding, an, the Son of God hath given us, 273.
Ungodly, the, and the sinner, can by no means escape judgment, 140; the, the barkings of, ought to be disregarded, 170.
Unjust, the, reserved for judgment, 400.
Unlearned, the, wrest the Scriptures, 424.
Unrighteousness, from all, God is faithful to cleanse those who confess their sins, 168; all, is sin, 270.
Unstable, the double-minded is, 284; the souls which are, are beguiled, 404; the, pervert the Scriptures to their own ruin, 424.
Upbraid, God does not, when he gives, 283.
Unspotted, to keep one's-self, from the world, is pure religion, 300.

V

VANITY, swelling words of, spoken by false teachers, 407.
Vengeance belongs to God, not to man, 91.
Vices, the seed of all, in man, 124; the, of youth, 184.
Victory, the, over impostors, gained only through God, 234; depends on faith, 254.
Vigilance, or watchfulness, enjoined, 150.
Virtue, we are called to, 369; is to be added to faith, 372.

Visit, to, the fatherless and widows, a part of pure religion, 299.
Visitation, the day of, its meaning, 79.
Voice, the, which came from the excellent glory, 383.

W

Wars and fightings, whence they came, 328.
Water, by or with, and blood, Christ came, 256.
Waver, to, we ought not, in asking, 283.
Waverer, the, compared to a wave of the sea, 284.
Waves, raging, the false teachers compared to, 442.
Way, the, of truth, evil-spoken of, 394.
Weak, the, an offence to, 393.
Wells without water, the false teachers were like to, 406.
Will, of his own, God has begotten us, 292.
Wine, the excess of, 120.
Wisdom, to be asked of God, 281; the, that is earthly, sensual, and devilish, 325, 326; the, from above, described, 326, 327.
Witness, a, Peter was, of Christ's sufferings, 144; the, of God, greater than that of men, 260; the, the believer has in himself, 261, 262.
Witnesses, the three, 256-259.
Wives, ought to be subject to their husbands, 95; ought not to give way to fear, 98; are the weaker vessels, 99; are heirs of the grace of life, 100.
Word, the, a mirror, 45; the, of God, abides for ever, 59; the, the sincere milk of, 62; the, unbelievers stumble at, 72; the, without, husbands may be won, 95; the, of God, a spiritual food, 144; the, of life, 157; the, of God, kept by those who know him, 175, 176; to love in, not sufficient, 221; the engrafted, able to save souls, 296; the more sure, of prophecy, 384, 385.
Words, with feigned, false teachers made merchandise of men, 394.
Works, good, means of conversion, 79; faith without, is dead, 311; by, Abraham was justified, 314; by, Rahab was justified, 316.
World, the, not to be loved, 185; the, the love of, excludes the love of God, 186; the, passes away, 188; the, hates the children of God, 204; the, has a wide meaning, 255; the, includes the whole human race, 272; a, of iniquity, the tongue is, 320; the, the love of, adultery, 331; the, the friendship of, is enmity to God, 331; the old, not spared by God, 397; the, the pollutions of, escaped through the knowledge of Christ, 410; the, perished by water, 416.
Wrath, we ought to be slow to, 294.

Y

Year, a, promised to themselves by the presumptuous, 340.
Years, a thousand, are as one day with the Lord, 418.
Younger, the, ought to submit to the elder, 147.

www.ingramcontent.com/pod-product-compliance
Lightning Source LLC
Chambersburg PA
CBHW071221290426
44108CB00013B/1253